The Routledge Companion for Architecture Design and Practice

The Routledge Companion for Architecture Design and Practice provides an overview of established and emerging trends in architecture practice. Contributions of the latest research from international experts examine external forces applied to the practice and discipline of architecture. Each chapter contains up-to-date and relevant information about select aspects of architecture, and the changes this information will have on the future of the profession.

The *Companion* contains thirty-five chapters, divided into seven parts: Theoretical Stances, Technology, Sustainability, Behaviorism, Urbanism, Parametricity, Professional Practice and Society. Topics include: Evidence-Based Design, Performativity, Designing for Net Zero Energy, the Substance of Light in Design, Social Equity and Ethics for Sustainable Architecture, Universal Design, Design Psychology, Architecture, Branding and the Politics of Identity, the Role of BIM in Green Architecture, Public Health and the Design Process, Affordable Housing, Disaster Preparation and Mitigation, Diversity, and many more. Each chapter follows the running theme of examining external forces applied to the practice and discipline of architecture in order to uncover the evolving theoretical tenets of what constitutes today's architectural profession, and the tools that will be required of the future architect.

This book considers architecture's interdisciplinary nature, and addresses its current and evolving perspectives related to social, economic, environmental, technological, and globalization trends. These challenges are central to the future direction of architecture and as such this *Companion* will serve as an invaluable reference for undergraduate and postgraduate students, existing practitioners, and future architects.

Mitra Kanaani is a Professor of Architectural Design, Research & Tectonics at the NewSchool of Architecture and Design, in San Diego, California, USA.

Dak Kopec is an Architectural Psychologist and Director of Design for Human Health at Boston Architectural College, Boston, Massachusetts, USA.

The Routledge Companion for Architecture Design and Practice

Established and Emerging Trends

Edited by Mitra Kanaani and Dak Kopec

NEW YORK AND LONDON

First published 2016
by Routledge
711 Third Avenue, New York, NY 10017

and by Routledge
2 Park Square, Milton Park, Abingdon, Oxon OX14 4RN

Routledge is an imprint of the Taylor & Francis Group, an informa business

First issued in paperback 2021

Library of Congress Cataloguing in Publication Data
The Routledge companion for architecture design and practice : established and emerging trends / [edited by] Mitra Kanaani and David Kopec.
pages cm
Includes bibliographical references and index.
1. Architectural practice. I. Kanaani, Mitra, editor.
II. Kopec, David Alan, editor.
NA1995.R68 2015
720.28–dc23 2015019455

ISBN: 978-1-138-02315-4 (hbk)
ISBN: 978-0-367-27803-8 (pbk)
ISBN: 978-1-315-77586-9 (ebk)

Acquisition Editor: Wendy Fuller
Editorial Assistant: Grace Harrison
Production Editor: Hannah Champney

Cover image: Ammar Alammar, Patrik Schumacher, Mitra Kanaani, Ken Yeang, Sean Ahlquist, Thom Faulders, Achim Menges, and James Carpenter.

Typeset in Bembo
by HWA Text and Data Management, London

Contents

Figures

Tables

Contributors

Sean Ahlquist, M.Arch, AA
Assistant Professor of Architecture
Taubman College of Architecture and Urban Planning
University of Michigan

Kathryn H. Anthony, Ph.D.
ACSA Distinguished Professor
School of Architecture
University of Illinois at Urbana-Champaign

Adenrele Awotona, Ph.D. (Cantab)
Professor and Director
Center for Rebuilding Sustainable Communities after Disasters
University of Massachusetts Boston

Nathaniel Quincy Belcher, AIA, NCARB
Professor of Architecture,
H. Campbell and Eleanor R. Stuckeman School
of Architecture and Landscape Architecture
Pennsylvania State University

Phillip G. Bernstein, FAIA RIBA LEED AP
Lecturer in Practice, Yale School of Architecture
Vice President, Autodesk Inc.

Georgia Bizios, FAIA, DPACSA
Professor of Architecture, NC State University
Bizios Architect, Durham, NC

James Carpenter, BFA
Founder and President
James Carpenter Design Associates

Ben Colebrook
Artist, consultant and researcher
Associate with James Carpenter over a twenty-year period

Jim Dator, Ph.D.
Former Director, Hawaii Research Center for Futures Studies
Professor Emeritus, Department of Political Science,
University of Hawaii at Manoa

Stephen D. Dent, AIA
Professor, School of Architecture and Planning
University of New Mexico
Partner, Dent & Nordhaus, Architects

Aniruddha Deodhar, MBA, BASc.
Senior Product Manager, Sustainable Buildings Solutions
Autodesk Sustainability Solutions

Eve Edelstein, M.Arch. Ph.D., Assoc. AIA, EDAC, F-AAA
Professor New School of Architecture and Design

Thomas Fisher
Director, Metropolitan Design Center
Dayton Hudson Chair in Urban Design
College of Design, University of Minnesota

Valerie Fletcher
Executive Director
Institute for Human Centered Design
US Counselor, International Association for Universal Design

Mark Foster Gage, B.Arch, M. Arch.
Principal, Mark Foster Gage Architects
Assistant Dean, Yale School of Architecture

Todd Gannon, BS, M.Arch, PhD, RA, NCARB

Robert Greenstreet, Dip. Arch. (Oxford), RIBA, FRSA, PhD., DPACSA, Int. Assoc. AIA

Laura L. Harjo, Ph.D.
Assistant Professor
Community and Regional Planning
School of Architecture and Planning
University of New Mexico

Robert F. Herrmann
Menaker and Herrmann LLP

Eve Hinman, Eng. Sc.D., PE | President
Hinman Consulting Engineers, Inc.
San Francisco, Washington DC, New York City

Geraldine Forbes Isais, DPACSA, Assoc. AIA
Dean and Professor of Architecture
School of Architecture and Planning
University of New Mexico

Mitra Kanaani, ARCH.D, MCP, AIA, ICC
Professor of Architectural Design, Research and Tectonics
NewSchool of Architecture and Design

Peter Katz
Consultant in Private Practice
Founding Executive Director, Congress for the New Urbanism
Board Member (Emeritus), Form-Based Codes Institute

Joseph F. Kennedy, M.Arch, MA
Professor of Environmental Design
NewSchool of Architecture + Design
Co-Founder of Builders without Borders

Ralph Knowles, ACSA Distinguished, ACSADP
Professor Emeritus, USC School of Architecture

Branko Kolarevic
Professor and Chair in Integrated Design
Faculty of Environmental Design
University of Calgary

Dak Kopec, Ph.D., MS.Arch., MCHES
Architectural Psychologist
Director of Design for Human Health, Boston Architectural College

Ted Landsmark, M.Env.D., J.D., Ph.D.
President Emeritus of the Boston Architectural College
Past President of the ACSA, and NAAB.

Hugh D. Lester
Fellow, Center for Complex Systems and Enterprises (CCSE)
School of Systems and Enterprises
Stevens Institute of Technology

Angus Macdonald, B.Sc. (Hons), Ph.D, FSA (Scot), Hon.FRSGS
University of Edinburgh

Marvin J. Malecha, FAIA, DPACSA
NC State University College of Design
Past President: ACSA, and AIA
Topaz Laureate: AIA/ACSA

Sharon Carter Matthews, AIA
International Architectural Education Consultant
Former Executive Director of the NAAB

Achim Menges, AA Dipl. (Hons.), Architect BDA
Professor and Director
Institute for Computational Design
University of Stuttgart

David E. Miller, FAIA
Professor and Chair
Department of Architecture
College of Built Environments University of Washington
Miller/Hull Partnership

Juhani Pallasmaa
Architect SAFA, HonFAIA, IntFRIBA, Helsinki
Professor Emeritus Helsinki University of Technology
Teacher, lecturer, writer

Vera Parlac
Assistant Professor
Faculty of Environmental Design
University of Calgary

Michael Pyatok, FAIA
Principal of Pyatok Architects in Oakland, California,
Professor Emeritus, University of Washington in Seattle

Meredith Sattler, M.Arch, M.E.M., LEED BD+C
Assistant Professor, Cal Poly San Luis Obispo

Patrik Schumacher, Dr.Phil., Dipl.Ing., ARB, RIBA
Partner Zaha Hadid Architects
Founding Director AA Design Research Lab
Architectural Association School of Architecture, London

Brett Steele
AA Dipl, Hon FRIBA, FRSA
Director of Architectural Association, AA, in London
Founder and former director of the AADRL Design Research Lab the innovative team-based M.Arch program

Kathleen Sullivan, Assistant Professor
Radford University
MFA Design Thinking

Linda M. Thomas, JD, Ph.D.
Director, Construction Management
Civil, Environmental and Ocean Engineering
Stevens Institute of Technology

Katie Wakeford, M.Arch
Bizios Architect, Durham, NC

David Wang, RA, Ph.D.
Professor of Architecture
Washington State University

Ken Yeang, Ph.D. (Cantab), AA Dipl., RIBA, FAIA (Hon.), APAM, FSIA, Dist.
Professor University of Illinois

Michael Young
Assistant Professor
Irwin S. Chanin School of Architecture at the Cooper Union
Partner Young & Ayata, LLC

Andrew Zago, B.F.A., M.Arch, AIA, NCARB, FAAR 2002

Designing Practice

A Foreword to the *Routledge Companion for Architectural Design and Practice*

The German philosopher Friedrich Nietzsche once wrote "Our tools are beginning to affect how we think." It was an opinion he formed and then expressed (in writing, I should add) late in his lifetime when, having been a lifelong letter-writer and hand note-taker and not only thinker, he found himself thinking differently—while sitting in front of a typewriter! Nietzsche expressed his view, interestingly, soon after he started using one of these strange, late-nineteenth century machines (which, equally interestingly, he felt himself forced to do beccause failing eyesight). In making that claim as he did, what Nietzsche was giving expression to is the consequences of what we today call being a "new adopter"; a person taking up for use in his or her life new ways of working, new technologies, artefacts, living and working habits.

I mention this small anecdote in part because this short preface sits above a compilation of kindred sensibilities related to the consequences of architects in our time turning towards entirely new ways of working (or "practicing," in the language of this book) which in turn give the four-dozen authors gathered together here the basis for articulating the many and provocative—dare we say trend-setting—architectural ideas, knowledge and experience which this handbook, edited by Mitra Kanaani and Dak Kopec, so suitably recommends. The following handbook of new kinds and forms of architectural practice has been assembled as a horizon-wide scan across many distinct channels, topics and interests that have come to take on distinguishing traits within architectural culture in these (still) early years of a new century of post- post-modern architectural life. Which (we should remind ourselves here at the outset) in recent years has jumped around in ways that are still giving form to architectural culture more broadly,.This fact alone, this book helps remind us, embodies perhaps the dominant quality of nearly all forms of culture today—that of their utter dispersion, across what were once hardened disciplinary boundaries,with astonishing speed, and interactivity between architects (and a growing number of other distinct yet related fields); all across, we must also recall. immense geographic distances.

What was once simply labeled as "modern" architecture has, in the century since, expanded in scope, breadth and practice to comprise something more resembling a sensibility than a discipline; architecture that is as much an idea, as it is a fixed, stable field of enquiry. Indeed, the very idea of architecture's "disciplinarity" is itself a sustained topic or thread that can be seen to move across many of the individual chapters making up the four sections of this book. "How," the reader might remind him- or her-self, "can modern architecture—itself now so old, and so predicated upon an idea of change—reconcile such a view with modern and experimental architecture's own, now-considerable, longevity?" If modern architecture was about a revolution and break from architecture's centuries-old past, what happens when that break (and its many modern successes, no less than failures) begins to attain an advanced age, and patina?

Without rehearsing any of the now well-rehearsed disciplinary dichotomies the reader already knows (i.e., "modern" v. "post-modern," or familiar formulae stressing complexities and their contradictions), what follows in this book is a more nuanced means of addressing this question. By appealing to not simply how architects "think" (or what they say), so much as this: *what they do*. What architects do—their various kinds of habit or routine; their regimes, their ways of work, their bundle of habits, the apparatuses of their workspace, their tools, concepts and often-unacknowledged routines—all of this, this book helps reveal are the "practices" of architecture in the broadest sense imaginable. And these points, these bundles of routine, habit and topic, are the focus of this companion. That's what makes it relevant today, and for this reason above all others: architects now find themselves suddenly, unexpectedly, and often unknowingly, working in bafflingly new, strange, unprecedented ways. That they are now expressing some of the interesting, fresh and unexpected ideas found in the texts that follow.

Ours is a world not only where the planet's natural resources are dwindling at rates never before witnessed. Where, in a time of staggering political strife and conflict, in an era of sweeping urbanization and building of all kinds, bodies and goods and materials are being transported at speeds, distances and costs never before seen. Architects and their worlds (including, especially, the worlds comprising their own most sacred of spaces, that of the architectural studio) are being utterly transformed by all of this, including most certainly the overlaying of all kinds of new communication technologies, design systems, and work regimes—so often, ones that are profoundly different from that of even their near, late-20th century ancestors (consider, for a moment, something as simply the difference in impact of the architectural studio of television or radio, versus the internet of network-distributed design platforms of the kind now used universally). The idea that such change is anything less than the material realities by which we are able to realize anew the fact that our mental ideas of architecture are themselves undergoing sweeping transformation, adjustment and evolution.

To cite this fundamental feature of our architectural era, however, has an added consideration, which the companion that follows also provides valuable context for: how might architecture and its own unique forms of knowledge, produced by the practices of architecture, yet endure—most especially (if not ironically) is a period of such exaggerated claims of change? How might architecture continue to not only endure (as a distinct field of human enquiry and experience) but also remain relevant beyond the direct and obvious ways it does as today's (increasingly industrialized) commercial conditions of a global architectural profession? Without trying to give away too much of the tale here in a few-hundred word preface, let me just say it this way: new ways of thinking and not only doing architecture proliferate and are permeating architectural culture in more ways than we know, and for evidence, scan the horizon of this book's table of contents.

Other critics have done with architecture what many have in so many other forms of contemporary culture. They have drawn our attention to the increasingly "expanded" idea of architectural culture itself. Undoubtedly this is the case, as architecture (like so many other cultural realms) finds itself tribalized, balkanized, and subdivided around and alongside so many other equally-specialized interests, fields, sensibilities and ways of working. Again, many of the chapters below document this reality convincingly.

My point here, given all that and so much more in the sheer breadth (and not only depth) of expertise emerging across so many different architectural interests today is that whatever else architects imagine themselves doing in the work they associate with their design, what they are always embodying, regardless are ways of working. And those, most definitely, are suddenly the stuff of entirely unexpected formations. How architects work matters today more than ever. Not because architects find themselves working in so many new and unexpected ways, but for this, the most disciplinary reality of all in architecture: architecture is a form of knowledge only ever learned one project at a time. By, that is, *its practice*. How projects emerge and unfold within an architect's studio (or, these days, across so many other kinds of collaborative spaces, only some of which are geographic locations, or rooms) provides the context, ultimately, for assessing and not only grasping how architectural thought is itself changing. It used to be said (of athletes and architects and other creatures) that "practice makes perfect." These days, practice simply is. Which makes anything else, if not a fiction, something that matters a whole lot less.

Brett Steele
Architectural Association
London. February, 2015.

Preface

The idea for this book originated in my mind while I was serving on the Board of the Association of Collegiate Schools of Architecture (ACSA), and on the steering committee for its Centennial Celebration. This was over a decade and half since the publication of *Building Community: A New Future for Architecture Education and Practice: A Special Report* also known as the *Boyer Report*. As an active educator for two decades, I felt the need to reexamine the vital professional and educational issues that the report so eloquently and poetically coalesced into. In brainstorming with my friend and colleague Dr. Dak Kopec the idea turned to the pursuit of an exciting journey into such collaborative ambitious project.

Throughout the past two decades, the need for architectural educational reforms based on valid points specified in the *Boyer Report* have been repeatedly brainstormed, debated and deconstructed by educators and members of the design collaterals. A trend toward engaged scholarship and renewal has already begun. However, at this juncture, we are encountering rapid ambiguity in design professions, which is increasingly complex and unnerving for many stakeholders. This is propelled by overwhelming social and political manifestations, consequential economic uncertainties, accelerated advancements in technology, all-encompassing globalization, and the trend toward integration of various disciplines and professional fields. Concurrently, the territory of design is expanding. While forms are increasingly becoming fluid, complex, and computational, professions and disciplines in the arts and sciences are broadening their scope. Designers in various fields now work not only within their own domain, but also create territories within the field of architecture. With such an ambiguous future for architecture with a concern for its fragmentation, the question arises: What are the professional prospects, and what is the role of the architect in this arena of design?

The *Boyer Report's* elaborate articulation of larger meanings provides a novel outlook for architectural education and practice. Its rendition of the evolving design values and larger relevance in a multidisciplinary intellectual framework were one of the sources of inspiration for this handbook. The explicit theme of "Established and Emerging Trends" became the intrinsic theme for each of the seven parts and 35 chapters. *Change* as a rapid evolutionary phenomenon and *integration* as an inclusionary process are the two constant themes, and interweaving elements relating design to each of the seven major tenors of the handbook, which are: theoretical tenets, tectonics and science, ecological sustainability, behaviorism, urbanism, practice of the profession, and societal issues.

One alarming concern in the *Boyer Report* has been the identified disconnect between architecture and other disciplines. Now, two decades later since its publication, the relationship between architecture and social and cultural mainstreams remains incohesive and uncoordinated. A couple of years ago, Lee Mitgang the co-author of the Boyer Report asked me to update him on changes in architectural education with respect to architectural practice since its publication. My response was that although little progress has occurred to address issues raised in the report, there is major consensus on the need for holistic strategies and inclusionary measures in design thinking. Current architectural design is more cognizant about the need for merging education and practice, while attracting a broad range of perspectives. Now, more than ever, we are keenly aware of the necessity to learn, adopt, borrow and exchange with other disciplines and professions.

The relationship between architecture as a discipline and a profession has transformed and evolved throughout time. Shifting viewpoints are easily traced in the adopted styles and architectural expressions of various philosophical, historical and political movements, and even in the indigenous architecture of global regions. This book aims to lay out a comprehensive inquiry into current persuasive modes, views and tenets, as well as novel emerging trends and fundamental values, dispositions and canons that are integral to good design and architecture of this time.

Looking back into history, the 19th Century saw tectonics gradually divorced from aesthetics. This was the time when an abstracted artistic design began to be prioritized and overly valued in architecture above all technically driven approaches. The Beaux Arts architectural philosophy in particular created a perception amongst architects that design piety and purity required a focus on form in abstraction and emphasis on aesthetic architectural education. This also disseminated public attitudes that viewed the architectural profession as luxurious and as less vital than other professions, thus initiating a crisis that further divorced the discipline from the profession.

However, many of the issues facing architects today are unique and directly related to the social, economic, environmental, technological, and globalization trends of our world. These challenges are central to the future direction of architecture that speaks about a prospect that involves complicated integrative approaches. I wholeheartedly echo Boyer's remark that the future belongs to the *integrators*. This sets the tone for novel roles, and augmented responsibilities for architects. Today's architects are expected to be visionary creators, artists, and idealists, as well as scientifically and technologically savvy problem solvers, communicators, socially responsible humanists and civil servants with intellect, knowledge and sensibilities beyond just building buildings. It may seem a tall order, but it is also a promising trend for the future of our noble profession as the most collaborative profession in the world. The solution lies in the magic of "integration" as a vehicle for playing inclusionary roles in the design arena, thus solidifying and stabilizing the profession. We cannot deny the fact that architects and designers have always been subject to influences from art, science, nature, and culture, as well as political and economic stances as a propellant for design thinking.

In an imminent future we will encounter a multiplicity of interweaving trends in architectural practice and education. There will be a multitude of evolutionary and transformative factors and forces influencing and demanding change in the profession, and within its related pedagogical educational requirements. Globalization, diversification, plurality and demands of flexible and interactive workforce environments, the profound and rapid influence of information technology in the form-making and interdiscipliniarity of design and practice, as well as emerging hidden facets of specialization will all serve as the impetus behind major transformations, which will undoubtedly affect the future direction of architecture in the coming decades.

This book considers architecture's interdisciplinary nature, and attempts to address its current and evolving perspectives. Chapters are choreographed to analyze topics that are propelling integrative practices and viewpoints within architecture and design. By investigating these newly developing issues we hope that readers will be inspired and stimulated to further push the envelope. We as architects and designers need to rise up! We have the ability, knowledge and the know-how to step forward as one agent of change to reconstruct a world in desperate need of help, and collaborate toward a more promising future for the inhabitants of Mother Earth.

The idea of this book would have not come to fruition without the support, encouragement and joint effort of my friend, colleague and co-editor Dr. Dak Kopec, and the sincere collaboration of Dr. James Dator, who has devotedly acted as an advisor since joining the team of authors. I would also like to extend my deep appreciation to the esteemed team of authors who enthusiastically dedicated their time, knowledge, and expertise in developing manuscripts with rich content, deep meaning, and scholarly arguments, contributing to a unique repository for various realms of design thinking. My final appreciation goes to Patrik Schumacher for his thoughtful and sincere contributions and mentorship, Lucy Campbell, the Librarian at New School of Architecture and Design for her valuable editing insight and expertise, and to my former BIHE students, Nasim Rowshan, Mona Shoghi and Pegah Roshan, as well as my son Arian Nadertabar for their sincere contributions to the production of this handbook.

Mitra Kanaani

Introduction

Established and Emerging Trends

Bob Greenstreet

The concept of change in architectural practice is not a new one; sweeping reforms and profound changes displacing well-worn conventions, paradigm shifts that rewrite the known landscape of practice or watershed moments that presage a crossroads in the profession seem to emerge regularly (and colorfully) in the ongoing discourse on future trends and have done since the emergence of the profession during the nineteenth century. Of course, change is not necessarily positive; it can imply advances and improvements in the field, but just as well signify a destructive, diminishing impact upon the status quo. Neither is change solely a reaction to outside phenomena. Within the established boundaries of a professional body, change may be prompted by outside forces—climate, construction culture, competition, etc.—but just as easily by internal pressures that could be striving for realignment to future needs or, conversely, retrenchment to established or previously held values.

Following the forging of a professional identity through institutionalization and ultimately registration, architecture has evolved steadily over time to its present status as it has struggled to resolve the contradictions between art and commercialism and align its role amongst the other forces affecting the construction industry. Internal change, often contentious, has focused on such issues as advertising, marketing and ethics, while the profession has contended with external forces challenging the status quo such as burgeoning legal liability, or the growth and perceived encroachment of rival professional fields such as town planning, engineering and, most recently, interior design.

While the consistency of the debate on professional change has been quite regular, the scale of change that the profession is facing within the construction industry has increased noticeably of late. Forces such as exponential growth in technological capacity, globalization and innovative delivery methods have challenged the prevailing concept of architectural practice more comprehensively than in the past and have inevitably led to more urgent reappraisals of the profession to ensure that it can maintain a relevant role within the process of future growth.

One thing is certain; the architect's skills may need to adapt to new circumstances and challenges, but the need for architectural input will not diminish. In fact, in both short-term and long-term perspectives, the prognosis for professional survival is promising. In the United States, for example, recent statistics generated by the Bureau of Statistics at the Department of Labor indicate that architecture is a growth profession, predicted to expand by as much as 24.5 percent by the year 2020 and resulting, by their calculation, in the creation of as many as 28,000 new jobs to meet demand. Looking further out into the century, the Brookings Institute has calculated that, based solely upon demographic need (and not factoring in economic feasibility), the physical infrastructure necessary to meet the needs of American society in 2030 is significantly underbuilt. They estimated that, in 2004, only half the physical environment necessary to live, work and play within the next few decades currently existed, meaning that the present building stock will need to double to meet demand, as the reduced pace of building during the recession did little to meet the projected demand. While not all this work will entail the services of the architectural profession, especially in the residential field where such involvement is limited, the growth and demand for a habitable environment in a rapidly urbanizing world has the potential to fuel the profession for the foreseeable future.

Periodically, the profession has reflected on its structure and purpose, looked to the future and has developed new rationales for change, an activity that has helped to promote and shape the debate on the evolution of the profession. That debate in the past has focused on the survival of the profession (*Crisis in Architecture*: MacEwan 1974), the status and role of architectural education (*Building Community*: Boyer and Mitgang, 1996) or a call to realignment for future practice (*The Changing Context, Business and Practice of Architecture*: AIA, 2013). Regardless of the stimulus of the initiative or its focus, the collective viewpoints on emerging or perceived trends always provide a useful, reflective exercise to enable the profession to take stock of its prevailing status and position itself for the future. In particular, bringing together a broad spectrum of respected voices commenting on future expectations within architectural practice provides a valuable opportunity to strategically approach the future, and all indications are that now is an opportune moment for such reflection. *The Routledge Companion for Architecture Design and Practice is* therefore a timely addition to the discourse.

Some components of architecture may not change. Demand for construction will not diminish, although the methods and materials of delivery, and therefore the role and relevance of the design profession will need to continue to evolve to survive. However, the basic, underlying skills of the architect, rooted in the right-brained, kinetic personae of most successful practitioners—creativity, problem-solving, collaboration, consensus building—will remain fundamental traits of the future professional. As to the structure of practice, its relationship to other components of the construction industry, its essential but sometimes uneasy relationship with architectural education and the role of institutional leadership to foster and guide meaningful change—all these factors are in play, challenged and transformed by rapid and often unpredictable change within the very industry that architecture seeks to define and, if not control, to at least effectively influence and coordinate.

Undoubtedly, it is an important time in the continued evolution of the profession, and an opportunity, if handled appropriately, to effectively manage the process of change instead of simply reacting to it after the fact.

The Routledge Companion of Architectural Design and Practice brings together the collective voices of some of the leading figures in current practice, addressing future trends and change from a wide spectrum of perspectives. The collective content of their cumulative musings provides an ideal forum for serious consideration of the future direction of the architectural profession and the role it will play in shaping the built environment for future generations. Change can be good or bad, but it is inevitable. Planned, managed change based upon a reasoned assessment of collective wisdom can only be positive in steering the evolution of the architectural profession towards its role and relevance in the built environment of the future.

References

AIA (2013) *Foresight Report: The Changing Context, Business, and Practice of Architecture 2013.* New York: American Institute of Architects.

Boyer, E.L. and Mitgang, L.D. (1996) *Building Community: A New Future for Architecture Education and Practice*. San Francisco: Jossey-Bass.

MacEwan, M. (1974) *Crisis in Architecture.* London, RIBA.

Part I

Architectural Design and Theoretical Tenets

This part incorporates multiple facets, ethos, and relevant meanings of the multidisciplinary framework of today's architectural design. It also expands on the meaning of cognitive design thinking, and the augmenting role of research trajectories, speculating on potential paths for design methodology.

The focus of this part is on the current duplicitous realms of *design and theoretical tenets of architecture;* one to be disciplinary and cultural, and the other, interdisciplinary, meaning technological and scientific, determining the vast boundaries of the design domains of this time.

1

Design Parameters to Parametric Design

Patrik Schumacher

Parametric design is a computer-based design approach that treats the geometric properties of the design as variables. The dimensions, angles and geometric properties (like curvature) remain malleable as the design progresses. Although at any time the "*parametric model*" displays a determinate shape according to the set of currently chosen values, the essential identity of the parametric design resides in the malleable object's topology rather than its momentary determinate shape. This means that the design consists in the relationships that are maintained between the various elements of the composition. In fact the parametric design model is conceived as a network of relations or *dependencies*. This way of building up a design has the important advantage that the build-up of complexity and the detail resolution of the design can progress while simultaneously maintaining the malleability to adapt to changing requirements as new information is fed into the design process. The generation of alternative options remains viable and economical deep into the detail design without requiring abortive modeling and drafting work. This parametric malleability is advantageous both for the sake of continuous design adjustments as the design progresses, and for the sake of the generation of options and variations. The parametric model can be conceived as general building plan or *geno-type* for the generation of many different versions or *pheno-types* that might co-exist (rather than substitute each other as options). Optioniering thus leads to versioning. Mechanical repetition is being replaced by mass customization. Versioning might also be applied within a single building design via the versioning of components, via "*generative components*". The components adjust their individual shapes in relation to their placement within the encompassing model. These components are small parametric models, i.e. sets of interdependent parts with adjustable shapes. The component adapts to (and fits into) local constraints via the adjustment of its internal parameters. For instance an array of façade components—complete with glazed openings, frames and fixing details—might be made to populate the surface of a volume with changing curvature. The components are to be set up in such a way that they auto-fit to the surface. Each component will assume an individually fitted "pheno-typical" shape, on the basis of the same underlying "geno-type" Thus parametric design is a powerful methodology to achieve a new architectural morphology, namely a morphology of *continuous differentiation*. However, the potential for such

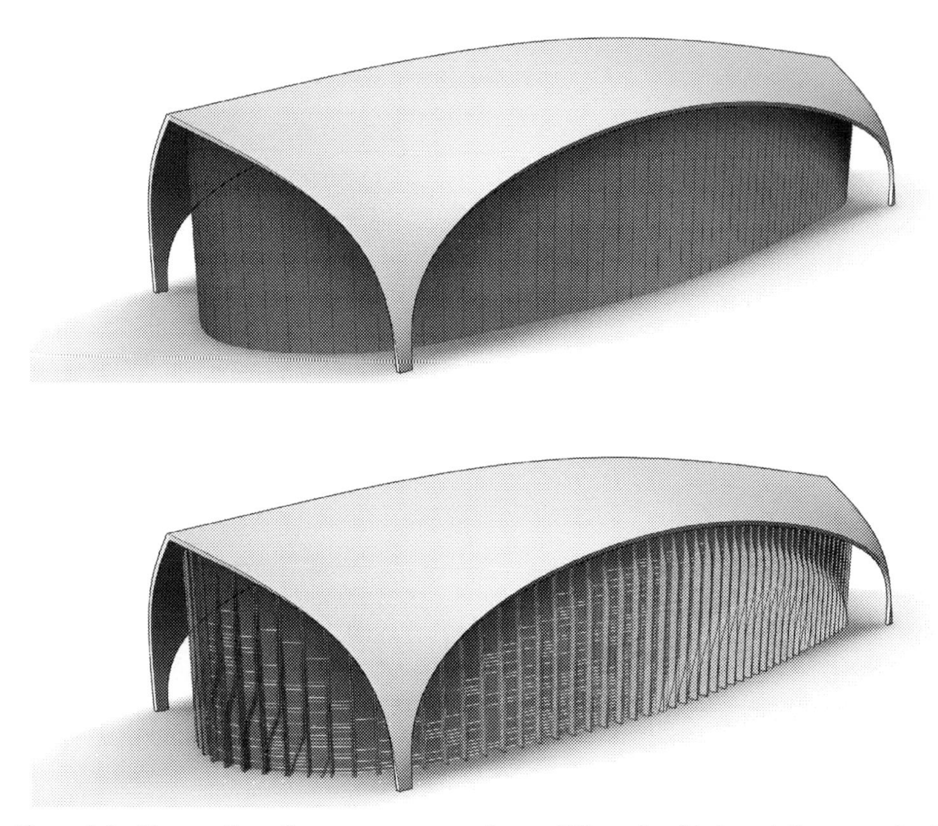

Figure 1.1 Transcoding of sun exposure map into a differentiated brise soleil pattern. Study for Soho China Wang Jing towers, Beijing by Zaha Hadid Architects.

differentiation is not confined to the achievement of scaling and geometric fit with respect to complex forms with continuously changing surface curvature. This kind of differentiation might also be driven by performance parameters like structural parameters or environmental parameters like sun exposure or wind-loads. For instance the opening within a façade panel or the shape of a shading element might vary according to the differential sun exposure of a curved façade at each point of its surface. The parametric designer might set up the following dependency: the higher the sun exposure of a certain surface patch, the smaller should be the opening of the façade component at this location. A sun-exposure map imported from an environmental analysis tool might then deliver the data input for the component differentiation. The sun-exposure map is thus being "*transcoded*" into a differentiated field of façade panels that "optimizes" the sunlight penetration within brackets set out by the parametric design. The resultant façade articulation is thus a function, mapping or indeed a *representation* of the façade's differential exposure to the sun.

Similarly, a designed architectural volume might be structurally articulated via the transcoding of structural analysis parameters into differentiated geometric components. For this purpose the results of a finite elements stress analysis might become the input for a framing pattern that differentiates either member density or member size or both. Again, the result achieves a relative structural optimization (if compared to an undifferentiated framing pattern) and the differentiated structure represents the underlying stress distribution.

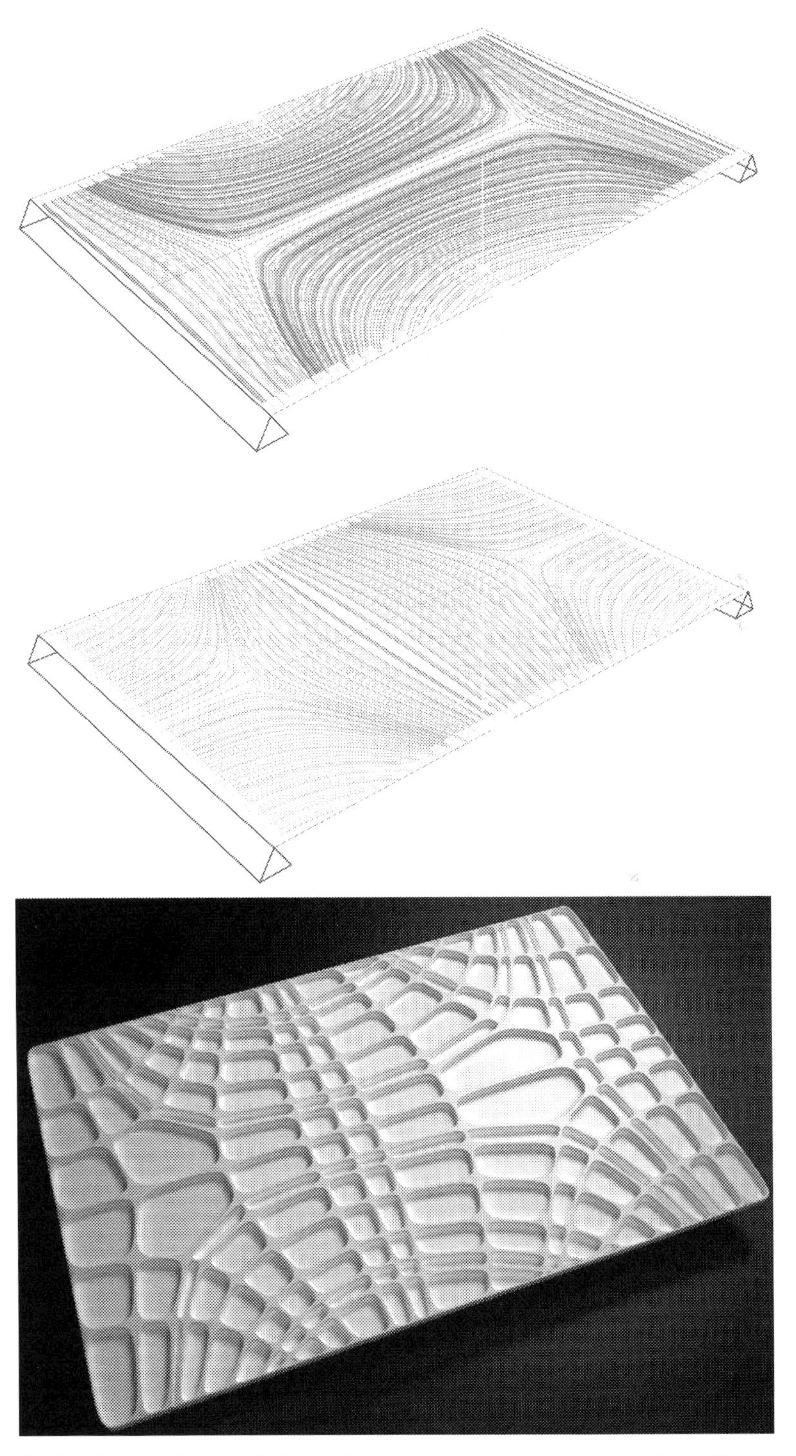

Figure 1.2 Studies in the translation of primary and secondary stress lines from structural analysis software Karamba into a configuraion of ribs reinforcing a slab with two linear supports and two point loads. Philipp Ostermaier, Zaha Hadid Architects.

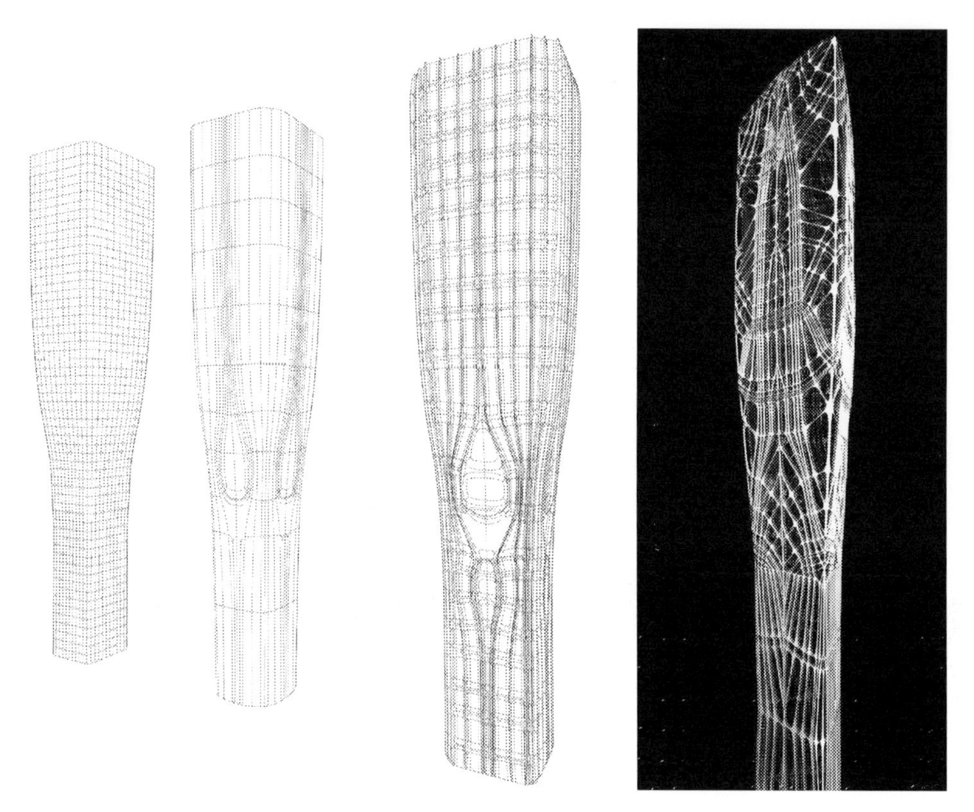

Figure 1.3 Studies in the translation of stress lines from structural analysis software Karamba into a configuration of a tubular skeleton for high-rise structures. Philipp Ostermaier, Zaha Hadid Architects.

Thus in a tall building a parametrically designed skeleton responds to and displays the differentiation of structural forces. Both compressive stresses due to the accumulating vertical loads as well as the moments due to horizontal wind-loads accumulate at the bottom of the tower which will thus be rather different from the middle and top of the tower respectively. The respective variation of performance parameters of the various subsystems of the building like envelope and skeleton thus translates into the morphological differentiation of these subsystems.

The way performance parameters might be transcoded into morphologies is an open question that calls forth the creative designer. Further: these subsystems—each adaptively differentiated according to its own performance logic—also might adapt to each other's differentiation. We might talk about subsystem "*correlation*." To the extent that the envelope's differentiation is responsive to the skeleton's differentiation according to a rule it becomes its "*mapping*" or "*representation*." The particular rule or mode of correlation is again open to design invention. The same principles of adaptive system differentiation and multi-subsystem correlation might be applied to urbanism which thus becomes "*parametric urbanism*." The initially considered subsystems here might be the circulation system (road network), the building fabric (massing) and the programmatic distribution (land use). The existing topography (topo-map) as well as the pre-existing roads might serve as underlying input data sets to be transcoded into a differentiated road network. The differentiation of the

Figure 1.4 Zaha Hadid Architects: Soho Galaxy, Beijing 2012. The project demonstrates the advantages of using parametric curves. Both volumes and urban spaces are easily identifiable, facilitating orientation and navigation despite the density and complexity of the urban scene.

urban massing might initially follow its own logic of block differentiation, initially conceived as internal product variation without as yet responding to external data inputs. This internal differentiation could in a second step be "*over-coded*" or correlated with the differentiation of the circulation network according to a certain rule. The fabric differentiation might be further adapted with respect to an agenda of morphological affiliation with the adjacent urban context. Each step requires the invention of a rule of differentiation or adaptive correlation. At the basis of these differentiations and correlations are the chosen geometric "*primitives*" (or components built up from those primitives) with their respective variables and respectively chosen *degrees of freedom*.

Parametric design thus delivers a new powerful adaptive capacity to architectural design. This new capacity opens up a new domain of creative design invention, namely the invention of transcoding rules and rules of subsystem correlation. Design thus becomes "*rule-based*" design. Critics unfamiliar with this new world of parametric design sometimes presume that the new algorithmic design operations, somehow replaces or dis-empowers the designer's creative freedom. The opposite is the case: a new realm of creative exploration with its new design challenges is opened up and calling for the designer's creative ingenuity. The more computational design tools free the designer from the drudgery of drafting and modeling, the more the creative essence of the design process as a process of invention and decision making comes to the fore.

To design is to generate and to choose. All design is decision making, i.e. the making of choices. Choice presupposes a set of alternatives to choose from. The design process thus comprises two fundamental sub-processes: the generation of alternative solution candidates and the selection of an alternative according to test results on the basis of posited evaluation/selection criteria. Thus, the overall rationality and effectiveness of a design process depends on two principally independent factors: its power to generate and its power to test/select. The design principle of "*generate and test*" conducted in a design medium or model in advance of physical construction stands in as economic (rational) substitute for the physical "*trial and error*" process that is the principle of the biological evolution as well as of all pre-architectural building, i.e. building without architectural design aided by drawing. Both powers of design rationality are being massively enhanced by the computational aids that constitute parametric and algorithmic design in comparison with traditional design based on drawing according to precedent or intuition. The more the processes of generation and selection are themselves automated via algorithms, the more powerful does the design process become, as the designer's creative choices shift to the meta-plane of choosing generative algorithms and evaluating selection criteria. These in turn might be looped into evolutionary algorithmic set ups. Parametric design and design via scripted rules is replacing design via the direct manipulation of individual forms. Computational processes can uniquely enhance both the design process's generative power and its analytical power. The techniques of variation and versioning as well as the differentiation on the basis of transcoding and correlation advance the parametric designer's efficiency as well as the rationality of his design.

The generation of design options can be opened up much further than the mere versioning proliferation of pheno-types on the basis of a pre-established geno-type. A much more open ended, generative technique of producing solution candidates is via an agent-based system whereby the elemental primitives (atoms) of a composition or multi-primitive components (molecules) are set free to roam within the modeling space where they aggregate and configure larger global structures according to local rules of attraction, repulsion, alignment, attachment, etc., set by the designer. Many of the properties of the resultant configuration are emergent and un-anticipated outcomes of the complex interaction of the rules. Prediction can only mean pattern prediction here in terms of general qualitative properties or in terms of quantitative brackets but hardly precise anticipation. Genuine surprise is possible. Some undesired properties might be prevented by giving the generation process respective constraints. Certain desired properties might be attainable in ways and to a degree that would have been difficult or impossible to attain via intuitive methods. Agent-based processes open up a huge field of exploration and arena for the designer's creative ingenuity. They can also be used in the agenda of multi-subsystem correlation described above. A structural skeleton or an urban path network might be configured via agent-based aggregation processes. Urban fabric particles (agents) might interact and configure over the substrate of a topographic map that biases the migration and self-organization process of the agent population in ways that produce a transcoding of the underlying topography not unlike the more direct transcoding via a simple rule of correlation. The result of the agent-based model might display many unexpected variants and properties that might or might not be advantageous upon further analysis. The general advantage of these less predictable processes is that they might deliver in-built criteria in new, unexpected ways and offer up unusual properties that might stimulate the designer's formulation of altogether new desires and criteria. However, the legibility of the transcoding as representation might be compromised relative to the technique with direct rules of correlation.

Parametric Software

By far the most widely used parametric design software in architecture is "*Grasshopper*" developed by David Rutten for Robert McNeel Associates (founded in 1980, McNeel is a privately-held, employee-owned company based in Seattle) and first released in 2008. Grasshopper is a freely available graphical associative logic modeler and algorithm editor closely integrated with McNeel's 3-D modeling tool "*Rhinoceros*." Grasshopper is a pertinent tool for the set-up parametric models as described here as networks of interdependent elements and manipulations. The network of relations is set up and visualized graphically so that the designer can keep track of and intervene in the relational network he is designing. The parametric designer usually opens two programs/windows: the 3D modeling space of Rhinoceros and Grasshopper's graphical algorithm editor. The designer can now move between the modeling and the scripting environment to build up the parametric design, e.g. creating objects in Rhino, make them interdependent and manipulate the parameters in Grasshopper and then view the behavior of the dynamic interdependent configuration in Rhino, etc. Grasshopper might become the primary medium and site of the design work while the 3D geometric model visible in Rhinoceros (passive visual control) is driven or executed by the active definition/script visualized and manipulated in the grasshopper window. That the design is all about the set-up of topological parametric geno-types defined via networks of relations (both internal to the building/artefact and external in relation to context parameters) is thus evident in the constitution of the primary design medium. That indeed most parameters/values are treated as variables is evident in the ubiquitous use of sliders (with designated ranges of values).

Rhino/Grasshopper has also become the preferred platform for scripted plug-ins and for a new powerful set of integrated tools that push architecture's design intelligence beyond the mere handling of geometry to include engineering logics and real time access to physics simulations that allow for sophisticated form finding and optimization processes to be seamlessly folded into the design process. Kangeroo is a physics engine created by Daniel Piker as a tool for interactive real time structural form-finding simulations like surface-relaxations. These simulations are implemented via particle-spring systems. With this particular tool Frei Otto's seminal physical form-finding experiments with tensile structures and shells via inverted catenary systems can be recreated in the much more versatile digital domain. Frei Otto's models represent but a small corner of the new space of possibilities that is put at the fingertips of parametric designers in a very intuitive, playful way that equals the intuitive play with real physical materials, however now unleashed from the narrow parametric bounds given by any chosen physical material. Karamba and Millipede are structural analysis and optimization tools for Grasshopper. They are interactive, parametric finite element analysis programs that display stress distributions and deformations of any geometric form under any imaginable load. Karamba was (and continues to be) developed by Clemens Preisinger and Robert Vierlinger a.o. within the structural engineering office Bollinger- Grohmann-Schneider. Millipede was (and continues to be) developed by Panagiotis Michalatos. These tools are allowing architects to design intuitively with immediate engineering feedback and intelligence. They also allow the articulation and characterization of spaces and elements to be guided by structural logics, i.e. they are tools for the architectural project of "tectonic articulation" (Schumacher, 2012a).For instance, both programs deliver vector-fields that depict the principal stress lines of any surface under specific load conditions. These principal stress lines (or moment lines) can then be used to generate beautifully adapted rib-patterns beyond the usual default grids. These might be used to articulate skeletons, waffle-slabs or grid-shells, etc. In addition, Millipede also offers structural form-generation via so called topology optimization, i.e. the iterative erosion of a solid form placed between any loads and support points to reveal an optimized truss-like dematerialization or framing pattern that might be substituted for the solid form.

Octopus is a multi-objective optimization tool for Grasshopper using genetic algorithms developed by Robert Vierlinger (from the Karamba team). Objectives might include both structural and environmental parameters at the same time, or any other further parameters. The program searches for the best trade-offs between the different potentially conflicting fitness criteria that need to be addressed. Or the designer sets a single fitness criterion but imposes diversity as a second objective to generate a multitude of possible approaches and solutions. Octopus displays the various (pareto-optimal) solutions within a 3D possibility matrix. In a multiple objectives search (within a multi-dimensional parameter space) that searches trade-offs between several goals a full range or spectrum of options is produced that spans between the extremes of each separate goal. (Note: a solution in a multi-objective optimization is called "Pareto optimal", if none of the addressed fitness values can be increased without decreasing some of the other fitness values. The set of Pareto-optimal solutions is called the "pareto front.") This tool is based on David Rutten's Galapagos User Interface. Galapagos is a general evolutionary solver that David Rutten has developed for the Rhino/Grasshopper design world. The computational harnessing of the principles of evolution—variation (mutation, recombination), selection (according to fitness criteria), and reproduction (as a basis for further variation)—is one of the most exciting new frontiers in computationally augmented design. The work with evolutionary algorithms accelerates the design process. Some worry about where the designer is in such a process. However, like all enhancements that are implied in the move from manual design to computational design, the use of evolutionary algorithms does empower rather than dis-empower the designer and enhances the designer's explicit design intelligence. All design might be construed as a trial and error quasi-evolution. With evolutionary algorithms the fitness criteria for design decisions have to be clearly stated. This enhances the clarity of design thinking. The author does not expect that the totality of the design process for a complex product like a (contextually embedded) building can be solved via a single evolutionary set-up. This is so because it is virtually impossible to state in advance all the criteria that might become relevant during the project development. The design process is a discovery process not only in terms of solutions but also in terms of the goals and potentials of the project. Computational design processes augment the designer's capacity of discovery in both dimensions. The proliferation of (intelligently pre-constrained) options boosts selection according to set criteria and stimulates the setting of new criteria. To summarize, the advantages of augmenting the design process with the computational tools are described above:

Contemporary, parametric and scripting-based design techniques allow for the establishment of a powerful design process/method. The unique power of this process/method lies in its ability to combine otherwise conflicting trajectories:

1 The combination and simultaneous increase in both the generative power and the constraining power of each design cycle.
2 The combination and simultaneous increase in both the breadth and depth of the solution search in each design cycle.
3 The combination and simultaneous increase in both the power of creative surprise discovery and analytic selective rationality.

Parametric Style

Is there a parametric style? Parametric design is a design methodology based on parametric modeling and scripting techniques. This methodology might be productively employed on any architectural design, independent of the architectural style the designer might be adhering to. All styles can benefit from the advantage of maintaining design malleability during the design's progressive resolution. Parametric design is thus equally applicable to all architectural styles and in this sense stylistically neutral.

Parametricism is the contemporary style that is most vigorously advancing its design agenda on the basis of parametric design techniques.

Conceptual and Operational Definition of Parametricism:

As a conceptual definition of Parametricism one might offer the following formula: Parametricism implies that all architectural elements and compositions are parametrically malleable. This implies a fundamental ontological shift within the basic, constituent elements of architecture. Instead of the classical and modern reliance on ideal (hermetic, rigid) geometrical figures—straight lines, rectangles, as well as cubes, cylinders, pyramids, and (semi-)spheres—the new primitives of Parametricism are animate (dynamic, adaptive, interactive) geometrical entities—splines, nurbs, subdivs, particle-spring systems, agent-based systems, etc.—as fundamental "geometrical" building blocks for dynamical compositions that react to "attractors" and that can be made to resonate with each other via scripts.

In principle every property of every element or complex is subject to parametric variation. The key technique for handling this variability is the scripting of functions that establish associations between the properties of the various elements. However, although the new style is to a large extent dependent upon these new design techniques the style cannot be reduced to the mere introduction of new tools and techniques. What characterizes the new style are new ambitions and new values—both in terms of form and in terms of function—that are to be pursued with the aid of the new tools and techniques. Parametricism pursues the very general aim to organize and articulate the increasing diversity and complexity of social institutions and life processes within the most advanced centers of post-Fordist network society. For this task Parametricism aims to establish a complex variegated spatial order. It uses scripting to lawfully differentiate and correlate all elements and subsystems of a design. The goal is to *intensify the internal interdependencies* within an architectural design as well as the *external affiliations and continuities* within complex, urban contexts. Parametricism offers a new, complex order via the principles of differentiation and correlation.

This general verbal and motivational definition of Parametricism can and must be complemented by an operational definition. It is necessary to operationalize the intuitive values of a style in order to make its hypotheses testable, to make its dissemination systematic, and to be exposed to constructive criticism, including self-critique of the Parametricist design work.

The operational definition of a style must formulate general instructions that guide the creative process in line with the general ambitions and expected qualities of the style. A style is not only concerned with the elaboration and evaluation of architectural form. Each style poses a specific way of understanding and handling functions. Accordingly, the operational definition of Parametricism comprises both a formal heuristics—establishing rules and principles that guide the elaboration and evaluation of the design's formal development and resolution—as well as a functional heuristics—establishing rules and principles that guide the elaboration and evaluation of the design's social functionality.

For each of these two dimensions the operational definition formulates the heuristics of the design process in terms of operational taboos and dogmas specifying what to avoid and what to pursue. At the same time these heuristic design guidelines provide criteria of self-critique and continuous design enhancement.

Operational definition of Parametricism:

Formal heuristics:

Negative principles (taboos):	avoid rigid forms (lack of malleability)
	avoid simple repetition (lack of variety)
	avoid collage of isolated, unrelated elements (lack of order)
Positive principles (dogmas):	all forms must be soft (intelligent: deformation = information)
	all systems must be differentiated (gradients)
	all systems must be interdependent (correlations)

Functional heuristics:

Negative principles (taboos):	avoid rigid functional stereotypes
	avoid segregative functional zoning
Positive principles (dogmas):	all functions are parametric activity/event scenarios
	all activities/events communicate with each other

The avoidance of the taboos and the adherence to the dogmas delivers complex, variegated order for complex social institutions. These principles outline pathways for the continuous critique and improvement of the design. The designer can always increase the coherence and intricacy of his/her design by inventing further variables (degrees of freedom) for the compositions' primitive components. There is always scope for the further differentiation of the arrays or subsystems that are made up by the elemental primitives. This differentiation can be increased with respect to the number of variables at play, with respect to the range of differences it encompasses and with respect to the fineness and differential rhythm of its gradients. There is always further scope for the correlation of the various subsystems at play in the multi-system set-up. Ultimately every subsystem will be in a relation of mutual dependency with every other subsystem, directly or indirectly. The number of aspects or properties of each subsystem that are involved in the network of correlation might be increased with each design step. Further, there is always the possibility (and often the necessity) to add further subsystems or layers to the (ever more complex and intricate) composition. Also: it is always possible to identify further aspects or features of the (principally unlimited) urban context that might become an occasion for the design to register and respond to. Thus the context sensitivity of the design can be increased with every design step. Thus the heuristics of Parametricism direct a trajectory of design intensification that is in principle an infinite task and trajectory. There is always a further possibility pushing up the intensity, coherence, intricacy, and beauty of the design. As the network of relations tightens, each further step becomes more elaborate, more involved as all the prior subsystems and their trajectories of differentiation should ideally be taken into account. Arbitrary additions show up conspicuously as alien disruption of the intricate order elaborated so far. Each additional element or subsystem that enters the composition at a late, highly evolved stage challenges the ingenuity of the designer, and more so the more the design advances. The complex, highly evolved design assumes more and more the awesome air of necessity or quasi-nature. However, the design remains open ended. There can be no closure. The classical concepts of completeness and perfection do not apply to Parametricism. Parametricism's complex variegated order does not rely on the completion of a figure. It remains an inherently open composition.

Parametric Society

In the perspective of architecture, and specifically in the perspective of contemporary parametric design, contemporary society is a vast panoply of parametrically variable event scenarios. (This formula spells the program dimension of the built environment.) But is parametric design really concerned with society?

Many critics of parametric design and Parametricism ask: What is the societal relevance of the complex geometries and intricate spatial compositions made possible by parametric design? Is this not an expensive, indulgent and self-serving narcissism on the part of designers that distracts from the social task of architecture? This question must be answered. In order to answer this question we need to clarify the specific social task (societal function) of architecture: the spatial ordering of social processes. The increasing density, diversity and complexity of contemporary social life processes require complex spatial configurations that allow a diversity of event scenarios to unfold in close proximity and awareness of each other. The required complex spatial organizations can only function if the participants that need to come together in the various event scenarios can successfully orient and navigate the spaces they encounter. This requires architectural articulation. The stylistic characteristics of Parametricism like curvlinearity, gradients and correlative resonances are potentially more effective in the legible articulation of complex relations—clustering, nesting, interpenetration—between multiple different spaces.

Without curves, smooth transitions and gradients the complex urban scene quickly degenerates into visual chaos. Above the correlative transcoding of external parameters into subsystem differentiations, and then the correlative resonances between different subsystem differentiations was introduced as a key concept and technique of parametric design. The urban subsystems that might be correlated via rule-based associative set ups or scripts might include the differentiated urban massing, topography, vehicular circulation, and pedestrian circulation. It is important to note here that establishment of systematic dependencies via transcodings—and indeed all associative logics—increase the information density of the built environment because every dependency chain can be traced back via inferences. The designer might choose and calibrate the adaptive correlations between the subsystems so that the different systems do indeed become "representations" of each other in the sense that users navigating the urban environment can not only follow the gradients or vectors of transformation in each of the subsystems but that whatever is visible from one of the subsystems gives clues about the other systems even if they are not directly visible, e.g. the silhouette of the urban massing will "represent" the topography and allow the street- and path network to be inferred. Similarly, within a mixed-use complex the differentially articulated structural system might represent or indicate the circulation path

Figure 1.5 Zaha Hadid Architects: Soho Galaxy, Beijing 2012. The built environment becomes a 360 degree interface of communication where densely layered interaction offerings come into view above, below and all around. This logic operates continuously from exterior to interior

and the program distribution, etc. This powerful enhancement of the communicative capacity of the built environment via rule-based parametric design goes to the heart of architecture's societal function of ordering the multitude of social interaction scenarios that make up contemporary society. Architecture is in charge of the social functionality of the designed/built environment. (Its technical functionality can become the responsibility of various engineering specialisms. However, here too the concept of parameter-based differentiation is relevant in the delivery of optimized solutions with respect to structural and environmental engineering.)

Here we can only point towards the promising potential of parametric design techniques—employed under the auspices of the heuristics of Parametricism—for the organization and articulation of contemporary societal complexity. The actual proof can only be delivered via individual designs and buildings. There are successful built examples of Parametricism. (The attempt to deliver this proof via the documentation of these designs and their ordering work would go beyond the scope of this chapter.) However, the parametric design community is still flexing its muscles rather than going to work with a clear social purpose. In many young design studios and schools of architecture the playful exploration of new parametric tools results in designs that cannot yet stand up to the critical scrutiny of the skeptics that demand to see the societal relevance and social performance of design efforts. The strategic social instrumentalization of parametric design becomes an urgent agenda that must be explicitly posed and addressed now with the parametric design movement. The credibility of

Parametricism is at stake. However, we must also protect the need for continued playfulness in the exploration of new tools, techniques and repertoires. Innovation requires the oscillation between open ended exploration and determinate testing leading to tangible improvements. The explicit formulation of the key task is crucial: the ordering of the complexity of social life processes via complex, legible, information-rich spatial orders.

A post-Fordist network society demands that we continuously browse and scan as much of the social world as possible, in order to remain continuously connected and informed. We cannot afford to withdraw and beaver away in isolation when innovation accelerates all around. We must continuously recalibrate what we are doing in line with what everybody else is doing. We must be networked all the time, so as to continuously ascertain the relevancy of our own efforts. Telecommunication via mobile devices may help, but it does not suffice. Rapid and effective face-to-face communication remains a crucial component of our daily productivity. The whole built environment must become an interface of multi-modal communication, as the ability to navigate dense and complex urban environments has become a crucial aspect of the agglomeration economies and synergies that are an important factor in society's overall productivity.

Parametric Semiology

In the agenda of parametric semiology the author's conception of society as the panoply of parametrically variable event scenarios comes together with Parametricism's conception of the built environment as a complex system built up from correlated subsystems: The event scenarios—simulated via agent-based crowd modeling techniques—are treated as one more subsystem in the multi-system parametric design model. However, this system of differentiated crowds should be the central, decisive system around which all the architectural subsystems revolve as so many contributing inputs to its patterned functioning. The principle of correlation, i.e. the establishment of rule-based dependencies also encompasses the relationship of the crowd behavior relative to its surrounding architectural subsystems, albeit with the additional complication that the pattern displayed by the crowds emerge bottom up via the behaviors of the individual agents (Note: crowd modeling must follow the principle of "methodological individualism."). These agents' behaviors are made dependent on where they are, guided by the encoded environmental clues presumed to be accessible to the agents' cognition. The space communicates its designation with its implied rules of behavior and interaction.

All design is communication design. The built environment, with its complex matrix of territorial distinctions, is a giant, navigable, information-rich interface of communication. Each territory is a communication. It gives potential social actors information about the communicative interactions to be expected within its bounds. It communicates an invitation to participate in the framed social situation. Designed spaces are spatial communications that *frame* and order further communications. They place the participants into specific constellations that are pertinent with respect to the anticipated communication situations. Like any communication, a spatial communication can be accepted or rejected, i.e. the space can be entered or exited. Entry implies accepting the communication as the premise for all further communication taking place within its boundaries. Crossing a territorial threshold makes a difference in terms of behavioral dispositions. Entry implies submission to the specific rules of conduct that the type of social situation inscribed within the territory prescribes. In this way, the designed-built environment orders social processes. This spells the unique, societal function of architecture: to order and frame communicative interaction.

Parametric design is able to increase the information density of the built environment. Everything must resonate with everything else. This should result in an overall intensification of relations, which gives the urban field a performative density, informational richness, and cognitive coherence that makes for quick navigation and effective participation in a complex social arena. Our increasing ability to scan an ever-increasing simultaneity of events, and to move through a rapid succession of communicative encounters, constitutes the essential, contemporary form of cultural advancement. Further advancement of this vital capacity requires a new built environment with an unprecedented level of complexity, a complexity that is organized and articulated into a complex, variegated order of the kind we admire in natural, self-organized systems.

The more free and the more complex a society, the more it must spatially order and orient its participants via perceived thresholds and semiotic clues—rather than via physical barriers and channels. The city is a complex text and a permanent (slowly evolving) broadcast. Therefore, our ambition as architects and urban designers must be to spatially unfold more simultaneous choices of communicative situations in dense, perceptually palpable, and legible arrangements. The visual field must be dense with offerings and information about what lies behind the immediate field of vision. The parametricist logics of rule-based variation, differentiation, and correlation establish order within the built environment, giving those who must navigate it the crucial possibility of making inferences. Employing associative logics correlates the different urban and architectural subsystems in ways that make them representations of each other. Everything communicates with everything. This is not a metaphysical assertion about the world, but a heuristic principle for parametric design under the auspices of Parametricism. The rule-based design processes that inform all forms on the basis of informational transcoding imply the possibility of information retrieval through the user, as long as human cognitive capacities are reflected.

Architecture's societal function—the framing of communicative interaction—can be broken down and concretized into three related subtasks: *organization, articulation*, and *signification*. Organization is based on the distribution of positions for spatial elements and their pattern of linkages. Articulation is based upon the constitution of morphological identities, similitudes, and differences across the architectural elements to be organized. Organization is instituted via the physical means of distancing, barring, and connecting via circulatory channeling. These physical mechanisms can, in theory, operate independently of all nuanced perception and comprehension, and can thus, in principle, succeed without the efforts of articulation. However, the restriction to mere organization without articulation, and without facilitating the participants' active navigation, severely constrains the level of complexity possible in the pattern of social communication thus framed. Articulation presupposes cognition. It enlists the participant's perception and comprehension, and thereby facilitates the participants' active orientation. The distinction of organization versus articulation is then based on the difference between handling the users as *passive bodies* and enlisting them as active, *cognitive agents*. These two registers relate in this way: articulation builds upon, and reveals, organization. It makes the organization of functions apparent. In so doing, it elevates organization into order.

The dimension of articulation includes two distinct subtasks: *phenomenological* and *semiological* articulation (signification). Their distinction is between the enlistment of behavioral responses from cognitive agents, on the one hand, and the communicative engagement of *socialized actors*, on the other. The phenomenological project enlists users as cognitive agents, perceiving and decomposing their environment along the lines of the principles of pattern-recognition or Gestalt-perception. It makes organizational arrangements perceptually legible by making important points conspicuous, avoiding the visual overcrowding of the scene, and so on. This is a necessary precondition for all semiological encodings that can only attach to the visually discernible features of the environment. In other words, users can only read, interpret, or comprehend what they can discern. However, the comprehension of a social situation involves more than the distinction of conspicuous features. It is an act of interpretation that presupposes socialization. It is an act of reading a communication: namely, the reading of space as both framing communication and the premise for all further communications to be expected within its ambit. (These framing communications are attributed to the institutions hosting the respective communicative events, i.e. they are attributed to the clients, rather than to the architects or designers.) Communication presupposes language, that is, a system of signification. The built environment spontaneously evolves into such a (more or less vague and unreliable) system of signification. The task of architectural semiology as design agenda, therefore, is to go beyond this spontaneous semiosis (that every talented designer navigates intuitively), and build up a more complex and precise system of signification.

Architectural semiology needs to be re-inaugurated as architecture's core competency under the auspices of Parametricism. After the failed attempts of the 1970s and 1980s, architectural semiology can now be effectively theorized and operationalized as *parametric semiology*. It is important to note that a semiotic system can neither be reduced to syntax nor to semantics. This was the mistake of the attempts in the 1970s. Eisenman's work had no semantic dimension, and Jencks had no syntax. The postmodern architects tried to build on the spontaneous semiosis of architectural history and were thus restricted to the recycling of clichés, and without the chance to build up a more complex syntax. Instead the refoundation of architectural semiology promoted here suggests a radical severance from all historical semiotic material, promoting the construction of a new, artificial spatio-visual language in analogy to the creation of artificial programming languages, taking full advantage of the radical arbitrariness of all languages. The construction of this language must proceed step by step, oscillating between syntactical and semantic advances. This is made possible via parametric agent-based modeling that realizes the signifying relations as associative functions that systematically make agent behaviors dependent on architectural features. At the same time the pragmatic layer is anticipated as the (never fully predictable) social appropriation process that commences when the design spaces are finally utilized and re-utilized.

In the second volume of the author's treatise, *The Autopoiesis of Architecture* (Schumacher, 2012b)· a set of axioms and heuristic principles are formulated that outline strategies for semiological projects conceived as complex architectural designs—for instance, the design of a university campus—as the design of a coherent visual language or system of signification. The first axiom restricts the domain of architecture's signified to the social events that are expected to happen within the respective buildings or spaces, defined along the three dimensions of function type, social type and location type. The second axiom states that the relevant unit of architectural communication, the architectural sign, is the designed/designated territory (just like the sentence is the minimal relevant unit of speech). Territorial thresholds mark differences that make a difference in terms of social situation. These differences in use constitute the meaning of architectural signs/communications.

Architectural semiology can be operationalized via agent-based crowd modeling. The scripting of the agents' specific behavioral dispositions, in relation to specific spatial and/or morphological features of the designed environment, allows designers to model and work on the signification relation. The domain of the signified—the patterns of social interaction expected within designed territories, can thus be brought into architecture's design medium as one more subsystem (the crucial subsystem) in the set of correlated

Figure 1.6 AA Design Research Lab: Agent-based parametric semiology, London 2012. This new methodology allows for the speculative simulation of new spatial configurations engendering innovative interaction patterns and event scenarios. Design: Yitzhak Samun, Sobitha Ravichandran, Di Ding, Anusha Tippa, AADRL Studio Schumacher.

subsystems constituting the parametric model. It therefore becomes possible, for the first time in the history of architecture, to model this life process, thus incorporating it into design speculation. This was made possible by the use of computational crowd modeling techniques, via agent-based models. General tools like "Processing," or specific tools like "MiArmy" and "AI.implant" (available as plug-ins for Maya), and "Massive" now make behavioral modeling within designed environments accessible to architects. Agent modeling should not be limited to crowd circulation flows, but should encompass all patterns of occupation and social interaction in space.

The agents' behavior might be scripted so as to correlate with the configurational and morphological features of the designed environment, i.e. programmed agents responding to environmental clues. Such clues or triggers might include furniture configurations, as well as other artefacts. The idea, then, is to build dynamic action-artefact networks.

Morphological features, as well as colors and textures that, together with ambient parameters (lighting conditions), constitute and characterize a certain territory can now influence the behavioral mode of the agent. Since the "meaning" of an architectural space is the (nuanced) type of event or social interaction to be expected within its territory, these new tools allow for the refoundation of architectural semiology as *parametric semiology*. The semiological project therefore implies that the design project systematizes all form-function correlations into a coherent system of signification. A system of signification, in turn, is a system of mappings (correlations) that map distinctions or manifolds, defined within the domain of the signified (here the domain of patterns of social interaction), onto the distinctions or manifolds, which are defined within the domain of the signifier (here, the domain of spatial positions and morphological features defining and characterizing a given territory) and vice-versa. This system of signification works if the programmed social agents consistently respond to the relevantly coded positional and morphological clues in such a way that expected behaviors can be read off the articulated environmental configuration. However, rather than modeling scenarios frame by frame, agent-based modeling works by defining the agents' behavioral dispositions and biases relative to environmental features. The event itself then becomes an emergent global pattern resulting from the local interactions of agents with each other inside the environment. If this succeeds, architecture will have done its job of ordering the event scenario. That is, the meaning of architecture, the prospective life processes it frames and sustains, will have been modeled and assessed within the design process as an object of direct creative speculation and cumulative design elaboration. In this way, architectural semiology can finally be operationalized; in this way, it will have a real chance of succeeding as a promising, rigorous design-research project.

Conclusion

Parametric design starts with parametric variation. Variation can be employed for the differentiation of a field, layer or subsystem. To the extent to which this differentiation is rule-based (and gradual) rather than random, it establishes an order that might allow for orientation and navigation along its vector of transformation. Gradients as well as more complex rule-based differentiations allow for inferences from what is visible to what is not yet visible. A differentiated field or subsystem might become the substrate upon which the differentiation of further subsystems might be made dependent via functions or transcoding rules. As rule-based mappings these subsystems are representations of each other that allow inferences from one to the other (Note: the German word for mathematical function—*Abbildung*—literally means pictorial representation). The technique of associative modeling allows the crucial program layer to be treated as one more correlated subsystem in the multi-system parametric set-up, via a program distribution rule that correlates with the spatio-morphological (typological) differentiation of the design. However, the heuristics of Parametricism interpret the programs as parametrically variable event scenarios whereby the number, type, density and configuration of participants are pertinent variables that make a difference. This conception allows for gradual variation as well as inbetweening or hybridization of programs or event scenarios. This program layer is thus much more pertinently displayed and elaborated via crowd modeling than via the usual labeling or color coding of areas.

The ordered pattern of crowd behavior and interaction, i.e. the social life process, will be a correlate of the spatio-morphological built environment. This built environment in turn becomes a function and representation of the life processes it accommodates. And its functioning as a legible representation that becomes a communication is part and parcel of its very functioning, i.e. of the functioning of the accommodated life processes themselves. These life processes indeed require the organized and articulated system of spatial frames as a necessary precondition of their very formation and regular reproduction. Parametric design can enhance the density, intensity, complexity and thus productivity of contemporary life processes via the systematic enhancement of the built environment as a well-ordered, information-rich, perceptually tractable, and intuitively legible system of signification. The ultimate criterion of architectural design success resides in the built environment's social performance. This criterion can be operationalized via parameters like encounter frequency and interaction diversity observed in the built environment and anticipated within the parametric agent model.

References

Schumacher, P. (2012a). Tectonics—The Differentiation and Collaboration of Architecture and Engineering. In S. Polonyi, *Bearing Lines—Bearing Surfaces*. London: Edition Axel Menges.

Schumacher, P. (2012b). *The Autopoiesis of Architecture*, Vol.2: *A New Agenda for Architecture*. Hoboken, NJ: John Wiley & Sons.

2

Tabloid Transparency

Looking through Types, Legibility, Abstraction and the Discipline of Architecture

Andrew Zago and Todd Gannon

Architecture can only be political, that is, contribute to the production of another world, by being relentlessly attentive to its own discipline.

R.E. Somol

Contemporary architecture is in the throes of an unprecedented expansion of practice types, areas of expertise, and topics of interest. Though similar proliferations of specialized niches have occurred in fields ranging from engineering to music, architecture's unique responsibilities to society as both a service profession and a cultural discipline have produced more, and more problematic, internal divergences than in other fields. Today, one is more likely to speak of the concerns of "sustainability architects," "interior architects," or "healthcare architects," than to speak of the concerns of the field as a whole. Indeed, articulating such overarching concerns has become increasingly challenging, just as constructing productive conversations between architecture's internal specializations has become more difficult.

At issue in any discussion of nascent tendencies within architecture is the status of the field's conventions of communication, its habits of speech, its discourse. The difficulty of communicating disciplinary concerns to popular audiences is well known. Less often considered is the difficulty of communication within the field, which often suffers from a similar lack of linguistic common ground. Failing to recognize important shades of meaning in familiar terms, members of specialized sub-groups in architecture —both established and emerging ones—often fail to recognize, and thus to understand and respect, the contrasting ambitions, roles, and responsibilities of architecture's varied specializations. In short, many architects today simply do not speak the same language. What follows is an attempt to clarify some basic terminological distinctions in architecture, to outline some of the field's generally accepted and less often acknowledged responsibilities to society, and to sketch the contours of a few promising developments in architecture's recent contributions to culture.

Discourse Communities

Fields of cultural production, like all social groups, develop unique vocabularies to articulate shared ambitions, to identify novel forms that emerge as the field progresses, and, perhaps most importantly, to signal an individual's membership in that group. When associated with geographical regions and socio-economic classes, these clusters of linguistic habits are commonly known as dialects. Think of Swiss-German, Québécois French, or the distinctive speech patterns of the American South. Social groups defined by shared professional responsibilities or cultural interests also develop specific dialects, which in many cases are known (often derisively) by their jargon, as in "legalese" or "art-speak." Though sometimes bewildering to outsiders (and occasionally to the initiated), the curious inflections of meaning, structure, and syntax found in all dialects are both common and necessary. This proliferation of linguistic complexity enables not only nuanced description of topics important to the group but also the construction of the group's self-identity. The sophisticated dialects of numismatists, oenophiles, and skateboarders, for example, not only capture the intricacies of the currency, wines, and aerial maneuvers those groups esteem but also structure the very substance of the groups themselves. Submission to a dialect's vocabulary of expertise, authority, and authenticity constitutes one's membership in a group, while an ability to manipulate and direct that vocabulary establishes one's expertise. In sociology and linguistics, such groups often are referred to as "discourse communities" (Wallace, 2006; Schmidt & Vande Kopple, 1992).

Like many large discourse communities, architecture has developed sophisticated dialects (and many sub-dialects) to govern its internal communications and to represent itself to society. Replete with jargon, neologisms, and obscure syntax, architecture's dialects are as necessary to the field's development and they are befuddling to the uninitiated. Consider, for example, architecture's use of the word "transparency." As Colin Rowe and Robert Slutzky famously pointed out, the word has two main meanings in everyday English, one pertaining to material pellucidity, the other having to do with intellectual clarity (Rowe & Slutzky, 1976). To structure a particular formal debate within architecture, Rowe and Slutzky developed further inflections of the term. In architecture (at least in one of its more common sub-dialects), literal and phenomenal transparency now signify contrasting surface effects, the former having to do with the transmission of light through building materials, the latter having to do with the registration of multiple abstract patterns and illusory depth on building façades. Of course, Rowe and Slutzky used these terms not just to make categorical distinctions. More importantly, they used them to make value judgments. Literal transparency, they argued, was associated with the oblique compositional tendencies they denigrated in the work of Walter Gropius and others, and phenomenal transparency with frontal compositions, primarily those of Le Corbusier, which they supported.

Such proliferations of meaning are rampant in contemporary architecture and contribute to the difficulty of speaking of the field as a whole. Nonetheless, certain general observations can be made. One relates to architecture's ability to productively engage other disciplines and the wider world. Another has to do with the unlikely reemergence of legibility in a field long thought to have traded representational concerns for abstraction. But before turning our attention to these inflections, we must first establish an important distinction within the field, that between the profession and the discipline of architecture.

Profession and Discipline

The *profession* of architecture concerns itself with the advancement of the field as a reliable, affordable, and sustainable commodity, the *discipline* with its advancement as an art form. While those architects active in the discipline may well provide reliability, affordability, and sustainability, it is the discipline alone that takes responsibility for advancing the public imagination. This is not to say that those engaged primarily with professional concerns do not on occasion participate in architecture's cultural project, simply that when they do, they have supplanted a professional posture with a disciplinary one.

Compounding architecture's disciplinary responsibilities with the sheer size, permanence, and ubiquity of its professional output produces a unique form of politics unavailable to other art forms that also advance the public imagination. Though a person might easily avoid painting, literature, and other cultural artifacts (indeed, many do), no such option is available with regard to built form. Architecture's ubiquitous presence in the quotidian affairs of contemporary life affords it a unique political capacity irreducible to other forms of engagement, such as policy, advocacy, and social responsibility, which obtain in architecture as well as in related fields such as the political and social sciences.

Figure 2.1 illustrates the relationship of the discipline to the profession. Notice that the discipline is much smaller than the profession, lies partially outside it, and has a porous boundary. Its porosity owes to the fact that some practices work at times within and at others outside the discipline and the overlap to the fact that some extra-professional work (writing, drawing, etc.) affects architecture without being building per se. As the discipline is capable of things that the profession is not, the relationship is hierarchical. The discipline provides the evolving set of artistic concerns that, inevitably, even the most prosaic practice must draw from. This dependency is rarely acknowledged by the wider profession.

As with the broader profession, the discipline has splintered into numerous sub-interests. In the past, internal specializations within architecture such as engineering, landscape architecture, and urban planning spawned new, autonomous fields of expertise. The current proliferation of specializations may well continue to produce such distinct fields. The discipline, on the other hand, is first concerned with the interrogation and reinvention of architecture's own potentials and self-definition and only later with instrumentality in the wider world. Proliferating specializations within the discipline remain embedded in the structure of the field.

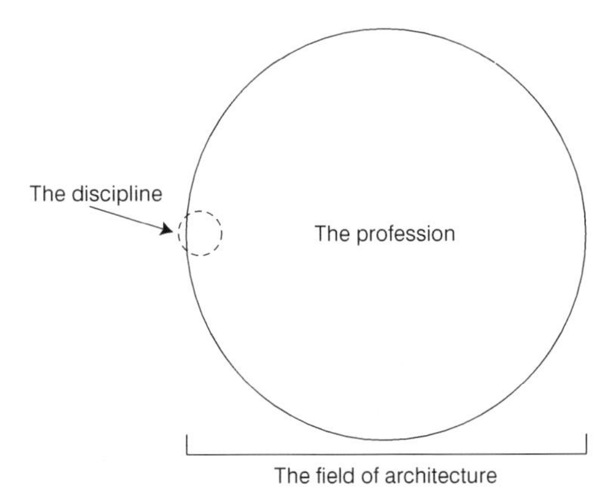

Figure 2.1 Diagram of the profession and the discipline, Andrew Zago

Though both the discipline and the profession organize social relations through the construction of buildings and both deploy drawings, models, diagrams, and other media to do so, their contrasting responsibilities to society point their activities in markedly different directions. The profession responds to society's immediate needs, where the discipline projects alternative possibilities for the future.

Most projects are presented to architects as problems to be solved at the level of the profession, that is, in response to society's immediate needs. Goals of course vary, but typically include functional and economic ambitions as well as site, budgetary, and programmatic constraints, among other concerns. To effectively address these challenges, architects apply the collective knowledge of the field as well as that of neighboring professions such as engineering and economics. Such relationships constructed between architecture and neighboring professions are commonly understood to be interdisciplinary. Within the discipline, on the other hand, interdisciplinarity is more complex. To project alternative possibilities to the public imagination, architecture often pursues interests parallel to those of other art forms, and at times finds itself allied with neighboring fields such as painting, literature, and philosophy, to project a shared cultural agenda. Interdisciplinarity in this sense operates not in the cause of pragmatic efficiency, but rather to open new avenues of interest for the field.

Despite these differences, it is important to insist that both the profession and the discipline be understood as advancing architecture as a *material practice*, even if the former's materiality is usually manifest in the durable physicality of buildings and the latter's often is found in more ephemeral media, including the seemingly (but not actually) immaterial flux of digital design software (Hayles & Gannon, 2012). Where the profession and the discipline deploy similar media, the former does so primarily in the cause of immediate societal needs (usually via constructed buildings), whereas the latter deploys architectural media (buildings included) as ends in themselves and to project alternative social relations. In other words, the profession instrumentalizes architectural media in order to serve society, while the discipline maintains the autonomy of those media in order to advance architecture's cultural ambitions.

Clients, Users, and Constituencies

There was a time when architecture was thought to address a single, general audience. Architects from Vitruvius to Le Corbusier imagined idealized subjects such as the Vitruvian Man and the Modulor Man as personifications of the collective audiences they wished to address. One of the more significant achievements of the past century of cultural production has been the critical demolition of such idealized subjectivities and with them, the hegemony of the generalized audiences they stood for. Recently, more vital groups have emerged around specific interests and proclivities within both the profession and the discipline. In the profession, increasingly complex demands have given rise to specialized service niches which address issues of programming, sustainability, accessibility, and branding as well as specific program types such as housing, prisons, hospitals, and schools. The clients who commission and finance such work, as well as the immediate users for whom the project is designed, may be understood as the direct recipient of a professional service.

The discipline, while it usually works at the behest of commercial clients and users, also addresses a broader constituency, which may or may not directly inhabit or use a building. The primary concern of such constituencies is not a *building's* accommodation of utilitarian functions but rather the *architecture's* contributions to ongoing cultural projects. Where a building's users and clients are usually proximate, architecture's cultural constituencies are increasingly dispersed. Effectively addressing them requires the discipline to be particularly attentive to the full range of architectural media. Not only is architecture's proliferation as and through media crucial to its ability to impact globalized cultural constituencies, but also, the integral role of such media in architecture's ontology must be taken into account if one wishes to take seriously questions of architecture's place in cultural production.

Where a building is a concrete physical object (as are drawings, models, photographs, texts, etc.), architecture as such, the dynamic complex of habits, techniques, biases, proclivities, and, importantly, values deployed by architects, is abstract, virtual, and ineffable. As literature is irreducible to books, architecture is irreducible to buildings. And, as a mode of cultural production as opposed to a class of buildings, architecture inhabits and activates an array of media, even if buildings remain a privileged focus of our efforts. Thus, to characterize the paper architecture of the 1970s or more recent forays by the discipline into the manipulation of digital environments, the construction of pavilions, or the programming of robots as somehow *less than* fully architectural, as some in the field do, is to fundamentally misunderstand architecture's ontology and woefully underestimate its potential as an agent of cultural production.

Such dismissive characterizations also fail to recognize the spectrum of constituencies that has arisen within and through architecture's recent disciplinary achievements. As in music, the diversity of audiences addressed by contemporary architecture has increased dramatically. In response, the discipline has evolved a host of specialized genres through which to address them. Given the breadth of interests, limitations of space, and the fact that many of these nascent tendencies are not yet fully formed, we will not attempt a comprehensive overview of such practices here. Instead, we will devote our remaining space to a discussion of themes with which the more promising of these new practices are all in some way grappling.

Legibility and Abstraction

The return to questions of legibility today can be seen in a wide sampling of contemporary work, including the neo-post-modernism of FAT (the now defunct practice led by Sam Jacob, Sean Griffiths, and Charles Holland), the frank clarity of typological forms in projects by Herzog and de Meuron or Atelier Bow Wow, and the regional symbolism deployed in recent projects by BIG, FOA (now split into AZPML and Farshid Moussavi Architecture), and others. At the same time, one sees a resurgent and diametrically opposed interest in overt, perhaps neo-modernist, abstraction, as in the fluid expressionism of Zaha Hadid Architects, the stark minimalism of John Pawson, or the seeming return to the themes of 1970s "paper architecture" in the work of young practices in Los Angeles, Chicago, and elsewhere.

In 2011, the principals of FAT made their case for a resurgent "Radical Post-Modernism" by calling into question Modernism's associations with abstraction. Citing observations by the novelist Gabriel Josipovici, they write,

> [T]he essential characteristics of Modernism can be limited to neither abstraction nor technological innovation and, indeed ... the kind of abstraction promoted by the likes of Abstract Expressionist high priest Clement Greenberg did not represent the essence of Modernism at all, but acted merely as a sign of it.

Modernism's key characteristic, they continue, was instead "the recognition of a loss of authority after the Reformation," which caused Modernist artists to adopt exactly the values pursued by the Post-Modernists of the 1970s, that is, "those of multiple authorship, multivalence, collage, quotation, and decentered authority" (FAT, 2011). Modernists, they claim, preached abstraction but in fact practiced Post-Modern legibility.

In this, the authors are half right. Though Greenberg certainly promoted Abstract Expressionists in the 1950s, he was by no means convinced of abstraction's necessity to Modernism. In a seminal 1960 essay, he wrote, "Abstractness, or the non-figurative, has in itself still not proved to be an altogether necessary moment in the self-criticism of pictorial art, even though artists as eminent as Kandinsky and Mondrian have thought so" (Greenberg, 1993). Indeed, it was self-criticism, not abstraction, that Greenberg saw as Modernism's essence. Self-criticism had to do primarily with self-definition, with establishing the "unique and irreducible" qualities of each art, which in painting issued from the flatness of the picture plane. For Greenberg, the key feature of Modern painting was not abstraction, but rather the *legibility* of a painting's irreducible flatness. Twenty years after Greenberg, Peter Eisenman addressed the question of Modernism in architecture and attempted a similar self-definition of the field. Once again, the central concern was legibility, not abstraction. Modernism, he argued, was distinguished by an "object's tendency to be self-referential" (Eisenman, 2004).

Indeed, for Eisenman, it was not just Modern architecture but architecture as such for which legibility was a necessary precondition. To distinguish itself from geometry, he argued, architecture required legible intentionality. To distinguish itself from sculpture, it required a legible relationship to function or use. Finally, to distinguish itself from building, architecture had to "overcome" its function through self-referential signification, as when a classical column both carries a load and simultaneously represents the act of structural support. Like Greenberg, Eisenman saw no need to include abstraction in his formulations. In his view, architecture does not, indeed *cannot*, deal in abstract forms such as planes and volumes. Rather, architecture's elements—walls, roofs, floors, et cetera—are always already legible signs associated with shelter, structure, or use. More than thirty years on, Eisenman's self-referential conception of Modern architecture remains more convincing than other views that understand Modern architecture as a visual style based on Platonic forms and blank surfaces. In Eisenman's (and, it turns out, Josipovici's) view, Modernism is not a style particular to a specific medium, but rather a pervasive cultural condition manifested across creative fields. As Eisenman put it, "Modernism is a state of mind" (Eisenman, 2004).

On this, the principals of FAT seem to agree, and indeed they see Post-Modernism not as a "disavowal of Modernism," but rather as "the continuation of it under different conditions and armed with new weapons" (FAT, 2011). They are also correct in their assessment that Modernist abstraction is not abstraction as such but rather a sign of abstraction. Their dismissal of abstract formal vocabularies on such grounds, however, is specious. The question is not whether abstraction has been achieved, but rather how to overcome architecture's pre-existing associations with shelter, structure, and use. FAT's neo-Post-Modernism works to overcome these associations by pointing beyond architecture toward other resonances with culture. Their outwardly referential project is served well by a formal vocabulary freighted with easily legible content. Eisenman's Modernism, on the other hand, works to overcome architecture's pre-existing associations by directing attention inward toward architecture's "unique and irreducible" qualities. At least through the 1970s, this self-referential project was best served by a vocabulary of elements with minimal symbolic associations.

The suitability of non-figurative vocabularies to disciplinary self-reflection by twentieth-century artists and architects is well known. Equally well known, is that by the 1960s, abstraction in both painting and architecture was on the verge of exhaustion. The reductive vocabularies of Mondrian and Corbusier, adopted by each as means to direct attention away from representational clichés toward core disciplinary questions in their respective fields, began, after decades of imitation, to appear as legible and clichéd as the symbolic vocabularies they had been developed to replace. By the 1970s, many architects had turned away from the Platonic forms of orthodox Modernism toward a vocabulary of legible historical types. For some, the use of identifiable typological forms was a means to counter Modernism's abstract self-reflections with overtly symbolic and often nostalgic outward associations (e.g. Jencks, 1977). Others wagered that an engagement with historical types offered the best chance to recover the exhausted disciplinary ambitions of Modernism. As Anthony Vidler explained in 1977,

> the issue of typology is raised in architecture, not this time with a need to search outside the practice for legitimation in science and technology, but with a sense that within architecture itself resides a unique and particular mode of production and explanation.
> (Vidler, 1998)

While Vidler claimed this new, "third typology" "refuses any 'nostalgia' in its evocations of history" (Vidler, 1998), subsequent productions demonstrated just how difficult it was to avoid nostalgia and sustain serious disciplinary reflection when using historical types. Indeed, even the formal abstraction of Eisenman and the New York Five was susceptible to charges of nostalgia, in their case for the historically identifiable vocabulary of Le Corbusier's *lait de chaux* villas of the 1920s and 1930s.

The dispute between "abstract" neo-Modernist autonomy and "legible" Post-Modernist engagement raged through the closing decades of the twentieth century. On one side, the unavoidable fact of legibility was embraced and used to sanction a broadly engaged populism. On the other, architects (particularly in the 1980s) allied themselves with philosophers such as Jacques Derrida not to evade legibility but rather to destabilize it an attempt to maintain architecture's inwardly focused autonomy. By the 1990s, new architectural interests rooted neither in populist legibility nor in autonomous abstraction began to come into focus. Terence Riley's 1995 exhibition, "Light Construction," at the Museum of Modern Art in New York, showcased an array of projects that focused instead on specific material effects, particularly those of glass. In 2008, the exhibition "Matters of Sensation," curated by Marcelo Spina and Georgina Huljich at Artists Space in New York, built on this renewed interest in material effects and directed attention toward architecture's affective, as opposed to representational, potential. The latter exhibition drew significant inspiration from the writings of Gilles Deleuze on Francis Bacon. In Bacon, Deleuze saw a painter who rejected both representation (what Deleuze referred to as "figuration") and abstraction as viable options for contemporary painting. Instead, Bacon deployed what Deleuze called "the Figure," which he described as "the sensible form related to a sensation; it acts immediately upon the nervous system, which is of the flesh, whereas abstract form is addressed to the head and acts through the intermediary of the brain" (Deleuze, 2003).

Through the 2000s, appeals to affective figures and visceral sensation (as opposed to indexical forms and conceptual intellection) were common in architecture, particularly among younger practitioners engaged in speculative projects executed in unbuilt work and gallery installations. At the same time, firms such as BIG and FOA began to make overt appeals to legible symbolic content, claiming to do so in order to seduce clients and competition juries. In an important 2005 text, Alejandro Zaera-Polo of FOA made a case for a "double agenda" that wedded the firm's longstanding interest in formal abstraction and indexical process with their clients' desire for legible symbolic identity (Zaera-Polo, 2005). Though Zaera-Polo attempted to distance his approach from the earlier Post-Modernist positions, his argument distinctly resonated with Charles Jencks' idea of "double-coding" (Jencks, 1977), and drew pointed responses from Sylvia Lavin and Jeffrey Kipnis. Lavin criticized Zaera-Polo's appeal to metaphors, which, she argued, were inevitably bound up with meaning and thus vulnerable to falsification. As an alternative, she proposed the use of seductive but ultimately meaningless forms "that have no logic of verifiability, truth, or even use," offering fishnet stockings and Pereira and Luckman's 1961 Theme Building at Los Angeles International Airport as examples (Lavin, 2005). Like Lavin, Kipnis also suggested non-signifying forms as an alternative to Zaera-Polo's mimetic paraphrase, arguing that these should aim to elicit irreducibly architectural effects. Though he offered Deleuze's reading of Bacon as a model for how such effects might be pursued (with the caveat that architecture could not achieve its ends by imitating painting), he noticed that Bacon's paintings did not fully overcome the legacy of abstraction due to the traces of the process of painting evident on the surface of his canvases. Better, in Kipnis's view, were recent works by Damien Hirst, Jeff Koons, and others that, by effacing all evidence of process, proved startlingly resistant to the clichés of both representation and abstraction. Works such as Koons' *Balloon Dog*, he argued,

> do not mean anything, they do not say anything, but neither are they silent. ... It is not that they have nothing to say, it is that they do not say; they belong to a world, to an ontology that has no place for saying, even as a possibility. This effect, made possible only by the figural, suggests an un-theorized power of the figure.
>
> (Kipnis, 2005)

Writing in 2005, Kipnis found little work on the figure in architecture beyond the writings of R.E. Somol. In the ensuing decade, a number of architects have taken up the problem. And if contemporary rehearsals of neo-Modernist abstraction and neo-Post-Modernist legibility appear ill-equipped to open new avenues of disciplinary exploration, these novel figural speculations signal just such a possibility.

Tabloid Transparency

To distinguish recent experiments with the figure in architecture from those pursued in painting and sculpture, we propose the term "tabloid transparency." In this, we take a cue from tabloid newspapers, in which the content is so vapid that it cannot possibly bear scrutiny as meaning. The presence of content provides raw materials to perception, while the vapidity of that content allows one's attention to shift toward the material fact of the tabloid as an object—to the letter forms, the patterning of dot-screen printing, the materiality of the paper, et cetera. Meaning in such works is so inconsequential that it collapses and, in effect, becomes transparent. In the object's absolute lack of ambiguity, questions such as, "What is this?" or "What does it mean?" are suspended. Thus, tabloid transparency does not proliferate ambiguities or otherwise destabilize meaning, but rather disarms it by rendering it insignificant. Where Deleuze aimed to bypass both abstraction and figuration via the Figure, tabloid transparency dissolves the obvious in order to access what might be referred to as the Abstract.

The Abstract, we submit, stands for an ineffable but nonetheless specific disciplinary condition, akin to Greenberg's "unique and irreducible" qualities, or Kipnis's "ontology that has no place for saying." Though closely linked to questions of form, the Abstract exceeds mere description of physical shapes. As an analogy, imagine an accomplished athlete, say, a competitive diver or gymnast. While such athletes are likely to be "in shape," their performance is ultimately judged in terms of good or bad "form." In this sense, form, as a function of the Abstract, *disciplines* physical shapes. Though a function of physical materials (e.g. paint and canvas, steel and glass) the Abstract cannot be reduced to its physical manifestation.

Where the distilled palettes of early twentieth-century painting and ideal geometries of early twentieth-century architecture were able, temporarily, to sustain the illusion of being "content-free," that is, of appearing to operate somewhere beyond language or indexicality, they ultimately collapsed into legibility. Ironically, abstraction precluded access to the Abstract. Equally ironically, tabloid transparency's awkward embrace of the banal legibility of cartoons, contortionists, funny faces, and other trivial figures points toward novel abstract achievements (i.e. Zago, 2010). Such projects do not attempt to evade meaning, but rather wager that overt triviality might render the question of meaning moot.

In the art world, the conundrum that links abstraction to figure is hilariously diagrammed in Mike Kelley's 1980 triptych, *Square, Tangents, and Cats*. The effect can also be seen in much of Kelley's later work as well as in Koons' *Balloon Dog* and other of his pieces. Koons and Kelley are typically understood as pursuing widely different, even antagonistic, ambitions, and both are well known for including overt narratives of their respective subjectivities in their work (cf. themes of autobiography and suppressed memory in Kelley and of seeming narcissism and ironic self-promotion in Koons). In the present context, however, both are notable for their keen understanding of their position within current and broader historical trends in the art world and for their cunning ability to leverage that knowledge toward the development of novel abstract effects. If the Post-Modern argument (in both architecture and art) holds that legibility is unavoidable and therefore should be embraced, works such as *Balloon Dog* and *Square, Tangents, and Cats* demonstrate that abstraction is equally ever-present and, in fact, more powerfully unavoidable. These works demonstrate that no amount of literalness can remove the fundamentally abstract nature of everything, and that the more obvious the content, the more efficiently it can offer access to the Abstract.

Since at least the late 1970s, a number of architects have deployed familiar forms to open similar avenues of exploration in architecture. Early experiments can be seen in James Stirling's use of typological forms at the Berlin Wissenschaftszentrum (1979–87). While one can easily identify the fortress, theater, and church forms in the building's plan and massing, the interior arrangement and façades both work to undermine the clarity of those type-forms. It is not that their historical significance is effaced, but rather that it is rendered inconsequential to Stirling's other organizational and material ambitions. This is particularly apparent in plan, where the interior organization often diverges sharply from the massing of the typologically legible volumes. With questions of quotation or meaning thus largely suspended, novel organizational and material possibilities, such as the axial connections constructed between the type-forms or the undulating shapes of the building's perimeter (rendered continuous with banded and cartoonishly flat stone surfaces) come to the fore.

Certain of Frank Gehry's projects from the same period operate similarly. At the Loyola Law School in Los Angeles (1979–84), Gehry deployed a collection of typologically legible forms—church, temple, basilica, et cetera—to accommodate a large expansion of the campus. Filtered through the lens of Modernist abstraction, Gehry's legible forms resonate with Vidler's idea of the "third typology." And, like contemporaneous works by Aldo Rossi, Georgio Grassi, and others, the strong associations between these forms and the programs they house (e.g., the relation of ancient basilica and temple forms to law courts) remain intact. In this, the project produces something akin to Jencks's idea of "double-coding," in which one's attention oscillates between the legibility of the shapes and the abstraction of their material and organizational effects. Gehry's Chiat/Day Building in Venice (1991), with its distinctive over-scaled binoculars by Claes Oldenburg and Coosje van Bruggen, comes closer to achieving tabloid transparency. The triviality of the binoculars undermines (but does not completely eradicate) one's ability to tie them to metaphorical narratives related to the program or context, and hastens a shift in attention to the object's unexpected voluptuousness. In more recent projects such as the Lewis House project near Cleveland, the Guggenheim Museum in Bilbao, or the Disney Concert Hall in Los Angeles, Gehry's formal sources, whether borrowed from painting, folded fabrics, billowing ship's sails, or allusions to the building's immediate context, are relaxed to the point of non-recognition. Though exhilarating, Gehry's recent work has become an identifiable signature, making it increasingly difficult to separate the abstract achievements of individual buildings from their legible associations with the architect. Something closer to the effect currently under discussion can be found in Gehry's serial use of various animal forms, such as fish and serpents, and more emphatically in his experiments with the form of the Horse's Head in the Lewis House, the DZ Bank in Berlin, and elsewhere (Lavin, 2006).

Herzog and de Meuron have conducted a similar series of experiments with the archetypal house form dating at least to their 1985 House for an Art Collector in Therwil, Switzerland. Here, as in their 1997 Rudin House in Leymen, France, the architects adopt the banal massing of a gable-roof house only to dissolve its prototypical associations through unconventional materials, detailing, and a curious disengagement from the ground. A number of other architects also have taken up the archetypal gable form in recent years, but in most cases, their projects fail to achieve the tabloid transparency found at the Rudin House. In MVRDV's Ypenburg Master Plan in The Hague (1998–2005) and Sou Fujimoto's House 7/2 in Hokkaido (2006), for example, clear associations to traditional ideas of "house" remain firmly intact and the projects ultimately fail to overcome the banality of their elements. These latter projects, and others like them, rely too strongly on reductive tactics, similar to the Platonic abstractions of the 1920s and 1930s, which have lost their efficacy and no longer offer a viable means of approaching the Abstract.

Herzog and de Meuron's achievements notwithstanding, most recent "typological" projects, as well as the commercial popularity and lack of significant disciplinary purchase of neo-Minimalism (whether manifest in John Pawson's luxury asceticism or *Dwell* magazine's fashionable populism), suggest that the discipline's reductive project of the early twentieth century, as well as its typological one of the late twentieth century, have been completed. Rather than rehearse well-known successes, today's more inventive practices have concerned themselves with other possibilities, particularly those that arise from complex geometries that superficially "look like something," left unexplored by earlier innovators. Johnston Marklee's House project for Ordos (2008), Jason Payne's Raspberry Fields project in rural Utah (2008), and Herzog and de Meuron's Vitrahaus in Weil am Rhein (2009) are promising examples. Though each begins with an archetypal gable form, each then aggressively manipulates that massing and deploys curious surface treatments to loosen familiar associations.

Whether deployed at the level of the element or the massing, the "content" of each of these projects is immediately apprehensible but, owing to its utter lack of ambiguity, quickly fades from attention to allow more sophisticated organizational and material effects to take over. In them, typological forms serve simply as a means of entry into a discussion of the Abstract. Of course, typology is but one way to enter into such discussions. Other methods,

Figure 2.2 Raspberry Fields (Jason Payne/Hirsuta, 2010)

such as cartoons or contortions, offer other ways, which Zago Architecture has explored in recent projects.

Though these latter tactics are sometimes nurtured as inevitable end-games by neo-Post-Modernists and are easily coopted by those interested in producing a kind of meta-critical irony, the projects to which we refer here deploy tabloid transparency and an interest in the Abstract to introduce a reinvigorated sense of *authenticity* into progressive architectural discourse. Tabloid transparency points toward the possibility of a post-ironic "stealth authenticity," which, by pressing the banal, the ordinary, and the dull into the service of the Abstract, avoids both the skepticism of neo-Post-Modernism as well as the well-known pitfalls of traditional authenticity.

Projecting Interdisciplinarity Outward

Armed with such a concept, architecture might finally begin to move beyond the longstanding insecurity felt by many architects over the field's relation to neighboring areas of cultural production. As we noted above, interdisciplinary collaboration has become a central feature of contemporary practice. Though it greatly increases the effectiveness of building design

Figure 2.3 Taichung City Cultural Center. Zago Architecture with Jonah Rowen, 2013

and construction, this very effectiveness has led to unfortunate consequences. Routine injections of efficacy from outside architecture have led many architects to view their own field as fundamentally inadequate. In the hands of some within the discipline, architecture has become little more than a thinly veiled paraphrase of philosophy, computer science, or studio art. In the profession, one finds engineering, sustainability, and humanitarianism overshadowing specifically architectural concerns. The effect is tantamount to draining the architecture from architectural projects. Feelings of disciplinary inadequacy have also inspired some architects to retreat from engagement with the broader world to aim exclusively at disciplinary concerns. Taken to extremes, this approach can result in isolation, acrimony, and, ultimately, irrelevance.

Today, though architecture enjoys a general admiration by society, it is difficult to find instances where a specifically architectural issue is recognized as making a valuable contribution to the world. This is not the case for law, engineering, medicine, or, for that matter, painting, music, literature, or any number of other fields. Though this state of affairs might be attributed to the fact that some of architecture's most potent effects operate beneath the threshold of conscious attention, a more convincing reason is that architecture tends to engage the world on the world's terms, not its own. As they generally are not seen to offer an immediate public health, safety, and/or welfare "service" to society, painting, music, literature, and other art forms are valued primarily for their specific disciplinary contributions, that is, for their form as opposed to their function. Architecture, on the other hand, though it offers society both functional "service" and formal enrichment, generally is understood solely in terms of the former, even though its greatest strengths issue from the latter. In short, most people (many architects included) miss architecture's point, and as a result, many architects have tacitly or explicitly accepted a position of apparent impotency and have constructed alternative constellations of values in compensation. R.E. Somol forcefully countered such tactics in a recent essay. "If architecture has lost its ability to operate in the world," he opines, "it's not because architecture has become too self-involved, but because it has not been attentive enough to its own protocols, techniques, and forms of knowledge." His argument hinges on the unrecognized potential of architecture's disciplinary abstractions. Too many architects, he continues,

> seem afflicted by the assumption that the abstractions of other fields are real (for example, the bookkeeping tricks that allowed Enron to count potential future profits as if they were actual—conceptual accounting?), while the abstractions of architecture are not. Architecture, if it is to operate in the world, first needs to overcome this reality envy of other fields, and take its own abstractions as literally as it accepts those of others.
> (Somol, 2012)

The form of disciplinarity we have outlined here, one not insulated by neo-Post-Modernism's ironic detachment but rather galvanized by stealth authenticity, offers a potent means to answer Somol's call to action. Though we respect architecture's very real and important professional responsibilities, we insist that the field's most valuable contributions to culture have been and will continue to be made in terms of architecture's disciplinary ambitions. Today, the discipline of architecture can best "serve" society by continuing to explore counterintuitive, risky, and abstract possibilities which for various reasons the profession is unable to explore. Only by taking seriously architecture's disciplinary responsibilities, and by relentlessly proliferating formal and rhetorical dialects through which to articulate them, can we meet architecture's obligation to "provoke other fields (ecology, law, economics, politics and policy, and so on) to challenge their own limitations that have been unconsciously and pervasively founded on ours" (Somol, 2012). Projecting architecture's abstractions on other fields, as opposed to absorbing those of other fields into our own, is a model for a new, more productive mode of interdisciplinarity, one founded not on pragmatic efficiency, aversion to risk, and the solution of known problems, but rather on counterintuitive experimentation, calculated risk-taking, and the invention of new problems from which new possibilities—of built form as well as political life—might emerge.

References

Deleuze, G. (2003). *Francis Bacon: The Logic of Sensation*. Minneapolis, MN: University of Minnesota Press.

Eisenman, P. (2004). Aspects of Modernism: Maison Domino and the Self-referential Sign. In P. Eisenman (Ed.). *Inside Out: Selected Writings 1963–1988*. New Haven, CT: Yale University Press.

FAT, Post-Modernism—An Incomplete Project (2011). Architectural Design: *Radical Post Modernism*. Hoboken, NJ: John Wiley & Sons, Inc.

Greenberg, C. (1993). Modernist Painting. In J. O'Brian (Ed.). *Clement Greenberg: The Collected Essays and Criticism, Volume Four, Modernism with a Vengeance, 1957–1969*. Chicago IL: University of Chicago Press.

Hayles, N.K. & Gannon, T. (2012). Virtual Architecture, Actual Media. In C. Greig Crysler, S. Cairns, and H. Heynen (Eds). *The SAGE Handbook of Architectural Theory*. London: Sage.

Jencks, C. (1977). *The Language of Post-modern Architecture*. New York: Rizzoli.

Kipnis, J. (2005). What We ~~Got~~ Need Is—Failure to Communicate. *Quaderns,* 245, 94–100.

Lavin, S. (2005). Conversations over Cocktails. *Quaderns,* 245, 88–93.

Lavin, S. (2006). Twelve Heads are Better than One. In B. Bergdoll & W. Oechslin (Eds.). *Fragments: Architecture and the Unfinished, Essays Presented to Robin Middleton*. London: Thames and Hudson.

Rowe, C. & Slutzky, R. (1976). Transparency: Literal and Phenomenal. In C. Rowe (Ed.). *The Mathematics of the Ideal Villa and Other Essays*. Cambridge, MA: MIT Press.
Schmidt, G.D. & Vande Kopple, W.J. (Eds.). (1992). *Communities of Discourse: The Rhetoric of Disciplines*. New York: Prentice Hall.
Somol, R.E. (2012). Shape and the City. *Architectural Design* 82, Special issue: City catalyst: Architecture in the Age of Extreme Urbanisation, 82, 5, 108–113.
Vidler, A. (1998). The Third Typology. In K.M. Hays (Ed.). *Architecture/Theory since* 1968. Cambridge, MA: MIT Press.
Wallace, D.F. (2006). Authority and American Usage. In *Consider the Lobster and Other Essays*. New York: Little Brown and Co.
Zaera-Polo, A. (2005). The Hokusai Wave. *Quaderns,* 245, 76–101.
Zago, A. (2010) Awkward Position. *"The Real" Perspecta 42: The Yale Architectural Journal* 205–218.

3

Spatial Choreography and Geometry of Movement as the Genesis of Form

The Material and Immaterial in Architecture

Juhani Pallasmaa

Complexity of Architecture

Buildings are usually regarded and conceived as material objects of differing degrees of functional, organizational and formal complexity. The design process is normally understood as a conceptual and rational problem-solving task, which develops towards an aesthetic resolution through a distinct rational design logic. Yet, architecture is a hybrid and "impure" discipline, as its practice contains and fuses ingredients from conflicting and irreconcilable categories, such as material structures and mental intentions, engineering and aesthetics, physical facts and cultural beliefs, knowledge and dreams, means and ends. This internal complexity is characteristic to architecture, and it calls for specific methods and approaches, which combine rationality and emotion, logic and intuition, scientific reasoning and embodied artistic creativity. Alvar Aalto (1898–1976), the Finnish master architect, acknowledges the complex and contradictory essence of architecture, and assigns the main role in the design process to an artistic synthesis.

> In every case [of creative work], opposites must be reconciled [...] Almost every formal assignment involves dozens, often hundreds, sometimes thousands of conflicting elements that can be forced into functional harmony only by an act of will. This harmony cannot be achieved by any other means than art.
>
> (Aalto, 1997a)

An architectural design task may extend from a single room to extensive and complex entities, such as manufacturing plants, airports and hospitals, for instance. In such extensive buildings, the design process itself is usually dominated by strict technical, functional, and performance requirements, arising from the specific purpose of the building, i.e. movements of people, materials, vehicles and services, or the detailed performance of various processes from the industrial production line to security systems, patient treatments, and surgical operations. In the case of a factory, the architectural envelope usually follows closely the outlines of the processes and machine lay-outs optimized by process engineers. An impressive example of the significance of spatial thinking in design is the case of the Varkaus Papermill designed by Gullichsen-Kairamo-Vormala Architects, Helsinki, in 1975–85. The architects were able to shorten the huge main volume of the papermill by nearly a hundred meters by redesigning the process three-dimensionally instead of the standard two-dimensional layout of the process engineers.

Yet, only structures with little daily human involvement in their operation, such as highly automated storage structures, or power plants, can be designed on the basis of their rationalized and mechanized operations. Usually architectural tasks contain both technical and rational aspects and various psychological, sensory and emotive requirements. In most types of buildings, human factors, such as ergonomic, physiological, psychological, atmospheric, experiential and symbolic issues actually guide the design process more than any purely mechanical, rational and measurable properties. However, research has made it clear, that the experiential qualities and ambience of any working place has an impact on work efficiency and the mental wellbeing of the workers. It is also evident that even hospitals serve their purpose best, if the experiential atmosphere of their architecture supports processes of healing. Yet, until our time, hospital designs have mainly been rationalized from the perspective of the medical processes and personnel, rather than the individual experiential reality of the patient. Alvar Aalto confesses that at the time he began the design of the legendary Paimio Sanatorium in Finland (1929–1933), he was ill himself and he realized suddenly that the hospitalized patient experiences the hospital setting primarily from a horizontal position. He decided to design the patient rooms for "the horizontal man": "The room design is determined by the depleted strength of the patient, reclining in his bed. The color of the ceiling is chosen for quietness, the light sources are outside the patient's field of vision, the heating is oriented towards the patient's feet, and the water runs soundlessly from the taps to make sure that no patient disturbs his neighbour" (Schildt, 1994). This simple empathic insight led Aalto to design a hospital that is uniquely supportive of healing processes. The architect himself suggests that the sanatorium was designed as "a medical instrument". The general layout and plan solution reflect contemporaneous medical ideas, such as locating the sanatorium in a pine forest, permitting the patients to be outdoors in the sunlight and take walks in the surrounding forest, whereas rooms, equipment and objects were designed for maximum hygienic requirements. Designing the spaces and objects ergonomically, experientially and aesthetically pleasing was yet another aspect of the architect's aspiration. Somewhat later, Aalto extended the lesson of his hospital project to architectural design in general: "Every decision is in some way a compromise which can be attained most readily if we concider human beings at their weakest" (Aalto, 1997b). Instead of supporting a purely intuitive artistic design approach, Aalto wanted to expand the rational method to include even phenomena explored in the fields of neurophysiology and psychology:

> My aim was to show that real Rationalism means dealing with all questions related to the object concerned, and to take a rational attitude also to demands that are often dismissed as vague issues of individual taste, but which are shown by more detailed analysis to be derived partly from neurophysiology and partly form psychology. Salvation can be achieved only and primarily via an extended concept of Rationalism.
>
> (Aalto, 1997b)

Respectively, educational buildings from minute school houses to university complexes, perform well as settings for learning only if they project an appropriately stimulating, inspiring and focusing ambience. Buildings for museums, concert halls and other cultural institutions, need to provide not only the technical and functional circumstances, such as appropriate illumination, air qualities, or acoustic conditions, but they also need to provide specific psychological, perceptual and sensory conditions for the appreciation and enjoyment of the art form in question. Finally, in order to serve as spaces for the purposes of religion and faith, religious buildings have to project an air of meditative focus and sacredness, in addition to the functional requirements largely determined by liturgical traditions.

Architecture, Mechanization and Performance

The architectural structure is a container and facilitator of given activities. However, in the technologized world, the tectonic and spatial structure has to be complimented by an increasing number of technical systems in order to create the required internal climate, and provide the required technical services from appropriate temperature and humidity to conditions of acoustics and illumination. This concerns practically all building types of the technological era. Since the nineteenth century, the role and relative cost of these technical systems have kept growing, and in his well-known essay "A Home is Not a House" of 1965, Reyner Banham (1922–88), one of the leading architectural critics of the time, predicted that the mechanical systems will eventually replace architecture as it has been historically understood (Banham, 1965).

New material technologies have expanded the notion of technical performance to various structural elements, materials and surfaces, sometimes functioning beyond the limits of human perception in a nanometric scale, such as the surface structure of self-cleaning glass. The recent concept of "intelligent buildings" refers to architectural structures whose intended performance is self-regulated to react automatically to different external and internal conditions and their dynamic changes. As architectural expression has largely been based on historically evolved typologies, structures and formal themes—the traditional architectural language—the fast development of technologies related with construction, challenges this inherited language. Although computerized design and production, as well as algorithmic, parametric and computational design processes have opened up entirely new possibilities for creating complex spaces and forms, these methods tend to weaken the experiential and mental meaning of architecture, although the use of computational methods does not exclude intuitive and empathetic judgement. The human fact is that architectural meaning cannot be invented or fabricated, as it is bound to echo the encounter of architecture and the human embodied and historically and culturally determined mind. Architectural meaning arises from the human experiential ground and existential themes, not formal inventions

Altogether, there are architectural tasks in which the rational, utilitarian and measurable realities dominate, and others were experiential, and mental properties and qualities are constitutive. Yet, any architectural structure that engages human beings needs to respond to relevant human needs and expectations—the structures have to become part of the reality of "the flesh of the world," to use a notion of philosopher Maurice Merleau-Ponty (1908–61) (Merleau-Ponty, 1969). Architectural projects cannot be predetermined, and we can conclude that every architectural entity arises from an interaction and dialectics of the material and immaterial, technical and human, action and structure, rationality and irrationality, definability and undefinability. Today's "performative architecture," a design approach that is methodically projected to respond precisely to carefully analyzed functions and requirements of performance, aspires to increase the definability, predictability and certainty in the design process, and consequently, the architectural entity itself. Also the currently crucial requirements for sustainability call for a precise identification, understanding and control of the countless aspects and consequences of the design process, both positive and negative, desirable and undesirable. The entire process from the resources and materials, fabrication and construction to use, eventual dismantling and re-use has to be understood and controlled.

Architecture as Meaning and Expression

An architectural design task aims at a physical structure that is appropriate for its utilitarian purpose. But at the same time of being an actual frame for the activities, the construction is also a mental depiction or metaphor of this very activity. Each aspect of a building channels, guides and articulates action and intentionality, often outside our consciousness, but it also gives these actions specific meanings and qualities. Architecture and built settings frame landscapes, urban settings and life situations, and establish specific horizons of experiencing and understanding them. Besides, architecture articulates and expresses our being in the world; every construction reveals the builders' views of the world although they are mostly unconsciously experienced. We experience ourselves as well as our culture and world articulated by architecture. Our built structures mirror both our internal mental world and our understanding of the external world around us. Every building is a microcosm, a constructed world. As Merleau-Ponty suggests, "We come not to see the work, but the world according to the work" (Merleau-Ponty, 2010). The philosopher speaks here of artistic works, but his claim applies equally to architectural works. Louis Kahn spoke of "human institutions", referring to the multitude of societal and cultural structures and values, which are brought to our awareness and made visible through architecture. The various institutions of political and economic power, production and culture, as well as social hierarchies, are legible in the architectural narrative of every city. Thus architecture is inherently an epic art form. We even understand the course of time primarily through the temporal layering of historical structures. Buildings are markers of the depth of time and they narrate the story of cultural development. We feel safe and invigorated in settings that speak of time and lived life, because they reinforce our confidence in the continuum of time.

Spatial Choreography

All architectural structures are forms of spatial choreography that guides action; space facilitates or prohibits, encourages or prevents, invites or inhibits. This choreography predetermines patterns of movement and behavior, but it also guides experiential characteristics, perceptions, imageries, emotions and feelings. A sensitive and empathic designer intuits human behavior and desire, and this intuitive architectural scripting resonates with the actual user/occupant's natural and instinctual needs and intentions. While designing a house, the designer lives, uses and feels the non-existent house in his imagination on behalf of the future dweller. A correctly placed window is located exactly where the occupant wishes to look out into the garden, or where daylight is needed. The stairway is located where the dweller wishes to enter the floor above or below. Successful architecture does not need manuals or signage for its use, as it reveals its very structure and use in a wordless embodied manner. A profound building is an extension of human bodily and mental actions and capabilities.

Architectural spaces, configurations and details are always invitations to specific actions, and they are also promises of distinct human fulfillment. Instead of being nouns, true architectural encounters are verbs which invite and guide action. The door frame, or the door as an object is not the essence of the door. Opening the door, sensing its protective weight and passing through the doorway from one spatial realm to another, reveal the essence of the door, its very "door-ness," and turns the encounter into a genuine architectural experience. Similarly, a window opening and the window frame are not true essences of the window; looking through the window at a tree outside, or a distant mountain range, and permitting light to enter, reveal the "window-ness" of the architectural device, and turn this active participation into a true architectural experience. The essences of the door and the window lie in their mediating tasks. Architectural elements have their motifs in practicalities of life and action, but they also have their mental projections and meanings. Architectural images echo their primordial and historical origins and they articulate conventions by giving them new meanings. The floor, roof, wall, stairway, hearth/stove, bath/shower, table and the chair have similarly their origins, architectural essences and specific emotive charges. The table is usually seen as a mere furnishing item outside the realm of architecture, but the table, particularly the table for meals or important encounters, has a powerful mental role as a focusing center, which gathers the people together and represents the nourishing meal and the collectivity of the family or the party.

Architectural images arise from the acts of dwelling and celebration. The first imagery expresses and articulates the utility of the structure, whereas the latter concretizes its mythical, cultural and symbolic values. Philosopher Ludwig Wittgenstein (1889–1951) makes a significant argument: "Architecture immortalizes and glorifies something. Hence there can be no architecture where there is nothing to glorify" (Wittgenstein, 1998). As our quasi-rational and materialist culture deliberately eliminates higher metaphysical and mental meanings from construction, the question arises, is there anything in our materialist life style to celebrate and glorify?

Primary Meanings

Ontologically, the floor is the first element of architecture. The floor invites us to stand up, or perhaps, to dance, or to place a table and a chair upright on this horizontal plane for a reunion or a meal. When Edmund Hillary was asked what was the most difficult moment in his first climb to the top of Mount Everest in 1953, his surprising answer was: to find a horizontal plane to set up the tent (Blomstedt, *c.* 1960). It is the horizontal plane that makes human life possible and horizontal planes in the landscape are frequently signs of human culture. The horizontality of the floor is also a powerful expression of its "floor-ness", whereas the roof creates a protective cover and shadow inviting us to calm down, feel safe, and rest under this protective gesture.

The stair is the heart of the house, the tireless muscle that keeps circulating inhabitants up and down between the floors of the house. But ascending and descending are not equal experiences. All ascension is eventually bound to lead to the heaven, whereas the ultimate end of all descent is the underworld. The primordial meanings of up and down as well as other spatial situations still carry an echo in our mental imagery. Sigmund Freud's and Carl G. Jung's dream symbolisms reveal these ultimate meanings of the stairway. It is crucial to understand that here we are not engaged with conventional symbolization, but the inherent and internal reactions arising from human embodiment, historicity and being in the world. Our embodied life situation gives specific and implicit meanings to spatial experiences, such as up and down, above and below, left and right, in front and behind, ascension and descent. Our existence in the world is structured by being integrated with the "flesh of the world," to use a notion of Merleau-Ponty (Merleau-Ponty, 1969).

The most powerful architectural experiences arise directly from our embodied way of existing. Such embodied meanings also have their inherent roles in the metaphoric meanings and structures of language, as Mark Johnson and George Lakoff have shown in their book *The Metaphors We Live By* (Johnson & Lakoff, 1980). Altogether, explicit symbols are cultural conventions and agreements, and they lack the innate emotive content and psychic power which could initiate and guide our emotions. Only reactions that arise from, or touch upon the primal, primordial and preconscious layers of our mind can release mental energies that move us deeply. They also help us to experience ourselves as whole and integrated beings.

One of the reasons why modern architecture has lost much of its expressive and emotional power, is surely that its "perceptual and experiential ingredients," or its "primary images," have lost their ontological identities and emotional charges; floor and roof have become identical horizontal planes, and the door and the window have turned into equal holes in the wall surface. The disappearance of the door and window frame have also decisively weakened their emotive impact. An automatically opening all-glass door does not project any emotive meaning, it expresses only instrumentalization and convenience. The obsession with comfort in modern life—today architecture is often identified with comfort—eradicates experiential meaning and turns life into a parody akin to Jacques Tati's cinematic portrayals of modernity. "Home has become mere horizontality," Gaston Bachelard laments (Bachelard, 1969), and he quotes Joe Bousquet's sad description of the modern man: "He is a man with only one story: he has his cellar in his attic" (Bachelard, 1969).

Another reason for the loss of meaning lies in the regrettable understanding of abstraction as a visual, stylistic and aesthetic quality instead of regarding it as an internal process of compression and condensation in the creative act. Artistic meaning is intensified through compressing meaning rather than reducing it. Constantin Brancusi, the master sculptor, states convincingly: "Simplicity is not an end in art, but one arrives at simplicity in spite of oneself, in approaching the real essence of things. Simplicity is at bottom complexity and one must be nourished on its essence to understand its significance" (Shanes, 1989).

Seamless functionality and perfect comfort are not self-evident aims in architecture. In his early Azuma House in Osaka (1975–1976) Tadao Ando (1941–) separates the living space and the bedroom of this tiny house by a courtyard obliging thus the inhabitants to cross the outdoor space several times every day in order to experience the climate and weather. He makes a significant comment on the dialectics of function and form: "I am interested in discovering what new life patterns can be extracted and developed from living under severe conditions […] I believe in removing architecture from function after ensuring the observation of functional basis. In other words, I like to see how far architecture can be removed from function. The significance of architecture is found in the distance between it and function" (Ando, 1982).

Geometry of Movement

Due to the nature of the processes of assembly, from which architectural structures arise, constructed spaces and forms are most often angular, as the inherent tectonic language of construction as well as furniture and other interior objects tend to be angular and rectangular. It is clear that human movement and action is hardly ever angular, and it follows flowing, fluid and continuous patterns. Movement and action has most often a dance-like smoothness and continuous pattern. In sensitive architecture this inherent conflict is turned into a positive contrast and friction. The spontaneous paths and rhythms of human movement are set in a positive tension with the angular and rigid boundaries of space. Contrary to hasty assumptions, human movement tends to lose some of its dynamic expressiveness when taking place in plastically molded spaces. This observation arises from the crucial significance of counterpoint in perceptual phenomena. Counterpoint is an essential perceptual and artistic device, which implies an expressive juxtaposition and dialogue between foreground and background, active and passive, plastic and planar, organic and geometric, container and contained.

The use of fluid, plastic and organicist forms, as in the case of the works of Antonio Gaudi, Hans Scharoun, Alvar Aalto, Frank Gehry, and Zaha Hadid has given rise to impressive spaces and forms, but this choice is stylistic and formal rather than motivated rationally by the fluidity of human movement and action. Today's computerized and computational design methods, as well as new technologies of construction have given rise to increasingly fluid and continuous spaces, forms and surfaces. Complexly plastic and organicist forms have even turned into a contemporary fashion, which is often associated with artistic radicality and the notion of the avant-garde. However, fluid spaces and shapes tend to strengthen the perceptual reading of a singular, continuous object or space, and this is bound to weaken the counterpoint of spatial and formal units, scales and details. Geometry and form, space and action, structure and construction, entity and detail, are essential dualities of architecture and they have their own internal logic and dialectics. It needs to be reminded that architectural constructions are not abstractions as they derive from and communicate with the users in their embodied and bio-cultural essence. Architecture is fundamentally a specific existential and aesthetic articulation and expression of our being in the world.

Empathic Design

A significant aspect of design, which is regrettably rarely talked about or taught in architecture schools, is the designer's capacity for empathy. As I studied architecture at the Helsinki University of Technology in the late 1950s and early 1960s, my professor and mentor Aulis Blomstedt (1906–1979) used to say in his lectures: "For an architect, the capacity to imagine human situations is more significant than the gift of fantasizing spaces" (Blomstedt, *c.* 1960). As an experienced architect he contrasted human interactions and architectural space, the experiential essence of space and its formal or aesthetic qualities. A direct aesthetic preoccupation tends to result in purely visual and often somewhat sentimental aesthetic quality, whereas true and mysterious beauty arises from other concerns and aspirations. Beauty should not be turned into a conscious aim in design; it usually arises unintentionally from a fully resolved entity. Joseph Brodsky even criticizes *Cantos* by Ezra Pound, another great poet, for his tendency to aim at beauty: "[...H]e hadn't realized that beauty can't be targeted, that it is always a by-product of other, often very ordinary pursuits" (Brodsky, 1992).

It is helpful to make a distinction between formal or projective imagination, on the one hand, and empathic imagination, on the other, in the design process. The first is capable of imagining a geometric shape, or a topological configuration in space, whereas the latter is also capable of imagining its perceptual, experiential, emotional, and mental impact. The first imagines the object itself, whereas the latter imagines it as a lived experience. The limited projective imagination tends to lead to formalism, whereas empathic imagination is capable of operating with form, material, texture, illumination, and human situations as lived realities in imaginative space. To imagine real life situations seems to be difficult for human imagination. "The composite city of your subconscious [...] is empty because for an imagination it is easier to conjure architecture than human beings," Brodsky (1995) argues. This seems to be often the case in architectural design; contemporary buildings are frequently formalist exercises that exclude life. Yet, writers, theater directors and filmmakers imagine vivacious life situations and human interactions. This capacity, in fact, is the very core of their art. The fact that the imagination of architects seems to focus on buildings as physical objects rather than the life taking place in them, may largely arise from the traditionally exclusive visual emphasis in the art of architecture. "Why is it that architecture and architects, unlike film and filmmakers, are so little interested in people during the design process? Why are they so theoretical, so distant from life in general?", the Dutch filmmaker Jan Vrijman asks provocatively (Vrijman, 1994). Are the limitations of imagination of the real life situations in architectural design also a consequence of the overly heavy burden of rational criteria extending from legal issues, regulations, and standards to logistical and technical complexities? Isn't architecture forced to become increasingly a problem-solving task rather than an existential and poetic exploration?

Designing for the Other

It seems to be a common assumption, that the architect imagines the reality of his/her project on behalf of the client, or the unknown other. I believe, however, that we can only imagine and sense our own feelings, and consequently, the designer has to internalize the client or the other and feel the impact of the imagined structures through him/herself in the momentarily adapted role of the other. The inevitable conclusion of this is that a responsible designer has to design the object or building for himself in the internalized role of the future user, and hand the completed work as a gift to the real occupant in the end of the process. I wish to suggest that profound architecture is always a gift, as it materializes ideals, intentions and dreams, which did not consciously exist before they became thematized and materialized in the building itself through the creative process. A profound building always achieves more than it has been expected to do.

Paul Valéry, the poet, makes a beautiful remark on the architect's sense of empathy in one of his dialogues. In the dialogue *Eupalinos, or The Architect,* Phaedrus describes the care by which Eupalinos proceeded in his design process:

> He gave a like care to all the sensitive points of the building. You would have thought that it was his own body he was tending ... But all these delicate devices were as nothing compared to those which he employed when he elaborated the emotions and vibrations of the soul of the future beholder of his work.
>
> (Valéry, 1956)

Later Eupalinos confesses, "My temple must move men as they are moved by their beloved" (Valéry, 1956). As in an affectionate human relationship, a significant architectural space stimulates and strengthens our most subtle and humane qualities.

Although we believe to be rational beings with a scientific world view, we continue to live mentally in an animistic world, and we feel the emotive essences of things and objects, as if we were dealing with other living beings. "Be like me," is the call of every poem, as Joseph Brodsky suggests (Brodsky, 1997). The recent neurological invention of mirror neurons helps us to understand how we are able to feel the emotions of another individual, and to experience deep emotion and existential meaningfulness when listening to music, contemplating an abstract painting, or confronting a profound piece of architecture. Indeed, great works of art and architecture enable us to experience emotions and feelings, which we would not be able to feel ourselves alone, and great architecture makes us more sensitive and responsible human beings.

During the past two decades, we have been living in the era of unforeseen architectural hubris and euphoria. The computerized methods of design and construction have made almost any imaginable structure and shape practically possible. At the same time, however, architecture has increasingly become an autonomous realm of formal and technical imagination and invention without connections with traditions, human bio-historical essence, or the realities of place and culture. My firm belief is that today architecture needs to be reconnected with its own origins and limits as well as the natural boundaries of human experience and feeling.

The responsibility of the architect is too wide and deep to justify an architecture that only aims at enticing imagery and the architect's self-expression. Fred Gage, neurobiologist and geneticist, makes clear the significance of the architect's work:

> While the brain controls our behaviour and genes control the blueprint for the design and structure of the brain, the environment can modulate the function of genes and, ultimately, the structure of our brain. Changes in the environment change the brain, and therefore they change our behaviour. In planning the environments in which we live, architectural design changes our brain and behaviour.
>
> (Gage, 2015)

References

Aalto, A. (1997a). Art and Technology. In Göran Schildt (Ed.), *Alvar Aalto In His Own Words*. Helsinki, Finland: Otava Publishing Company, 174.

Aalto, A. (1997b). Rationalism and Man. In Göran Schildt, (Ed.), *Alvar Aalto in His Own Words,* Helsinki, Finland: Otava Publishing Company, 92.

Ando, T. (1982 May). The Emotionally Made Architectural Spaces of Tadao Ando, *The Japan Architect*, 9.

Bachelard, G. (1969). *The Poetics of Space.* Boston: Beacon Press, 27

Banham, R. (1965, April). The Home is Not a House, *Art in America*, Vol. 53, 70–79.

Blomstedt, A. (c.1960). Memorized quote from a lecture at The Helsinki University of Technology.

Brodsky, J. (1992). *Watermark.* London: Penguin Books, 70.

Brodsky, J. (1995). A Place as Good as Any, *On Grief and Reason* New York: Farrar, Straus and Giroux, 38, and 43

Brodsky, J. (1997). An Immodest Proposal, *On Grief and Reason.* New York: Farrar, Straus and Giroux, 206.

Gage, F. (2015). Neuroscience and Architecture, as quoted in Melissa Farling, From Intuition to Immersion, *Mind in Architecture,* Sarah Robinson and Juhani Pallasmaa (Eds). Cambridge, MA: MIT Press, 183.

Johnson, M., & Lakoff, G. (1980). *The Metaphors We Live By*. Chicago, IL: The University of Chicago Press.

Merleau-Ponty, M. (1969). In C. Lefort (Ed.), *The Intertwining—The Chiasm: The Visible and the Invisible.* Evanston, IL: Northwestern University Press.

Merleau-Ponty, M. (2010). As quoted in Iain McGilchrist, *The Master and His Emissary: The Divided Brain and the Making of the Western World.* New Haven, CT and London: Yale University Press, 409.

Pallasmaa, J. (2002). The Lived Metaphor, *Primary Architectural Images*, seminar Document 2001/2002, St. Louis, MO: School of Architecture, Washington University in St.Louis, 2–10.
Schildt. G. (1994). *Alvar Aalto A Life's Work—Architecture, Design and Art.* Helsinki, Finland: Otava Publishing Company, 69.
Shanes, E. (1989). *Constantin Brancusi,* New York: Abbeville Press, 106.
Valéry, P. (1956). Eupalinos, or the Architect, *Paul Valéry: Dialogues*, trans. William McCausland Stewart. New York: Pantheon Books, 74.
Vrijman, J. (1994, January). Filmmakers, Spacemakers, *The Berlage Papers*, 11, pages unnumbered.
Wittgenstein, L. (1998). *Culture and Value*, G.H. von Wright in collaboration with Heikki Nyman (Eds.). Oxford: Blackwell, 74.

4

Cognitive Design Thinking and Research in Design and Practice

Evidence-based Design

David Wang

The terms "design thinking" and "evidence-based design" are all well known in the literature. This chapter addresses architectural research with these terms, as a function of cognition, in mind. There is increasing recognition in the design fields that intuitive design activity is aided by cognitive processes. This chapter addresses ways in which this linkage holds true.

The dictionary defines research as "studious inquiry or examination; especially: investigation or experimentation aimed at the discovery and interpretation of facts, revision of accepted theories or laws in the light of new facts, or practical application of such new or revised theories or laws" (Merriam-Webster Dictionary, n.d.). Four features stand out in this definition, and it would be good to itemize them before we consider how they can be adapted for architectural research.

First, we can take "studious inquiry or examination" to mean *systematic* inquiry; indeed, other dictionary definitions for research use the word system (for instance, the OED) (Oxford English Dictionary, n.d.). Research, then, is not simple fact finding, as in going to Sweet's Catalogue and identifying all the manufacturers for window walls. This is not to demean the design professional's responsibility to be educated about available product lines for a particular application. But this is fact finding. If we are to be serious about what architectural research entails, we must respect what research has been taken to mean in wide swaths of the professional and academic domains. It means a mode of inquiry such that the process of research is itself a systemic framework; it is itself an ordered, logical process generating new knowledge; it is itself, therefore, the subject of theory and analysis (hence this chapter).

Second, then, research aims at "new facts ... new or revised theories or laws." The emphasis here is on *new*. It may be argued that by learning about window walls in Sweet's, I have gained new knowledge. But new knowledge in a research context does not just mean new knowledge for me (or for you) of existing facts we did not previously know. It means knowledge that does not yet exist in the literature. Thus the results of research yield new knowledge for all. Hence it is knowledge that the researcher contributes to, and hence expands, the literature on that subject. To be more grandiose, knowledge coming out of research is new knowledge the researcher gives to the world.

The third feature: research stands in intimate relation to "theories and laws." Almost all research builds on existing theories. This means getting to know those theories and laws—otherwise known as getting to know the relevant literature—well; and critically appraising those theories and laws for ways in which they can be added to, or modified. One of the decisive challenges for architects doing research is what I call the "let there be light and there is light" mentality. The architectural mind is fundamentally a creative mind. Creative minds tend to say that something is so, therefore it just is so. Creative minds instinctually see no merit in systematically learning about existing findings when approaching a design problem. For instance, Bryan Lawson has observed that designers prefer the "thinnest information possible" when it comes to design briefs (Lawson, 2005). This kind of inclination is usually a deterrent to disciplined research which, again, builds on established theories and laws to expand, revise, or otherwise enrich, our knowledge. I will explain in what follows that the design-oriented mind is not antithetical to research; the need is to find how the latter can enrich the former. Suffice it now to say this: when we use the well-traveled term "evidence-based design," evidence means something empirical—that is, something measurable, something observable, something documented, something other than the designer's purely subjective inclinations—by which a design decision is informed. Researchers use the word *intersubjective* to denote this requirement: research findings are based upon data that is mutually (read: intersubjectively) understandable among at least a peer group of persons, if not among a much wider general audience.

The fourth feature of the above definition: the "practical *application* of such new or revised theories or laws," italics added. Research yields knowledge that applies beyond a single case of X; instead, the new knowledge can be applied to, or is relevant for, many or all cases of X. The term for this is *generalizability*. And because researchers want their findings to be generally applicable to cases beyond the case under study, they are concerned with *internal validity* (i.e., that the logic of the research framework itself is sound) and *external validity* (i.e., that the outcomes of the research can be confidently applied to similar cases in an inductive manner).

Given the four features of research just outlined, the chart in Table 4.1 displays the inherent tensions that exist between design activity and research inquiry.

Overall differences between design outcomes and research outcomes should be self-evident in the chart. But perhaps the second pair best encapsulates the tension. While research thinking relies heavily on deduction and induction, design thinking prominently features abduction. In his book *Design Thinking,* Nigel Cross cites the philosopher C. S. Pierce in regards to abductive logic: "Deduction proves that something *must* be … abduction suggests that something *may*

Table 4.1 Differences Between Design Outcomes and Research Outcomes

Design	*Research*
Asks what to do?	Asks what is the case?
Action based on abduction or polemics	Action based on deduction and induction
Results in a material object	Results in a conceptual system
Site-specific	Independent of locale
Outcome is one-of-a-kind	Outcome fits into a literature
Presumes human freedom	Presumes a causal (at least a systemic) world

be" (Cross, 2011). Explained another way, Kees Dorst describes deductive and inductive logic as explaining and predicting "phenomena already in the world," while in the abductive logic of the design professions, the goal is to "create valuable new things" (Dorst, n.d.). Hence Lionel March has called abductive logic a *productive* logic, productive in the sense of creating something that had not existed previously—architecture, for instance—but after it is created, in the words again of Cross, the solution is a "match" to the problem it was meant to solve (Cross, 2011). Thus an ongoing challenge for architectural research is to accommodate the abductive/productive logic that is embedded in creative acts, on the one hand, while also achieving the rigor of systematic inquiry and generalizability of findings, on the other. In what follows, six factors related to this goal are outlined. The conclusion addresses the impact of the computer on architectural research. When Linda Groat and I published the second issue of *Architectural Research Methods* (2013), it is safe to say that the most significant elements needing to be updated from the first issue (2002) had to do with advances in computer technology. Only the future can tell how the computer revolution will ultimately change the givens of our world overall. But the computer's impact on design thinking is already palpable. And the conclusion itemizes some ways this impacts architectural research.

Architectural Research Recognizes that Creative Design has Spontaneous Qualities that May Be Out of the Reach of Systematic Research Frameworks (Figural Generation Resists Prediction)

A tremendous amount of research has been conducted in recent years to comprehend the design process, more specifically, the *moment* design happens. The names of Rowe (Rowe, 1987), Schon (Schon, 1983), Lawson (Lawson, 2005), Darke (Darke, 1979), Duerk (Duerk, 1993), Jones (Jones, 1992), Buchanan (Buchanan, 1992), and of course Cross (Cross, 2011), among others, come to mind immediately. Arguably, the entire mission of the journal *Design Studies* focuses on this juncture. Advances in computer technology have also enabled rule-based computation to play key roles in the earliest stages of design production (Iwamoto, 2009). But it is one thing to have ever more powerful computer programs doing the work of design; it is another to think that human creativity itself can be comprehended by rule-based operations *en toto*. The creative act—that is, figural conception and generation—remains something uniquely human, of which computerized versions of figural production still require human creative input.

With respect to design creativity, then, architectural research can take two tacks. One is to hypothesize that creativity itself can be eventually mapped as a rule-based operation, and hence harnessed as such. This approach echoes earlier attitudes in Western ideas, for example, when Enlightenment thinkers proposed that our experiences of beauty were "immature" sensations that cannot be completely understood until they could be empirically measured and explained (Barnouw, n.d.). Or at the beginning of the twentieth century, there was the search for a "covering law" for history, to wit, that at some point our scientific prowess will develop to a point that can predictively map historical processes (Hempel, 1942). The failure of these earlier views should suggest that this first tack has limited promise. Again, while the computer may someday replicate creative spontaneity with rule-based formulas, it is difficult to imagine that such a technology will replace (or, perhaps more importantly, *explain*) human creativity completely.

The second tack is to hold research inquiry and design activity as distinct domains of human experience, but that they are not antithetical, but complementary. As my co-author Linda Groat states, "we take the stand that design and research are most appropriately and usefully understood as relatively distinct kinds of activity, but they indeed embody many important similarities, including many complementary and overlapping qualities" (Groat & Wang, 2013). Foremost among these is logics-in-use, a term that recognizes that, at the operational level, intuition and logic work in tandem in both design and research activity. This second tack is more useful because a) it does not seek to implicitly negate the legitimacy of creative design as its own domain, but rather b) seeks to mine the rich boundaries and overlaps between creative design and "research" as it is traditionally understood in the natural and social sciences. Creativity, of course, is not limited to architectural figural production only, but infuses so many, if not all, of the modes of human endeavor. So this second tack is tantamount to saying that design research is an interdisciplinary endeavor that can enrich knowledge of so much of our life experiences. The factors for architectural research to follow all assume this starting point.

Architectural Research Recognizes that Creative Design Activity Does Have Measurable Dimensions

In his recent doctoral research, Alhusban (2012) sought to measure the rate at which "creative leaps" occur in first-year through fourth-year architecture students, and also to compare this phenomenon with the rate creative leaps that occur in architecture professionals, and also in university students in non-design programs. By tracking subjects as they complete a given design problem, Alhusban was able to measure the "limited commitment mode (LCM)"; this term refers to the unique decisions a subject makes, which has been shown in the literature to relate to design creativity (Kim *et al.*, 2007). The tracking was done by filming the subjects, recording what they said aloud during the process, and then meticulously analyzing the spoken/filmed data with the drawn design material over units of time. Alhusban found that the number of creative leaps per unit of time increased steadily from first-year to fourth-year students, and it is dramatically higher in professional architects and design faculty. One applied outcome from this research is a recommendation that senior faculty teach first-year design students, thus pairing those with high creative leap capacity with entry level students (as opposed to having "intro" classes taught by teaching assistants, for instance, or even by junior faculty). This is one example of using a research framework to comprehend human creativity. Alhusban showed that, while human creativity may seem mysteriously spontaneous, at least its frequency can be correlated to training and education.

Here is another example. Several years ago, with Ali O. Ilhan, I co-authored an article addressing architecture's "body of knowledge" (Wang & Ilhan, 2009). We surveyed many examples in the literature that tried to define the exact boundaries of this body of knowledge. We came to a startling conclusion: architecture doesn't have a body of knowledge per se, because it's very ontology traffics in all bodies of knowledge. (Our cases also included the interior design and industrial design professions.) We then generated a logical framework that discerned a fundamental difference between design professions in comparison with non-design professions (accounting, for example). Specifically, design professions must maintain their identities with "sociological wrapping," focusing outwards towards the general society, in ways that non-design professions tend not to do. Wrapping around what? Wrapping around the creative act which is what gives design professions their uniqueness. It raises the larger question of how design activity must be "packaged" so that it can have a place in cultures that are fundamentally driven by measurable constructs such as monetary value, societal pressures equating professionalism with esoteric knowledge, and utilitarian measures of worth. The above are just two examples illustrating how human creativity can be understood more deeply by identifying measurable factors surrounding it.

It is encouraging to see academic standards for what constitutes "research" shifting to accommodate research related to (and in) design. I am referring to Elison and Eatman's *Scholarship in Public: Knowledge Creation and Tenure Policy in the Engaged University: A Resource on Promotion and Tenure in the Arts, Humanities, and Design*. This document explicitly encourages creative activities as research: publicly engaged academic work is scholarly or creative activity integral to a faculty member's academic area. It encompasses different forms of making knowledge "about, for, and with" diverse publics and communities. Through a coherent, purposeful sequence of activities, design contributes to the public good and yields artifacts of public and intellectual value (Ellison & Eatman, 2008).

On the other side of the ledger, design practice is also embracing research, thus affirming its value for the design professional. This can be evidenced in the increased attention the American Institute of Architects has given to research in the last 10 years or so. Within this time frame, the AIA has held three Research Summits (in 2007, 2012, 2013), and began the Upjohn Research Initiative which provides grants for joint research projects between practitioners and academics (American Institute of Architecture, n.d.). The AIA Knowledge Communities also disseminate research knowledge. These communities identify knowledge domains and, in the words of one of its leading proponents, Bruce Blackmer, "provide peer review needed in the validation of potential knowledge contributions" (Blackmer, 2005). Peer review is one way to assess the internal and external validity, addressed earlier, of research projects. In sum, what we are witnessing is an increased awareness for the need for research in the design fields, more methodologies being developed for conducting such research, and standards by which design research can be evaluated as rigorous scholarship.

Architectural Research Encompasses both Research about Buildings/Built Environments and Research about the Cultures that Spawn, Build and Experience those Objects

When the first edition of *Architectural Research Methods* was being written, the default assumption by friends and even colleagues was that the book would be about buildings as such. This is always a hurdle to be surmounted in defining the far greater scope of architectural research. Even if research is centered around buildings, buildings, in turn, are among the most complicated objects created by human hands. And the agglomeration of buildings—namely, a city—is arguably the most complicated humanly-made object we have. Thus if architecture is taken to mean the organized efforts by which humans have altered nature for the purposes of shelter and community, then it is difficult to conceive of any area of the inhabited world that has not been impacted by architecture.

So the moniker "architectural research" encompasses an enormous range of human experiences. It not only includes buildings as such, it includes the profound cultural worldviews that motivate their construction, and then in their ongoing presence in the cultural values they evoke and signify. One way to sort this range is to ask: is a research topic directly about buildings themselves, or is the topic related to how a built object is situated in some way in relation to cultural processes? Or is the topic somewhere in between? The kinds of evidence architectural researchers look for, then, depend upon where in this broad range a research study is situated. As I write this, I happen to be giving a seminar on architectural research methods to doctoral students at the Huazhong University of Science and Technology in Wuhan, China. Their various topics of research were mapped on this slide used during the seminar (see Figure 4.1)

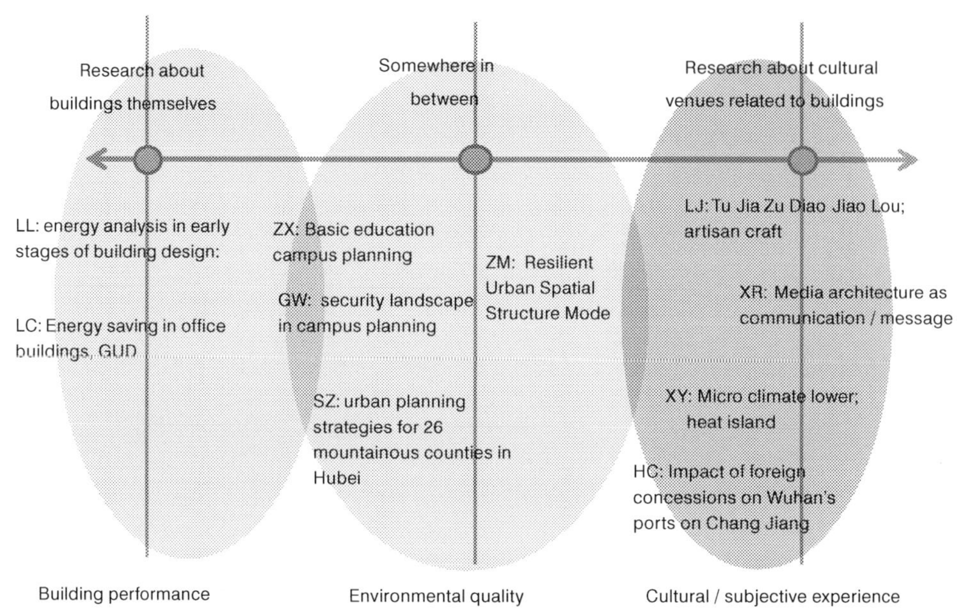

Figure 4.1 Range of research topics of doctoral students at the Huazhong University of Science and Technology, Wuhan, China, Spring 2014. Chart by author

On the left, modeling energy efficiencies in the schematic design phase is research that concerns buildings themselves. But on the right, architectural research also encompasses the impact of foreign concessions on the urban morphology of the city of Wuhan, specifically along the Chang Jiang (Yangzi) River. Also on the right is a project that seeks to understand the impact of buildings used as media (for example, digitized façades that change in response to real-time inputs). In between are research topics ranging from developing guidelines for campus design to strategies that help to sustain rural communities at a time when large percentages of China's population is migrating to the cities. As a whole, this grouping is representative of the scope of topics that can be subsumed under "architectural research."

The challenge, then, is to conduct research that fits the four criteria outlined at the outset of this article, on the one hand, with research methodologies that are appropriate for an enormous range of possible topics, on the other. It follows that this large range of topics necessarily requires an equally broad range of research methodologies—and also a concomitant breadth of types of evidence for evidence-based research. This is what the next sections address.

Architectural Research Embraces a Broad Interdisciplinary Range of Research Methodologies—Which means Understanding What Non-design Peers Understand by "Research" and Harnessing their Methods for Design Inquiry

The projects listed on the left side of Figure 4.1 deal with energy consumption in buildings. These make use of experimental research and simulation modeling, both familiar methodologies in the sciences and in engineering. Experimental research isolates the object under study into units of test, and then manipulates independent variables to see how dependent variables respond. It often makes use of control groups for comparison; these are units of test that are not manipulated (or manipulated with a placebo) to clarify the impact of the real independent variable(s) on the tested units. In all, experimental research tries to identify causal factors, knowledge of which can yield applications in similar contexts with a high degree of predictability. Simulation research contrasts with experimental research in that it seeks to include all possible variables in its units of test, which are replications of real-world contexts. Simulation seeks to replicate a future real-world scenario (or a past real-world scenario) (Galea, *et al.*, 2008). So that the multivariate outcomes of that scenario can be studied without endangering actual lives, or ethically compromising actual persons, or otherwise suffering from the consequences of the actual event. In energy simulations, the goal is obviously to minimize fuel expenditures for the actual cases.

Projects on the right side of Figure 4.1 call for very different methodologies. In the top right case, the researcher wants to document the artisan techniques of the *Tu Jia* minority people (China has over 50 minority populations among its citizenry), particularly in the relationship between calligraphy and their vernacular building typology (called the *Diao Jiao Lou*) before this vernacular craft tradition fades into history. This calls for extensive ethnographic methods, in which he will reside on-site among the *Tu Jia* people, conversing with them, witnessing and documenting their craft techniques, doing the crafts himself, understanding the rituals associated with their praxis, and so on. In the lower right project, the impact of foreign concessions on Wuhan ports along the Chang Jiang will necessarily require history research, including interviews of subjects who can get close to memories of that period. This researcher must learn the subtleties of historical narrative, writing in what Arthur Danto calls narrative sentences (Danto, 1985). Another project at this end of the spectrum is buildings as a new mode of media communication. As of this writing it is not clear what direction this researcher might go. Analyses of media behavior can make use of correlational research strategy, in which certain variables are shown to have significant statistical relationship to other variables. Some simple examples come to mind. How do digitally responsive building façades relate to the amount of pedestrian traffic in urban plazas? Does showing news real-time on building façades increase awareness of current world affairs among demographic segments of the population with typically lower awareness? But a topic such as this can be approached by methodologies of a much less statistical, and a much more interpretive, nature (which is where I suspect this researcher's interests really lie). For instance, she can draw from Bourdieu's theory of *habitus* to examine how media communications, as a social practice, can play a significant role in shaping sense of place (Bourdieu, 2005), or from Lefebvre's theory of space as a political production (Lefebvre, 1992), to create a logical framework explaining how digital media communications alter social constructions of space. The point is that topics on the right side of the spectrum in Figure 4.1 make use of substantially different methodologies from those on the left side. And yet all are encompassed within architectural research.

In the middle region of Figure 4.1 are various topics that fit well with case study research. Linda Groat adapts Robert Yin's definition this way: "A case study is an empirical inquiry that investigates a setting within its real-life context, especially when the boundaries between phenomenon and context are not clearly evident" (Yin, 2013). Take for instance the project "urban planning strategies for 26 mountainous counties in Hubei Province" listed at the bottom of the middle region in Figure 4.1. Case study research seeks to develop theory from in-context engagement, with the goal of applying that theory in a generalizable manner to other similar cases. Here, the researcher can identify several representative cases for theory development, on the way towards developing planning guidelines for all 26 counties. Or, it might work to conduct in-depth research in just one case, as Herbert Gans famously did in his study of Levittown (Gans, 1982). An aspect of what architects are trained to do already resembles case study research: theorizing about specific projects towards fitting them into a generalizable "typology," for instance. (Historically, what architects were typically *not* trained to do, at least in their schooling, is to engage with clients and the general public with interviews, focus groups, survey questionnaires, and other social science research tactics, which case study research often requires.)

In sum, "architectural research" makes use of the full range of research frameworks found across the spectrum of disciplines that conduct research, from the sciences to the humanities, and into the fine arts. It is a daunting task to be familiar with what all of these research methods entail and how they work, and then harnessing them for research related to architecture. But it is also stimulating work to think through research possibilities with all of these tools at hand. This interdisciplinary diversity affirms the very nature of architecture, which was recognized early on by Vitruvius in the first architectural theory to have come down to us in the West. In the first of his *Ten Books on Architecture,* Vitruvius held that the competent architect must be trained in philosophy, music, medicine, the law, astronomy, and so on (Vitruvius, 1914). To say no more, these represent quite a few disciplinary domains. Vitruvius's insight is that the architect's role is essentially to create something that not only reflects the full-orbed cultural worldview of his or her times, but in doing so to elevate the quality of social life with a creative production that reflects the highest aspirations of those times. The next section addresses how to organize this diverse array of research methodologies.

Architectural Research can be Organized Around Strategies and Tactics

We often hear of research described as either quantitative or qualitative. But this is too broad-brushed, and does not really capture the subtleties of the range of methodologies described above. It is not unusual for qualitative researchers to make use of rigorous statistical analyses—which those who favor the quantitative/qualitative divide usually consider quantitative. Conversely, experimental (read: quantitative) researchers sometimes make use of qualitative tactics to operationalize their processes. *Architectural Research Methods* organizes research methodologies with a more nuanced set of factors, taking into account the researcher's own predilections on how he/she views the world. Readers can refer to *ARM-2* for our review of the literature regarding broad systems of inquiry (and also a detailed assessment of the limitations of "quantitative / qualitative") (Groat & Wang, 2013).

Suffice it here to describe the distinction between research *strategies* and research *tactics*. Strategies are broad ways of knowing the world. For example, experimental research, in its search for causal linkages and its reduction of its study subject into isolated units of test, reflects commitments to how knowledge can be ascertained, backed by convictions for how reality works. In contrast, qualitative research rejects reducing its study subject; instead it seeks to understand it in its real-world context. And rather than looking for causal linkages, it often narrates its findings to achieve "thick description (i.e. Geertz 1973), that is, offering an account of the subject phenomenon from multiple perspectives with layers of meaning any social-cultural phenomenon or venue contains, making the resulting narrative "thick" (note: this is a term usually associated with Clifford Geertz, but Geertz cites Gilbert Ryle). In *ARM-2*, research strategies are identified as historical, qualitative, correlational, experimental and quasi-experimental, simulation, logical argumentation, and case studies/combined strategies.

The distinctive feature of research strategies is that they can be conceived of without taking action. To put it more colloquially, one can sit in one's armchair and think through his or her research, at the level of strategy, without leaving one's room. Because strategies reflect ways of knowing the world, they are themselves "merely" conceptual. Given a topic of research, we can easily discuss the appropriate strategy for it over coffee. What might make the discussion more interesting is that, given a *general* topic, a variety of strategies might be a fit. It depends on how clearly defined the topic is; and discussing various strategies for the right fit always goes some way towards focusing a topic.

Almost all research designs make use of a single strategy; if multiple strategies are used, they are usually used in sequence. For example, an experimental researcher might first conduct qualitative interviews to determine his or her sample subjects. But strategies used in tandem synchronically usually signify an unclear topic. This is a warning for students who often like the idea of using "mixed methods." I often say that "mixed methods" ought not to actually mean "mixed-up methods." If a research proposal says it uses mixed methods, and what it means is that two strategies are conceived as being deployed at the same time, it almost always signals an unclear goal, because the research question is unclear.

In contrast to research strategies, research tactics are anything but "armchair." Tactics exist at the operational level; they are actions taken so that samples can be found, subjects can be identified, interviews can be conducted, data can be collected and analyzed, and so on. Refer to Figure 4.2. The vertical columns are strategies. The horizontal bars are tactics (and only a handful of all possible tactics are shown in Figure 4.2). Again in contrast to strategies, note that for any single strategy, multiple tactics are typically used. Researchers use the term *triangulation*. This means that several different approaches result in outcomes that logically reinforce each other; or that a single outcome is arrived upon by different routes. These approaches and routes exist at the tactical level. Another way of saying this is that using multiple tactics assures greater triangulation.

Note also how something "quantitative," such as statistical analysis, can easily intersect more qualitative strategies such as historical research *at the level of tactics*. The strategies/tactics distinction is stronger than the quantitative/qualitative distinction precisely for this reason. The latter distinction, although much more common, does not distinguish between how a researcher looks at the world; or how he or she conceives of a research approach ontologically. The world, and experience of the world, is simplistically divided into quantitative and

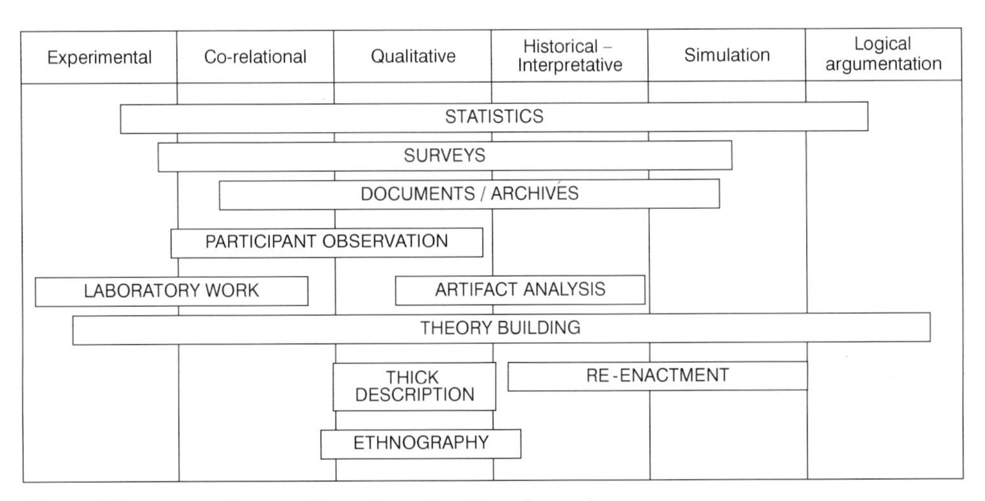

Figure 4.2 Research strategies and tactics. Chart by author

qualitative. The strategies/tactics distinction is a closer match to reality: the quantitative and qualitative dimensions of human experience are interspersed in very nuanced ways.

All of this is to say that architectural research is necessarily a crossroads of research approaches found in other disciplinary endeavors. The way forward is to respect those other approaches, and find ways they can be harnessed for robust research in architecture and related design fields.

Architectural Research is Itself a Creative Endeavor

In brief, if a research *topic* is likened to a destination, a research *methodology* is the vehicle that will drive you there. The research *design* is the map for how to get there—which is akin to the research *strategy*. The research tactics are all the *actions* entailed to get there. But there is one more element missing in this analogy: you have to have an *engine* that drives the car; this is the thing that actually makes the wheels turn, that allows you to make actual progress towards the destination. What do I mean by this? Well, here is an example from Clare Cooper Marcus. Early in her career, she wanted to understand how her subjects felt about their homes. But the methods she used were somehow not getting to where she wanted to go. She wanted her subjects' *immediate* feelings about their homes; but what she was getting were reports that seemed second-hand. She then happened upon Martin Heidegger's writings, and here she is in her own words:

> I attempted to approach this material via what philosopher Martin Heidegger called "pre-logical thought." This is not "illogical" or "irrational," but rather a mode of approaching being-in-the-world that permeated early Greek thinkers at a time before the categorization of our world into mind and matter, cause and effect, in-here and out-there had gripped ... the Western mind. I firmly believe that a deeper level of person/environment interaction can be approached only by means of a ... process that ... eliminates observer and object
> (Copper Marcus 1995).

This insight led Cooper Marcus to ask her respondents to draw their feelings about their homes, thus circumventing the need to frame their feelings into words. Cooper Marcus's approach falls in the domain of qualitative research; specifically, it is a kind of phenomenological inquiry (Groat & Wang, 2013). The point for us is that the engine, for Cooper Marcus in this case, was the insight to do the sketches. A researcher can talk about "qualitative research" all she wants, but unless she has a particular "in," she is still standing on the outside looking in; she does not yet have a specific means—the engine, as it were—to actually implement the study and take her where she wants to go.

For any research project, conceiving of this specific means takes as much creativity as figural design work. Like figural designs, it often comes as a flash of insight, a novel idea for an approach that was not obvious before, and often not found in existing literature as such. This is from John Zeisel (2006), author of one of the most enduring books on design research: "Creative researchers invent and discover ... In the beginning of a project, emerging concepts are *visions* defining what data to gather ..." I italicize the word *vision* because the word does a fair job in describing how an idea for a research design comes. I have avoided this term "research *design*" until now because we have been addressing the separate (but complementary) domains of design and research. But "research design" is a standard term describing how a researcher devises his or her framework for a particular research project. And thus we come full circle back to design. Zeisel further uses words like "inspiration," "imagination," and "intuition" to describe the tools a researcher uses for his or her work; these words obviously apply to figural design activity as well. So cultivating good research ideas is not unlike fostering good design ideas. One has to be immersed in a community of like-minded researchers, or designers who see that research can enhance design praxis. Just as designers are always on the lookout for new designs, design researchers must continuously update themselves on the latest design research; this is done in part by being constantly updated on the relevant literature. It also means cultivating an ability to sense the research implications in any or every bit of news one becomes aware of. And just as it helps for designers to be at centers of design, where resources are available and exemplars are abundant, so researchers should be connected to sources, archives, databases, and so on, for easy access. All of this is for convenience and facility, yes. But all of it also helps in waiting for that next flash of creative inspiration.

Conclusion

The computer's impact on architectural practice and, more fundamentally, on design education and design thinking, has already been profound. Advancements in computer technology heightens the sophistication in how the research and design domains overlap. This is perforce because computer technology rasterizes reality into numerical bits of data. The levels to which this technology has already begun to do this rasterizing of reality blurs some boundaries that have traditionally been taken to be fixed.

For example, theory and practice have typically been regarded as separated domains. Add to this the "third-something" domain of research, which relates to both theory and practice but is arguably neither. Now think of these three domains in terms of *time* and *space*. It was assumed that a temporal gap must exist between thinking about design (*theoria*) and actual design implementation (*praxis*). And research has only loosely related to both theory and praxis because in a way it stands apart—"apart" being a spatial construct—from both theory and practice. But rapid prototyping technology challenges these temporal and spatial separations *by uniting them in ways that approach simultaneity*, so much so that Michael Speaks writes of a new kind of design intelligence. He cites a design for an extension of the city of Utrecht in which a computer program was able to "transform the 'software' of public and private policy directives into the 'hardware' of buildings and infrastructure" (Speaks, 2006). In this instance, it seems that theorizing as a separate *a priori* activity was circumvented by inputting data, open-ended, into a rasterizing process which directly resulted in design options. With regard to research, Speaks quotes architect George Yu:

> The traditional distinction between research and doing or making is something that's becoming blurred for us. Doing has become research and research has become doing at this point. For us, research is not something that comes *before* doing—it's maybe even the other way around. Doing is in fact a kind of research [italics added].
>
> (Speaks, 2006)

Yu's rejection of research as its own category does not mean there will be an erasure of research. But it is the computer's ability to blur the lines between theory, practice (read: design) and research that opens up new avenues for research as such. Consider:

Simulation in relation to experimentation

Earlier we noted that experimental research reduces to essential variables and isolates into units of test, while simulation research incorporates all possible variables. With the computer's ability to crunch volumes of data that approach modelings of reality in real-time (Speaks, 2005), it is not surprising that simulation research can overtake experimental research as an important means for understanding our world, especially in visioning possible future scenarios of the world in built forms. If experimental research has always been an uncomfortable fit with the creative architectural mind, simulation research is quite resonant with what architects have done from time immemorial: building models. Now, static models usually do not meet the standards of simulation research (Groat & Wang, 2013). But computerized simulations capturing dynamic interactions of multiple real-world variables certainly do. The upshot is that, in the simulational powers of the computer—as expressed, for instance, in building information modeling (BIM) platforms, or geographic information systems (GIS), to name just two—architectural practice and education now have a strong connection to what has traditionally been a kind of research not often accessible to architects.

Open source and qualitative research

The computer not only processes enormous amounts of data quickly, but also offers enormous access. This year I serve on a student's Masters of Architecture thesis committee the focus of which was to allow open source data gathered from the internet to determine the program of a mixed-use commercial/residential building, and then to use parametric factors in determining a range of possibilities for the building's form (see Figure 4.3). The work is ongoing and the outcome is uncertain (Rideout, 2015). But the point is this: if the program is generated by open source access on the internet, and the architect is one who programs parameters rather than envisions form, it portends profound changes in what "client" and "architect" can mean. And yet we have a sense this is where the future of design is headed. The relation between the architect's conception and users' input has traditionally been weak, as intimated in Lawson's point cited at the outset of this chapter. Architects have rarely made use of surveys, focus groups, questionnaires, and other tools of qualitative research, in the design process. But open source input via the computer again changes the game, not only for developing the initial program, but also for gathering ongoing client responses to design decisions, and for post-occupancy evaluation. In short, the computer brings the design process closer to many of the traditional tactics of qualitative research. Future success in practice will most likely depend on knowledge of these qualitative tactics and how to harness them to inform the design process.

Customized cases versus "generalizability"

Another feature of computational power is its ability to tailor solutions for specific and localized applications. Speaks writes of "swarms of little truths appearing and disappearing so fast that ascertaining whether they are really true is impractical if not altogether impossible" (Speaks, 2005). This of course is spoken from a post-structuralist point of view and can be debated philosophically elsewhere. What matters for research is to consider how traditional measures of generalizability (which presumes repeatable, or replicable, facts if not truths) may need to accommodate various forms of one-of-a-kind creative works as examples of research. The student example cited above is the culminating project of a design degree. And yet its research dimensions are clear: the inquiry is systematic in scope; it results in new knowledge; it builds on theories and laws; and it is generally applicable—not in the sense of repeating the same project over and over again, but in demonstrating a process that is generally applicable while the outcome itself, a building, is customized for location-specific

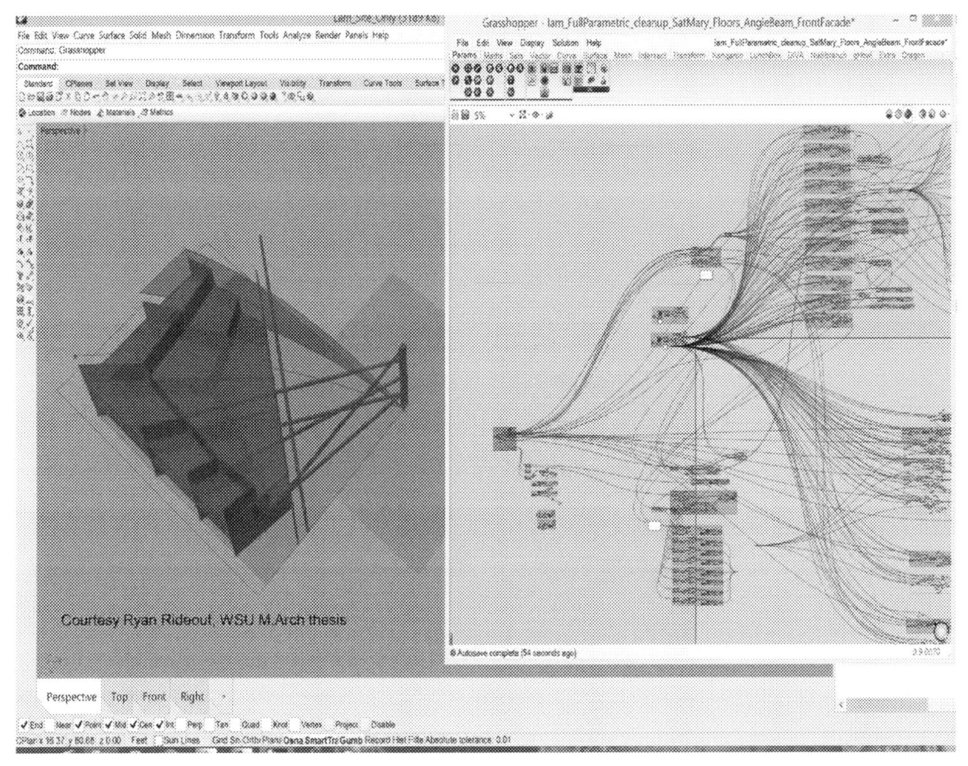

Figure 4.3 Parametric factors determining the form of a building. Courtesy Ryan Rideout

factors. The same can be said of Speak's example of the project to extend the city of Utrecht, cited earlier. Open source computer technology transforms non-design data (like policies) into the forms of buildings and infrastructure in customized applications.

Virtual reality

This term can be defined in various ways, but in essence it describes scenarios that erase the distinction between what is and what could be into one seamless experience. Computer technology enables this possibility in various ways, and all of them are subjects for rigorous research. Sentient buildings are one example. These are buildings that automatically respond to human presence in customized ways, for instance, in adjusting internal climatic conditions to specific individuals or groups of individuals. Sentient buildings go one step beyond modeling energy performance in buildings because the buildings themselves are in a real sense the models, thus mingling the real with the virtual.

Another example of "virtual" is the Wikihouse initiative (Wikihouse, n.d.). This is an open source platform for the design and construction of buildings predicated on the proposition that "the factory is everywhere … the design team is everyone" (Parvin, 2013). Anywhere in the world, anyone can order a kit of parts for a house, provided that a 3-D printer on site can cut out all of the parts. The structure can then be assembled without tools, by people without design or construction training. If virtual reality is indeed the erasure between what is and what could be, initiatives like Wikihouse democratize the availability of architecture for enormous numbers of people, real-time. Another example can be viewed in the videos titled "A Day Made of Glass," by Corning (Corning Incorporated, 2011; Corning Incorporated, 2012). Both videos present a world in which glass blurs time and space. Dinosaurs can be viewed "live" in the wild, through glass. More remarkably, a glass wall seemingly integrates two distant hospital surgery rooms into one virtual space, in which the doctor remote from the patient nevertheless operates on him. Finally, even history research benefits from "virtual" computer technology. Anne Kelley Knowles, of Middlebury College, has done extensive modeling of environments in history to bring them to life once again. In this way she has modeled the Gettysburg battlefield on the day of battle. She and her colleagues have also used GIS technology to model the arrival of prisoners at Auschwitz (Knowles, Jaskot, & Harvey, n.d.).

These are only a few examples of how the computer is integrating architecture practice, and design practice in general, with research. Simulation research will increase in relevance for design practice. User and occupant needs will more and more become real-time inputs in the design process, thus ushering qualitative research tactics right into the realm of design thinking and praxis. Architects will need to engage with "open source" computer technology, not only for generating design programs, but also for ways to make their designs publicly accessible. Finally, virtual reality, in its various forms, will impact design research profoundly in the foreseeable years to come. But with all of these new possibilities for research, the measures for what *constitutes* robust research do not change: a systematic research framework; new knowledge as outcomes; engagement with the extant literature; and generally applicable results.

References

Alhusban, A.A. (2012). What does the architectural creative leap look like through a conceptual design phase in the undergraduate architectural design studio? Doctoral Dissertation, Washington State University, Interdisciplinary Design Institute.

American Institute of Architecture (n.d.). A History of Research at the AIA. Retrieved June 5, 2014 from: http://www.aia.org/practicing/akr/AIAB081882.

Barnouw, J. (n.d.). The beginnings of 'aesthetics' and the Leibnizian conception of sensation. In P. Mattick Jr (ed.), *Eighteenth-Century Aesthetics and the Reconstruction of Art,* 52–95. Cambridge: Cambridge University Press.

Blackmer, B. (2005). Knowledge on Knowledge, *Journal of Interior Design*, 31, 1, vii–xii.

Bourdieu, P. (2005). Habitus, In J. Hillier and E. Rooksby (eds.), *Habitus: A Sense of Place*, 43–52. London: Ashgate.

Buchanan, R. (1992). Wicked problems in design thinking, *Design Issues,* 8, 2, 5–21.

Cooper Marcus, C. (1995). *House as Mirror of Self*, 10–11. Berkeley, CA: Conari Press.

Corning Incorporated, (2011). A day made of glass 1. Retrieved November 21, 2014 from: https://www.youtube.com/watch?v=6Cf7IL_eZ38&feature=kp.

Corning Incorporated, (2012). A day made of glass 2: same day. Expanded corning vision. Retrieved November 21, 2014 from: https://www.youtube.com/watch?v=jZkHpNnXLB0&feature=kp.

Cross, N. (2011). *Design Thinking*. Retrieved July 26, 2014. From: http://books.google.com/books?id=F4SUVT1XCCwC&printsec=frontcover&dq=nigel+cross+design+thinking&hl=en&sa=X&ei=VM_TU_jtEaStigLH7oGQCQ&ved=0CDcQ6AEwAA#v=snippet&q=abduction&f=false.

Danto, A. (1985). *Narration and Knowledge, 152*. New York: Columbia University Press.

Darke, J. (1979). The primary generator in the design process, *Design Studies* 1, 1, 36–44.

Dorst, K. (n.d.). The nature of design thinking, 132. Retrieved May 24, 2014 from: http://www3.nd.edu/~amurniek/assets/DTRS8-Dorst.pdf.

Duerk, D.P. (1993). *Architectural Programming: Information Management for Design*. New York: John Wiley.
Ellison, J. & Eatman, T.K. (2008). *Scholarship in Public: Knowledge Creation and Tenure Policy in the Engaged University*. Syracuse, NY: Imagining America.
Galea, E.R., Sharp, G., Lawrence, P.J. & Holden, R. (2008). Approximating the evacuation of the World Trade Center North Tower using computer simulation, *Journal of Fire Protection Engineering* 18, 85–115.
Gans, H. (1982). *The Levittowners*. New York, NY: Columbia University Press.
Geertz. C. (1973). *The Interpretation of Cultures, 6–9*. New York: Basic Books.
Groat, L. & Wang, D. (2013). Does design equal research? In L. Groat & D. Wang (eds.), *Architectural Research Methods*, 2nd edition. New York: John Wiley & Sons.
Hempel, C.G. (1942). The function of general laws in history, *Journal of Philosophy*, 39, 35–48.
Iwamoto, L. (2009). *Digital Fabrications: Architectural and Material TechniqueS*. New York: Princeton Architectural Press.
Jones, J.C. (1992). *Design Methods*, 2nd edition. New York: Van Nostrand Reinhold.
Kim, M., Kim, Y., Lee, S., & Park, A. (2007). An underlying cognitive aspect of design creativity: Limited Commitment Mode control strategy. *Design Studies*, 28, 6, 585–604.
Knowles, A.K., Jaskot, P.B., & Harvey, C. (n.d.). In L. Groat & D. Wang (eds.), *Architectural Research Methods*, 2nd edition. New York: John Wiley & Sons.
Lawson, B. (2005). *How Designer's Think*, 4th edition, 183. Amsterdam: Elsevier.
Lefebvre, H. (1992). *The Production of Space* [1974] trans. Donald Nicholson-Smith. New York: John Wiley and Sons.
Merriam-Webster Dictionary, (n.d.). Research. Retrieved May 1, 2014, from: http://www.merriam-webster.com/dictionary/research.
Oxford English Dictionary, (n.d.). Research. Retrieved May 3, 2014, from: http://www.oxforddictionaries.com/us/definition/american_english/research?q=research.
Parvin, A. (2013, February). Architecture for the people by the people. TED Talk. Retrieved July 16, 2014 from: http://www.ted.com/talks/alastair_parvin_architecture_for_the_people_by_the_people.
Rideout, R. (2015). Design of a mixed use program with open source and computational strategies, Master's thesis, Washington State University School of Design and Construction.
Rowe, P. (1987). *Design Thinking*. Cambridge, MA: MIT Press.
Schon, D. (1983). *The Reflective Practitioner*. New York: Basic Books.
Speaks, M. (2005). After Theory. *Architectural Record*, June, 15.
Speaks, M. (2006). Intelligence after theory. *Perspecta 38, "Architecture After All": Yale Architecture Journal*, 106.
Vitruvius, (1914). The education of the architect. In M.H. Hicky Morgan (trans.) *The Ten Books on Architecture* I.1.3. Cambridge, MA: Harvard University Press.
Wang, D. & Ilhan, A. (2009) holding creativity together: a sociological theory of the design professions, *Design Issues* 5(1) 5–21.
Wikihouse, (n.d.). Open Source Construction Set. Retrieved July 16, 2014 from: http://www.wikihouse.cc.
Yin, R.K. (2013). Case study research: design and methods. In L. Groat & D. Wang (eds.), *Architectural Research Methods*, 2nd edition. New York: John Wiley & Sons.
Zeisel, J. (2006). *Inquiry by Design*. New York: W.W. Norton.

5

Minimalism and the Phenomenological Fold

Michael Young

Since Heinrich Wolfflin's *Principles of Art History* (1915), there has been a tendency to read aesthetic shifts in art and architecture as a cyclical recurrence between restraint and exuberance. Renaissance and Baroque, Art Nouveau and International Style Modernism, Brutalism and Pop Post-Modernism, Digital Formalism and Neo-Modernism. Although this last cycle is still too close to fully see, one can put forward several observations to consider this most recent pair in a different relation. As Tom Conley observes in the work of Henri Focillon, "the Romanesque and Gothic, two dominant and contrastive styles, often inflect each other. They crisscross and sometimes fold vastly different sensibilities into each other" (Conley, 1993). The pairing of Digital Formalism and Neo-Modernism is similar in this regard. They are less cyclical responses than simultaneous reflections of each other.

During the 1990s, the label "Neo-Modernist" described a simplicity of form and clarity of tectonic expression that echoed back to the heroic phase of International Style Modernism. As this chapter will discuss, this title is misleading. A better one might be "Light Constructors," in honor of the 1995 exhibition at the Museum of Modern Art *Light Construction*. The other side has had several monikers, the most prevalent being "Digital Formalism," "Blob Architecture," or "Single Surface Architecture." From here on in this chapter it will be referred to as "Digital Folders" in honor of the 1993 AD publication *Folding in Architecture*. These architects exploited the potential of the computer to create complex topological forms that blurred tectonic differences through smooth folds.

In many public forums during the 1990s, these two architectural positions, the "Light Constructors" and "Digital Folders," vehemently attacked each other (i.e., Lynn, 1996). There are many instances that one can point to, for example, Greg Lynn, "Why Tectonics is Square and Topology is Groovy" from the Any 14 Conference of 1996 as an attack on "Light Construction" and Juhani Pallasmaa, *The Eyes of the Skin* from 1996 as an attack on the digital. Key components of these arguments crystallized around issues of physical building and digital representation. One side built more, was grounded in material construction and its experiential phenomena. These architects attacked the use of the computer in architecture as damaging to the human experiential qualities of design, encouraging extravagant formal indulgence. The other side focused on experimentation in form through computational techniques that pushed the boundaries of architecture aesthetically and conceptually. These architects attacked the conservative values that the "non-digital" architects professed, describing their tectonic purity as a reactionary position to the undeniable changes in contemporary society. The presence of the computer in architectural design seemed to be the main destabilizer of the decade, but in hindsight from our position in 2014, with the profession fully digital, it appears that there must be something else at the heart of this debate.

The two positions can be defined without reference to computation as follows: the Light Constructors designed architecture with simple form, legible tectonics, modular repetition, and phenomenological experience; the Digital Folders designed architecture with complex forms, blurred articulation, continuous variation, and affective sensation. These descriptions would also seem to place the two positions decidedly against one another, until we consider a third actor: Minimalist Art. If we compare our two 1990s architectural movements to aspects of Minimalism, we find interesting alignments. All three use formal languages described as abstract; through a reduction of formal complexity, diagrammatic abstractions of phenomena, or the directness of a blunt object in space. All three suppress the articulation of the joint; through the reveal, the fold, or the flush alignment. All three share a desire for apparent objectivity through procedural constraints; through modular repetition, geometric transformation, or serialism. Around questions of phenomenology we find all three imbedded in phenomena; through the human subject's relation to the natural world, the natural world itself as an emergent process, or the temporal contingencies of bodily perception in space. This comparison identifies four shared concerns between Minimalist Art and 1990s architecture: reduced formal expression, suppressed joint articulation, serial procedure, and perceptual phenomena.

One of the most prominent debates in the second decade of the twenty-first century is between architects that profess a phenomenological influence and those who are aligned with the technologies of parametric software. This contemporary debate is the direct offspring of the debates of the 1990s. The possibility that the Light Constructors and Digital Folders share several crucial underlying similarities holds an intriguing promise to alter the prevailing interpretations of these arguments today.

Four Years: 1992–1996

*1992—*Zone 6: Incorporations *(Crary & Kwinter, 1992)—edited by Jonathan Crary and Sanford Kwinter*

Zone 6 collected writing from Gilles Deleuze, Felix Guattari, Francisco Varela, Manuel Delanda, Diller/Scofidio and Peter Eisenman among others. Eisenman draws several influential connections in his article titled "Unfolding Events." "In the idea of the fold, form is seen as continuous even as it articulates possible new relationships between vertical and horizontal, figure and ground, breaking up the existing Cartesian order of space" (Eisenman, 1992) The article tied four themes together. First, that the electronic paradigm in media manipulation is different from the mechanical, requiring a shift in the conceptual discourse; second, the writing of Gilles Deleuze can provide ideas that help describe this shift; third, one idea put forward by Deleuze that engages aspects of this new mode can be described through the metaphor of "the fold"; and fourth, that folding is related to temporality, to processes, to becoming, which Eisenman associates with the architectural event. This fourfold between Deleuze (theory), becoming (event), folding (technique), and the digital (technology), will be repeated in various versions over the next two decades of architectural discourse.

Another essay within this collection from biologist Francisco Varela titled "The Reenchantment of the Concrete" is also of interest. Varela's argument bases reality on the emergence of order through the phenomenological interactions of subjective perception.

> Reality is not cast as a given: it is perceiver dependent, not because the perceiver "constructs" it at whim, but because what counts as a relevant world is inseparable from the structure of the perceiver. Such an approach to perception is in fact one of the central insights of the phenomenological analysis undertaken by Maurice Merleau-Ponty in his early work.
>
> (Varela, 1992)

This article was one of the first examples of Varela that an architectural community would read. Varela along with Humberto Maturana introduced the concept of emergent self-replicating systems through a process they termed "autopoiesis." This word would be used again in Patrik Schumacher's two part manifesto for "Parametriscim" as an architectural style titled *The Autopoiesis of Architecture* (2012).

1993—AD Issue Folding in Architecture *(Lynn, 1993)—edited by Greg Lynn*

Folding in Architecture was one of the first challenges to the formal language of postmodern deconstruction from within the discourse of formalist theory. As Mario Carpo pointed out in his introduction to the 2004 re-issue, these "folding" concepts were initially viewed as extensions of post-structuralism (Carpo, 2004). Peter Eisenman's early 1990s work dominated the first part of the publication and included designs for the Alteka Office Building, the Rebstock Park Masterplan, and the Emory University Center for the Arts. But a number of new voices were also introduced including Greg Lynn, Reiser+Umemoto, Asymptote, and Stan Allen, all of whom would play pivotal roles at Columbia University's Graduate School of Architecture and Planning as design professors of the paperless studios beginning in 1994. Dates are important, for none of these architects were working in a fully digital manner when *Folding in Architecture* was published. The aesthetic agenda of the digital paradigm was forged prior to the use of the computer. Greg Lynn articulated several aspects of this brew in his introductory essay "The Folded, the Pliant and the Supple." "Curvilinearity can put into relation the collected projects in this publication, Gilles Deleuze's *The Fold: Leibniz and the Baroque* and René Thom's catastrophe diagrams. The smooth spaces described by these continuous yet differentiated systems result from curvilinear sensibilities that are capable of complex deformations in response to programmatic, structural, economic, aesthetic, political and contextual influences (Lynn, 1993)." Gilles Deleuze was published here for the first time in a purely architectural setting with the excerpted chapter "The Pleats of Matter" from *Le Pli: Leibniz and the Baroque* (Lynn, 1993). Jeffery Kipnis's "Towards a New Architecture" essay in particular was prophetic in stressing the importance of deformation as continuous transformation, an issue that would dominate digital design for the next two decades. Kipnis was able to spot architectural possibilities in Deleuze's writing through the production of new effects and techniques, not as applied philosophy for critical interpretation. "Neither pure figure nor pure organization, folds link the two; they are monolithic and often non-representational, replete with interstitial and residual spaces, and intrinsic to non-developable surfaces" (Kipnis, 1993).

1994—A+U Issue—Questions of Perception *(Holl* et al., *1994)—* *featuring Steven Holl, Alberto Pérez-Gómez, Juhani Pallasmaa*

Questions of Perception gathered architectural interpretations of phenomenology through the design work of Holl, a historical reading by Pérez-Gómez, and an interpretation regarding craft from Pallasmaa. This triad pulled the discussion of phenomenology in architecture away from the spirit of place as presented by Norberg-Schulz's book *Genus Loci: Towards a Phenomenology of Architecture* (1980). This was a shift from the late writings of Martin Heidegger, such as "Building, Dwelling, Thinking" (1951), towards an emphasis on sense perception as inspired by Maurice Merleau-Ponty's *Phenomenology of Perception* (1945) English translation (1962). The architectural interpretation of phenomenology that followed would be defined through bodily sensations in response to the materially crafted world. It was these concerns that would steer architectural phenomenology into conflict with the technology of digital mediation. The critique claimed that the digital as an extension of a visually dominated technocratic culture separated the body and its senses from the richness of the world.

> As buildings lose their plasticity and their connection with the language and wisdom of the body, they become isolated in the cool and distant realm of vision. With the loss of tactility and the scale and details crafted for the human body and hand, our structures become repulsively flat, sharp-edged, immaterial, and unreal. The detachment of construction from the realities of matter and craft turns architecture into stage sets for the eye, devoid of the authenticity of material and tectonic logic.
>
> (Pallasmaa, 1994, p. 29)

1994—The Presence of Mies *(Mertins, 1994)—edited by Detlef Mertins*

The Presence of Mies documents a series of papers first presented in 1992 in Toronto at a symposium of the same name. Two key essays for the current argument are Rosalind Krauss's "The Grid, the /Cloud/, and the Detail" and Ignasi de Sola-Morales Rubio's "Mies van der Rohe and Minimalism."

Krauss was a key art critic in the late 1960s identifying a link between Minimalism and phenomenology (Krauss, 1966). These were important arguments in that they allowed Minimalist art work to be understood as a positive interaction with real space and the embodied perceptions of the subject, not as a nihilistic abstract formalism. Krauss begins her essay "The Grid, the /Cloud/, and the Detail" with an observation on how architects have picked up on this phenomenological implication in Minimalism.

> What this second reading underscored was the way geometric shape was shown to be entirely context dependent, ... and thus open to the cat's cradle of the interface between viewer and viewed ... Minimalism produces the paradox of a center-less because shifting geometry, in objects with no fixed armature, objects that can be rearranged at will (Morris). Because of this demonstrable attack on the idea that works achieve their meaning by becoming manifestations or expressions of a hidden center, Minimalism was read as lodging meaning in the surface of the object, hence its interest in reflective materials, in exploiting the play of natural light.
>
> (Krauss, 1994)

Krauss would expand and alter this theme in this essay by situating the connection between Minimalism and the architecture of Mies van der Rohe squarely between the haze of phenomenology and the structural signification of the grid. Mies becomes linked to Minimalism less through box-like forms, or surfaces of reflective materials, but through an aesthetic tension between the singular object and the variable vagaries of loosely associated qualities. This tension is what Krauss identifies in the shifting readings of Anges Martin's paintings that move from material mark, to cloud like atmosphere, to blank signification; perceptual difference in tension with conceptual difference.

Ignasi de Sola-Morales Rubio draws a different connection between Mies and Minimalism.

> Mies's art, like the work of Donald Judd or Dan Flavin, has a material component that delimits it. The concrete materiality, which these have in common, makes them not general but particular. Their works are not the expression of a general idea, but tangible physical objects, the producers of perceptions and affections.
>
> (Sola-Morales Rubio, 1994)

Sola-Morales Rubio supports this reading of Mies through two references to the philosophy of Gilles Deleuze. The first is the idea that art produces a block of sensations, the combination of perceptions and affections. This idea comes from Deleuze and Guattari's last collaboration titled *What is Philosophy?* (1991). The second Deluzian reference is from *Difference and Repetition* (1968).

> Repetition as innovation, as the mechanism of liberation, of life and death; repetition as will, as the opposite of the laws of nature; repetition as a new morality beyond habit and memory; repetition that only attains tension and creativity with the fissures of difference, with disequilibrium, innovation, opening, and risk.
>
> (Sola-Morales Rubio, 1994)

It is important to recognize the simultaneous influence of Deleuze for both the Light Constructors and the Digital Folders. Questions of sensation, affect, and repetition will become crucial concepts for both sides, even though handled in different manners.

1995—The "Light Construction" exhibit at the Museum of Modern Art—curated by Terry Riley with accompanying catalog publication (Riley, 1995)

The "Light Construction" exhibit was the first major exposure in the United States for an emerging Neo-Modern aesthetic in architecture that tended toward simplified form and dematerialized matter. A partial list of participants includes; Steven Holl, Kazuyo Sejima, Toyo Ito, Jean Nouvel, Peter Zumthor, Herzog & de Meuron, Renzo Piano, Tod Williams/Billie Tsien, and OMA. This is an eclectic group if one considers the work that these practices would produce in the following 20 years, but in 1995 there was a strange alignment that brought together Japanese minimalism, Swiss tectonics, Dutch abstraction, and American craft. By paying closer attention to the projects included in the exhibition several initial assumptions can be questioned. This architecture was not articulated through the mechanical paradigm of expressed structure and construction assembly. Rather, structure was often hidden, joints reduced to a minimum, and material denied of any apparent "natural" origin. What bound these architects together was a combination of simple form and dematerialization, a combination that privileged a phenomenological response. As Terence Riley in the catalog introduction suggested, "The tension between viewer and object engendered by the use of veil-like built-up membranes parallels a tension between architectural surface and architectural form that is evident in many of the works presented here (Riley, 1995)." To support this introductory argument Riley quoted Rosalind Krauss's "The Grid, the /Cloud/, the Detail." "Rosalind Krauss has recently described a phenomenological reading of minimalist sculpture, on the part of certain architecture critics, which effects a shift in meaning that closely parallels the shift from form to surface evident in the projects presented here" (Riley, 1995).

1996—The Return of the Real *(Foster, 1996)—Hal Foster*

The Return of the Real is a collection of essays evaluating the influence of certain strands of 1960s art on contemporary art in light of the post-structuralist critiques produced during the 1970s and 1980s. One issue Foster grappled with was how to understand the shifting relevance of Minimalism for art production. There were several pieces to the argument, but one key moment was his identification of the phenomenological project in Minimalism as being in tension with the conceptual legacy of appropriation art.

> In this way the stake of minimalism is the nature of meaning and the status of the subject, both of which are held to be public, not private, produced in a physical interface with the actual world, not the mental space of idealist conception. Minimalism thus contradicts the two dominant models of the abstract expressionist, the artist as existential creator (advanced by Harold Rosenberg) and the artist as formal critic (advanced by Greenberg). In so doing it also challenges the two central positions in modern aesthetics that these two models of the artist represent, the first expressionist, the second formalist. More importantly, with stress on the temporality of perception, minimalism threatens the disciplinary order of modern aesthetics in which visual art is held to be strictly spatial.
>
> (Foster, 1996, p. 40)

For Foster, the provocation of Minimalism was that the art was simultaneously literal, serial, and phenomenological. This critique contains the suggestion that the most important quality of Minimalism was not abstraction as a formal essential ideal, but instead the manner in which it challenged conventions of artistic mediums.

> In this way the object of critical investigation becomes less the essence of a medium than "the social effect (function) of a work" and, more importantly, the intent of artistic intervention becomes less to secure a transcendental conviction in art than to undertake an immanent testing of its discursive rules and institutional regulations. Indeed, this last point may provide a provisional distinction between formalist, modernist art and avant-gardist, postmodernist art: to compel conviction versus to cast doubt; to seek the essential versus to reveal the conditional.
>
> (Foster, 1996, p.58)

It was in the "tension between different specific objects and repetitive serial ordering" that Foster finds a powerful folding of the aesthetic and social, the high and low, the industrial and mass-cultural made available in Minimalist Art (Foster, 1996). The chapter titled "The Crux of Minimalism" concludes with a quote from Gilles Deleuze's *Difference and Repetition*, referenced here not for the ideas of affect or sensation, but rather for the discussion of how Minimalism created aesthetic difference through the serial repetition of modern industrial processes. The artwork demanded a singular subjective experience of the temporal phenomena in which the body encountered it, and at the same moment it recoiled into the endless repetition of identical representation produced not through the hand crafted or expressive gesture but through mechanical, industrial manufacture. Understood in this way, Minimalist Art is not about a reduced formal essence, but closer to an aesthetic representation of the surface conditions of modernity. This places Minimalism in the lineage of realism.

1998—Folds, Bodies & Blobs: Collected Essays *(Lynn, 1998)—Greg Lynn*

The writing collected in the publication *Folds, Bodies, & Blobs* ran exactly the length of this four year time period from 1992 to 1996. There are three important recurring themes: first, an attempt to establish a position in opposition to Deconstruction, especially in its most prevalent visual representation as the *Deconstructivist Architecture* exhibition at MoMA in 1988; second, an attack on Neo-Modern tectonics, especially as represented by the *Light Construction* exhibition of 1995; and third, an argument for a formally novel architecture. This last theme referenced several different influences from physics, biology, information theory, differential geometry, and digital technologies. The prime references were to René Thom's catastrophe theories (Lynn, 1998) (pp. 85, 115, 144), Gregory Bateson's studies on evolutionary variation (Lynn, 1998) (pp. 67, 69, 113), D'Arcy Thompson's geometric deformations (Lynn, 1998) (pp. 38,46, 85,1 21,153), Edmund Husserl's *Origin of Geometry* (Lynn, 1998) (pp.43, 83, 118, 136, 208), and the writings of Gilles Deleuze (Lynn, 1998) (pp. 42, 47, 83, 111, 115, 130, 139, 223, 226). This combination of sources shows a newfound interest in the natural sciences especially biology, through the metaphors of mutations and variations in evolutionary nature. Architectural design was understood as an instance in a process of becoming; form was contingent on internal and external pressures. Context was translated as a field of forces, geometry was understood as continuous transformation, and matter was the manipulated terrain. The formal language was folded, curved, supple, and adaptable. These forms offered architectural effects that seemed to be ever-changing and dynamic, not dissimilar from the phenomena of sensation, the speed of technology, and the variations of the biological.

Minimalism

Minimalism as an aesthetic category in the 1960s catches ABC Art, Literal Art, Process Art, the Light and Space movement as well as Minimal Art. The artists referenced here are from two slightly different camps; East Coast and West Coast. Donald Judd, Dan Flavin, Tony Smith, Robert Morris and Sol Lewitt are representative of the New York school, Robert Irwin, Doug Wheeler, Craig Kauffman, and Ken Price from Los Angeles. There has been a tendency to read the New York Minimalists as more conceptual and the Los Angeles Minimalists as more phenomenological. It is important here to present a description of this artwork not based on geographical biases, but instead based on the four categories suggested above; reduced formal expression, suppressed articulation, serial procedure, and perceptual phenomena. Although these artists have very different material palettes and formal qualities they all share these categories in some way.

The first of our four characteristics states that in Minimalism, formal expressivity is reduced. Donald Judd took issue with the claim of reduction. He argued that new sculpture was producing new complexities. "Simple form and one or two colors are considered less by old standards. If changes in art are compared backwards, there always seems to be a reduction, since only old attributes are counted and these are always fewer" (Judd, 1965). Judd discusses how this new art form of specific objects, neither painting nor sculpture, contains qualities that are "strange and dangerous" (Judd, 1965), "intense and narrow and obsessive" (Judd, 1965), and how "an image has never before been the whole work, been so large, been so explicit and aggressive" (Judd, 1965). These comments provide a different platform from which to understand the simple geometric forms that Judd uses in his sculpture. These are not a "reduced" art, only a reduction in the formal expressivity associated with illusion and gesture in the conventions of Western Art. Minimalism is a challenge to conventions, both formal and conceptual. To interpret Minimalist form as abstract ideal geometry is a mistake often made by architects. The formal vocabulary of Minimalism, as Barbara Rose notes, is a combination of appropriation art from Marcel Duchamp and the Suprematism of Kazimir Malevich.

> It is important to keep in mind that both Duchamp's and Malevich's decisions were renunciations—on Duchamp's part, of the notion of the uniqueness of the art object and its differentiation from common objects, and on Malevich's part, a renunciation of the notion that art must be complex.
>
> (Rose, 1965)

Dan Flavin used off-the-shelf lengths of fluorescent light tubes. Donald Judd used standard industrially manufactured materials. Sol Lewitt for the majority of his sculptural career worked with variations of partially defined cubes, always exhaustively incomplete. Robert Irwin reduced the formal element of his art so far that he eventually gave up his studio, as the necessity of a physical space for the production of his art became superfluous. Ken Price sculpted objects as lumps that resisted expressive gesture not through abstract geometry but through soft informality.

Related to this reduction in formal expressivity is the suppressed articulation of the joint between materials. The joints are not hidden, yet are also not expressed. Donald Judd reveals the industrial material of his sculpture, the joints left in a matter of fact simplicity. Surface material is often folded, as in the sheet metal wall boxes; or the mechanical fasteners counter sunk producing edges perfectly flush in alignment. Another example is Robert Irwin's incredibly crafted and constructed slightly curved canvases. The assembly is completely sublimated by the experience of the perceptual phenomenon that they trigger, the craft hidden on the canvas's underside. Craig Kaufman's plastic and resin sculptures are smooth in all their transitions; formal smoothness of shape, tectonic seamlessness of casting, and optical translucency of material.

Tony Smith's sculptures are constructed from sheets of steel, which reproduce the folds in paper that Smith uses to develop the projects at a small scale. Even though these sculptures are assembled from a base tetrahedral unit, the unit is never legible in the final construction, only the smooth black surface that kinks and folds in unexpected ways.

Many Minimalist artists worked through multiple iterations, the process itself gaining as much importance as the final piece. This is clear for Sol Lewitt in both his *Variations of Incomplete Open Cubes* (1974) and his lifelong development of the wall drawing. These projects exist between the written instructions as a set of iterative procedures understood conceptually and the physical output experienced perceptually. Hal Foster describes repetition as one of the most important aspects in Minimalism. "In this way minimalism rids art of the anthropomorphic and representational not through anti-illusionist ideology so much as through serial production. For abstraction tends only to sublate representation, to preserve it in cancelation, whereas repetition, the (re)production of simulacra, tends to subvert representation, to undercut its referential logic" (Foster, 1996). In Minimalism, process is often rule-based with the appearance of objectivity or mechanism. This aspect is responsible for the undue emphasis placed on the "conceptual" aspects of Minimalist Art. Clear procedural rules are often understood as a tribute to mathematical rationality; as the height of abstraction. But, as Rosalind Krauss points out in the work of Sol Lewitt, the artwork is absurd, not rational (Krauss, 1985). The aesthetic result creates excessive affective qualities *through* abstraction, not the abstract representation of a conceptual idea. Repetition in Minimalist Art is both thematic in single works as well as in the production of series or runs of nearly identical pieces. Donald Judd worked through series of wall objects, floor boxes, and concrete frames. Dan Flavin held true to the possibilities of the standard length evenly-illuminated fluorescent tube for thirty-five years.

These artists also all pulled the artwork off of the wall (or as with Lewitt made it literally *the* wall) and into the space of the gallery. This art is often an object that edges closer to architecture than to the pedestal traditions of sculpture. The observer engages this art through movements of the body, shifts of light and perceptual distortions. This is one of the key components in a discussion connecting Minimalism with phenomenology. Minimalist Art is conditioned by the experiential observation of a subject encountering an object perceptually (Krauss, 1977). Donald Judd's sculptures are literally objects that the beholder must negotiate as a changing physical presence in real space. Doug Wheeler creates rooms of infinite luminous glow where the viewer loses all sense of depth. The color combinations in Ken Price's sculptures are structured around Joseph Albers *Interaction of Color* (1963), producing a flickering sensation through color contrast. Tony Smith's sculptures lean and shear forcing the inclination of the observer's body out of balance, yet resisting anthropomorphic identification.

The role of subjective bodily experience is crucial if we wish to engage the most prominent critique of Minimalism penned by Michael Fried. For Fried in "Art and Objecthood" (1965), Minimalism is critiqued for its literalness; an equivalency with everyday non-art objects (Fried, 1998). It is also critiqued as theatrical; it requires the subjective performance of the body moving in relation to the object in space in order to complete its meaning (Fried, 1998). Both of these aspects were deemed by Fried to be detrimental to the art qualities of the work. In his book *Nothing Less than Literal* (2004), Mark Linder argues that for Fried, the literal is a stand-in for the architectural (Linder, 2004). This reading implies that Fried is worried about more than the literal and theatrical; he is worried about the possible contamination of art by architecture. By pulling art away from the plane of the wall with its framed window-like view for transcendent contemplation, art enters into the everyday realm of real space, and for Fried is no longer "Art" (Krauss, 1999). Fried was opposed to the phenomenological aspects of Minimalism, aspects that would make Minimalist Art very appealing for architecture. The discussion that commonly follows is how Minimalism changed art practices, but this shift into real space, real objects, and real material, also radically affected architecture.

Two Birds

Although the categories are generalizations and the architects in each often changed over their careers, it is helpful to specify a list of architects comprising each category during the mid-1990s.

- *The Light Constructors*: Steven Holl, Kazuyo Sejima, Toyo Ito, Jean Nouvel, Peter Zumthor, Herzog de Meuron, Renzo Piano, Williams Tsien.

- *The Digital Folders*: Greg Lynn (FORM), Reiser+Umemoto, Asymptote, UN Studio, Mark Goulthorpe (dECOi), Lars Spuybroek (NOX), Kas Oosterhuis, Sulan Kolatan and William MacDonald (Kol/Mac), Zaha Hadid Architects.

Let us now examine these two architectural positions through the four categories suggested above in relation to Minimalist Art; reduced formal expression, suppressed articulation, serial procedure, and perceptual phenomena.

The formal language of the Light Constructors is easy to identify in the sculptures of Donald Judd, Tony Smith, and Robert Morris. Likewise, there are formal similarities between the Digital Folders and the art of Craig Kaufmann and Ken Price. But it is more than visual similarity of form that is at stake. In the catalog introduction for the *Light Construction* exhibit, Terrence Riley writes,

> In telling contrast to the ultimate importance given to architectural form in both historicist postmodernism and deconstructivism, many of these projects exhibit a remarkable lack of concern for, if not antipathy toward, formal considerations. In fact, most of the projects could be described by a phrase no more complicated than "rectangular volume."
>
> (Riley, 1995)

Topology is often evoked in relation to the continuous deformed rubber sheet like surfaces of 1990s Digital Folds. However, from a geometric point of view we could just as easily use topology to discuss Minimalist Art as generic boxes of "rectangular volume." Topology is the simplest, most reduced geometric classification focusing on sequence and continuity, not specific shape or form. In this manner it is also the most abstract geometric condition. As mentioned earlier, the formal languages for both sides are abstract. The Light Constructors saw in Minimalist Art the perceptual effects of simple abstract form. The Digital Folders derived form via abstract procedural notations of temporal geometric transformations.

The Light Constructors and the Digital Folders used different methods to suppress the articulation of the joint. The Light Constructors sublimated flat panels into planes that met magically in the small gap of the reveal, as if never physically connected. The Digital Folders suppressed articulation through the fold of one surface continuously into the other, creating a smooth flow between wall and floor that challenged notions of horizontality and verticality. This issue of tectonics was a hotly contested zone for both sides during the mid-1990s, and remains so today. Greg Lynn addressed tectonics specifically in opposition to the Light Constructors in "Differential Gravities" (Lynn, 1998) and "Why Tectonics is Square and Topology is Groovy" (Lynn, 1998). Pórez-Gómez and Pallasmaa have the reverse critique, arguing that digital architecture lacks the sensibility built through the contact of hand with material; a sensibility that provides the richness of the crafted world. However, a closer inspection of the architectural projects included in the *Light Construction* exhibit opens questions regarding this cliché of expressed construction and clear materiality. Steven Holl bounces colored light through apertures from unknown origins (D.E. Shaw and Company Offices). Kazuyo Sejima floats reflective materials past each other with no indication of assembly (Saishunkan Seiyaku Women's Dormitory). Herzog & de Meuron details a wood truss building to appear as if it is floating massive concrete, sandwiched between frosted illuminations of solid light (Goetz Collection). The small gap reveal, the concealed fastener, frosted translucent luminosity, and multiplied reflection all serve to dematerialize architecture. When examined in this light, the Digital Folders are more interested in material

Figure 5.1 Bregenz Kunsthaus—Peter Zumthor Architect. Completed 1999. Photo by author

Figure 5.2 NMR Facility, UN Studio Architect. Completed 1997. Photo by Christian Richters

matter than the Light Constructors. The formal folds often intensify the sensation of forces struggling through their materialization, rather than their de-materialization. This desire for morphogenetic formal articulation of material process suggests a tectonic that resists the articulation of assembly as discrete fragmented parts. The folded surface was used to create a formal continuity between multiple orientations of surfaces, expressive of forces other than the resistance of gravity.

As previously discussed, Minimalism is connected with ideas of process art and serialism as aesthetic tactics that used repetition or rule-based systems to distance the hand of the author from the resulting work. The Light Constructor's use of serialism as an aesthetic motif in architecture often betrays the conceptual desire to make a system of design legible in the repetition of its parts. In this way, the rationality of the building's appearance is in direct relation to the rationality of the process of design. Robin Evans noted this feature in the work of Mies van der Rohe. "Conceptual structures are notable for their independence from material contingency ... In order to look like a conceptual structure, a load-bearing structure must brazenly deny the fact of its burden" (Evans, 1997) This reading of Mies not as a tectonic rationalist, but as a conceptual rationalist in his use of abstract grid organizations, is one of the many ways in which Minimalism was tied to modern architecture. The Digital Folders, emphasized a more algorithmic aspect of procedure. For these architects it was a formal transformation that changed step by step. Even if the final result was smoothed as a continuous deformation, there was a latent history of procedural transformation. This process could be written as code, as a step by step recipe for the generation of form. At its most computational level, the locus of the architectural work became the script of transformations rather than the origin or outcome. These scripting procedures often achieved an absurd visual complexity from simple recursive rules akin to the dense buildup of a Sol Lewitt wall drawing.

Many of the Light Constructors treated the phenomena of perceptual experience as crucial components in the production of meaning in an architectural design. Phenomenology had a huge spread of influence across twentieth-century architecture through a number of different interpretations. It is important to note the difference between the *Genus Loci* phenomenology of Norberg-Schulz as an interpretation of late Martin Heidegger (i.e. Norberg-Schulz, 1980) and the material craft readings of Pallasmaa, more influenced by the writings of Maurice Merleau-Ponty (Pallasmaa, 1996). The Light Construction group combined these interpretations, shifting the conversation around place away from the earth bound site and into the atmosphere of light.

> Transparency and sensations of weightlessness and floatation are central themes in modernity. In recent decades a new architectural imagery has emerged, which employs reflection, gradations of transparency, overlay and juxtaposition to create subtle and changing sensations of space, movement and light. This new sensibility promises an architecture that can turn the relative immateriality and weightlessness of recent technological construction into a positive experience of place and meaning.
>
> (Pallasmaa, 1996, p .21)

The architecture of the Digital Folders was equally enamored with phenomena, although the source lineage was slightly different. The philosophical questions regarding phenomena are those surrounding affect and sensation drawn primarily from the writings of Gilles Deleuze. Deleuze is often understood to be anti-phenomenology due to his refutation of Hegel, but the philosophical debate regarding his relation to Husserl and Heidegger is complex and is anything but settled (i.e., Shores, 2012). A number of phenomenological issues run through his writings influential for the digital architecture discourse in the 1990s. Among the most widely read included: *A Thousand Plateaus* (1980) written with Felix Guattari, *Cinema 1: The Movement Image* (1983) and *Cinema 2: The Time Image* (1985), *Le Pli: Leibniz and the Baroque* (1988), and *Francis Bacon: The Logic of Sensation* (1981). The following descriptions by Deleuze of Francis Bacon's painting exemplify this phenomenological luster:

- "Sensation is vibration. … the state of the body 'before' organic representation: axes and vectors, gradients, zones, kinematic movements, and dynamic tendencies, in relation to which forms are contingent or accessory" (Deleuze, 2003, p. 30).
- "Color-force: Figures, flows, and broken tones" (Deleuze, 2003, p.116).
- "The phenomenological unity of the senses: sensation and rhythm" (Deleuze, 2003, p.31).
- "The action of invisible forces on the body" (Deleuze, 2003, p.36).
- "Deformation: neither transformation nor decomposition" (Deleuze, 2003, p.48).
- "Abstract painting, code and optical space vs. Action painting, diagram, and manual space" (Deleuze, 2003, p.81)

Architects interpreted Deleuze's writings as a way out of the fragmentary and into the dynamic flux of the material and energetic world, physically and virtually. Architecture was no longer the static end object, but instead evolved and emerged from a confluence of forces existing both externally and internally. The concepts of emergence, field, intensity, and dynamic force were tied to abstract graphic notations of these phenomena, translated into fields of vectors, flows, and gradients to gain a formal articulation. These diagrams represented an aesthetic agenda that predates the use of the computer in architectural design. The introduction of computation accelerated the ability of designers to handle larger quantities of information in more facile ways. This aspect is often mistakenly thought to make complex design simple, which is not the case; digital modeling was and continues to be as laboriously difficult as any other mediation. But, digital interfaces and output did provide a precise numeric calculation of forms that were outside of common architectural expertise. This aspect of precision was crucial for how computation entered the pragmatics of the building industry, but for the 1990s design discourse, the impact was to distance the artisanal hand from the mediation of architecture. A distancing that some architects felt as positive, some as negative, but as discussed above, this issue was a fundamental aspect for Minimalist Art.

Francis Bacon: The Logic of Sensation was originally published in French in 1981. Excerpts from three chapters; "Becoming Meat," "Painting and Sensation," and "The Diagram," were translated into English as part of *The Deleuze Reader* in 1993 (Deleuze, & Boundas, 1993). The first full English translation was in 1992, but it was published independently with an extremely small print edition. The only copy I have seen belongs to Peter Eisenman, which is a crucial connection. Through his reading, Eisenman developed many of the ideas that he would use to transform his post-structuralist critique towards a digital paradigm (Deleuze, 1992). The distancing of the hand of the author is an important crossover concept. It is interesting to see a significant amount of this transitional discourse in Eisenman's personal annotations on the text. "Diagram a critical tool," "figure vs. figurative" and "digital scrambler" are a few of the notes made in the margins of the text. When viewed in this light, Delueze's text on Bacon becomes a key document for deciphering a major transformation in formal discourse that occurred in the 1990s. This observation only occurs in hindsight though, for the full text was read by very few people at the time as a complete English translation was not available in broad publication until 2003. This distance from the mid-1990s Eisenman reading is important, for the interpretations in the new millennium lead toward a different discourse. In the 2000s the text was read not through post-structualist signification, but rather through the lens of affective qualities.

One Stone

A new version of the argument between the Light Constructors and the Digital Folders is being fought in the second decade of the twenty-first century by architects who follow a phenomenological agenda on one side and digital architects associated with "parametricism" on the other. This disagreement is as heated and antagonistic as its forbearer with many similar points of contention. But, as seen previously there is a fundamental level of shared issues. Both sides share a belief in the existence of fields of forces translated by an abstractly mediated version of context. These can be environmental (sun, wind, rain, climate, vegetation), cultural (techniques of craft, material, construction, and patterns of use), and/or perceptual (light, color, material texture, atmosphere). The parametric architect will find a manner in which these variables can be described mathematically in order to drive the associated parameters constraining the design. The phenomenological architect will find an intuitive equivalent through the perceptual feedback of drawing and modeling. Both sides believe that the architectural project comes from a close attention to the forces surrounding it through a process of abstraction that translates these forces into a visual or numerical language. Architecture is the crystallization or the inflection of these forces.

> To move through such a field would be akin to being thrown into a deep forest where trees have no name and where thickets and clearings emerge and fade gradually, and where topographic features are translated and accentuated by shifts in vegetation … Here everything is structured via intensities such as climatic gradients and shifts in vegetation. Here the lines or trajectories of movement following the vectors of intensity/transformation are prior to any points that might be encountered on these paths.
>
> (Schumacher, 2012, pp. 424–425)

On first reading this quote drips with phenomenological overtones. We would expect the phenomenology of Norberg-Schulz (Norberg-Schulz, 1980) instead of the "parametricism" described by the actual author, Patrick Schumacher. The apologies for parametric architecture as a style that Schumacher puts forward are largely built out of the late 1990s digital discourse. It is curious that the two-decade distance of *The Autopoiesis of Architecture* (2012) seems to reveal the phenomenological inclinations harbored in much of the digital design discourse in a manner that was more difficult to see in the 1990s.

The word "autopoiesis" was first used in biology by Humberto Maturana and Francisco Varela to describe "the self-producing nature of living systems" (Schumacher, 2012). In Varela's writing we find a number of this essay's recurring themes. First is a theory related to biology and the life sciences regarding the emergent properties of cellular life and their ability to self-replicate through an inner logic, a genetic code. Second these self-generated properties are part of the way in which an organism structures its perception of the world, which is generated by an interaction between external stimuli and internal actions related to sensorial abilities. This means that there is no "picture" of reality without the creative interjections of the perceiver. Varela describes this as a phenomenological idea pulled from both Merleau-Ponty and Heidegger (Varela, 1992). This reference completes the circle suggesting the depth to which phenomenology is woven into contemporary architectural thought.

Considered in this light, it is understandable that such a volatile disagreement exists, for like the Light Constructors and Digital Folders before them, both the "phenomenological" and "parametricist" share several similar beliefs. Both positions are deeply tied to abstraction and phenomenology. One side posits abstraction in form, allowing the phenomena of perception to become the focus of human experience. The other side locates abstraction in computational processes as a parallel of natural processes, form is contingent to the constraining parameters that translate these phenomena. The disagreement becomes a stalemate in that the terms are agreed upon but the interpretations as architecture are inverted, leading to frequent misunderstandings and a generation of architects talking past each other. By identifying this shared lineage, the hope is that we can swerve around this argument into other promising implications that stem from Minimalism, namely the strange possibilities of the aesthetics of realism.

References

Carpo, M. (2004). Ten Years of Folding. In G. Lynn (ed.), *AD Folding in Architecture*. Chichester, UK: John Wiley and Sons.

Conley, T. (1993). Translator's Preface. In G. Deleuze, *The Fold: Leibniz and the Baroque*. Minneapolis, MN: University of Minnesota Press.

Crary, J., & Kwinter, S. (1992). *Zone 6: Incorporations*. New York: Urzone Inc.

Deleuze, G. (1981) *Francis Bacon: The Logic of Sensation*. Annotated by P. Eisenman, New York: Portmanteau Press.

Deleuze, G., & Boundas, C. (eds.) (1993). *The Deleuze Reader*. New York: Columbia University Press.

Eisenman, P. (1992). Unfolding Events. In J. Crary & S. Kwinter (eds.), *Zone 6: Incorporations*. New York: Urzone Inc.

Evans, R. (1997). Mies van der Rohe's Paradoxical Symmetries. *Translations from Drawing to Building and Other Essays*. London: AA Publications.

Foster, H. (1996). *The Return of the Real*. Cambridge, MA: MIT Press.

Fried, M. (1998). In Art and Objecthood (1965) Chicago, IL: University of Chicago Press.

Holl, S., Pallasmaa, J., & Pérez-Gómez, A. (1994) *Questions of Perception*. Tokyo, Japan: a+u Publishing.

Judd, D. (1965). Specific Objects. *Art Papers* 8.

Kipnis, J. (1993). Towards a New Architecture. In G. Lynn (ed.), *AD Folding in Architectur,*, Chichester, UK: John Wiley and Sons.

Krauss, R. (1966). Allusion and Illusion in Donald Judd, *Art Forum 5,* New York.

Krauss, R. (1977). *Passages in Modern Sculpture*. New York: Viking Press.

Krauss, R. (1985). LeWitt in Progress. In *The Originality of the Avant-Garde and Other Modernist Myths*. Cambridge, MA: MIT Press

Krauss, R. (1994). The Grid, the /Cloud/, and the Detail, 133–134. In *The Presence of Mies,* D. Mertins, (ed.) New York: Princeton Architectural Press.

Krauss, R. (1999). *A Voyage on the North Sea*. London: Thames & Hudson

Linder, M. (2004). *Nothing Less than Literal*. Cambridge, MA: MIT Press.

Lynn, G. (ed.) (1993). *AD Folding in Architecture*. Chichester, UK: John Wiley and Sons.

Lynn, G. (1998). Differential Gravities. From Any 5 Conference 1994, *Folds, Bodies and Blobs: Collected Essays*. Brussels and London: La Lettre Volée.

Lynn, G. (1996). Why Tectonics is Square and Topology is Groovy. From Any 14 Conference 1996, *Folds, Bodies and Blobs: Collected Essays*. Brussels and London: La Lettre Volée.

Mertins, D. (ed.) (1994). *The Presence of Mies*. New York: Princeton Architectural Press.

Norberg-Schulz, C. (1980). *Genus Loci: Towards a Phenomenology of Architecture*. New York: Rizzoli.
Pallasmaa, J. (1994). An Architecture of the Seven Senses, 29. In *Questions of Perception*. Tokyo, Japan: a+u Publishing.
Pallasmaa, J. (1996). *The Eyes of the Skin*, London: Academy Editions.
Riley, T. (1995). *Light Construction*. New York: MoMA.
Rose, B. (1965). ABC Art. In G. Battcock (ed.), *Minimal Art: A Critical Anthology*. New York: E.P. Dutton & Co.
Schumacher, P. (2012). *The Autopoiesis of Architecture*. Chichester, UK: John Wiley and Sons.
Shores, C. (2012). Body and World in Merleau-Ponty and Deleuze, *Studia Phenomenologica* Vol. XII. Bucharest: Romanian Society for Phenomenology.
Sola-Morales Rubio, I. (1994) Mies van der Rohe and Minimalism. In D. Mertins (ed.), *The Presence of Mies*. New York: Princeton Architectural Press.
Varela, F. (1992) The Reenchantment of the Concrete. In J. Crary & S. Kwinter (eds.), *Zone 6: Incorporations*. New York: Urzone Inc.

6

Design Emulating Biological and Organic Forms

Morphogenetic Design

Ralph Knowles

At this critical time of unprecedented energy use, worldwide migration and urbanization, architects are being challenged by such leaders in the field as Edward Mazria who has called for "a dialogue with nature" to answer at least some of our problems. This chapter explores some possible outcomes of such a dialogue.

What might buildings and cities look like if we accepted the challenge to have open and honest cooperation with nature? What patterns would they display? Would we meet them with recognition and empathy or pass them by with indifference? Would they interest us, please us and bring us joy, or would they be ordinary and lacking in quality? These are questions with practical meaning for a sustainable life.

This chapter focuses specifically on how architectural form responds to the forces of sunlight and heat for energy and enhanced quality of life. The fascination with this subject extends from antiquity to our own time, from naturally occurring shapes to designed forms that promise particular modes of solar performance. The studies shown here as illustration extend over a period of thirty-five years, from 1967 to 2002, at the University of Southern California's School of Architecture.

A desire to learn and to teach more about biological and organic forms led in 1967 to the establishment of the USC Natural Forces Laboratory. With a grant from the Design Arts Program of the National Endowment for the Arts, the laboratory was first set up as an essential part of the third-year architecture design studio. Three kinds of simulation tools were designed, built and used by students as integral to the design process. Sun machines, wind tunnels, and water tables of various types occupied the studio space along with traditional drafting tables. This team-taught integrated function of the laboratory was subsequently transferred to a bigger space occupied by the USC Graduate Program in Building Science. Now, computers have mostly replaced the earlier equipment of physical simulation and testing.

This chapter is organized in two major parts. The first part goes back in history to describe how the pueblos of the Southwest emulated biological and organic forms in response to the sun. The second part of the chapter gives an account of how a modern city may be zoned as a morphogenetic field in which each individual property may interact with others for access to the sun.

Found Form: Long House, Mesa Verde, CO

Long before modern technology opened the chance for designers to examine certain performance aspects of their projects as part of the creative process, there was the recognition that some natural forms behaved in helpful architectural ways. An example is Long House.

In the extreme southwestern corner of Colorado lies a deeply eroded tableland called Mesa Verde. Its geology consists of deep layers of sandstone on a slate base. Over millennia, water has worked its way downward through the sandstone, settling on the slate base and flowing outward toward the cliff face where continuous water action formed shallow caves with broad openings. The caves have sloping floors of slate; the sandstone overhead rises steeply to the cliff edge. In the bright summer sun of the region these edges cast deep and mobile shadows, leaving the impression of a furled brow on the remains of some ancient Cyclops.

There is evidence that people lived in the region for twelve to 14,000 years, working their fields on the mesa above while often taking refuge at night in the caves. Their permanent houses on the mesa were one story, built side by side in crescent-shaped rows opening to the south. Around A.D. 1100 the region fell under attack from marauding nomads. The inhabitants then retreated to the caves where they built permanent dwellings while continuing to farm the mesa above. By A.D. 1500 an extensive drought diminished their ability to withstand further attack and the culture died. An impressive record remains today behind the stone prosceniums of the caves.

The anthropologist Douglas Osborne has examined this permanent record with particular attention to the one called Longhouse. This settlement occupies a cave 500 feet across and 130 feet deep. At the face of the cliff the cave rises 200 feet in a long vaulting arch. These large dimensions provided ample space for a settlement of considerable size. With stone from the cave, short timbers from the mesa above, and clay from the river below, living spaces were enclosed in a terraced arrangement, the roof of one space becoming the terrace of the one above and further to the rear of the cave.

There are other large caves among the hundreds in the Mesa Verde area. Many of them have access to the agricultural land on the mesa and are defensible because of difficult access. Although most of them, including Longhouse, are subject to water action and flaking from above, those showing signs of past settlement are numerous. On-site observations indicate that most of the caves open to the east or west and do not feel as comfortable through the year as Longhouse with its south orientation. Those facing east tend to feel too cold in winter. Others opening to the west seem too hot in summer. This first-hand knowledge must have been well recognized by the original builders.

In Longhouse, the most important mechanism that performs in response to the sun is its great overhanging brow. Buildings were arranged in south-facing tiers so that their vertical stone walls and horizontal terraces received great benefit from the low winter sun while being protected during the hot summer sun by shadows cast from the upper edge of the of the cave opening.

In combination with the sun's dynamic geometry at latitude 37 degrees north, the brow increases the desirability of Longhouse as a place to live comfortably year round. Summer sun barely enters the cave. The sun rises at about 30 degrees to the north of east. It circles to a high noontime altitude of 78 degrees, and when it disappears at sunset its path has taken it 30 degrees to the north of due west. The consequence is that the high desert summer sun is shadowed from the south-facing cave and building surfaces; the cave remains comfortably cool. By contrast, winter sun floods the cave. The winter sun first appears at 30 degrees to the south of east. Its noontime altitude is only slightly over 30 degrees above the horizon and sunset occurs 30 degrees to the south of west. The winter sun shines on most cave and building surfaces all day long, rendering them pleasantly bright and warm.

Designed Form: Pueblo Bonito, Chaco Canyon, NM

While the dwellers of Longhouse recognized sheltering advantages in a particular natural setting, the builders of Pueblo Bonito purposely created a freestanding structure to perform in particular relation to the sun. Planned and constructed in two stages by ancestral pueblo peoples, for defense reasons and for spiritual motives, Bonito appears to have been the center of the Chacoan world.

Today Pueblo Bonito evokes the image of a great amphitheater, with a stage surrounded by curving rows of seats too big for people—the Greek theater of Epidauros transplanted and scaled for gods. Even today, one can sense in the powerful half forms of the ruins some pulsing affirmation of life (as illustrated in ink drawing by Gary S. Shigemura) (Knowles, 1974).

The history of the pueblo can be read in changes of form as interpreted and first recorded by archeologist N. M. Judd. Chaco Canyon had been occupied long before the pueblo was begun. During this early time people lived in small huts, isolated from one another. Then around A.D. 919, the people collectively built a large two- and three-tiered crescent structure with doors and windows opening off terraces facing mainly to the southeast. Judd dubbed this first structure "Old Bonito" (Judd, 1964; Judd, 1954).

Judd reports that around A.D. 1050–1060, strangers to the original Bonitians were welcomed into the region, bringing a quite different culture. Their influence must have been extraordinary if modifications to the original building form are any indication. During a 20-year period, these skilled and apparently self-confident builders tripled the size of the original pueblo. Not only was their use of materials refined but also their understanding of solar dynamics shows a high degree of sophistication. Judd called this later structure "New Bonito."

Figure 6.1 Pueblo Bonito: N.M. Judd unearthed Pueblo Bonito in Chaco Canyon, New Mexico during seven National Geographic Society expeditions, 1921–1927. Ink drawing by Gary S. Shigemura in Ralph L. Knowles, *Energy and Form.* (Cambridge, MA: MIT Press, 1974) 34

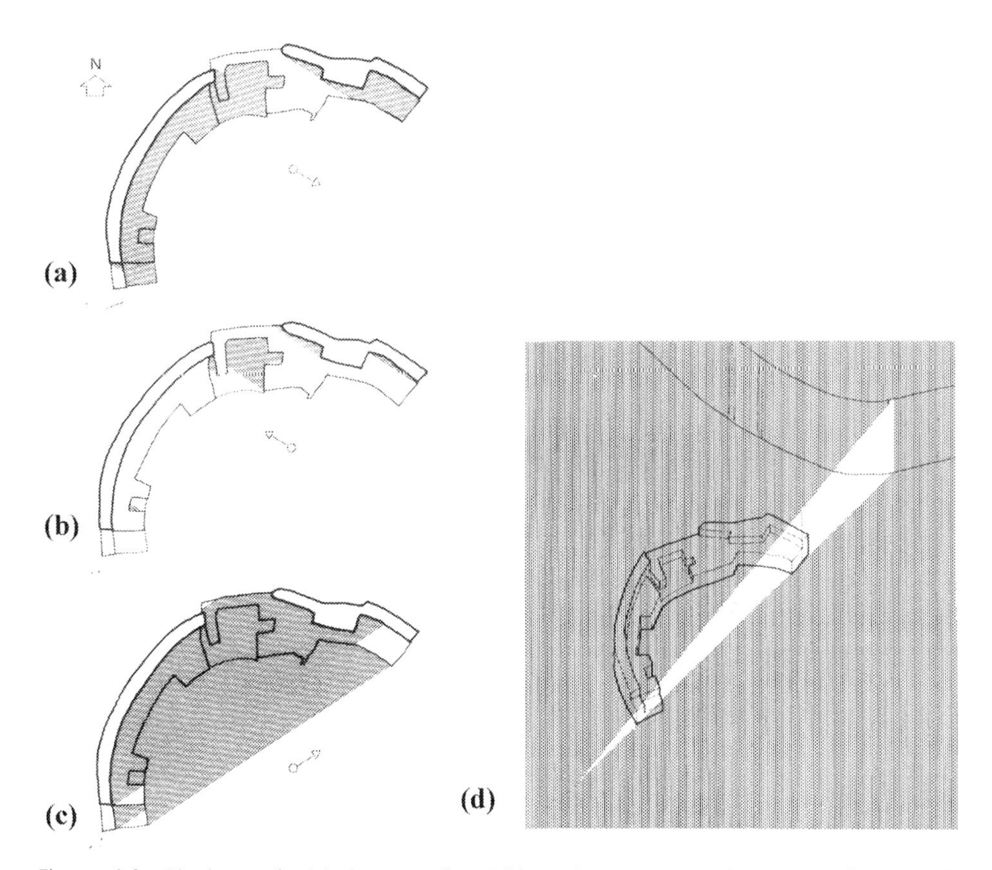

Figure 6.2 Shadows of critical sun angles, Old Bonito. Arrows indicate critical sun angles: (a) sunset, summer solstice; (b) sunrise, winter solstice; (c) sunset, winter solstice; (d) sunrise, summer solstice

As with the southern exposure of tiered construction at Longhouse at Mesa Verde, the forms of both Old and New Pueblo Bonito suggest the possibility of a special relationship to the sun. Careful examination demonstrates that the way they both received sunshine on their south-facing walls and terraces and then transferred the heat to interior spaces tended to equalize seasonal temperature differences—i.e. they tended toward a steady thermal state.

Both Old and New Bonito also performed as solar observatories. The outlines of Old Bonito have long-since been obscured by the great walls of the larger New Bonito but model studies have shown that Old Bonito accomplished this by the way sunlight interacted with the overall building shape to identify sunrise and sunset on both the summer and winter solstices.

Several later studies by others have shown that New Bonito appears to have depended on how sunlight entered strategically placed openings as well as on overall shape to keep solar time.

New Bonito, in addition to being an early trading center of considerable importance was probably designed as a temple to honor the sun and was very likely a background for ritual celebrations that occurred not only at special times of the year but perhaps every morning and evening with the rising and setting of the sun. Daily and seasonal rhythms were not only the beat of pueblo life, they were causes of celebration.

Simulating changes in patterns of sunlight and shadow conveys some sense of this spiritual dimension of Bonito. The result of the sun's daily migrations is a shift in the shadowed portions of the great courts and a related shift in the unlighted portions. That daily shift always takes place in the east-west direction. The summer-winter shift occurs in a north-south direction.

The daily shift in the shadows from east to west occurs at all times of the year, but the shadowing of the north and south portions of the court varies with seasons. The result is a kind of segmentation of each court into spotlighted areas where it is easy to imagine ritual activities taking place at different locations in the courts at different times of the day and year. Such rituals occur today on the terraces and in the courtyards of modern pueblos.

This practice of ritually following the patterns of light and dark was probably well developed by the time of Bonito. Morning ritual dances might have taken place in the glaring light of the western portion of each court, while evening dances would have shifted their stage to the east. Summer celebrations might have occurred in the southern portions of each court, while the winter celebrations shifted northward to gain exposure to the sun (Scully, 1975)

Historically, ritual has served to intensify our awareness of recurring natural events. The rites of spring, fall, and Thanksgiving, morning flags and evening trumpets, all remind us of natural time. Of course, Bonito may not have functioned precisely as described, but the images are strong. The notion that ritual activities may have migrated upon Bonito's stage, following the movements of the sun, only strengthens the perceptual link between form and performance.

Solar Envelope

The sun is fundamental to all life. It is the source of our vision, our warmth, our energy, the rhythms and rituals of our lives. Its movements inform our perceptions of time and space and our scale in the universe. Assured access to sunshine is thus important to the quality of our lives.

To use the sun, you must have access to it. To have access, there must be a public recognition of the right of access—a solar policy. Access can be achieved by private design or development initiatives, but a commitment expressed as public policy best assures access on an equitable, comprehensive and long-term basis. The process of developing a public policy also provides a forum for public expression of the value of urban solar access.

It is a simple fact that tall buildings cast long shadows. A 50-story tower in Los Angeles casts a shadow about 1,000 feet long (305 m) between 1 and 2 pm in December. By 3 pm, that building's shadow is close to 1,800 feet long (549 m), with an area equivalent to two city blocks. Its leading edge cuts across the swimming pool of a popular downtown hotel isolating a few sunbathers in a narrow strip of warm sunlight. The rest of the pool area is shadowed, cold and empty.

There is an ethical issue here, as well as an issue of quality of life. While I may choose to stand in shadow, I resist a developer's mandating it. If I occupy a building in the wake of another's shadow, I will resist that violation of my right to the sun's light and heat. I can always create shade for myself but access to the sun must be guaranteed.

There are recent energy-conscious building designs that accomplish their efficiency goals at the expense of their neighbors. A building that publicizes its use of the sun to save energy but deprives its neighbors of the same opportunity is clearly on questionable ethical ground. By using a concept of solar zoning called *solar envelope*, which describes the volumetric limits to development that will not shadow its neighbors, we can address the ethical issues of a right to sunshine in cities. We can also reclaim the accents, meter and tempo of nature in our lives.

The solar envelope represents what urban planner Frederick R. Steiner, in a general reference to planning, describes as "a philosophy for organizing actions that enable people to predict and visualize the future of any land area … that gives people the ability to link actions on specific parcels of land to larger regional systems" (Steiner, 1991).

In that philosophical sense, the solar envelope represents what may be called a *Meta-control* on performance, applied at a higher level of abstraction than, for example, building and safety codes. It does this by setting limits on the size and shape of a building volume on a given site to assure the sun-rights of surrounding properties. Within the envelope architects and developers are free to make their own choices. Because sunshine is mutually assured to all properties, designers can make use of the changing directions and properties of light without fear that a taller building will one day cancel their ideas. The potential exists to conceive of architecture in other than static terms of form and space.

As a public zoning mechanism, the solar envelope liberates and challenges the architect to design with nature. Architects can commit to building and urban form in response to orientation. One side of a building will not look like another and one side of a street will not look like another. Development will tend to be lower on the south side of a street than on the north where a major southern exposure is thus preserved. Streets take on a directional character where orientation is clearly recognized. Buildings and streets assume separate identities, providing a basis for what Kevin Lynch has called "way finding" (Lynch, 1960).

What Is a Solar Envelope?

The solar envelope is not a physical thing. It is a set of imaginary boundaries, enclosing a building site, that regulate development in relation to the sun's motion. Buildings within this envelope do not overshadow their surroundings during critical energy-receiving periods of the day and year.

Consider a biological analogy: while the solar envelope is not a physical thing, it nonetheless can be viewed in biological terms as the basic theoretical unit in the differentiation and growth of a morphogenetic urban field. It interacts with other units (properties) to guarantee solar access. When applied uniformly, as the basic structure of an urban field, it has the effect of preserving the solar rights of others that you would claim for yourself.

The idea of an imaginary envelope is common to all zoning in the United States. Conventional zoning mostly uses an envelope shaped like a simple box with four sides and a top to establish setbacks and heights. In contrast, the moving rays of the sun generate solar envelopes, resulting in forms like multi-faceted crystals or even a series of warped surfaces. Adjacent envelopes can be quite different, depending on their site and particular surroundings. Consequently, buildings made within the solar envelope are more likely to have unique shapes than to repeat box-like designs.

The solar envelope is a construct of space and time: the physical boundaries of surrounding properties and the period for which access to sunshine is assured. The way these measures are set decides the envelope's final size and shape (Knowles, 1981).

Shadow Fences

First, the solar envelope guarantees sunshine to others by preventing shadows above designated boundaries along neighboring property lines; these boundaries have been called *shadow fences*. A shadow fence is an imaginary wall that rises from a property line. The solar envelope is then configured to meet the top of the fence rather than the ground, thus allowing the solar envelope to rise and gain volume. Different heights of shadow fences will affect the shape and size of the envelope.

Shadow fences, being imaginary, do not actually cast shadows but instead allow shadowing of adjacent properties within limits set by community values. The height of the shadow fence can be set in response to any number of different surrounding elements such as windows, party walls, or courtyards. The height of the shadow fence may also be determined by adjacent land-uses. For example, housing may have lower shadow fences, and thus less overshadowing, than some commercial or industrial uses where rooftop access for solar collectors may suffice.

Cut-off Times

Second, the envelope provides the largest possible building volume within time constraints, called *cut-off times*. The envelope accomplishes this by defining the largest theoretical container of space that would not cast shadows on neighboring properties between specified times of the day. Cut-off times that are specified very early in the morning and late in the afternoon will result in smaller volumes than would result from later times in the morning and earlier times in the afternoon.

When shadow fences are set at all property lines (sides as well as front and back), including any adjacent streets or alleys, solar envelopes are shaped with tilted facets defined by the sloping rays of the sun. Each separate face of the envelope is defined by a different time of day or season of the year. And because the wintertime sun angles are lowest, they are usually the main determining factor of envelope form.

Realizations

Motivated by objections from architects and developers, studies conducted in USC's Solar Studio have tested the proposition that *the solar envelope will not overly constrain either development or design*. Developers have objected to the possibility that they might lose freedom to use their property as they see fit while architects have complained about the possible loss of design choices. Over a period of ten years, 1983–1993) the USC Solar Studio challenged these expressions of opposition (Knowles, 2006).

A design-studio project to test that proposition is shown on the diagonal Spanish grid of downtown Los Angeles, achieving densities of 80 to 100 du/ac (198 to 247du/ha). The solar envelopes are generated to provide four hours of sunshine in winter and eight hours in summer; they slope downward to a 20ft (6.1 m) shadow fence at all property lines to accommodate a base of street-front shops under housing. The envelopes are consistently higher on the south than on the north with the exception of tower-like shapes that project upwards at some corners where shadows are allowed to extend further northward into streets, but not onto properties across the street.

When building designs fill the solar envelopes, they contain many traditional elements. Roof terraces appear where the rectangular geometry of construction meets the sloping envelope. Courtyards center many designs to achieve a proper exposure for sunshine and air. Façades are enriched by porches, screens, and clerestories—all differentiated by orientation to the sun and wind. Beyond the appearance of such time-honored means that respond to nature, adjacent buildings meet each other gently, across sloping spaces, not abruptly

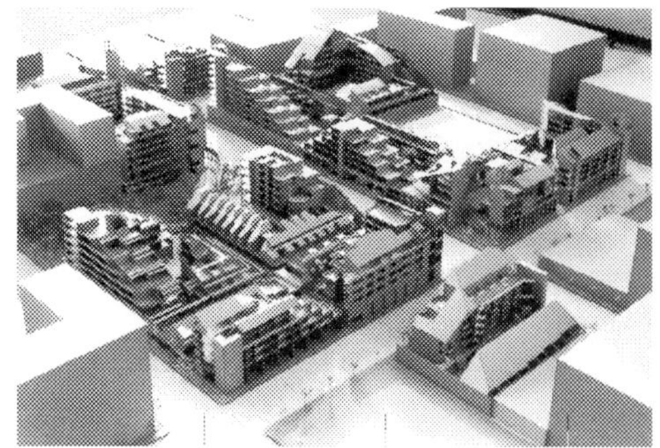

Figure 6.3 Housing project on the Spanish grid, viewed from the east: (left) the solar envelopes appear crystal-like while existing buildings are rectilinear blocks; (right) housing designs under the envelope achieve a density range of 80 to 100 du/ac (198 to 247 du/ha) over street-front commercial (the old Spanish grid runs at about 36 degrees off the N–S axis of the US Land Ordinance of 1785). Source: Ralph L. Knowles, *Ritual House* (Washington, DC: Island Press, 2006) 134

across property sidelines and alleys. The resulting spaces, not confining and dark but rather liberating and filled with light, allow distance views and the free flow of air through the city.

When shadow fences are set only at front and back property lines but not at sidelines, solar envelopes run continuously to allow for an unbroken façade along a typical suburban street. A studio project that tests this condition replaces suburban densities of 5 to 7 du/ac (12 to 17 du/ha) with higher densities of 25 to 45 du/ac (62 to 111 du/ha). The solar envelopes rise and fall with changes in street orientation and lot size. Envelope rules provide longer periods of sunshine than in the first project: six hours on a winter day, ten hours in summer. They are generated to a 6ft (1.8m) high shadow fence across streets at neighboring front yards and at rear property lines. Since envelopes do not drop at property sidelines as in the first project, buildings are free to run continuously along the street.

When building designs replace the envelopes, the result is remarkable innovation within harmony. The continuous envelopes allow a smooth flow of street fronts. At the same time, building types range from town houses and courtyard clusters to apartments. Individual designers are clearly exploring separate formal ideas from one parcel to another. The consequence is an enormous range of diversity and choice within a neighborhood.

We have seen that the basic solar envelope, especially when applied at higher urban densities, tends to produce roof terraces, a real benefit for urban living. When the right angles of most building construction meet the sloping geometry of the solar envelope, stepping roofs are a natural result. Instead of abandoning these terraces as left-out roofs, they can be designed spaces for enriching urban life. They can also replace the ground level covered by the building: "green roofs" for gardening, growing fruits, vegetables and flowers, and for small trees—absorbing carbon dioxide and releasing oxygen into the atmosphere, attracting birds, bees, and butterflies. But municipalities that limit the building envelope, usually by applying only winter sun angles, preclude some important dynamic possibilities for design. While such amenities definitely benefit urban living, more recent studies have explored the possibility that the size and shape of the envelope need not be limited by winter boundaries, thus expanding even further morphogenetic design possibilities.

Figure 6.4 Housing project on curving streets, viewed from the south: (left) solar envelopes run continuously along the street, dropping to shadow fences only at the front and back of lots; (right) housing designs under the envelope achieve a density range of 25 to 45 du/ac (62 to111 du/ha), much higher than normal subdivision densities. Source: Ralph L. Knowles, *Ritual House* (Washington, DC: Island Press, 2006) 135

Interstitium

"Works that are dynamic and based on systems in these times of dynamism and systems... invite our participation in their lives." Thus, architect Eduardo Catalano speaks of a great mechanical flower, *Floralis Generica* that he designed for the Plaza Naciones Unidas in Buenos Aires. The flower, based on the hibiscus, opens and closes giant petals with the days and seasons "to integrate the creations of man with the creations of the earth." The work is now a popular reality in a civic space where people of all ages gather around and are reminded of their connection to nature (Catalano, 2003).

Catalano's flower, by opening and closing daily, symbolizes a morphogenetic vision for architecture. Traditional modes of sheltering have always corresponded with nature's rhythms and, at the same time, evoked rich patterns of social behavior. A dynamic interpretation of solar-envelope zoning can advance the integration of such traditional methods and, at the same time, support the dynamism of a new architectural paradigm—one based on a dialogue with nature that will give architecture its identity.

The solar envelope has been earlier defined as the largest theoretical volume on a building site that does not critically overshadow neighbors, but the size and shape of the envelope need not be fixed. It may contract in winter and expand in summer while still allowing the same period of solar access to adjacent properties. Between the winter envelope and the generally higher summer envelope is an intervening space, a region of temporality that can accommodate seasonal adjustments to program and climate. Analogies drawn from nature have provided a name for this region: *Interstitium.*

The term "interstitium" is borrowed from human anatomy. The interstitial space of the lung is that area of tissue between the alveoli (tiny air sacs) and the capillaries that carry the blood. When we breathe in, the alveoli expand with air, and the interstitium stretches into a very thin layer. In this way, alveoli and capillaries are brought into close proximity so the oxygen has less distance to travel in its diffusion from outer world (alveolus) to inner world (capillary). When we breathe out, the process reverses and the interstitium contracts. Like Catalano's flower, architecture can also expand and contract in response to the cycles of nature.

An architectural interstitium expands the morphogenetic role of the solar envelope by responding to changing seasons. A building might, for many good reasons, transform from a tighter, compact winter mode to a looser arrangement in summer. Flexible structures, comprising either the whole or some part of a building, might expand and contract, making use of different seasonal envelopes. And all surrounding properties comprising a morphogenetic field can enjoy these same design choices as well.

The functional needs of buildings quite often change with the seasons. This sort of cyclic behavior may include advertising, selling, entertaining, manufacturing, sports, and gardening. Some changes can be accommodated within the fixed boundaries of the basic envelope. Others, as for example temporary housing for summer tourists or a theater under the warm nighttime sky, can benefit from a flexible structure. Summer cafés, market fairs, art exhibits and expanded common rooms for apartment dwellers are other possible uses.

The interstitium provides the space for adding open trellises, lattice structures for supporting deciduous plants and vines that shed their leaves in winter, gaining them back in spring for summer shade. It even allows for the summertime addition of folding rooms, screened for warm-weather sleeping or recreation. When combined with roof gardens, the result is an important enrichment of urban life.

The interstitium, besides accommodating the flexible use of space, can act as a shield, a zone of defense against climatic extremes. Shading devices that rise during the summer months for comfort in outdoor spaces or to cool the roof and reduce air-conditioning loads can come down in winter. In some climates, such as Hawaii, rain catchers might rise for protection from downpours and to catch precious fresh water. Such shields might be as small as a parasol or as large as a circus tent, operated manually or completely automated with a kinetic device responding to sun, wind or water.

Courtyard buildings, because they are so common throughout the world, deserve special attention for the design advantages provided by the interstitium. The traditional courtyard houses of southern Spain gain comfort by means that transform space by day and by season. John Reynolds has described how Spanish courtyard houses typically use several rhythmic adjustments to nature. One example is the house of Victor Carrasco in southern Spain where extremely hot and dry summers make cooling the major objective. The adjustments he describes modify the courtyard space that centers the house. They also match up with family rituals, private and often joyous (Reynolds, 2002).

Shading for the patio depends on a movable horizontal white translucent canvas cover or *toldo*. Like a large tree, the toldo casts shade over the entire patio during a hot summer day; unlike a tree, it is swept away in the early evening to facilitate both ventilation and cold-sky radiation at night. Winter reverses the cycle. As falling leaves permit warming rays of the sun to pass through a mantilla of bare branches, so the toldo is folded back during the day to let sunlight flood the patio; then at night it is closed to retain the heat that was collected during the day.

Adjusting the toldo provides desirable shade but we can also imagine how it changes the feeling of space. Open, the toldo extends the view to the sky, shrinking pupils to pinpoints. Leaves of a tree or of a vine appear in dark outline; wind stirs shadows across the patio floor. The sounds of neighborhood children, passing cars, and barking dogs remind the family of a wider world. In contrast, the closed toldo limits the view, darkens and quiets the space. Sharp contrasts give way to suffused light; moving shadows, to still shade. The atmosphere is more protective, more intimate. Only at the edges of the courtyard, where the toldo does not quite meet the walls, does there remain a trace of the outside brightness.

Using the interstitial space of the solar envelope can expand the potential of courtyards, offering architects a powerful tool for designing in cities. With so many possible functions and endless variations of size and shape, there are numerous ways to make courtyards serve as dynamic spatial intersections, domains of choice that are both culturally and climatically responsive.

Building on the example of the Spanish toldo, a white translucent canvas covering, modern ways can be found to achieve comfort in courtyards. John Reynolds points out that, as traditionally applied in Spain, the toldo nearly fills the sky opening of the courtyard, interfering with ventilation. It might thus be seen as disadvantageous despite its obvious advantage for shade. However, by taking advantage of the interstitium, a courtyard cover can rise above the building to shield from summer sun and, at the same time, to direct cooling winds downward to the patio floor. In winter, the cover withdraws so that the courtyard can receive full sunshine and less direct wind. Another possibility is that wind scoops may rise into the interstitium as a separate mechanism from the toldo.

Los Angeles, like Spain, has a long history of courtyard buildings. The era of courtyard buildings in Los Angeles dates from the eighteenth-century Spanish Missions to elegant housing of the 1920s. Then the building boom after World War II mostly rejected this history in favor of air-conditioned tract houses and high-rises. Now, concerns for earthquake safety and for energy conservation, as well as the need for greater density, have awakened interest in mid-rise courtyard buildings for many different applications.

More recent studies at USC's Natural Forces laboratory have explored the urban possibilities for combining sun control and ventilation under the interstitium. Besides the courtyard cover, ventilation stacks can rise above the winter roofline allowing for interior heat to be vented in summer. Structures resembling large awnings or umbrellas can shade and ventilate the courtyard. Hence, the summer landscape might unfold with clusters of diamond-shaped sails or kites floating motionless and weightless above the rooftops. The winter landscape might collapse inward, appearing lower and smoother than in summer. All such means are expansions of ways people have traditionally achieved comfort while conserving energy.

Large deciduous trees, valued for both climate control and beauty, can be accommodated by the interstitium. Studies have shown a summertime difference of as much as 42F (23C) in urban surface temperatures between those well shaded by trees and those in direct sun. Unfortunately, conventional solar-access zoning can work against trees. Clearly, evergreens do need to be limited to the winter envelope to avoid harmful overshadowing of neighboring properties. Otherwise, for trees that lose their leaves in winter, there is no reason why they shouldn't rise in maturity to fill summer boundaries of the interstitium.

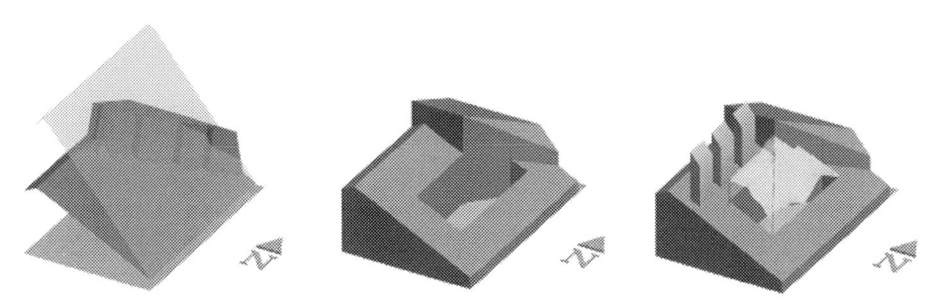

Figure 6.5 Climatic adaptations: (left) winter and summer envelopes; (middle) diagrammatic building winter mode with courtyard open; (right) diagrammatic ventilation stacks and courtyard cover—summer mode (computer modeling by Karen Kensek). Source: Ralph L. Knowles, *Ritual House* (Washington, DC: Island Press, 2006) 157

Looking to the Future

The benefits of solar-access zoning can be realized around the world. The results of the Los Angeles studies, done at 34 N, can apply directly to any city at approximately the same latitude either north or south of the equator. Some of these are Baghdad, Tehran, Kabul, Lahore, Osaka, Tokyo, Buenos Aires, and Santiago. For cities at other latitudes, the size and shape of the solar envelope will vary, but the basic principles hold.

Investigations of the solar envelope have also been done in places at latitudes other than 34 N. The most northerly location is Bratislava at 48 N, where a mixed-use study was made in 1993 at the Slovak Technical University. The most southerly site is Honolulu at 21 N where, between 1999 and 2000, two separate hillside-housing studies were made at the University of Hawaii at Manoa. Design and development requirements were met in each case, confirming the value of solar-access zoning within a broad belt from at least 50 N to 50 S.

The interstitium of the solar envelope adds measures of time to the fixed dimensions of older zoning frameworks. It offers a dynamic reference in which buildings may change: growing, decaying, moving or disassembling with the seasons. Designers and dwellers alike thus have the opportunity to explore new possibilities for self-expression that derive from the rhythms of a place.

With boundaries that pulse, urban designers may conceive a kinetic landscape. In winter, the lowest envelopes outline a compact and undulating landscape. Spring and fall bring an additional layer of architectural space. Finally, summer adds a third layer of space into which sheltering systems can expand to complete a yearly cycle for seasonal programming and for climate control. The effect is a collective rising and falling of the scene—like breathing.

References

Catalano, E. (2003). *Floralis Generica*. Cambridge, MA: MIT Press.
Judd, N.M. (1954). *The Material Culture of Pueblo Bonito*. Washington, DC: Smithsonian Institution.
Judd, N.M. (1964). *The Architecture of Pueblo Bonito*. Washington, DC: Smithsonian Institution.
Knowles, R. L. (1974). *Energy and Form*, 34. Cambridge, MA: MIT Press.
Knowles, R.L. (1981). *Sun Rhythm Form*. Cambridge, MA: MIT Press.
Knowles, R.L. (2006). *Ritual House*. Washington, DC: Island Press.
Lynch, K. (1960). *The Image of the City*. Cambridge, MA: The Technical Press & Harvard University Press.

Reynolds, J.S. (2002). *Courtyards: Aesthetic, Social, and Thermal Delight.* New York, NY: John Wiley & Sons.
Scully, V.J. (1975). *Pueblo: Mountain, Valley, Dance.* New York, NY: Viking.
Steiner, F.R. (1991). *The Living Landscape: An Ecological Approach to Landscape Planning.* New York, NY: McGraw Hill.

Part II
Architectural Design and Tectonics, Materiality and Sciences

This part focuses on architectural design as a marriage of arts and sciences, or poetic innovations and tectonics. It expands on the current architectural design methodology as an assertion of epistemological frameworks in design thinking, and a thought process that demands a creative transition from "*immeasurable, to measurable and ultimately back to immeasurable*" (Kahn, quoted in Green, Louis I. Kahn, Architect, 3).

7

Performativity

The Fourth Dimension in Architectural Design

Mitra Kanaani

This chapter expands on the meaning of *Design Performativity* as an emerging trend in architectural design methodology, and discusses the ways it is transforming architectural practice. The chapter argues that performative design is not a novel concept, but instead has a long legacy in the history of architecture and vernacular design around the globe.

Performance-based design theory asserts *building performance* as a guiding principle and approach toward the creation of intelligent and novel architectural form-making. Analyzing the roots, current practices, and broad paradigm of *performativity* within the context of architectural principles will shed light on its meaning as a seemingly emerging approach in architectural practice. By exploring the relevance of *performativity* with respect to known design parameters and principles, this chapter examines multiple facets of performativity with respect to the three fundamental design principles of architecture as identified in Vitruvius theorem: *firmness*, *commodity* and *delight*. It also investigates the manner in which these parameters have been utilized in creating novel forms related to the expected performance of buildings. In fact, these principles relate to the three embedded relationships at the heart of architecture. These three, include how a building relates to the earth, to man and to itself (Abercrombie, 1984). Through sophisticated use of novel design tools and emerging materials, performative architecture can be considered both a new approach to design thinking and a historical practice.

The term, Performativity as the Fourth Dimension was also used by Chris Lubkeman as "4D Design" in his keynote address under the topic of "Between Research and Practice, The Practice of Research," in the 2004 joint conference of ARCC and EAAE in Dublin School of Architecture, in Ireland.

Performativity—a Novel Trend or an Old Concept

Performance in design is broad and multi-faceted, consisting of a wide range of factors including environmental, social, cultural, physical, and emotional concerns. These must be analyzed in conjunction with the performance of systematic building elements including

Figure 7.1 Stonehenge, Wiltshire, UK. Sketch credit: Nasim Rowshanabadi

structural, environmental, and acoustical factors. Together, these become determinants in form-making.

A survey of precedents in history of architecture and urban design reveals an inevitable depth of attention to structural, environmental, and ecological factors in the design and siting of buildings. The most extraordinary aspect of prehistoric architectural sites is the presence of highly utilitarian design considerations, reflecting the inherent symbiotic nature of architectural form-making and performative design thinking. For instance, the intricate circular plan of Stonehenge mirrors and captures the revolution of the cosmic/lunar circuit as a giant sundial. Scientists believe the structure was intended to act as an astronomical computer, predicting both solar and lunar eclipses. The remarkable design intent of Stonehenge reveals the presence of performance-based thinking for a unique functionality (Trachtenberg & Hyman, 1986) (see Figure 7.1.).

Similar performative thought processes can be traced throughout architectural history. For instance, the derivation of architectural forms during the Gothic era of the Middle-Ages was based on spirituality and attention to heaven. This necessitated tall, slender and spacious monuments, which could not be executed without paying attention to the structural performance of the form and its relationship with the resolution of lateral forces. The outcome was the emergence of flying buttresses for lateral resistivity of the building, included in the architectural vocabulary of the façade which in combination with tall, slender columns and vaulted ceilings, give the impression of lightness and spaciousness. Flying buttresses simultaneously address a multitude of performative objectives, including the admittance of daylight and transparency (see Figure 7.2).

Tracing performative thought processes in low-tech vernacular architecture around the globe reveals diverse performance-based design approaches, which are unique to each region and locality. For instance, the intelligent designs of traditional Thai houses in Southeast Asia are perfect performative responses to their regional climatic conditions. Interestingly, Thai houses have various forms based on their specific climatic, cultural, and geographical circumstances (Chaichonrak *et al.,* 2002). Performance-based design considerations include

Figure 7.2 Notre Dame, Paris, France. Sketch credit: Nasim Rowshanabadi

Figure 7.3 A vernacular Thai house. Sketch credit: Nasim Rowshanabadi

usage of high platforms and terraces as a response to severe flooding resulting from tropical monsoons, and modular systems of prefabricated wall panels for ease of erection and transportability for the purpose of relocation. These houses are methodically built to respond to existing environmental influences, as well as the customs and beliefs which have influenced the performative expectations of the building (see Figure 7.3).

In another part of the world, low-tech vernacular performative design thinking is vividly evident in two historical villages in northern Iran: the village of Masouleh, situated on the outskirts of the Alborz Mountains facing the Caspian Sea, and the village of Kandovan, located on the opposite side facing east toward the mountain. In the village of Masouleh, the moist air blowing southwest from the Caspian Sea is blocked by the Alborz Mountains, creating heavy precipitation and fog (see Figure 7.4).

However, the landward side of the Alborz receives much less rainfall and rapidly becomes arid. These two opposite eco-systems have resulted in the development of two unique types of performative architecture. In Masouleh, buildings are built into the mountain in a stepping manner, and are interconnected. Courtyards and roofs serve as both pedestrian areas and narrow streets. Houses have rooms specially designed for winter and summer, with a small veranda extending at the front for summer use. The winter room is at the far end of the house, and receives little daylight. A central fireplace acts as an oven, while providing a source of energy for warming the space (see Figure 7.4).

Figure 7.4 Houses of Masouleh, Iran. Sketch credit: Nasim Rowshanabadi

Figure 7.5 Houses of Kandovan, Iran (a) and (b). Sketch credit: Nasim Rowshanabadi

On the contrary, Kandovan is known for its unique rock-carved troglodyte houses, dating back more than seven centuries. Originally conceived as hideouts dug to escape invading Mongols, these spaces slowly became complex homes, offering comforts including kitchens, hallways, bedrooms, and family rooms with beautiful colored glass windows allowing for the admittance of daylight, air, and spectacular views (see Figure 7.5).

Another interesting example of low-tech performative architecture is the historic city of Yazd situated in the heart of Iran's central plateau with a heritage of more than 3,000 years. One of the distinctive features of its adobe architecture is the attractive and dominating wind catchers (see Figure 7.6).

Wind catchers are towers carefully arranged above a system of aqueducts called Qanats. By using existing wind energy, the air rising from Qanats is cooled by convection and evaporation. Air is drawn into the Qanat from channels, as a low-tech cooling system, and then systematically disseminated across the entire building. As air warms, it rises into the tower and is pushed out by the incoming cool air. In the entire historical quarter of Yazd, structures were methodically built along this system of Qanats as a natural cooling system. The ancient concept of wind catchers is one of the most advanced city-wide low-tech cooling systems, working in harmony with the Qanats system (Figure 7.7). Buildings of antiquity did not enjoy today's technological advantages, however, in traditional building designs, there are thoughtful examples of usage of natural resources, based on specific conditions and locality. In the most low-tech approach, buildings were elaborately equipped with architectural solutions that could not only address ecological challenges and utilitarian needs, but also the aesthetic interests of architects.

Centuries of global architectural heritage revealing various lifestyles, traditions, rituals and attitudes of people are reflected in architectural forms. This reinforces the argument that performativity has always been an inherent approach in their design thinking methodology.

Sources of Performative Design Thinking in Modern Architecture

The architects of antiquity were master builders who successfully combined the art, science, culture, and technology of their time. They were physically involved in construction, but were also philosophers, artists, craftsmen, engineers, mathematicians, and chemists. Their

Figure 7.6 City of Yazd Wind Catchers, Iran. Sketch credit: Nasim Rowshanabadi

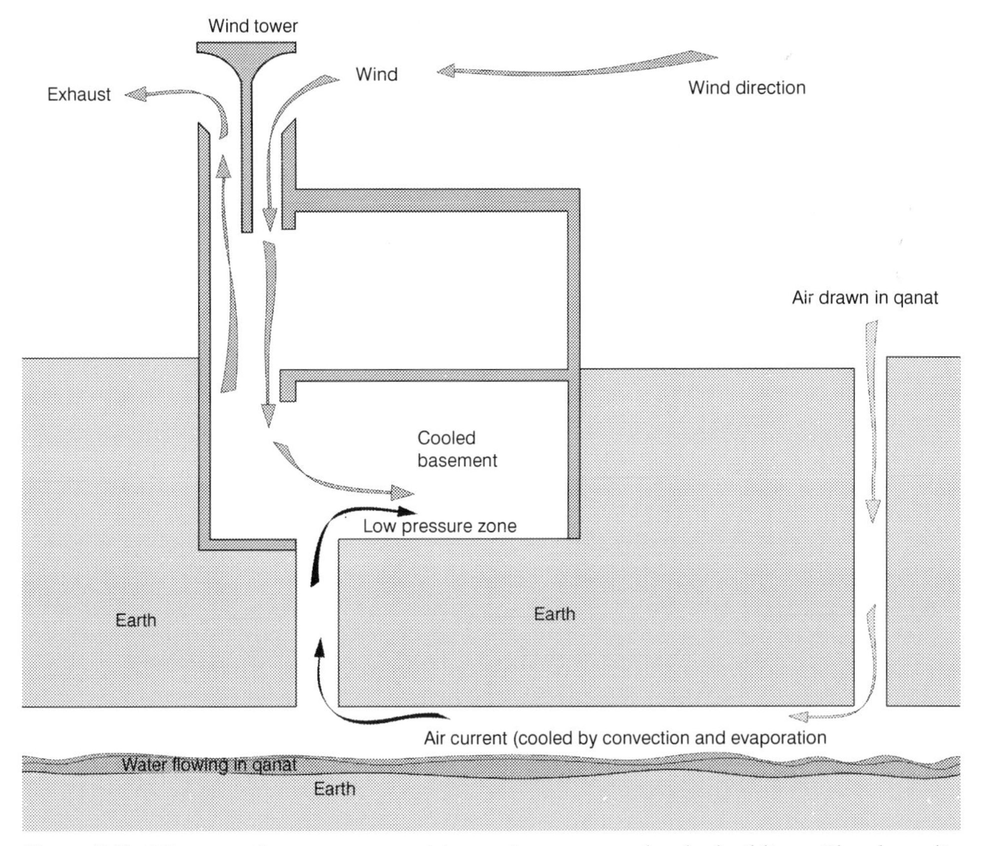

Figure 7.7 Diagram of qanat system, with running water under the buildings. Sketch credit: Nasim Rowshanabadi

in-depth understanding of the properties and performance of building materials rendered them to be evidence-based designers. Major transformations during the industrial revolution of the nineteenth century created a drastic divorce between arts and sciences. It was the dawn of a new era in the practice of architecture, when architects played the role of intellectual artists and designers, while an emerging group of professionals known as engineers became responsible for making dream designs come to a practical reality.

This division had major consequences. On one hand, it triggered major advancements in structural and mechanical aspects of building design. On the other, it gave the architect an excuse for poor understanding of the technical requirements of form-making. This became a prohibiting factor in architects expanding their scope of creativity to more atypical *forms*. For a long time the philosophy that, "practical purpose comes first, and physical necessity follows" (Torroja, 1987) became a limiting factor for designers attempting to break the grid or the box. Attention was instead focused on architectural expression, and sought in the meaning of *beauty* inside and outside of the box.

One positive ramification of this disconnect was the rising interest among architects in sociology, philosophy, physiology, environmental psychology, biology, and even physical science. Ironically, once technological grounds were provided, this drove designers and architects to develop novel geometries and unprecedented concepts in form-making.

In combination with these new attitudes, the advent of modernism allowed the liberation of building's expressive elements from constructive constituents—in particular, with the invention of the curtain wall system. Architecture is now confronted with two alternative possibilities in form-making: one in which form follows its structural armature and largely takes the shape and pattern of its structure, where the structure is considered as a component of the aesthetics and poetics of design as well. In this approach the selection of the structural system demands intuitive sensibility for aesthetics of architecture, as well as technical knowledge of the materials and the system. The alternative possibility is when structure plays supportive and stabilizing roles in maintaining the integrity of the form, but has a minimal or non-existent role in the aesthetics of design and form-making.

The role of Bauhaus and functionalist views in the development of rational and objective thought processes toward performative design thinking is undeniable. Similarly, performative forms are built on factual information, following sequences in which the functions unfold. An aesthetic agenda and poetic preferences is one of the three items of the main design principles. However, the emphasis is on deriving an optimum form from the precise spatial parameters of the desired action. The final optimized form is a compromise between "the amount of space, the costs, the convenience of use, all of the above at the same time, or something completely different" (Jormakka, 2011).

Meaning of Function and Performance in Architecture

Architecture, and in a broader sense "world of design, … (is) both of the world, and about the world" (Mau, Institute without Boundaries, 2004), which its meaning, content and purpose transcend its constituent elements contributing to its make-up. It initiates from exalted aspirations for humanity, art, environment, culture, and society, and ties directly to the history of civilizations, innovations, and environmental differences, as well as changes in political and economic factors. Aristotle famously stated that architecture imitates human action and life (Shields, 2014), while modern philosophers have reinforced the idea that design in architecture should serve a purpose, and a *function* related to the needs of its users (Zalta, 2009). This was further expounded upon by the twentieth-century functionalist expression of Louis Sullivan, who stated: *form follows function*. However, technological advancements in the latter decades of the twentieth century, such as the emergence of atypical geometric and morphogenetic forms, demonstrates that *form* does not necessarily have to follow the *function*, as long as the purpose is not lost or sacrificed.

The concept of *function* implies a utilitarian meaning: a role, purpose, or assigned duty; whereas *performance* refers to a continuous process to begin and carry through to completion. By the same token, performance is a series of actions that intertwines function and time into one essence. For instance, in the case of a ballet dancer, who has a role in dancing, the term used is *performance*.

On the other hand, the factor of *time* was introduced by Einstein in his Theory of Relativity as an abstract and independent element intertwined with *space* to conceive the fourth dimension, meaning *space-time*. According to the Merriam-Webster dictionary, the word performative was first used in 1955 by a British philosopher of language, J. L. Austin (1911–1960) with respect to what constitutes performance of specified act by virtue of its utterance. In architecture, the meaning of performativity has various implications. With respect to the concept of time and space in the design of buildings, it relates to an approach in architectural design thinking that predates the post-occupancy design considerations, and equips the building with the capacity to reformat itself in the *continuum of time*. According to this theory of design, space as part of the building's programmatic requirement is simultaneously charged with the potential to adjust itself to *foreseen and unforeseen external contingencies* (Leatherbarrow, 2005).

Architectural design is expected to enable a building to perform a sustained role, meeting the requirements of its intended use and beyond. By applying the theory of space-time to performative design, it is appropriate to draw the conclusion that performative architecture promotes and incorporates any and all philosophies of change and adjustability. This philosophy has been interpreted by different design theoreticians around the globe. However, performance-based buildings are generally designed, constructed, and assessed as part of a dynamic and living organism or system, which may be environmental, technical, social, or even financial. From the formal point of view, it is an approach in design thinking that visually and inherently defies any resemblances of stagnation and inertia. This methodology promotes dynamism by considering strategies of adjustment and allowing contextual flows and forces to influence the morphing of form and the physical aspects of buildings. By the same token, with the current performative trend in design thinking, it would not be inappropriate to make a *slight but daring* modification to the Sullivan's famous functionalist quote: *Form Follows Function*, to: "Form Follows Performance!". The origin of this quote is: "Whether it be the sweeping eagle in his flight, or the open apple-blossom, the toiling work-horse, the blithe swan, the branching oak, the winding stream at its base, the drifting clouds, over all the coursing sun, *form ever follows function*, and this is the law" (1924).

Scope, Paradigm, and Parameters of Performativity

The most challenging aspect of a design process is to achieve a *homogeneous* whole through a *heterogeneous* process. Approaches, strategies, and methodologies are for the most part influenced by the designer's own experiences, pre-occupations, socio-cultural background, technical understanding, and socio-economic conditions. In performative architecture, the designer establishes a *function* or a *continuum of dynamic relationship* between a *subject (user)* and an *object (spatial formal entity)*. In the current logic of formal conception, the three main elements of Function-Form-Subject are considered the drivers for performance-based

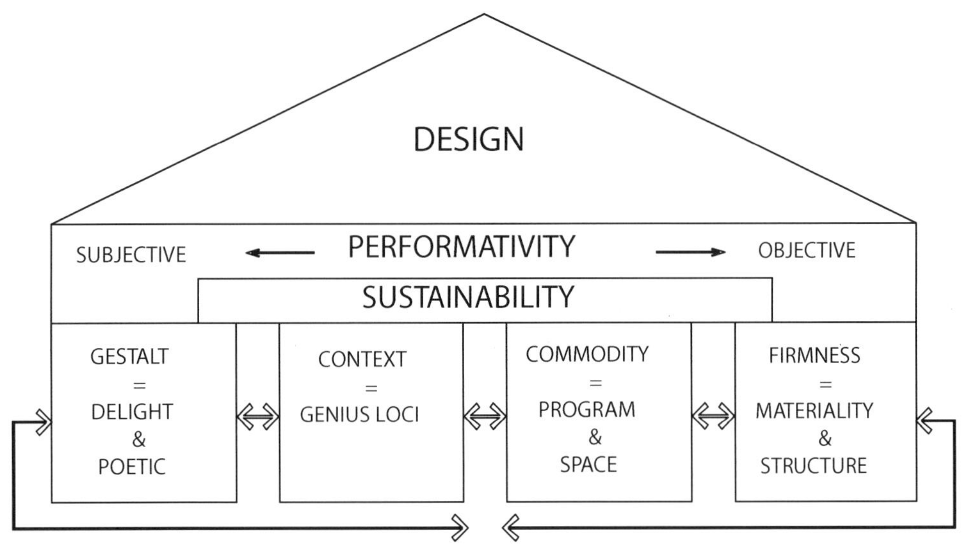

Figure 7.8 Design Pyramid Diagram. Sketch credit: Nasim Rowshanabadi

architecture. However, in performative design the role of computers to transform function to performance is inevitable (Grobman, 2012).

Simultaneously, for the architecture to perform certain functions, and meet certain expectations, it must incorporate known design parameters. The Vitruvian triad of architecture principles, *Firmness (Materiality & Structures), Commodity (Program & Spatial Qualities), and Delight (Gestalt & Poetics)*, are considered the main parameters in performative design thinking. How and in what manner these design ingredients are combined to compose the *whole* differentiates buildings. Most importantly, in performative architecture the element of *context* or *genius loci*—the prevailing spirit or character of a place—has risen to a higher level of importance and relevance, in line with the three main parametric concepts. Current transformations in design thinking and technological advancements in design-skills have provided opportunities to include *contextual* factors with increased scientific precision in design methodology. Hence contextual studies have constituted a major design tool in form-making assessments, thus transforming the three-part *triad* of architectural principles to a four-part *quadrad* (see Figure 7.8).

In retrospect, architectural *meaning* has undergone major transformations, with complexity of formal expressions and demands for novel functionalities. There is a drastic shift in the meaning and scope of beauty, and an obvious move toward isolation of form. While form can now be completely liberated from firmness (structure), technological advancements have provided potential for daring and dynamic collaboration between the *quadrad* of architectural elements. However, the process of design has become more scientific and complex, as the variables in each element have increased. The elevated expectations for each element of the quadrad and the augmented number of participant variables and determinants of each realm have added more depth to the complexity of the design process. Performativity of design, in its current meaning relates to the status and level of performance of each element and coherency within the *quadrad* of design principles.

Genius Loci and the Contextual Factors in Performative Design

One key difference between current architecture compared with historical practices is the complexity of operations, and the expected coherency between the four elements of design principles. Emerging typologies have complicated programs and more dynamic forms. The *context* is comprised of natural and man-made constituencies. Historical, social, and cultural attributes of the context are among the multitude of diverse factors that influence design options and characteristics.

The factor of site, or genius loci, harbors the most justifiable and rational factual information for form-making. Genius loci refers to the attributes of a specific site that contributes to certain spatial types and characters, such as physical elements, dimensions, materials, cultural influences, and considerations for sustainability (see Figure 7.8).

In performative design, context plays a major role in formation of the form. Most decisions originate from mandates arising from contextual factors and genius loci. Climatic and environmental factors are the first level of interface, physically relating a building with its context and respective setting. In performative design, there are various climatic factors related to sun, wind, humidity, and light that inevitably determine the formation of the building. These factors contribute to a building's thermal, solar, aerodynamic, and luminous performative conditions.

In a broader sense, according to Leonard Bachman, contextual influences in design form-making associate to three tiers of elements; this includes: Macro-scales, Local scales, and Micro-scales. Macro-scales relate to cosmos (solar and lunar influences), ecology (sustainable design), and climate (environmental influences). Local scales relate to site (setting and surrounding), envelope (filters, barriers, switches, and interventions), and interior (human comfort). Lastly, Micro-scales relate to bacterial (indoor air quality), chemical (fire and material aging toxicity), molecular properties of materials, elasticity, thermodynamics), and subatomic (light, electricity, heat and radiation), (Bachman, 2003).

By defining the three-scaled interrelationship of building elements, systems and subsystems with respect to the three-tiered range of context, Bachman (2003) makes a reference to a "complexity science," or a gamut of influences stemming from common examples of nonlinear behavioral complexities in nature. There is a deep rooted order and logic behind these seemingly erratic patterns. As any site and context is unique to itself and subject to influences of the three scales of nonlinear dynamic interrelationships, the outcome of design for the same typology will never be identical, because the manner in which the designer combines the factors is always different.

As we move forward, the multitude of genius loci influences are leading design methodology toward sustainable-based ecological thinking. This negates fixation on any design solution as a fixed model or prototypical approach, and demands buildings to be perceived as elements of the cosmos, with the potential to adjust themselves with solar and lunar influences, as well as ecological and climatic factors, while making the least impact on their local settings and surroundings. Establishing a harmonious relationship between the spontaneous inspiration of the artist, tradition and the laws of nature for the man-made systems within the natural environment is a key shared point between performative and sustainable design thinking (Van der Voordt & Van Wegen, 2005).

Similar to ancient and vernacular architectural practices, the ecological approach to design thinking is now transformed to a design methodology which considers climatic and ecological data highly important in form-making. The siting of a building, its orientation, and its relationship to *context* begins with a series of formal responses. These responses include but are not limited to, thermal, solar, and aerodynamic factors. While responding to contextual attributes, and in line with sustainable design thinking, performative architecture focuses on preserving and promoting such attributes.

The siting of a building inevitably impacts its context and changes the form of its surrounding. However, in performative design, a building is expected to establish harmonious relationships with its contextual forces and flows, toward creating balanced and healthful sensory, physical, and emotional relationships between man and the man-made environment. This is the area where poetics of design, or *Delight* and *Commodity*, share views toward common goals of sustainability.

In *A Pattern Language,* Christopher Alexander (1977) makes simple, yet meaningful recommendations with respect to the siting of buildings:

> On no account place buildings in the places which are most beautiful. In fact, do the opposite. Consider the site and its buildings as a single living eco-system. Leave those areas that are the most precious, beautiful, comfortable, and healthy as they are, and build new structures in those parts of the site which are least pleasant now.

Performative Design and Current Meanings of Commodity

Today the meaning of Commodity, as it refers to building functionality has expanded far beyond the simple idea of use. Instead it signifies the extent to which a building can serve and satisfy the needs of its occupants. The expectation of a building to be useful has augmented far beyond references made by classical philosophers, such as Plato, Aristotle, and Socrates. Giving a superficial meaning of usefulness as it relates to the functionality of design is too rudimentary and insufficient to convey the gamut of subjective and objective views in design expectations. The twentieth century unfolded various views with respect to the utilitarian aspect of design.

Throughout the twentieth century the meaning of use in architecture has challenged Kant's thesis that all arts only express aesthetical qualities and ideas for the pleasure of the beholder. According to Adrian Forty: "The interrelationship of architecture and use *is* now presented as the primary content of architecture, not just in opposition to the aesthetic but taking its place to constitute a wholly new meaning to that concept" (Forty, 2000). The architect Bruno Taut has also made reference to the relationship of these two concepts by identifying beauty as the outcome of a structured and organized utilitarian state of use: "The aim of architecture is the creation of the perfect and therefore most beautiful, efficiency" (Taut, 1929).

With respect to commodity, there is an increasingly complicated web of elements, directly related to the lifestyle of the building occupants. With all the advancements in scientific inquiry, formulating man's physical and psychological needs into an objective and quantifiable strategy is still at the experimentation stage.

Meaning of Flexibility of Form and Functionalism in Performative Design

> If the designers focus only on the low-hanging fruit of functionalism or usability, the human experience with designed objects is destined to a level of mundane Banality.
>
> (Kolko, 2009)

We are in an era in which the meaning of *use* is in constant transition. Contrary to the views of *Functionalists*, there are certain philosophers who strongly reject defining the meaning of use solely from the standpoint of function. Conversely there are certain theorists who believe: "Flexibility is, of course, in its own way a type of Functionalism" (Shields, 2014). During the early 1950s, the concept of *flexibility* was introduced in the meaning of *use*, as an architectural principle for accommodating the dynamic features of modern life. One of the main forerunners of this approach among the international Modernist architects, Mies van der Rohe, used this concept as the core of his design explorations. Ironically his approach to universal, or "All-Purpose Space" was against massaging the form to the function. As Leland Roth refers to Mies' elaboration of this approach: "Today this is the only practical way to build, because the functions of most buildings are continually changing, but economically the building cannot change" (Zalta, 2009).

In the early part of the twentieth century, some prominent architects initiated the concept of *open plan* spaces. This concept opened the door for liberation of building inhabitants from box-like enclosed environments. The concept of transparency for the indoor-outdoor relationship was also developed, hand in hand with the concept of free and flexible forms. This was a shift toward abandonment of opacity, the admission of daylight, and the provision of adjustability in space for various indoor needs.

According to Adrian Forty there are three types of transparencies resulting in arousal of three types of senses in humans. First, *Literal transparency* refers to how the physical construction of a building allows for the occupant to experience daylight and gain exposure into and through the enclosure of the building. Second, *Phenomenal transparency* refers to the simultaneous perception of different spatial entities, which for the most part relates to flexibility within spaces. According to Forty, the third type of transparency had roots to an article by American Critic, Susan Sontag in *Against Interpretation* (1966). It is called *transparency of meaning,* which refers to space having inherent luminosity of its own. In other words, the form and its contained parts allow an unambiguous, *un-camouflaged and undisguised* constructive appearance, while representing its sense of identity in all honesty. "This idea that there should be no distinction between form and content, between object and meaning, lies at the very heart of modernist aesthetics" (Forty, 2000).

In performative architecture the notion of transparency has a canonical meaning and application in all three senses. The Domino House of Le Corbusier (1914–1915) was based on the same simplicity of the concept of open floor plan of a concrete slab supported on four columns that has the potential to be adapted to various functions and settings (see Figure 7.9).

Undoubtedly, twentieth-century structural solutions allowed greater flexibility to architectural forms. However, it is worth noting that flexibility does not necessarily bear the best results, if the form and all its systematic constituents are not coherent and fully integrated. The main goal in design flexibility is to anticipate all prospective possibilities of the form. It must allow the opportunity for the space and its container to be used for various settings toward an optimal solution.

One of the potentials provided by the concept of flexibility in architecture was an inherent meaning of performativity, allowing the designer to project ideals of design performance on to specific future timeframes. This "allowed the architects the illusion of projecting their control over the building into the future, beyond the period of their actual responsibility for it" (Forty, 2000). The flexibility of the plan is considered a delayed programming opportunity toward any arising future needs.

Nonetheless, ironically, the twentieth-century modernists believed in universality of human needs, to the extent that Le Corbusier had the strong notion that there is a possibility of having one design type for all nations and climates (Roth, 1993). However, the notion

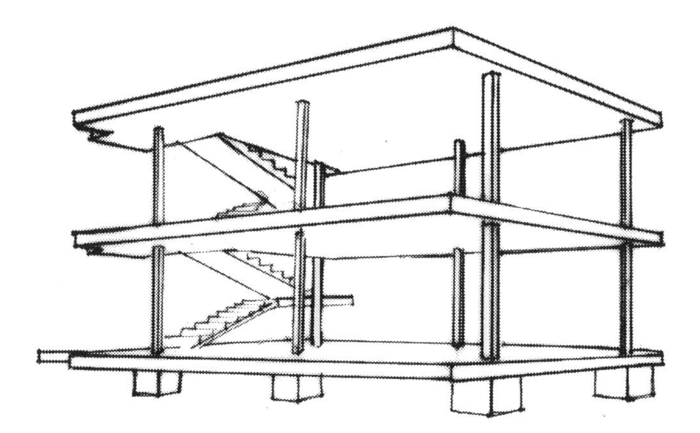

Figure 7.9 Domino House, Le Corbusier. Sketch credit: Nasim Rowshanabadi

of flexibility in performative design does not lend itself as a one size fits all form-making in architectural design. Adrian Forty identifies three distinct strategies for design flexibility:

1 *Flexibility as Redundancy*. As Forty refers to Rem Koolhaus as interpretation of this kind of flexibility, which is related to the "creation of margin—excess capacity that enables different and even opposite interpretations and uses ... Deterministic coincidence between form and program" (Forty, 2000).
2 *Flexibility by Technical Means*. When there are attempts for flexibility through making elements of the building—walls, windows, even floors—movable. ... and, when morning use of the building can be converted for afternoon and evening use.
3 *Flexibility as a Political Strategy*. Flexibility not as a property of buildings but of spaces, a property characteristic they acquire through the uses to which they are situated (Forty, 2000).

Advances in technology, and the liberation of form from structural constraints, has provided opportunities for maximum flexibility of space planning and building function. Currently, there are various approaches for the positioning of the structural elements to allow for interior architectural flexibility with various cost related ramifications. Nonetheless, the concept of *free-form* in reference to the lay out and the building enclosure, has opened the door for more innovative concepts in spatial qualitative transformations.

The Current Meaning of Firmness—Firmitas and Performativity

Structure, as the main element providing stability to form has a long history of usage as a space definer. Throughout history, the potential of structural systems has been utilized to provide organization and unification of architectural forms.

Each approach comes with a certain degree of compromise with respect to optimization. However, in performative architecture optimal practice is one of the key considerations that demands coherent and integrative design thinking with respect to the building's systematic elements. Frequently, what we perceive as an apparent structural armature is not in reality utilized for that purpose. This is what Leland Roth refers to as *physical structure*, versus *perceptual structure* (Roth, 1993).

The world of design tectonics is shifting toward weightlessness, dematerialization, and efficiency in usage of materials. In many ways, it is through the structural elements of buildings that today's designers are challenging the emotions of the beholders. Throughout the ages, building structure has been used to personify architectural design and convey meaning and conceptual ideas. By using provocative and dynamic expressive architectural forms that defy gravity, and pushing creativity to extreme levels of scientific rivalry, architects today are showcasing their aspirations for advancement and progress. Structural innovation in these types of architectural endeavors plays a major role in the creation of dynamic and symbolic forms.

Since post-World War II industrialization and the emergence of new structural materials, a major shift in the methodology of architectural design and form-making has occurred. Computer information optimization and novel approaches has become synonymous with systems thinking, or understanding how to make systems work properly and efficiently. As the complexity of building systems has increased, architects must be cognizant of identifying the best approach to integrate structural systems with other building systems. Advancements in structural materials, such as higher grades of steel, Ferro-Concrete with its possibilities for prestressing, and emergence of more lightweight concrete, such as *Polymer*, have opened the door for new opportunities toward fluidity between architectural design and structural systems.

This is the era in which expression of technological manifestations has become central to architectural vocabulary, allowing architects to make daring gestures through the use of steel and concrete. The choice of material is of great importance in conveying the message of architectural character. Currently, trends in architectural design with respect to design engineering are taking a multitude of directions. Current close collaborations between architects and engineers in parametric design, is allowing engineering technologies to entrust the final design vision to more sophisticated, complex and enriched design solutions than traditional architectural approaches could deliver.

One extreme approach for an architect would be to ignore structural considerations in the process of form-making, and camouflage the structural armature through various architectural claddings and finishes. This approach creates consonant forms, "where the architectural and structural forms neither synthesize, nor … contrast" (Charleson, 2005). Notwithstanding how the structure has been considered, it has to perform to provide stability and firmness for the building to stand up.

The other extreme is where entire buildings are nothing but structural armature. This is most common in tall buildings and long span form or resistive shape structures. In such cases, the performative role of the structure is expanded to connect formal architectural ideas with rules of gravity and stress flow of building structural armature by transforming its architectural form from a geometrical form to a structural system.

There are many variations between the two extremes, which determine the level and nature of integration between architectural form, structure, expected role, and performativity. Among these levels is a concept, which Angus McDonald (2001) terms *Structure as Ornament*. Recently this approach has been used extensively to create modernistic high-tech building characteristics. In this approach, the design process is driven by visual rather than technical considerations to convey a modernistic high-tech characteristic. As a consequence, "the performance of these structures is often less than the ideal, when judged by technical criteria" (McDonald, 2001) (see Figure 7.10).

The different ways in which structure can contribute to visual vocabulary includes a gamut of tools for design, such as: indoor-outdoor relationships, creating a sense of entry,

Figure 7.10 Renault distribution center, Swindon, Sir Norman Foster. Sketch credit: Nasim Rowshanabadi

rhythmic and hierarchal modulation, variation of depth for playing with natural and artificial light and texture, façade treatment by screening and filtering, aesthetic modulations to façade, and more.

Additionally, functional flexibility, and the directive and disruptive functionality of the space subdivisions, have become achievable through methodical elimination of structural constraints. For instance, by positioning the structural elements outside the building, and aligning the structural grid with the programmatic grid pattern determined by the typological use of the building, the performative role of structure coincides with the utilitarian aspects of design in providing programmatic requirements.

The trend of celebrating structural innovations in design concepts began during the last decades of the twentieth century and has maintained momentum. However, structural and architectural collaboration is bringing design to higher levels of sophistication and intelligence in firmness and overall physical and systematic functionality. An in-depth review of many noteworthy and spectacular architectural manifestations, where buildings act as intelligent biospheres, reveals sophisticated performative achievements. The role of the computer in integrating geometries and forms with mathematical relevance is undeniable. The trend of design performativity has situated engineering in a creative space between architecture and technology with the potential to converge the two. Presently, digital modeling and complex simulation of complete buildings allow for informed decisions in form-making based on the integration of various systems. Analyses are also considered from a monetary perspective, which include the economy of means, materials and time.

Today, *performative* design is an analytical process, requiring extensive research into building technologies, where designers move from subjective concepts to technical and practical solutions. Choosing the right set of design objectives and criteria is central to the design, while revealing the viability of selected criteria and the outlook of its performance in real time.

The Current Meaning of Beauty and Delight—Gestalt and Design Performativity

In contemporary architecture, form is one of the triads of space and design. There is in *form* an inherent ambiguity between its *shape* on one hand, and on the other *idea* or *essence*. "While one describes the property of things as they are known to the senses, the other describes properties as they are known to the mind … *Gestalt* generally refers to objects as they are perceived by the senses, whereas *form* usually implies some degree of abstraction from the concrete particular" (Forty, 2000).

The difference between the meaning of architecture and building has been discussed repeatedly. Considering that "architecture is the making of space" (Pevsner, 1963), building can be considered the place, or what incorporates the space.

Various attributes and qualities contribute to provision of the meaning of delight and poetry for the space. The configuration of spaces can set the tone for the pattern of behaviors that are created within them. Every competent designer knowingly or inherently uses these design attributes in composition and expression. Spaces, as behavioral settings are developed and arranged by the designer based on specific functions. However, these decisions can impact the mood, performance, and well-being of the users.

There are various thoughts behind space development: *Physical space* refers to a spatial volume that is measurable and inevitably computable. *Perceptual space* is practically impossible to quantify, yet can be perceived and seen. *Conceptual space* can be defined, perceived, and developed in the mind. *Behavioral space* is intended for a specific use. *Interweaving spaces* refer to connected fluid or flowing spaces that have a high degree of usage in design flexibility. *Static space* contrasts with interwoven space, and does not offer the potential for fluidity in functionality. A *directional space* is an obvious path, which contrasts with *non-directional space* that provides no direction. There are also positive and negative spaces, which concern spaces that are void or contained and surrounded by a built form. Lastly, *personal space*, relates to the space and distance humans need to maintain between each other (Roth, 1993).

There are other categorizations for space distances that are based on the nature of relationships, and the manner in which humans become aware of each other's presence, by seeing, hearing, smelling, and touching. The classification of human distances can be based on normal distances for public formal performances, social/business interactions, and personal or intimate relationships. These may be different based on cultural variations. Bryan Lawson (2003) refers to these spaces as intimate, personal, social, and public distances. The importance of space perception and tolerance for the presence of others has recently been brought to the forefront of design objectives. The meaning of space and the way our senses convey a pleasant or unpleasant feeling to us is to a great extent related to the appropriateness of these distances.

In performative architecture, it is important to pay close attention to the phenomenology of space—as it is perceived in human consciousness. Our perceptional awareness can directly stimulate our senses and emotions. David Leatherbarrow (2005), while referring to this condition as perceptual intentionality, alludes to the fact that, "attention to performance will contribute to a new understanding of the ways buildings are imagined, made and experienced."

It is important to note that without the *human* aspect of performativity, the theory of performative architecture is not any different from *Functionalist* design thinking. Architecture is about human lives and thus should accommodate people and be responsive to their needs. In *Performative Architecture* poetics of the form are derived from and involved with concepts in conjunction with social responsibility, as well as scientific and technological advances. However, the beauty of the form is not sacrificed for the sake of performance. The usage of prototyping of building systems and building simulation techniques allows for the examination and systematic interpretations of marginal conditions toward formulation of different alternatives and solutions, which by no means camouflages or undervalues the meaning of beauty.

Poetic of Light and Transparency in Performative Architecture

Light is the most encompassing natural phenomenon that gives meaning to space. Scientific inquiries have proven the psychological and physiological effects of light on humans. Light has a beneficial effect on the mood, physical well-being, and productivity of people.

The usage of light has deep roots in the history of architecture. The most successful architects are those who have mastered the sculpting of architecture with light, particularly natural light. From the Pantheon of Rome with the 27-feet diameter oculus that serves as the source of natural light and ventilation (see Figure 7.11), to the transparent high glass walls of the Gothic era merging poetics of design with spirituality, to the twentieth-century high-rise curtain walls that take advantage of panoramic views and daylight, the meaning of light has been intertwined with the delight of architecture. Light is today synonymous with the concept of transparency, which ties with other programmatic design concepts, such as free-form, open plan, indoor-outdoor, natural ventilation, and efficient energy consumption.

The technical potential of transparency has become more sophisticated with developments in glass and plastic production. Architects and designers have a rich palette of transparent materials at their disposal, providing the opportunity for sculpting delightful manifestations by using daylighting effects. Performative designers have exploited solar energy and daylight for heating and lighting spaces through combining transparency with materials that have potential for thermal storage. The challenging aspect of natural lighting is how to achieve excellent light quality without sacrificing indoor air quality, overheating or giving rise to excessive energy consumption.

Today's performative designers are able to create ingenious design elements that allow indirect luminous radiation to enter the building, while simultaneously screening direct sunlight, and avoiding excessive heat gain for interior spaces. Two holistic examples of this performative method are Renzo Piano's creation of leaves in the design of the Menil, and Louis Kahn's barrel structure for Kimbell museums (see Figures 7.12 and 7.13).

Double façade skin is another innovative performative design solution with several advantages. While the outer glazed skin acts as a screen against wind and offers natural ventilation, the interior layer with sun shading allows for proper maintenance and cleaning, while protecting the interior and acting as thermal storage for the building (see Figure 7.14).

The poetics of transparency in modern times has assumed various utilitarian and performative roles toward integrating the multiple facets of design parameters. Form in modernity is transformed into a more dynamic, fluid and even provocative concept, in which the usage of light and transparency is a major contributor to design sophistication.

The Theory of Design Performativity

So, with all that being said, what is the approach to a performative design methodology? In practice, performance-based design still conveys ambiguous meaning for many in the design field. This results from the breadth, depth, and scope of performance-based design concepts. Many designers selectively focus on certain aspects of performativity, based on their potential and area of interest. It is through the success of a multitude of interested practitioners that the

Figure 7.11 Pantheon, Rome. Sketch credit: Nasim Rowshanabadi

Figure 7.12 Menil Museum, Houston, TX. Renzo Piano Workshop. Sketch credit: Nasim Rowshanabadi

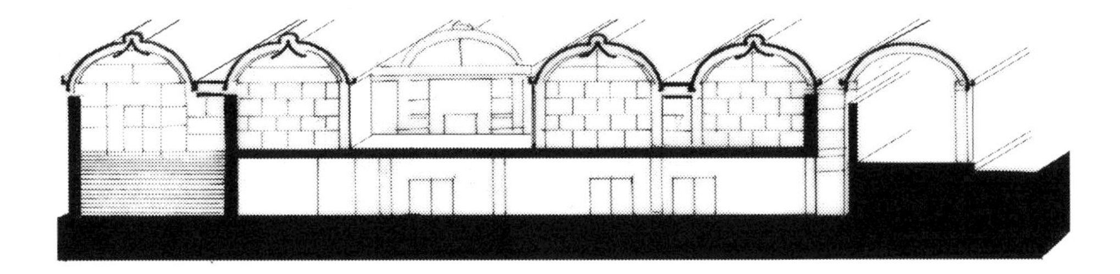

Figure 7.13 Kimbell Museum, Dallas, TX. Louis Kahn. Sketch credit: Nasim Rowshanabadi

concept of performativity has been transformed and indoctrinated to a school of thought in design thinking. The positive attributes of performative architecture will only be manifested as an integral component of a comprehensive vision that takes advantage of a constantly evolving and expanding technology. *Performative architecture* has created a web of systems that allow users to participate in interactive relationships with internal spatial elements, building systems and the external elements of the surrounding eco-system. This constitutes a continuous circuit of reactive and interactive web of systems, resulting in occupants being considered as instrumental *players* rather than *users.*

With all the emerging technological changes, the building industry has kept a slow pace in implementing changes. This may relate to architecture requiring reinterpretation of the novel technologies with respect to human and social norms and conventions. In fact, architecture has the capacity to humanize technology by way of its inherent utilitarian quality. However, toward restoration of human organic purpose in this expeditiously growing mega-technical

Figure 7.14 Cité Internationale, Lyon, France, Renzo Piano Workshop. Sketch credit: Nasim Rowshanabadi

civilization, today's architecture must possess capacities to constantly reformat itself toward developing livable communities with dynamic healthful indoor/outdoor spatial entities. Along this line, Lewis Mumford in his book of articles, *Values of Survival* (1946) argues about humanization of technology and the hope that the organic depths of human nature, in the passage of time, might provide the basis for a transformation of mega-technical civilization, which he considers is essential toward creating balanced human beings. The question would be how architects and designers can contribute to the creation of healthful environments that nurture balanced human beings.

Today, *performative design methodology* lays out a milieu of opportunities for designers and architects to explore innovative constructs and building systems, as well as emerging materials and morphogenetic forms, from the pragmatic and conventional to the organic and esoteric. Thus, "the first step in the development of a performative architecture is to outline strategies of *adjustment*, for unforeseen manifestations toward development of a reformatable architecture in the trajectory of time" (Leatherbarrow, 2005).

Conceptually, the meaning of adjustability applies to the design of architecture that incorporates opportunities for buildings to adjust to nuances of contextual settings. It applies to various factors and meanings, and many expected and unexpected situations. On this note, Leatherbarrow (2005) offers an analogy with musical or theatrical improvisational performances that require the ensemble or actors to continuously stay attuned with each other and be accommodating to various unexpected conditions. Similarly, in the performance of architecture, buildings must be equipped and charged to act as one web of systems and yield to unforeseen contingencies. The concept of adjustability is broad and encompassing. Strategies can incorporate manually and mechanically movable elements of the building, as well as considerations for certain design features, including structural elements.

In essence, the theory of performative design focuses on morphogenetic design practices and any and all sorts of innovative ideas for building transformation from one state to another in the trajectory of time and space, and as part of a dynamic living system. The integration of scientific inquiries in the design process has opened the door for many immeasurable aspects of buildings to become measurable. Performative design methodology encompasses objective and scientific exploration on issues related to energy efficiency, thermal comfort, lighting / day-lighting, air quality, sound and acoustics, as well as considerations for hybrid environmental systems, integrating both, active, passive, and mechanically driven systems. There is a level of complexity of the systematic integration in performative design thinking that is demanding more than just intuitive thinking from architects. The resultant high level of concentration on work performance requires tools and measurements that are scientifically calculated and objectivized.

Today performance-based design uses techniques in virtual reality, digital modeling, and rapid prototyping to integrate multiple contributions, and encourages close collaboration in the evolution of building systems design. This results in the proliferation of numerous morphogenetic forms. It is a process-product-based design practice, revolving around manufacturing, tectonics, and the art of detailing. The concept of a building is manifested even in its smallest details. From the stand point of *practicing* performance-based design, architecture demands a transparent approach and mode of operation from pre-design to post occupancy evaluation. By using tools for performance experimentation, opportunities are presented to move the post occupancy assessment to the present allowing a pre-post occupancy evaluation in real time. The Igus Factory of Nicholas Grimshaw in Cologne is one of the best examples, which had the post-occupancy assessment conducted at the time of its design by allowing a pre-post occupancy evaluation performed in real time. (See Figure 7.15)

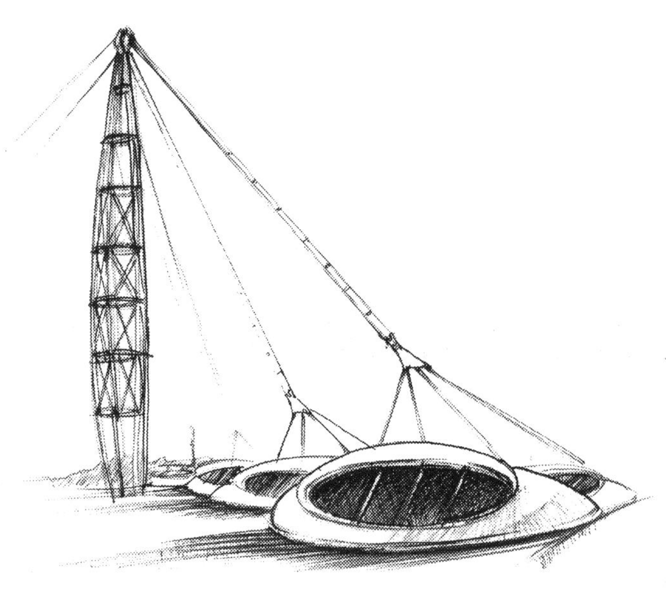

Figure 7.15 Igus Factory, Cologne, Nicholas Grimshaw. Sketch credit: Nasim Rowshanabadi

Performative Architecture and Research for Design

In his book, *Creation is a Patient Search*, Le Corbusier referred to the pursuit of design in architecture as a *patient search* (Le Corbusier, 1960). The concept of performativity has become a form of *research by design* and is usefully pursued in various current design investigations, as performative design that allows the form to be found rather than made. It is an architectural design that is not limited to the constraint of conventional techniques. Instead, it is envisaged, manipulated, and adapted to the selected design concepts through various three-dimensional experimentations. Performative designs involve research, analysis, trial and error, use of computer simulations, teamwork, and client participation toward systematic and methodical arrival of optimal architectonic forms. According to Branko Kolarevic (2005):

> It is important to note that performance-design should not be seen as simply a way of devising a set of practical solutions to set of largely practical problems ... The emphasis shifts to form generation based on performative strategies of design grounded at one end in intangibilities such as cultural performance and, at the other, in quantifiable performative aspects of building design, such as structure, acoustics, or environmental design.

Performative design methodologies have created a new synergy between architecture and engineering, which guides design by following the laws of physics, the cosmos, and natural elements. The work of architects who have pursued performative design reveals sensitivity, exploration, and research into today's vital aspects of design such as cultural, social, ecological, climatic, contextual, and even behavioral and perceptual values, which demand informed knowledge of scientific inquiries from the designer's perspective.

For some architects, performative design is only at the level of form conception in the design process. This process does not inform the development of parameters for the final architectural expression of the building. Other designers focus on manufacturing the form, and the investigation of strengths and weaknesses through potentials provided by the computer. This is a sophisticated back and forth procedure for the investigation of form with respect to a given program and environmental factors. In this digitized approach simulation tools model forms initially developed through traditional approaches. Other designers may focus on an intended specific form based on: "original genius, nature, and geometry" (Jormakka, 2011). This approach requires searching and data gathering that justifies and corroborates the reasoning behind the selection of certain form and geometry. Typically, the form is originally symbolic and beyond function. However, performative thinking directs designers toward a painstaking process of rendering the form becoming functional and performative. This is a reverse process, as form is made, before being found.

There are still other designers who focus on the tectonics of architecture and exploring the form through a formal logic related to the firmness parameter of design. In this approach, "form is generated through the deployment of three different types of matrices: armature, smart skin, and interface" (Grobman, 2012). At some point, the environmental, ecological, and perceptual aspects inform the final formal outcome.

Some other designers focus on computational methodology and integration of mathematical equations by making physical models and development of digital modeling for subjective and objective assessments of the form. This is a cross-disciplinary design process, in which researchers focus on self-assembling technologies to establish meaningful relationships across the disciplines of science and industry, including biology, materials, aerospace, and transportation engineering, through the application of various software, robotics, manufacturing, and various areas of the arts. These researchers draw inspiration from processing tools by using coding graphics and simplified syntax to construct randomized collages of images. Complex forms are developed through analysis of the association of craft and computation based on parametric information for performativity.

Finally, some designers may use performativity solely to arrive at sustainable ends and objectives. The main purpose of this design thinking is to allow the building to act as a biosphere and be a friendly participant in the natural processes of the eco-system (see Figure 7.16). The main challenge for these architects is integration of hybrid active and passive systems toward creation of forms that are self-regulating and self-organizing, as well as an intuitive optimization in design and form-making.

Conclusion

Performative design is more an attitude than a methodology, and though in its introductory stages, it represents a renewal of an ancient mentality. Performative design is revolutionizing conventional thinking about the future of design and the practice of architecture. Its broad interdisciplinary paradigm is entirely transforming the closed-minded manner of perceiving design forms. It is a movement that incorporates many types and styles of forms, and is the outcome of a global demand with respect to current societal, ecological, and environmental needs. It is not associated with a specific designer's taste, interest or innovation. It is a trend, which is unlikely to become old fashioned, but will instead evolve to become a major player in future innovations, undoubtedly transforming the discipline and profession of architecture. Lastly, performative design in architecture inherently possesses highly ambitious globalized objectives that are increasingly transforming and transcending meanings of architecture discipline, for the highly interconnected and interdisciplinary world of the future.

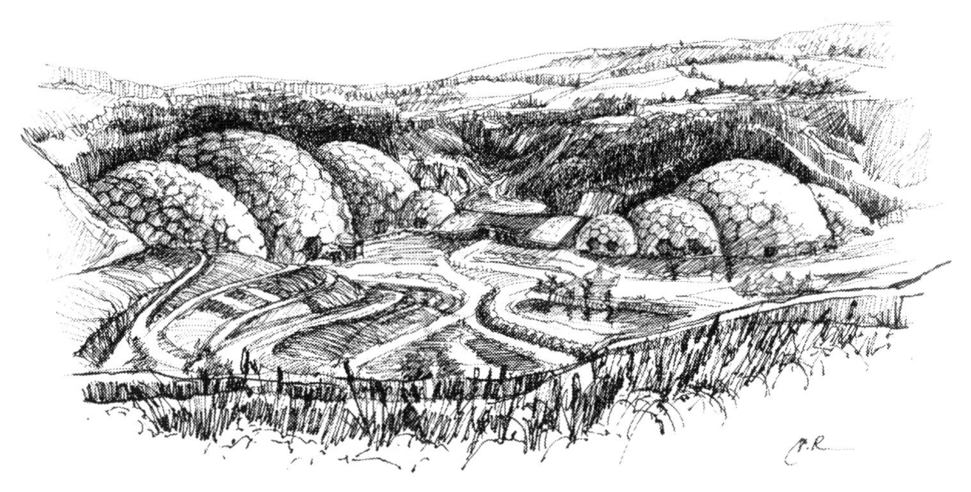

Figure 7.16 Eden Project, Cornwall, UK, Nicholas Grimshaw. Sketch credit: Nasim Rowshanabadi

References

Abercrombie, S. (1984). *Architecture as Art.* New York: Van Nostrand Reinhold, pp.125, 165–169.

Alexander, C. (1977). *A Pattern Language*. New York: Oxford University Press, p. 511.

Bachman, L.R. (2003). *Integrated Buildings—The System Basis of Architecture*. Hoboken, NJ: John Wiley & Sons, p.12.

Chaichonrak, R., Nil-athi, S., Panin, O. & Posayanonda, S. (2002). *The Thai Houses, History and Evolution*. Trumbull, CT: Weatherhill Inc., p. 11.

Charleson, A. (2005). *Structure as Architecture*. Burlington, MA: Architectural Press, p. 34.

Collins, P. (1965). *Ideals in Modern Architecture.* London: Faber & Faber, p. 234.

Forty, A. (2000). *Word and Buildings, A Vocabulary of Modern Architecture.* New York: Thames & Hudson, pp. 142–148, 9, 143, 183, 239–242, 48, 286–288.

Grobman, Y. (2012). Performalism: A Manifesto for Architectural Performance. In Y. Grobman and E. Neuman (Eds.), *Performalism, Form and Performance in Digital Architecture*. London: Routledge, p. 5.

Jormakka, K. (2011). *Basics, Design Methods*. Boston, MA: Birkhauser, pp. 9, 42.

Kolarevic, B. (2005). Computing the Performative. In B. Kolarevic & A. Malkawi (Eds.), *Performative Architecture: Beyond Instrumentality.* New York: Taylor & Francis Group, p. 195.

Kolko, J. (2009). *Thoughts on Interaction Design*. San Francisco, CA: Morgan Kaufman, p. 83.

Lawson, B. (2003). *The Language of Space.* Boston, MA: Architectural Press, pp.109–120.

Leatherbarrow, D. (2005). Architecture's Unscripted Performance. In B. Kolarevic & A. Malkawi (Eds.), *Performative Architecture: Beyond Instrumentality*. New York: Taylor and Francis, pp.7, 13, 15.

Le Corbusier, C.E.J.G. (1960). *Creation is a Patient Search*, J. Palmes (trans). New York: Praeger.

Mau, Bruce, & the InstituteWithout Borders. (2004). *Massive Change*. New York: Phaidon.

McDonald, A. (2001). *Structures and Architecture.* 2nd ed. Oxford, UK: Elsevier, pp. 77–78.

Mumford, L. (1946). *Values for Survival,* New York: Harcourt Brace.

Pevsner, N. (1963). *An Outline of European Architecture*, 7th ed. London: Penguin Books, p.15.

Roth, L.M. (1993). *Understanding Architecture, Its Elements, History, and Meaning*. Boulder, CO: Westview Press, pp.10, 19, 45–54.

Shields, C. (2014). *Aristotle*. New York: Routledge.

Sullivan, Louis (1924). *Autobiography of an Idea*. New York City: Press of the American Institute of Architects, Inc., p. 108.

Taut, B. (1929). *Modern Architecture*. London: The Studio, p. 9.

Torroja, E. (1987). *Philosophy of Structures*. Oakland, CA: University of California Press, p.3.
Trachtenberg, M. & Hyman, I. (1986). *Architecture: from Prehistory to Post-Modernism*. Upper Saddle River, NJ: Prentice Hall/Abrams, p. 51.
Van der Voordt, T.J.M. & Van Wegen, H.V.R. (2005). *Architecture in Use, An Introduction to Programming, Design and Evaluation of Buildings*. New York: Routledge, p. 37.
Zalta, E. (2009). *Stanford Encyclopedia of Philosophy*. Stanford, CA: Stanford University.

8

Structure and Architecture

Tectonics of Form

Angus Macdonald

Introduction

This chapter is concerned with architectural structures: those parts of buildings which are required to provide the support necessary to resist load. The structure is a fundamental part of any building as it is of any artefact which exists in the physical world: without structure there is no solid object; without structure there can be no building.

Structures are bulky objects which occupy a significant part of a building's volume and which are present in every part of a building. They have a similar shape to that of the building which they support. Their performance is determined by their form, so the act of designing a building is also an act of structural design. Structure and architecture are therefore very intimately related (see, for example, Figure 8.1).

The great theorist of the Italian Renaissance, Leon Battista Alberti, regarded architecture as the queen of the arts, because it was concerned with the fusion of art and science. For him, the perfect building was one in which artistic meaning and physical fabric were combined in the most elegant way. In this vein, it has often been argued that the seamless harmonization of meaningful form with shapes which produce good structure is an essential characteristic of the best architecture—a meeting of art and science through design. This has been a recurring theme of the theory, if not always the practice, of Modern architecture, which has been concerned to develop a visual vocabulary which is celebrative of technology.

There has never been a time when a coming together of art and science was more important in architecture. We live now in an age of climate change (almost certainly anthropogenic), which is but one manifestation of the current abuse of the Earth's operating systems being chronicled by the scientific community. If we are to move towards a way of living which is based on a more sensible and considered use of resources, architecture will undoubtedly have to play its part. The problem of building for an environmentally sustainable future is largely a technical problem, albeit one with socio-economic and political implications. If buildings are to be created which satisfy the need for enclosure without contributing to the ongoing destruction of the ecosphere, they will have to be designed in such a way that purely technical issues concerned with the development of form, selection of materials and ease of

Figure 8.1 [Upper] L'Oceanogràfic, Valencia, F. Candela, with S. Calatrava, A. Domingo and C. Lázaro. Long-span, form-active shell structures by architect/engineers achieved a seamless fusion of art and technology (Rauenstein / Wikimedia Commons). [Lower] Riverside Museum, Glasgow, Z. Hadid and Buro Happold. This building has a structure appropriately configured for its span: a reasonable compromise between art and technology (E. Z. Smith / Hawkeye).

fabrication are accorded an appropriate level of priority. In the Modern period, structural technology has been developed to the point at which almost any form can be realized and this fact offers the possibility of a harmonious fusion of art and technology in the creation of an environmentally sustainable architecture.

In the Modern period until now, however, the recent, increased freedom to invent form has rarely produced the happy combination of art and technology which it has theoretically made possible. This failure has been due, largely, to the design methodologies which have been adopted by architects. This chapter is concerned with the relationship which has existed between structure and architecture in the Modern period and concludes with some hopes for the future in the light, particularly, of current environmental concerns. The discussion is preceded by a brief account of the factors which affect the relationship between structural form and structural performance.

The Relationship Between Form and Performance

This section is concerned with the relationship between the shape of a structure and its *efficiency*, which is taken here to be the ratio of the load which is carried divided by the quantity of material specified. (An *efficient structure* is one in which a high load-carrying capacity results from the use of a small amount of material.) The consideration of this leads to a wider discussion of the effect of structural form on the consumption of resources overall.

The principal reason why the shape of a structure affects its efficiency is that it determines the *types of the internal forces* which occur when a given load is applied. The important distinction is between *bending-type internal force* and *axial internal force*. The following simple examples serve to illustrate the differences. If a plank of wood is laid horizontally across a stream to create a bridge, the action of a person standing on the plank will be to cause it to bend. An alternative way of using the plank to assist crossing the water, if the stream is not too large, is to use it to form a kind of stepping stone by driving it vertically into the bed of the stream at midstream and fixing a small platform to its top. In either case the primitive structure must be strong enough to bear the weight of a person. The size of the cross-section required to provide adequate strength is markedly different between the two cases, however: the plank laid horizontally needs a cross-section approximately eight times larger to provide the same weight-carrying capacity as the stake driven vertically to provide a stepping stone. The *strength* of these two simple structures is the same—sufficient to carry the weight of a person. Their *efficiencies* are markedly different. The significant difference is in the *type* of internal force which was present—*bending* in the case of the horizontal plank, *axial* in the case of the stepping-stone stake.

The very simple example of the stream crossing demonstrates one of the great truths of structural engineering: that the efficiency with which load can be resisted depends on the *type* of internal force which it generates. *Axial internal force can be resisted more efficiently than bending-type internal force, by an order of magnitude (a "power of 10").* The type of internal force which occurs is determined by the form of the structure in relation to the *pattern of applied load*; the latter is therefore a vitally important consideration in the design of any structure.

Buildings are enclosures and so the structures which support them involve a horizontal span. The most onerous loads to which buildings are normally subjected are gravitational loads due to their own weight and that of their contents, and these all act vertically downwards. The basic scenario of load and form in an architectural structure favors resistance to load through a bending-type action. Most architectural structures are therefore of the bending type and thus rather inefficient in their use of material. Two factors in relation to the shape of a structure can mitigate this unpromising situation: one is the adoption of an overall form which is such that the internal forces caused by the vertical load acting on a horizontal span generates only axial internal forces, and the other is the use of shapes for the cross-sections and longitudinal profiles of structural elements which allow bending-type internal forces to be resisted with optimum efficiency. A simple comparison demonstrates the first of these two possibilities.

Perhaps the simplest structural arrangement is that of the horizontal span carrying a single concentrated load at the mid-span position. A practical example of this is the bridge mentioned above: a plank of wood spanning a small stream and carrying the weight of a single person. The plank here is loaded in pure bending and its structural efficiency is low.

A more efficient structure results if the plank is replaced by a length of tightrope (similar to a circus high wire). Because a tightrope is flexible it is incapable of resisting bending. The only kind of internal force which it can sustain is axial tension. Assuming that the person keeps their balance, the rope bridge will take up a form, that of an inverted triangle, which allows it to transfer the weight of the person to the bank of the river through internal force which is pure axial tension. This requires much less material than the rigid plank of wood and so the rope bridge is much lighter and therefore more efficient. It must, of course, be more securely attached to the riverbank, so a requirement for a more complicated support is an unavoidable penalty accompanying the increase of efficiency.

This extremely simple example illustrates a very important point concerning the relationships between the overall form of a structure and its performance: *the type of internal force which occurs is dependent on the form of the structure*. In this example the horizontal plank produces bending-type internal force and the inverted triangle produces axial internal force, in this case axial tension. A mirror image of the rope structure, with the triangle pointing upwards rather than downwards, built in timber, would result in internal force which was axial compression.

This example also illustrates another key point concerning the relationship between the form of a structure and the type of internal force involved: for any load pattern, there will be a form, the *form-active shape*, which will allow the load to be resisted by purely axial internal force. There are in fact two versions of this form-active shape which, in the context of vertically acting loads, are mirror images about a horizontal axis. The downward-acting form will carry axial tension and the corresponding upwards-acting form will carry axial compression.

Both versions of that form have a unique shape, in this case that of a triangle, which is dependent on the pattern of applied load. A different load pattern would require a different form to achieve the axial-internal-force condition. The shape concerned, in each case, may be deduced by imagining the form taken up by a flexible rope or cable—that is a structure which is incapable of resisting bending—when the pattern of load is applied to it. Two equal, concentrated loads applied to the one-third-span points of the rope, for example, produce the form of a trapezium. If the rope is suspended under only its own weight, with no external load applied, a condition of fully distributed load occurs and the shape adopted is that of a catenary curve (a catenary curve is simply the shape which a rope takes up when suspended horizontally by its ends and subject to no load other than its own weight).

The above considerations apply to arrangements of two-dimensional surfaces as well as to linear elements. The equivalents of the single rope or cable are the cable network and the fabric membrane. These, too, always take up the tensile form-active shape when load is applied and will change shape to remain form-active under the action of varying loads. The dome and the vault are their compressive equivalents. The latter must be rigid and cannot therefore change shape in response to varying load; they are therefore form-active for one load condition only.

Just as there is, for any given load pattern, a shape which produces purely axial internal force in a structure, there is also a unique shape which produces only bending. This is the *non-form-active* shape. In the case of horizontally spanning structures carrying vertical loads (the normal condition for architectural structures supporting enclosures) the non-form-active shape is a straight horizontal line. The plank of wood acting as a simple bridge described earlier is an example. There are, therefore, for any given load configuration, two unique structural forms, the form-active shape and the non-form-active shape. All other shapes produce structures in which a combination of axial and bending-type internal force

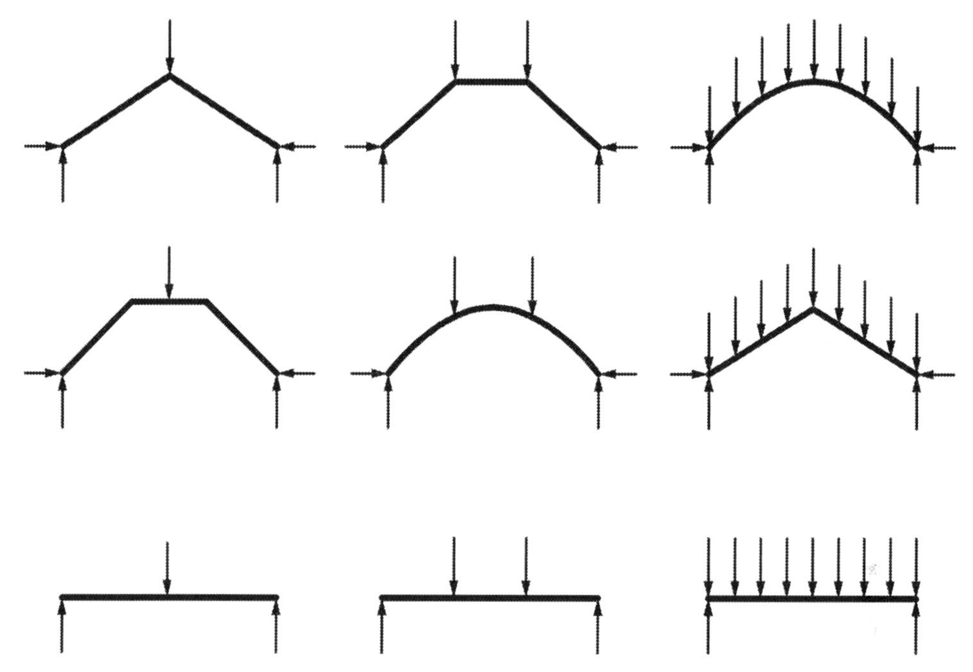

Figure 8.2 The structures in the top row are 'form-active', those in the bottom row 'non-form-active', and those in the second row 'semi-form-active'—all in response (and this is significant) to the particular loads shown (A. Macdonald with A. Siddall).

occurs. Such shapes are said to be *semi-form-active* shapes (see Figure 8.2). Form-active shapes are the most efficient: they provide the strength required to resist given loads using the least amount of material. Non-form-active shapes are the least efficient. Semi-form-active shapes achieve intermediate levels of efficiency: they are more efficient the closer they are to the form-active shape (see Macdonald, 2001, Chapter 4; Engel, 2013).

Although the form-active shape is unique to the load pattern, it is also dependent on the configuration of the supports. This means that in complex three-dimensional arrangements, such as cable networks and shells, the designer can vary the form by altering the layout of the supports, including the positions of masts in cable structures. For a given load and arrangement of supports, the form-active shape is unique.

A measure of the difference in efficiency between form-active and non-form-active shapes is provided by a further example. A very commonly used structural element is the solid reinforced-concrete floor slab spanning horizontally between beams. Under the action of distributed floor loading this is a non-form-active structure in which only bending-type internal forces occur. To achieve adequate strength over a span of 10 m, under normal floor loading conditions, a reinforced-concrete slab requires a thickness of around 300 mm. If the slab were arched upwards in the shape of a parabola it would become a form-active structure and the same strength could be achieved with a thickness of 50 mm. In this case, therefore, the form-active version is more efficient by a factor of six.

If efficiency in the use of material were the only consideration in structural design, form-active shapes would always be used. It will be readily appreciated, however, that there are many situations in which it is not possible or even desirable that a form-active shape be adopted, and that there are many structures in which a non-form-active or a semi-form-active geometry must be used. The ubiquitous post-and-beam building form, in which horizontally spanning floor and roof structures are carried on vertical walls or columns, is a non-form-active configuration. Such arrangements are potentially highly inefficient in their use of structural material, as demonstrated above, but their efficiency can be greatly enhanced by the use of *"improved" shapes of cross-section and longitudinal profile*, as described below.

The reason why bending-type internal force can be resisted less efficiently than axial is that the pattern of stress, which occurs where bending action is taking place, undergoes considerable variation within the cross-sections of the structural elements involved. The sizes which are adopted for structural elements must be such that the maximum stresses are not greater than the strength of the material concerned although, for efficiency, the peak stresses should be only slightly less than the strength of the material. The fact that bending-type action involves variation of stress results in significant quantities of material being present which are carrying low stress and which are therefore not providing full value for their weight. This is the reason for its inefficiency. It is possible, however, to improve the efficiency of non- or semi-form-active structural elements by adopting shapes of cross-section which minimize the amount of under-stressed material.

The distribution of stress in a structural element which is subjected to bending is such that low stress occurs near the centers of cross-sections and high stress at their extremities. If a shape of cross-section is adopted which eliminates most of the material near its center, this will not be significantly weaker than a solid cross-section. Thus, a beam with a cross-section which is I-shaped is almost as strong as one with a solid rectangular cross-section with the same overall dimensions because it is the material at the top and bottom extremities, in the solid rectangular cross-section, which is actually carrying most of the load. The removal of the material towards the center does not therefore significantly weaken the beam. The I-shaped cross-section has a strength which is almost the same as the solid rectangular cross-section but contains significantly less material and so is more structurally efficient.

A generally applicable principle is that, where structural elements are subjected to bending-type loads, their potentially low level of structural efficiency can be improved by the adoption of shapes of cross-section which concentrate material at their extremities. Thus, elements with cross-sections which have I, T or channel shapes, and tubes with rectangular or circular hollow cross-sections, make more efficient elements for resisting bending than those with simple solid rectangular or circular cross-sections. Equally, slab-type structures which have corrugated or folded forms or voided interiors are more efficient than those, which are solid. A very commonly used form of such "improvement" is *triangulation*. The triangulated girder or space framework is more efficient than the solid-core beam or slab because its interior contains less material. The potential for "improvement" of non- and semi-form-active elements, based on the principle of eliminating under-stressed material from cross-sections and longitudinal profiles, is in fact very high and a wide range of shapes are used in structural engineering for this purpose.

It should be clear from the above that the vocabulary of structural form which is available to the structural designer is considerable and offers a wide range of possible structural efficiencies. The most efficient structures, as explained, are those with form-active geometries. Semi-form-active types offer a varying degree of possible efficiencies depending on their closeness to the form-active shape for the pattern of load which they carry, and non-form-active shapes are the least efficient. Within all configurations a range of efficiencies is possible depending on the extent of the "improvements" which are used. A structure with an overall form which is not form-active can nevertheless, therefore, achieve a high level of efficiency if suitable "improvements" are applied to its cross-sections and/or longitudinal profile.

Increased efficiency does, however, involve increased complexity of both overall form and element shapes—another axiom of structural engineering. The disadvantages of efficient configurations are that they are more difficult to make and that the structural calculations are considerably more elaborate. They are thus more expensive to design and to construct than simple, inefficient structures and this consideration may outweigh the saving in the cost of material used.

All structures therefore involve a compromise. Complexity is desirable because it improves efficiency but is undesirable because it makes design and construction more difficult. This raises the question of which level of efficiency (and so of complexity) is appropriate or justified for a particular structure—that is, of which particular structural configuration represents the best compromise for a particular application. This is one of the most interesting aspects of structural design and it has significant implications for the creation of environmentally sustainable architectures. It also provides a basis for the critical appraisal of structures.

In order to make a reasoned assessment of the performance of an architectural structure, in anything other than superficial stylistic terms, the critic should first "read" the building as a *structural* object. The structural parts of the building must be distinguished from those which are non-structural, and the concepts outlined above should be used to make judgments concerning its likely structural behaviour. The relevant questions are: is its overall shape form-active or otherwise, and to what extent have the various forms of "improvement" been incorporated? Consideration of these factors allows a judgment to be made concerning its likely structural efficiency.

The next question to arise concerns whether the level of efficiency achieved is appropriate, given the particular circumstances of the structure. This question relates to a long-held tenet of engineering: that the principal objective of structural engineering is to provide a structure which performs its function with maximum *economy of means*. Economy of means is not simply a matter of achieving high levels of efficiency in the use of material. It requires economy with respect to all aspects of the input to the structure, such as the energy and resources required for design and construction, and the long-term durability of the structure. It is the need to achieve overall economy of means which determines the nature of the most structurally appropriate compromise of complexity/simplicity for a particular case.

It is worth noting at this point that structures which perform well when judged by these criteria are also likely to consume the least of the world's resources and therefore to perform well in environmental terms. This topic is discussed more fully on pp. 130–2.

A difficulty in attempting to compare alternative schemes and thus determine the best arrangement for overall economy of means may arise because the various quantities concerned—weight of material, time spent on design, energy expended in manufacture—are measured using different parameters. There is no simple total calculated figure which can be reached to compare one scheme with another.

One parameter which may be applied universally is of course monetary cost. Everything involved—material, time, energy—may be assigned a monetary value. The resultant overall figure is obviously not an absolute quantity: it depends on the socio-economic system within which the structure is designed and constructed. The latter has a significant effect on the nature of the generally perceived "best compromise" between simplicity and complexity, principally because it influences the relative costs of materials and labor.

In a modern industrialized society, with a high-wage economy, structural complexity is expensive. The use of simple inefficient structures thus tends to be favored because material is cheaper than labor. Most architectural structures in industrialized societies are therefore of the inefficient beam-and-post type, making the least efficient use of material. An energy- or eco-based economy, in which the environmental costs of materials were the principal consideration, would, by contrast, favor a trend towards more efficient use of material because the labor costs involved in achieving the necessary complexity would be lower relative to those of materials. Such a situation is already seen in non-industrial societies where traditional forms of construction are often more complex and sophisticated than their equivalents in industrialized societies. The Bedouin tent of Africa or the yurt of Central Asia are traditional examples, as are the many variants of mud, pisé-de-terre-based, or complex wooden vernacular architectures and their more recent derivatives. In any society the majority of structures which are erected conform to the best compromise, from the point of view of that society, for achieving economy of means. Simple observation of what is built under normal circumstances therefore gives a good indication of the type of structure, which has been considered best suited to a particular economy.

The principal factor which determines the best compromise *for a given economy* is *length of span: the longer the span, the greater the level of efficiency, and therefore of complexity, which is economically "justified"* (see Macdonald, 2001, for a discussion of the reasons for this). The effect of economic regime is to vary the particular span at which increased complexity becomes expedient. This is why the considerable structural complexity of a fabric tent, with its tailored membrane, guy ropes and poles, is justified for short spans in the context of traditional societies but not in industrialized societies in which such forms tend only to be used for long-span or flamboyant temporary structures.

The most important conclusions from this section may be summarized as follows:

- the efficiency of a structure is dependent on all aspects of its form—its overall form and the shapes of the elements at a detailed level
- high levels of structural efficiency can only be achieved with high levels of complexity of form
- complexity of form gives rise to high design and construction costs
- almost all structures are a compromise between complexity, for efficiency, and simplicity, for ease of construction
- the principal factor which determines the "best compromise" is length of span
- the best compromise will produce maximum economy of means in the total input of resources to the structure
- the job of the structural designer, in engineering terms, is to find the best compromise for a particular application.

The Nature of the Architecture/Structure Collaboration in the Modern Period

Throughout the Modern period, largely as a consequence of great advances in structural technology, architects have been able to exercise great freedom of expression in the matter of form. The relationship between art and technology, in the context of tectonics, has not, however, always been a satisfactory one, and has often resulted in the creation of buildings which, although considered distinguished architecturally, have not performed well technologically. As the twenty-first century progresses, and more consideration requires to be given to the issues of environmental impact and sustainability, the freedom exercised by many present-day architects to allocate a low priority to technical matters, when determining form, may have to be relinquished in favor of a more balanced approach to design.

The most significant structural development to influence the forms of Modern buildings was the introduction of the "new" structural materials of steel and reinforced concrete in the late nineteenth century: this development freed the designers of buildings from many of the constraints associated with the "traditional" materials of masonry and timber. In particular, due to their ability to resist high levels of bending, these new materials greatly extended the span possibilities of non-form-active and semi-form-active structures. Their much greater strength also allowed them to be used in the form of skeleton-frame structures rather than loadbearing-wall structures and thus permitted greater freedom of architectural expression by freeing walls, both exterior and interior, from any structural function and consequent technical constraint.

Changes in manufacturing technology were also important. From the mid-twentieth century the application of computers to structural analysis enabled more accurate calculation of the internal stresses and strains in complex structures. The resulting greater certainty over the strength provided in structures allowed factors of safety to be reduced, with consequent reductions in the bulk of elements and savings of material. The more sophisticated calculation techniques also increased confidence in the ability to build, safely, ever more complicated structural geometries. Towards the end of the century, as well as facilitating highly sophisticated calculations, the application of computers to the control of manufacturing allowed structural and cladding components of very complex shape to be made economically. Computer control of manufacturing also made possible the creation, by mass production, of components which were not identical, and this freedom from standardization, in the context of mass production, was a further factor in enabling the manufacture of structures and envelopes with highly complex geometries. By the beginning of the twenty-first century it was possible to construct buildings of virtually any shape, irrespective of technical performance, and architects therefore enjoyed a level of freedom in relation to form which could hardly have been imagined in pre-Modern times.

This novel freedom was exercised in the context of theories of architecture which sought to create visual vocabularies which were appropriate for the Modern age. These new architectural theories contributed, in the twentieth century, to the development of an uneasy relationship between architects and those who were responsible for the technical performance of buildings. There is insufficient space here to go into the many arguments and counter arguments which surround this controversial subject. It is sufficient, in the context of this chapter, to make a few observations on how these have affected the relationship between structural design and architectural design.

The pioneers of early Modern architecture were in pursuit of a new visual vocabulary, not related to any previous styles, which would be a symbolic embodiment of a "new world" and therefore appropriate for the Modern age. Such a visual vocabulary was intended to express the mood of the age, and to embrace the Modernist ideals of rational thought and a related belief in the beneficial effects of material progress, both of these realized through buildings, or at least building components, which were created by industrial machinery and process rather than by the hand-crafting methods of the past. Above all, the aspiration was to develop a visual vocabulary which would celebrate technology as the instrument of social and economic progress.

In the book which was perhaps the most influential of all of the works of Modernist architectural theory and polemic (Le Corbusier, 1923/1927), Le Corbusier included a profusion of illustrations of all types of technical objects, drawing his examples from aeronautical, automotive and marine engineering as well as from the technologies of building. The message seemed to be clear: it was from images like these that the new visual vocabulary of Modern architecture would be derived. It was also implied that the new Modern architecture would be created by adopting the methodology of the engineers. New architectural forms would be devised, in other words, by a logical process of considering which technological shapes would best fulfil the functions of buildings. The abstract rectilinearity of early Modern buildings, so expressive as it was of the idea of a machine age, also had its origins in the theories of art and architecture which were developed in the early twentieth century by writers such as those in the De Stijl group, in which symbolic meaning was attached to such forms.

From the first, most of the images of Modern architecture were certainly evocative of the machine. The rectilinear geometries with their compositions of straight edges and smooth, plane surfaces looked as though they had been made by machines rather than by the human hand. The rectilinear building forms were also uncannily well adapted to the use of steel and reinforced-concrete post-and-beam frameworks. The level of complexity, and thus efficiency, which was achieved with these were acceptable for the short-to-medium spans involved and so the structures performed reasonably well when judged by purely technical criteria. There seemed therefore to be an ideal relationship between the visual forms desired by the architects and the structural forms found satisfactory by the engineers. It may be argued, however, that although the building forms appeared as if they had been derived logically from a consideration of function, this was, to a large extent, a coincidence rather than the result of a conscious desire to merge architectural and technical thinking in the early stages of a design. Although it is difficult to be precise about the causal relationships in any particular case, it seems likely, from an examination of these parallel historical developments, that the reality of the relationship between aesthetics and technology in early Modernism has been, to a large extent, obscured by the temporal coincidence of the technology of the post-and-beam framework in steel or reinforced concrete with the development of the preference for rectilinear forms favored by the architectural theory of the time. It was the image which was of principal interest to the architects rather than the technology itself.

In the later Modernism of the second half of the twentieth century and the early twenty-first century, as techniques for the design and fabrication of buildings became ever more sophisticated, it became increasingly easy to make structures which were actually technically deficient in the sense that they made an extremely wasteful use of material. The true nature of the relationship between art and technology in Modern architecture then began to become more apparent. A particular manifestation of this may be identified in the mid-twentieth century in the field of large enclosures requiring long-span structures. The history of the Modern long-span enclosure with a metal or reinforced-concrete structure derives largely from the vast, utilitarian, train sheds constructed in iron and glass which began to appear from the mid-nineteenth century. The equivalents of these in the mid-twentieth century tended to be built in reinforced concrete and took the form of thin-shell structures. Like their nineteenth-century predecessors, these were designed entirely by structural engineers and were works of more-or-less pure engineering unaffected by architectural theory. The early structures of Pier Luigi Nervi and Eduardo Torroja from the 1930s are prime examples, and the tradition has been continued by engineers such as Felix Candela, Heinz Isler and Santiago Calatrava in more recent decades (see Figure 8.1) (see Adriaenssens *et al.*, 2014).

Most of these long-span buildings, which were designed by engineers working without architects, or rather *as* architects, were appropriately balanced in respect of efficient use of material and ease of construction. The reinforced-concrete shells were remarkable for their spectacular forms and for their extreme efficiency in the use of structural material. Shells with thicknesses of as little of 100 to 150 mm could span 100 m or more. The high level of efficiency achieved was due to their being given very specific form-active shapes.

The spectacular forms of these long-span enclosures were very striking visually: they were featured in the architectural media and their designers were accepted and even lauded in the narrow world of architectural criticism. The long-span shells rightly came to represent the most advanced structural technology of their day and were attractive to architects wishing to produce forms associated with the idea of combining art and science through a tectonically inspired architecture. They were therefore much imitated but most architects who were not also trained as engineers failed properly to understand or interest themselves in the technology involved. The designers concerned regarded such structures simply as an opportunity to experiment freely with curvilinear form. The results, at least in terms of technical performance and cost, were often disastrous.

Perhaps the most spectacular and well known of the architect-designed free-form shell-like buildings was the *Sydney Opera House* of 1973 (see Figure 8.3). The intended shapes of the "shells" which are the dominating feature of this well-known building were not generated by the architect (Jørn Utzon) from a knowledge of the principles of form-action. Rather, his original concept sketch was supposedly inspired by the forms of sails (which are, ironically, *tensile* form-active structures—but crucially, structures in which the loads

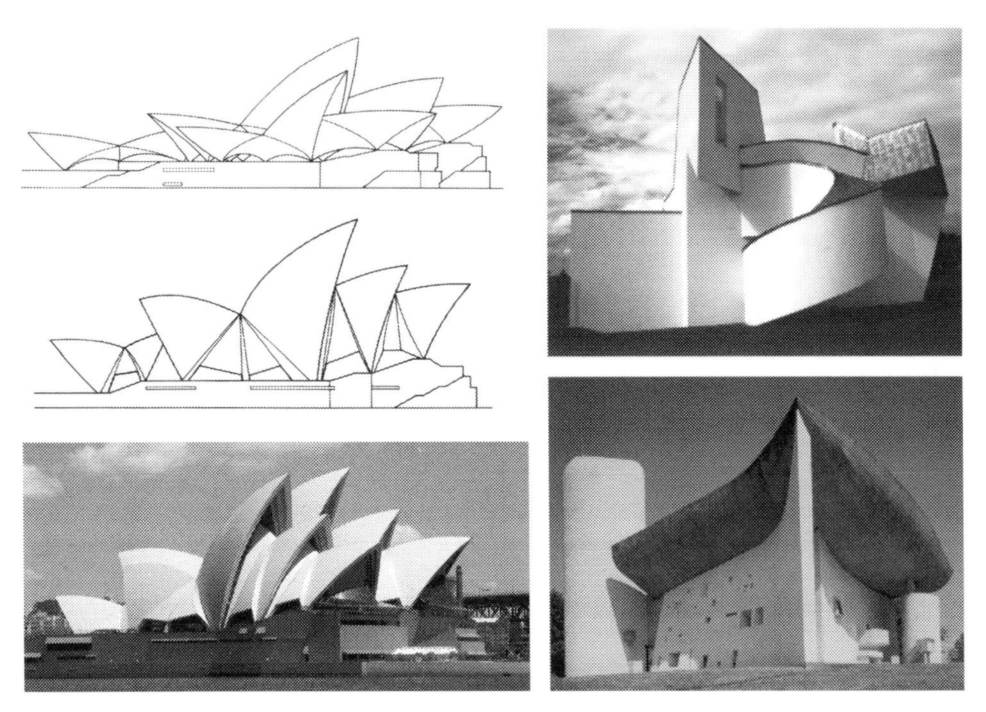

Figure 8.3 Structurally inefficient 'free-form' architecture based on semi-form-active reinforced concrete 'shell' structures: [left] Sydney Opera House, showing realised form [middle left] which was quite different from that initially intended [top left] ([bottom left] B. Sorensen / Wikimedia Commons; [middle & top left] A. Macdonald with S. Gibson); [upper right] Vitra Design Museum (E. & F. McLachlan); [lower right] Chapel of Notre Dame du Haut (P. Macdonald).

involved are horizontal, not vertical, as they must be in a building enclosure, and which also involve masts and other supporting spars). The proposed (*compressive* not tensile) shapes for the Opera House had to be radically modified subsequently into sections of a sphere in order to make the huge building technically and economically feasible. The final shapes achieved are only semi-form-active and generate large intensities of bending. Vast quantities of reinforced concrete were required to provide adequate strength and the building, contrary to its appearance, is not composed of efficient thin shells but of massive reinforced-concrete frameworks—extremely strong but highly inefficient and wasteful of material, but the only possible technology that could, at the time, approximate to the desired shapes. The project, unsurprisingly, ran massively over budget. Economy of means, in any sense, was far from being achieved; only the use of appropriate, true form-active geometries could have made this possible. The problems at Sydney arose from a failure by the architect to understand the structural principles which were crucial to the realization of his design. That such an inefficient structure could be built at all was due to the advanced state of contemporary reinforced-concrete technology. Another memorable building of which the same comment could be made is the *TWA Terminal* (now *Head House, Terminal 5*) of 1962 by architect Eero Saarinen at Idlewild (John F. Kennedy) Airport in New York.

It should perhaps be mentioned, that the principal difficulties which arose at the Sydney Opera House were caused by the sheer scale of the building. Had it been significantly smaller, the bending moments generated in the semi-form-active forms of the original concept would have been smaller and could probably have been effectively resisted by reinforced concrete, albeit with a structure which would have been highly inefficient. The *Vitra Design Museum* (1989) by Frank Gehry is one example of such a smaller building which was successfully realized, and the renowned *Notre Dame du Haut* chapel at Ronchamp (1954), by Le Corbusier, is another.

This tendency, just described, to evolve architectural form without paying due regard to its structural consequences has continued to be particularly noticeable in all styles of architecture in which the imagery of engineering is used as a visual vocabulary. The most obvious examples in recent decades are to be found in the creations of the "High Tech" movement of the late twentieth century.

The *Centre Pompidou* in Paris (1978—architects Piano and Rogers; engineer Peter Rice of Ove Arup and Partners) serves as an example (see Figure 8.4). This is a large building, requiring long-span areas, and has a steel structure of unconventional layout. The principal floor girders, which span across the building, are attached to the columns through cast-steel "gerberette" brackets which form a prominent, and widely celebrated, feature of the building's exterior. This is not however, an efficient structural arrangement: it sends 25 percent more force down each column than is needed to support the weight of the floors, with ongoing consequences for the excessive weight of steel which had to be specified. Other features of the frame, concerned with architectural rather than technical performance, contribute to its inefficiency. A further problematic, although visually dramatic, decision was the placing of a large proportion of the steelwork outside the weatherproof skin of the building, resulting in an ongoing maintenance problem. The specification of an all-glass external envelope, which forms a poor environmental barrier between the interior and the exterior—although not a structural feature—is a further technical deficiency in a permanent building, and there are many others.

Economy of means, in terms of efficiency in the use of structural materials and of subsequent maintenance and running costs, was therefore only achieved to a limited extent in this building. Despite these technical shortcomings, the building undoubtedly made a

Figure 8.4 Buildings with steel structures which are inefficient because visual considerations were given precedence over technical efficiency (economy of means): [left] Centre Pompidou (P. Macdonald); [top right] Central China Television headquarters (J. Montrasio / Wikimedia Commons); [lower right] Walt Disney Concert Hall (Arturoramos / Wikimedia Commons).

significant addition to late twentieth century architecture, but it should nevertheless not be regarded, as many critics have claimed, as an example of good architectural technology. It is ironic that it is one of the most significant examples of what has become known as "*High Tech*" architecture. Similar criticisms can be made of most examples of the High Tech style, which clearly demonstrate that where engineering motifs are used principally or purely as visual imagery, the result is rarely satisfactory technically: the technical reality of the building is usually precisely the opposite of its intended message of technical innovation and excellence.

By the later twentieth and into the early twenty-first century, as described above, due to significant developments in design and construction technologies of steel-framework structures and cladding, it became increasingly possible to make curvilinear structures in steel on a large scale. This method of working is favored by such architects as Frank Gehry (for example the *Walt Disney Concert Hall*, Los Angeles, 2003—see Figure 8.4), and Daniel Libeskind, who exercise a freedom of expression in form unavailable to Utzon and Saarinen. A related approach was adopted by the architects (Rem Koolhaas and Ole Scheeren, with the East China Architectural Design and Research Institute; engineers Ove Arup & Partners) of the *China Central TV (CCTV) Headquarters* building in Beijing of 2012 (see Figure 8.4). The building is notable, not only for its novel shape, but for the extreme quantities of structural steelwork which were required to realize it.

A survey of current and recently built architecture (e.g. Jodidio, 2013), reveals, as would be expected, an enormous variety, worldwide, of building shape, size and appearance. The examples featured range in scale from short-span domestic enclosures, through a wide variety of commercial and public buildings, to very long-span enclosures associated with, for example, sporting arenas and concert halls. It is clear that in virtually all of these, very close collaboration has taken place between architects and structural engineers. The relationship between the two professions nevertheless remains similar to that which has characterized the whole of the Modern period. Visual concerns dominate and, if the structural technology is appropriate, this unusual circumstance is normally found only in the context of small-scale buildings in which post-and-beam structures have been employed.

The uneasy and unequal relationship between architects and engineers which developed in the architecture of twentieth-century Modernism continues, therefore, into the present day. The dominating influences on the form and general arrangement of most buildings in which architects have a central involvement remain an adherence to a chosen architectural theory and the attachment of an overwhelming importance to appearance, often to the detriment of technical performance. Although the recently-developed technical mastery of built form can enable the realization of almost any project, technical factors are still only rarely granted a high priority in design.

The Future—Structure in an Environmentally Sustainable Architecture

In the present day, as mentioned in the previous section, there is less reason than there has ever been for architects to feel constrained by the technical requirements of structure, and consequently either to be concerned personally with consideration of technical matters, or to need to collaborate in design teams with structural engineers in the early stages of the form-determination process for a building. Many currently prominent architects have chosen to exploit this freedom to the full and to evolve fantastic forms, which bear little relationship to either structural efficiency or simplicity of construction. Such buildings are often exceedingly wasteful of both material and energy despite attracting considerable attention from the architecture media.

We are perhaps, therefore, further than ever from the Albertian ideal of a fusion of art and science in architecture than has been the case since the time of the Gothic cathedrals, and this at a time when the need to design buildings which function well technically, so as to be environmentally sustainable, has never been greater. If architects are to play their part in the creation of a sustainable society, the currently widespread, unhealthy, and almost total preoccupation with the visual will need to be replaced by design methods which unite the visual more sympathetically with the technical. It is important to recognize that such a change will require a fundamental shift of attitude on the part of architects, who have hitherto tended to protect themselves in a self-congratulatory world where they remain aloof from the opinions of the rest of society.

A broader range of solutions, successful in different ways, will have to be valued by the design community generally, along with a holistic approach to design which does not favor one single, "sanctified" aspect, and an acceptance that compromise is necessary in order to achieve a form which offers the best overall solution. Appearance, and the expression of chosen philosophical ideas, will remain extremely important, but not to the exclusion of all other considerations.

In future, due consideration will have to be given in structural design to the resources which buildings consume. Greater attention will have to be paid to the obvious factors which affect structural performance, including selection of materials with appropriate structural properties and levels of embodied energy, and the adoption of forms which are the most suitable for the spans and the loads carried. Structural arrangements will be needed which can be constructed without undue difficulty, and which are durable in service. Always, emphasis will have to be placed on the achievement of the engineer's maxim of economy of means. All of these factors will affect both the overall form of structures and their general characteristics and, unlike in the recent past, they will have to be given an appropriate priority in the design process. Such a new approach to design will require a greater emphasis on the generation of form from first principles, and less reliance on the use of forms which have either become the accepted practice for common applications or which are simply architecturally fashionable.

The priorities of the building-components industry will also have to be challenged in the direction of the manufacture of products which have smaller embodied energy and better ecological credentials overall. It will also be advantageous to evolve a better system of training for builders with perhaps a return to a more rigorous apprenticeship system so that people recover, or re-develop, the ability to actually make things, rather than simply assemble them. Alongside these developments there will have to be a trend away from high-embodied-energy construction systems, which minimize time spent in building—which favors the use of mass-produced elements which can be quickly assembled on site—towards more environmentally friendly methods of building.

These types of change may already be observed in the growing number of buildings designed by architects seeking to evolve building forms which are appropriate for the present world situation (see Figure 8.5) (Marta, 2010). These are, however, mostly small-scale

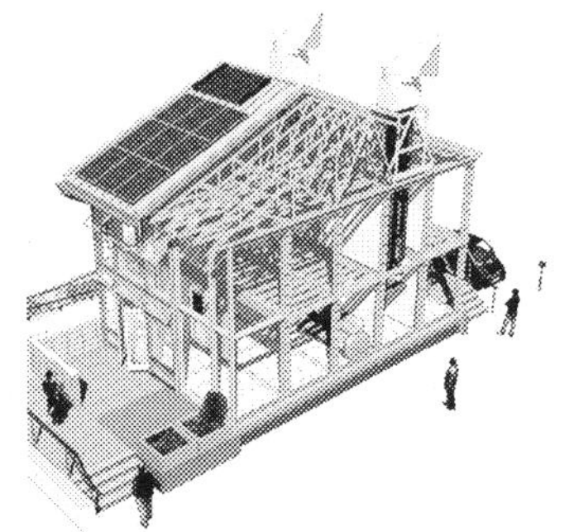

Figure 8.5 Buildings (currently mostly small-scale) designed for economy of means, so as to minimise environmental impact, represent an increasing architectural trend: [upper] The Houl, Dalry, Scotland, S. Winstanley, 2009 (A. Lee); [lower left] RuralZED House, UK, ZEDfactory, 2003 (ZEDfactory); [lower right] Gamlingay Eco Hub, UK, civic Architects, 2012 (civic Architects).

buildings, and very few examples exist to date of buildings on a large scale which attempt the kind of radical shift of approach which is required. Most mainstream architects, even those who acknowledge the need for a "greener" approach, continue to apply Modernist solutions based on the now obsolescent Modernist scenario of adopting increasing amounts of "hard" technology involving, for example, sophisticated, but high maintenance, interactive cladding systems. A rare exception is the *Riverside Museum* in Glasgow of 2011 (architect: Zaha Hadid; structural engineers, Buro Happold) which is of complex ("folded") geometry and which has a (triply "improved") structure that is appropriately configured for its span (see Figure 8.1).

All of the considerations earlier, if implemented, are likely to have a profound effect on architectural form, which may be expected to evolve away from the theoretically determined forms of mainstream Modernism. In the present day, in which basic priorities are undergoing rapid change in the light of unavoidable environmental concerns, a new visual vocabulary may be expected to emerge. Such a new vocabulary, for the current century and beyond, should be both expressive of the current state of human knowledge and understanding, at a philosophical level, and compatible with the technologies required to create an environmentally sustainable architecture. This is the most significant and exciting challenge facing architecture today, as much for those whose specialism is in the visual aspects of architecture, as for their collaborators whose expertise lies in the structural and technical spheres.

References

Adriaenssens, S., Block, P., Veenedaal, D. & Williams, C. (Eds.) (2014). *Shell Structures for Architecture.* Abingdon, Oxon: Routledge.

Engel, H. (2013). *Structure Systems,* 5th Edition. Ostfildern, Germany: Hatje Cantz.

Jodidio, P. (2013). *Architecture Now*. Cologne, Germany: Taschen.

Le Corbusier (1923/1927). *Vers une architecture (Towards a New Architecture).* London: Architectural Press.

Macdonald, A. J. (2001). *Structure and Architecture,* 2nd Edition. Oxford, UK: Architectural Press.

Marta, S. (2010). *150 Best Eco House Ideas*. New York: Collins Design/Loft.

9

Designing for Net Zero Energy

From Low-tech to Mid-tech to Hi-tech and to Eco-tech

Ken Yeang

Preamble by Stephen D. Dent

For those of us who designed, built, or taught in the area of "energy-efficient design" in the 1970s and 1980s, the interest in our buildings, writings, research, and conferences seemed to fluctuate yearly with the price of oil. We understood the waste of resources, the inefficiency, and the environmental degradation caused by most buildings at that time, but our design movement to Solar Architecture was largely driven by the "energy crisis" that dramatically increased oil prices starting in 1973. However, as the encompassing issues of climate change and the long-term sustainability of our developed societies came into focus in the 1990s, we came to see that the issues were much broader and much, much more important.

For many, their first exposure to the potential scope and reality of climate change and environmental degradation came from reading *The End of Nature* in 1989. In it, Bill McKibben showed clearly that the hand of man is felt directly or indirectly on natural systems everywhere on the planet. We did not set out to do this, we were sure that the natural world was too big to influence. "But, quite by accident, it turned out that the carbon dioxide and the other gases we were producing in our pursuit of a better life—in pursuit of warm houses and eternal economic growth and of agriculture so productive it would free most of us from farming—*could* alter the power of the sun, could increase its heat. And that increase *could* change the patterns of moisture and dryness and breed storms in new places breed deserts." (as we have learned since, the qualified *could* has been replaced by an emphatic *will*). Unfortunately, it is taking too long to marshal our forces to address these problems. Meanwhile, climate change and environmental degradation seems to be progressing faster than initially predicted.

The historian Thomas Berry writes in *The Great Work* that

> History is governed by those overarching movements that give shape and meaning to life by relating the human venture to the larger destinies of the universe ... the Great Work now, as we move into a new millennium, is to carry out the transition from a period of human devastation of the Earth to a period when humans would be present

> to the planet in a mutually beneficial manner ... This is our Great Work and the work of our children.

It is important to note that no generation specifically asks for their Great Work—it is thrust upon them by the forces of the time and that in this case the transition to an "ecological enlightenment" in our economic, social, and governmental systems will probably take at least several generations—and will also forever change how we design the built environment now and in the future.

The essential root of climate change is in our production of what are called greenhouse gases, over 70 percent of which is carbon dioxide, but also methane and nitrous oxide. As of 2011, the worldwide production of carbon dioxide for power production was over 35 billion tons! Edward Mazria and his Architecture 2030 organization has been pivotal in pointing out that buildings are critical factors in the problem and setting goals for the alleviation of the problem. Approximately 48 percent of the energy consumed in the United States comes from heating, cooling, lighting, and operating the equipment and appliances within our buildings; making the materials that go into the construction of buildings; and the processes of construction of our buildings. Consequently, architects have a major role in addressing our Great Work.

Our long-term love affair with the ever expanding wonders of technical innovations and the numerous household products that reduced the drudgery of household chores and blessed us with nearly limitless mobility also blinded us to the evolving ecological disconnect with natural systems. Architects and architecture have had a crucial role in the creation of this problem—though few could ever have foreseen its global implications. Modernism in architecture had strong social roots as its major early practitioners and theorists believed that technology could be directed by design to solve such major social issues as affordable housing for all. Unfortunately, this seldom was the result, but our buildings did get larger and more complicated and less and less connected to the climate in which they were located and more and more dependent on their mechanical systems. The awareness of the scope of the problem occurred roughly in sync with the High-Tech movement in architecture, practiced principally in Europe. The expression of materials, connections, and building systems was a natural base on which to develop a new architecture that addressed the ecological imperative that has been called eco-tech. The expression of the systems for solar shading and daylight control, power generation, and water harvesting, for example were a logical extension for the new sustainable buildings.

The newest design software allows (encourages?) the making of building forms and enclosures that have not been possible before. We can now create truly new and innovative forms and, by connecting directly to computer controlled manufacturing processes, actually construct what was previously impossibly complex in form or assembly. This is especially true of the building enclosure system. I believe that the attraction of creating buildings that are just different for aesthetic reasons is missing a great opportunity for creating a new architecture that addresses the need for ecological connections and sustainable development. For example, a *purposeful differentiation* of facades by orientation and exposure to environmental forces leads to highly variable and differentiated surfaces that have purpose. This approach will lead to more ecologically responsive forms and surfaces, but also to a dynamic architecture that responds to the endlessly variable forces of sun, wind, and light.

However, there is a great conundrum in designing more technologically sophisticated buildings. The technology can solve, or at least ameliorate, the provision of comfortable conditions at lower energy input levels, but at what long-term cost in embodied energy in materials and products, energy for transport to market, environmental impact, and higher and higher expectations for building performance? As we spread prosperity to currently underprivileged societies, won't they too rightly expect the equivalent buildings with their accompanying economic, aesthetic, and functional performance, thus further enlarging humankind's devastating environmental footprint? (If everyone on Earth consumed resources like Americans, we'd need five more planets to provide for us.) Can we ever answer E. F. Schumacher's question "What is enough?" in his classic text *Small is Beautiful*? Solutions are not easy unless human to environmental relationships are at the forefront, i.e., we must move quickly to an ecological vision that puts climate-responsive design as our first step in any design due to its ability to drastically reduce energy and materials use *before* we apply our high-tech or even the highest performing eco-tech solutions. This is the path described in detail by Ken Yeang's following chapter.

Fossil Fuels Energy vs. Renewable Energy

Cheap energy is of course an expeditious way to improve society's living standards, and certainly it has lifted millions of people (as in China) out of poverty—not through use of renewable sources of energy such as wind turbines or solar energy, but with huge amounts of cheap coal. However, this endeavor to improve society's living standards comes with a high environmental cost—the price to pay is atmospheric pollution leading to global warming.

Global warming is caused by CO_2 emissions from burning fossil fuels to generate power to provide this cheap energy. Fossil fuels power just about everything we like about modern life: they feed us, warm and cool us, transport us and keep the lights on while powering our industries, our economies, our cities, including the internet. Global warming has become a key issue besetting our planet's health—an issue that comes from human beings demanding a standard of life, which is dependent on the availability of cheap, convenient and immediate source of energy.

Despite much talk about renewable energy such as wind or solar, we still get 82 percent of our energy from fossil fuels, and it is predicted that in 2035, fossil fuels are expected to provide 80 percent of a much higher amount of society's energy consumption. Herein lies the challenge—what steps can we take to reverse this?

Discussed here is a set of strategies for reducing the use of non-renewable energy and reducing carbon emissions in a progressive design process that starts from first optimizing "low-tech" strategies and options to "mid-tech" to "high-tech" heading to our ultimate objective of "eco-tech," being the reduction of non-renewable energy use and carbon emissions to an eventual net zero energy and carbon neutral human society.

We need, at the same time, to be aware of the fact that the designing of net zero energy and carbon neutral buildings, addresses only one aspect, being the engineering aspect of eco-design from a host of other environmental issues. Eco-design is defined here as the seamless and benign bio-integration of four strands—first, the eco-infra-structures being the ecology of the site and environmental biology of the biosphere; second, the activities of our human society being everything that we do and make on the planet; third the clean-tech eco-engineering and our built environment including the management of material flow and achieving zero waste; and finally water management in seeking to conserve and close our built environment's water cycle.

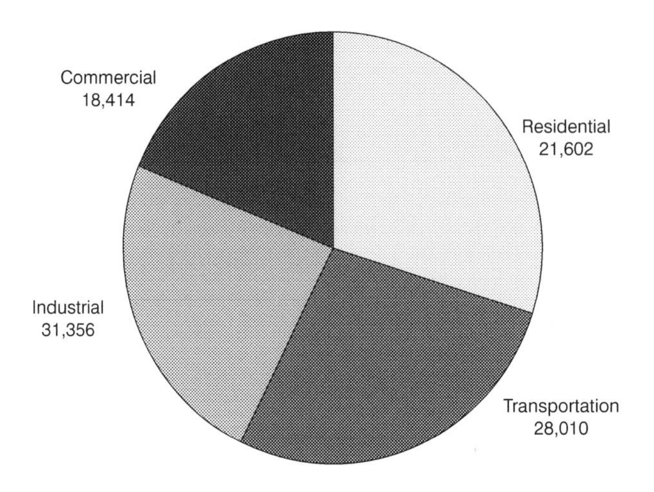

Figure 9.1 Energy consumption, USA, 2008 (trillion BTUs)

Buildings and Energy Consumption

To rectify climate change, we need to take large and radical steps to reduce our consumption of fossil fuels. We need to change the existent systems and hardware that we are currently using to meet our demands for a high standard of living that is tied to our society's consumerist and wasteful lifestyles and the systems that drive our economies, manufacturing, industries, food production, education, recreation, storage and distribution, transportation, etc., all of which callously consume huge amounts of energy.

Over 50 percent of non-renewable energy use is in our buildings (in Wikipedia) from construction, to its operation, to its demolition and its reuse, recycling and its eventual benign reintegration back into the natural environment. Buildings are essentially significant contributors of greenhouse gases. The designing for reduction in the use of non-renewable energy in buildings has to be one of the key design actions that we must take.

Moving toward Net Zero Energy Building (NZEB)

Net Zero Energy Buildings (NZEB) is defined as an energy-efficient built environment with zero net (non-renewable) energy consumption, meaning the total amount of energy used by the buildings is roughly equal to the amount of renewable energy created on the site.

NZEB uses the electrical grid for energy storage but some are interdependent of grid. Energy is usually harvested on-site through combination of renewable energy producing technologies like solar and wind while reducing the overall use of energy with highly efficient, clean-tech and lowered embodied-energy technologies (e.g. for HVAC, lighting, etc.).

The term, 'net' emphasizes the energy exchange between the building and the energy infrastructure. By the building-grid interaction, the NZEB becomes an active part of the renewable energy infrastructure. The need for connection to the energy grid reduces seasonal energy storage and oversized on-site systems for energy generation from renewable sources.

Energy conservation starts with us and our expectations of the level of comfort in buildings. This needs to be reconsidered. Buildings provide an enclosure as protection from the outside elements for a variety of human uses and activities (e.g. whether for habitation, commerce, industrial, recreation, storage, etc.). All of these demand a required level of internal environmental conditions determined at the early onset of design and not after.

It is at the early stage of a project at its design process, whether for cities, communities or buildings, that the issue of environmental impairment needs to be planned, addressed and implemented. It is also at the design stage where we have the most options and flexibility. Our options become increasingly limited as we head towards implementation and after construction.

An example is the motorcar industry. Much effort had gone into seeking to produce cars that are energy efficient that consume less fossil fuel. This is enhancing energy use efficiency after the car has been produced, however we should look beyond the production line and seek solutions that at the outset reduce and eliminate the use and need for cars in entirety. This, calls for a critical review and change in our city planning patterns.

Essentially, our environmental problems need to be addressed early on at the design stage rather than after. In the case of building, rather than seeking energy efficient and carbon neutral hardware solutions after the built-form has been designed, we need to make prudent early design decisions to minimize non-renewable energy demand before seeking to improve the performance of buildings in enhancing their energy systems efficiency and durability. The life of a building should continue after its commercial period of use. We need to design in flexibility such that it will enable the adaptation to using less energy consuming systems in future refurbishment (e.g. using skeleton-infill building systems) and to facilitate future energy and material conservation in the reuse and refurbishment of the building.

Standards of Internal Environmental Conditions

The energy consumption of buildings is determined by its internal environmental conditions, and by their use and the expected comfort level of the buildings' occupants.

These expected internal environmental conditions become determining factors in the design of the environmental engineering systems in our buildings. The higher the expected level the greater the demand for energy to achieve these conditions for comfort and use. The question then is do we need to design to meet conventional internal environmental standards (e.g. ASHRAE standards, etc.)? What if we adopted in buildings for habitation and work such internal environmental conditions that are a bit hotter in the summer (in temperate zones) and a bit colder in winter? The lowering of even a few degrees in internal environmental conditions can significantly reduce the consumption of energy.

For buildings of human habitation, we need to ascertain the level of environmental comfort as the basis for design, and on a space by space basis. We need to reduce our current expectations of lifestyle and use in our built environment whether residential, commercial, retail, recreational, industrial, etc.

Addressing this will involve other lifestyle changes, for example, encouraging, seeking and demanding our building's occupants to adopt habits that avoid wasting energy, to use energy-efficient electrical appliances, to wear warmer clothing in winter to lower the heating level, to have shorter hot showers, to recycle waste, to reduce the consumption of water, etc. An acceptable zone of thermal comfort for most people in the UK lies roughly between 13°C (56°F) and 30°C (86°F), with acceptable temperatures for more strenuous work activities concentrated towards the bottom end of the range, and more sedentary activities towards the higher end.

Low-Tech Design—Designing to Optimize Passive Mode Options Without the Use of Any Engineering Systems

Building design starts by designing with low-tech strategies which is to optimize all passive mode means, prior to the inclusion of any active engineering systems (such as its Mechanical and Electronic (M&E) systems).

Low-tech design strategies involve designing in relation to the local climatic conditions. This includes—appropriate built-form shaping and massing, built-form orientation, layout of the internal "served" spaces and the "serving" spaces, façade design, use of ambient energies of the locality, etc. There is a need to apply these design strategies for all built-form types and uses—whether for high-end building or a low-cost affordable building or industrial building. The desired outcome is a low-energy passive-mode built-form and envelope.

Passive-mode design is an effect climate-responsive design, where we maximize the use of all non-technological active responses to the climatic conditions of the locality.

Climatic conditions of course vary depending on where the built-form is located, for example in temperate, cold, tropical climates, etc. Different climatic zones demand the appropriate set of bioclimatic passive-mode responses.

Generally stated, design needs to start as low-tech, before we bring in the active M&E engineering systems, whether partially as in mid-tech design (mixed-mode systems) or high-tech design (using full-mode active systems). The rationale is that if our design starts out with poor or non-climate responsive attributes, then any subsequent active M&E systems that we put in afterwards will need to first alleviate and compensate its poor passive energy performance and rectify any earlier erroneous or inappropriate non-passive mode design decisions. The outcome then requires the increases in the extent of active systems (hardware)

Figure 9.2 Menara Mesiniaga Tower

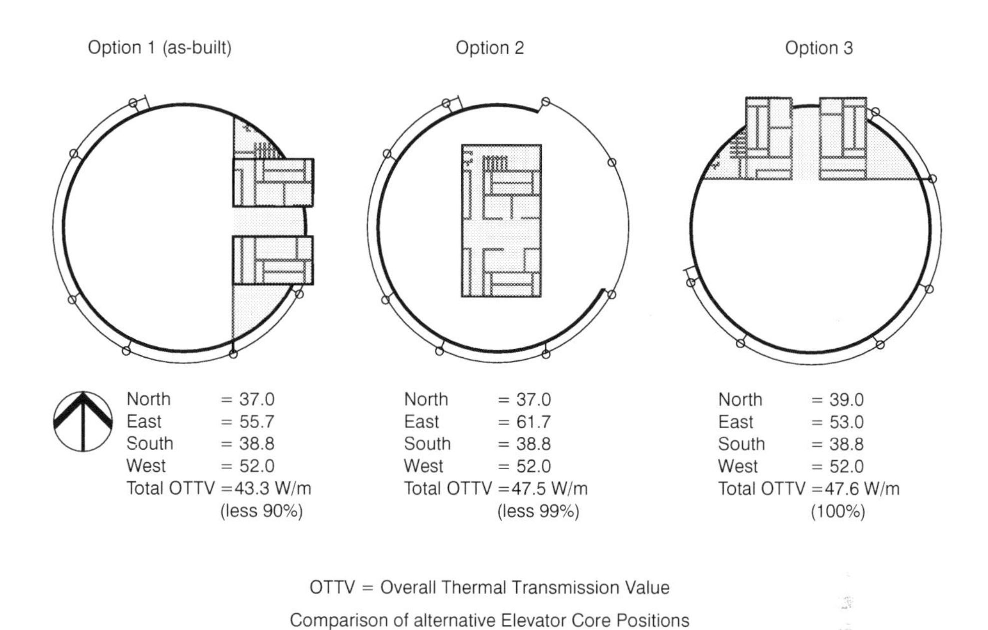

Figure 9.3 Evaluation of alternative service-core configurations for Menara Mesiniaga tower

to be provided. This then makes the built-form and its engineering systems counteractive in our endeavor for a net zero energy design in the first instance.

Passive mode as a climate-responsive design is essentially 'bioclimatic design'. This is an approach in design that makes use of the built-form's thermal mass or the configuration of the built-form, its layout and its orientation, as well as the building components, such as its façade and roof's design to respond to the climate of the locality. This can also be achieved by adoption of certain constructional strategies such as having a higher level of insulation, the reduction of thermal bridging, a higher level of air tightness, etc., toward mitigating and simultaneously harmonizing with the effect of the local climatic elements and factors such as sun, wind, humidity, temperature, and rainfall. In essence, the goal is to take advantage of the ambient energies of the locality. Bioclimatic design as "low-tech" design involves no active engineering systems

Bioclimatic design can start by looking into the effects of the sun and responding to its particular solar path for that latitude on the built-form and its surroundings. The later includes the influence of shadows of adjacent and surrounding structures, of topography, etc. All these can have an impact on the façade and the internal comfort conditions of the occupants of the building. The solar path for a locality is not the same for different latitudes and this also varies depending on the time of the year and the time of the day. The appropriate built-form configuration and orientation can reduce the solar radiation on the building.

In the hot humid tropics, the sun path generally moves from the east to the west over the day, whereas in temperate and cold climates being higher up in their latitudes, the sun path is considerably lower and varies more depending on the season and time of the year. In temperate and cold climates the built-form's configuration and orientation and disposition of its internal spaces can be shaped and laid out to maximize the sunlight entering the built-form in winter to bring in warmth into the internal spaces, whereas the façade needs to be designed to reduce solar radiation in the summer.

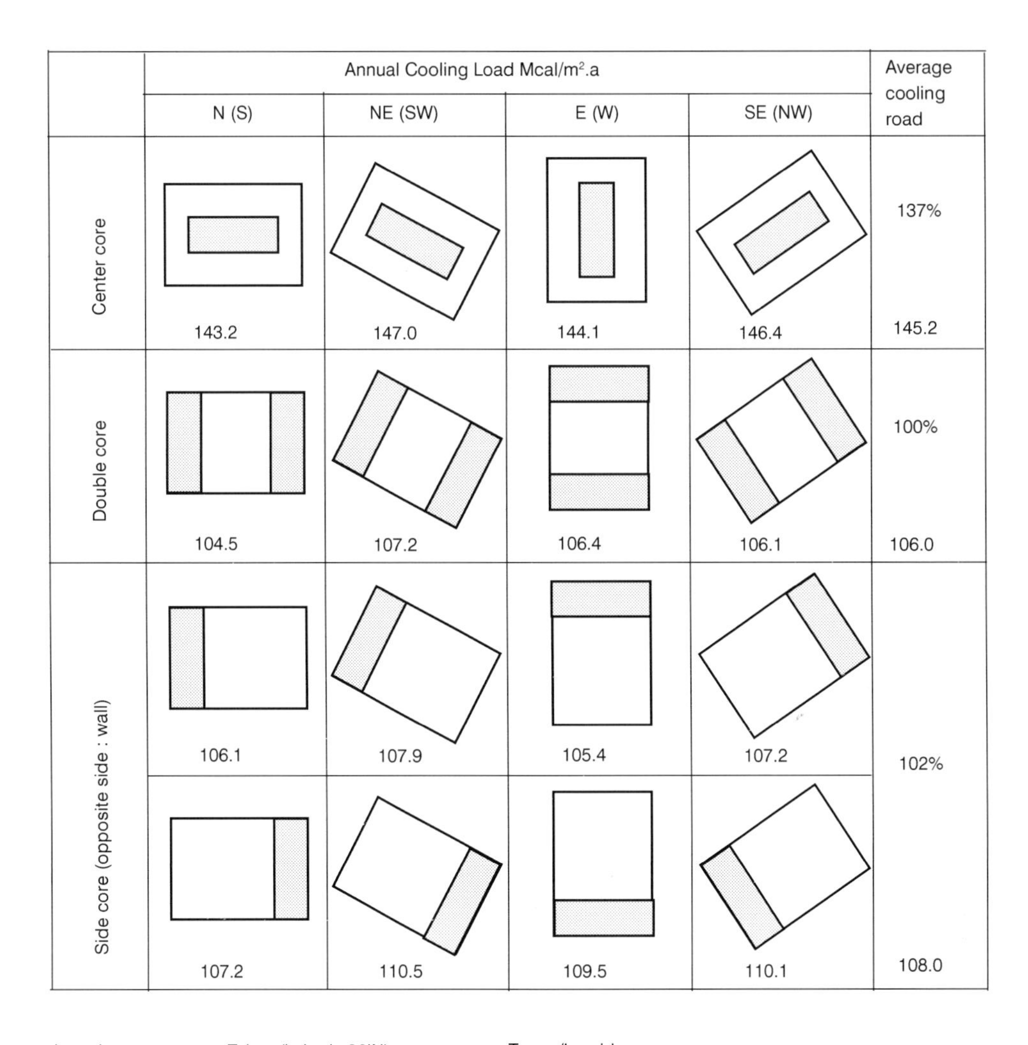

Location	: Tokyo (latitude 36'N)	Temp./humid	
Typical floor area	: 2,400 m^2	Cooling	: 26°C 50
Floor height	: 3.7 m	Heating	: 22°C 50
Window-wall ratio	: 60	Air cond. floor area ratio	: 65
Lighting	: 30W/m^2	Outdoor air intake	: 4.5m^3/m^2h
Infiltration	: 1 change/h	Length-breadth	: 1 : 1.5
People	: 7m^2/p	ratio insulation	: Foam polysthyrene 25mm

Elevator core position and annual cooling load

Figure 9.4 Impact of orientation, service core positions and cooling-load in office buildings for Tokyo [@ Lat. 60°N]

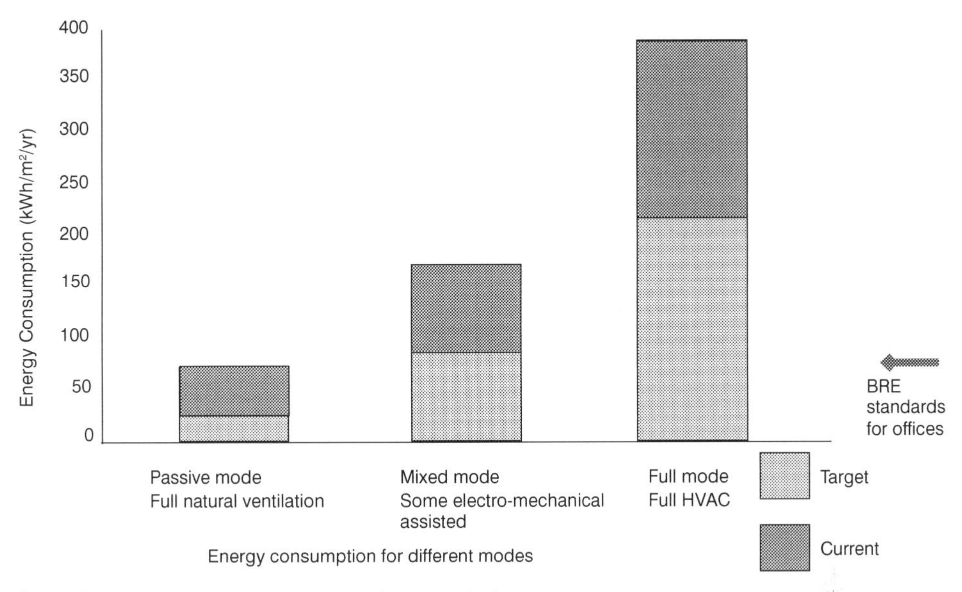

Figure 9.5 Comparative operational energy indexes

Another example of the bioclimatic design strategies is considering the effects of wind on the built-form and its surroundings. Wind, like the sun can have a significant impact on the occupants' comfort level inside the building and on its surroundings. The wind direction and its intensity vary depending on the time of the day and year and its location. It is also influenced by the conditions of the site such as the topography of the terrain, the elevation of the site, surrounding structures, etc. The appropriate configuration and orientation of the built-form can enhance natural cross-ventilation and the cooling effect of the internal spaces, as well as the external spaces around the built-form. This strategy can be used to eliminate the need for mechanical ventilation of the rooms with no window openings and provide natural ventilation through controllable openings for the night-time flushing.

In the temperate zones, during the mid-seasons (spring and autumn), the ambient energies of the locality can create a natural buoyancy between the inside and the outside of the built-form. Natural ventilation can be enhanced through a flue, or an atrium or an air-gap in the façade. Natural ventilation strategy can be used to extend the pleasant conditions during the mid-seasons into the other extreme seasons of summer and winter to reduce the period for heating in the early and later parts of the winter months, and to reduce the need for cooling in the early and later parts of the summer months, thereby reducing the overall energy consumption of the building.

Passive mode also includes the use of devices such as light-pipes to bring in natural daylight without the use of electricity, the use of light shelves and holographic glass to cast natural daylight to the inner parts of buildings to reduce the use of electricity for artificial lighting.

Appropriate passive mode design is generally best carried out by the designer responsible for determining the disposition of the internal spaces, as well as shaping and positioning of the built-form in relation to the climate and conditions of the site and locality (e.g. its topography, ecology, etc.). He has to work in tandem with the designer of the active engineering systems on the passive mode systems and strategies adopted for the built-form. For example, natural ventilation can be implemented combined with mechanical heat recovery strategies.

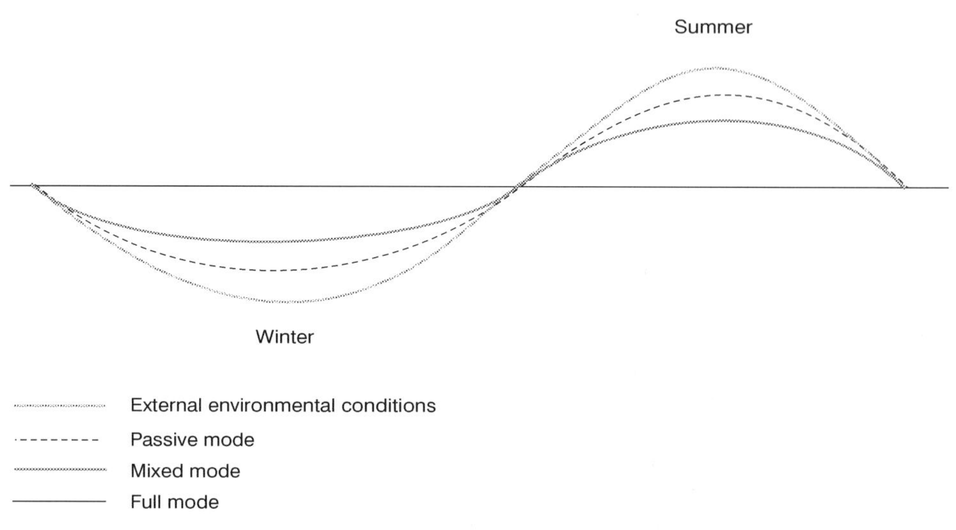

Figure 9.6 Comparison of comfort conditions

Mid-Tech Design—Designing to Assist Passive Mode Options with the Partial Use of Engineering Systems

The immediate next design level of net zero energy design, pursuant to exhaustion of all passive mode low-tech design options, is to optimize the "mid-tech" strategies.

"Mid-Tech" design is the intermediary stage between "low-tech" and "high-tech" design. This involves the use of 'mixed-mode' environmental systems being the partial use of engineering (M&E) systems.

Examples include:

- The use of ceiling or wall-mounted electric fans at times of low or inadequate wind flow to achieve cooling effect on building inhabitants;
- The use of mechanical extraction turbines to enhance natural ventilation in atriums;
- The use of flues;
- The combined use of cooling (or heating) systems together with fan cooling systems;
- The use of solar-tracking devices to angle the sun-shades to let in sun during the winter months and to cut out the sun in the summer months to avoid heat build-up and glare;
- The use of overhead extractor fans to reduce heat-build-up in plazas, in the uppermost floors and ceiling voids in the hot months;
- The use of venting extractors (e.g. in toilets and bathrooms);
- The use of 'double-switching' artificial lighting systems at the periphery of the floor plate to reduce artificial lighting levels when external daylight conditions are adequate, etc.

As is the case in passive mode design, we need to maximize all possible mid-tech mixed-mode opportunities in our design. This is especially in the built-form's transitional spaces such as corridors, infrequently- intermittently-used spaces (such as store rooms, meeting rooms, toilets, etc.) and spaces that do not require full-mode lighting, ventilation, cooling or heating.

All the low-tech and mid-tech design steps need to be adopted in aggregate to enable the built-form's design to head towards an increasingly net zero energy solution before the incorporation of active high-tech systems.

High-Tech Systems—Designing with Clean Tech Full Mode Active Engineering Systems

Following our maximizing of the low-tech and mid-tech options, we can then look into the adoption of active full-mode environmental engineering systems as high-tech solutions to provide the desired level of internal environmental conditions. These need to be the most efficient state-of the-art energy-saving clean technology (i.e. minimized carbon emission) with the lowest embodied-energy engineering systems, whether for cooling or heating, lighting (e.g. LED), hot water heating systems, off-plug energy-saving appliances (whether domestic or commercial appliances). At the same time, the designer needs to ensure the discontinuance of the use of ineffectual and inefficient systems. The high-tech systems must extend and not diminish the built-form's lifespan.

At the same time we need to be aware that the more technology, and the higher the level of engineering hardware is used in the built-form, the greater is the embodied energy inherent in the hardware, thus, driving up its carbon emissions content. A balanced holistic energy management system must be considered, not just in the design and selection of the hardware, but also in the energy use in the system's operations. The reduction of energy use can include, for instance, the use of automation and monitoring systems that provide crucial operational energy-saving roles, the use of energy recovery systems, as well as occupancy control of common area systems by users.

High-tech solutions include the use of efficient internal and external artificial lighting systems such as the use of ultra-low energy LED lighting, the use of advanced power management systems, hydrogen fuel cells, elevators with reparative motors for energy efficiency.

Eco-Tech Design—Designing in the Productive Mode and with the Other Aspects of Eco-Design Being the Green Eco-infrastructure (Ecological Considerations) and the Blue Eco-Infrastructure (Water Management)

The final stage in net zero energy design is eco tech, which involves the use of 'productive engineering systems; involving the use of renewable sources of energy for the active systems inasmuch as possible and with the other aspects of eco-design being the green eco-infrastructure (ecological considerations) and the blue eco-infrastructure (water management).

Productive mode simply means the autonomous production of energy by renewable sources of energy through maximizing on-site energy sources such as earth energy ground-source heat-pumps, solar hot water heaters, district cooling systems, combined heating and cooling systems, solar (PV systems), wind, geothermal, tidal, hydraulic, and biomass energy.

It is important to recognize that till this day, much of the energy derived by renewable sources of energy is still not generally commercially competitive. A quantum leap in green technologies is needed. Despite renewables not being commercially competitive, their use remains an ethical decision and should not inhibit their adoption. In eco-mimicry, we are made aware that nature's prime source of energy is primarily from a renewable source being the sun.

Use of Eco-Materials and Methods of Assembly

Beyond energy conservation in the engineering systems, we need to ensure that the built-form's materials and structural content and its method of construction are carbon neutral using eco-materials, which reduce CO_2 emissions. This includes maximizing resource efficiency in the material's extraction, manufacturing transportation, fabrication and eventual deconstruction, reuse and recycling. We need to ensure that the materials used have low environmental impact and low embodied energy, as well as optimizing the use of reused and recycled materials from local and regional sources to reduce transportation energy cost. Additionally we need to ensure that at the end of the useful life of a building and its materials at their disposal, we are able to reuse and recycle the building's materials inasmuch as possible. This demands an approach at the outset in the way the materials are connected in the built-form at its construction, ideally as DFD ("designing for disassembly").

Design must seek to reduce off-site CO_2 emissions; this is only achievable when on-site CO_2 emission reductions are optimized. An example is to use certified wood to help reduce amount of CO_2 emissions. Reduced CO_2 off-site emissions contribute to attaining carbon-neutralization as a whole while maintaining flexibility in design.

Carbon Credit and Lifecycle Management

'Carbon credits' is an approach where credits can be acquired for the balance of residual energy and carbon emissions for the procurement of off-site renewable energy sources with 'Certified Emission Reductions' to allow the built-form to conclude its reduction of CO_2 collectively. This does not actually resolve the issue of carbon emissions but is simply the transfer of the emissions from one locality to another elsewhere within the biosphere not acknowledging that the biosphere is a closed system.

The designer needs also to develop and use systems of lifecycle management applied consistently throughout the life of a building. An effective lifecycle management system

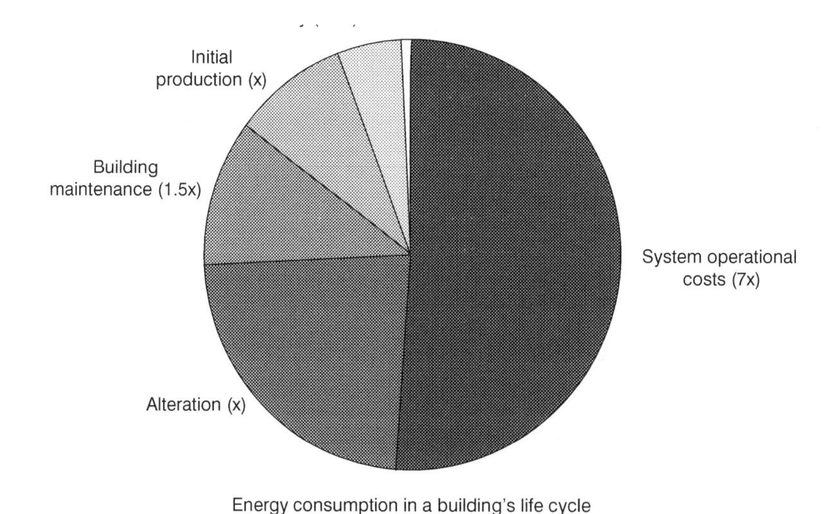

Figure 9.7 Projected life-cycle energy costs (from extraction production, operation to reuse and/or recovery

covering the entire life of a building, includes designing, construction, operation, renovation and disposal. This needs to be developed and implemented.

Master-planning for Net Zero Energy

Net zero energy design must not be restricted to the design of a single built-form but must be addressed at the urban and regional level of design and master-planning. Energy conservation design must not be at the site-specific scale of design but at the biome.

For instance, master-planning layouts should adopt compact (as against dispersed) urban forms, use regional or district energy supply, use unused and/or renewable energy, reduce energy use for transportation by appropriate master-planning layouts and disposition of land use for shortened travel distances. Travel distance can be shortened from home to residential amenities where the community master-plan is based on a maximum practical walking distance (e.g. "7 minute walking distance" planning concept) to schools, local provision shops, cafés, doctors, dentists, recreation, etc.

As with building design, master-planning and urban design, must also focus first on low-tech or bioclimatic climate-responsive-passive-mode concepts. Passive town-scaping must conform with building design to respond to local climatic and micro-climatic elements. This integrated approach in design thinking will reduce the energy demands for heating and cooling through appropriate building layout, street alignment, building forms and configuration, as well as proper application of building features and elements, such as roof and façade color, and so on. Each city, region and society, over time, needs to implement a long-term energy conservation planning and greening vision, to extend measures to counteract global warming, linked to social reform.

Master-planning must incorporate green areas, forests, public parks, local planting for carbon sequestering. Citywide landscaping and greening measures need to be adopted to mitigate the heat island effect of urban areas. Greenery and forest-stored carbon should be used and nurtured in a long-term program. For example, the lumber used in buildings functions to become a carbon sink over the life of the building, as forest carbon storage achieved through appropriate use of wood in buildings.

Our design thinking and master-planning processes demand further consideration for the provision of a *healthy living environment* for all users and occupants throughout their entire lives and to create a lifestyle for people in the cities to be in harmony with nature, towards a natural-human-made environment that uplifts their spirits and enable a happy and pleasurable way of life for their citizens.

Eco-Education

Generally stated, our human behavioral habits, lifestyle, economies and industries must change to one that has a lower reduced energy consumption and lesser waste of energy. For example in Japan in 2005, the Ministry of the Environment (MOE) in Japan widely encouraged businesses and the public to set air conditioning thermostats in offices to around *28°C during summer*. MOE has been promoting summer business styles to encourage business people to wear cool and comfortable clothes. In 2005, from a survey of 562 respondents where their offices set the thermostat higher than in previous years, CO_2 emissions were reduced by approximately 460,000 tonnes in 2005.

This is, however, a major undertaking, which requires an encompassing change in our entire society with unanimous consensus.

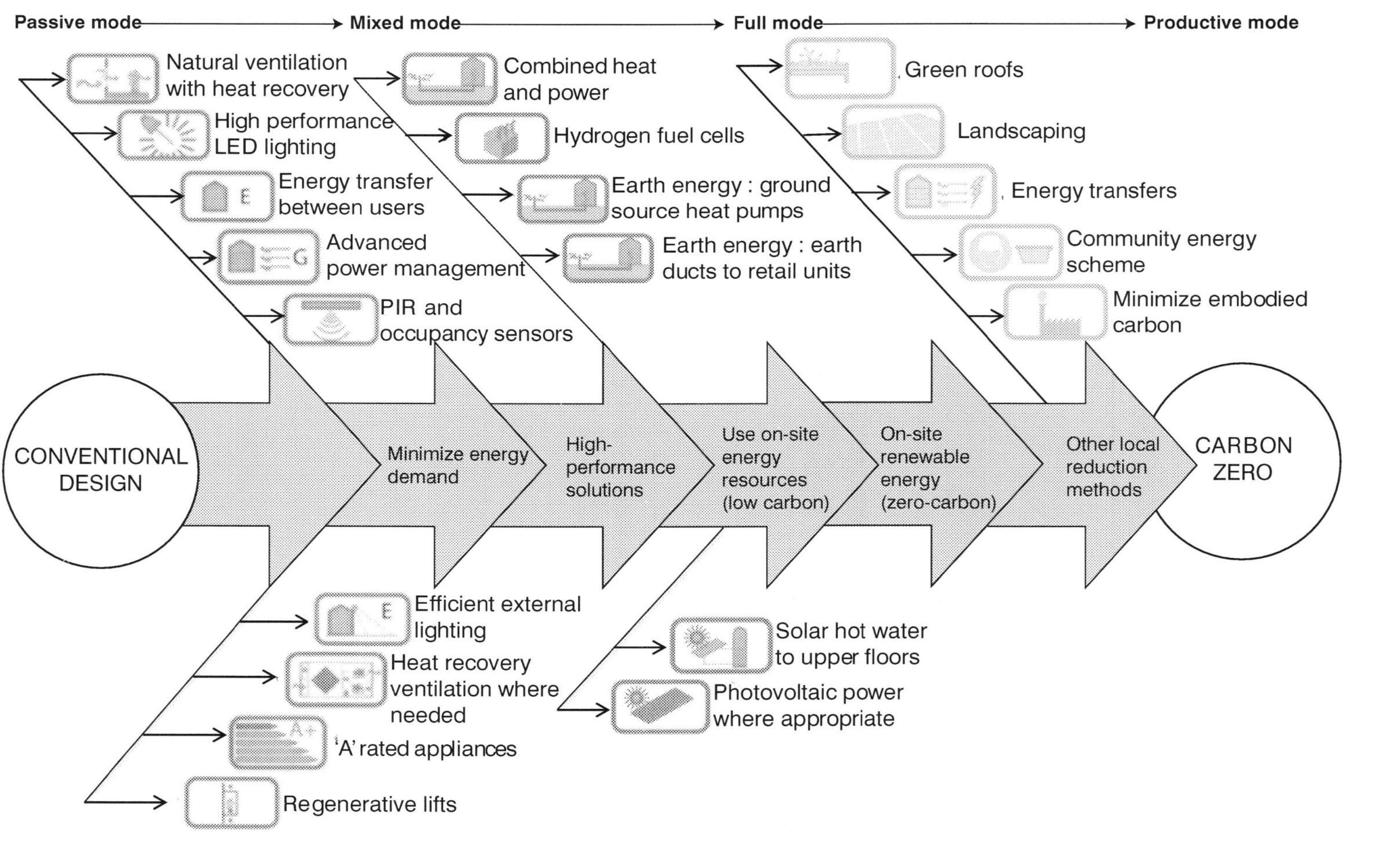

Figure 9.8 From passive mode to productive mode

Society needs to recognize that for a net zero energy, carbon neutral and zero waste community, major societal and lifestyle reforms are crucially needed. Society needs to adopt lifestyles which do not rely on carbon energy. We need to adopt a more visceral and less wasteful and less consumerist behavioral pattern in the consumption of energy, materials and goods. Designing for energy conservation starts with us humans effected with an environmentally-driven public educational system.

Part of eco-education is the use of a universally standardized eco-labeling and evaluation system for products and goods giving immediate access to vital eco information, such as the extent of the products' and goods' greenhouse gas emissions, their green credentials and performance. The use of certification, carbon credits, and credit procurement will create for the public a system towards reducing CO_2 emissions for each community and building.

Conclusion

While the use of cheap non-renewable energy had improved much of society's living standards, this cannot be perpetuated due to its non-sustainable high consequences on the environment.

Our human society needs to extend the energy and greening vision discussed here for buildings, cities and regions. This requires the adoption of effective net zero energy, zero carbon emissions and zero waste strategies for all building types and uses, including changing our existent businesses, industrial production and distribution, agricultural, recreational, transportational, retail, and urban entities in all aspects of the city's active life.

The above discussion covers a set of strategies starting from low-tech through mid-tech to hi-tech and to eco-tech for the design of constructs of our built environment toward the sustenance of a healthy planet Earth being the only one we have.

10

Materiality and Computational Design

Emerging Material Systems and the Role of Design Computation and Digital Fabrication

Sean Ahlquist and Achim Menges

Architecture is undoubtedly a *system*, the on-going mediation of vast matter/material hierarchies to social, economic, historical, contextual and environmental influence. Whether passive, active or impartial, *materiality* defines pivotal aspects towards the governing and engagement of an architectural system. When defined as a material-*inherent* system, the methods and technologies for material formation are investments of both a literal and conceptual nature. Modes of fabrication, as the processes of *materialization*, are the literal agents in defining physicality, dictating the means by which the system operates as a spatial material form. More critically, where form itself is a dynamic system, its materialization simultaneously imparts the conceptual qualities and capacities for how one engages architecture. The depths of material hierarchy at which modes of fabrication can be instrumentalized determine the potentials and precision of the architectural system to be cognizant and reactive to its critical stimuli.

Architectural form as a system of material logics and assemblages relies upon the coordinated understanding of materiality and materialization. Materiality encapsulates, in simple terms, material quality, its physical tactile nature. Materialization defines the efforts by which such qualities are formed. In collapsing the distinction between materiality and materialization, architectural form is, at once, an endeavor of creating its material quality and forming its spatial condition. This occupies the definition of morphology, which is, at once form, a consequence of its material make-up, and a repercussion of specific steps of material organization. Morphology is the apparatus at which both design and manufacture are synchronous and explicit, in how material organizes and produces a resulting definition of spatial descriptor and mediator.

Introduction

A critical facet of architecture is its material make-up. The level of depth at which material make-up is designed determines the level of articulation in architecture, as a spatial, functional and contextual experience. Often, individual aspects of material quality are confined to

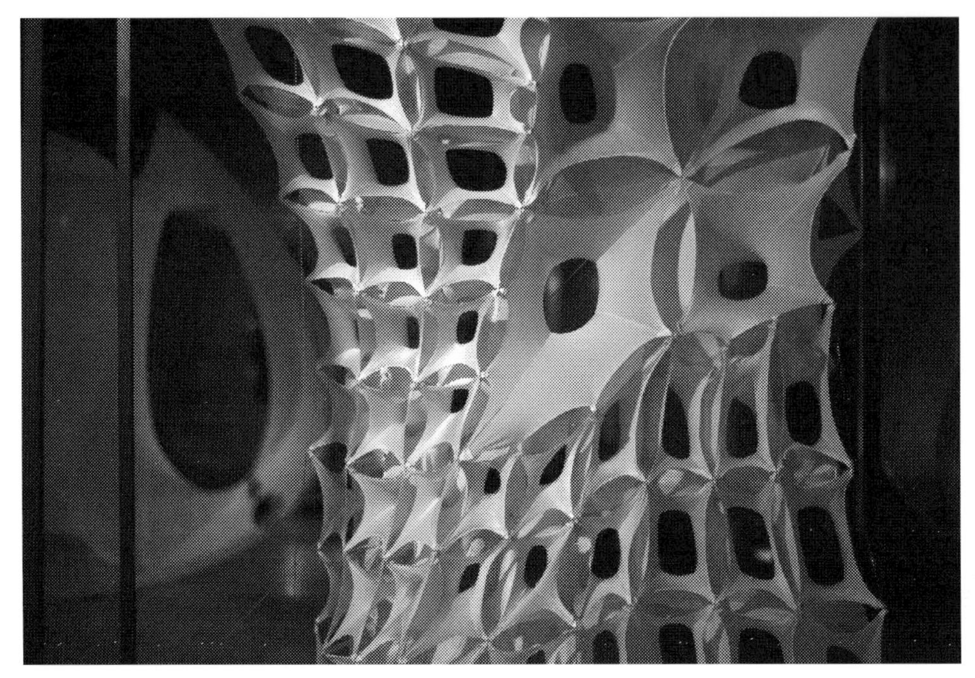

Figure 10.1 Cylindrical deep surface morphologies, Michael Pelzer, Christine Rosemann (University of Stuttgart—Institute for Computational Design, Achim Menges, Sean Ahlquist), 2010

isolated applications of spatial, functional *or* contextual and experiential objectives. This is a consequence of design process, and the degree by which form is segregated from materiality. The degree of influence upon *explicit* material descriptions judges the ability of design process to simultaneously consider form and materiality. Is materiality an imposed condition within a design process or an observed capacity emerging from a design process? Operating upon the nature of a material offers the opportunity to both discover and amplify its imposition to architectural form. This means interrogating materiality at multiple scales: making, manipulation, and as a part of a larger hierarchical assembly. Aspects of material composition become vehicles for synthesizing an array of architectural intentions and performances. While design synthesis of form and materiality is the intent of a design process, such a complex palette of material parameters and architectural intentions demands a sequential methodology.

Therefore, design process is more effectively understood when constructed as an extensible *framework*. Rather than a succinct set of procedures, *framework* implies a sequencing of interoperable design events, able to be agile and repositioned to shifting design inquiries and constraints. Such events allow for the encapsulation and, ultimately, integration of form, its architectural meaning and operation, and the materiality, which constructs it. These events are, in essence, modes of design, which span both real and virtual computation.

A design process, which studies material computation, relies upon the understanding that material form in its physicality is a computed condition. The soap film studies of Frei Otto are evidence of a material's ability to compute its own form. The soap film generates a minimal surface in distributing forces equally through surface tension within a given boundary. In close examination, the force distribution is so equally resolved that the surface molecules are in constant flow, causing the additional phenomena of animated iridescence and refraction. Such an exercise offers definition to the concept of a *material system*. The constituents of the system, the soap film and the boundary condition, work in feedback with each other to generate specific behaviors, in force distribution, form and visual quality. This helps delineate the input parameters from the computed conditions. The design of a material system operates on the level of the input parameters but only does so at the observation of the outward behavior. Features, as morphological moments of the outward behavior, are consequences, designable only after the parameters, magnitudes and degrees of interaction are identifiable. Thus, it is a learned process in simultaneously understanding how components of a system interact and to what nature the resulting system operates. Ultimately, this becomes inverted where the educated process can state specific input parameters for a desired system behavior.

A key factor in this methodology is the absence of a geometric constructor as a part of the design process. Referring to the soap film precedent, when given a singular geometric description of the boundary condition, a mathematical solution could be utilized to determine the resulting minimal surface. Yet, design exploration is not singular. Rather, it is a mapping of design possibilities. To encapsulate all minimal surface solutions driven by variable boundary conditions, a singular mathematical description is not possible. A helicoid may be transformed mathematically into a catenoid. But to accomplish a wider range of forms, different mathematical approaches are needed, such as with Costa's minimal surface emanating from a toroidal topology. But, if we seek to define the properties which organize the material system, then we accomplish a robust set of methods to exhaustively explore the design space of the material system. To codify the minimization of energy across a surface of specific topology with the definition of an input boundary, a design process would be able to explore a multitude of soap film and minimal surface forms. Such an approach, eschews the concern with explicit calculation of geometry, freeing up the design process by pursuing the manner in which material organizes from individual parameters and their basic means of interaction. While codifying *interaction* is often a complex process unto itself, operating with such generalized rules allows for a range of specificities in materiality and form to emerge through enacting the design process.

The complexity of a material system lies with its operation, its emergent behavior being at once material and form. Yet, as mentioned, it is not the emergent behavior that is to be explicitly described within a design process. Rather, it is the building blocks and agents of interaction, which are to be made explicit, accessible and variable. Such properties of a material system can be broken down through distinct definitions of topology, action and materialization, allowing for simple generalized rules to be tunable into specific emergent conditions (Ahlquist & Menges, 2013). *Topology* defines count, type and relation of material elements. *Action* defines the physical phenomena at play. *Materialization* defines the constraints of material formation. Compiling these definitions establishes the character of a material system. It outlays a matrix of both variable and deterministic parameters, constituting the axes of a design space. From the soap film example, the topological description is quite simple as a boundary condition and surface topology. Materialization of the soap film describes the parameters in tuning viscosity. The primary action implemented is the equalization of surface tension. When employing the action of force distribution across a soap film of specific viscosity within a given boundary and surface topology, the behavior of the material system as a singular minimal surface is realized. While the distinct definitions of topology, action and materialization aid to unravel complexities of material behavior, it is only at the activation and resolution of all parameters that system behavior is established.

A critical limitation of the soap film study is its temporal nature, the evaporation of water content thinning the structure to eventual fracture. Great value can be gleaned from soap film experiments in understanding forms, which make capable equalized force distribution. But the very nature of the material system is only that of a model. It serves as an exemplar to specific rules and behavior, but not a scalable simulation to a more permanent material strategy. This professes the need for a design framework at which multiple scalar modes of exploration allow for the full description of a material system. Where soap film study is a mode of physical design exploration, the action of force distribution can be digitally explored. Calculating forces via Hooke's Law of Elasticity can successfully approximate a surface of force minimization, without the need to fully replicate the molecular bonds that define the surface tension of a soap film.

Positioning the modes of design is critical as the intent is to accumulate a multifaceted understanding of the material system. The digital endeavor need not be a replication, nor a replacement of the physical experiment. Rather, each mode should effectively weight different aspects of the material system against desired conditions of form and behavior. Such a framework functions through shifts between relative, prototypical and absolute depictions of the input parameters and subsequent outward features of a material system.

From Geometric Shape to Computational Systems-Based Processes

From Computerized Design to Design Computation

The shift from design approaches based on representational design techniques to design methods that actively engage material processes has profound repercussions to our established modes of design thinking, and as a consequence also to the role we allow computers to play in design. Since the Renaissance, the distinction between designer and maker, which was most prominently postulated by Alberti, together with the development of perspectival and projective techniques over the ensuing centuries, geometry has become the primary modality for architectural design. This primacy of geometry in architectural design thinking in concert with the development of representational design techniques still dominates our conceptualization of the design process itself. Deeply entrenched in our understanding how architecture should and can be conceived, this has also profoundly influenced most architects' take on employing computer technology.

Until this day, the predominant use of computers in architectural practice is merely a digital extension of representational design techniques. Most commercial drafting and modeling software is conceived as a computer-based equivalent to previously manual techniques of drawing or modeling. As a consequence, they have neither challenged our conception of design nor have they been understood as a potential instigator for rethinking the role of the material. They remain what one may refer to as merely computerized design (Terzidis, 2003).

Simultaneous to the rapid adoption and ubiquitous use of computerized design techniques that architectural practice has experienced, a much smaller number of academic researchers and avant-garde architects have explored an alternative approach to employing computers in design. It is interesting to note that these pioneering investigations, which have been pursued since the mid-1960s, have actually preceded the commonplace logic of CAD packages that only took off with the wider availability of personal computers since the mid-1980s. More importantly, these explorations offer a fundamentally different perspective on how the computer can be engaged in the design process, where the machine's capacity is not merely reduced to

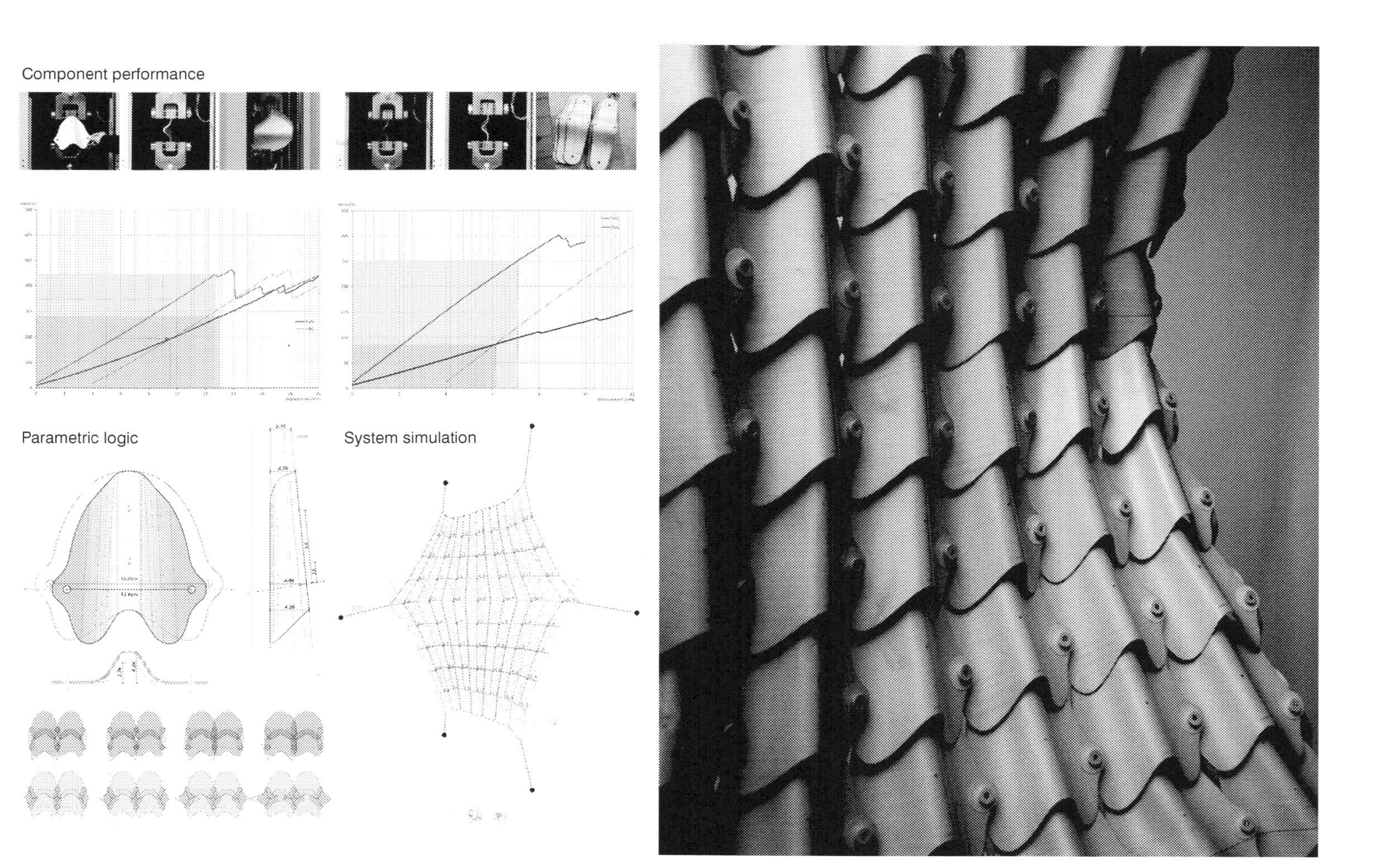

Figure 10.2 Differentiated tensile wood-laminate morphologies, Bum Suk Ko (University of Stuttgart—Institute for Computational Design, Achim Menges, Sean Ahlquist) 2011

a more efficient or partially automated workflow, but understood as an enabling device that allows engaging aspects in design that previously remained too complex or too far lodged away from the designer's sense and intuition (Kwinter, 2003). Instead of computerization, such an approach gives rise to design computation, and thus accounts for the computer's capability of not only processing a limited set of inputs, but generates more information than it is initially supplied. Such computational design thinking has profound repercussions for the way we engage complexity and reciprocity in design (Ahlquist & Menges, 2011). It also enables us to rethink the *material* in architecture through the *computational*.

Overcoming Representational Design Techniques

With the introduction of the first CAD system, *Sketchpad*, by Ivan Sutherland at MIT in the 1960s, the foundation was laid for a parametric approach towards design (Sutherland, 1963). Having roots in the then burgeoning concepts of general systems theory, design is envisioned, by Sutherland, as the means to iteratively resolve the relationships between consistent and conflicting rules (Chrisman, 2006). As mentioned above, this vastly pre-dates what are now the conventional design programs popularized in the 1980s. Yet, this rule-based approach, while in its infancy mostly applied to solving complexities of space planning, gives rise to what are more appropriate means for dissecting the complexities of material-driven design. The value in this approach is the primacy of *association* over geometry, meaning the relationship of parts has agency over the geometric definition of the parts themselves. While, with the parametric model, in Sutherland's case as well as with contemporary environments for parametric design, *association* defines the constrained (*metered*) relationships by which a solution can be formed. Such constraints avoid the *explicit* definition of geometry, and present a case for form as the deduced and calculated outcome rather than the predicated factor. Parametric design unfolds the approach at which process is an information generator; rules of association *generate* instances of geometry, where the instances are of an immense array of possibilities based upon the initial ruling inputs.

Dissecting parametric design through the concept of *General Systems Theory* provides a specific framework at which complexities of a systems-based approach can be disentangled. Established by Ludwig von Bertalanffy, the most basic intention of the theory is the "formulation and deduction of those principles which are valid for 'systems' in general ... whatever the nature of their component elements or the relations or 'forces' between them" (von Bertalanffy, 1950). It is the latter dissection of system parameters, in components, relations and "forces," that aids in a generalized proposition for the methods of parametric design. Bertalanffy defines three constituents of a system: count, species and relation. This allows for such parameters to be constructed in isolation of each other, while introducing a feedback schema allows for exploration of their integration, variation and resulting degrees of success in operation. The basic feedback schema established by Bertalanffy is stated as a *receptor* for an input stimulus, translated by a *control apparatus* to send the appropriate signal driving an *effector* (von Bertalanffy, 1969). The output from any given stimulus is addressed in its success for meeting particular criteria. This type of system structure and feedback schema is oriented towards success in self-regulation and homeostasis. In this sense, the receptor can easily emulate aspects of materiality determining how it is affected by other influencing parameters. Yet, more interestingly, the feedback schema can apply to Sutherland's concept for a parametric model defined via a graphical interface. Design input can be the instigating stimuli where the feedback mechanism processes the value of such inputs to system performance. This enables the comprehension of a material system and a design system to be addressed through a common conception of a feedback schema and the operators of count, species and relation.

Overcoming the Primacy of Geometry

Goethe in his doctrine on *Morphology* emphasizes the *logic* of form, rather than the geometry of form itself (von Goethe, 1989). Form is understood as the resultant condition, where its range of geometric states can only be deciphered through the means of formation. Where the definition of form is in fact a system of governing processes, we can then translate Bertalanffy's parameters of count, species and relation into more specific categories of *topology*, *action* and *materialization*, all as drivers of form *generation*. A key aspect in this system-based structuring of formation is the shift of geometry as a global input to that of local association. In describing system parameters, geometry is relevant only at the level of *materialization*. *Topology* encapsulates the number of elements and their networks of association. *Action* describes the phenomena that will drive formation. *Materialization* then is the primary operator for geometric constraints, determining how the influence of *action* will organize a particular construct of *topology*. But, there is only the possibility to provide geometric information at the level of detail in which the topological construct allows. More simply, topology dictates the number of units and the manner in which one unit associates with another. Geometric material input can only be provided at the scale of such units and unit-to-unit associations. There are no geometric variables in this systems-based approach, which operate globally, since form is a consequence of interaction and interaction is a realization of actions applied across a series of interconnected units.

D'Arcy Thompson describes form as the output of a system of processes; ones which can be mathematically defined for a specific instance of form and parametrically collated across a family of instances (Thompson, 1961). Thompson's desire is to encapsulate the relationship of physical forces to structure and pattern within a mathematical construct, which he defines as *homologies*. The value of Thompson's homologies is its representation of *families* of possible outcomes. Such an approach ultimately codifies *transformation*, in not only forming the single instance, but more importantly morphing across a field of potential interrelated instances.

Thompson's studies of the pelvis geometries of Archaeopteryx and Apatornis are a keen example of a constructed *homology,* representative of a parametric model. Transforming a Cartesian grid allows Thompson to trace existing pelvis structures. Interpolating between transformed grids allows for the projection of undiscovered pelvic types. With transformation as a primary agent in form generation, known forms can be used to seed unknown forms through a process of mathematical rigor.

Towards Integrative (Non-procedural) Computational Processes

Where Thompson's parametric model generates a translational tool between two geometric states, John H. Holland introduces means for understanding transitions between states of a dynamic model. A dynamic model is simply understood as one with "changing configurations," where the pursuit is to decipher the underlying laws, which drive reconfiguration. In the context of our discussion, this means codifying the functions of *action* that induce changes in *topology*, based upon a particular palette of material constraints. Holland states "To build a dynamic model we have to select a level of detail that is useful, and then we have to capture the laws of change at that level of detail," defining these laws of change as "transition functions" (Holland, 1998). It is important to understand Holland's definition of a *model*, not as a singular instance, but actually the compilation of processes. A more fitting example is the weather model over the conventional understanding of the architectural model. By introducing the transition function between states of a model, we now have means for integrating, and more importantly, *updating* the parameters of the systems-based method. Action is implemented to define a particular state, yet it also must house the methods to encapsulate all states. Referring back to Thompson's examples, the deformed coordinate system and Cartesian grid generate a particular state. The interpolative function defines all states within the model.

A fundamental intent for Holland's definition of the dynamic model and its transition function is to provide means for predicting systems with emergent properties from simple rules and agents. James Crutchfield nicely defines emergence as "generally understood to be a process that leads to the appearance of structure not directly described by the defining constraints and instantaneous forces that control a system" (Crutchfield, 1993). Therefore, in finding the *useful* level of detail in which to operate, the ability to identify outward system features is as necessary as deciphering the simple rules driving the emergence of such features. Because these two ends of the spectrum are not explicitly linked, distinct methods are involved in first *observing*, and second, *exploring* the parameters of the emergent system. Again, referring to the studies of pelvis geometries by Thompson, the observational tool is the Cartesian grid, finding its particular distortion to match an existing precedent. The explorative tool is the *transition function* of interpolating between precedent grids. Christopher Alexander conjoins these efforts defining the framework as *systems generating systems*. Alexander indicates the two scales as (i) "a particular holistic view of a single thing," and (ii) "not [referring] to a single thing at all, but to a kit of parts and combinatory rules capable of generating many things" (Alexander, 1968). This is extrapolated as a constructed framework involving the multi-scalar resolution of observed behavior, parameterization of individual componentry and functions defining the agents of interaction.

Integration of Materiality and Materialization as Generative Design Drivers

Design approaches based on the shift from explicit towards associative geometry, and from static models representing cerebral design intent towards dynamic models negotiating multiple design criteria and influences, open up the possibility to rethink the *material* through the *computational*. Here, the machine's capacity to process complex interrelations can be employed to embed material data in the form generation process. This data may include particular characteristics of material behavior, the specific topology and anatomy of the material make-up, as well as the constraints and affordances of processes of materialization, which include production, fabrication, assembly and construction. Beyond the established linear logic of CAD-CAM chains, such an approach to design is based on iterative feedback with material properties and materialization environments. Thus computation can become an interface between the virtual realm of the digital and the physical domain of the material in architecture. The embedding of system-intrinsic material data provides a critical process constituent, one on which system external influences and forces can then act to derive specific form. Most importantly, such a conceptualization of computation promotes an understanding of material not as a passive receptor of predefined, or more precisely pre-designed, shape, but rather as an active agency in design.

Material Agency in Design and Multi-Modal Computational Frameworks

Material as an Active Design Generator Instead of Passive Recipient of Shape

Thompson's studies of pelvis geometries and his Theory of Transformation focused primarily on deducing transitional logics through extrapolation of geometric states. This provides a critical understanding of the parametric model, as the embodiment of processes and functions. Materiality is inherent in these studies, but it is confined to a mathematical, geometric and precedent-based understanding. If the level of detail were to operate on the formation of bone, could Thompson's parametric model generate geometries for a much wider array of bone structures? To answer this, the model would have to embed means for describing the factors of external influence, as this is a primary engine for bone formation. The Theory of Transformation states, in simple terms, that geometric rules can be found to represent processes of formation, thus implicitly embedding the physical forces and material properties, which produce structure and pattern. In this case, the level of detail in the parametric model indirectly refers to forming processes and external pressures. To embed materiality, such factors need to be explicit. The parametric model must operate at a level of detail where material's imposition upon state change, as a response to external factors, can be constructed in the simplest terms possible. Thompson's references to the glass-blower reiterate this; all possibilities of glass forming are transformations of the simple tube through the external influence of unequal heating and cooling. Holland expands the *transition function* in this context so that it "provides a correspondence between each possible (state, input) pair and the state that results." He cites Newton's equations as helpful examples that "define the dynamics of gravity via a transition function that relates mass and acceleration (states of a particle), and force (an input)."

We are now presented with the means to institute materiality as a generative function within the parametric model. This is primarily at the moment at which external influence is allowed to operate upon the form generating process. Ernst Mayr contributes an important understanding of the design space that arises, examining in evolutionary terms the relationship between input parameters (genotype) and outward performance (phenotype). Mayr advances Thompson's definition of *homologies* by citing the difficulty for willful inflexible means of formation to find equilibrium with contextual pressures. To address this, Mayr poses that it is *only* at the interaction of external influence that the processes of formation can be understood (Mayr, 2001). There is no intent at the level of the genotype. The robustness of the input parameters can only be determined at the understanding of the phenotype in relation to its environment. The degree of success in relation to environment can only be judged comparatively. Success of the parametric model operates at the level of *many* phenotypes, or in evolutionary terms, with the robustness of the population. It is at this level of population thinking where designing the parametric model is about generating and evaluating the vast scope of the design space that it produces.

Precedents of Material-informed Design Thinking

The initial example in this chapter of Frei Otto's soap film studies offers a clear depiction of extrapolating design knowledge through material exploration. Knowledge is gained in finding the geometric rules of minimal surfaces and a desired equalized distribution of force.

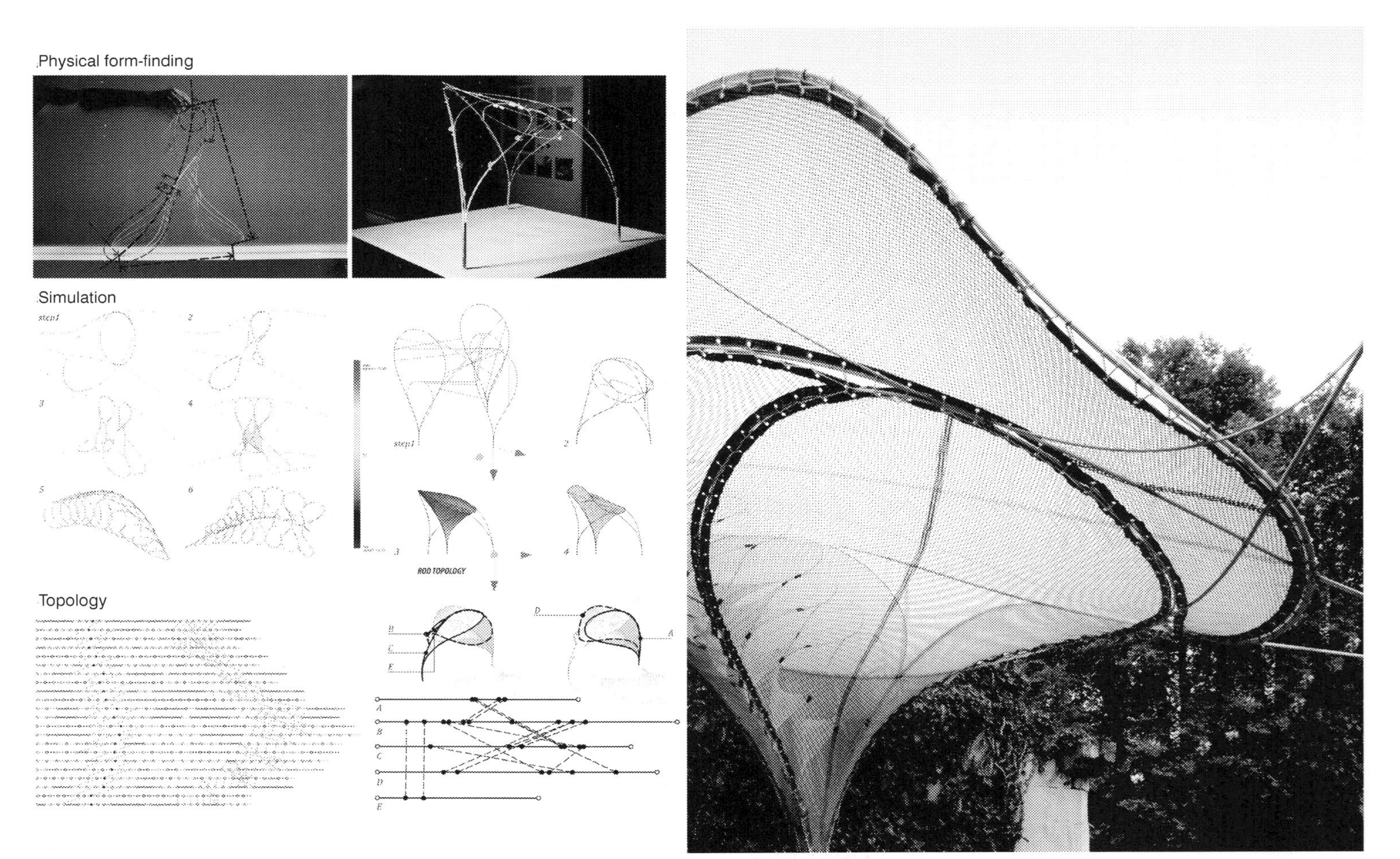

Figure 10.3 M1 textile hybrid at La Tour de l'Architecte, Sean Ahlquist, Julian Lienhard (University of Stuttgart—Institute for Computational Design, Achim Menges, Institute for Building Structures and Structural Design, Jan Knippers) Monthoiron, France, 2012

Figure 10.4 M1 textile hybrid at La Tour de l'Architecte, Sean Ahlquist, Julian Lienhard (University of Stuttgart—Institute for Computational Design, Achim Menges, Institute for Building Structures and Structural Design, Jan Knippers) Monthoiron, France, 2012

What is key, though, is designing of the processes of formation. This is where the initial soap film studies lead to more explicit avenues for material-informed design thinking. The soap film studies eschew Thompson's approach of codifying mathematical means to implicitly describe shapes and patterns formed of external pressures. As described in Section 1, a range of mathematical equations are needed to catalog the extent of minimal surfaces. Otto simply allows the material behavior of the soap film to provide information for the geometric description of the minimal surface. Yet, what this particular approach necessitates is a *translational* step. Soap film is not ultimately the material of construction, and the parametric studies are not at the desired scale. In practice, materialization would now include the means of translating the output of the parametric model towards specific material properties of an architectural scale and constructional logic. While behavior is instituted for means of design study, the soap film precedent adds an additional moment of state change in transforming the temporal model into a differently scaled and materialized architecture.

Frei Otto embeds both the discovery of form and articulation of construction logic in the timber lattice gridshell of the Mannheim Multihalle. To develop a doubly-curved form, a geometry which can be structural with the use of minimal material means, a hanging net model is initially utilized. Following the precedent of Gaudi's hanging chain models to physically compute catenary arches; Otto utilizes gravity to hang a mesh with fixed nodes within a fixed boundary to generate a structural surface based upon the principle of thrust surfaces. If the geometry of such a mesh in pure tension is inverted, a compression-only shell is derived, and as there are no bending moments under self-weight in the shell, the structure can be very thin. We again see the use of a translational model. It stands as a *model* in the sense of being a system of materials and processes at which form is realized under the external loading of gravity. Yet, it is also a translational model where the materials of the hanging chain model are in tension, which ultimately represents a geometry for the constructed architecture which operates in compression. Gaudi's experiments in stone exploited the ability to invert the tensile catenary arch into a compression one. But, in Otto's case, he is materializing a gridshell instead of a continuous surface structure. This is based on the recognition that in a particular geometric range, the catenary line quite closely resembles the elastica curve, the curve a slender element generates under elastic bending. So at this moment, Otto makes the significant turn in employing a forming process as the means of form-finding in both: the process of design and the process of construction. The gridshell is constructed of a double layer of interconnected timber lathes. The grid of lathes is initially assembled loosely as a flat plane. But once the regular and planar lattice is hoisted at a few strategic points, the structured form is realized at the moment when the lattice finds its structurally stable, double curved form based on the elastic behavior of the wood elements. With the Multihalle, the constructed model *is* the parametric model.

Physical Form-finding Integrated with Computational Form Generation Based on Material Behavior

In Otto's work with the Mannheim Multihalle, primacy is placed upon the scaled form-finding of the hanging net model and, ultimately, the full-scale form-finding of the construction logic. While Otto engages material behavior and form-finding at the scale of the constructed system, the means of design, the hanging net model, is still a translational step away from the material logic of the timber lathe grid shell. Two important aspects are exposed at this moment, the necessity for multiple modes of design in order to generate the abundance of information necessary to execute the material system, and the desire for explicitness in each mode. The hanging net model is explicit in its topological and geometric depiction of an inverted pure compression shell. The study at full-scale of the construction logic assesses the material parameters to resist buckling in the global form yet allow elastic bending to achieve the double curved geometry. Each mode of design is accumulative to the overall dataset, rather than substitutive in only sequentially providing specificity. Specificity is gleaned across the scope of design modes.

Thus far in the chapter, material-informed computational design has been explained via means of physical study, allowing explicit material behavior to compute form. For each study, it is helpful to recognize it as a *prototype*. We refer to *prototype* not simply to the result, but the set of processes and particular parameters which led to the formation of that specific result (Coyne *et al.*, 1990). It is a single moment within the design space of the parametric model. Yet, to establish the expansiveness of the design space, as Mayr's population thinking applies, the value of the input parameters from the single prototype can only be established at the assessment of *many* results. This is a critical moment in defining computational design as a material-driven endeavor. Where *action*, the state-altering transition function, is based in materiality, there are inherent limits with the single prototype to predict collective behavior beyond its own specific scale. The methods which generate the exemplar remain solitary to a narrow set of possibilities and material choices that might be inferred from the single prototype. We move then to a *meta*-prototypical approach, where the parametric model envelopes multiple design spaces, to enable exploration of an ever-broadening range of material-based schema. This establishes criteria for a mode of design, which must be able to operate upon an intense variety of physical and material phenomena. This is where we overtly define the digital component of computational design as a mode, which operates at once as the hanging net model and also as the engine for generating specific material constructional logics. Computational design is thus a synthesized endeavor, acquiring specific prototypical material conditions through physical computation, combined with exploration of an exhaustive design space through digital computation.

Evolutionary Means of Computational Design

The parametric model is a paradigm which suits the various modes of design, *virtual* and *real*, involved in establishing a framework for computational design. *Parametric design*, in an architectural context, often has the narrow connation of studying systems through the transformation of geometric primitives via variations in dimensional values. We institute *model* as the operative term, instead of *design*, to guarantee the study of systems through processes, associations and the metrics of both. Peter Trummer poses the shift from *object* in favor of *assemblies* in order to center the methodology on "physical systems, whereby the addition of parts defines a space of possible change" (Trummer, 2007). He cites Manuel DeLanda's term of *degrees of freedom* to define a system's transformational limits (DeLanda, 2002). DeLanda expands upon this to provide an understanding of what constitutes limits. He delineates *properties*, *capacities* and *tendencies* as means to sort what is individual to the part, what arises when interactions are exercised, and what behaviors are possible at the scale of the part and the assembly (DeLanda, 2007). DeLanda describes the tendencies of a simple knife to liquefy in an environment of certain heat, while the capacities of the knife, such as the event of cutting, are only realized at the moment of coming into contact with an object that can be cut. Tendencies are multivalent yet finite, while capacities are less measurable because they involve an interaction in order to be realized.

What we arrive at is an understanding of *associations* within the parametric model as requiring descriptions of *interactions*. It is in the execution of these interactions that the capacities of a system emerge. John Holland poses that "rules (transition functions) that are almost absurdly simple can generate coherent, emergent phenomena" (Holland, 1998). With this cue, we can look to processes which similarly emulate the formation of natural systems. This is to deal with the inevitability of a design space where a single emergent capacity is multivalent, and a multitude of emergent capacities are probable. The genetic algorithm (GA), initially developed by John Holland in 1975, codifies the processes of natural selection to evolve solutions of certain fitness (Holland, 1992). This functions upon the blindness of genetic code to produce systems whose degree of effectiveness is determined at the moment it interacts with its environment. In technical terms, GAs produce populations of individuals, where the parameters of each individual are defined as the genotype and its outward functions defined as the phenotype. The most effective individuals in response to the imposed environment are bred, through means of cross-over (intermixing of the genotypes), to produce new generations. This cycles multiple times until populations converge with individuals of all similar levels of fitness and traits. A critical question, which returns us to the focus of the parametric model, is the representation of *action* within the GA. Peter Bentley introduces the step of *embryogeny* as the "growing function" which "decodes the genotype" in order to produce the phenotype (Bentley & Corne, 2002). He poses the critical consideration between *explicit* and *implicit* embryogeny as a way to remove bias from the process of "growing" individuals. Eschewing explicit methods such as Lindenmayer systems or shape grammars, Bentley shifts to a rule-based approach used iteratively at the level of each gene. This allows for great scalability, where the "growth" method does not need to expand in complexity in order to accomplish more complex individuals (Bentley & Kumar, 1999). What Bentley opens up with this proposition is an evolutionary approach, which seeks to discover possible *capacities*, rather than optimize for known properties.

Designing Material Systems

Material System vs. Common Conception of Building Elements/Systems

Speaking more directly to materiality in architecture, the parametric model affords not only materiality as the initiator of design exploration, but a computational structure which spans from the formation of a component, to the interaction between components, the assembly into an emergent system and, ultimately, the capacities of the emergent system to operate in a specific context. This realizes the understanding of a material system as inherently *integrated* across its *properties*, *tendencies* and *capacities*. This gives rise to a significant distinction between the concept of a material system and that of a conventional building system. A material system is innately born of material characteristics, means by which it is made, and logics by which it is assembled. There is no description of geometry or form until these interrelationships have been expressed. Expression is formed in response to specific stimuli external to the system itself. In the complexity of the external stimuli, it is self-evident that differentiation will evolve in the material system. Differentiation, as a repercussion of setting materiality and materialization as an *a priori* instigator, is in stark contrast to the common conception of building systems, which prioritize shapes (rather geometries) elusive of material resource (Menges, 2008). In such a scenario, materiality is resolved as an additive characteristic. Standardization becomes the means to address materiality where the parameters of manufacturing are present in the design process only as general principles rather than specific rules. The critical distinction is in shifting from typological thinking to morphological processes. As such, the material system is not generated as a derivative of a given system-type, but rather through processes driven by system-internal capacities and constraints, and system external influences and forces.

The New Affordances of Digital Fabrication and Robotic Production

Today, innovations occur not only because of our ability to design and fabricate digitally, but our capacity to think computationally. In combination, digital fabrication and computational design thinking opens up a new perspective on our understanding how our built environment is produced, both in the intellectual process of designing and the physical process of making. This may entail a profound shift for architectural thinking and design culture, one that is now becoming ever more tangible after a gestation period of almost half a century. In this way, the development of computer aided design and manufacturing is no different from many other technological advancements. In the history of architecture, groundbreaking technologies were often initially employed to facilitate long-established design concepts and construction logics, and only after the lengthy process of overcoming the considerable inertia of architectural design thinking and well-established construction principles were able to play out their transformative character (Menges, 2008). One of many examples can be found in the way that the structural layout and connection of the first cast-iron bridges of late eighteenth-century England mimicked previous timber constructions, or, in a similar way, the early reinforced concrete

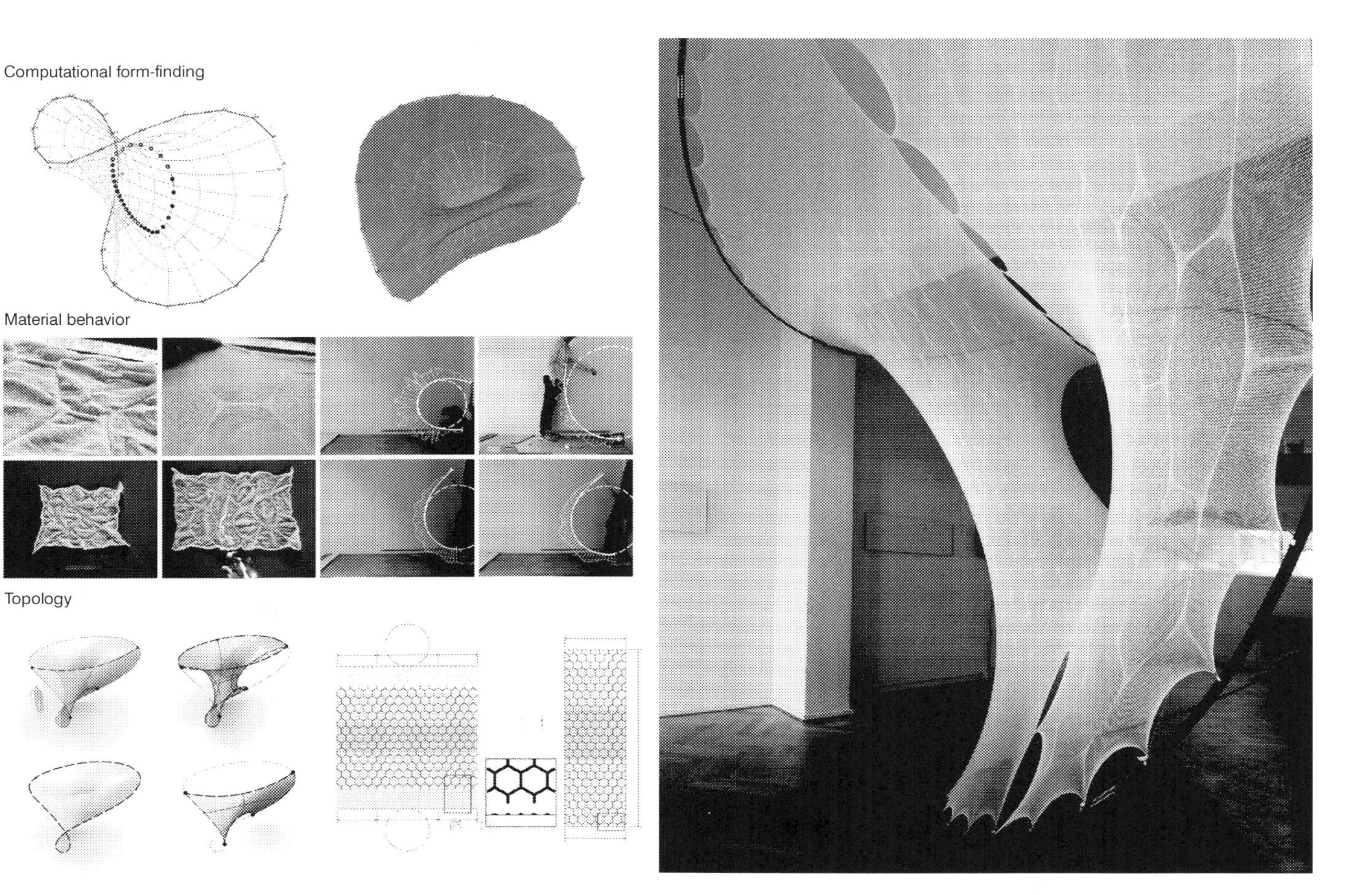

Figure 10.5 Semi-toroidal textile hybrid morphologies—installation at ggggallery, Sean Ahlquist (University of Stuttgart—Institute for Computational Design, Achim Menges) Copenhagen, Denmark, 2012

structures of the late nineteenth century were conceived and constructed in a similar way as previous iron and steel frame buildings. It is interesting to note that it took approximately half a century for the amorphous character and structural capacity of reinforced concrete to have a real impact on design, a period spanning from the initial patent in the 1860s to manifestation of innate material traits in Robert Maillart's bridges and the shell structures of pioneers such as Franz Dischinger in the early twentieth-century.

While the nature of digital fabrication renders the production of a vast range of varied parts a feasible proposition, the underlying conceptualization of fabrication remains unaltered. It is still mainly conceived as a facilitative step in going from digital construct to physical realization. The preservation of the facilitative character of digital fabrication is most symptomatic in terms like "mass customization," which fundamentally remain extensions of long-established design processes based on a hierarchical conception of form and material. However, digital production cannot only be deciphered as a mere extension of well-known protocols, but it can also serve as a radical departure towards novel, integrative design methodologies. Robotic production offers a particularly fascinating opportunity in this regard, because in contrast to other digitally controlled machinery the robot is initially not process specific. While common CAM-machines mainly are the computer-numerically controlled equivalent to known processes such as sawing, milling, etc., the industrial robot constitutes a generic piece of hardware that only becomes specific through the control software and the effector. This has a number of profound repercussions on the way we think about materialization in the robotic age. If we consider the design of the effector and the design of the control software not as the execution of a facilitative service, but rather as one critical constituent of the design domain, we shift towards an extended understanding of design, one that actively incorporates the "design" of processes and protocols from which material form emerges. Here fabrication is not merely the execution of predetermined, or rather pre-designed instructions, but the set of procedures and constraints innate to a machine environment. Computation allows capturing these procedures and constraints of digital fabrication, and turning them into active design drivers.

Computation and Digital Fabrication as New Means to Designing Across Multiple Scales

As the aptitude with techniques of computation and digital fabrication proceeds, the opportunity arises to operate materially at finer and finer levels of detail. Arguably, this is simply a consideration of scale, but poses profound consideration of what constitutes a material system and the designing of it. The level of detail at which the componentry sits is what challenges the conception of a material system. *Componentry*, as a collection of elements, which self-organize through the negotiation of internal properties and external impositions, will always exist. This is to be distinguished from a kit of parts approach where a component is standardized and conceived in isolation. The component is simply a designation for the level of detail at which materiality is addressed in the design of the material system. Often, the design of the material system occurs through the relationship of geometrically varied components. Variation is produced through the manipulation of homogenous materials. A generic material is manipulated to be made specific. In this methodology the lowest scale of interrogation of the material system is at the meso-scale of elements, assembled into the macro-scale of the architectural system. As a result, the organization of the macro-scale system is of a rigid topological structure, with variation only evident geometrically at the level of the meso-scale componentry.

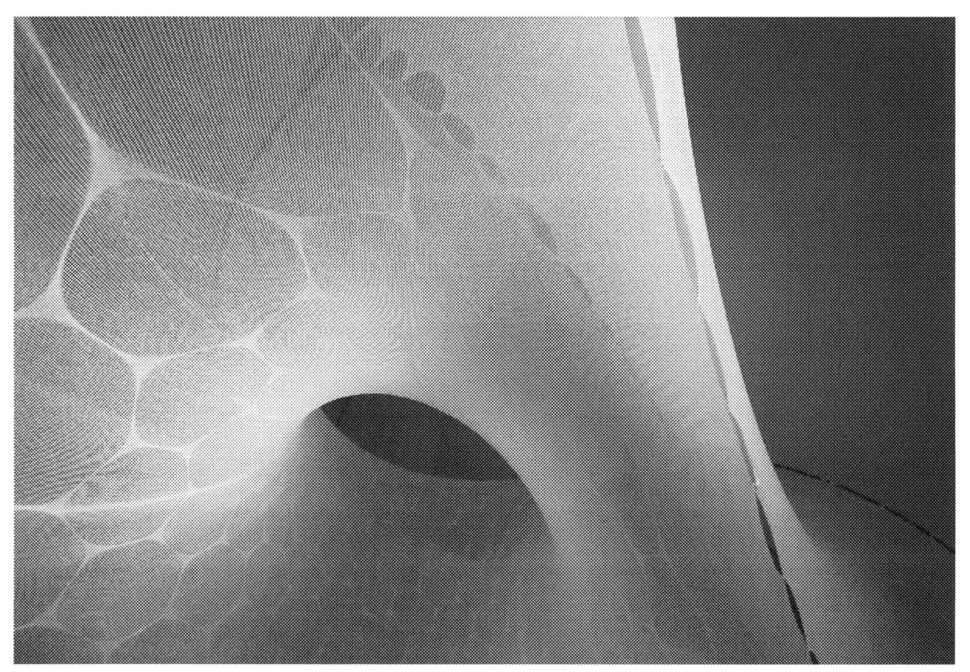

Figure 10.6 Semi-toroidal textile hybrid morphologies—installation at ggggallery, Sean Ahlquist (University of Stuttgart—Institute for Computational Design, Achim Menges) Copenhagen, Denmark, 2012

If heterogeneity is a desired trait, the formation has to occur at the micro-scale of materialization. The component is more abstractly defined at levels such as chemical bonds and fibrous orientations. The material system is now truly founded upon processes, which span all scales, noticing that the component is defined in the realm of *actions*, needing to be *bonded* or be *oriented*. Material properties are no longer discreet factors but are now *capacities* in and of themselves. To be *oriented* means orientation in comparison to another, returning us to DeLanda's proposition that *capacity* is realized only at the moment of interaction. The behavior of the system is now a scalar construct, yet the application of the parametric model to access and compose this complexity still applies. The level of iteration across the scales of the system becomes expanded; feedback is a shifting modality where context at one scale may simply be the influence of properties at a subsequent scale. Where the perception of a material system shifts is at the collapse of material properties and material formation. As design is addressed from the capacities of a material logic, the processes of formation are the concepts of design. This is significant in that a representative view of architecture is now dismissed in favor of form as an explicit expression of material processes.

A Novel Synthesis of Form Generation and Materialization

The moment at which the *action* of materialization becomes the genesis of form, we find correlation with the logics inherent in the evolution and development of natural systems, in particular biological structures and organisms. George Jeronimidis, a world-renowned expert in composites engineering, indicates the most fundamental tenet of a natural system is recognizing the absolute inextricability of material and structure. He states, "in the morphogenesis of biological organisms, it is the animation of geometry and material that produce form" (Jeronimidis, 2004). This is not to say that the pursuit of material systems is only in regards to structure. Rather, it is in the growth of differentiated anisotropic materials that the material system is made multivalent. Jeronimidis indicates how in biological structures this is done with an extraordinarily small number of materials, working as simple polymers. The concept of natural morphogenesis, the evolution of growth and form, provides a conceptual understanding for the design and formation of a material system. Yet, a material system is not a biological construct. Jeronimidis establishes a critical distinction between the attempt to replicate or represent biological concepts, and the more appropriate approach where the *technological transformation* of a biological concept enables the pursuit of material systems.

Reliance upon the concept of evolutionary development brings a significant level of complexity to the design of a material system. This outlays an inherently non-deterministic process. The effort is to initiate form generation at the lowest level of detail with the simplest terms for describing the means of interaction, internally and externally. To shape the results of these fundamental operators, the means of evaluation and feedback span a great number of scales. System formation is at the hands of the terms of interaction as well as with the functions of evaluation and feedback. J. Scott Turner (2007) poses that some aspects of an evolved system can be disentangled from the cyclical stepping of evolution, where they operate as *self-governing* agents in pursuit of homeostasis with their environment. Turner's study of termite mounds cite specific instances of these actively operating features of a system; "the mound captures wind energy at a particular rate that is matched to the colony's metabolism, which makes it an organ of homeostasis" (Turner, 2007). Turner argues that the formation of the termite mound is not an explicit consequence of hard coded evolved genetic information, but rather through reactive mechanisms for the colony of termites to operate in efficient and effective means with its environment. Evolution relies on a certain memory of performance through genetic code. Turner gives rise to how Jeronimidis' simple polymers form life, driven in part by "thermodynamic machines" which actively drive physiology and genetic code which carry means for "good fit" to environment across generations (Turner, 2007). Interactions in forming the material system can be parsed between evolved features and active operations.

Emerging Material Culture

Matter turns into material when it is engaged in the human activity of making. The way we make things, and more importantly the way we conceptualize this process as both an intellectual and technical activity specific to its context in space and time, is what defines material cultural. Today, advancements in computation and fabrication suggest a profound transformation of the way the built environment is conceived and materialized, with profound repercussions on the way we think about the interrelation of form, material, structure, process and performance. *Form* has been used in the description of a material system throughout this chapter as means to emphasize the priority of formation, the depiction of *making* form over the description *of* form. Geometry is merely a state, where formation is the transference through many states. What is critical, but possibility not obvious, is the intention for form to describe a lack of finality. Form is not simply physicality. In that sense, the material system is form, which continually changes in its identity *after* the step of assembly. It is not merely defined by its physical elements, but the milieu in which, and through which, it performs. It is the considering of the extra-systemic that is not only about formation, but is always about inflection and response. While responsiveness in an architectural sense is portrayed as a passive, intelligent, learned condition, the material system should be asked to actively engage and contribute. The material system is not just a more efficient and integrated version of the building system. Rather, the material system is a vehicle to augment, adapt and *be* adapted to the environment, individuals, contexts, societies, deficiencies and disabilities that it engages. A culture of contemporary material engagement is the architectural implementation of Turner's "living structures [that] are not distinct from the function they support; they are themselves the function, no different in principle from the physiology that goes on there" (Turner, 2007).

References

Ahlquist, S. and Menges, A. (2011). Computational Design Thinking. In A. Menges and S. Ahlquist (eds), *Computational Design Thinking*. pp 1029. London: John Wiley & Sons Ltd.

Ahlquist, S. and Menges, A. (2013). Frameworks for Computational Design of Textile Micro-Architectures and Material Behavior in Forming Complex Force-Active Structures. In P. Beasley, O. Khan and M. Stacey (eds), *ACADIA 13: Adaptive Architecture Proceedings of the 33rd Annual Conference of the Association for Computer Aided Design in Architecture,* pp. 281–292. Cambridge: ACADIA.

Alexander, C. (1968). *Systems Generating System: Architectural Design Theory*. London: John Wiley & Sons Ltd.

Bentley, P. and Corne, D. (2002). An Introduction to Creative Evolutionary Systems. In P.J, Bentley and D.W. Corne (eds), *Creative Evolutionary Systems*. San Diego, CA: Academic Press.

Bentley, P.J. and Kumar, S. (1999). Three ways to grow designs: a comparison of embryogenies for an evolutionary design problem. Paper presented at Genetic and Evolutionary Computation Conference (GECCO '99), Orlando, FL.

Chrisman, N. (2006). *Charting the Unknown: How Computer Mapping at Harvard Became GIS*. Redlands, CA: ESRI Press.

Coyne, R.D., Rosenman, M.A., Radford, A.D., Balachandran, M. and Gerö, J.S. (1990). *Knowledge-Based Design Systems*. Reading, CA: Addison-Wesley Publishing Company.

Crutchfield, J.P. (1993). The calculi of emergence: computation, dynamics, and induction. *Physica D* special issue on the Proceedings of the Oji International Seminar Complex Systems 'From Complex Dynamics to Artificial Reality'. Numazu, Japan

DeLanda, M. (2002). *Intensive Science and Virtual Philosophy*. New York: Continuum.

DeLanda, M. (2007). Real virtualities. In A. Menges and S. Ahlquist (eds), *Computational Design Thinking*. London: John Wiley & Sons Ltd.

Holland, J. (1992). *Adaptation in Natural and Artificial Systems: An Introductory Analysis with Applications to Biology, Control and Artificial Intelligence*. Cambridge, MA: MIT Press.

Holland, J. (1998). *Constrained Generating Procedures, Emergence: From Chaos to Order.* Reading, MA: Perseus Books.

Jeronimidis, G. (2004). Biodynamics. *Architectural Design*, 74(3): 90–95.

Kwinter, S. (2003). The computational fallacy. *Thresholds – Denatured*, 26, 90–1.

Mayr, E. (2001). *Variational Evolution: What Evolution Is*. New York: Basic Books.

Menges, A. (2008). Integral formation and materialisation: computational form and material gestalt. In B. Kolarevic and K. Klinger (eds). *Manufacturing Material Effects: Rethinking Design and Making in Architecture*. New York: Routledge.

Sutherland, I. (1963). Sketchpad: A man–machine graphical communication system. In *Proceedings of the AFIPS Spring Joint Computer Conference.* Detroit, MI: Joint Computer Conference.

Terzidis, K. (2003). *Expressive Form*. New York: Spon Press.

Thompson, D.W. (1961). *On Growth and Form*, abridged edition. Cambridge: Cambridge University Press.

Trummer, P. (2007). Associative design from type to population. In A. Menges and S. Ahlquist (eds), *Computational Design Thinking*. London: John Wiley & Sons Ltd.
Turner, J.S. (2007). *The Tinkerer's Accomplice*. Cambridge, MA: Harvard University Press.
von Bertalanffy, L. (1950). An outline of general system theory. *The British Journal for the Philosophy of Science*, 1(2): 134–165.
von Bertalanffy, L. (1969). *General System Theory: Foundations, Development, Applications*. New York, NY: George Braziller.
von Goethe, J.W. (1989). *Formation and Transformation*, translated by Bertha Mueller. Woodbridge, CT: Ox Bow Press.

11

Transparency

The Substance of Light in the Design Concept

James Carpenter and Ben Colebrook

Introduction

Architecture, by enclosing space within the public realm, physically obstructs views and diminishes the urban dweller's intuitive understanding of their physical and social environment. Architecture by its physical nature cannot be wholly transparent but can gain a transparent relationship to its surroundings by its responsive surfaces, intuitive program and clarity of form. Transparency as the substance of light is the ability of the architecture's solids and voids to reveal light information and it is this information that simultaneously connects us, consciously and subconsciously, to the specificity of a local context and the astonishingly expansive nature of the universe.

To reframe the idea of transparency as the substance of light, this chapter approaches transparency in architecture with an emphasis on glass and its ability to encompass light and its presence at an urban scale. The attributes and development of glass are woven through the chapter to better understand and think beyond this material's current counterproductive assignment as the material of literal transparency. This chapter's approach to transparency in architecture is defined by light as it is light that informs us about our context. Glass, or a conceptual approach based on an understanding of glass, is presented as the opportunity to embed contextual light information within the architecture itself.

This chapter refers to select examples of architecture across the centuries that represent innovations in structural design and corresponding developments in glass production. These examples and their approach to glass represent the drive toward entirely glass buildings but stand in contrast to the current predominantly banal treatment of glass.

Transparency—Void or Materiality?

In the absence of light, there is no transparency. It is through the body's sensitivity to the spectrum of energy we call light that our visual spatial experience is activated. It is interesting to note that the term "seeing" in astronomy refers to the sky's level of atmospheric instability and the consequent distortions to the imagery of celestial events. Similarly, transparency is in fact always a nuanced state affected by atmospheric conditions. Only a perfect vacuum allows light to travel unimpeded. The photons we perceive have been cumulatively affected over time by the atmosphere's gases, pollen and particulates, all of these in constant non-linear motion generated by topography, geography and meteorology. Our visual perception of color, saturation and every other visually qualitative aspect of the world around us is from the interaction of photons and the materials that transmit, diffract, diffuse, absorb and reflect those photons. What sense do we make of this information? Research has shown that our brain processes and stores much more visual information to the point of recognition than we are consciously aware of (Sanguinetti, Allen & Peterson, 2013).

Our senses are intertwined and it might be that their complex coordination, from which our brain resolves a 'complete' sense of the world useful for conscious determination, requires a vast array of very detailed, subconscious and unedited sensory information. Transparency needs to be thought of more as an extension of materiality. Beyond the concrete fact of any work of architecture's occupation of space and obstruction of sightlines, and beyond any actual or implied views in or through the architecture, architecture is really defined by its response to light.

At its origin, transparency in architecture may have represented the void. Early linguistic references such as the Old Norse "vindauga" (Skeat, 1963), literally "wind-eye" or Old English eagbyrl, literally "eye-hole" describing unglazed openings in the roof are suggestive of the roots and evolution of transparency as a concept in architecture. This original conception of the window as the physical eye of the architecture, an aperture in its "body" that provides access to air and light, suggests a foundation for current ideas about transparency as the reading of architectural tectonics across spatial divides. The "eye-hole" in the ceiling of an otherwise enclosed space would however offer a particular experience—one defined by the stream of light coming through it. This isolated experience of light diminishes the reading of a view and heightens observation of light's variability, to the point where it becomes pure information.

Light has always been the basis of a broader physical and temporal orientation within our world. Icelandic Sagas tell of the Vikings' journeys by sail from Norway to Iceland and Greenland and the American continent at Newfoundland around 700–1100 AD. In the 1960s, Danish Archaeologist, Thorkild Ramskou (Ramskou, 1967) posited the theory that the Vikings used "Sunstones," polarizing crystals, to orient themselves when clouds obscured the sun.

The use of the sunstone is conceivable but one principle holds true: Vikings were skillful navigators in a time before compasses and so had to have been able to interpret and orient themselves using light phenomena such as the subtle, yet distinct volume of brighter sky in the lower atmosphere caused by light reflected off Greenland's ice cap. Thinking of the Viking ship as a vessel connects it to architecture—a vessel open to the air. The openness of this architecture keeps the sailors connected to nature through all their senses and the specific information conveyed by the light informs their spatial relationships, even beyond what view they can "see."

The Development of Glass and Transparency

The impulse to develop the possibilities of glass can be traced more than 4,000 years back in history. Obsidian, fulgurites, moldavites and tektites are all natural glassy materials, and the use of obsidian, a volcanic glass, can be seen at multiple Paleolithic sites in the form of cutting tools or ritualistic objects. This first use of these glassy materials is considered a critical development in human evolution as it represents a technological breakthrough. For example, obsidian dated to 6000 BC has been found in Turkey, its black opaque surface polished into an extraordinary mirror presenting a simultaneous presence and absence of light.

From this earliest known exploitation, glassiness has been valued for its ability to reflect the world with optical accuracy yet imbued with a contemplative sensation—a luminous materiality. Glass can present a spectrum of qualities including reflectivity, transmittance, diffusion and diffraction, but for thousands of years transparency was its rarest, and maybe therefore its most desirable attribute. This may explain the vast investments in capital expended to develop and produce it at larger and larger scale. Surveying the history of glass, it appears that wherever civilizations and empires built wealth, they developed glass.

The wide ranging economy of the Roman Empire (27 BC to 476 AD) encouraged the development of glass compositions for ceramic glazes, as well as glass and glass blowing, mostly of beads and vessels. The use of translucent glass was very limited, but its non-transparent properties were also being widely exploited in the built environment as a material for pavements, walls, drainpipes—all applications that use glass as a surface for its color and impermeable properties (McGrath & Frost, 1961).

The surviving architecture of the earliest civilizations demonstrate the structural advances such as the post and lintel, the arch, vault and dome that still surprise us today, yet, at an architectural scale, glass played only a minor role. The Romans adopted and created the incentive for the further development of many labor and resource intensive technologies such as glass—yet their formulation and manufacture of concrete is probably their greatest contribution to creating the larger openings associated with transparency in architecture, their production of glass remaining within the realms of small vessels and rarefied objects. Even the small amounts of glass used in Roman architecture were not optically transparent and so direct views would still only be associated with unglazed openings. That is not to say that the translucent window lacking transmitted views, was considered worthless as a form of enclosure and simultaneous connection to the outside world—only that it was not one defined by optically transparent materials.

Stained glass is one glass type that found early adoption in architecture, evidence of which was found in the villas of wealthy Romans preserved by the volcanic eruption of Mount Vesuvius in Pompeii in 79 AD. Beginning with the simple, latticed glazing of the Romanesque Period (sixth to tenth centuries) stained glass became increasingly in demand as an architectural element of Christian structures. By the fifteenth century, the Seine-Rhine region (McGrath & Frost, 1961) was supplying demand for window glass for the Gothic cathedrals and their soaring openings and the cooling climate. By end of Gothic period (the sixteenth century) the art of the stained glass window was perfecting the merging of light and imagery on a large scale. Although a window, the image within the window aperture becomes more important than the view beyond, which is subjugated by the glass's strong color, graphic images and patterns. However, stained glass demonstrates the possibilities of transparency as the substance of light because of its ability to filter and project the information within the closed vessel of the cathedral, cinematically embedding the space with the sum total of mythic narrative. The materiality of the glass, its very chemistry and how it responds to light is an alchemical expression of light and matter. This immersive arrangement transforms the experience of the interior into a transcendent vessel, a vessel maybe not so unlike the Viking ship isolated in the ocean, removed from land and cast beyond the borders of self and daily life. Vikings were masters of observing and interpreting light, the builders of cathedrals of channeling and revealing this light.

This Middle Ages (fifth to fifteenth centuries) saw primarily two methods of glass making (McGrath & Frost, 1961), the crown glass method and the cylinder blown sheet method, but each required transforming a blown shape into a flat panel through a labor intensive process. The cylinder method was more widespread but the crown was considered of higher optical quality. As larger glass became available by the seventeenth century, it drove a desire and demand for glass that was larger than was possible by these methods. The breakthrough that led to the larger scale glass was made in France by the glassmaker Bernard Perrot in 1687 but the next year Louis XIV gave exclusive rights of this technique, and provided the enormous investment necessary, to Abraham Thevart and Louis Lucas de Nehou who set up proto-industrial glassworks that ended up at the Chateau de Saint-Gobain (McGrath & Frost, 1961). The purpose was to develop this process further and satisfy the king's demanding architectural applications for large panels of glass and mirrored glass which would represent a leap in the idea of light and transparency in architecture. The scale, quality achieved and tremendous cost had never been seen. The new process was essentially a scaled up casting process, with large ovens heating the glass for twenty-four hours before being poured onto a table with iron rulers set to limit the glass's spread. A roller was then run across the edge of the rulers to flatten out the glass before being replaced in the oven for days of annealing. Of interest to us now is the fact that the clear glass that emerged from the oven was still not perfectly flat and that a series of grinding and polishing operations were integral to the finished product. The scaled up operation and product of this glass was still essentially a craft, with the artistry of the polishers defining the final result, the best known example of which can be seen in the Hall of Mirrors at the Palace of Versailles, built between 1678 and 1684. The brilliance of the glass found in the crown glass could not be reproduced by this technique due to the flat glass' contact with the table. The subtle differences in glass characteristics were understood but considerations of size and manufacture were and still are primary due to the investment of resources and labor necessary to the process.

Jules Hardouin-Mansart's Hall of Mirrors at Versailles represents the first large-scale use of glass mirrors (Albanel, Arizzoli-Clementel & Coppey, 2008). Located one storey above the ground overlooking the formal gardens, water features and formal landscape, the hall is centered on the primary northwest-southeast axis of the Versailles plan. Monumental arched windows frame this grand view while identical arches on the wall facing the windows feature inset mirror, doubling the perceived scale of the space and embedding a perceived transparency within the body of the architecture. Glass and light exist in a rich interplay with a spatial play on transparency that would become a significant concern of Modernism over 200 years later. The use of mirrors was not a casual one, as their scale, quantity and cost were enormous. The mirrors are about double the size of the window panes, which suggests the goal was to have them be as monolithic and seamless as possible. Charles LeBrun, commissioned to produce the wealth of painted imagery within the hall, could have applied a trompe l'oeuil treatment for a fraction of the cost, but evidently there was a tremendous desire to go beyond the illusion and toward the authentic architectural experience of light. It is important to note that the hall had been a terrace and was built upon and enclosed to be transformed into the Hall of Mirrors. The vestige of its role as a terrace with commanding views of the landscape is integrated into its new heightened ceremonial role as a passage between the royal apartments that it connects.

Despite these initially prohibitively expensive applications, the ultimate functionality of glass in general and glass in architecture enabled production to persist with further technical improvements. An economic breakthrough was James Hartley's 1847 patent for a thin cast rolled plate technique perfected by the Chance Brothers in Birmingham who rolled the

Figure 11.1 Ziegler and Co, Versailles Palace. Hall of Mirrors, 1858, albumen print, 8.8189 × 11.2205 in., courtesy of Cornell University Library

glass between two rollers. This inexpensive thin rolled glass (McGrath & Frost, 1961) was never supposed to have a clear polished finish, could feature additional surface treatments transferred from textured or patterned rollers onto the glass, opening the door for the application of a wide spectrum of specifically molded optical properties.

Horticulturalists supported and pushed these and other material and structural developments toward a proto-modern architecture. Originating in the formal building type known as an 'Orangerie' and often built into the side of a hill, these buildings were designed to seasonally shelter climactically sensitive plants.

Greenhouses in the eighteenth and nineteenth centuries drove the demand for progressively larger glass sheets manufactured through the cylinder process, the use of cast iron and later wrought iron, standardization, mass production and prefabrication as well as structural innovations such as space frames and shell structures. Such breakthroughs are encapsulated in the glass and wrought iron frame domes and semi-domes created by J. D. Loudon and George McKenzie between 1817 and 1820 (Kohlmaier & von Sartory, 1986).

The chronological achievement of more efficient and larger glass structures culminated with Joseph Paxton's Crystal Palace in London's Hyde Park built to house the Great Exhibition of 1851. This all glass and iron building covering an extraordinary 990,000 square feet, and measuring over 100 feet at its central transept, merged technology and art to achieve the demand for a low cost, temporary, demountable and recyclable building to be completed in less than a year. A horticulturalist and garden designer, Paxton's design was based on his experience with greenhouses and the advances that were based on the primary concern with functionality and cost efficiency. It is interesting to note that an important factor in the development of greenhouses' curvilinear structural advances was driven by the desire to maximize diurnal and seasonal illumination, presenting the greatest area with the most ideal angle to the sun. Light was the foundation of these buildings down to their decorative filigree detailing which was primarily about reducing obstruction to light as well as reducing material, weight and cost. As established in greenhouses, the entire design of the Crystal Palace was based on a single module of measurement defined by the most challenging material to manufacture at larger sizes—glass. Using a blown glass cylinder process, the manufacturer, Chance Brothers of Birmingham, was able to produce at 49 inch × 10 inch glass lites through his experienced glass blowers' skills (many of them from France), a specially designed kiln, the use of diamond cutting tools and the flattening of the glass on a bed of polished glass instead of the usual iron plate and sand (Kohlmaier & von Sartory, 1986).

The nearly 300,000 pieces of glass were uniformly produced in this dimension and the parameters of mass production, prefabrication and on-site assembly of the other parts followed from it (Kohlmaier & von Sartory, 1986). The basic element of the four-foot pane of glass was multiplied by six to produce a twenty-four foot module. The plan, columns and beams are all multiples of twenty-four and this determined the design approach for the space frame. The space frame was refined to feature a minimum number of parts to streamline fabrication, assembly and disassembly.

No building had ever been seen like this, where an enclosure of light encapsulated a merging of industry and nature. As an engineering breakthrough the Crystal Palace was, and still is, largely ignored as a seminal work that expanded opportunities for transparency, let alone, economical production of large-scale architecture in an urbanizing world. Another important early breakthrough of proto-modern architecture should also in retrospect include the Oriel Chambers designed by Peter Ellis and built in 1864 in Liverpool in the United Kingdom where it still stands. Though only five storeys it is one of the first buildings to feature a metal framed curtain wall. The structure presents a bay window-like arrangement that captures light. Facing the courtyard this arrangement is unadorned and the façade steps back as it rises, allowing greater availability of daylight at the lower levels. Despite the adornment featured on the street side, added to make it culturally acceptable at the time, the building was harshly criticized by the architectural press of the day.

As manufacturing methods for glass advanced, another independently minded man, Freidrich Steiff, was behind another seminal building. As director of the Margarete Steiff AG toy producers in Giengen, Germany, he visited Chicago to represent Steiff toys at the 1893 World's Columbian Exposition. It is not known if seeing early steel skyscrapers, such as John Wellborn Root's Reliance Building (1889) (possibly informed by Root's time spent in Liverpool where the Oriel Building is located), inspired Steiff's own groundbreaking 1903 expansion of the company's factory. In response to the large orders for plush toys he acquired on his trip to the United States, Steiff contracted Eisenwerk München AG to rapidly design and build the structure, the first entirely unadorned steel frame building with a glazed curtain wall, furthermore, it stands as the first double-skin façade. It is unknown if the 3 mm cathedral glass, a rolled glass that features texture on one side, was selected for its cost advantages or because of its optical and thermal properties. Considering every other aspect of the structure's focus on utility, it may have been due to the glass' capacity to significantly increase light levels throughout the work space. The light within the building has a particular resonance by its interaction with the two layers of glass and the void that separates them as well as by being isolated from direct views (Murray, 2013). What should

Figure 11.2 Ignacio Fernández Solla, present day view of the Steiff factory building, Giengen, Germany, 2011, courtesy of Ignacio Fernández Solla

have been a celebrated marvel in its day was ignored by the architectural community, perhaps due its uncompromisingly functional approach, lack of an architect, its factory typology or most likely just for the lack of dissemination. Still standing, it is a timeless structure defined by the client's desire for a building that would be functional in every way, particularly the need for a specific quality of light.

The 1909 Boley Building, designed by Louis Curtiss completed six years later in Kansas City, Missouri also exploited and embodied engineering and architectural breakthroughs motivated by light, in this case light as promoter of commerce. The glazed curtain wall was the first in the United States. The use of glass was extended into the building with glass counters and display cases and glass-enclosed elevator shafts as well as with the use of mirrored walls and columns reflecting the boundary's brightness within the space. Louis Curtiss also instituted the innovation of setting back the posts and beams by nearly six feet from the curtain wall, cantilevering the floors which support the plate-glass panels, creating a volume of light for products to be both highly visible within the store and from the street. By its transparency, the visibility of its display could extend the architecture's presence within the public realm, obviating the need for architectural surface decoration. The desired effect for a crystalline experience of the interior was successfully achieved by Curtiss and promoted as a key attraction for the retail space. Despite the brilliant engineering of the curtain wall, Curtiss' Boley Building curtain wall is visually framed at its corners by white glazed terracotta pilasters, a detail that gives the mistaken impression of supporting the expanse of glass between them.

Nine years later, many of Curtiss' innovations including the curtain wall can be found in the Willis Polk designed Hallidie Building in San Francisco California, then owned by the University of California at Berkeley. Completed in 1918, the focus on light was transferred and refined to the commercial/office typology (Murray, 2009).

It is unknown if Polk was aware of Curtiss' achievements, but the Hallidie Building presents a more horizontal expression with smaller-scale external details interacting with the curtain wall. The vertical expression of the columnar corners found in Curtiss' Boley Building is here transformed into the delicate suspension of filigree fire escapes that instead emphasize the floating crystalline plane of the façade. The result heightens the presence of the glass and more clearly reveals the slightly set back interior columns revealing the structural logic of the building.

In the earliest phase of modern architecture at a point when electrical lighting was still in its infancy, as the massive solidity of the structural façade was replaced by steel framing, the façade could now be considered as a lightweight porous membrane largely devoted to the transfer of light. Building upon the light-redirecting glass developed for greenhouses in the nineteenth century, prism glass products produced by such manufacturers as the American Luxfer Company, capitalized on the opportunity for more effective daylighting above ground through the façade or below ground through the sidewalk. Transparency here was manipulated for the exploitation of an essential resource—daylight as a source of illumination.

These developments in structural engineering and the possibilities of inserting daylight within the workplace led to much excitement about the benefits of daylight itself on the human experience, both in terms of productivity and general welfare. From the end of the nineteenth century a growing body of literary and popular articles responded to the advances in glass with a utopian vision of a world improved by a literal sense of this transparency. Glass, its strength and impervious surface, could be imagined as a transformative medium that would turn every aspect of the designed world into an opportunity for brilliance.

Meanwhile the glass industry continued to develop methods that would reduce the cost of the material and satisfy a growing demand. The breakthrough of drawing flat sheets was invented in the early 1900s by Fourcault in Belgium. Fourcault developed a glass furnace built into the floor of the factory where under pressure the glass rises and is bonded with a steel bar which pulls it up vertically to rollers that vertically draw a continuous sheet of glass. This method was further developed by several manufacturers including Libbey-Owens and the Pittsburgh Plate Glass which achieved additional economies of scale. However these methods produced glass which lacked the flatness of the ground and polished cast plate glass. There was still the search for glass that would have all the best characteristics of the various approaches: the economical continuity of the drawn process, the flatness and scale of the cast plate process and the brilliant surface of the crown glass (McGrath & Frost, 1961).

The further development of casting directly into rollers and grinding and polishing both surfaces ultimately culminated in the improvement of a fire polished surface, or float glass process. In 1952, Pilkington Brothers achieved a continuous stream of glass flowing across molten metal which, with the additional heat, achieved a polished surface. This process might best be envisioned as exploiting the phenomenon of 'oil floating on water', where the molten glass literally floats upon a shallow pool of molten tin where it finds a remarkable flatness and, due to the heat, brilliance.

These developments are the foundation of the current manufacture of glass with the great range in composition, size, thickness, hardness, color, clarity, reflectivity, etching, acoustic and thermal performance, complex shape and unitizing. The economic barriers and limits of manufacturing that kept glass a carefully guarded process and costly material have diminished but inversely, the properties that make glass such a valuable medium have become largely ignored.

Transparency as A Connection to Nature

Electrical lighting altered ideas about transparency in architecture in subtle but significant ways. Instead of being a source of light, the façade openings would solely serve as an access to views. As the workplace could be artificially illuminated and therefore closed off or isolated from the façade, those views would become commoditized as a luxury. As the view became more valuable than daylight, the incentive was to develop glass that would not interfere with those views. The progressive mastery of glass as the material of this transparency has resulted in today's abundance of ill-considered glazed façades. Treating glass as purely the absence of materiality, as if it were a material that could cancel any differentiation between inside and outside, denies the opportunities it affords in using daylight to define and enrich both the private and public realm. It is by its materiality that glass has a special ability to surprise, delight and engage us with our environment in a way that no other material can quite achieve. Glass, as a powerfully responsive material, is particularly suited to revealing the substance of light in the public realm, but ironically, glass today is mostly considered for its least engaging characteristic: uninterrupted views; a banal notion that ignores the complex interaction of light and glass, or more importantly, light and architecture.

The language of glass materiality is useful because of its mutability. All materials and material treatments can at some level be explored for their ability to transmit, refract, diffuse, absorb and reflect light. Treating any material for the potential responsiveness of its surface has led my design studio James Carpenter Design Associates (JCDA), known for its particular sensitivity to light, to develop new material and structural innovations.

JCDA was founded on my work as an artist using 16 mm and 8 mm film projected on the uniquely responsive surface of glass. This cinematic work from the early 1970s exploring image transmission and reflection led me to a particular interest in light and its significance in our experience of life—not so much in the sense that it allows us to see the world outside ourselves, but in its capacity to accumulate information along its journey to the eye. Out of this gallery film installation practice a desire developed to engage with the wider community by reintroducing this exploration of experiential qualities of light back into the public realm.

The Luminous Glass Bridge was one such seminal project from 1985 which proposed aligning a pedestrian bridge with the course of the river. To "cross" the bridge, pedestrians would access each end of the 100-foot long glass deck along the cantilevered abutments emerging from opposite shores of the river. The surface of the bridge would be composed of a lightly etched laminated glass composition that would capture the caustic reflections from the surface of the water below; in essence transposing the imaging of the river's transparent surface onto the translucent underside surface of the bridge. Instead of being purely about convenience, this bridge would allow a direct interaction with the river, slowing the individual down and immersing them in the specific ecology of their environment, allowing the close observation of the presence and substance of light.

Transparency and seeing are often thought of in tandem when observing and understanding our discrete experience, but transparency as the substance of light extends vision beyond the uninterrupted sight line and brings us closer to subconscious vision and the paradox of our own transience. This more complete "sense" of the world slows the usual instant process of seeing and broadens it until we have a less certain, but far richer, feel for the depth of our sensory experience. Transparency in architecture can focus upon integrating light and its many phenomenal expressions within urban environments, interior and exterior.

Functioning at a domestic scale, the Periscope Window is a window with a view limited by an adjacent wall and building. Commissioned by the client, JCDA sought to redefine the

Figure 11.3 James Carpenter Design Associates, Aerial view of the Luminous Glass Bridge model, Marin County, California, 1987, courtesy of JCDA

idea of a window and view with substantive optical layers, presenting a transparency based on the substance of light that would gather a layered experience of the sky and trees and passage of the sun and moon. The effect was achieved within the 12-inch depth of the insulated glass device. Horizontally suspended inclined mirrors and eighty glass lenses are arranged to gather and broadcast the landscape beyond what would be a typical window's outlook. The interior glass of the insulated unit is a specially treated and acid-etched laminated composition. This element acts as a projection screen that resolves and embodies the various light effects gathered by the assembly.

The Periscope Window redefines the singular idea of the window, as a framed absence within the solids of the architecture, and instead extracts light information that exists in the environment well beyond the window frame's limit. In a sense, this device uses optics just as the Versailles Hall of Mirrors did. In this case the mirrors, lenses and etched glass compress a divergent array of imaged views and light effects and project them within the boundary of the threshold itself. Multiple properties of light, view and content are collapsed and superimposed to create a new hybridized view—an expanded and cumulative transparency.

Transparency and Performance

The Periscope Window is a device that expands the window and its view by pushing its optical performance. Free from architecture's academic and stylistic conventions, Paxton's Crystal Palace also approached the possibilities of transparency through performance, applying the greenhouse's principals to the habitable space, encapsulating a sense of nature by radically merging boundary, structure and light, not for the purposes of transparent access to views, but to create large interior spaces that harvest light as a synthesis of nature in an urbanizing

Figure 11.4 JCDA, Brian Gulick, Interior view of the Periscope Window, Minneapolis, Minnesota, 1997, Courtesy of JCDA

world where clean air, light and space were becoming inaccessible to the majority of citizens (Schoenfeldt, 2008).

For visitors, the connection between interior and exterior and vice versa, was not experienced through the materiality's absence but by its very presence and relationship to light. The result at Crystal Palace is described by Lothar Bucher as follows:

> the eye projects on to an endless perspective which disappears into a blue haze. If we let our gaze slowly descend again it meets the discontinuous blue-painted girders, first in the wide intervening spaces, now advancing even closer, then interrupted by a shining strip of light, finally merging into a distant background.
>
> (Kohlmaier & von Sartory, 1986)

Bucher's sense of wonder is underscored not only by the extraordinary scale but by the primacy of light and the presence of light within the very fabric of the architecture. He does not dwell on views or make a reference to an image-related connection to the outside. It is a pure sense of light and its specificity to the site. This is no accident, as the development of greenhouses was a highly technical search based only on the performance of every element. The transparency of this architecture is about transposing and deploying light to establish a synthesis of nature within the architecture.

The investment in greenhouse design, materials and assembly, followed from performance goals responsive to the very specificity of the building's location. The glass could be tinted, textured or clear, the angle of the glazing and structural form of the building could vary, but all these choices would be in the service the greenhouse plants' particular life cycle and in response to the specific latitude of the building. Often the performance parameters would even include the need to maximize light and heat gain exactly when the greenhouse's particular plants would be bearing fruit. From the outside, greenhouses also appear veiled, the various orientations of glass presenting complex merging of reflected and transmitted views. Even as the largest greenhouse structures create a spectacular impression by their scale, it is the combination of their scale and their embodiment of light and performance that makes them appear to transcend the solid and void of architecture and present the substance of transparency—light.

Operating at a greenhouse's level of performance, both structural and optical, the Sky Reflector-Net is an integrated artwork for the Fulton Center, a transit hub in Lower Manhattan. JCDA was commissioned by Metropolitan Transportation Authority Arts for Transit and Urban Design and MTA Capital Construction Company. The artwork uses no glass, but explores the properties we associate with glass and transparency, in this case through the use of aluminum with specific optical properties, a specific program of perforation, and the articulation of the form-found structural net. Tensioned within the atrium's conical form, the artwork folds the image of the sky into the core of the building, essentially expanding the boundary of the skylight window and transposing the sky's presence within its thin, taut and lightweight surface. JCDA, working with engineer Schlaich Bergermann und Partner, developed the form-finding cable-net structure that is held in tension within the atrium. The form of the two-way cable-net, an eccentric toroid, was selected for its calculated ability to harvest and redirect light from the skylight oculus.

Figure 11.5 JCDA, Richard Kress, Sky Reflector-Net during installation, New York, 2013, courtesy of JCDA

As in the Crystal Palace, this public space is defined by an accumulated experience of light. The artwork embodies the very substance of light within its matrix, unfolding the sky's expanse and temporal qualities beyond the skylight's oculus and transposing a moment of contemplative observation *within* architecture's boundaries. As in greenhouses, the form is a perfect merging of structure and programmed light distribution, operating like a periscope to bring light, and the experience of the sky-dome from above and down into the depths of the transit center.

Embedding Transparency

Colin Row and Robert Slutzky's seminal work on transparency in architecture breaks down transparency into two main components, Literal Transparency and Phenomenal Transparency (Rowe & Slutzky, 1963). Literal Transparency relates first to the absence of obstacles allowing views through the body of the architecture, second to the use of latticed, punctured or other veiling assemblies of materials and third to the use of inherently transparent materials such as glass. Phenomenal Transparency describes the spatial arrangements that are out of view but that are implied by the formal articulation of the architecture's visible surfaces, their example being Le Corbusier's villa at Garches (Rowe & Slutzky, 1963). Transparency as the substance of light collapses the distinction between literal and phenomenal transparency, uniting them in the goal of inserting the mutable presence of light within the architecture's envelope.

A conceptual example that presents the idea of transparency derived from a performance driven process is Joseph Paxton's 1855 proposal for the Great Victorian Way, which used the same engineering approach as the Crystal Palace (Kohlmaier & von Sartory, 1986). The Great Victorian Way represents a radical urbanism, merging transport, commerce and residential functions, all built around a 108 foot high and 72 foot wide, 11-mile glass-enclosed pedestrian arcade. As in Paxton's Crystal Palace design, the architecture is purely defined by the requirements of its function, essentially a bridge-like structure connecting the West End of London with the City of London in a loop. The pedestrian arcade is at its center, a steel arched frame onto which the commercial, residential and transportation elements are attached. What are usually interior functions/spaces are applied to the building's exterior, while the boundary and façade of the urban building system is inserted into its center. Retail spaces open on to the arcade at ground level while residential spaces are above the retail spaces and look out into the arcade. The elevated rail lines delineate the outer wings of the structure. The highest point of the structure is the arching glass vault above the arcade harvesting and transmitting light within the ceramic-clad volume of the arcade. The continuous structure traverses the Thames three times along its 11 mile loop. Free of the architect's priorities, Paxton approaches transparency mainly as a function of the building's purpose. The sky and daylight are harvested by the glass vault, the surface treatments reflecting light to create a luminous volume penetrating the full height of the structure and running its length (McGrath & Frost, 1961). From this volume of light, the other habitable spaces access daylight.

Considered a viable project, but abandoned due to a financial crisis, this proposal anticipates by over 100 years, Peter Cook's 1964 purely conceptual project with Archigram titled Plug-In City. Like the Great Victorian Way, this is a self-contained megastructure that is defined by circulation at an urban scale. As in Paxton's approach it creates a structural framework onto which elements are affixed and a systematic hierarchy by which elements could conceivably be "plugged in" or "unplugged," the whole expanding or contracting in response to the needs of its users (Sadler, 2005).

Both these conceptual projects dispense with the typical idea of the façade all together. Here, the idea of architectural transparency is almost irrelevant. Light is considered a far more important resource, be it from a utopian or dystopian point of view.

Conclusion

Solids and voids or the transparency of a façade are hardly relevant to Paxton's Great Victorian Way or to Peter Cook's Plug-In City. A contemporary approach to the built environment, essentially a more urban infrastructural approach to architecture, requires an updated conception of transparency at an urban scale.

Literal transparency is commonly thought of in terms of a simple material absence but considering transparency as the substance of light reverses this idea. Beyond the visible light that we are able to perceive, there is also light, such as x or gamma rays that pass right though the body and in a sense define the human body itself as transparent. What is most interesting about transparency is not so much that the eye has access or is obstructed, rather that transparency is inseparable from all the other operations that affect light and our ability to "see" or sense the world around us. Transmission, diffraction, diffusion, absorption and reflection are the basic actions that affect light and its visual or bodily perception, and these actions conceptually give substance to the light, freighting it with information. Light reaches us across space, from the surface of the sun in about eight minutes, but light, reaching us from more distant stars can have travelled for billions of years and is in its essence light from the distant past. Light can reveal a history both fleeting and deeply rooted in the origins of the universe and our place in it. Though mostly unnoticed, this information registers subconsciously in significant ways. This vertiginous experience of light makes transparent our connection to the vastness of space and time. Our memories are made up of the light information we are most consciously aware of whereas the unconscious recording of the full unedited range of light informs our dreams, for our dreams and the universe have a similarly unfathomable and confounding nature.

Rowe and Slutzky's 'Transparency: Literal and Phenomenal' (1963) is rooted in the formulation of Cubism's collapsed and multiple expressions of space and time. Transparency as the substance of light pulls us away from the academic concern with problems faced by painters depicting three-dimensional space on a two-dimensional surface and returns us to the primary source that inspired those very artists: the nature of space and time, at the center of which is light.

In architecture today, the idea of implying transparency through a façade's articulation or of achieving literal transparency by treating glass as the absence of materiality is simply not interesting, nor is it effective at providing the urban dweller with an essential sense of their environment. Glass, even optically clear glass, is not necessarily transparent. Under most conditions glass reveals its multitude of properties—properties defined by light. It is the articulation of this light that offers the opportunity for architecture to achieve a transparency that connects us to our context, both immediate and far reaching. When glass is understood for the entire range of its properties, it is supremely well suited to producing transparency as the substance of light. Expansive, poetic and performative, glass has the potential to capture and represent many local and distant levels of light information simultaneously, and this information can be orchestrated across the depth of the material's matrix, presenting a phenomenal transparency that, as a transcendent experience of light, has the potential to be a bridge between our experience of the built environment and a profound connection to nature.

As a design approach, transparency as the substance of light updates Aristotle's conception of vision as requiring a 'medium' connecting the object of vision with the eye. The contemporary conception of transparency in architecture assigns the space between the object and eye as a void while transparency as the substance of light reassigns the particles in the atmosphere and the context that uniquely affects them, to the role of "medium." The "substance" of light is accumulated by its path across the "medium" and this depth of accumulated information borne by the photon is what informed and responsive design can unpack and reveal thereby connecting the urban dweller to a profound sense of nature. Even the densest urban environment can be re-imagined as the simultaneously open vessel and the enclosed cathedral by which to observe and engage the breadth and depth of life's passage.

References

Albanel, C., Arizzoli-Clementel, P., & Coppey, P. (2008). *Hall of Mirrors: History and Restoration.* Easthampton, MA: Hudson Hills Press.

Enoch, J. M. (2006). Historical perspective, history of mirrors dating back 8000 years. *Optometry & Vision Science*, 83, 10, 775–781.

Kohlmaier, G. & von Sartory, B. (1986). *Houses of Glass, A Nineteenth-Century Building Type*. Cambridge MA: MIT Press.

McGrath, R. & Frost, A. C. (1961). *Glass in Arch and Decoration*. London: The Architectural Press.

Murray, S. C. (2009). *Contemporary Curtain Wall Architect*. New York: Princeton Architectural Press.

Murray, S. (2013). *Translucent Building Skins: Material Innovations in Modern and Contemporary Architecture*. New York: Routledge.

Ramskou, T. (1967). Solstenen. *Skalk*, 2, 16.

Rowe C. & Slutzky. R. (1963). Transparency: Literal and phenomenal. *Perspecta 8: The Yale Architectural Journal*, 45–54.

Sadler, S. (2005). *Archigram: Architecture without Architecture.* Cambridge, MA: MIT Press.

Sanguinetti, J. L. Allen, J. J. B. & Peterson, M. A. (2013). The ground side of an object: Perceived as shapeless yet processed for semantics. *Psychological Science*, 25,1, 256–264.

Schoenfeldt, H. (2008). The Crystal Palace, environmentally considered. *Architectural Research Quarterly,* 12, 3–4, 283–294.

Skeat, W. W. (1963). *A Concise Etymological Dictionary of the English Language.* New York: Capricorn Books.

Part III

Architectural Design and Ecological Sustainability

This part focuses on design for the projection of livable built environments and the requisite knowledge and understanding of ecological sustainability for preserving the planet Earth and its residents. It expands on the relevance of architectural design with a diverse range of meanings of ecological manifestations from the natural and social sciences, extending into the design process as integrative systems thinking. This part looks at sustainable design as a meaningful approach toward harmonizing various interrelated flows of forces between the building and its natural environment.

12

Situating Meanings of Sustainability Within the Architectural Discourse

Meredith Sattler

Figure 12.1 Hand-held Hasselblad photograph of Earth from Apollo 17. Courtesy of NASA. Image AS17-148-22727

On December 7, 1972, as the crew of Apollo 17 left Earth's orbit for the moon, they took the first ever photograph of the entire planet. In the instant the camera shutter was released, a new holistic paradigm was unleashed, manifest in the image of Earth as one continuous sphere, undivided by boundaries, political or otherwise. It took the Apollo 17 crew a short five hours and six minutes to arrive at this vantage point, but it has proven a lengthier and less calculated journey for those on Earth to unpack the meaning of this image, and ultimately begin to address its implications in terms of environment, equity, and economy.

Sustainability implies continuity, by definition. It requires an extended (holistic) view of space and time in order to comprehend, and ultimately facilitate, relationships and feedbacks between seemingly disparate, yet operationally continuous environmental conditions and circumstances. Humans maintain a somewhat complicated relationship with continuity and change. We cultivate changes we value or desire, but are generally risk-averse, preferring slow steady change or no change at all, to general uncertainty or sudden, unanticipated change. Likewise the built environment, which is predominantly static in nature, is particularly demanding of stable conditions. So sustainability, at its core, becomes an exercise in mitigating and managing change, typically slowing and steadying its pace.

Globally, we have experienced implicating events, some explosive, others sneakily silent, that demonstrate we are not just actors upon an environmental stage, but co-creators of the environment with the "natural" world. In 2002, Nobel Prize winning chemist, Paul Crutzen, identified the current age as the *Anthropocene*, a "human-dominated, geological epoch supplementing the Holocene" (Crutzen, 2002). In retrospect, it is clear that human endeavors such as the development of agriculture and urbanization, which catalyze Global Warming, are the products of a creative and dynamic partnership with natural processes. As architects we are particularly active agents in this partnership, which has resulted in the transformation of the Earth's surface, through the process of development, into a hybrid constructed environment.

It was concern over environmentally devastating issues such as the Manhattan Project and widespread DDT usage that seeded the Sustainable Development movement in global politics in the early 1970s. This political movement seeks to address over-population, resource depletion, industrial expansion and processes, energy, food security, the resilience of species and ecosystems, urban challenges, management of the commons, and the relationship between conflict and environmental degradation (Sitarz, 1993). In the last half century, increasingly international organizations such as the United Nations, the World Bank, and the Intergovernmental Panel on Climate Change have turned their attention to these issues, and it is from this arena that today's most widely accepted definition of sustainability originates: "Sustainable development is development that meets the needs of the present without compromising the ability of future generations to meet their own needs" (World Commission on Environment and Development, 1987).

While the above 1987 Brundtland Report definition is indisputably accurate in its formulation, it is frustratingly ambiguous for designers and consumers, resulting in a plurality of interpretations of sustainability today. Though highly theoretical, it does identify two critical factors for framing any sustainable solution, regardless of its geographic influence:

- sufficient needs—definition of both the quantity and quality of human needs
- temporal continuum—understanding cause and effect relationships (feedbacks) and their limits, between present and future generations.

Originally architecture arose from the need "to lift the raw load of the physical environment from our backs and to create [the mediated environments] required by civilization" (Fitch & Bobenhausen, 1999). As architects, we have always been deeply implicated in the creation and management of anthropocentric environments that perform in relationship to the above criteria, regardless of the extent to which these are consciously incorporated into the design process. Today, as external environments shift, they increasingly dictate our lifestyle and threaten our security, which demands we develop more robust architectural solutions to mitigate and adapt. This further positions architects, as not only creators of autonomous, programmed spaces, but simultaneous co-creators of multi-scalar spatial and temporal environmental systems. Therefore, only design processes that satisfy needs both spatially and temporally situated within their socio-environmental constructs are ultimately capable of fulfilling Brundtland's definition.

Yet the discipline has largely shifted its attention away from these larger environmental concerns since the mid-twentieth century, just as environmentalism was beginning to propagate globally. Instead it turned within, focusing primarily on formal considerations. If architecture is to continue to be relevant, the discipline can no longer afford to address the multitude of contextual forces thrust upon it in a piecemeal manner. As our understandings of these physical and socio-cultural forces become more sophisticated, so does the complexity of the issues to be addressed. This requires an evolution in design process that can accommodate both definable and bound problems with discrete solutions, such as those found in the natural sciences, and those that are less definable and rely on judgment and temporal iterative solutions, such as those found in the social sciences (Rittel & Webber, 1984).

In particular, it is imperative that architecture address the temporal and extra-disciplinary considerations urgently affecting living organisms' health and wellbeing, particularly those that provision the ecosystems services we rely on for survival. Today, the built environment, by and large, does not support a planetary ecology necessary to sustain human survival. In order to create and construct long-duration life enhancing systems, the discipline must look beyond the purely technological to incorporate emergent knowledge that facilitates situated hybrid technological solutions. The American counter-culture movement of the 1960s catalyzed the development of numerous disciplines that reevaluated equity and socio-environmental relationships. Together these have initiated a trajectory of increasingly sophisticated systems of environmental and social valuation, which offer architecture productive forward-looking influences.

The current developed world, post-growth, post-peak oil context has evolved from a multitude of cascading advances in technology, socio-cultural influences, and economics. These produce built forms that behave as concentrating cocktails of information, materials, and energy that feedback into ecological patterns and processes resulting in varying environmental outcomes across different geographies at different spatial and temporal scales. These outcomes are not necessarily definite or even clearly identifiable, which exacerbates our incomplete understanding of anthropocentric environmental impacts. This has resulted in a plurality of sustainable or green solutions designed to mitigate specific, and often isolated problems existing within a broader range of interconnected issues such as carbon based energy usage and accumulated environmental toxicity. Because the influence of these forces (both central to the discipline of architecture and contextual) is growing in scope and complexity, the discipline has struggled to address these systemic environmental concerns, which are ultimately sustainability concerns. Today, we are confronted with the resultant pluralistic and fragmented expressions of sustainable, green and ecologically responsive architectural design.

In an attempt to structure this plurality, architecture has adopted the more generally utilized sustainable framework of the 3 Es: Environment, Equity, and Economics. The 3 Es have been referred to as a "triangle of competing interests" (Moore, 2007) whose priorities align, shift, and realign through temporally morphing circumstances. Because we now know ourselves to be the catalysts of accelerating rates of environmental change on an already dynamic planet, this knowledge not only brings formerly established pragmatic design solutions into question, but also a host of operational and ethical issues for both humans and non-humans as we hone our abilities to serve each other's needs via mutualistic relationships. This chapter defines, contextualizes, and hierarchies the 3 Es in order to

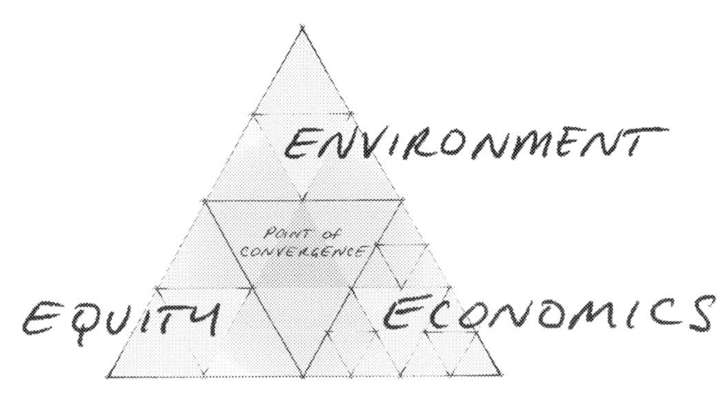

Figure 12.2 Sierpinski Sieve diagram illustrating relationships between the 3Es of sustainability. Drawn by Author

explicate the theory and practice of actualizing sustainability within an increasingly complex and self-aware context, and utilizes the 3 Es to demonstrate how the creation of meaning within this context has proven particularly plural, rendering it one of the most ambiguous and confused architectural concerns of our time.

Environment: Living Systems and the Support of Ecosystem Services

We begin with *Environment* because it is not only the living dynamic context within which architecture is physically situated, but also provides the life-support services (ecosystem services) that humans rely upon for survival. Essentially it is the baseline driving condition from which architecture and culture must operate. The environment can broadly be defined as the *lithosphere*, the thin crust of the Earth containing the atmosphere, water, land, and all living organisms that receive energy inputs primarily from the sun. This living space is first and foremost the domain of *ecology*, the etymology of which stems from the Greek *oikos* meaning *house, household, dwelling,* or *family*, combined with the suffix *logos* meaning *word, language of reason* (Schwartz & Jax, 2011). Therefore, the meaning of ecology can be understood as *the logic of Earth's household* (fitting for architecture), which today encompasses all species, constructions, and processes within the hybrid natural-built environment.

Increasingly we understand the interconnected behavior of the lithosphere, and all its components, through the discipline of Systems Ecology. Its methodology of tracing energy/matter stocks and flows through the environment emerged in the late 1950s in order to create an integrative language to describe relationships between large-scale ecosystems. The systems approach facilitates an understanding of the lithosphere that is driven by thermodynamic, multi-scalar, relational patterns and processes between living things and their environment. These processes result in the evolving environmental forms and circumstances we read as landscape that comprise the matrix within which architecture intervenes. In order to engage in a more sophisticated understanding of the logics of temporal environmental change, a preliminary understanding of systemic dynamic ecological patterns and processes is necessary. These include patterns and processes that catalyze change, that physically and chemically shape the environmental matrix, that influence the composition of communities, and that maintain the overall stable state of the larger climactic system.

Disturbance regimes are drivers of pronounced change in ecological systems over time. They are predominantly external, acting upon an existing system to induce changes either slowly via *press* disturbances such as climate change, sea level rise, or nutrient loading, or quickly via *pulse* disturbances such as fire, drought, or storms (Collins *et al.*, 2010). These regimes drive physical and chemical fluctuations in the environment, including the concentration and mobilization of anthropogenically produced toxins and pollutants, which in turn, influence the composition of communities that ultimately effect the larger environment or climate regime.

Ecological succession, by contrast, is a predominantly internally driven process whereby the species structure of a community will impact its own environment creating change over time. In the successional process a community of pioneering species, with low diversity and complexity, colonize an area and begin to alter the biogeochemical conditions until other species, more suited for these new conditions (more diverse and complex), move in and take over, again altering the biogeochemical conditions and further increasing the complexity of the system. This pattern continues until a relatively stable and complex *climax community* emerges, an external disturbance emerges, or the community exceeds its *carrying capacity*, the ability of a community to feed itself and effectively process its own waste. In these cases succession may decrease rather than increase in complexity.

Communities typically follow one of two patterned growth curves in relationship to their carrying capacity. They either increase in population exponentially until they approach their carrying capacity, and then maintain their population at or just below the tipping point, creating a stable "S curve" graph of sustainable population maintenance through time. Or they continue to increase their population exponentially, exceeding their carrying capacity in a "J curve" graph, resulting in either complete mortality or significant reductions in their population. In the "J curve" scenario, if there are reproductive survivors, these communities may be able to regenerate as long as they do not once again exceed their carrying capacity, duplicating an unsustainable environment.

The above factors contribute to the stability, or lack thereof, of large-scale environmental systems. This stability can be described according to several factors: *reliability* in maintaining little variation in levels of functionality, *robustness* or "ability to deliver service in conditions which are beyond [their] normal domain of operation" (Anderson, 1988) ability to *persist* or maintain functionality over long periods of time via closed loops of production and feedbacks, and *resilience* or ability to buffer disturbances or adapt quickly in response without changing state. When the whole environmental system, including both living communities and the nonliving processes that support them, exceed the capacity of these stabilizing mechanisms "instabilities can flip a system, into another regime of behavior" (Gunderson, 2000) abandoning the conditions and functionality of the original state altogether. This phenomenon is referred to as *system state change*. The new system state may or may not be an *alternate stable state*. If a stable state is available, *adaptive capacity* describes the property of an ecosystem to facilitate this flipping into another stable state versus flipping into a series of variable conditions (Gunderson, 2000). Adaptive capacity is also a term increasingly utilized to describe thresholds of architectural performance.

Maintenance of our current climactic system state is critical because it is the stable context within which the species that provision ecosystem services have evolved to thrive. In 2005, the Millennium Ecosystem Assessment defined the term *ecosystem services* as "the benefits people obtain from ecosystems" (Millennium Ecosystem Assessment, 2005) including *supporting services* such as nutrient cycling and primary production, *provisioning services* such as food, fresh water and fuel, *regulating services* such as climate and disease control, and *cultural services* such as aesthetic and educational. At that time, approximately 60 percent of the ecosystem services critical for human health and wellbeing were found to be degraded and unsustainably utilized (Millennium Ecosystem Assessment, 2005). This relatively recent occurrence roughly correlates with the American post-World War II Golden Age of Capitalism when petrochemical energy usage increased dramatically, deeply implicating pre-peak oil architecture and development patterns in environmental decline.

In the last twenty years, *mitigation* and *adaptation* strategies have been consistently rehearsed by designers, engineers, and politicians to address the implications of climate change, in particular. Today, conversations surrounding the efficacy of mitigation, the act of reducing the amount of greenhouse gases released into the atmosphere, are decreasing in frequency while exploration of adaptive strategies is increasing. It appears there is growing consensus that significant global mitigation of carbon-based emissions is not feasible, and that adaptation will be the primary mode of addressing changing environments. Adaptive strategies facilitate systemic hybrid human-natural transformation of circumstances in response to harmful environmental stimuli or their effects. Within the discipline of architecture specifically, adaptation describes the utilization of technologies to adjust the structural, behavioral, or resource demands of habitation, in response to climatic stimuli. Increasingly the term is utilized as a surrogate for sustainable architecture.

Historically, sustainable architectural practices were embedded within the practice of architecture. The production of long-duration shelters to mitigate environmental elements was the main function and preoccupation of the discipline. It is only in the last two centuries, particularly since World War II, that sustainable practices have decoupled enough to be identifiable as a subset. Architecture, pre-abundant petrochemical fuel, once had less complicated yet more complex (Moe, 2013) physical relationships with the thresholds, lags, limits, and discontinuities (Holling & Goldberg, 1971) inherent in *the logic of Earth's household*. Buildings relied on temporal energetic exchanges between Earth and Sun for interior lighting while mitigating external temperatures via the use of passive enclosure systems, wind, and sometimes water. These temporally responsive strategies that cycle with natural processes while leveraging renewable fuel sources have been referred to as *bioclimactic* or *climate responsive design* and utilize a set of *passive design principles* that include *solar geometry* and *daylighting, natural ventilation, thermal collection* and *lag, adiabatic heating* and *cooling, acoustic attenuation, freshwater harvesting* and *gravity conveyance*, and *wastewater reclamation*.

Increasingly, architecture is expanding the scope of bioclimactic design, through the utilization of systems ecology approaches for mapping and budgeting material and energy stocks and flows. These include matter/energy optimizations that consider not only the materials and performance of the designed object itself, but also their environmental impact. A *net-zero* energy building is designed to produce as much energy as it consumes over the course of a year thereby leaving a zero-operating energy footprint on the environment. There are multiple classifications of net-zero, each draws its energy footprint boundary differently. The two most common are net-zero site and net-zero source. *Net-zero site* determines the energy usage of the building at the site boundary, based primarily on downstream energy quantities whereas *net-zero source* draws the energy usage boundary at the power plant or on upstream energy quantities. *Upstream energy*, the energy required to mine fuel, transport it to the power plant, power the power plant, and transmit the energy across the grid, is much less efficient than *downstream energy* which is the energy use from its last point of conversion (usually the wall outlet) through the equipment it operates. Therefore, net-zero source buildings must produce significantly more energy than net-zero site buildings.

Embodied energy tallies the amount of energy utilized throughout the building lifecycle, not just the operational phase. It traces and quantifies energy usage beginning with material raw extraction, through manufacturing, transport, and the construction process, into operational performance, and ultimately demolition and end of life disposal. *Design for Environment (DfE),* a methodology developed by industrial designers, employs simulation to compare quantities of embodied energy versus building *operational energy*, and their environmental impact, facilitating more informed design decisions about the materials, form, and services a building design will engender. Due to the dramatic rise of global material sourcing, DfE analysis increasingly examines matter/energy efficiencies in order to reduce travel distances, quantity, and multiplicity of materials utilized, while increasing their ability to be recycled locally.

The systems approach also provides a framework for determining the *renewability* of building materials. William McDonough and Michael Braungart have proposed *cradle to cradle* design strategies which feed infinitely renewable materials through industrial ecologies modeled after natural ecologies. In these scenarios the waste of one building becomes the food of another through recycling processes. Cradle to cradle proposes a sustainable alternative to the current *cradle to grave* system where most construction demolition is routed to landfills.

These design methodologies fall under the larger umbrella of *performative design* which has also recently become a surrogate for sustainable design. Performative design is loosely defined as a design process that incorporates behavioral criteria to generate an integrated operational and formal design product. Ancient in its origination, the types of performance most frequently considered today are technical in nature such as energy or water usage, solar control, interior environmental comfort, or resiliency/adaptation, but theoretically any criteria that can be defined, modeled, and measured could be utilized. Performative design is heavily reliant on *simulation*, the process of modeling, testing, and iterating performative capacity during the design process. Modeling and testing can happen physically, digitally, or both. As software capabilities continue to evolve and become more ubiquitous, and the ability to model complex behaviors such as computational fluid dynamics becomes more sophisticated, advanced computational digital models are increasingly utilized.

Parametric design is a design process that utilizes performative criteria to not just test design iterations, but employs that criterion in the conceptual design phase as a generative design tool. Today parametric design is most frequently utilized to produce complex geometries, but increasingly designers are folding in additional criteria related to site context, fabrication/construction, and building performance. Organisms and natural systems deploy their own version of parametric design, embedded in evolutionary process. This "design process" occurs via the act of surviving to reproductive age, then passing on and recombining genetic information through sexual reproduction to create new, unique beings.

When designers look to the desirable formal or performative qualities within evolved organisms for inspiration, this is called *biomimicry* or *biometrics. Biophilia*, a hypothesis developed by entomologist E. O. Wilson which implicates human interest in biomimicry, suggests that there is a deep, instinctual bond between humans and other living systems. The Biophilia theory was subsequently utilized to develop the discipline of *Restorative Environmental Design* which takes the position that architecture must not only reduce its harmful environmental impacts, but should leverage humans' "innate affinity for the natural environment as an essential source of physical and mental wellbeing and productivity" (Kellert, 2004). Restorative environmental design is comprised of both design and research arms in order to utilize physiological, psychological, and ecological data to develop and justify its design principles.

Architecture was once inextricably linked with the environment. Vitruvius's *Ten Books on Architecture* include chapters whose titles demonstrate the importance of harnessing and using desired natural forces in the production of architecture: "On Climate as Determining the Style of the House," "The Proper Exposures of the Different Rooms," and "The Directions of the Streets; with Remarks on the Winds." In our era of climate change, as architecture redefines relationships with environmental conditions, looming, temporal questions emerge for environmentally driven design. How can architecture support and enhance ecosystem services over long durations? Is it possible for architecture to successfully adapt, and ultimately thrive, through massive environmental system state changes? What are the relationships between architectural, geologic, climactic, and ecological timescales, particularly in this era of accelerating environmental change?

Equity: Ensuring Equality and Justice for All Beings

Equity falls second within the 3 E hierarchy because it signifies the role of humanity within the larger activity of negotiating environmental conditions. Because humans innately experience environment through the perspective of the human body it is difficult to construct a clear separation between environment and equity. Equity is synonymous with the state of being equal or fair. Human history has been rife with political inequality, much of it originating from control over natural or other resources, or disinterest in accommodating or embracing alternate viewpoints. Within sustainability theory, the function of equity is so critical because it promotes respect for diversity and shared control of resources which leads to their increasingly even distribution. Together these create of a sense of *community*, the socio-political structure which tends to circumvent short-sighted, resource costly conflict, ultimately enabling long-duration cultivation and equitable, balanced resource use.

Though the American and French Revolutions of the late eighteenth century are seen as conical moments in the western world that formulated attention around political inequalities, issues related to equity in social, cultural, and political arenas have been addressed periodically throughout global history. But the theoretical trajectory that led directly to equity as it is understood by sustainability today was not articulated until the late-twentieth century. Its direct roots lie in Ghandi's socio-environmental practice of non-violent protest in the South African and Indian self-rule movements, which were, in turn, translated into King's leadership of the American civil rights movement beginning in the mid-twentieth century. These political movements, and others related to the liberation of oppressed groups of people, seeded the development of disciplines and movements such as ethnic studies in the late 1960s, deep ecology and ecofeminism in the early 1970s, green politics and post-colonial studies in the late 1970s, environmental justice in the early 1980s, and posthumanism and transgenderism in the 1990s. These practices have contextualized understandings of the complexities of cultural form as it relates to the structuring and management of equitable relationships between self-expression, space, resources, mobilized toxic concentrations, and all human and non-human species.

Despite these advances, today the incompatibility of human generational and environmental timeframes, particularly geologic timescales, is the root of significant environmental disturbance. The human generation of 20–35 years defines periodic durations of attention, timescales of action, and continuums of memory. This generational timeframe is further subdivided as cultural, political, economic, and technological cycles that accelerate human actions which feedback into the larger environment. Rapid and continuing global urbanization fueled by unprecedented resource availability and accelerating economic reporting cycles is one example of the kind of anthropocentric activity that is currently catalyzing the de-stabilization of the climactic system that supports the global collective.

As political concern over destabilizing human-environment interactions emerged in the 1970s, particularly in reference to growing *resource inequity* between the global north and global south, the seeds of sustainable development were planted. In the 1950s–1960s symptoms of environmental impacts in the developed global north catalyzed the environmental movement to focus on numerous issues, including DDT concentrations in the food chain, post-atomic detonation radiation, and the socio-environmental devastation caused by large dams and other energy generating strategies. In the developing global south, where basic physiological and safety needs are still generally not met, the environmental issues continue to be dramatically different. Equitable access to and distribution of resources such as food, fuel, and shelter in relationship to environmental carrying capacities are priorities, particularly as developed world lifestyles migrate to developing world consumption patterns putting increasing pressure on already stressed resources. Basic safety and security instigated by environmental change is another critical issue as more and more people become environmental refugees. This situation is exacerbated by the fact that environmental degradation, in the form of airborne greenhouse gases, toxins, and hazardous wastes, is primarily initiated by industrialized nations of the global north while their impacts are experienced most dramatically in the global south.

In order to reconcile these divergent environmental contexts and needs, in 1987 the UN World Commission on Environment and Development linked issues of environmental protection to the seemingly unrelated topics of equity and global growth and development (Sitarz, 1993). These resulted in the Brundtland Report which birthed the current definition of sustainability, and several years later the United Nations Agenda 21 series of voluntary non-binding environmentally, socially, economically, and culturally sensitive implementation plans. From these, movements such as *environmental justice* emerged, which seeks to empower people disproportionately exposed to environmental risks and harms. Critical to the success of such movements is the identification of all *stakeholders*, groups or individuals who have vested interest in particular aspects of the socio-environmental condition, particularly those who are oppressed such as women, children, and minorities, and those with alternative viewpoints. By working collaboratively with all stakeholders to build *consensus*, general agreement and harmony among all parties, through the utilization of consensus decision-making processes, more equitable outcomes are facilitated.

Issues related to the equity of stakeholders and consensus become increasingly complicated as they extend into diverse populations, including minorities, children, and those that are physically and mentally challenged. *Universal design* is a design approach that ensures that products and buildings can be utilized by the full population, regardless of their abilities or disabilities. Ultimately the equity of stakeholders is most challenged by the inclusion of all living beings (non-human others), particularly those that produce the ecosystem services humans rely upon for survival. Without shared languages to facilitate consensus, how are we to better provide for their needs while simultaneously mining their by-products without exploitation? *Posthuman* theory further explicates the logistical and ethical complications inherent in structuring mutualistic relationships between ourselves and non-human others as technologies increasingly permeate the collective matrix.

Architecture is, by definition, a *technology*, one that exists ubiquitously within this matrix. Therefore, as architects design they create operational mash-ups of technologically facilitated services, both high and low-tech, that intentionally serve clients while typically unintentionally impacting others and the environment. The larger ethical implications of technological use often remain unconsidered because “technologies belong to the realm of means and morality to the realm of ends” (Latour, 2002). Equity, within the context of sustainable design, seeks to further links between the "realm of means" and the "realm of ends" by tempering and balancing technological usage with *traditional wisdom*, hybrid ethical-practical forms of knowledge which have been tested and filtered through multiple generations, thereby ensuring sustainability. The Great Binding Law of the Iroquois dictates a procedure for deploying traditional wisdom which has come to be known as the *seven generation sustainability principle*. It has commonly been interpreted as "looking ahead … to make every decision that we make relate to the welfare and wellbeing of the seventh generation to come" (Lyons, 1994). This requires understanding and consideration of the long-term effects of technological usage on the larger collective matrix.

Today, American architects typically design for one generation, approximately thirty years, which conveniently correlates with the timespan of a residential mortgage. In order to facilitate more sustainable and equitable forms of architecture, the pre-design phase would incorporate the formation of design parameters that consider the increasingly equitable socio-environmental conditions of *user*, and timeframe, so that *program* may be realigned to the specific interface of user, culture, and socio-ecological context of site. As the discipline of architecture engages in more sophisticated conversations related to socio-environmental equity, Louis Kahn inspired questions relating to *who is serviced and who is servicing?* gain expanded relevance and meaning, triggering others including: Who are architecture's clients through time? How does architecture provide access for all of these clients? How are program and site redefined given more equitable socio-environmental understandings? How can architecture accommodate, or better yet, support the full diversity of the collective of all beings?

Economy: Calibrating Relationships Between Natural Resources and Socio-Economic Systems

Economy resides third in the 3 E hierarchy because today it is exceedingly difficult to accomplish sustainable performance without its influence. Socio-environmental responses were occurring before humans developed collective systems that negotiated and bartered value; however, the global economy is currently the facilitating and mediating force through which almost all activity is accomplished, including architecture. Economies, by definition, are comprised of the collective production, use, and transfer of capital that facilitates the management and consumption of resources to meet household and community needs. Until the early 1960s, when the sub-discipline of environmental economics was born, economists did not consider the environment. Since then, disciplines and movements linking conceptual frameworks and actual economic market forces to the environment have proliferated. These have created new modes of valuation that not only capture previously non-market environmental and social goods and services, but greatly further equity and expanded sustainability agendas.

Environmental economics came into its own in the wake of the American environmental movement initially to analyze the cost benefit ratios of scarce natural resources. The discipline utilizes the concept of *externality* extensively, a cost to the marketplace that is not factored into the market price. Externalities include raw materials and ecosystem services, anything that is extracted from or damages earth systems that is not paid for via reinvestment, such as oil, pollution, or the hydrologic cycling/cleaning of water. Externalities are considered market failures in economic terminology. Up to a point, humans do not experience the symptoms of environmental degradation resulting from these activities, so there is little reason for their cost to be factored into market prices. Additionally, the value of these materials and services can be difficult to quantify, rendering them problematic to price within the marketplace. So, often they are simply not paid for, until the resource becomes scarce and the market price goes up, or the quality of the service is degraded to the point that humans must intervene, as in the case of constructing costly wastewater treatment plants.

As environmental economists struggled to capture the measurement of environmental and sustainability indicators within gross national product (GNP) they developed additional tools such as *net national product (NNP)* which more accurately measures human wellbeing. This spawned the development of numerous other indicators including: *green gross domestic product (green GDP)* which is an index of economic growth that factors in environmental consequences, and *gross national happiness (GNH)*, developed by the Bhutanese Government to measure their national success not exclusively in terms of economic output.

Also central to the theory of environmental economics is the ability to classify and control shared environmental goods or resources. Economists identify four categories of goods based on their ability to be exclusive and obtained via rivalry. *Private goods* are excludable and rivalrous, and are therefore easily discernable within the marketplace; examples include food, clothing, and residential architecture. *Club goods* are also excludable, but non-rivalrous, and are relatively easily controlled within the marketplace; examples include private parks and cable television. *Common goods* or *common-pool resources* are non-excludable and rivalrous, which renders them difficult to control in the marketplace; examples include fisheries and timber. Common goods present unique environmental challenges in terms of sustainability because they are easily over-harvested, which may produce immediate abundant yields, but ensure future yields will be minimal or nonexistent; a recent example is the collapse of a major Atlantic fishery. *Public goods* are non-excludable and non-rivalrous, therefore they are non-market goods that are exceedingly difficult to police; examples include clean air and national defense. Public goods also present unique environmental challenges for sustainable development. Solving common and public good issues requires increasing basic standards of living for all, often despite increasing populations and finite resources, without causing further environmental degradation. "Economic and environmental sustainability depends upon redressing global inequities of income and material well-being" (Hawken, Loving, & Lovins, 1999). This is a monumental task that is only accomplished collectively.

Ecological economics emerged in the 1980s in response to the more mainstream economic analytical approaches of environmental economics. Inspired by a pioneering article presented in 1966 by Kenneth Boulding titled "The Economics of the Coming Spaceship Earth," ecological economics assumes earth systems have a finite carrying capacity and attempts to develop economic systems that respect this carrying capacity while preserving natural capital. It is an interdisciplinary, and more radical economic approach that borrows extensively from ecological systems modeling.

While ecological economics adopted a top-down approach, *natural capitalism*, which emerged a decade later, took a more grassroots approach. Calling for the valuation of all forms of capital framed within a pragmatic approach, natural capitalism outlines four central strategies that support living systems and perpetuate abundance: 1. radical resource productivity, 2. biomimicry, 3. service and flow economy, and 4. investing in natural capital (Hawken, Loving, & Lovins, 1999). By repositioning the capitalist market to first and foremost value socio-environmental systems, and then generate the next industrial revolution based on the development and deployment of sustainable and green eco-technologies, this approach has significant potential to impact the discipline of architecture. In 2011, this was made explicit in Jeremy Rifkin's proposed Third Industrial Revolution. His manifesto deeply implicates architecture via power generation and distribution mechanisms that transform "the building stock [and infrastructure] of every continent into green micro-power plants to collect [and store] renewable energy on-site" (Rifkin, 2011). While this alternate economy currently exists as a scenario, this and other proposals of sustainable futures are laying the foundation for the continued transformation of green architectural design.

As hybrid socio-environmental-economic drivers facilitate and mediate architectural production, which in turn feeds-back into the global economy, economic and regulatory architectural design drivers nudge the discipline toward more sustainable forms and technologies. Today, increasingly sophisticated financing mechanisms, along with the growing political concern for global equity, and proposals related to the re-valuation of architecture within the expanded field have grown. Yet value-engineering is still the predominant mode of interface between design and the marketplace. These contradictory modes of operation inspire questions related to expanding the potential sites of architectural agency and valuation within the marketplace. Other questions emerge relating to the roles and value of the use of human labor vs. material excess, the potentials for increasing resource productivity within architecture's domain, and the roles architects might play in developing new sustainable technologies and operational methodologies. Ultimately, we must ask how will socio-environmental valuation affect architecture's form and performance in the twenty-first century?

Future Prospects for Sustainable Architecture: Scope, Meaning, and Relevance for Sustainable Design in the Twenty-first Century

The millennium brought with it a legacy of siloed thinking, evident even within the interdisciplinary environmental movement. Historically environmentalists have partitioned themselves within four camps of thought and operation: the quantifiable arena of the laboratory (the eco-techs), the socio-ecological construction of the landscape (the counter-culture movement), the political arena of sustainable development (green parties), and the socio-economic arena of corporate environmentalism (the Googles). Each approach has had major impacts on environmental health globally, but none has successfully circumvented or solved the increasingly complicated socio-environmental issues we experience today. Climate change, for example, is classified as a *wicked* problem (Rittel & Webber, 1984), i.e. one that is difficult to define, and contains no discreet solution. Wicked problems require the application of diverse knowledge sets and approaches which necessitate a blurring of boundaries between disciplines. Sustainability theory, through its holistic construction, hierarchizing, and dynamic blending of the 3 Es, provides a framework that facilitates this deeply interdisciplinary incorporation.

Architecture, by definition, is a situated endeavor. As the discipline globalizes, the contexts of global north versus south present radically different sets of problems and potential solutions. Today, these disparate contexts collide with increasing frequency, ultimately merging, which further complicates the design process. Currently, the north exists within a post-growth economy, requiring architectural responses to shift toward the transformation of existing building stock, renovating and retrofitting both structures and brownfield sites. As architects expand their scope of services and increasingly work at infrastructural scale, this context requires the stabilization of aging infrastructure and the hybridization of existing and new technologies. In contrast, significant portions of the south are in growth economies where new construction dominates, potentially facilitating the innovation of material sourcing and modes of construction. New, intelligent, lightweight, infrastructural technologies dominate. Going forward, architects equipped with increasingly diverse knowledge sets and hybrid high/low-tech capacities, who are interested in balancing their application with intelligence and wisdom, will likely produce the most innovative, effective, and appropriate sustainable solutions.

Despite the seemingly insurmountable rift between the global north and south, it is becoming clear that certain temporally responsive, multi-scalar approaches, such as ecological frameworks, are effective bridging constructs. Ecological systems modeling provides mechanisms to capture and test flows of energy and matter. This tool can be mapped to complex systems that share structural and relational typologies with natural systems, including the built architectural environments already operating within these ecological systems, and the socio-environmental constructs that channel them. When a temporal lens is applied to architecture, the building envelope appears as a device of feedback, in perpetual transformation, subject to ecological frameworks of change such as disturbance regimes, population dynamics, successional process, and system state changes. Climate change, adaptation, and ultimately sustainability are only comprehensible through this temporal lens. As environmental stimuli become increasingly dynamic via patterns and processes native to different geographies, the premises upon which we base architectural production expands in scope and scale. Geographies heavily impacted by climate change such as coastlines may ultimately require shorter-duration, inexpensive, biodegradable, disposable building types, while more stable geographies may require long-duration, more expensive, durably constructed, programmatically adaptable building types. Many geographies would benefit from building types that support natural systems and increase natural capital such as the soil-based *Living Architecture* proposed by Rachel Armstrong. Ultimately, all geographies and inhabitants would benefit from architectures that have been conceptualized as larger systems, from their raw material extraction through their operable useful life and into their end of life disposal or renewal/rebirth, generating a more sustainable disciplinary conversation.

When an interdisciplinary, multi-scalar lens is applied to architecture, the building envelope appears as a device of mediation between humans' and the larger environment's health. We can zoom into the human body and apply current physiology to better understand how the body most effectively receives inputs and produces outputs such as thermal energy and physical/chemical compositions of air. We can zoom out to the global scale and apply current climate change science to better understand how thermal energy, carbon, and other chemical concentrations are interacting and circulating through the environment. Finally we can focus on the mediating building envelope and apply cutting-edge building science and engineering to better understand how the envelope should be redesigned to better provision the services of equity, comfort, and health to both the body and the planet. This framework would effectively replace traditional building technology and construction industry approaches which have not kept pace with the technological advances in most other sectors over the last 100 years.

Instead, today we categorize the sustainable production of architecture into four relatively static methodologies or categories: vernacular structures or those inspired by bioclimactic strategies, green guidelines which are essentially "prescriptions" of best practices for sustainable design, rating systems which utilize pre-determined valuation or benchmarking strategies to determine a quantification of sustainability, and signature sustainable buildings which are so low in quantity that they are essentially demonstration projects of sustainable strategies (Addington & Kilbert, 2006, 2012). Compounding the problem, most metrics for determining or quantifying sustainability utilize energy efficiency as a significant indicator, which is based on a false and pessimistic pretense of thermodynamics (Moe, 2013). These current paradigms leave the discipline of architecture little territory for innovating or integrating sustainability at the depth and scale necessary to create long-duration productive relationships between bodies, buildings, culture, and global environmental systems.

In order to support this next level of integration, architecture must construct a platform that supports necessary increases in research and development, not just project delivery. The profession's current business model is unsustainable. Profit margins are exceedingly low which creates crippling instability within firms. Liability is excessive, and whole generations of architects cannot enter, or are forced to leave the discipline when the economy downturns, taking valuable expertise and experience with them. In order to shore up the practice of architecture, architects need to increase their scope of services and value those services comparably with other professions (Bernstein & Ramos, 2007).

The pursuit of sustainability creates opportunities for innovation and collaboration with allied disciplines to develop design expertise in service sectors such as retrofit and rehabilitation, material technology and recycling innovation, supply chains, service oriented design, natural capital generation, ultra-performative constructed environments, and performance evaluation mechanisms. Each of these sectors is multi-disciplinary in nature, and will require a continuing retooling of architectural pedagogy to supply this workforce.

In the age of the Anthropocene the discipline of architecture has daunting constraints which ultimately produce incredible opportunity. As we increasingly understand our species as simultaneous client and agent of environmental change, it is architecture's role to spatially and temporally construct built relationships between the medical, the cultural, and the ecological, utilizing the tool of economics. Through the innovation of design approaches, funneled through tried and true architectural design processes, architecture has the potential to transform, while stabilizing the form and performance of the lithosphere. The deployment of core disciplinary knowledge integrated with innovative strategies and technologies can facilitate the achievement of contextualized, balanced, intelligent, and wise architectural approaches that will ensure an increasingly cohesive continuum of sustainable understandings and applications in the twenty-first century and beyond.

Acknowledgments

The author would like to thank Aron Chang, the Santa Fe Institute, and Carey Clouse for their assistance in writing this chapter.

References

Addington, M. & Kilbert, C. (2006, 2012). Lectures.

Anderson, T. (1988). *Resilient Computing Systems*, Volume 2. New York: John Wiley & Sons, Inc.

Bernstein, P. & Ramos, J.P. (2007). Lectures.

Collins, S.L. *et al.* (2010). An Integrated Conceptual Framework for Long-Term Social–Ecological Research. *Frontiers in Ecology and the Environment*: doi:10.1890/100068.

Crutzen, P. (2002). Geology of Mankind. *Nature* 415. doi: 10.1038/415023a

Fitch, J.M. & Bobenhausen, W. (1999). *American Building: The Environmental Forces that Shape It*. Oxford: Oxford University Press.

Gunderson, L. (2000). Ecological Resilience—In Theory and Application. *Annual Review of Ecological Systems* 31: 425–427.

Hawken, P., Loving, A. & Lovins, L.H. (1999). *Natural Capitalism: Creating the Next Industrial Revolution*. New York: Little, Brown and Company.

Holling, C.S. & Goldberg, M.A. (1971). Ecology and Planning. *Journal of the American Institute of Planners* 37(2): 221–230.

Kellert, S. (2004). Beyond LEED: From Low Environmental Impact to Restorative Environmental Design. Keynote Address at the Greening Rooftops for Sustainable Communities Conference, Portland, Oregon.

Latour, B. (2002). Morality and Technology: The End of the Means. Trans. Venn, C. Theory, *Culture & Society* 19(5/6): 247–240.

Lyons, O. (1994). An Iroquois Perspective. In C. Vecsey& R.W, Venables (eds), *American Indian Environments: Ecological Issues in Native American History*. New York: Syracuse University Press.

Millennium Ecosystem Assessment. (2005). *Ecosystems and Human Well-being: Synthesis*. Washington D.C.: Island Press.

Moe, K. (2013). *Convergence: An Architectural Agenda for Energy*. New York: Routledge.

Moore, S. (2007). Models, Lists and the Evolution of Sustainable Architecture. In K. Tanzer & R. R. Longoria (eds), *The Green Braid*, New York: Taylor and Francis, Inc.

Rifkin, J. (2011). *The Third Industrial Revolution: How Lateral Power is Transforming Energy, The Economy, and the World*. New York: Palgrave Macmillan.

Rittel, H. & Webber, M. (1984). Planning Problems are Wicked Problems. In *Developments in Design Methodology*, ed. Cross, N. New York: John Wiley & Sons.

Schwartz, A. & Jax, K. (2011). Etymology and Original Sources of the Term 'Ecology.' In A. Schwartz, & K. Jax (eds), *Ecology Revisited: Reflecting on Concepts, Advancing Science*, Dordrecht: Springer.

Sitarz, D. (1993). *Agenda 21: The Earth Summit Strategy to Save Our Planet*. New York: Nova Publishing Company.

World Commission on Environment and Development. (1987). *Our Common Future* (The Brundtland Report). Accessed July 10, 2014, http://www.un-documents.net/ocf-02.htm#I.

13

Social Equity and Ethics in Design of Sustainable Built Environments

Geraldine Forbes Isais and Laura L. Harjo

Introduction

Social equity is a term fraught with value and meaning that can strike anxiety in the hearts of many developers and designers. In this chapter we consider the ways that enacting social equity can function as a win-win venture for all parties. We also introduce social equity and contemporary conversations, related aspects of power, agency and capital. We then proceed with ideas of co-creation as a design approach to social equity and introduce case studies from Los Angeles and New Mexico. Each respective case study illustrates the conditions within which a win-win venture can happen and, conversely, an inadvertent win-lose case can occur. One Los Angeles example focuses on the "LA Live" development in the University Park/downtown area of Los Angeles. It demonstrates examples of equity carried out in an intentional way through community benefit agreements with a set of actors that might have otherwise engaged in an oppositional trajectory of LA Live's development. While equity does not have to emerge from an oppositional scenario, inequity can emerge quietly and unintentionally. The second case study, the Tribal Services Center at Isleta Pueblo, is an example of precisely that, the unintended consequences of designing places within a community space with insufficient understanding of the subtle cultural symbols of the community. This then demonstrates how designers and developers can misinterpret a differentiated program requirement and a community symbol. This symbol, visible on the landscape, becomes a misinterpretation of a community value.

In writing this chapter we do not presume to have all the answers to this complex social dynamic. We do wish, however, to identify and describe methods of practice in which developers, architects and community members can design a working methodology that decentralizes the gaze and production from the position of the creator/designer, to consider the subjective position of the community member, hence that of the collective, leading to a co-creative development process.

Concepts of Equity

Sustainability is not limited to the support of ecological systems, nor to judiciously parsing out resources. It is also tied to people and their deeper needs, both physical and psychological. It considers the question of how alienation from equitable places where communities dwell dilute the very practices and rituals that sustain them (Littig & Griessler, 2005). For example, in Taos Pueblo it is important to the members to create and maintain a community that enables them to perpetuate cultural practices that have existed for centuries. There are, however, outside pressures and challenges to these cultural practices. Both the fields of architecture and planning have codified standards of social equity and ethics, requiring these standards in the practice of their licensed professionals. We should, however, consider this the floor and not the ceiling when applying these minimums in a practice situation.

There are multiple subjectivities at stake here—the developer, the design team, the client, communities of difference, communities that reside on or adjacent to the site, invisible and visible communities involved in projects, communities within the commodity chain of the project. Our primary focus is on how the design process is practiced by architects and planners and its impact on the community.

Equity

David Harvey's "Right to the City," argues for the democratic participation in the condition of the city. He builds his argument for this by tracing the polarization of economic classes (Harvey, 2003). The elite and wealthy class, or in more contemporary terms, the 1 percent, are the controlling class, lording over how and in what ways space(s) is developed. Harvey continues, the political and economic elite are shaping the city and its spaces. If we move forward from this claim that the contemporary city is experiencing increased control and oversight by private firms instead of state or local governments, then the problem is in part that there is no requirement to allow local input or control. Furthermore, history has demonstrated that people who do not feel they have some level of power and or control over their living conditions, especially those living in marginalized situations, eventually organize and advocate for themselves. The type of organizing and advocacy is predicated on the level of inclusion they feel from those in power—owners, developers, legislators, design professionals and others with decision-making power over their space in the Commons.

For instance, the Los Angeles riots of 1992, were initially a response to the Rodney King verdict, which was a high profile case wherein white Los Angeles police officers were found not guilty after Rodney King, a black motorist was brutally beaten (Baldassare, 1994; Navarro, 1993). In this complex case the oppositional response resulted from the belief that proper justice was not delivered. It was the responsibility of the state to deliver justice, however, the private sector was subjected to the repercussions. Initially a political riot, it eventually turned into a bread riot, predicated on poverty and anger that resulted in stores being looted (Pastor, 2010). Further, rioters targeted Korean businesses hence transferring a sense of ethnic and class difference, thus furthering the polarization of class and power in all their neighborhoods (Chang, 1993).

Los Angeles is a city known for its social movements, societal upheavals and community-driven response to undesired and unsustainable living conditions. People want equity; they do not want decisions and conditions foisted on them by small groups of decision-makers. Citizens have responded accordingly from labor protests, to Watts and the 1992 Rodney King riots, to the spin-off of the 2011 Occupy Wall Street movement—Occupy Los Angeles.

People feeling that they have no power over a crisis, or a set of unacceptable conditions, respond.

Social Equity

As professionals, the larger question then is what motivates us to respond in ways that support justice and fairness in our work? We start with the concept of social equity which we must disentangle from equality. Equality means that citizens are entitled to equal access under the law, while equity postulates the idea of fairness. Equality is often conflated with fairness. Race Forward: The Center for Racial Justice Innovation, stresses the idea of focusing on impact rather than intent (Race Forward, 2014). While one might not explicitly intend to impact a community in an undesirable manner, unintentional development outcomes can result in unfair or inequitable impacts. Thus as the focus shifts to impacts and outcomes, it also moves toward methods of development and design that empower stakeholders and encourage those in power to share, thus enabling decisions where all stakeholders win.

Social equity is guided by the principle that members of certain classes are protected by United States law, while other groups still seek recognition, power and rights within the American legal system. According to the Race Forward: The Center for Racial Justice Innovation, social inequity is distinguished as unfairness. Thus, social equity implicates the alienation of groups based on difference, which can mean, for example, economic class—rich, working class, age, gender, race, ethnicity, familial status, ability/disability.

Cultural Equity

The following three terms, race, ethnicity and culture, tend to be slippery and are often conflated as they can overlap and be inclusive of each other. At the crux, is the underlying concept that these constructs operate as apparatuses of difference within modern society. These tend to be defined as received wisdom of the group in power, hence one of the tasks in thinking through what the concepts of race, ethnicity and culture mean is to look to writers and how they discuss them. Omi and Winant conceive of race as a socially constructed identity (Omi, 1994). They argue that race is a fairly recent construct of the modern world, and that it is a response by European explorers encountering groups of people that did not look like them (Omi, 1994).

Cultural equity, is distinguished as "the right of every culture to safeguard, express, and develop its artistic and expressive heritage," is another type of equity to be considered (Association for Cultural Equity, 2014). While cultural manner and artistic expression might not always be protected under civil rights law, there is a responsibility to know and enable the perpetuation of folk life at all scales (Association for Cultural Equity, 2014).

Another task required of the planning and design team is to review the individual and project team assumptions relative to what socio-cultural means in every new project context. This is particularly important in the early stages of a project as the design team enters and engages a community and begins its work. Reflecting on the case studies examined by Lisa Findley in "Building Change; Architecture, Politics and Cultural Agency" she states that "in order to respect, promote and symbolize the clients' agency and in order to respond to the evolving political and cultural context, architects had to rethink many of the usual processes and products of design" (Findley, 2005). Defining and redefining standard terms and practices for every new project is necessary, yet it requires the difficult task of translating community ideas and developer requirements into built form. This situation reveals conditions under which inequity might occur, while also, as in the cases studies examined by Findley, presents opportunities to take equitable action in all stages of the design process.

Contrasting Case Studies: You Decide, Who Wins, Who Loses?

Gratts Primary Center and Early Education Center, Los Angeles, California

West of downtown Los Angeles, just north of the busy Wilshire Boulevard corridor, lies an older neighborhood of primarily multi-story wood frame apartments that continue to house waves of immigrant families from Latin America and beyond. This densely populated urban area was identified by the Los Angeles Unified School District (LAUSD) as one that was in need of an educational center to strengthen the bond between the local school and the community. In order to accomplish this objective LAUSD sought to establish a joint-use project, including multiple educational and community programs. LAUSD identified community partners, New Schools/Better Neighborhoods, A Community of Friends, who teamed-up throughout the process to ensure a balanced working relationship between the project's educational leaders, Jubany Architecture, the developer of a new adjacent affordable housing project which housed a Boys and Girls Club and the surrounding neighborhood. What evolved was a campus designed for both student and after-school public access, including sports events, community meetings and public gatherings.

The design team was challenged by the 30-foot elevation change across the site, the traffic, urban noise and pollution and limited budget. However, the slope was used to create three school entrances, one on the southern edge for the Early Education Center accommodating separate drop-offs for pre-school, second graders, the second for the Primary center which shifted northward with impressive downtown skyline views. The third view was a ramp designed as a special entrance for the community. This entrance allowed community members to go directly to the multi-purpose room without crossing paths used exclusively by the children. This path also gave the community access to the school's fields for after-school recreation activity. From inception the project goal was to design an educational resource for the community. The intention allowed the architects to innovate a solution.

Isleta Pueblo Tribal Services center, Isleta, New Mexico

The indigenous people of New Mexico trace their history to a time so long ago that for them place, space and cultural history are inextricably intertwined. The Puebloan people were builders. They constructed adobe dwellings, meeting spaces and sacred structures that acknowledged and aligned with sacred astronomical phenomena. The Pueblo of Isleta evolved from that tradition. It is located just south of Albuquerque, New Mexico and is one of the nineteen pueblos situated in New Mexico's Rio Grande Valley. In 2010, the tribal leadership at Isleta Pueblo decided to build a Tribal Services Facility that would house the Tribe's fire, police, emergency 911, courts, council and administration functions in one complex. Situated in a natural depression that lies between the Rio Grande Bosque and the Manzano Mountains, the architects designed a two-level facility, with four distinct volumes. The buildings are finished with finely detailed white stucco corten steel framing a bold central plaza. From the nearby freeway the only visible form is the facility's council chamber, a place designed by the architects to be of cultural significance. Accordingly, it is a curved glazed structure, exquisitely wrapped, by beautifully finished stainless steel tubes that are in a woven pattern much like a traditional "jacal" structure. Ironically, many tribal members are confused by the allusion as they read the symbol to represent a woven basket. In discussing the council chamber a tribal member explained that he and other tribal members are mystified by their interpretation of the symbolic meaning, as he stated " um ... we make pottery not baskets" (Isleta Tribal Member, personal communication, January 4, 2014).

The LA Live Case Study

LA Live is an entertainment development that broke ground in 2005. In the southern downtown area of Los Angeles, nestled between the University of Southern California and downtown, AEG was the developer and initially there were plans to develop a large entertainment complex which would host shops, restaurants, theaters, a large concert venue and the Grammy Museum. The Staples Center, home to the Los Angeles Lakers, was also part of LA Live. Before the development could get started it faced opposition in the local neighborhoods. A continuous concern of local residents was jobs, adequate parking when local residents returned home after work, affordable rent and places to recreate, such as soccer fields.

Developers and decision-makers embarked on this large-scale development with very little to no input from local residents who would be impacted by this large and imposing development. This drew the ire of the local community and organizations. In particular, Strategic Action for a Just Economy (SAJE), zeroed in on the situation and responded by organizing community members that opposed the project. Consequently, the community waged a battle in opposition to the development and the lack of inclusivity. SAJE secure, legal representation to expedite their agenda of community input in the development process (Saito, 2012; Leavitt, 2006). AEG yielded to a set of demands from the community which materialized as community benefits (Peña & Parshall, 2001). What eventually became negotiated were allowances, jobs and green space. The community maintained that the development was going to take land and they asked for green space that would have soccer fields (soccer is a popular sport in the neighborhood). Furthermore, they asked that AEG provide employment opportunities for local residents, and they asked that this be carried out in a meaningful way that did not promise and not deliver.

We will now examine this case study in terms of power, agency and capital, as these are important concepts in equity and justice, in the practice of developing, planning, designing and building the physical environment. By power we mean who has the authority to act, by agency we mean who has the ability to act, and by capital we mean who has the economic assets to support the actions. These are three interlocking ideas that can be difficult to separate but we see how the community was able to draw upon the numbers of concerned residents, and legal counsel to create power and agency. They may not have initially had the power to act nor the agency to enact their idea, however after uniting as a group and moving forward with their demands that favored the community they took possession of transformative power and agency at the front end of the development process. The community still lacked capital; however they overcame this shortcoming via astute community organizing and action. We find in this case that the party with the capital does not always hold all the power, even in the case of a private developer (Cummings, 2006). If the developers had been willing to work upfront with the community or were cognizant and responsive to community concerns at the outset they would have saved themselves money and time. In a different case, this could have involved a sincere community input phase in which people could feel that their objections had been recognized and responded to within the developer's best abilities.

Conclusion

William Peña, first published *Problem Seeking: An Architectural Programming Primer* in 1969 (Peña & Parshall, 2001). This celebrated work was "the text" for years in determining the steps one took to develop an architectural project program. The five steps were: 1. establish goals; 2. collect and analyze facts; 3. uncover and test concepts, 4. determine needs; 5. state the problem. In addition, one was advised to additionally consider the following four design determinants: function, form, economy and time. After evaluating the aforementioned one would compose a "premise for the design" leading to design criteria which later would be used to "evaluate the design solution." To his credit, Peña codified the notion that a programmer had to expand the levels to include "the political considerations of urban problems." Included among six others of these considerations are "client structure and decision-making" and "user involvement." Hence the seed was sown for an analysis of "user involvement."

The struggle for a voice in the design process has been hard fought. In 2007 Craig Wilkens writes in his book *The Aesthetics of Equity,*

> Architecture—which has a long history of being used to perpetuate dichotomy and marginalization—has since the 1960's overtly viewed the urban condition as an inevitable illustration of the pathologies of its residents, becoming a place to mitigate, not to cultivate.
>
> (Wilkins, 2007)

Yet today the conversations that precede development and design often recognize the politics associated with spatial and building realities. Fifty years after William Peña alluded to the legitimacy of the user's or community's voice, contemporary architects have the opportunity to embrace social equity thus re-framing the definition of a successful building project.

References

Association for Cultural Equity. (2014). Association for Cultural Equity. Retrieved June 10, 2014, from http://www.culturalequity.org/ace/ce_ace_index.php

Baldassare, M. (Ed.). (1994). *The Los Angeles Riots: Lessons for the Urban Future*. Boulder, CO: Westview Press.

Chang, E. T. (1993). Los Angeles Riots and Korean-African American Conflict. *Korean and Korean-American Studies Bulletin*, *4*, 3, 10–11.

Cummings, S.L. (2006). Mobilization Lawyering: Community Economic Development in the Figueroa Corridor. *UCLA School of Law*. Los Angeles: UCLA School of Law. Retrieved from: http://escholarship.org/uc/item/1ht5s8nj

Findley, L. (2005). *Building change: Architecture, Politics and Cultural Agency*. London: Routledge.

Harvey, D. (2003). The Right to the City. *International Journal of Urban and Regional Research*, *27*, 4, 939–941.

Leavitt, J. (2006). Linking Housing to Community Economic Development with Community Benefits Agreements. In Ong, P. & Loukaitou-Sideris, A. (Eds.), *Jobs and Economic Development in Minority Communities*, 257–276. Philadelphia, PA: Temple University Press.

Littig, B., & Griessler, E. (2005). Social Sustainability: A Catchword between Political Pragmatism and Social Theory. *International Journal of Sustainable Development*, *8*, 1, 65–79.

Navarro, A. (1993). The South Central Los Angeles Eruption: A Latino Perspective. *Amerasia Journal*, *19*, 2, 69–85.

Omi, M. (1994). *Racial Formation in the United States: From the 1960s to the 1990s*. New York: Psychology Press.

Pastor, M. (2010). Contemporary Voice: Contradictions, Coalitions. In W. Deverell and G. Hise (Eds.), *A Companion to Los Angeles*. Oxford: Wiley-Blackwell, 257.

Peña, W. M., & Parshall, S. A. (2001). *Problem Seeking: An Architectural Programming Primer*. Hoboken, NJ: John Wiley & Sons.

Race Forward: The Center for Racial Justice Innovation (2014). Moving the Race Conversation Forward: How the Media Covers Racism, and Other Barriers to Productive Racial Discourse. Retrieved September 9, 2014, From: https://www.raceforward.org/research/reports/moving-race-conversation-forward

Saito, L. T. (2012). How LowIncome Residents Can Benefit from Urban Development: The LA Live Community Benefits Agreement. *City & Community*, *11*, 2, 129–150.

Wilkins, C. L. (2007). *The Aesthetics of Equity: Notes on Race, Space, Architecture, and Music*. Minneapolis, MN: University of Minnesota Press.

14

Integrative Design Practices

Twenty-First Century Building for Sustainability

Marvin J. Malecha

Integrative strategies in the design professions have been generally defined by a rubric that is characterized by the alliances of people and resources fostering a holistic decision process. Sub measures within this rubric include success in bringing together the necessary talents to accomplish a successful project, the optimization of project objectives, a cost benefit ratio that is attractive to the project financial interests, the meeting of environmental aspirations and general sense of efficiency and timeliness. It is a process that is focused on bringing content to deliberations in a timely fashion making it possible to determine significant directions much earlier in the design process. Integrative practices ensure that as much attention is given to the development of an appropriate project program stressing client and user need as to developing the criteria by which the success of the project will be determined. In short integrative practices, whether for integrated project delivery or for integrated project design, constitute a way of seeing.

Constituting a Way of Seeing: A Metacognitive Approach

Design practices have tended toward sparking innovation from particular client or user needs. As a result the introduction of technology continues to be understood as a direct response to the perceived needs of a particular course of behavior. Henry Ford (2012) observed, "If I had asked people what they wanted, they would have said faster horses." It was the leap of imagination; the abductive choice to consider what does not yet exist that led Henry Ford to the development of the automobile. It can be argued that Henry Ford's efforts to develop the Model T were nothing more than the recombination of existing technologies. In the case of the manufacturing processes developed by Henry Ford, it was the recombination of existing technologies with new approaches including a moving assembly line that constituted the innovation that was realized. Generally held concepts of time and speed of the late nineteenth and early twentieth centuries were as dramatically altered by the automobile as by the early introduction of social media in the late twentieth century. John Dewey (1980), perhaps the most important American philosopher on the matter of imagination further observed in his book *Art and Experience*,

> all conscious experience has of necessity some degree of imaginative quality … that experience becomes conscious, a matter of perception, only when meanings enter it that are derived from prior experiences. Imagination is the only gateway through which these meanings can find their way into present interaction; or rather, the conscious adjustment of the new and the old is imagination.

This is the situation that has arrived in the conduct of the design professions. What was first understood, with the introduction of Building Information Modeling systems, as an enhancement of practice has transformed the conduct of the design professions not only by enhancing practice but also by reconstituting what is practice. It is true that software applications such as Revit have transformed the manner of practice. But it is important not to confuse enhanced capabilities with the essence of what is really underway. Like the efforts of Henry Ford, the first stages of the understanding of integrated practice were little more than the recombination of the stages of practice as they were experienced and generally understood by design professionals. The American Institute of Architects (AIA) along with AIA California Council in the publication *Integrated Project Delivery a Guide* (2007), captures the essence of the transformation beyond software and hardware development.

> Integrated Project Delivery (IPD) is a project delivery approach that integrates people, systems, business structures and practices into a process that collaboratively harnesses the talents and insights of all participants to optimize project results, increase value to the owner, reduce waste, and maximize efficiency through all phases of design, fabrication, and construction. IPD principles can be applied to a variety of contractual arrangements and IPD teams can include members well beyond the basic triad of owner, architect, and contractor. In all cases, integrated projects are uniquely distinguished by highly effective collaboration among the owner, the prime designer, and the prime constructor, commencing at early design and continuing through to project handover.

What has become clear is that the root of integrated design practices is a dramatically altered way of seeing. To understand the implications of integrated practices, it is necessary to consider the very nature of design thought. Designers have long understood the non-linear nature of the creative process. Yet, the means by which the artifacts of this process have been realized were woven into an essentially linear model from schematic design to project realization. Every aspect of design practice from decision matrices to contracts and agreements followed this construct. Integrative practices reconfigure this understanding. A general model is postulated that places information in a three-dimensional frame. Components of a project with respective bits of critical data are placed in context with decision levels articulating not only specific user and client consent but also the related approvals from various government and funding agencies and in context with project program expectations. The frame of critical data, decision metrics and project program expectations assures the ability of the designer and the design team to become highly cognizant of meaningful choices from the earliest steps of the project. The nature of design cognition has been transformed in this model.

Upon reflection it can be discerned that this decision process alters design cognition and transforms the nature of the conceptualization of the building dramatically. It can be observed that this process renders obsolete the traditional approaches to the drawings, maquettes and documents that constitute the earliest conceptions of a project. It is a truism that traditional representation does not capture the vitality of a process that places conception in a three-dimensional frame with the ease and speed of manipulation that is only possible with the most advanced technology. The maquettes once carefully crafted by hand can now be produced by a process of rapid prototyping rendering decisions visible far exceeding the capabilities associated with traditional drawings. When properly embedded in the design process digital tools become an extension of the human hand. The digital and the handmade need not be in conflict. Each has a place and purpose in the integrative design process. Just as integrative design practices have reconstituted the design thought process so too have they created an even more important space in design thought for that which is the result of the most ancient human thought tendencies. It has become clear that integrative processes incorporate traditional thought inclinations as much as they push into the frontiers of thinking and conceiving. Kieran and Timberlake (2008) writing in the monograph *The Loblolly House* provide a concise observation of this aspect of integrative design processes,

> When architecture is simulated through parametric modeling, it becomes counterproductive, even painful to work in a disaggregated manner, where each contributor produces separate design documents ... Each collaborator—builder, owner, architect, engineer, fabricator supplier—contributes to a unified vision of a building to come, already simulated in a solid model.

What is clear is that integrative methods have been at play in various ways for some time. The master builder standing with the masons on the site of a cathedral was in fact employing integrative strategies. Building materials and methods were in harmony with the time and the place. The skills of the workers, the purpose of the structure, the nature of the materials and the design that evolved were brought together in such a fashion that a culture of building evolved with a high degree of sophistication. Because of this interaction with and trust for the skills of the craftsman the documents necessary to initiate construction were of a far simpler and more direct nature than the hundreds, even thousands of pages of documents that such a structure would require today. Similarly, the drawings that Louis Sullivan produced for the incredible decorative spandrel panels of the Carson, Pirie Scott Department Store of Chicago were wonderfully simple because of the capability of the craftsman and a well-developed familiarity of the building process. What pulled the process apart are the modern tendencies toward the separation of the builder and the army of subcontractors from the architects, the increasing complexity of building types and related performance expectations requiring an ever more vast array of consultants, the legal implications of codes, standards and covenants, and the separation of owner from user. The complexity of this process and the related mounds of information led to the formation of stages of development and the creation of silos of decision stages. The resultant linear process of programming, schematic design, design development, construction documents and specifications, bidding, and construction observation and administration was as much a mechanism to provide a means to manage information leading to decisions in a deliberate fashion as it was a way of thinking. This was further accentuated by practices that often changed the individuals responsible for the project from stage to stage. A design mystique evolved from this culture whereupon the terms "the creatives" and "the adults" of offices evolved indicating the dreamers and those who focused on the realization of projects. The evolution of integrative design practices has dramatically changed this understanding of professional design practice.

To understand this transformation, it is necessary to understand the dramatic development of visualization tools as the tip of the iceberg of integrative design practices. Too much time has been spent on only the aspect of parametric modeling that has been the most obvious example of transformed thought processes. To remain focused on this aspect of the capability of ever advancing tools is to lose sight of the metacognitive aspects of integrative design processes. Examples abound of prominent work that is developed with the new tools that is really not very different from the work produced in the old linear format. The images are more seductive and new paths in thought generation are implied but in many instances it is work that is simply passed along to an associated practice to see to the realization of the project. How is this different from the model of the "creatives" and the "adults" of past linear processes?

If integrative design practice can be understood as a metacognitive transformation of design practices then a genuinely new path is being forged. Integrative design practice is a new frame of mind. It is essentially a socialization of the pursuit of inquiry. It is a blending of scientific inquiry, humanistic inquiry and the intuitive inclinations of design inquiry. As such, it is as much about the rigorous testing of ideas and questions and the need to understand deeply the cultural and environmental context focused on the human condition as it is about the guiding conceptual vision that inspires the work. Michael Schrage (2000), a professor at the Harvard Business School observes in his book, *Serious Play*,

> This process made me painfully aware that I wasn't just playing with these various versions for myself. These models and prototypes were essential to how I worked with others. Innovation was more social than personal. Innovation would be a by-product of how well or poorly I played with others. Behavior—not knowledge, not insight—would drive innovation.

It can be argued that it should be unnecessary to place the word integrative before the word design as a qualifier. Design by its nature is an activity that intends to connect disparate information into previously unseen patterns. It is an activity that cannot take place without special insights into the questions and opportunities posed by the project to be addressed. Therefore the importance of the qualifier integrative is not that it accentuates what is already part of the nature of design as much as it is an indicator of a form of disruptive innovation. An expression of Ancient Rome comes to mind, "not new but new." There is freshness and vitality implied by integrative design practices that signals a new approach toward design and the realization of designed artifacts from clothing and transportation to buildings. It is an approach born of big data interpreted to inform the design process and the nurturing of social networks of work that give new definition to the complex teams of subcontractors and consultants necessary to bring a project to life. It is this understanding that constitutes a way of seeing.

Constituting a Way of Practice

In 2008 during an American Institute of Architects National Board discussion the then President Marshall Purnell (2008) observed that Integrated Project Development (IPD) was best described as an attitude toward practice rather than as a suite of technology and software options. He further observed that while IPD seemed to be evolving most rapidly in relation to large-scale projects it could just as easily be employed as a strategy for a simple structure. His point was clear. The intentions of those designing the process by which a project will be addressed will nurture the adoption of an integrative strategy.

The nature of practice is such that it is always affected deeply by the project brief to be addressed. Obviously the challenges to the practitioner range along a scale from easy to solve to those for which there is no ideal solution—the wicked problems. On this scale individuals may address the easiest challenges guided by personal experience. In this instance the iteration of alternatives is likely to be assessed in a simple structure of issues, options and recommendations. As the difficulty of the challenge increases the necessity of a team of qualified individuals becomes apparent and case studies must be identified. The breadth of experience brought to the process by each will provoke the interpretations necessary to guide the iterative problem resolution process. In this situation iteration remains closely related to previous case experience and the belief that the challenge can be met utilizing the strengths of a team. When the challenge approaches the scale of the wicked problem, teams of teams will be required and entirely new strategies will have to be configured. The notion of perfect closure will be abandoned and the iterative process is more likely to be related to the development of a scenario articulating choices among systems and the context of culture and environment. In this case resolution rather than solution is the expected outcome. It is through the experience gained by addressing the wicked problems that the notion of integrated design is best realized as a social network of work. This is the frame of reference that constitutes integrative design practice.

It is no surprise that the design practice organization is profoundly influenced by the nature of the challenges to be addressed. What was once easily described as a pyramid of management varying in its character by the size of the organization is now an organism that readily reconfigures, joins and separates as the challenge demands. The vitality of the design practice is measured by its ability to transform and reconfigure with an agile spirit. This is made possible by advances in information technology and related software applications. But it is most likely, even in the absence of any form of information technology that it is inspired by the complexity of the problem. Different from an academic context that seeks to pose questions and then seek best prospect answers, the practice environment is problem solution oriented. Because of this, aided by integrative design practices the professional design office is in continual reconfiguration. This reconfiguration is the cause of considerable reflection. What has emerged from the tradition of small-, medium- and large-office practice models is a form of organic organizational structure where even the large organization can configure itself as a small practice and the smallest practice through creative combinations and associations can be networked into a large collaboration. The tools of integrative practice make this possible by increasing the interconnectivity among groups located across the globe.

In a model that is becoming familiar it is not unusual to bring consultants considered exemplary in their fields together with architectural teams from across state and national borders for a project that is then accomplished by distributing work tasks from illustration and animation to the development of construction details to associated offices or service bureaus. The architectural team closest to the project may in fact only be a small branch office of a large organization.

In the first case of such a strategy the team that is assembled to accomplish the work may only hold together as long as the project requires. In this manner the organization is not unlike the structure of a team assembled to make a Hollywood film. The director and actors, specialized technicians and marketing people may never work together again once the film is complete. Several of the individuals may come together on another project but under entirely different circumstances. A team is assembled, a goal is identified and the work is accomplished. With the goal achieved the team disperses.

In the second case of such a strategy there are many examples of large organizations making acquisitions of small practices in emerging markets simply to provide a marketing and business development foothold in a region. It is also through this plan of action that the large organization can acquire particular specialized talents and skills to broaden the portfolio of experience allowing penetration into markets such as medical or laboratory work. In this model teams of teams are brought together with each aspect of the office contributing to a greater whole. In such a model one sub office of the greater organization may be focused on urban design while another on sports, commercial or hospital facilities. In this model one branch office may engage another to enhance its capabilities and thereby build the kind of team that would otherwise be composed of many independent consultants.

As a further elaboration of the second case, a third is emerging that reconfigures traditional relationships between architects and builders and financial partners. Tasks that would otherwise be assigned to specialists with no direct relationship to decision processes are brought back into the core team. In this model the architect becomes the builder, the construction advisor, the developer and the leader of the finance team. This model is an extension of what is known as a design-build process. The organization that is formed is assembled as a grouping of interrelated practices sharing the same core of management oversight. In this fashion the organization can configure itself to address specific building types, particular services such as project management, financial investment or software development as specialty services. With the organization structured in this manner it is entirely possible that the services may be provided to other architectural teams in a specialty rather than as a whole. This amoeba-like organizational concept allows the organization to grow and change and breathe with the climate for architecture and design services.

This organizational concept is elaborated upon in considerable detail in the "family" of contract documents developed by the American Institute of Architects developed for Integrated Project Delivery. This family of documents provides for a variety of arrangements that exemplify the agile nature of the approach. This approach to contract development is explained as an elaboration of the complex nature of the social collaborations that must be defined in legal terms.

> Integrated project delivery is a collaborative approach that utilizes the talents and insights of all project participants through all phases of design and construction. The AIA (2014) provides agreements for three levels of integrated project delivery. *Transitional Forms* are modeled after existing construction manager agreements and offer a comfortable first step into integrated project delivery. The *Multiparty agreement* is a single agreement that the parties can use to design and construct a project utilizing integrated project delivery. The *Single Purpose Entity* creates a limited liability company for the purpose of planning, designing and constructing the project. The single purpose entity allows for complete sharing of risk and reward in a fully integrative collaborative process.

These three tiers of legal construct demonstrate the necessity of building a framework for interaction that brings together primary team members and consultants such as architects and builders with secondary consultants such as programmers and special purpose consultants including acousticians, community organizers and specialized building type or material installation consultants.

What is true of each of these examples is that the traditional tripartite organization of architect, client and construction management with consultants and subcontractors attached to each, has evolved into an organization without firewalls. This is what constitutes the integrated design practice perspective. It is only possible because of changed attitudes toward working relationships, the management of information and the willingness to challenge the traditional phases of work. Perhaps what is most intriguing about this transformed model is that the content of action is becoming more important than the form of action.

That is, information is brought into the process when it is required rather than when a predetermined phase of work would specify it to be inserted. While the most schematic sketches are being developed, very sophisticated notions of material and building system choices can be introduced. In the most natural form how construction will proceed can influence early schematic design choices. In the very same moment knowledge derived from ethnographic and ethographic studies may also indicate the preferences and social networks of the local users and building managers regarding choices that impact issues of budget and time to construction while also further influencing fundamental decisions.

Perhaps the most important aspect of integrated design practice is the imperative for an easy and timely flow of information. In an age when vast amounts of information are available from an array of references both from highly qualified researchers and consultants and from on-line anecdotal references the flow of information and its veracity are critical to design practice. Gehl (2014) in a presentation to the Design Futures Council made this imperative clear. In response to what exactly his firm provided in the form of professional services he responded that his practice, Gehl Architects, was most concerned with the human dimension and specifically with regard to master planning with people in mind. To this end, he is committed to the development of urban environments that account for the pedestrian and bicycle pathways. His office does this not by providing traditional architectural services but by enriching the foundation of information fostering understanding among the architects and planners who will use his research. He does this by building a rich body of knowledge that can be translated to use in various urban situations. His emphasis encourages a system of values derived from rigorous research and observation which will guide design decisions. Similarly, there exist equally vital and important resources for information regarding building and material performance, building typologies, demographics and many more aspects of a project. This one example provides a critical case study for the importance of verifiable research to the design process. It further emphasizes the critical need for this research to be undertaken by architects for use in architectural settings. This need for directly applicable information is growing in an environment when design professionals are being held accountable for performance metrics. No longer can an architect or designer make a comment such as "student performance will improve with enhanced day lighting" without being asked to substantiate this conclusion with established research outcomes and then prove it through student performance in the finished classroom. How this information comes to the project at the right moment becomes the responsibility of the architect in this new format. In another presentation to the Design Futures Council, Ringelstein (2014) of SOM provided insight into the complexity of undertaking an urban design project. His framing of the process emphasized the role of the designer to orchestrate a flow of information that is dependent on large amounts of data including understanding of urban systems, cultural factors, economically viable design, the need for extensive collaboration and the value placed upon rigorous research. From a third perspective the nature of the documents being developed to guide construction is experiencing considerable transformation. These documents, once compiled in document sets of considerable similarity from project to project, are now undergoing change related to content, context and technology. It is not unusual to see advanced information technology on a construction site with workers reading information from tablets, accessing information through applications designed by the architectural firm along with the building in the midst of the fabrication process. The interior of the pickup truck of a construction manager or a subcontractor is as likely to be home for a printer, scanner and monitor as for muddy boots. Finally from a fourth perspective, Mr. Bill O'Brien of O'Brien Atkins Architects in

Durham North Carolina shared an observation regarding three projects underway within walking distance of each other in the center of Raleigh, North Carolina for which his office had substantial responsibility. Each of these projects was comprised of different professional associations, different contractors, subcontractors and consultants and vastly different public clients. The legal contracts guiding the relationships among these complex teams were similarly vastly different. This example brings with it the realization that just as integrative practice implies a revitalized flow of information so too does it bring with it a dynamic social network of work that requires a legal framework that cannot be the same from one project to the next. The "family of Integrated project delivery contracts" already referenced in this chapter reflects this vitality. A series of documents has been crafted to engage issues from project liability to the formation of limited liability companies addressing project specific necessities. In every instance of the contract development what is being constructed in legal terms is the "social network of work" articulated by Hesselbein & Goldsmith (2002), in the book *The Organization of the Future*.

These four examples together make, in the strongest terms, the case for a metacognitive process that places the designer in the lead because of the effective orchestration of information. This is perhaps the most important lesson for education. It signals the need for design professionals to not only be familiar with the continuous changes underway in how work is produced and how contracts are configured but also in how information must be managed. The entire endeavor that constitutes the integrative design process, with the associated diverse perspectives of clients, design professionals, funding and regulatory bodies, is better understood as an integrated enterprise.

About Sustainability

As a result of the adoption of integrative processes a heightened awareness of the imperative for sustainable practices has emerged. The ability to incorporate building performance measures early in the conceptualization process informs the designer regarding material choices, building program dimensions, surface area and use patterns and the implications of building system choices. Software programs have been developed to provide the designer with energy performance estimates at the earliest stages of design deliberations. With such information the designer can seek alternative strategies and explore entirely new building types. For the more complex project, teams of individuals can be brought to bear in real time exchanges that amplify the implications of particular design choices on energy consumption. It is during this process that the metrics for the performance of the building can be established to assess building performance in a fashion that is both rigorous and replicable. Through an integrative design process strategy the experience of one project can be directly transferred to the development of another by linking early programming aspirations, design strategies, commissioning and continuing building performance. Integrative processes result in an enriched database formed from the collective work of architects and builders.

In 2010 Weyerhaeuser introduced a DNA modified lumber into the framing of the Chancellor's Residence at NC State University. This new product was developed to reduce the warping of the studs thereby minimizing the waste factor caused by the rejection of members during the framing inspection and reducing the problems later evident in making true the finishing of interior walls. Each tree cut down for the residence project was individually documented with a gigabyte of information. Each stud was specifically identified with the tree from which it came. Any problem studs, and there were very few, were sent back to the plant for further testing. In this case the experience of the construction site was directly connected to the experience of the tree farm from which the material originated. Compare this with the experience of the architects and project faculty of the John T. Lyle Center for Regenerative Studies at Cal Poly Pomona who in 1989 made it their primary goal to develop a leading edge environmental model. Green design strategies and green products were little known. Literature connecting environmentally responsible manufacturing processes was simply unavailable and building products made no reference to such a standard. Every aspect of the Center was developed from a base of almost no information. Just as the work of Gehl places emphasis on the role of research in design decisions so too do these examples engaging environmental imperatives signal that research must provide the foundation upon which design decisions are made while reaching for sustainable design outcomes.

Rybczynski (2014) writing in a New York Times Style Magazine article makes a point that cannot be overlooked in a discussion of sustainability.

> Architecture, however, is a social art, rather than a personal one, a reflection of a society and its values rather than a medium of personal expression. So it's a problem when the prevailing trend is one of franchises, particularly those of globe-trotters; Renzo, Rem, Zaha and Frank. It's exciting to bring high-powered architects from outside. It flatters a city's sense of self-importance, and fosters the perception of a place as a creative hotbed. But in the long run it's wiser to nurture local talent; instead of starchitects, locatects.

This attitude toward design is made increasingly possible by integrative strategies that bring the wisdom and experience of a world culture to the desk of every design practitioner. It shuns the notion of architecture practiced as a personality driven idea factory without real relationship to people, culture and place. This is the farm to table mentality of sustainable restaurant practices brought to professional design practice. It is a strategy with the promise to give back a feeling of place and scale to the community.

Integrative practices have not only raised the awareness of design strategies to a greater scale but also have elevated the understanding of the connection of design choices to environmental sustainability. This experience fosters the understanding of the metacognitive character of design thought. Projects conceived through the filtering process of integrative thinking are more likely to be of their place and derived from the people and cultures they are intended to serve. This is the essence of sustainability.

Constituting a Way of Learning

Just as integrative design practice implies a way of seeing, it also implies a way of learning. Individuals who will be called upon to manage the intricacies of integrative practice will seek out strategies that involve new practice models. These models require the ability to sort out vast amounts of data and to interpret and apply this material to increasingly complex challenges. Such challenges require a commitment to a continuous learning path. Just as information comes to a project from many sources requiring discernment so too learning patterns will be influenced by content rather than by coursework. Traditional course work models, not unlike the long established phases of design and construction model, articulate a specified sequential path for learning. This model has not taken into account neither the varying ways people learn nor the need to know information element of problem resolution. The process of learning has become deeply affected by the ubiquitous sources of information that satisfies the gregarious learner as well as those who choose to investigate on a need to know to answer a question basis. All the information is now available at the touch of a screen. What is required is the maturity to assess what is appropriate for the work at hand. The content orientation of a way of learning is a reflection of the importance not only of accessing design research outcomes from a variety of references but also of leading the identification of new research areas so that relevant experience can be translated into a body of knowledge. It is this commitment that will transform the professional design office into a learning organization. A commitment to continuous learning enriches the individual: a commitment to the development of rigorous research enhances the design disciplines. The attention given to integrative design practices with embedded learning experiences has transformed the work of architects and designers. The very same technologies and alliance forging strategies that have changed design practice are now also changing the education experience. A professional education must be characterized by the necessity of the facility to manage information and relationships among diverse and often contradictory sources of information and disciplinary orientations. There must be a bit of an orchestra conductor in every design professional. This skill to access, interpret and apply the information and talents of a broad range of sources and people must be developed as a primary directive of a design education. Those who wish to teach in the design studio must themselves have experienced this role in the realization of constructed work. Too often abstractions and explorations distract from this imperative. There is a hard edge to this reality. Students must be taught to factor in the possibility of realization in the work they are expected to accomplish as design professionals. This ability is apparent in the work of the very best architects and designers. How often does the observer stand before a complex structure and marvel not only by what has been realized but also by how it was realized. The integrated project delivery process not only encompasses the utility of what is made but it must also facilitate the story that it tells as a built representation of culture.

These strategies transforming the design and realization of projects also have merit as the individual, the designer, is seeking to reconfigure himself or herself against the rubric of a self-imposed learning and development plan. This tendency toward the development of a learning plan has certainly been further encouraged by life-long learning requirements to maintain state licensure or membership in a professional association. However, it is also the case that many offices are seeking to connect the professional development of staff to learning plans that serve the interests of the practice. This strategy builds the capability of an office by devoting time and resources to its most precious commodity, its people. In the context of a study on the subject of teaching offices, Alan Baldwin, FAIA, observed,

> A teaching firm values learning, conducts a structured in-house learning program, is committed to allocating resources for a structured program, and is characterized by a completely supported upper-management team. Most of all a teaching firm community believes that not only is a learning program the means to foster individual professional growth, it is also a vehicle to achieve a greater vision.
>
> (Malecha & Baldwin, 2005)

The ultimate lesson of this aspect of integrative practices is that it is not only information and commodities that must be joined; it is also the very people who are the players in any design and realization process. It is always about people. It is about the play, as Shakespeare (n.d.) wrote, “all the world is a stage.”

Constituting the Search for the Magic

The creative experience is measured by the magic that is engendered in those who come into contact with its outcomes. There is no question that everyone wishes to be elevated in some fashion by where they live work and worship. The Imagineers of Walt Disney understand this and have a simple way of expressing it; "everyone must leave the park with a smile on their faces." We all seek the magic. Yet there is a distrust of the elevated awareness implied by a process that brings together vast amounts of information gathered through etho and ethnographic methods with the exigencies of budget and program brief demands. It is as though this exercise of informed action undermines the special qualities that a designer brings to the project. Dewy (1980) in the publication *Art and Experience* addresses this concern,

> Wherever social divisions and barriers exist, practices and ideas that correspond to them fix metes and bounds, so that liberal action is placed under restraint. Creative intelligence is looked upon with distrust; the innovations that are the essence of individuality are feared, and generous impulse is put under bonds not to disturb the peace.

Intuitive actions are not hindered by the rigorous pursuit of either scientific or humanistic inquiry. Kahneman (2011) writing in his book *Thinking Fast and Slow* articulates the difference between utility theory and prospect theory. The difference between these modes of action is found in the dreams and aspirations of the individual. This is where magic is found. Integrative design practice provides the slow and deliberate preparation necessary to establish the context for the fast and magical aspect of intuitive thought. It sets the stage for magic.

References

American Institutes of Architects (2014). *Contract Documents: Integrated Project Delivery (IPD) Family*. Retrieved December 14, 2014 from: http://www.aia.org/contractdocs/index.htm.

American Institute of Architects National and American Institute of Architects California Council, (2007). *Integrated Project Delivery: A Guide, Version 1*. Washington, DC: American Institutes of Architects.

Dewy, J. (1980). *Art and Experience, John Dewy: A Perigee Book*. New York: Berkeley Publishing Group.

Ford, H. (2012). *My Life and Work, Henry Ford*. New York: Snowball Publishing.

Gehl, J. (2014, June). Comments Made to the International Meeting of the Design Futures Council. Copenhagen, Denmark.

Hesselbein, F., & Goldsmith, M. (2002). *The Organization of the Future*. Hoboken, NJ: Jossey-Bass.

Kahneman, D. (2011). *Thinking Fast and Slow*. New York: Farrar, Straus and Giroux.

Kieran, S., & Timberlake, J. (2008). *The Loblolly House*. New York: Princeton Architectural Press.

Malecha, M.J., & Baldwin, A. (2005). *The Learning Organization and the Evolution of Practice Academy Concepts. Testimonial Review*. Raleigh, NC: North Carolina State University College of Design Publication.

Purnell, M. (2008). Comments made to the Fall Board Meeting of the American Institute of Architects. Vancouver, Canada.

Ringelstein, D. (2014, June). Comments made to the International Meeting of the Design Futures Council. Copenhagen, Denmark.

Rybczynski, W. (15, June, 2014). The franchising of architecture. *New York Times Style Magazine*, 57–58.

Schrage, M. (2000). *Serious Play*. Boston, MA: Harvard Business School Press.

Shakespeare, W. (n.d.). *As You Like it*. Act 2, Scene 7.

15

Architecture of Change

Adaptive Building Skins

Branko Kolarevic and Vera Parlac

As the external socio-economic, cultural, and technological context changes, so do conceptions of space, shape, and form in architecture. Over the past decade, we have seen an increasing interest in exploring the capacity of built spaces to change, i.e., to respond dynamically and automatically to changes in the external and internal environments and to different patterns of use. The principal idea is that two-way relationships could be established among the spaces, the environment, and the users: the users or the changes in the environment would affect the configuration of space and vice versa; the result is an architecture that self-adjusts to the needs of the users.

A common thread among the projects described in this chapter is a vision of an architecture in which buildings can change their shape, their form, the configuration and appearance of space, and environmental conditions—on the fly—in response to patterns of occupation and contextual conditions (and shape those, in return, too). Buildings will become adaptive, interactive, reflexive, responsive ...

Arduino, Mems and Alive Buildings

In 2005 an inexpensive open source microcontroller board called *Arduino* was released in Italy. It could be connected easily to a variety of sensors detecting light, motion, touch, sound, temperature, etc., and by reading input from them could be made to "sense" the environment. It could also be connected to all kinds of actuators, such as lights, motors, and other devices, and could control them to "affect" that same environment. It also came with a simple development environment for writing software that could interpret the received input values from the sensors and produce output instructions that would control the operation of the actuators. Since its release, hundreds of thousands of these inexpensive electronics boards have been sold worldwide, enabling enthusiasts to create all sorts of interactive objects and environments. *Arduino* boards also found their way into the schools of architecture worldwide, sparking the imagination of students and reigniting the vision of dynamic built environments that could change on the fly. Buildings could thus become "alive" by sensing what was happening in and around them and by adjusting their spatial configuration and the environmental conditions on the fly. The dynamically changing buildings, imagined in science fiction novels from the 1960s and 1970s started to emerge as a not-so-distant technological possibility. Ruiz-Geli's Media-TIC building, described later in this chapter, features a number of control systems based on over a hundred networked Arduino boards that can sense various changes in the environment and then produce a corresponding reaction not only in shading but also how the building is lit, etc.

While Arduino boards require wires to supply them with electricity and connect them with sensors and actuators, another interesting, emerging thread of technological development is Micro-Electro-Mechanical Systems (MEMS), tiny electro-mechanical devices made of miniaturized structures, sensors, actuators, and microelectronics. For example, Siemens has created micro-sensors for heat changes that could be embedded in glass to measure solar heat gain and trigger appropriate action, such as darkening the glass by applying electricity to its coating. Of particular interest are wireless micro-sensors, which could sense changes in air temperatures, humidity, CO_2 levels, and other inputs and transmit that information to the building's management system. With the size of several millimeters, they could eventually be "sprinkled" on building surfaces in thousands; such "dense network sensing" holds the promise of turning building envelopes into actual "skins." A building skin will no longer be a poor biological metaphor, but increasingly a layer that can sense and react.

It All Started in the 1960s

The first concepts of an adaptive, responsive architecture were born in the late 1960s and early 1970s, primarily as a result of parallel developments in cybernetics, artificial intelligence, and information technologies, in general, and as a response to architecture's rigid, inflexible articulation of space and its configuration.

Gordon Pask set the foundations for interactive environments in the 1960s; he was one of the early proponents of cybernetics in architecture, whose concept of *Conversation Theory* (Pask, 1969), as a comprehensive theory of interaction, is particularly applicable today as various attempts are made to create constructive relationships between humans and machines (as in interactive architecture). Pask's ideas had a tremendous influence on both Cedric Price and Nicholas Negroponte, whose pioneering work in the 1960s continues to inspire; Pask worked with both Price and Negroponte.

Cedric Price was the first to adopt concepts from cybernetics and use them to articulate a concept of "anticipatory architecture," manifested in his *Fun Palace* and *Generator* projects. Nicholas Negroponte was among the first to propose in the late 1960s that computing power be integrated into buildings so that they could perform better. In his book *Soft Architecture Machines* (1975), he moved beyond the "architecture machines" that would help architects design buildings and proposed that buildings could be "'assisted,' 'augmented,' and eventually 'replicated' by a computer" (Negroponte, 1975). The ambition was to "consider the physical environment as an evolving mechanism." In the last chapter, he made a prediction that "architecture machines" (in the distant future) "won't help us design; instead, we will live in them."

At roughly the same time that Negroponte was working on his "architecture machines," Charles Eastman (1972) developed the concept of "adaptive-conditional architecture" (Eastman, 1972), which self-adjusts based on the feedback from the spaces and users. Eastman proposed that automated systems could control buildings' responses. He used an analogy of a thermostat to describe the essential components: sensors that would register changes in the environment, control mechanisms (or algorithms) that would interpret sensor readings, actuators as devices that would produce changes in the environment, and a device (an interface) that would let users enter their preferences. That is roughly the component makeup of any reactive system developed to date.

Adaptive Building Envelopes

In 2011 the "Adaptive Architecture" conference was held at the Building Centre in London. At this seminal event, convened by Michael Stacey, presentations were grouped into four thematic categories: *Dynamic Facades*, *Transformable Structures*, *Bio-Inspired Materials* and *Intelligence*, which could be considered as a taxonomy of current research efforts in this area. Chuck Hoberman and Craig Schwitter (of Buro Happold) launched in 2008 the *Adaptive Building Initiative* (ABI), with the aim of "designing a new generation of buildings that optimize their configuration in real time by responding to environmental changes"; most of their initial efforts were aimed at creating environmentally responsive building façades (for more information visit www.adaptivebuildings.com).

The key focus in designing adaptive envelopes is better management of energy flows, both from the exterior environment into the buildings and from the interior spaces of the building to the outside, with the goals being the improvement of the building's performance and the user comfort inside the building. The adaptive behavior of the envelopes can be visible or invisible (or both); in addition to components that move literally, such as the shades or vents, air (or water) would move as directed, and thermal energy would flow through different materials as designed. The visible adaptive behavior could lead to an urban spectacle that can add performative dimensions to the project that go beyond the scale of the building. While the literal movement of components is not an end in itself, it is often exploited to make the buildings appear "alive."

The building envelope can act as a "living" part of the building—its "skin," a semi-permeable membrane that mediates between the building and the environment. It is a layer—or more precisely a set of layers—where architecture and environmental engineering intersect as disciplines. As the building industry developed new materials and technologies, many of them found initial application in building envelopes, leading to a never-ending tectonic evolution in façade engineering: curtain walls, shading systems, double-skin facades, etc. In the late 1990s, the double-skin facades with a controlled vented air cavity and operable, integrated shades or blinds became popular. With the greater incorporation of electronically controlled, mechanically activated shading and ventilation systems came the kinetic or dynamic facades, active and high-performance building envelopes. Whatever term is used, the principal idea behind these new systems is that buildings need to respond in dynamic fashion to constantly changing environmental conditions and do so in energy efficient ways. Whereas the focus is traditionally on blocking heat gain or heat loss—effectively creating energy barriers—the new façade designs attempt to harvest energy from the environment and channel it where it is needed. For example, in double skins, the air contained in the space between the two layers is heated by sun during the winter months; conversely, in summer months, cold air is drawn at the bottom of the cavity and as it heats up, it is exhausted at the top using natural convection. The dynamic control of energy flows (manifested as light and heat) is at the center of innovation in adaptive building envelopes, facilitated by new materials and the latest advances in sensing, control, and actuation systems.

The broad development in hardware and software found their applications in the building management systems (BMS) that were installed in buildings to control their mechanical and electrical equipment. The overall goal behind the deployment of BMS is to monitor and manage the buildings' energy demands, which extended to the building envelopes as they started to incorporate kinetic components that affect buildings' thermal performance, i.e. the heat loads.

There are essentially four different methods of actuation: motor-based, hydraulic, pneumatic, and material-based. Most of the automated adaptive façade systems that were deployed to date rely on motor-based, i.e. mechanical actuation. Recently, we have seen increasing use of pneumatic actuation, primarily with the use of ETFE-based systems. There are, however, ongoing experiments in material-based actuation, which offer the promise of "zero energy" dynamic building envelopes.

Mechanic Actuation

A mechanized Venetian blind system inside an air cavity, often in a double-skin façade system, is the most common motor-based actuation system in use today. It can reduce significantly glare and solar heat gain. It is often automated, whereby a central building management system (BMS) tracks the location of the sun and monitors the light conditions and can lower and tilt (or raise) the blinds as needed. The blinds are housed between two layers of glass, one on the outside providing protection from the elements, and the one on inside protecting it from potential damage or interference with its operation (and both providing protection from particulate matter).

Other automated, active shading systems sandwiched between two sheets of glass were developed and deployed in the past. Jean Nouvel's *Institut du Monde Arabe*, completed in 1989 in Paris, was the first significant, large-scale building to have an adaptive envelope (Figure 15.1). The building's kinetic curtain wall, a technological interpretation in glass and steel of a traditional Arab lattice screen called a mashrabiya, is composed of tens of thousands photosensitive diaphragms that control light levels and transparency in response to the sun's location (the system no longer works due to mechanical problems).

Hoberman Associates (led by Chuck Hoberman) is perhaps one of the best-known contemporary practices to have designed several kinetic, performance-based adaptive shading systems in collaboration with the New York office of Buro Happold, a global design and engineering firm, with whom they allied to form the Adaptive Building Alliance (ABI). One of the systems they designed is based on "adaptive fritting" that produces movable patterns of varying density and could be thus used to control transparency, light transmission, solar gain, and views. The variable patterning is accomplished by shifting several layers of fritted glass relative to each other. The fritting is a pattern of ceramic glazing fused to the glass layer; this is well-known surface treatment for solar control. The glass layers are housed in an integrated glazed unit; their motion relative to each other is accomplished with a simple motor-based actuation. The shading patterns are highly customizable and could be uniform or non-uniform, repetitive or not, etc.

In collaboration with Zahner Metals from Kansas, ABI has developed an adaptive façade system called *Tesselate*, a self-contained, framed perforated screen that consists of stacked panels that move and overlap, creating kaleidoscopic patterns, which control light and solar gain, ventilation and airflow, privacy, and views. The changing pattern density is accomplished in the same way as in adaptive fritting, by shifting the patterned layers relative to each other. In this case the perforation patterns are CNC-cut from sheets of metal (or other material). The perforated sheets are then housed in an integrated unit with a motor that provides for the rotational translation of the sheets, resulting in a constantly changing light-diffusing screen.

Figure 15.1 Kinetic curtain wall at Jean Nouvel's Institut du Monde Arabe. Image: Branko Kolarevic

The *Tesselate* dynamic perforated screen system was incorporated by the architectural firm WORKSBUREAU in the façade design for twin luxury spas that should become the gateway to the King Abdullah Financial District in Riyadh (construction is scheduled to begin in 2014). The system's modules consist of three layers of perforated color-interference titanium, two of which are motorized, so that the perforated patterns create overlaps and thus regulate light and heat in a continuous reaction to external conditions. According to the designers' estimates, this façade system should reduce the cost of cooling the building by 15 to 20 per cent.

Some of the motorized adaptive façades are applied externally to the building façade, i.e. they are external to glazing units. Many of them involve some kind of retractable mechanism that can either expand or contract the shading surface. The *Strata* adaptive shading system, also designed by ABI in collaboration with Zahner Metals, is made of modular units that consist of telescopic fins that can retract into a single slender profile or extend to form a nearly continuous surface. The HelioTrace System, which ABI has developed in collaboration with SOM and Permasteelisa, is based on the telescopic motion of stacked fins that can retract to a slender square shape or expand to an almost closed square surface. This kinetic shading system could be programmed to follow the location of the sun and adjust its square aperture as needed. The fins do not need to be completely opaque; they could be perforated, fritted, and made from different kinds of materials. According to ABI, the system is capable of reducing the heat gain by up to 80 percent. The *Strata* adaptive shading system was supposed to be deployed on several projects in the Middle East, which, however, had to be put on hold during the last financial crisis.

Active adaptive shading systems could be either internal, i.e. embedded into the building façade or external to it. Whether they are internal or external depends on the scale, materials, means of actuation—and the maintenance regime. Encasing the shading system between two sealed layers of glass eliminates dust particles (and sand), which can get into lubricated areas that reduce friction in mechanized assemblies. Mechanically activated systems that are external to the façade are not only exposed to the elements but particulate matter could get into the mechanisms causing greater wear and tear and thus resulting in shorter lifespan of the systems; there is also increased chance of malfunction in the system, resulting in more frequent and more costly maintenance than is the case with the internal, embedded systems.

The *Q1 Headquarters* building for ThyssenKrupp in Essen, Germany, completed in 2010 and designed by JSWD Architeketen, is shaded by an external kinetic system that consists of 1,280 feather-like motorized louvered shades made from stainless steel. The "feathers" come in different shapes, from triangles and rectangles to trapezoids, that can move from open to closed positions (and in between) as the control system tracks the sun moving across the sky. Besides shading the building's interior, reducing its solar heat gain and modulating daylighting, the "feathers" produce a finely textured façade. The feather-like pivoting elements can move in unison or independently, i.e. they could be individually controlled.

Another notable, recently completed building with an external adaptive shading system is the Abu Dhabi Investment Council (ADIC) towers, two 29-story buildings designed by AHR and completed in 2012. According to AHR's design team, the responsive façade is based on a traditional Arab lattice screen, a mashrabiya. It consists of approximately 1,000 triangular "umbrellas" organized into hexagonal units, which are attached to a conventional glass façade. The umbrellas can change their configuration from open to closed through linear actuation and origami-like folding, which is controlled by the building's management system that tracks the movement and location of the sun. According to estimates by AHR, the external shading system should reduce cooling loads by as much as 25 percent. AHR's Computational Design group developed a parametric geometric description of the external system and simulated its operation under different incidence angles over the course of a year, measuring its impact on the building's thermal and energy performance. By minimizing the solar heat gain the system reduces cooling requirements thus reducing the energy consumption. It also diffuses direct sunlight with its translucent, fiberglass surfaces, which don't block the views of the surrounding cityscape. It performs in multiple ways, as is the case with most active shading systems.

Gardens by the Bay in Singapore has a conservatory complex designed by Wilkinson Eyre Architects and completed in 2012, featuring a double-glazed roof with a mostly horizontal external shading system that is composed of triangle-shaped fabric shades (Figure 15.2). Each shade can be fully extended or rolled up depending on solar conditions, thus modulating daylight and reducing heat gain in the glazed buildings. Sensors inside the conservatories monitor the environmental conditions, i.e. the temperature, humidity, and the light levels. As light levels increase and reach a certain threshold, the external shading system is deployed. The shades, which when deactivated are rolled up and concealed under structural members on one side, are pulled by a cable towards the opposite side, creating a visually dynamic "pineapple" pattern when fully extended. The adaptive shading system also provides a degree of spectacle for the visitors as it expands and retracts across the glass surfaces of the conservatories.

The *Ocean One* pavilion for Expo 2012 in Yeosu, South Korea, designed by SOMA from Vienna, Austria, features an external kinetic façade system that mimics the movement of the gills of a fish. The kinetic façade, developed in collaboration with engineering consultants

Figure 15.2 Conservatory buildings in Gardens by the Bay in Singapore are covered by an automated fabric-based external shading system. Image: Branko Kolarevic

Knippers-Helbig from Stuttgart, Germany, is 140 meters long, with height changing from 3 to 13 meters. It consists of 108 vertical lamellas made from glass-fiber reinforced polymer (GFRP). The lamellas are both strong and flexible, allowing for reversible elastic deformations; when actuated by motors along the top and bottom edge, the lamellas bend asymmetrically, creating gill-like openings that allow light into the buildings and afford views to the outside. Each lamella is individually controlled; the bending of the lamellas is choreographed to create wave-like patterns as they open and close along the length of the façade, producing a dynamic effect that animates the building's organic form.

In 2010 our research group, Laboratory for Integrative Design (LID), created *iConic*, a prototype of a building façade system comprised of mechanized, electronically controlled truncated conic modules (Figure 15.3) that rotate independently, altering the orientation of elliptical apertures and producing different performative effects during the course of a day, from dynamic sun shading and regulating outward views to urban-scale performances across the exterior field. Even though various tests were performed on the rotating conic modules, the prototype started producing squealing, whirling, and scratching noises soon after it was publicly exhibited. The main challenge in its design was not the geometry, electronics, or the actuation, but *friction*, which to this date remains an issue in almost all mechanically, i.e. motor-based actuation systems. Friction, i.e. the required frequent maintenance of malfunctioning apertures, is the primary reason that the kinetic façade on Jean Nouvel's

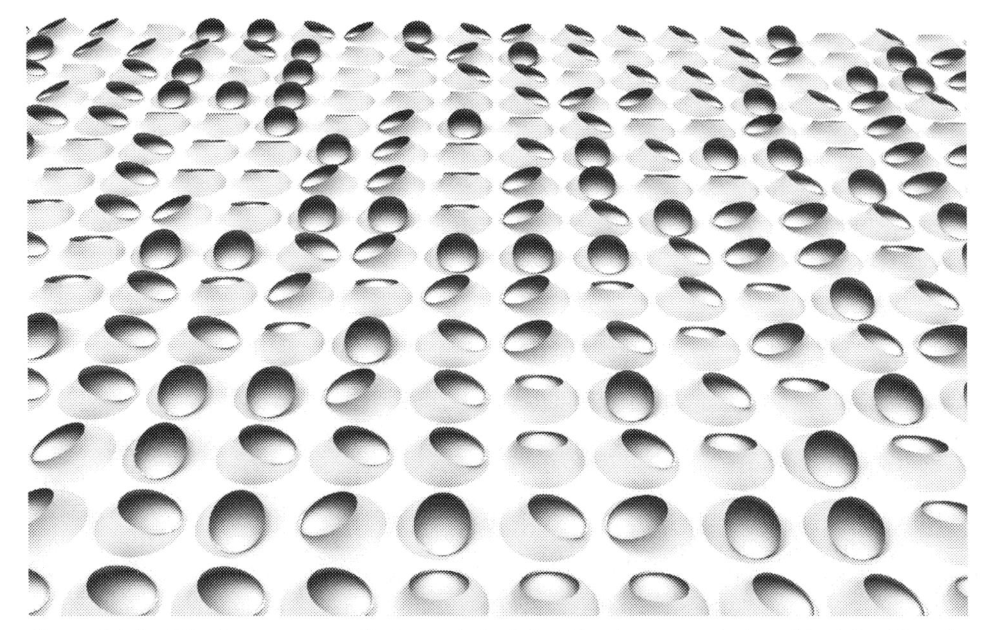

Figure 15.3 iConic, prototype of a dynamic building façade system designed by Matt Knapik, Eric and Mike Kryski from Laboratory for Integrative Design (LID), University of Calgary. Image: Matt Knapik / University of Calgary

Institute du Monde Arabe building is now "permanently frozen." It is also why designers of adaptive systems are looking into other ways of actuation besides motor-based ones, such as hydraulics, pneumatics, or material-based actuation.

Pneumatic Activation

The *Media-TIC* building in Barcelona, designed by Enric Ruiz-Geli of Cloud 9 and completed in 2011, features a dynamic façade made of lightweight ETFE (ethylene tetrafluoroethylene) air cushions that provides for pneumatic sun shading (Figure 15.4). The cushions consist of three layers of plastic with two air chambers between them that could be inflated or deflated as needed; the first layer is transparent; the second and third layers have a reverse pattern that creates shade when inflated and joined together. On the west side of the building, the ETFE air cushions are filled with nitrogen (mixed with tiny oil droplets) in the afternoon, transforming a transparent into a translucent façade that blocks 90 percent of the sun radiation, thus reducing substantially the building's heat gain. In addition, the building features a number of other control systems (based on over 100 networked Arduino boards) that can sense various changes in the environment and then produce a corresponding reaction not only in shading but also how the building is lit, etc.

ETFE cushions were previously used in the Nicholas Grimshaw designed *Eden Project*, completed in 2003, and in the *National Aquatics Center* (the "Watercube") in Beijing, designed by PTW Architects from Sydney in collaboration with Arup, and completed in 2008 for the Summer Olympic Games. ETFE is an incredibly lightweight, inexpensive, and thermally effective building enclosure that weighs about 1 percent of glass with the same area. Typically the sheets of ETFE are precisely cut using CNC cutters, heat-welded along the edges and then

Figure 15.4 Media-TIC building in Barcelona, by Enric Ruiz-Geli, features a dynamic façade made of "breathing" ETFE air cushions. Photo by Manuel Kretzer

inflated to create "cushions." The cushions need to be inflated continuously by air pumps, which consume energy and may require periodic maintenance. The cushions also require a separate support structure, which was given a honeycomb pattern on both Grimshaw's and Enric-Geli's buildings; the *Watercube* in Beijing features hexagons and pentagons. ETFE is finding increasing use in all types of buildings, from school courtyards to football stadiums (such as Bayern's stadium in Munich designed by Herzog and de Meuron).

Hydraulic Actuation

The *Council House 2* (CH2) building in Melbourne, completed in 2006, features an external adaptive shading system that consists of pivoting timber shutters that are moved by a computer-controlled hydraulic system. The shutters respond to the amount of direct sunlight hitting the western façade; they open fully in the morning and then slowly close up as the sun moves overhead to the west. This adaptive shading system is a rather simple, straightforward way to reduce solar heat gain. The building also features other systems that control lighting and ventilation, further reducing building's energy footprint, making it one of the "greenest" buildings in Australia. Its wood-textured façade provides for noticeable, yet subtle presence along one of the main streets in downtown Melbourne.

Material-based Actuation: Embedded Low-Energy Responsiveness

Several researchers are looking into "organic" or biological paradigm of kinetic adaptation, which relies on material instead of mechanical actuation. Much of that work shares John Fraser's observation from his *Evolutionary Architecture* book, published in 1995, that "natural ecosystems have complex biological structures: they recycle their materials, permit change and adaptation, and make efficient use of ambient energy" (Fraser, 1995). For example, Achim Menges has recently designed *HygroScope*, a prototype that relies on intrinsic properties of material to produce an actuated response. As described on his website (Menges, n.d.), "the dimensional instability of wood in relation to moisture content is employed to construct a climate responsive architectural morphology. [...] Mere fluctuations in relative humidity trigger the silent changes of material-innate movement." As Menges notes, "the material structure itself is the machine." Joanna Aizenberg at Wyss Institute at Harvard University has been experimenting with adaptive building materials, such as superhydrophic surface materials that can prevent or slow ice formation, can adapt from hydrophobic (non-wetting) to hydrophilic (wetting), and can collect rainwater efficiently; light-sensitive materials that control transparency and thermal gain; surface materials that can harness energy from the environment, etc.

Another trajectory in material-based activation is to work with two (or more) materials that react to environmental changes at dimensionally different rates. For example, Doris Sung is experimenting with bimetallic panels in which two laminated sheets of metal expand and contract at different rates when exposed to heat, i.e. direct sunlight. If one end of the laminated sheets is fixed, the different rates of thermal expansion or contraction result in deflection, which can be then exploited in different ways, depending on intended performance of such material assemblies. This method of material activation is rather old: the thermally induced bending of bimetallic strips has been used in thermostats for decades to produce an "automatic" electronic contact. What is novel in Sung's work is the scale of application, which has shifted tenfold from millimeters in thermostats to centimeters in the canopy project called *Bloom* she designed, produced and installed in 2012 in Los Angeles (Figure 15.5). The canopy consists of tens of thousands of laser-cut bimetallic components assembled into over 400 hypar-shaped panels that create a self-supporting structure when assembled. When exposed to sunrays, the panels start to open in the morning as temperature raises and then begin to close in the afternoon as the sun sets, i.e. as temperature drops. The bimetal assembly used by Sung in the *Bloom* relies on molecular bond between two different manganese-based alloys (i.e. there is no adhesive). The bimetallic panels are thermally very sensitive, with almost real-time deflection when exposed to solar heat. They could lead potentially to the development of dynamic, "zero-energy" building envelopes in which bimetallic-based components could open up vents for the hot air to escape or could move other elements into proper position to shade the spaces from direct sunlight.

Other researchers are working with shape-memory materials, in which deformation can be induced (and recovered from) through temperature changes. David Benjamin has experimented early-on with shape-memory alloys (SMA) and Nick Puckett has used various shape-memory polymers to create material actuated prototypes of building façades. In the "Living Glass" prototype, David Benjamin and Soo-in Yang (whose firm is called "The Living"), created a cast silicone membrane in which slits were lined with Flexinol, SMA wire manufactured by Dynalloy, which shrinks when electrical current is applied to it—and then returns to its original shape when the current is cut off (i.e. it "remembers" its shape).

Figure 15.5 Doris Sung's Bloom canopy in Los Angeles is made from thousands of bi-metallic components. Image: Doris Sung / DOSU studio architecture

When the Flexinol wire shrinks it forces the silicone "gills" to open and then closes them as it returns to its original length. Nick Puckett experimented with strips made from shape-memory polymers that bend when exposed to sunlight, thus creating apertures, and then return to their original shape when the sun is no longer present.

The so-called smart or designed materials that can change their shape based on external stimuli are of increasing interest to researchers in the building industry. Besides shape-memory alloys and polymers that change shape based on temperature, there are magnetic shape alloys, in which magnetization affects shape, then photomechanical materials, in which light affects shape, electroactive polymers, pH-sensitive polymers, etc.

None of these examples required sophisticated sensory, control, and actuation systems to produce a dynamic response to changing environmental conditions; instead, they cleverly exploited the embedded, intrinsic properties of the materials. Challenges, however, do exist before systems that rely on material-based actuation are fully developed. Most of the prototypes that make use of the designed materials are small-scale; in fact, *scale* remains a principal challenge in developing such smart material-based systems, for the simple reason that materials behave differently, i.e. in non-linear manner, at different scales. So, what works at a one-meter scale will not work at a ten-meter scale. It is highly likely that most adaptive systems (at the scale of building) that rely on shape or volume changes in smart materials will be based on some kind of hybrid actuation, such as mechanic amplification of material-based actuation. For example, in the *Hylozoic Ground* installation, Phillip Beesley used mechanical levers to amplify contractions in "muscle" wire (i.e. shape-memory alloy) used in the assembly that produce real-time dynamic behavior. Such hybrid actuation, combined with proximity sensors and controlled through a network of Arduino microcontrollers, produced what looks like a living, breathing forest of acrylic fronds that change shape as people move through the installation.

While these experiments are harbingers of future building skins that will look "alive," Arup's engineers developed collaboratively (with SSC Ltd. and Colt International) a photo-bio-reactive façade prototype called "SolarLeaf" that is actually alive. It features a layer of microalgae between two sheets of glass that generates biomass and heat as renewable energy resources. The four-story *BIQ House*, built for the 2013 International Building Exhibition (IBA) in Hamburg, has 129 of these bioreactor panels installed on the southeast and southwest façades, each measuring 2.5m × 0.7m. Solar thermal heat and algae are harvested over approximately 200m^2 of surface area in a closed loop system, in which they are stored and then fermented to generate hot water.

The future of dynamic building skins will likely belong to low-energy systems that can harvest the heat from the sun or the kinetic energy of the wind. In many experiments described in this section, the "sensing" and "actuating" capacities were built into the material, eliminating the need for complex mechatronic assemblies. Such passive systems of dynamic activation that rely on intrinsic properties of materials are perhaps the most promising direction for developing adaptive building envelopes.

Dynamics Using Simple, Lo-tech Strategies

The notion of adaptive environments is not new. In a traditional Japanese house any room could be a living room or a bedroom (or a dining room). What makes this adaptability in use possible are two key features: first, all furniture is lightweight and could be removed into large storage closets; second, the size of a *space* could be easily changed using sliding partitions (*fusuma*) that separate adjacent rooms. Such spatial porosity is also present in traditional Korean houses.

The Modernist *Open Plan* is based in large part on these East Asian precedents, as were the associated notions of adaptability and flexibility. Gerrit Rietveld's seminal *Schröder House*, built in 1924, features on the upper floor an adaptive large space that can be left open or subdivided using sliding and revolving partitions into four separate rooms, i.e. three bedrooms and a living room. Similarly, Steven Holl's apartment complex in Fukuoka Japan, completed in 1991, relied on hinged wall partitions to create adaptive apartment units in which spaces could change daily or on a larger timescale as family size changes. A similar use of hinged panels created an incredibly effective, puzzle-like transformable façade of the *Storefront for Art and Architecture* in New York, which was designed jointly by Steven Holl and Vito Acconci and built in 1993.

As more and more designers and firms begin to experiment with innovative sensing, control, and actuation technologies to create kinetic, adaptive spaces and systems, it is worth remembering that wheels and hinges—if used imaginatively—could create very potent transformable environments that need not rely on any fancy mechatronic setups. The *Naked House* in Kawagoe, Japan, designed by Shigeru Ban and completed in 2000, features four movable rooms on wheels inside a large, shed-like space. The six square-meter rooms are open on two sides and can be located anywhere within the large interior space or even moved outside; they could be also joined to form larger spaces if needed. The *Sliding House* in Suffolk, UK, designed by dRMM and completed in 2009, features an enclosure that can move along recessed tracks to cover or uncover different buildings along its 28m-long linear

Figure 15.6 dRMM's Sliding House (2009) in Suffolk, UK. Image: de Rijke Marsh Morgan Architects (dRMM)

path (Figure 15.6): the house, garage or the annex (and a swimming pool that could be added in the future). The four electric motors that move the enclosure are integrated into its wall thickness; each motor is powered by car batteries that are charged by mains or PV solar panels.

We should not lose sight of lo-tech solutions in our current quest for adaptive systems infused with the latest sensing, control and activation technologies. Oftentimes, simply adding wheels and tracks (and/or hinges) to elements that are then moved by people is all that is necessary for some adaptive designs to be effective spatially and programmatically. Buildings used to have adaptive façades with hinged and louvered shutters fixed outside the windows that were used to provide security, privacy, or to modulate light. Such simple solutions still have a place in contemporary architecture that seeks to provide user-controlled adaptability in buildings.

There is also a good chance that any mechatronic solution that depends on the current state-of-the-art technologies could become obsolete relatively quickly. One way of addressing this challenge of obsolescence is to rely on solutions that are already seen as "obsolete"; as such they won't become obsolete—they already are. For example, Jan and Tim Edler from realities: united, who took on the challenge of designing the media façade for the Kunsthaus

Figure 15.7 The sunscreen of the Children's Museum of Pittsburgh (2011) by Koning Eizenberg is made from tens of thousands hinged resin flaps. Image: Ned Kahn

in Graz by Peter Cook and Colin Fournier, considered all kinds of the latest and the greatest contemporary technologies, such as LEDs, plasma screens, projections systems, etc., but were concerned with their potential life span. In the end they settled for the humble but utterly "obsolete" round neon-lights that were ubiquitous in the kitchens in 1960s. They discovered that the intensity of those lights could be controlled with a simple capacitor that could be connected to a custom-designed controller board with a user-friendly screen interface. Thus, a lo-tech, low-resolution monochrome "BIX façade" (BIX stands for the "building pixel") made from technologically obsolete components was devised to withstand these inevitable challenges of time and technological progress.

Any cutting-edge technological system of today becomes an obsolete technology rather quickly. This dimension of time is rather critical for the designers of adaptive, responsive, interactive building systems of tomorrow.

The new pavilion added to the *Children's Museum of Pittsburgh* (Figure 15.7) offers a compelling example of a dynamic yet tectonically and technologically simple façade. Koning Eizenberg, architects of the pavilion, deployed a sunscreen called "Articulated Cloud," designed by Ned Kahn, that consists of tens of thousands of hinged resin flaps that flutter in the wind; during the day, their color depends on the sky conditions; at night they are illuminated, emanating bright white light like a large lantern. The architects have managed to produce a dynamic building skin that registers and responds to environmental conditions (light, wind) without any sophisticated mechatronics. It represents an excellent example of minimalist, simple tectonics producing complex, subtle spatial and surface effects. Such simplexity—complexity attained through simple means—is perhaps another promising trajectory for dynamic building skins.

The Challenges Ahead

Another critical issue in the design of any highly automated adaptive, responsive system is the user-override. For example, louvers in an automated, "high-performance" façade could automatically come down in bright sunlight to shade the interior spaces but that action could not only be distracting to people who might be in an important meeting but could also block a highly desirable and attractive view to a nearby park or lake. If an installed, automated system requires frequent manual overrides by annoyed users, its "life" is not going to be that long; a simple, people-activated "high-performance" and lo-tech solution would probably more than suffice in such cases. Social and cultural factors need to be taken into account in setups that rely on automated systems to attain certain technical performance goals. We shouldn't be blinded by technologies of the day and should not lose sight of the qualitative, i.e. non-quantifiable performative aspects of the project and whether they could be better served by no-tech or low-tech solutions. The overall issue of control is critical; in *Smart Architecture*, Ed van Hinte warns that "sometimes a simple and hence ostensibly 'dumb' building is smarter than a technology-dominated living-and-working machine over which the user has lost control" (van Hinte *et al.*, 2003).

There is also the ever-present danger of creating "gimmicky" architecture that becomes boring very quickly. The primary goal of constructing a truly responsive, adaptive architecture is to imbue buildings with the capacity to interact with the environment and their users in an engaging way. Architecture that echoes the work of Nicholas Negroponte could be understood as an adaptive, responsive machine—a sensory, actuated, performative assemblage of spatial and technical systems that creates an environment that stimulates and is, in turn, stimulated by users' interactions and their behavior.

When it comes to designing adaptive, responsive environments, the "software" side does not seem to present as many challenges as the "hardware" side, the building itself, whose majority of systems is inherently inflexible. That is perhaps where the biggest challenges and opportunities exist, as buildings would have to be conceptually completely rethought in order to enable them to adapt (i.e., to reconfigure themselves). Then there is the "middleware" that sits among the software and hardware and the users as devices that facilitate the feedback loops between the components of the system.

There are also some fundamental questions that have yet to be adequately addressed. For example, while Beesley and his colleagues predict, "the next generation of architecture will be able to sense, change and transform itself" (Beesley *et al.*, 2006). They fail to say clearly towards what ends. Even though they ask what very well may be the key question—how do responsive systems affect us?—they do not attempt to answer it explicitly. Similarly, Fox and Kemp, in their *Interactive Architecture* book (Fox & Kemp, 2009) avoid explaining fully—and admit as much—why interactive systems are necessary, meaningful, or useful, and simply state, "the motivation to make these systems is found in the desire to create spaces and objects that can meet changing needs with respect to evolving individual, social, and environmental demands." Fox and Kemp position interactive architecture "as a transitional phenomenon with respect to a movement from a mechanical paradigm to a biological paradigm," which, as they explain, "requires not just pragmatic and performance-based technological understandings, but awareness of aesthetic, conceptual and philosophical issues relating to humans and the global environment" (Fox & Kemp, 2009).

In short, much remains to be done: we would argue that change in architecture is far from being adequately addressed or explored theoretically, experimentally, or phenomenologically. As we probe and embed adaptability, interactivity, and responsiveness into the buildings and spaces, we must not unconditionally and blindly chase the latest technological advancements. As we have argued in this chapter, an effective adaptive, responsive system—including building envelopes—could be based on simple, lo-tech, low-energy solutions. It could be actuated by users, who could push, pull, turn, flip, move things … and it could be intelligently augmented with sensors and an Arduino board here and there, as needed.

References

Beesley, P., Hirosue, S., Ruxton, J., Trankle, M., & Turner, C. (2006). *Responsive Architectures: Subtle Technologies*. Cambridge, Ontario: Riverside Architectural Press.

Eastman, C. (1972). Adaptive-Conditional Architecture, in N. Cross, ed., *Design Participation, Proceedings of the Design Research Society Conference*. London: Academy Editions, pp. 51–57.

Fox, M., & Kemp, M. (2009). *Interactive Architecture*. New York: Princeton Architectural Press.

Fraser, J. (1995). *Evolutionary Architecture*. London: Architectural Association.

Hinte, E. van, Marc, N., Jacques, V., & Piet, V. (2003). *Smart Architecture*. Amsterdam: 010 Publishers.

Menges, A. (n.d.). *HygroScope*. Retrieved December 14, 2014 from: http://www.achimmenges.net/?p=5083.

Negroponte, N. (1975). *Soft Architecture Machines*. Cambridge, MA: MIT Press.

Pask, G, (1969). Architectural Relevance of Cybernetics. *Architectural Design*, September 1969, pp. 494–496.

Part IV
Architectural Design and Behaviorism

This part focuses on architectural designs originating with relevance to interaction of humans and their perceptual understanding, as well as their physical experience with the built environment. The chapters of this part expand on impact of design with occupants' interactions, and behavioral manifestations and ultimately, the physical and psychological well-being of people within their man-made environments. This part will also argue on the current public recognition of architects' approaches and roles in branding architecture.

16

The Intersection of Design Psychology Theories with the Elements and Principles of Design

Kathleen Sullivan

A typical day can involve home, work, perhaps shopping, eating out, driving, and then returning home. During the first visit to an establishment or the first time we take a new route to a destination, our senses are acutely tuned to the environment, gathering as much information as possible in order to safely accomplish our mission. Available cues make the mission pleasant, difficult, or something in between, and may dictate whether we enthusiastically patronize an establishment, tolerate it, or never return. For example, you have extra time running errands Saturday afternoon and decide to venture into that specialty food store you pass all the time. You hold preconceived notions that the products are out of your price range and you will feel out of place, but once you enter, your mindset begins to change. The interior is pleasant, with generous aisles and a high, sky-lighted ceiling flooding the space with natural light. Ah, the atmosphere fills your senses with delight; you see products that arouse your curiosity, and you explore the open-market-style layout. The staff are friendly and informative, the prices reasonable; you put a few items in your basket and then check out, feeling that you fit right in! As you drive away, you say, "Why didn't I go there before? I think I just met my new best friend!"

Many factors affect how one feels about a space. Environmental design psychology theories provide a starting point for understanding people's reactions. In this case, you initially associated the store with a social stratum of which you felt you were not a part. The positive multi-sensory experience triggered by the ambience of the space, user-friendly layout, variety of products, and interactions with the informative and courteous staff, led to an unexpected sense of all-around satisfaction, thereby changing your perception of this store.

Environmental design psychology is the study of symbiotic relationships between humans and their environments. This holistic approach separates environmental psychologists from other professionals in the field of design and social science (Kopec, 2012). Just as plants form symbioses in their environments, so humans form symbiotic relationships with their environment, fulfilling functional and emotional needs.

Environmental design psychology utilizes social and physical science perspectives and views human environment behaviors as derivative of a combination of social, cultural, and biological factors. Environmental psychologists consider biological and sociological influences, and how to use methods of environmental modification and design strategies to enhance preferred actions and reduce undesirable behaviors. For example, simple crowd control belt stanchions in banks are cues for people to wait their turn.

Interaction with the Environment and Psychological Processes

When humans interact with their environment—composed of physical structures (massing, furniture), physical stimuli (light, noise, temperature, smells), and symbolic artifacts (meaning of the setting)—psychological processes commence. For example, a preconceived negative perception about the food store vanished upon interaction with that environment. The distal cues (characteristics of the setting, building style, interior layouts, and physical stimuli like natural light and savory aromas) and the proximal cues (subjective impressions of the setting, a feeling of fitting in and having functional needs met) combined to leave the shopper with a comfortable feeling and overall positive experience.

Results of Environmental Interaction

The five components of the psychological process in environmental interactions produce *arousal* (psychological readiness for activity), *overload* (excessive arousal or stimulation), *affect* (emotional reaction), *adaptation* (process of changing and adjusting), and issues of *personal control* (ability to control the environment)—all fundamental psychological processes.

Outcomes of Environmental Interactions

Outcomes of these interactions then fall into categories of performance, interpersonal relationships, satisfaction, health, or stress. *Performance* is the manner in which one responds to stimuli; *interpersonal relationships* refer to how well the environment facilitated interactions of individuals occupying the space; *satisfaction* is determined by how pleased the individual is with the respective environment; and *health or stress levels* are determined by the overall fundamental psychological processes.

By approaching design solutions from multiple perspectives, environmental design psychology is poised to explain why humans engage in particular behaviors in relation to their environment, and how they perceive the environment that they occupy.

Needs assessments and a keen understanding of a space's functional intent are imperative in the pre-design phase of the built environment. Taking the time to consider and then match the appropriate theories to the needs of the people who will occupy the space, along with consideration of the functional requirements, is a good start to creating a positive experience for the end user. Environmental psychology should inform the manipulation of the elements and principles of architecture and interior design, to facilitate the intended function of the space and fulfill the emotional needs of the end user. For example, every interior designer (professional or DIY) knows that a low ceiling, dark colors, and insufficient lighting foster feelings of claustrophobia and disorientation; incorporating better lighting and color into a room moves the perceived planes further apart and changes how the space makes one feel.

A Day in the Life

We are going to analyze several interviews in which individuals share their perceptions and feelings about a space that they frequent. How the subject processed their interaction with the respective environment, followed by outcomes and the categories into which they fall, are detailed in tables in the interview, illustrating how these terms are present in "A Day in the Life."

Choosing an Assisted Living Facility

Over the span of fifteen years, our family watched our mother slowly physically decline after our father's death. It became evident that she needed closer monitoring in that she was falling, a lot. You never think that the day will come when family discussions turn to "What do we do to take care of mom?" Mother is now in a facility. She is 92 years old and sharp for her age. The only problem she has is that she loses her balance and falls. She needs assistance so that she does not fall. This facility does just that, they assist her.

> [The family's] criteria were: cleanliness, food quality, caring staff, activities, appearance, openness, natural light, security, no institutional odors, views to the outside, and a private suite and bathroom. It is hard to prioritize the criteria; they are all important. We did not want to see people left sleeping in wheelchairs in the hallways; we wanted staff who would take residents back to their rooms ...The family made the decision to put her in the one we selected ...Would these criteria have been as important to mom? We will never know, but there is a smile on her face every time we visit.
>
> A big criterion when selecting a facility was odor; if we walked into a building and it smelled of body odors, wastes, sanitizing, or had a musty feeling, we did not consider it. ... Here there is absolutely no odor and it is immaculate. This [home was] built twelve years ago, looks nice when you pull up, and has lots of trees and flowers, well-manicured grass ... It is easily accessible from a main road ... the lobby ... has a three story open atrium with a skylight...[the] receptionist is not behind a glass window but behind a counter. Other places that we visited felt like an office where the ceiling was all one level with acoustic ceiling panels, with mostly fluorescent lighting. In the main lobby, there are plenty of comfortable sofas and chairs. You perceive it as grand hotel; it has a large fireplace off to the left side. In this facility, there are only two hallways off the center lobby; finding yourself disoriented is impossible ... the layout is so simple that no signs are required to direct you to wherever you need to go. You just can point to all of the areas for directions.
>
> [In the] dining room, the tables seat four people, have tablecloths, folded napkins, and real floral centerpieces; it feels like a high-end restaurant. Servers wait on residents; menus posted each week allow the residents to know what their menu choices are. The food is excellent.
>
> Her room ... has high ceilings, two large windows and she has all the amenities she needs ...: a beautiful private bathroom, a kitchenette, and personal temperature controls. [W] e furnished her room with the items from her house. Mom wanted personal photos of the family on the wall and her plants from home ... her room is a vignette of the home in which we were raised!
>
> We wanted to see an atmosphere where you are motivated to leave your room; there is a main street feel on the first floor where there are various types of shops and

destinations. On all of the landings in the atrium, there are places to sit to look out into nature. The colors are calming. The hallways ... are very wide and have hotel-style corridor carpeting. You can lock your own door but most do not, even at night; the residents feel very secure. They have a great activities program; she gets out of her room and socializes. Because of these activities, she made friends quickly. She is more active here than she was at home.

The most satisfying part of this is that when we take her out for the day, when she gets tired she states that she wants to go home. She means her home at the assisted living facility. We know we made the right decision.

Environmental Components, Psychological Processes

The family shared a psychological construct, a conceptual representation of what an assisted living facility should look like, how it should function. There is an overarching Comfort Theory that applies to this family and the mother; a facility reminiscent of their family home and life style makes them feel at home, and comfortable (Guthrie, 1997). In addition, the family desired a facility that would encourage their mother to leave her room. The commons area providing social destinations for activities, a variety of sitting areas providing socio-pedal and socio-fugal seating, and a strong activities program fulfilled the environmental component of arousal to the family's satisfaction. The atrium and lobby enhance the aesthetic and provides a node for human interaction. Large windows allow natural light to fill the space and afford residents the opportunity to function in the effortless attention mode by staring into nature as a means of restoring attentional capacity (Kaplan & Kaplan, 1982). The environment posed neither excessive arousal nor stimulation. Meeting, exceeding, and perpetuating daily the family's conceptual representation of the ideal assisted living facility has provided them with utmost satisfaction. The family feels that their mother's adaptation to living in a nursing home has been smooth; they feel their criteria successfully fulfilled. Their satisfaction is enhanced by observations of their mother in the environment; she has adapted well. Both the family and their mother have freedom to come and go at any time, permission to personalize the room, and participate in activities, thereby exhibiting personal control.

The categories of performance, interpersonal relationships, satisfaction, health/stress, into which the environmental components fall into are positive. The family responded

Table 16.1 Snapshot of Environmental Interaction: Nursing Home

Snapshot of environmental interaction	*As rated by family members*
Arousal (psychological readiness for activity)	Fulfills image family had in mind
Overload (excessive arousal or stimulation)	Perfect for their mom
Affect (emotional reaction)	Exceeded expectations, very happy
Adaptation (process of changing and adjusting)	Went smoothly
Issues of personal control (one's ability to control the environment)	Very satisfied

Table 16.2 Snapshot Outcomes of Environmental Interactions: Family Reaction

Performance (manner in which one responds to stimuli)	The facility engages her
Interpersonal relationships (how well the environment facilitated the interactions of the individuals who occupy the space)	Has increased mom's interaction with people, this makes us happy
Satisfaction (how pleased the individual is with the respective environment)	Our homework paid off
Health/Stress (determined by the overall fundamental psychological processes)	Our family can sleep at night knowing our mom is treated with respect and care

holistically to the environment, which includes the approach to the facility, the exterior, the interior space, furnishings, and amenities. The lack of certain stimuli (institutional odors and effluents) contributed to their satisfaction. The built environment and the engaged staff facilitate residents' interactions, and the family observes these are keeping their mother alert and happy. The family's overall pleasure with the environment reduces their caretaking stress levels.

I Avoid Your Store, Would You Like to Know Why?

Fibromyalgia is a disorder that causes pain all over the body. People with fibromyalgia can have "tender points" throughout their bodies, specific places on the neck, shoulders, back, hips, arms, and legs that hurt when pressure is put on them. People with this disorder are hypersensitive to their environment. Fibromyalgia affects as many as 5 million Americans aged eighteen and older. Eighty to 90 percent of sufferers are women, but men and children also can suffer from the disorder (Office on Women's Health: U.S. Department of Health and Human Services, 2012). The following interview may help inform designers, architects, and storeowners, in their efforts to attract a population that otherwise would avoid their stores.

> I have certain ... cognitive, physical, and psychological issues and understand that most spaces are built to accommodate the public at large; they cannot be designed to facilitate every human condition, so I acquiesce to spaces. I have moderate to severe cognitive and memory problems. It is painful to stand and wait; I need to move freely through a space. As a former interior designer ... I can tell when my responses are caused by my conditions and when they would be a universal response from people without the same challenges.
>
> I have already eliminated all but a few stores [at the mall] because the layout and environmental conditions make me miserable. The department store that I do frequent visits, possesses many attributes that make it an overall positive experience. I love the atmosphere of this store and it calms me. I know the sales staff is friendly, "findable," and helpful. [T]here is carpet; it feels good. [T]here is lounge seating in case I need to rest; I am able to shop longer when I have an opportunity to rest ...The racks are

Table 16.3 Snapshot of Environmental Interaction: Desired Environmental Conditions

Arousal (psychological readiness for activity)	Unless the store meets basic criteria, I dread going there
Overload (excessive arousal or stimulation)	What other people call normal is generally excessive to me
Affect (emotional reaction)	It can take days to reconcile a shopping trip if it is not pleasant
Adaptation (process of changing and adjusting)	I don't adapt easily; if at all, so the environment must have certain design features in place
Issues of personal control (one's ability to control the environment)	The most important features are – can I sit, clearly navigate, and how easy is it to find what I am looking for?

spaced widely enough apart that two people can pass each other without one having to move for the other one. The lighting is pleasant ... it is warm and designed ... to help me navigate through the store; not just rows of 2 × 4 fluorescents. I am hypersensitive to noise and odors. If there is music playing in this store, the volume is low enough that I am not aware of it or it is pleasant enough that I can enjoy it and still focus on my own thoughts. Be it the quality of the merchandise or the air handling system that removes odors, whatever, the store does not reek of cheap dyes and sizing. This store is open enough that I can clearly identify where everything is ...I would be able to tolerate most shopping environments for a short amount of time regardless of environmental conditions if I were able to quickly find what I want, pay for it, and leave. Signage and distinguishing architectural features directing one to an area are very important for me. In other department and clothing stores ... I struggle with trying to think in the presence of over stimulation; I am at my threshold for what I am able to tolerate. When this happens, I feel worse mentally, emotionally, and physically; all I want to do is leave. For someone with fibromyalgia, a few simple errands can be draining and take days to [recover]. [S]imple adjustments could make all the difference in the world for the end user and the business owner who wants to make money! Perhaps someone without these issues would have the same observations but not have the same stress levels.

Table 16.4 Snapshot Outcomes of Environmental Interactions: Impact

Performance (manner in which one responds to stimuli)	No excessive stimuli afforded a positive shopping experience
Interpersonal relationships (how well the environment facilitated the interactions of the individuals who occupy the space)	Architectural and interior design features are calming and interaction with the sales associates is satisfying
Satisfaction (how pleased the individual is with the respective environment)	The social and physical experience provided a high satisfaction level
Health/Stress (determined by the overall fundamental psychological processes)	Low stress, no negative impact on health, a positive experience

The individual determined through prior visits that this department store would not cause her stress. The categories of performance, interpersonal relationships, satisfaction, health/stress, into which the environmental components fall—all positive—keep her coming back. With a robust laugh, she stated, "If I could only be beamed up to the store rather than dealing with traffic, this would be a perfect shopping experience."

The Little Girl Still Inside Me

The following interview reveals how the physicality of a space experienced by an individual when they were in preschool affected them for their entire life. More so, how the sociological experiences affiliated with these spaces contribute to adult behavior and attitudes regarding spaces.

> As a 5-year-old in Iran, I was placed in preschool; this experience affected me for the rest of my life. I [have] vivid memories of how the space made me feel ... A woman who had an interest in preschool/kindergarten education founded the school; she rented a house and converted it to an educational environment ... [but]the owner never understood the consequences of how space affected attitude and mood.
>
> My first classroom at the neighborhood preschool was dark, and lighting was poor. It had built-in bookshelves, remnants of its residential history. The color of the walls was a light neutral, [but] the lack of daylighting made it feel dark ... dingy. The pervasive smell of the house was ... what I imagine a dungeon would be. There were no [good] smells ... the humidity was awful. Daylight was minimal at best.
>
> [I]t became evident that I was well ahead of my fellow students in my age group ... [and] the principal and teacher proposed that I move up to the next level. Th[is] room [had] the same feeling, but in this space, I was bullied and not welcomed. In spite of the fact that both rooms shared the same physical properties, I felt better in the first room in that I was not bullied. The denseness and busyness of the first room made me feel good; in the new room, miserable ... my positive interaction with my fellow classmates [in the first room] created a feeling that I was in control ... Persistently being bullied in the second space left me feeling helpless and unhappy. Nothing in the second room stimulated me, it was a negative experience.
>
> I was and still am a high achiever and exhilarated about learning, this atmosphere haunted me for the rest of my life. [T]o this day, working in offices that have poor lighting is not acceptable. When given a choice, I will always choose the office with the most daylighting, the bigger the window, the better. I will compromise on other factors, but not natural light and good artificial light.
>
> I [can] find myself in situations that evoke specific memories of my preschool days. I recently attended a conference at Harvard University, passing through a corridor whose smell elicited a ... memory of my elementary school. In Iran, lunch boxes were collected at the entrance to the school and then distributed to their owners at lunchtime. These sat for hours, unrefrigerated, and the combined odors were not pleasant. The room had a musty and repugnant smell. I hadn't thought about that[room] for years, but in an instant, it all came back in that corridor at Harvard.
>
> I understand that a mindset affects how I feel about an environment. We have technical means to control emotional reactions. Architects and designers need to use these tools to help people control the space ... in order to have a positive experience.

Table 16.5 Results of Environmental Interaction: As I Recall...

Arousal (psychological readiness for activity)	All classrooms fell short of engaging me
Affect (emotional reaction)	Negative feelings follow me throughout life and impact the decisions I make today regarding the environments that I occupy
Adaptation (process of changing and adjusting)	I tolerated all of the environments
Issues of personal control (one's ability to control the environment)	In the first classroom, I was able to control the environment because I was not bullied, not the case in the second classroom

Table 16.6 Snapshot Outcomes of Environmental Interactions: Impact at The Time

Performance (manner in which one responds to stimuli)	Because I was intelligent and highly motivated, I circumvented the negative stimulation
Interpersonal relationships (how well the environment facilitated the interactions of the individuals who occupy the space)	Sociological factors impacted how the environments were utilized
Satisfaction (how pleased the individual is with the respective environment)	Neither classroom satisfied the me, but interpersonal relationships impacted my attitude towards the space
Health/Stress (determined by the overall fundamental psychological processes)	My ability to see beyond the immediate environments and social factors, while they were stressful at the time, did not lead to negative health

Elements and Principles of Design Aren't From Mars and Theories Aren't From Venus: They Can Learn to Speak to Each Other!

Designers and architects design environments to fulfill programmatic needs and make every attempt to create an aesthetically pleasing space. Considering and then matching the appropriate theories to the needs of the people who will occupy the space, along with functional requirements, is a good start to creating a positive experience for the end user—but will not necessarily please everyone. These interviews indicate how the application of environmental psychology theories affects the perception of spaces. According to the adaptation theory, someone expecting a low stimulation level in a space would have a positive experience if the aggregate of the elements and principles of design present spoke to the anticipated calming mood. Conversely, if someone was expecting a highly stimulating space, this same environment would prove a letdown and be underwhelming; in other words, a negative experience.

Environmental design psychology theories should inform the manipulation of the elements and principles of architecture and interior design, to facilitate the intended function of the space and fulfill the emotional needs of the end user. For example, the orientation of a line affects its role in a visual construction. While a vertical line can express a state of equilibrium with the force of gravity, symbolize the human condition, or mark a position in space, a horizontal line can represent stability, the ground plane, the horizon, or a body at rest (Ching, 2007). The shape, size, color, texture, position, orientation, and visual inertia of the form, arranged per the principles of design, affect the perception of a space. The six ordering principles—axis, symmetry, hierarchy, rhythm, datum, and transformation—are very important factors in the overall satisfaction of the assisted living and shopping experience. The occupants are able to quickly understand the space and navigate through it, taking cues from size, placement, and density of the structural components and furniture. Linking the psychological perception of the elements and principles with theories such as the stimulation, affordance, preference model, and elements of legibility, the end user is highly satisfied with the space(s).

Color, applied to the built environment, has an impact on the psyche of the occupants. Culturally, color has different symbolic meanings, so designers need to research these meanings in order not to offend. Meaning, as ascribed to color, is based first on physical associations we take from the natural world around us. For, example, we "see red" because people actually do show an increase in blood pressure when viewing the color red. These responses to color are ingrained deeply into our brains and biology (Dorosz & Watson, 2011). Associations are created by selecting a combination of a picture plane (portrait, landscape, square, and round), shapes (regular, irregular), and colors (value, saturation, temperature). Designers can use certain formulas to better create a connection between the message of color and shape, having it speaks to an environmental design psychology theory. For example, a horizontal picture plane, irregular flowing lines, high key values, and desaturated tinted cool analogous colors result in a calming essence in the environment. Conversely, fear and intimidation could be conveyed by the use of strong verticals, sharp angular irregular shapes, the use of predominantly low-key values, and fully saturated and complementary colors (Dorosz & Watson, 2011). Not fully understanding the inherent visceral properties of tools used to manipulate space and the link to the success of environmental modification while speaking to theories steering their use, can result in spaces that do not fulfill the needs of the end user.

Conclusion

Environmental design psychology should use a holistic approach in which environmental psychologists consider biological and sociological influences, and how to use methods of environmental modification and design strategies to enhance preferred actions and reduce undesirable behaviors. Designers and architects need to pay close attention to their use of the basic elements and principles. The pervasive, recurring theme in the interviews is how a space made the subject(s) feel. Buildings and interiors should serve their occupants functionally, aesthetically, and emotionally. To that end, environmental design psychology theories thoughtfully intersected with the elements and principles of design and architecture might provide a positive experience for all who occupy a space.

References

Ching, F.D.K. (2007). *Architecture-Form, Space, and Order*, 3rd ed. Hoboken, NJ: John Wiley and Sons, Inc.

Dorosz, C. & Watson, J.R. (2011). *Designing with Color.* New York: Fairchild Books.

Guthrie, S.E. (1997). Anthropomorphism: A definition and a theory, in R.W. Mitchell, N.S. Thompson, and H.L. Miles, eds. *Anthropomorphism, Anecdotes, and Animals* Albany, NY: State

University of New York Press, pp. 50–58. As cited in Kopec, D. (2012). *Environmental Psychology for Design*, 2nd ed. New York: Fairchild Books.

Kaplan, S. & Kaplan, R. (1982). *Cognition and Environment: Functioning in an Uncertain World*. New York, NY: Praeger. As cited in Kopec, D. (2012). *Environmental Psychology for Design*, 2nd ed. New York: Fairchild Books.

Kopec, D. (2012). *Environmental Psychology for Design*, 2nd ed. New York: Fairchild Books.

Office on Women's Health: U.S. Department of Health and Human Services (last updated: 2012, July 16). *Fibromyalgia Fact Sheet*. Retrieved July 22, 2014 from: http://www.womenshealth.gov/publications/our-publications/fact-sheet/fibromyalgia.html

17

Inclusive/Universal Design

People at the Center of the Design Process

Valerie Fletcher

Design as a Social Art

We episodically remember that architecture—and all of design—is a "social art" by people for people. Our definition of "social" evolves and shifts in response to the current context. With Vitruvius' treatise on architecture in the first century, a perfectly proportioned young athletic male was the starting point for a rational architecture that aligned human symmetry with the perfect geometries of the circle and the square. More than 1,400 hundred years later Leonardo da Vinci created the drawing that defined that perceived harmony between the idealized human body and the physical world (Froyen, 2012).

In the Middle Ages, the mingling of architecture and devotional practices emphasized every aspect of the mind and body's involvement in pilgrimage. The Abbey at Cluny and the Cluniac monasteries throughout Western Europe created magnificent vaulted stone structures that were perfect complements to the sound of chanted psalms. The effect was so compelling that the monasteries drew crowds of pilgrims hundreds of miles, some making the trek at the end of their lives to the splendor of that multisensory experience as the ideal transition to the afterlife (Conant, 1978).

Early modernists Marcel Breuer, Le Corbusier, Walter Gropius, and Mies van der Rohe took up the reformist stance of the Arts and Crafts movement and "embraced the philosophy that good design might, by bringing unity to the arts, operate as a tool for social change" (Barter, 2001). For them, the opportunity for standardization of quality would make good design available to everyone across the economic spectrum.

The mid-twentieth century called for a new modernism that explored the relationship between architecture and human needs as well as synthesizing social science disciplines that could enhance architecture's positive impact on people. The College of Environmental Design at the University of California at Berkeley pays homage to its founders from that era and quotes William Wurther's vision expressed in an essay on architectural education in 1948 in the *Journal of the AIA*. Wurther extols the importance of emphasizing architecture for the social and public good over personal expression and promotes the incorporation of scientific knowledge from the social sciences and economics (College of Environmental Design, University of California at Berkeley, n.d.).

Intersections between social trends and architecture, from Vitruvias' foundational ideas about the body as a base element for form to industrialization as an opportunity to extend good design to everyone, have defined the sequential iteration of architecture as a social art.

Twenty-first Century Demographics as a Catalyst

In the twenty-first century, another intersection of cultural trends poses a radical challenge to architecture and design. This time, it is a demographic tsunami competing for attention in a world still newly awakened to a shared responsibility for sustainability. Twentieth-century inattention, if not blatant irresponsibility, to the protection of the planet's finite resources demands a sense of urgency that few would question today. For those designers of the built environment who make choices about materials and energy, there is a special onus. A weekly bounty of lectures, publications, conferences, and symposia sound the alarm of the risk to life as we know it. They assert the critical role of designers to find ways to stem the damage and uncover new methods of making places and things that not only do no harm but contribute to the restoration of balance. Opportunities abound in design education to pursue undergraduate and graduate degrees and certificates in environmental sustainability. Though some programs offer a more expansive attention to social sustainability, it's rare to find attention to design for a world more diverse in age and ability than ever before.

Global Aging

The dramatic extension of the human lifespan is an equally dramatic by-product of the twentieth century. Longer lives—worldwide—are an irreversible fact of the twenty-first century with profound implications for architecture and design. A recent joint publication from the United Nations Population Fund and HelpAge International, *Ageing in the Twenty-First Century: A Celebration and A Challenge,* makes the point that global aging is the most stunning accomplishment of the last hundred years but also that it demands a comparable sense of urgency to green if we are to make it work.

The hallmarks of development worldwide are that the population lives healthier and longer lives and that each woman has fewer children. As development progresses, the population age cohorts shift dramatically. Today, only Japan has a population where the percentage of people aged 60 and over is 30 percent of the population. By 2050, it's expected that 64 nations will have 30 percent or more of their population over 60 (United Nations Populations Fund, Help Age International 2012). The longer lives in the developed nations are no surprise where there are resources to ensure safety, adequate nutrition and good healthcare. But the phenomenon of aging is at least as extraordinary a story in the developing nations. Today 50 countries have more than 10 million people aged 60 or over; seven of them in developing countries (United Nations Populations Fund, Help Age International, 2012).

We don't have the option to cheer our good fortune and our 30-year 'longevity dividend' and get on with our longer lives. If we do nothing, our demographic bonus catapults us into untenable social and economic conditions in which a sizable portion of elders are physically and economically dependent. With the reduction or eradication of infectious and parasitic diseases and with safer drinking water, we now live long enough for a high proportion of us to experience chronic conditions and non-communicable diseases. Our challenge is to figure out how to design a world that can accommodate an increasing volume of episodic and persistent functional limitations and allow as many people as possible to be independent and thriving as contributors for all of their lives.

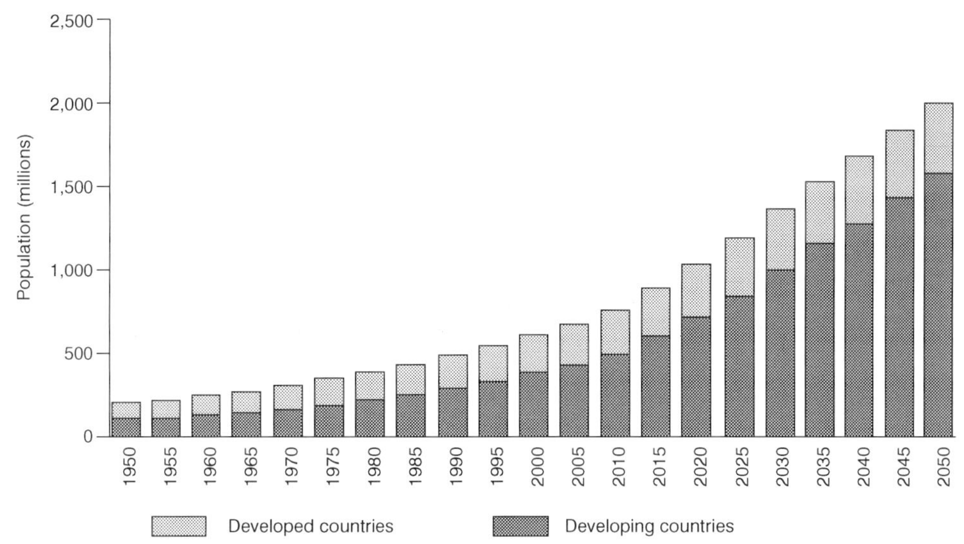

Figure 17.1 Chart of world population aging depicts the identical trajectory of developed and developing countries. Chart courtesy: HelpAge International

A Global Shift in the Etiology of Disability

The extraordinary boon in lifespans is not the only by-product of the global public health successes of the twentieth century. Disability has changed fundamentally in etiology and in the shift from a focus on diagnosis as destiny to an appreciation that functional impact is what's significant to understand and to mitigate. We once assumed disability to be the fixed state of a minority who had congenital impairments, birth trauma, or who acquired significant functional impairments from injury or illness. Now, with longer lives and high survival rates, difference in ability has increased to become a predictable human experience, at least episodically, for everyone.

Arthritis, not surprisingly, in all its manifestations from the common osteoarthritis to rheumatoid arthritis, lupus, fibromyalgia, and gout leads as the most common reason for disability in the U.S. Though it is common among people over 65, two-thirds of people with arthritis are under 65. The symptomatic joint pain and stiffness can dramatically impact both dexterity and the ability to walk or climb stairs (Centers for Disease Control and Prevention, 2013).

Hearing loss is another example of a rising incidence condition related to aging. This observation is borne out by recent epidemiologic data reporting 26.7 million Americans 50 or older have hearing loss, a substantially higher number than those who self-report hearing loss. Fewer than 15 percent of that number own hearing aids with a far smaller proportion who use them (Lin, 2012). We have yet to grapple with the design of environments for work or leisure that anticipate this new reality.

Changing Perspectives on Disability Impact Data

As a demographic category, disability is a human characteristic similar to race or gender. An individual may or may not choose it as part of their personal identity. For some, there is a sense of community that can be a source of pride and strength. For many others, especially those with non-apparent conditions, there is little impetus to disclose a disability. It is likely that the sharp global shift away from categorization by diagnoses was made possible by the many thousands of people who reinvented the experience of disability by living unique self-directed lives because they were free to do so for the first time. With the shift in focus to a continuum of health and function, we leave behind notions of a sharp line between health and disability and recognize the mutability of individual limitations.

In order to understand better whom we are designing for, it's helpful to know the four questions on disability in the U.S. Census Bureau's American Community Survey (ACS), all of them soliciting a yes or no answer about a set of functional limitations of whatever cause:

- Is this person deaf or does he/she have serious difficulty hearing?
- Is this person blind or does he/she have serious difficulty seeing even when wearing glasses?
- Because of a physical, mental, or emotional condition, does this person have serious difficulty concentrating, remembering, or making decisions?
- Does this person have serious difficulty walking or climbing stairs?
- Does this person have difficulty dressing or bathing?
- Because of a physical, mental, or emotional condition, does this person have difficulty doing errands alone such as visiting a doctor's office or shopping (U.S. Census Bureau, 2013)?

The U.S. Census Bureau annually issues a report to coincide with the anniversary of the passage of the Americans with Disabilities Act on July 26 in 1990. Their 2014 report indicated that there are 56.7 million Americans with disabilities, about 19 percent of the non-institutionalized population. That's 8 percent of children under 15; 21 percent of people 15 and older; 50 percent of people 65 and over.

What is the functional profile of this large slice of the population? The Census Bureau reports that the most common impairment for people 15 and over is movement limitation, such as walking or climbing stairs with 30.6 million reporting it (U.S. Census Bureau, 2014). Most within that big number use no visible assistive devices, not even a cane. As any built environment designer knows, the primary focus across all accessibility standards is design that accommodates people who use wheelchairs or other wheeled mobility. Though many others who report difficulty walking can benefit from designs for wheelchair access, the actual number of people who use wheelchairs in the United States is 3.6 million today, projected to grow to only 4.3 million by 2030.

Children and Disability

The changes in childhood disability are at least as dramatic as for adults. Many of the most common conditions causing disability in the twentieth century have been eradicated (e.g., smallpox, diphtheria, polio, rubella). Families have fewer children. Over the last century the population in the United States tripled but the birth rate declined dramatically, from 32.2 to 14.4 per 1,000 persons (Halfon *et al.*, 2012). The United States has a higher fertility rate than other developed nations but still averages just one or two children per woman and less than the 'replacement rate' of 2.1 births that maintains the existing population (Livingston & Cohn, 2012).

The United States led the world in modeling legal mandates for non-discrimination for children with disabilities but, even more significantly, was the first nation to ensure the provision, regardless of cost, of integrated education for children with disabilities. The 1975 Individuals with Disabilities Education Act (IDEA) mandated that children and youth ages 3–21 with disabilities be provided a free and appropriate public school education in an integrated setting to the maximum extent possible, paid primarily, like all preK-12 public education, from local property taxes and supplemented with federal and state formula grants (U.S. Department of Education, n.d.). The U.S. commitment to integrated education has transformed the experience of growing up with a disability in America as well as guaranteeing that every student is exposed to peers with functional differences.

The most recent Department of Education statistics reports that 95 percent of 6- to 21-year-old US students with disabilities were served in regular schools. Only 3 percent were served in a specialized school for children with disabilities with 1 percent placed in private schools by their parents. Less than 1 percent of children with disabilities between 3 and 21 were served a separate residential facility, educated at home, in a hospital, or in a correctional facility (Halfon *et al.*, 2012).

Inclusive schools are normative in the U.S. But accessibility standards for the design of schools hasn't caught up with the changing profile of childhood disability. Until the 1960s, the typical image of childhood disability was of a child with polio using leg braces and crutches. Rates of childhood disability are increasing but they are due primarily to emotional, behavioral, and neurological conditions (Livingston & Cohn, 2012). The United States also experienced much higher survival rates of very fragile preterm births, some of whom will have complex physical, sensory and cognitive limitations all of their lives. The design interventions for children on the Autism Spectrum and others such as learning disabilities and sensory processing disorders are being explored in small studies around the world but not yet widely known.

One constant remains in place: the disparity in rates of disability between poor and non-poor families. Poor households have rates of disability 150 percent of non-poor families (Salmen, 2001).

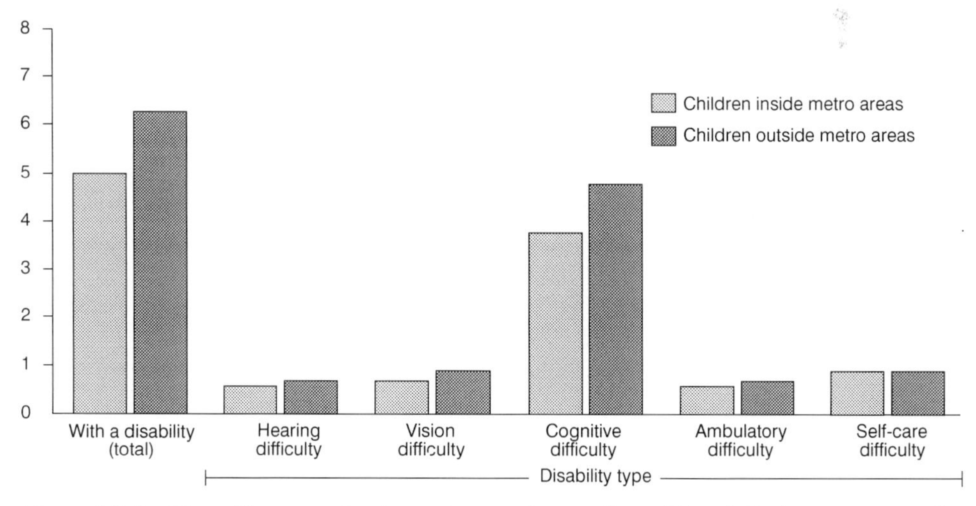

Figure 17.2 Chart illustrates the dramatic prevalence of cognitive difficulty as a reason for disability among school-aged children. Image courtesy: International Copyright, 2016, U.S Department of Commerce, U.S Government

In the twenty-first century, the social art of design must find ways to respond to a new world shaped by our collective good fortune in which we can expect to live longer and survive more than at any time in human history. Design is a key to that being a celebratory challenge and not a shared burden.

Requirements for Accessibility

United States Legal Infrastructure for Accessibility

The United States was an early adopter of mandates for accessibility that date to the early 1960s. The American National Standards Institute (ANSI) issued the first standards for accessibility in 1961 with ANSI A117, initiating a continuing practice of public/private collaboration. It became the basis for model building codes. At the federal level, the Architectural Barriers Act of 1968 referenced ANSI A117, the first of a sequence of laws with regulations and standards that became the framework for legally mandated accessibility in the U.S. (National Council on Disability, 2003).

The passage of the Rehabilitation Act in 1973 marked the first time that people with a range of functional limitations were considered a "class" that could be identified as having a shared experience of discrimination. It built upon the 1964 Civil Rights Act. In a time of social ferment and activism, people with disabilities shared strategies and tactics with the anti-war, women's, and gay right's movements.

Section 504 of the Rehabilitation Act was designed to promote and expand opportunities for persons with a broad range of disabilities and offer protection from "unwarranted discrimination stemming from prejudice, social stigmas, and negative assumptions about their ability to fully participate in the mainstream of society" (U.S. Access Board, 2004). Previously, people with developmental disabilities, blindness or low vision, mental health conditions, who were Deaf or hard-of-hearing, veterans, polio survivors, and others were considered separately in the nation's laws and policies. For the first time anywhere, design was identified as a civil right, making the case that equal opportunity for people with disabilities is contingent on accessible environments.

From 1984 to 1990, a sequence of three federal laws expanded the rights of the newly protected class of people with disabilities, all with stipulations for accessible design. The 1984 Voting Accessibility Act mandated that polling places be accessible or that alternative ways be identified that would enable older adults and people with disabilities to exercise their right to vote. The 1988 Amendments to the 1968 Fair Housing Act (FHA), expanded the original protections of the Act that prohibited discrimination based on race, national origin or family status to include people with disabilities and requirements for accessible design and construction in multi-family housing regardless of public money and applicable to both owned and rental properties.

The landmark Americans with Disabilities Act (ADA) was signed into law on July 26, 1990, the most sweeping legislation regarding the equal rights of people with disabilities to date worldwide. It prohibited discrimination on the basis of disability in employment, state and local government, public accommodations, commercial facilities, transportation, and telecommunications. The ADA expands beyond the condition of federal financial participation in the Rehabilitation Act and establishes responsibilities for nearly all public and private organizations. The ADA Accessibility Guidelines (ADAAG) set a new bar for mandated accessible design requirements for new construction and alterations but also provided clarity about expectations for existing conditions in private places of public accommodation.

The U.S. Department of Justice issued revised 2010 ADA Standards for Accessible Design in the Federal Register on September 15, 2010. The U.S. Access Board generates the design standards that are then issued in final form with the force of law by the U.S. Department of Justice. In these revised ADA standards, the Access Board prioritized "harmonization" to state building codes and worked closely with the International Codes Council (ICC) and the American National Standards Institute (ANSI) in order to reduce the confusion of meeting the requirement of federal standards deriving from civil rights legislation with state buildings code accessibility requirements (Goldsmith, 2000). Though helpful in some ways, the emphasis on harmonization with building code risks occluding the civil rights vision of the federal legislation that challenged designers to use their skills to create integrated settings.

The United Kingdom's Legal Infrastructure for Accessibility

The United Kingdom's commitment to accessible design has followed a similar but not identical pattern to the United States. The Royal Institute of British Architects (RIBA) published *Designing for the Disabled* in 1963 that became a standard textbook for architects. The Polio Research Fund commissioned Selwyn Goldsmith, registered architect and polio survivor, to write it (Staintons, 2014). Second editions were published in 1967 and 1976.

U.K. minimum standards for accessibility were issued in 1992 as Approved Document M of the Building Regulations and modified in 1995 and in 2004. Compliance with Part M initially required Access Statements to be developed and provided as part of the pre-schematic, design development, and construction documentation phases for major developments. It required an innovative Access Statement that involved people with disabilities. If needed, the Access Statements could be used to identify constraints to typical compliance and to describe alternatives (Equality Act 2010, C.15, Chapter I. 2010).

The Disability Discrimination Act of 1995 used a human rights approach similar to Section 504 and the ADA, and focused on people with disabilities as a protected class. It was superseded, along with other anti-discrimination laws, by the Equality Act 2010. The anti-discrimination focus remained but with a much broader set of social conditions covered under a single umbrella law (Equality Act 2010, C.15, Chapter I).

Both the United States and the United Kingdom had extensive history with mandates for equal rights and design standards primarily focused on architectural access by wheelchairs users. It had become clear that many other people benefited from the standards despite that narrow focus. Curb cuts, ramps and accessible vertical access made wheeled luggage the rational choice for everyone. Few people used wheelchairs but ten times that number had difficulty walking.

Universal Design Leadership Evolves from Accessibility

Two figures emerged at approximately the same time in the 1990s with a shared perspective that it was time to think more expansively about designing for everyone. Both Selwyn Goldsmith, born in 1932 in Nottinghamshire, and Ronald (Ron) Mace, born in 1941 in North Carolina, were licensed architects who had survived polio and used wheelchairs. Both had the credibility of being wheelchair users bent on summoning attention to a bigger idea. For them, mandated accessibility was a valuable floor but too narrowly focused for an increasingly diverse world.

Universal Design

Ron Mace, FAIA was a key figure in the development in the United States of the Principles of Universal Design in 1997. Ten authors (Bettye Rose Connell, Mike Jones, Ron Mace, Jim Mueller, Abir Mullick, Elaine Ostroff, Jon Sanford, Ed Steinfeld, Molly Story, and Gregg Vanderheiden) from five U.S. organizations compiled the Principles. They were copyrighted to North Carolina State University's Center for Universal Design. The definition of universal design introduces the principles: "The design of products and environments to be usable by all people, to the greatest expect possible, without the need for adaptation or specialized design." The seven principles follow with a key concept and definition. The full set also includes brief guidelines and key elements.

- *Principle One: Equitable Use*: The design is useful and marketable to people with diverse abilities.
- *Principle Two: Flexibility in Use*: The design accommodates a wide range of individual preferences and abilities.
- *Principle Three: Simple and Intuitive Use*: Use of the design is easy to understand, regardless of the user's experience, knowledge, language skills, or current concentration level.
- *Principle Four: Perceptible Information*: The design communicates necessary information effectively to the user, regardless of ambient condition or the user's sensory abilities.
- *Principle Five: Tolerance for Error*: The design minimizes hazards and the adverse consequences of accidental or unintended actions.
- *Principle Six: Low Physical Effort*: The design can be used efficiently and comfortably and with a minimum of fatigue.
- *Principle Seven: Size and Space for Approach and Use*: Appropriate size and space is provided for approach, reach, manipulation, and use regardless of user's body size, posture, or mobility (Mace, 1998).

The original publication closed with a note that the Principles address only universally usable design and that the practice of design must also integrate other considerations such as economic, engineering, cultural, gender, and environment.

In June 1998 the first international conference on universal design was held in New York, *Designing for the 21st Century: An International Conference on Universal Design* with participants from 30 nations. Ron Mace delivered a keynote on June 19, *A Perspective on Universal Design*. He expressed his concern that there be clarity that accessibility and barrier-free design were not universal design. He stressed that terminology mattered and described accessibility as focused on people with disabilities, a useful baseline but only a floor. He clarified that assistive technologies like wheelchairs and white canes solve problems at the individual level and universal design at the general level (Staintons, 2014). Ron died suddenly of post-polio syndrome ten days after his lecture.

Just two years later, in 2000, Selwyn Goldsmith published *Universal Design* with PRP Architects. He critiqued the traditional practice of accessible and barrier-free design as "top-down" dictates of special provisions for people with disabilities. He posited that we need a shift to a "bottom-up" way of thinking that would reframe normal to include all potential users, requiring that anticipating diversity of ability should be a given in good design (Froyen, 2012). Goldsmith stressed that his publication focused solely on information that could be conveyed with diagrams, well short of the plethora of details like acoustics, finishes, and heating and cooling systems that comprise a universally designed environment.

A dozen years later, another architect with a disability, Hubert Froyen, explored a frontier area in universal design. A professor of architecture in Hasselt, Belgium, Froyen was a diligent student of modernism, studying in the Netherlands with John Habrakan and at the University of California at Berkeley with Christopher Alexander. Deeply involved in the global movement called by a variety of terms by that time: universal design, inclusive design, design-for-all, Froyen developed a narrative that tied modernism to the movement's radical reversal of focus from designing for a person who needs to be accommodated to designing an enabling environment for all.

Professor Froyen mounted a long-term research project to investigate what we know and don't know about the needs and desires of an increasing proportion of the population with functional limitations. He acknowledged that we knew a great deal about people who used wheelchairs but that there was scant information about what failed and what worked for the great majority of people who experienced physical, sensory or cognitive differences.

The principles of universal design had been in use globally for fifteen years. Froyen diagnosed a knowledge gap that designers needed filled in order to be able to design the deeply creative and high quality solutions that needed better empirical evidence to inform design. Unlike environmental sustainability that derives data from measurable use of energy and materials' life-cycle costs, universal design needed more data about human experience. He recognized that filling the gap required generating substantial new information about a large number and diversity of users interacting with a multitude of detailed elements within the built environment.

Froyen also called for designers to heed the complementary work of other disciplines that could inform and compel inclusive design. He tied it to the pervasive commitment

Figure 17.3 A simple touch is all it takes to activate the flow of water in Delta kitchen faucet with Touch20 Technology. Photo courtesy: Delta Faucet

Figure 17.4 The tactile Bradley watch, named for blind paralympian swimmer, Brad Snyder, is as esthetically compelling as it is functional. Photo courtesy: Eone Timepieces

to the environment/economy/equity foundation of sustainability. He linked not only the obvious resonance with equity in considering equal opportunity and equal participation. He also makes an economic argument that societies will suffer the economic cost of caring for dependent people unless we can design a world to support independence and life-long contribution. He pointed to the pertinent explosion of the growth of neuroscience that has revealed the extraordinary plasticity of the nervous system, opening the door to a radically new potential for recovery from illness and injury.

If universal design is ever to have the kind of impact that radically alters how we design and how we think about the consequential power of design, Froyen argued that we must invest in research as a central priority. He called for interdisciplinary research through the creation of a dynamic open content community development model of research by and with diverse users. Having tested the method for seven years, he had proven that user data could illuminate patterns about design that could minimize limitations and enhance strengths for people across a wide range of functional abilities (Guimarães, 2011).

Universal/inclusive design builds from a floor of accessibility that has an abundance of fixed standards within a larger vision of equal rights. Those standards vary little from nation to nation. While establishing awareness and appetite for universal design, it's important to gather precedents that demonstrate universal design that is satisfying esthetically as well as environmentally and economically sustainable. Though vital, precedents cannot obviate the critical task of additional research that will give architects and designers the information about user experience that can drive and inspire innovation.

Pervasive accessibility requirements have resulted in an unintended negative consequence of just-tell-me-what-I-have-to-do that is an impediment to universal design. Brazilian architect and professor of architecture Marcelo Pinto Guimarães laments that his nation has some good examples of inclusive design but misses the chance to integrate it in Brazil's rapid development. He describes the basic catalogue of accessible solutions as "grammar" as opposed to creative writing of the "poetry" of design for inclusion that we need now (World Health Organization, 2001).

Global Policy Responds

The United Nations' World Health Organization (WHO) spent ten years building consensus among 192 U.N. member states for a more accurate definition of disability appropriate to the twenty-first century's seismic demographic shifts. They published the International Classification of Functioning, Disability, and Health (ICF) of 2001 with a dramatic new definition of disability that has shaped an evolving consensus across the globe. It suggested that disability is "an umbrella term for impairments, activity limitations, and participation restrictions" (World Health Organization, 2002).

The new WHO's ICF offered a common language that reflected the demographic transformations of the twenty-first century. With greatly extended lifespans worldwide and dramatically improved survival rates from congenital conditions and from illness and injury, WHO mainstreamed functional limitation as a universal human experience. WHO also succeeded in equalizing physical and mental reasons for impairments.

Most significantly for designers, the new definition described disability as a contextual variable. Functional limitation becomes disabling at the intersection of the individual and her or his multiple environments: physical, information, communication, social or attitudinal and policy. Designers, significant shapers of the human context, have the power to minimize disability despite a rising tide of functional limitation.

Given the advances of the twentieth century and substantial experience of people with disabilities living fully integrated lives in the community, it had become clear that diagnosis of a condition did not predict the level of disability. With decades of experience with mandated accessibility standards in the U.S. and E.U., there was ample evidence that barrier removal benefited people with and without disabilities. But accessibility was not enough to minimize limitations for the extraordinarily varied and changing profile of functional limitations at the start of the twenty-first century. Even removing familiar barriers in all environments would fall short of a new WHO vision of designing facilitating environments.

The World Health Organization specifically identified universal design as the most promising framework for identifying facilitators. It assumed that universal design was the starting perspective but that work would be required to assess needs, identify potential solutions, test them with users, refine them, and gradually to develop guidelines for facilitating environments for a mix of sectors (United Nations Populations Fund, 2012).

With focus on creating a policy and action agenda for an aging world, the Second World Assembly on Aging convened in Madrid in 2002. Building on the ICF and its contextual definition of disability, it focused on catalyzing policies that would go beyond the too modest goal of barrier removal and "ensure enabling and supportive environments" (*Political Declaration and Madrid International Plan of Action on Ageing,* 2002). The policy repeatedly emphasized multi-generational living and design that enhances individual capabilities and supports the contribution of older people (United Nations, 2006).

The most recent international policy also builds on ICF and responds to the growing proportion of the world's population with functional limitations by establishing a global commitment to equity and participation. The U.N. Convention on the Rights of People with Disabilities (CRPD) was completed and enforceable in 2006. This is the third supplement to the 1948 Universal Declaration of Human Rights. The CRPD established accessible design as a human right and emphasized universal design as a preferred goal. It also affirmed that these issues must be integrated into global strategies for sustainable development (Convention on the Human Rights of People with Disabilities, Preamble).

Catalysts to Inclusive Design Practice

A baseline of accessibility standards has grown steadily for both new construction and existing conditions in much of the world. There is also a growing tier of practitioners around the world that recognize the limits of fixed standards for people with disabilities and strive to redesign a context for our lives that aligns with the demographic facts of our time. They are creating solutions inspired and informed by human diversity without sacrificing esthetics or delight.

Urban design sometimes leads, with connectivity between places, shared outdoor gathering places, and seamless public transit as lynchpins of designing for people. Great public spaces, like London's South Bank or Los Angeles' Grand Park, illustrate that inclusive public spaces generate the social capital that occurs when people connect in a place they want to be across social, economic, age, ability, and cultural differences.

United Kingdom

The United Kingdom's Commission for Architecture and the Built Environment (CABE) was created in 1999 as a public body to help elevate the quality of public design. By helping decision-makers and professionals to create great spaces and inspire the public to demand good design, CABE committed to integrating environmental sustainability and inclusive design, intent on creating places that work for people (Bonnett, 2013). Until 2012 when more than 90 percent of funding for CABE was cut, CABE set a high and very visible bar for inclusive design in the United Kingdom. Through training designers to bring these values to the local planning tables, fostering participatory planning with local people with functional limitations, and capturing detail in case studies, they helped to instill inclusive design into ordinary design practice.

David Bonnett Associates authored valuable guidance in a 2013 publication by the British Standards Institution, *Inclusive Urban Design*. They make the case for an approach and the use of detailed considerations to deliver inclusive design solutions without adding dozens of fixed standards. Bonnett advises consulting with local users with functional issues in order to understand their perspectives before moving to design development. The guide stresses the significance of legibility and wayfinding as central to places that work and includes recommendations for consistency, lighting, touch, smell, and sound as well as signage (Bonnett, 2013).

Singapore

Singapore, with a population of only 5.4 million, has built an identity as a global design powerhouse. They envision design as a means to economic growth as well as a way to make lives better. They moved very rapidly from establishing requirements for accessibility to exceed compliance by building capacity and creating incentives for universal design. Government engaged leaders in the design community as well as developers. A national green design strategy evolved first and wins international recognition and awards for its smart density and livability strategies. Singapore is now using similar top-down promotion to stimulate innovation in universal design. Good examples grow annually of impressive green and universal projects. Platinum 2013 Universal Design Mark winner, the United World College of South East Asia (East Campus), also won the 2012 Platinum Green Mark Award. The campus' elevated landscape connects four academic blocks with a main plaza, playing fields, and other amenities while distinctive cultural motifs and colors make wayfinding intuitive and seamless (twenty-six winners for the first BCA Universal Design Mark Award).

Housing

Across the world, a sense of urgency is growing that we must reinvent typical housing that will work for a large proportion of the population with some level of functional limitations. With rising prevalence of functional limitations, traditional solutions of specialized funding or housing types is proving inadequate and outmoded. In the United States, the doubling of the 65+ population over the next 40 years is finally setting off alarms. Too little attention has been paid to a looming misfit between the housing we have and the housing we need (Lipman *et al.*, 2012).

The London 2012 Olympic Park, now the Queen Elizabeth Olympic Park, has resulted in an international exemplar of inclusive design in the public realm but also in housing. Starting with the 2,828 homes of the Olympic Village, there will be a total of 6,800 housing units, as well as health, retail, and community spaces, all of them green and universal. Guidance and oversight are provided by the London Legacy Corporation with strong support from the Mayor (London Development Authority, 2010). This massive development in East London illustrates the fundamental shift to designing for the physical, sensory, and brain-based variations in ability and over the course of a lifetime. One hundred percent of units align with the London Housing Design Guide of 2010 (London Development Authority, 2010) including thoughtful features detailed in the remarkable chapter on "Home as a Place of Retreat."

Culture

Tourism, particularly cultural tourism, has become another driver for universal design especially in Europe. The European Commission hosts conferences on accessible tourism and annually sponsors a conference for cities to compete to be the most accessible city in the European Union. France, perennially one of the most popular destinations for cultural tourism, has struggled to make its historic environment more welcoming to more people and prioritizes its design-for-all investments in culture.

An outstanding example of inclusive design is in Nantes, France, the former capital of Brittany. The Castle of the Dukes of Brittany (le Château des Ducs de Bretagne), a museum of the history of Nantes, offers a vigorous solution to vertical access designed by Jean-François Bodin. Rather than tucking an elevator out of sight in this fifteenth-century tufa rock castle, he celebrates it in deep bold red, just one of countless details that enrich everyone's experience well beyond concern for function.

DeafSpace Design Guidelines

Gallaudet University in Washington, D.C. offers an example of what's possible when people with functional limitations get involved in identifying design details that facilitate their performance and experience. Through a series of six semester-long courses and additional workshops, Gallaudet students, faculty and staff learned design and research skills sufficient

Figure 17.5 Dramatic dark red elevator makes a strong design statement while also creating vertical access in the sixteenth century castle which is now the Museum of the History of Nantes, France. Photo permission: Château des ducs de Bretagne

to give them the tools to generate design insights. In this case, users were all Deaf and focused on translating to the environment their Deaf culture and their needs related to their visual language, life experiences, and cognitive sensibilities. Hansel Bauman, AIA, Gallaudet's Executive Director of the Design and Planning Department, organized the insights into a pattern book called DeafSpace Guidelines in an initial 2010 draft describing five major points: space and proximity, sensory reach, mobility and proximity, light and color, and acoustics and electromagnetic interference (Bauman, 2010).

Incorporating the DeafSpace Guidelines, LTL Architects designed a new five-storey 60,000 square foot residence hall that opened in 2012. Though a strong design with exposed steel, wood and bamboo, polished concrete and rich color, its real drama is in its function. As Hansel Bauman noted in an article in Metropolis in July/August of 2013: "It's about creating empathy between the individual and the building" (Hales, 2013).

Conclusion

It's time for a sense of urgency that the good fortune of our longer lives and resilient survival demands action as surely as stopping environmental degradation and restoring our planet to health. We have a shared set of global policies, a near complete global understanding of at least rudimentary barrier removal and accessibility, and a framework and precedents for inclusive

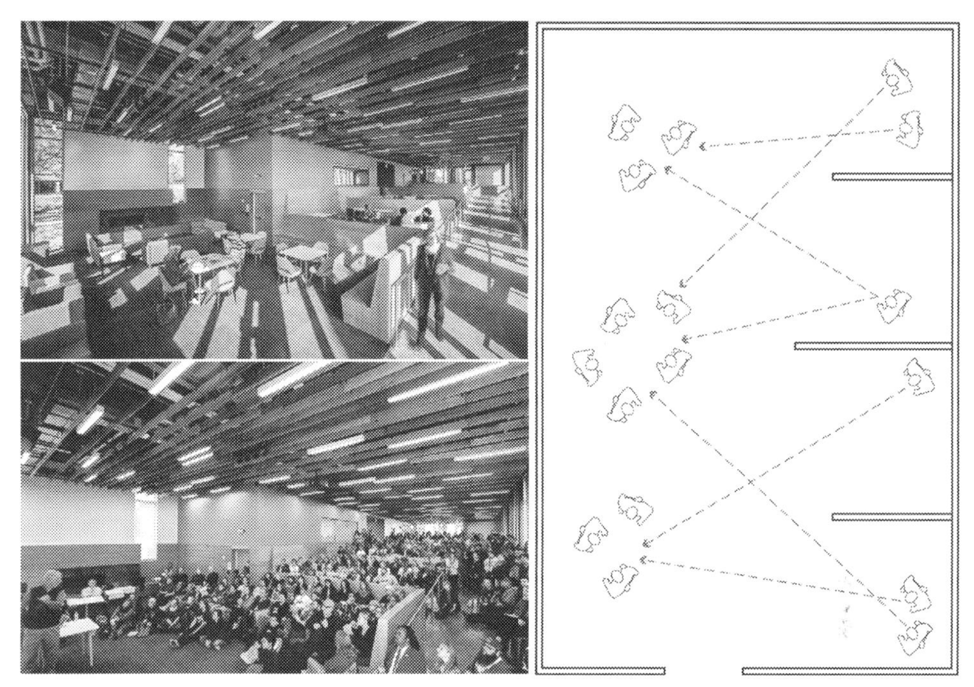

Figure 17.6 DeafSpace Guidelines informed the design of the dormitory by LTL Architects at Gallaudet University. Photo courtesy: LTL Architects; Illustration courtesy: Hansel Bauman, AIA

design that we can build upon. Even the richest societies among us cannot accommodate a steadily expanding population of dependent fellow citizens cut off from independence let alone contribution. We have the frontier of the brain just beginning to reveal what's possible if we design environments to support how our brains develop and function. John Zeisel calls for an Environment/Behavior/Neuroscience (E/B/N) paradigm could contribute to not only quality of life but to survival (Zeisel, 2006).

There is a great deal of research to be done to understand the patterns that reveal the elements that make the most difference to people. "Personas" do not generate insight or detail. We will need to make mining the experiences of real and varied people easy to do anywhere and compelling to people with talent and drive. And we'll need to find ways to make that data an inspirational part of design education and practice. Designing for people in the twenty-first century must be understood as a calling, a vocation. Susan Szenasy, editor-in-chief of Metropolis, has written as much as anyone summoning designers to be more. "We are interested in more than just the fulfillment of the design brief. We want to know how the user, the earth, and the client are served by the design. We want to know what the design says about us as a people" (Hudner, 2014).

References

Barter, J.A. (2001). Designing for democracy: Modernism and its utopias. *Art Institute of Chicago Museum Studies*, 27, 2, 7–10.

Bauman, H. (2010). *DeafSpace Design Guidelines,* Working Draft. Washington, DC: Gallaudet University.

Bonnett, D. (2013). *Inclusive Urban Design: A Guide to Creating Accessible Public Spaces*. London: The British Standards Institution.

Building and Construction Authority (2013). *Twenty-six winners for the first BCA Universal Design Mark Award*. (2013). Retrieved March 16, 2014 from http://www.bca.gov.sg/Newsroom/pr08052013_UDMA.html.

Centers for Disease Control and Prevention (2013). *Arthritis: Meeting the Challenge of Living Well*. Retrieved May 26, 2014 from: http://www.cdc.gov/chronicdisease/resources/publications/aag/arthritis.htm.

College of Environmental Design, University of California at Berkeley (n.d.). *Environmental Design/A New Modernism, Homage to Founders*. Retrieved May 26, 2014 from http://ced.berkeley.edu/cedarchives/exhibitions/exhibits/show/new-modernism/college-and-campus.

Commission for Architecture and the Built Environment (2008). *Inclusion by Design: Equality, Diversity and the Built Environment*. (2008). London: CABE. Retrieved July 20, 2014 from: http://webarchive.nationalarchives.gov.uk/20110118095356/http://www.cabe.org.uk/files/inclusion-by-design.pdf.

Conant, K.J. (1978). *Carolingian and Romanesque Architecture, 800–1200*. New Haven, CT: Yale University Press.

Equality Act 2010, C.15, Chapter I. (2010). *The Protected Characteristics*. Retrieved July 1, 2014 from http://www.legislation.gov.uk/ukpga/2010/15/section/4.

Froyen, H. (2012). *Universal Design: A Methodological Approach*. Boston: IHCD Books.

Goldsmith, S. (2000). *Universal Design*. Oxford: Architectural Press.

Guimarães, M.P. (2011). Writing Poetry Rather than Structuring Grammar: Notes for the Development of Universal Design in Brazil. *Universal Design Handbook*, Second Edition. New York: McGraw Hill.

Hales, L. (July/August 2013). Clear Line of Sight. *Metropolis*, 33, 1, 52–58, 82–83.

Halfon, N., Houtrow, A., Larson, K., & Newacheck, P.W. (2012). The changing landscape of disability in childhood. *Children with Disabilities*. Princeton, NJ: Princeton/Brookings. 22, 1, 13–42.

Hudner, A.S. (2014). *Szenasy, Design Advocate*. New York: Metropolis Books.

Institute of Education Sciences, National Center for Educational Statistics. (2013). Fast facts: Students with disabilities. Retrieved May 26, 2014 from: http://nces.ed.gov/fastfacts/display.asp?id=59.

Lin, F. R. (2012). Hearing Loss in Older Adults: Who's Listening? *Journal of the American Medical Association,* 307, 11, 1147–1148.

Lipman, B., Lubell, J., & Salomon, E. (2012). *Housing an Aging Population: Are We Prepared?* Washington, D.C.: Center for Housing Policy.

Livingston, G., & Cohn, D. (2012). U.S. Birth Rate Falls to a Record Low; Decline is Greatest among Immigrants. *Pew Research Center Social & Demographic Trends*. Retrieved June 30, 2014 from: http://www.pewsocialtrends.org/2012/11/29/u-s-birth-rate-falls-to-a-record-low-decline-is-greatest-among-immigrants/.

London Development Authority (2010). *London Housing Design Guide*. Retrieved March 16, 2014 from http://queenelizabetholympicpark.co.uk/~/media/LLDC/Policies/LLDCInclusiveDesignStandardsMarch2013.pdf.

London Legacy Development Corporation, (2013). *Inclusive Design Standards*. London Legacy Corporation. Retrieved February 23, 2014 from http://queenelizabetholympicpark.co.uk/~/media/LLDC/Policies/LLDCInclusiveDesignStandardsMarch2013.pdf.

Mace, R. (1998). A Perspective on Universal Design (excerpt). Retrieved July 7, 2014 from http://www.ncsu.edu/ncsu/design/cud/about_us/usronmacespeech.htm.

National Council on Disability (2003). *Rehabilitating Section 504*. Retrieved May 1, 2014 from: http://www.ncd.gov/publications/2003/Feb122003.

Political Declaration and Madrid International Plan of Action on Ageing. (2002). Second World Assembly on Ageing, Madrid, Spain. New York: United Nations.

Salmen, J.P.S. (2001). U.S. Accessibility Codes and Standards. *Universal Design Handbook*. New York: McGraw Hill.

Staintons, D. (2014). Part M of the Building Regulations, Approved Document Part M Building Regulations, Minimum Standards. Retrieved July 13, 2014 from http://www.disabledaccess.co.uk/Access_Requirements/partm.htm.

The Center for Universal Design. (1997). *The Principles of Universal Design*, Version 2.0. Raleigh, NC: North Carolina State University.

United Nations. (2006). *Convention on the Human Rights of People with Disabilities, Preamble*. New York: United Nations. Retrieved May 25, 2014 from http://www.un.org/disabilities/convention/conventionfull.shtml.

United Nations Populations Fund. (2012). *Ageing in the Twenty-First Century: A Celebration and A Challenge*. Retrieved February 6, 2014 from http://unfpa.org/ageingreport/

United Nations Populations Fund, Help Age International. (2012). *Ageing in the Twenty-First Century: A Celebration and a Challenge*. Retrieved May 25, 2014 from http://www.unfpa.org/ public/op/edit/home/publications/pid/11584.pdf.

United States Access Board. (2004). Harmonization Benefits, Chapter 3 in *Regulatory Assessment: Executive Summary of the Final Revised Accessibility Guidelines for the Americans with Disabilities Act and Architectural Barriers Act*. Retrieved April 10, 2014 from: http://www.access-board.gov/guidelines-and-standards/buildings-and-sites/about-the-ada-standards/background/regulatory-assessment/chapter-3.

United States Census Bureau. (2013). *American Community Survey: Question on Disability*. Retrieved November 2, 2013 from: http://www.census.gov/acs/www/Downloads/QbyQfact/disability.pdf.

United States Census Bureau. (2014). *Facts for Features, Anniversary of the ADA: July 26*. Retrieved June 29, 2014 from: https://www.census.gov/newsroom/releases/pdf/cb14ff-15_ada.pdf.

United States Department of Education, (n.d.). Building the Legacy: IDEA 2014 Retrieved July 12, 2014 from http://idea.ed.gov/explore/view/p/,root,dynamic,TopicalBrief,18.

World Health Organization (2001). International Classification of Functioning, Disability and Health. Retrieved April 3, 2014 from: http://www.who.int/entity/classifications/icf/icf_more/en/index.html.

World Health Organization. (2002). *Towards a Common Language for Functioning, Disability and Health ICF*. Geneva: World Health Organization.

Zeisel, J. (2006). *Inquiry by Design, Revised Edition*. New York: W.W. Norton.

18

Neuroscience and Architecture

Eve Edelstein

Introduction

The term "*neuroarchitecture*" has long been used to denote the brain's form and function. Increasingly, architects have adopted this term to describe a new field of study that explores how the form of architecture may better serve human function and generate delight. In common with discourse by Vitruvius and the Greek philosophers, the study of neuroarchitecture seeks to expand our understanding of the influence of buildings on the brain, body and behavior. The emergence of new modes of study and research-based design approaches now offer to reconcile the arts and sciences. A large body of neuroscientific research demonstrates how specific physical attributes influence sensory, perceptual, kinetic, emotional, cognitive or behavioral functions. Further, studies reveal that exposure to built settings may change the brain and thereby the experience of architecture itself.

It has been suggested that architectural phenomena are too complex to be reduced to the study of their parts. However, the scientific method and even reductionist approaches allow for the study of great complexity in the context of holistic philosophies. Just as an architect considers an entire building within its site and social context, as well as the structural impact of each penny-nail or screw, so too does a neuroscientist think in terms of behavioral interactions as well as the specific neural interactions that underlie the human experience of design. Thus, the interpretation of neuroscientific research enables us to look beyond intuition.

Conceptual Frameworks and Emergent Paradigms

A "*neuroarchitectural process*" utilizes rigorous biomedical studies to derive design hypotheses, describe design principles, and inform research-based design decisions (Edelstein, 2013). This "inside-out" perspective provides an essential design rationale that is too often overlooked if the primary focus is on exterior form. The scientific method provides the conceptual framework that relates built form to human function. The process reveals how physical stimuli of the built environment (input), influence psycho-physiological reactions (responses) associated with behavioral, economic and ecological results (outcomes) (Edelstein & Marks, 2007).

With knowledge of the interconnected synchronous parallel, serial and feedback systems that comprise the brain, a more informed set of design principles may be derived. With such

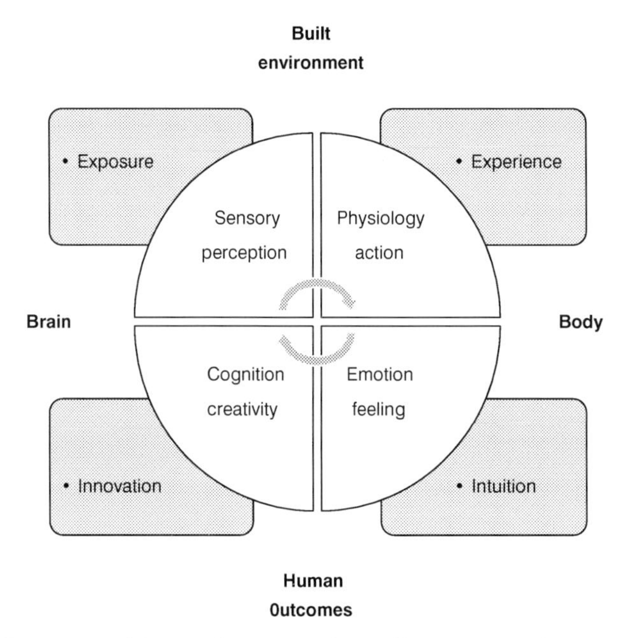

Figure 18.1 The neuroarchitectural process relates all interactions between the brain, body and buildings. Credit: Mona Shoghi

specificity, understanding of the biological bases of sensory, perceptual, emotional, visceral and cognitive responses may be incorporated into design guidelines.

For example, the neurophysiological principles of color perception provide the basis for understanding color preference in terms of brightness and contrast in addition to recommendations based on trend and culture. Similarly, recent advances in studies of the neurophysiology of hearing, refines our understanding of how central neural systems feedback to modulate the sensory cells in the hearing organ in order to enhance detection, discrimination, and comprehension of speech in noisy settings. Such data add to long-held acoustical principles, and suggest design changes to enhance wall systems for greater speech confidentiality. Knowledge of the complex system that links the eyes, ears, touch, proprioceptive and the vestibular balance organs advances understanding of how hardscape materials and textures should be used to encourage physical activity, reduce fall risk, and provide visual vertical stimuli to serve those fearful of heights or overhangs. Wayfinding strategies may incorporate emerging studies of how brain cells map location and direction, and the neural substrates of emotion and cognition may be used to guide design for all uses, regardless of ability or onset of dementia.

A "*neurouniversal approach*" includes Universal Design (UD) principles as outcome measures. A universal human experience reflects the dynamic change in ability that each person encounters across their lifetime. Therefore, one of the most profound opportunities is to incorporate information about how exposure, experience, aging, diseases or disorders alter the human response to design elements. Universal Design sets out a framework for the use of places, things and policies that serve the widest range of people and situations without special or separate designs (Preiser & Ostroff, 2001). Seven principles focus on a responsibility to the experience of the user: equitable design must not disadvantage or stigmatize any group of users; flexible design should accommodate a wide range of individual preferences and abilities; simple and intuitive design should be easy to understand for a broad range of cognitive abilities; perceptible information must communicate effectively regardless of ambient conditions or the user's sensory abilities; the design must have tolerance for error to minimize adverse consequences of unintended actions; and design should be used efficiently and comfortably with low physical effort. There must be appropriate size and space for use, regardless of the body size, posture, or mobility. Their universal approach points out that variation in human ability is not a "special need," but affects most of peoples.

Design must therefore take into account the continuum of human abilities, and embrace the most gifted as well as the least able. The translation of findings from developmental, cognitive and clinical neurosciences offers an expanding wealth of data to document specific physiological, mental, and social interactions with built settings for all ages and abilities (Edelstein & Sax 2013).

Practice-based Research

"Translational design" applies such knowledge to the art of design practice (Edelstein, 2006). The inclusion of clinical neuroscience expands the evidence available to inform global policy change. Critical analysis of the many competing stimulus-response functions may be set out in a translational design grid to establish priorities based upon research rigor. Design decisions may be ranked in terms of physical health and safety, enhanced mental function, emotional wellbeing and socio-political factors. With the addition of environmental and economic analyses a more holistic understanding of brain-building interactions reveal the risk, cost and human value of design.

Neuroarchitectural Methods

Recent advances in neuroscience over the past decade alone have begun to change our understanding of human physiological, psychological and behavioral needs. In merging a reductionist approach with holist perspectives, the impact of specific components of design may be understood in terms of their measurable influence on specific human responses. By incorporating electrophysiological through behavioral metrics, a finer scale of information may be linked to specific design parameters. A practical way forward integrates individualized biological and environmental sensors to synchronously log environmental exposure associated with neural and behavioral responses. Brainwave, visual attention, and heart-rate variability monitors may be used to track cognitive, sensory and emotional responses. Biosensor data aggregated across numerous individuals reveal the interactions between people and places from cells to cities. Immersive virtual design simulations offer new paradigms for testing, where the design team may engage with user/experts and clients to *experience* design before build begins or the first brick is laid. Such technology enables pre-design research evaluations (PRE) and provides baseline data that may be compared to post-occupancy evaluations (POE) results in order to validate the efficacy of built solutions.

Research-based Practice

Consistent with the concept of integrated-project delivery (IPD), the design team need not expect architects or designers to be schooled in clinical or neuroscientific disciplines, or practiced in technological research. Instead, a neuroarchitectural approach brings in user/experts, scientific and clinical consultants who offer evidence, research, and innovative

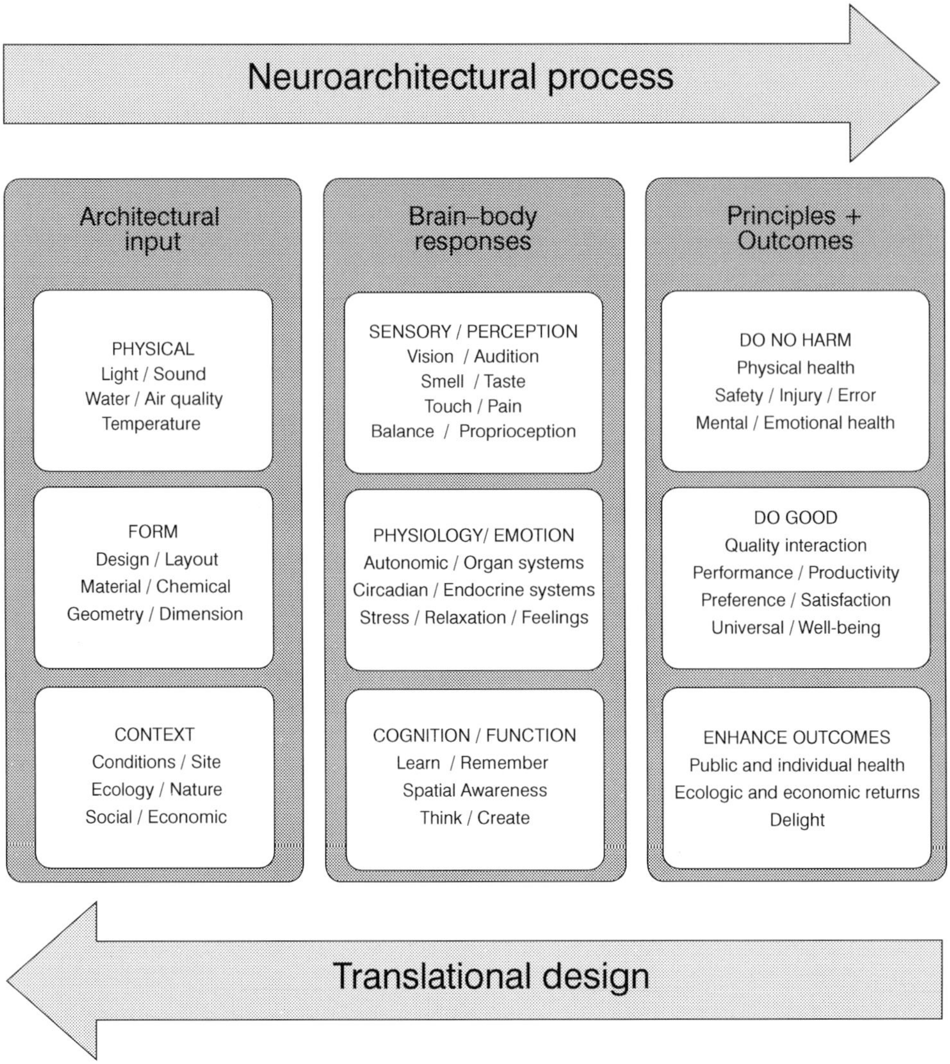

Neuroarchitectural process

Architectural input

PHYSICAL
Light / Sound
Water / Air quality
Temperature

FORM
Design / Layout
Material / Chemical
Geometry / Dimension

CONTEXT
Conditions / Site
Ecology / Nature
Social / Economic

Brain–body responses

SENSORY / PERCEPTION
Vision / Audition
Smell / Taste
Touch / Pain
Balance / Proprioception

PHYSIOLOGY/ EMOTION
Autonomic / Organ systems
Circadian / Endocrine systems
Stress / Relaxation / Feelings

COGNITION / FUNCTION
Learn / Remember
Spatial Awareness
Think / Create

Principles + Outcomes

DO NO HARM
Physical health
Safety / Injury / Error
Mental / Emotional health

DO GOOD
Quality interaction
Performance / Productivity
Preference / Satisfaction
Universal / Well-being

ENHANCE OUTCOMES
Public and individual health
Ecologic and economic returns
Delight

Translational design

Figure 18.2 A translational design grid may be expanded to map how each design topic relates the built environment (input), neural principles (responses) and the impact of design on outcomes. Credit: Mona Shoghi

options from the earliest stages through the final test of design efficacy. Rigorous research is among society's most valuable tools for laying the foundations of better strategies to improve human outcomes. Anticipatory analysis will reveal the effects of climate change, new technologies and the new competencies required (Burton, 2010).

Design and Health Benchmarks

This practice-based approach provides the "*human performance benchmarks*" needed to inform and document improvements to the planning and design of our cities, neighborhoods and buildings. Together with "building performance" benchmarks, rigorous data that links environmental factors to escalating health burdens may thus drive significant changes in policy and practice (Edelstein, 2014).

Over the past decade, calls for policy changes that support both healthy and sustainable cities have been disseminated globally. The World Health Organization (WHO), the American Institute of Architects (AIA) Design + Health Research Consortium, the International Academy of Design and Health (IADH), and the Center for Health Design (CHD), as well as initiatives in United States of America, Canada, Singapore, South Africa, China and others identify a number of environmental determinants of health risk that are within the scope of the building and design professions. The WHO reported that urbanization, land use, spatial planning, occupational exposure and exploitation of natural resources are among the main environmental determinants of health. Economic inequity further amplifies these health risks and drives the need to consider design and health together (WHO, 2012).

In 2012, the WHO reported that over 17 million deaths per year with some relationship to environmental conditions. Worldwide, there were 8 million deaths related to air quality and respiratory ailments, 7 million related to exercise, stress and cardiovascular deaths, 6.2 million strokes, 1.9 million deaths related to water quality and diarrhea, and 1.3 related to road injuries and transportation systems. All of these deaths may not be directly related to environmental exposure in each individual case. Nonetheless, these data do not include non-fatal conditions, and likely underestimate the total possible impact of the built environment on human health and wellbeing. Statistics on the number of errors, near-misses, injuries, impediments and preventable adverse events are now being gathered to reveal a more realistic picture of the impact of the built environment on human outcomes. The potential scale of mental health issues was revealed in the 2014 WHO global report on mental disorders. They estimated that approximately 400 million people are affected by depression, 60 million by bipolar disorder, 35 million by dementia including Alzheimer's disease and 21 million by schizophrenia. The impact of developmental disorders that affect mental health and intellectual ability, including pervasive developmental disorders such as Autism Spectrum Disorder, persist from childhood into adulthood (WHO, 2014).

Building processes and materials may have direct and measurable impact on neural function in those cases where the production or release of neurotoxins increase the risk factors associated with some of the 1 billion people who are affected by neurological disorders worldwide (Society for Neuroscience, 2012). Yet, human-centered data is absent from many of the current benchmark initiatives. Many regulations and guidelines fail to incorporate the past decade of progress in which neural science has revealed a great deal about the brain's sensory, perceptual, motor, emotional and cognitive responses. As more recent data from social, psychological, physiological and clinical sciences are included, the impact of the environment on mental wellbeing as well as physical health becomes clear. Continued systematic efforts are required to verify the association between specific environmental factors and human health and wellbeing. Drawing data from across design, planning, landscape, and architectural disciplines, specific physical attributes of the built and natural environment may be correlated with physiological, psychological and clinical interactions. Knowledge of social and cultural engagement, community, education, enterprise and employment should also be included. Finally, the impact of climactic and environmental changes must be integrated, as all of these factors influence global and human outcomes. For example, neural, physiological and physical health may be improved by planning and design that reduces exposure to toxins and tobacco, supports physical activity, and makes readily available healthy food and water. Policy and guidelines that enhance these components of the built environment may directly reduce the prevalence of non-communicable diseases that give rise to respiratory, cardiovascular (ischemia and stroke), digestive (diarrhea, obesity), diabetes and associated disorders (obesity), and road injury. Together, these factors fall into the top ten causes of death worldwide, estimated in 2011 to be associated with over 25 million fatalities (Edelstein, 2014).

The Emergence of Neural Science

The history of neuroscience reveals a quest to understand neural function shared by the fathers of Greek philosophy and medicine, the masters of anatomy and architecture such as Leonardo da Vinci, and the emergence of empirical scientists across many centuries. Investigation of the human nervous system can be said to date back at least to ca. 2700 B.C., when Shen Nung is credited with describing acupuncture and the distribution of dermatome patterns similar to the peripheral nervous tracts. It is suggested that hieroglyphics provide the first written record of the nervous system in the time of Imphotep, an Egyptian royal physician and architect of the pyramid in Sakkara (seventeenth century B.C.). However, the brain may not have been considered an essential organ in these times, as it was often not preserved as part of the burial process. More than a thousand years later, Greek philosophers still mused over the anatomical location of the mind. Plato (427–347 B.C.) believed that the brain was the seat of mental processes, and Hippocrates (460–379 B.C.) postulated that the brain was involved with sensation and was the seat of intelligence. Yet Aristotle (384–322 B.C.) later proposed that the heart was the primary organ of the mind, cooled by the fluid system that surrounds the brain. Galen (130–200 A.D.) identified sensory and motor systems, but still considered fluid "humors" to drive the mental function.

Over one thousand years later, and spanning the Renaissance, anatomists and philosophers continued to consider that a fluid neural communication systems linked sensory and motor functions. Descartes (1596–1650) proposed that the mind and body act as separate dual entities. In the 1600s, new methods were applied to anatomical studies of the brain that challenged such beliefs, but the few techniques available limited understanding to the study of gross anatomical neural structures. Important discoveries in the seventeenth through nineteenth centuries revealed the role of electricity in the nervous systems. The propagation of electrical changes along bundles of neurons (nerves) and the simulation of sensory mechanisms were explored in the eighteenth and nineteenth centuries. However, it was advances in microscopy and histology at the turn of the twentieth century that heralded the age of contemporary neuroscience. Santiago Ramón y Cajal and Camillo Golgi won the 1906 Noble Prize in Physiology for their work demonstrating the Neural Doctrine. They illustrated how discrete nerve cells formed the basic units of the nervous system, the presence of synaptic gaps between neurons, and the direction of information flow from dendrites to axonal outputs.

Today, the field of neuroscience has grown to encompass a broad range of sub-disciplines and methods. Chemical, molecular, cellular, anatomical, physiological, psychological, sociological and computational approaches and technologies are deeply integrated in both scientific studies and clinical practice. Cognitive neuroscience considers classical philosophy and psychology to frame questions about mental function in light of knowledge from modern cellular and molecular biologic research. Controlled laboratory studies and "ecologically" relevant studies in natural contexts are supplemented by modeling and simulation to investigate the neurobiological basis of cognition and behavior. Systems neuroscience, network analysis and engineering explore normal function as well as neurological and psychiatric disorders. Predictive computational models test ideas about neural components and large-scale neural networks to reveal various representations of human function, and to explore the how biological processes give rise to consciousness. Thus, a broad neuroarchitectural approach may span studies of individuals through social organizations, and include data from intracellular studies through whole brain images in order to reveal the brain's neural representation of the environment (Kandel *et al.,* 2013).

Dynamic Complexity of The Brain

It has been suggested that the human brain may be one of the most complex living structures known. Recent studies approximate that the human brain is comprised of 200 billion neurons and up to ten times as many glial cells, and that each neuron may give rise to up to tens of thousands of connections (Micheva *et al.,* 2010). Genetic instructions guide the development of the basic architecture of these neural connections. A complex network of parallel and overlapping systems travel from one side of the brain to the other, feeding forwards and back, to integrate sensation, perception, action, emotion and cognition.

Despite this genetic developmental substrate, the brain is no longer considered to be a fixed or hardwired body of connections. Since the 1980s, numerous studies have demonstrated that the brain grows new cells (neurogenesis) and makes new connections throughout life (neuroplasticity). New neural networks may be formed during experience, enhanced during learning, lost due to lack of use or injury, thereby changing perception and function (Fuchs & Flügge 2014). A number of factors including stress and aging as well as conscious attention, repetition and reward may influence these neuroplastic changes (Kempermann & Gage, 2000). We now understand that the brain rewires itself, growing connections and enhancing signal transmission with repeated activities or environmental cues (Koehl & Abrous, 2011). These discoveries inspired the American Institute of Architects to join with neuroscientists to explore how enhancement of the built environment may change the brain and thereby alter perception of built form and human outcomes.

Principles and Myths

Over the course of the past several decades of brain research, many long-held myths and commonly-held beliefs have been refuted. Whilst an in-depth treatise on contemporary neuroscience is beyond the scope of a single chapter, a general understanding of the biological basis of the human experience provides important insights for those seeking to translate neuroscientific findings into design solutions.

Buildings Modify the Brain

- Environmental exposure and experience of the environment may lead to measurable changes in brain anatomy and function.
- The brain regrows (neurogenesis) and rewires (neuroplasticity) itself in response to its own experience.
- The form and function of each individual's brain is not fixed.
- We no longer think of the brain as a fixed hardwired computer.
- Neurons may be lost or grown, and new connections established, retained, or enhanced to improve function.
- Each individual's brain function and anatomy may differ from others and vary within their own lifetime.
- The exact anatomy and physiology of each individual brain changes with experience, learning and loss of use.

- Gross brain structures are similar in their cellular architecture and function across most individuals, but may differ with an individual's genetic makeup and experience.
- Developmental patterns slow neural growth in adulthood and create barriers between central and peripheral regeneration. Recent discoveries are beginning to reveal that the brain may overcome these limitations.

Interpretation of the Sensorium

- At the periphery, where the body and the physical world interact, multiple mechanisms modulate perception before passing information to higher brain centers.
- Modulation of physical input may occur within the sensory organs themselves.
- Information may be further integrated or modulated at the level of the brainstem, across both sides of the brain, and as it ascends through perceptual, cognitive, motor or associative processing centers.
- Sensory information rarely flows via a "one-way" system alone.
- Information about interactions between the body and the physical world integrate local "bottom-up" and central "top-down" processes.
- Complex neural mechanisms may tune, excite or inhibit sensory responses.

Integration of the Brain, Mind and Body

- Much of the brain is active all at once.
- We do not accept that only a small percent of the brain is active at any one time.
- Brain imaging and electroencephalography (EEG) demonstrate that most of the brain is active, to continually assess the importance of incoming information, provide multi-modal associations, and control body functions.
- The brain synchronously controls essential body systems (respiratory, cardiovascular, muscular systems), sensory systems (audition, vision, touch, temperature, smell), and modulates cognition (conscious thoughts and subconscious functions), emotions, feelings and actions.
- Brain imaging pictures usually highlight only the *difference* in brain activities that occur under different conditions rather than showing only active areas.

Functional Neuroanatomy

- Neuronal information is modulated by many mechanisms.
- Neurons and glial cells comprise the essential elements that form the gross anatomical structures of the central, peripheral and autonomic nervous system.
- Chemical, gaseous and electrical changes modulate the transmission of information from one neuron to another.
- Glial cells also contribute to the integration of electrical potential differences across neural membranes, mediated by electrochemical and gaseous exchanges.
- Neural activity and neurotransmitters may be inhibitory or excitatory.
- A massive network of interconnected pathways connect the different functional regions in feed-forward and feedback systems up and down the brain, and across from one side to the other.
- The brain is segmented into functional regions that follow general genetic instructions that guide their growth, form and function.

- The brain is asymmetric, such that certain functions tend to occupy the right side and others the left side.
- Many neural systems receive and send neural projections to the same (ipisilateral) and opposite (contralateral) sides.
- There is great redundancy in the neural structures and functional networks of the brain.
- Most systems send information in parallel (multiple pathways sending information to different locations at the same time), and in series (information proceeding from relay station to relay station).
- This neural redundancy provides resiliency by enabling the brain to rewire functions in other locations or networks in order to overcome damage or enhance function.

Form and Function of the Nervous System

Essential Elements

The essential unit of the human nervous system is the neuron. Glia cells, which may outnumber neurons ten fold, provide scaffolding for nerve growth, modulate neural interactions, form connections with vasculature and other cellular systems, contribute to the formation of synapses, insulate axons, ensheath synapses, and control extracellular and neurotransmitter concentrations. Glia determine how rapidly electrochemical signals flow along neurons by insulating their axons (forming white matter). Uninsulated neurons form nuclei and interconnected masses of gray matter that integrate signals from many cells.

Neural Doctrine

In general, signs flow through neurons via a common mechanism. Dendrites receive electrochemical input from other cells. If all inputs exceed a threshold level in the cell body, discrete electrical pulses flow out along the axon and stimulate the release of neurotransmitter chemicals, change electrical charges across tight gap junctions between cells, or modulate soluble gases that change extracellular conditions or second chemical messengers. Over 100 chemical messengers have been identified including acetylcholine, glutamate, gamma-aminobutyric acid (GABA), dopamine, serotonin, norepinephrine. The influence of each neurotransmitter depends on interconnected systems that add great complexity to each chemical's action. Repeated neural activation may lead to dramatic neuroplastic changes in cell structures, thereby stimulating new cell growth (neurogenesis) or the biomolecular basis of learning.

The Nervous System

Whilst recent studies show that the precise anatomy of each individual's brain differs, the human genome guides the development of an organized neuroanatomy that is similar across most people. The nervous system is comprised of the central nervous system (CNS) formed by the brain and spinal cord, the peripheral nervous system (PNS) that innervates the body, and the autonomic nervous system (ANS) that automatically (autonomously) controls the internal organs and body processes without conscious effort.

The spinal cord receives, processes and sends sensory information from the skin, joints and muscles of the limbs and body, sends motor fibers that control the movement of the limbs and trunk, and feeds back signals to the skeletal muscles and the autonomic involuntary muscles and visceral organs. The autonomic nervous system is subdivided into two divisions.

The sympathetic division that mediates fear, flight and fight responses, increases heart rate, blood pressure and blood flow to muscles, and dilates the pupils. The parasympathetic division prepares the body for rest, decreases heart rate, blood pressure and blood flow to muscles.

The brain is further divided into the brainstem (medulla oblongata, pons, cerebellum), the midbrain (diencephalon), and the forebrain (cerebrum). The brainstem, densely packed with neural centers responsible for vital functions, controls breathing, heart rate, and digestion, and sends information about the force and range of movement and motor learning modulated by the cerebellum. The brainstem and pons transfer information from the sensory and motor systems of the body, head and neck, and the reticular formation conveys information that regulate arousal and awareness.

The midbrain passes information from sensory, motor and interneurons that control eye movements, and coordinate visual and auditory reflexes, among many other functions. The thalamus integrates and relays information to the cerebral cortex. The hypothalamus and pineal gland regulate autonomic, endocrine and visceral functions that release hormones into the blood stream to modulate target organs function. The basal ganglia regulate motor performance, while emotional reactions are mediated by the cingulate gyrus and the amygdala.

The forebrain comprises the two outer hemispheres of the cerebrum, each divided into four lobes. In general, the frontal lobe is largely responsible for short-term memory and movement planning. The pre-central ridge (gyrus) forms the motor cortex, while the somatosensory cortex sits on the post-central gyrus. The parietal lobe is involved with somatic sensation, the formation of a body image and orientation to extra-personal space. The occipital lobe is concerned with vision, and the temporal lobe is involved with language and audition. Deep within the temporal lobe, the hippocampal formation is involved in learning and memory. Interneurons flow across the cortex, connecting primary and association regions on the same side. Just underneath the layer of gray cells, the corona radiata forms a crown of white matter that speeds information within each lobe and across the corpus callosum to the other side. New findings indicate the segregation of separate streams, with upper and lower cortical layers playing separate roles in processing sensory information. This suggests that long-held concepts about a serial flow of information from thalamus to cortex does not adequately describe processes that drive our thoughts, decisions and actions (Constantinople & Bruno, 2013). Rather, our complex neuroarchitecture should be thought of as an interconnected systems of synchronously active parts.

Sensory Systems

The human experience of the sensorium is central to an architect's scope of influence. In addition to the visual sense, architecture simulates auditory (sound, speech, noise), and vestibular organs (angular, linear and gravitational movement and a sense of balance). Smell and taste inform programmatic layouts, the design of ventilation systems, air-flow and landscape architecture. Somatosensory systems are equally important in providing the brain information about the body's interaction with physical form (touch, temperature, stretch and pressure). Whilst an overview of all sensorial, perceptual and cognitive interactions with built space deserve lengthy consideration, this singular chapter focuses on a few topics that demonstrate the relevance of neural systems and mechanisms.

The architecture of each sensory organ also reveals how the physical world is transduced into electrochemical signals. Sensation is derived from neural representations of the physical world, and perception is the interpretation of sensory signals modulated by several layers of "bottom-up" as well as "top-down" modulation from higher brain centers that add memory, and emotional salience.

Auditory System

The cellular architecture of the hearing system exemplifies how a complex form transduces "physics into physiology." Sound is heard when air-borne pressure waves are transferred through air, to bone and then to fluids. This filters the amplitude, frequency, phase and pattern of sound waves, oscillating the basilar membrane on which the hearing organ sits. Within the hearing organ, pyramidal cells form a rigid fulcrum on which a cantilevered membrane holds outer hair cells with cross-gridded scaffolding that contracts and modifies the fluid dynamics around the inner sensory cells, altering their communication with the brainstem. Frequencies that fall outside of the most important sound and speech ranges are modulated by these mechanics. Edelstein-Williams (2000) demonstrated in intracellular animal recordings and extracellular measures of human cochlear responses, that signal perception in background noise modulates this system via an efferent feedback loop from the brainstem to the outer hair cells. In addition to this top-down neural system, multiple bilateral pathways between the cochlea and the cortex control attention, adapt and habituate responses to sound. Disruption of these systems by noise damage or other injuries alters the exquisite sensitivity to sound, and reduce the ability to understand speech in noisy environments.

Neuroarchitectural Principles in Practice

Current architectural regulations and guidelines do not take into account many recent neuroscientific findings. The time course and function of efferent feedback and more recent data on noise-induced hearing loss are yet to be integrated into standard metrics. Guidelines and legislation that limit sound exposure to prevent noise-induced hearing loss (Directive by the European Union (2003/10/EC) continue to base the maximum averaged continuous noise levels on the ISO 1999:1990 standards. Further, the limits set for impulse sound (140dB including hearing protection) fails to take into account the frequency or duration of sound and lacks scientific validation (Buck *et al.,* 2012). Yet, there is a great need for such data to be incorporated in acoustic design where communication is critical. In 2013, Edelstein recorded almost continuous impulse noise levels from 85–120 dB are more than 60 dB above conversational speech in urgent healthcare environments. A survey of over 100 medical leaders indicated that noise-related stress was among the most important design issues to be addressed for clinician and patient outcomes (Edelstein, 2013) Such data supports specification of enhanced wall systems, floor and wall finishes, room geometries and installations. It should be noted that material performance described in sound absorption tables are often provided by the manufacturer, and rely on careful installation to achieve performance standards. Sound readily travels through any air gap, along connecting wall structures, and bounces over suspended ceilings. Therefore, the minimum standards for speech privacy rarely meet the needs of users who require confidentiality.

Visual System

The eye modulates light even before it reaches the sensory cells. The cornea, lens, iris and muscles of the eye change the focus of light and regulate how much light falls upon the retina where several layers of cells, photoreceptors and ganglion cells collect visual information from the built world. The rods, responsive in dim light have less sensitivity to color. Cones have greatest acuity in bright conditions, with differing peak sensitivities to red, green or blue wavelengths that overlap, combining to convey information across visible colors. In addition to sending signals along the optical nerve to the visual nuclei, retinal ganglion nerves send fibers to the supra-chiasmatic nucleus (SCN) that drives the circadian clock. (See *Circadian Systems* below.)

As sensory information ascends from the retina to the brain, a number of complex neural systems extract and analyze the amount of light, contrast, form, movement and color of objects. Binocular vision and depth perception are formed as higher centers in the brain fuse the signals from both eyes. Percepts are incorporated according to the brain's rules, while attention and memories are integrated to form cohesive and meaningful neural representations. Intermediate-level processing identifies contours (visual primitives), fields of motion and the representation of surfaces. In general, visual information is anatomically organized and transmitted along different streams: the dorsal pathways analyze image size and position; the ventral pathways discriminate color and shape; primary visual cortical cellular layers are organized and grouped according to their responsiveness to bars or edges at particular angles, orientation or direction. Neurons in the temporal lobe are most sensitive complex stimulus features, including faces, expressions and hands.

It is estimated that over 30 cortical areas participate in visual processing of objects, faces and places. The highest stage of visual processing in the inferior temporal cortex integrates information from a vast region of visual space. This convergence with cognitive processes identifies similar objects regardless of different viewing conditions, lighting, angle, position and distance. Perceptual constancy allows objects to appear the same despite changes in size, position or rotation. Form-cue invariance refers to the constancy of a form even though the cues that indicate its form change, including changes in contrast, color or texture. Viewpoint invariances maintain recognition of three-dimensional objects from different vantage points.

Visual Memory and Attention

In general, meaningful attributes and visual recognition are informed by previous sensory experiences and acquired associations via projections to the hippocampal formation. The prefrontal cortex responds to objects that are physically different but semantically related, and play roles in visual perception, visual working memory and recall of stored memories. Connections via the perirhinal cortex to the amygdala attach emotional valence.

Repeated exposure or practice may yield pronounced improvement in visual discrimination and object recognition ability (implicit or perceptual learning). Explicit learning occurs with the storage of facts or events related to visual memory. It is thought that continued neural firing in the inferior temporal cortex is associated with short-term storage of visual patterns and color information. Activity in the prefrontal cortex encodes spatial and other sensory information that is not eliminated by the appearance of another image and likely involved in long-term memories and the coding of expected or associated objects. Visual priming may occur when subjects respond more rapidly following repeated visual exposure, even without conscious awareness of the stimuli.

Areas within the hippocampus and medial temporal lobe are essential for acquisition of visual associative memories and may facilitate neuroplastic reorganization of the neuronal circuitry. It has been suggested that the brain forms a "visual priority map" that directs focus according to the relative importance of objects. The inherent characteristics of an object and significant features such as sudden movements or color patterns attract "bottom-up" attention, whilst the importance and previous experience attract "top-down" attention. It is thought that inhibitory processes suppress visual fields where an object has been viewed to minimize continual fixation on a known object. Object recognition is improved by surround suppression inhibiting visual areas adjacent to an important object to enhance slight differences between areas of the visual field to highlight motion and unusual features. Albright and colleagues demonstrated that the response of inferior temporal neurons to paired objects became more similar and consistent with behavioral changes dependent on successful learning (Albright, 2012).

Neuroarchitectural Principles in Practice

The perception of visual stimuli depends on several complex systems that process information about shape, color, movement, location, spatial organization and the recall of memories. Visual illusions reveal the brain's computational rules. Brightness and contrast may convey more information than color in the perception of movement, depth, perspective, shading, texture and the relative size and movement of objects. However, the visual system occasionally makes errors in reconstructing images. For example, the brain may interpret objects in shadows as brighter, and items next to darker ones may be seen as lighter.

Whilst such complexity may appear to confound design guidelines, vision science offers one of the most comprehensible sources of information to guide design. Lighting, brightness, contrast can be modified to change the perception of materials, objects and spaces. The rules of depth perception and view angle may be used to modify the perception of distance, depth and volume. Subconscious visual priming may be used for recall of visual priorities and wayfinding strategies.

A review of the most common visual disorders reveals how architectural openings, material reflections, color pallets and electrical lighting systems may meet a broader range of needs. For example, as people age or develop ocular disorders, the color of the lens may yellow, become less transparent, or light may enter the retina in a manner that limits full vision. Therefore perception of color and the effectiveness of contrast and light intensity that differ with age or cognitive decline make it more difficult to discern and comprehend the visual stimuli and clinical conditions must be taken into account in design.

Circadian Systems

The visual system serves more than the transduction of light into sight. Decades of rigorous research demonstrates that light is the primary stimulus that regulates multiple physiological systems in the brain, mind and body that change in synchrony with the time of day (circadian rhythms) or time of year (circannual or seasonal rhythms). Light and darkness turn on and off an intricate system of genes and proteins that control the internal clocks that drive activity, alertness, attention, performance, learning, mood, and vigilance. The supra-chiasmatic nucleus serves as the "master clock" of the brain and synchronizes neural, endocrine and exocrine function (e.g. melatonin, cortisol, etc.) that modulate sleep-wake cycles, body temperature and metabolic, digestive, cardiovascular, immune and even aging processes that cycle in regular patterns. In a constantly dark environment with no other behavioral or time cues, human rhythms run slightly longer than 24 hours, but are reset by the solar cycle.

Exposure to light at night can disrupt this spontaneous rhythmicity and has serious implications for human health. The American Medical Association House of Delegates adopted a policy that concluded that the strongest epidemiologic evidence links breast cancer to light at night and circadian disruption (Stevens *et al.,* 2013). The potential carcinogenic effect of melatonin suppression has been the focus of much research. In addition, nighttime lighting has been associated with adverse health effects including metabolic, DNA damage, hormonal and cell cycle regulation influencing growth, development and tissue function. It has been estimated that sleep-related disorders may affect over 70 million adults in the US alone, and insufficient sleep is linked to an increased risk of chronic diseases like high blood pressure, diabetes, depression, bipolar disorder and seasonal affective disorders. Recent studies revealed that flight crew had reduced temporal lobe volume along with deficits in spatial learning and memory (Nicolaides *et al.,* 2014). A large-scale study of long-term night shift workers had lower scores on tests of memory and processing speed. Impaired cognition was stronger for shift-work durations exceeding 10 years, and recovery took at least five year to reverse (Marquié *et al.,* 2014).

Recent studies have revealed the effectiveness of a broader range of colors beyond short wavelength blue light in modulating circadian rhythms. Whereas the majority of recent studies have focused on the efficacy of blue light in stimulating melatonin, fewer studies have explored the influence of other spectral intensities present in the visible range in sunlight. For example, Edelstein *et al.* (2008) showed how heart-rate variability (HRV) and EEG changed even with brief exposure of less than 15 minutes when comparing light with different peak spectra and intensities. HRV in response to bright white light with a blue peak was highly significantly different to variability in red light when the subject was at rest, but not when engaged in a memory task. The cardiovascular system is driven by both sympathetic and parasympathetic input that controls cortisol levels, stress and relaxation and reminds us that melatonin is not the only circadian endocrine (Edelstein, 2008b).

Neuroarchitectural Principles in Practice

Despite expansive evidence on the pervasive influence of light and darkness on human function and health, recent knowledge has rarely been communicated between designers, engineers and physiologists or incorporated in design practice, recommendations and guidelines. The Special Conference on Light and Health revealed that designers, engineers and physiologists had yet to combine their knowledge in practice guidelines (Edelstein, 2008a). Several general principles may be adopted. Both lightness and darkness are required to most effectively stimulate circadian rhythms. It is the control of light, not simply more light, that is necessary. Therefore, rather than using a "one size fits all" lighting strategy, a variety of light zones and systems may provide for safety and egress as well as individual circadian status and visual acuity needs. The distribution of light at the level of the floor can accommodate safe egress while minimizing circadian disruption and fall risk. Further, solar lighting and ceiling lighting systems should be controlled when supplementing individual lighting zones. Together, these strategies may minimize energy and maintenance costs, and support measurable improvements in human outcomes.

Somatosensory and Proprioceptor Systems

The body's sensory system is comprised of a number of different receptors that innervate the skin and epithelia, skeletal muscles, bones and joints, internal organs, and the cardiovascular system. Somatic and skin receptors include thermoreceptors (temperature), nociception receptors (pain, extreme heat, cold, pressure chemicals) and mechanoreceptors formed by axon terminals encapsulated in non-neural structures that transduce mechanical forces (touch, vibration or pressure) by opening ion channels that generate electrical signals. The proprioceptive sensors in muscles and connective tissues (stretch or tension and pressure or movement) give a sense of body position. These signals travel in fibers via the spinal cord or cranial nerves to the brainstem, and ultimately to the somatosensory cortex in the parietal lobe to create a map of the body that represents the concentration of receptors. Connections to the anterior cingulate cortex modulate the emotional response to pain.

Neuroarchitectural Principles in Practice

The sense of touch and perception of texture are important sensual components to architectural materials. Texture, absorption and the insulation qualities of floor and wall materials are equally important to ceiling finishes when speech perception in noise, or privacy and confidentiality are critical. The textures of materials underfoot become very important to those with abnormal ambulatory proprioception. This may arise from dysfunction of the visual, vestibular or proprioceptive systems. Rough or sandy surfaces underfoot are difficult or impossible for those with balance disorders or dysfunction in muscles and joints. Both the sight and touch of certain textures afford connotations and meaning. Thus, wooden wall panels connote warmth and may demonstrate recent findings that reveal connections between tactile and visual networks.

People experience architecture in four dimensions, thus movement through place and across time modifies how volume is perceived, how sight-lines yield different perspectives, and the kinetic experience of materials. Design must address both perception of and movement through space given the increasing prevalence of people with one or more mobility impairment, cardiovascular or respiratory disorders, or increased levels of obesity that decrease activity. The American with Disabilities Act (ADA) legislated minimal design considerations, but broader consideration is warranted to provide design that serves *more* than mobility disorders. The 2008 Behavioral Risk Factor Surveillance System estimated that up to 1 in 3 adults (18 to 30 percent) in the United States self-reported a disability (CDC, 2013).

Cognitive Systems

As sensory information is deconstructed into meaningful constituent parts it retains a physical order as it is conveyed from the sensory organ to the brainstem, through relay stations, to the thalamus and then to separate primary regions of the cerebral cortex. These primary cortical areas process one modality, and are organized in physical layers that map the deconstructed components. An integrated percept is formed via multi-modal association across a vast network of pathways that spread across the cortex from primary to associated cortical areas that combine sensory and motor information according to the brain's general rules of perception, attention, memory processing, decision strategy and conscious experience.

The neuro-anatomical arrangement reveals how each region processes the components of stimuli. Sensory information in is extracted in a series of unimodal processes of increasing complexity arising from the primary visual, auditory or somatosensory areas. The frontal association cortex and prefrontal areas are involved in the executive control of behavior. The dorsolateral prefrontal cortex maintains intention, organization and focused attention. The orbital-ventromedial cortex associates motivational values to objects and consequences of action. The temporal association cortex links multiple sensory systems and the ventral frontal lobe concerned with emotion and cognition, storing knowledge that serves recognition, semantic memory and speech comprehension. Within the temporal lobe, the hippocampal formation, cingulate and limbic association cortex play important roles in memory formation. A dorsal stream of the parietal association cortex processes spatial information and behavior. The ventral stream to the temporal association cortex processes feature information for stimulus identification. The parietal association cortex links multiple sensory systems to motor areas in the dorsal frontal lobes, and in humans informs body awareness, motor control, visual guidance of behavior, spatial vision and spatial cognition. Multisensory integration plays many important roles in achieving optimal sensitivity, perception and comprehension during interaction in the physical environment. For example, visual and haptic information combined enables finer size estimates than is possible with either vision or haptics alone (Gepshtein & Banks, 2008).

Neuroarchitectural Principles in Practice

Cognition reflects all of the processes that interpret multisensory input to generate perception, emotion, thought, language, memory and action. The myth that only a fraction of the brain is used is inconsistent with the reality of this great complexity. Therefore, a neuroarchitectural process considers more than programed space (an office, an operating room, a classroom), and focuses instead on the environmental qualities that support sensation and perception, modulation of emotion, effective communication and movement, as well as spaces for focused concentration and collaboration. Neural imaging, eletrophysiological brainwaves, psychometric reactions and behavioral observations help to reveal how specific elements of the environment may serve these mental functions.

Spatial Cognition

The brain's rules for understanding and remembering the physical environment are of particular interest to architects, designers and planners. Somatosensory, visual, auditory and motor memories are integrated with hippocampal analysis to form spatial percepts of objects within and outside of a person's space. Parietal lesions produce deficits in personal and peripersonal spatial perception, visuomotor integration and selective attention. "Place cells" within the hippocampus in the temporal lobe are responsive to previous experience in a specific location, direction and orientation (O'Keefe & Nadel, 1978). A hexagonal network of "grid cells" in the nearby entorhinal cortex associates memories of landmarks and self-motion in an neural "cognitive map" of places and events. Early research focused on egocentric versus allocentric (bird's eye) mental mapping methods. Continued studies reveal multiple factors that may influence an individual's neural navigation strategy. Disoriented patients with temporal lobe disorders revealed that some are unable to recognize or perceive landmarks, while others have no deficits in object or spatial perception, but cannot associate landmarks with directional information, relying heavily on maps and plans that they may draw for themselves (Aguirre & D'Esposito, 1999). Changes in the speed of visual cues was found to be associated with large-scale reorganization of spatiotemporal contrast sensitivity, unlikely to arise from changes in attentional or decision strategies. These findings may be generalized to many stimuli and tasks, and may impact cue effectiveness (Gepshtein *et al.,* 2013).

Neuroarchitectural Principles in Practice

Immersive stereoscopic virtual reality simulations at full scale have been used to test the effectiveness of visual and auditory cues in forming a memory of space and place. With synchronous recordings of brainwave activity, independent component analysis (ICA) revealed differences in brain dynamics of the parietal and occipitotemporal cortexes when subjects were lost or knew their location. A significantly stronger synchronization in theta waves and stronger desynchronization in the lower alpha band of EEG frequencies was observed. This pattern likely reflects analysis of visuo-spatial information from a first person perspective, and parietal and occipitotemporal areas involved in processing heading changes and planning of future paths. Disorientation in spaces with less visuo-spatial information was associated with increased alpha wave desynchronization, likely reflecting increased attentional demands (Edelstein *et al.,* 2008). With the advent of wearable, wireless microsensors, studies of movement and memory of place may now inform wayfinding strategies with buildings and across an urban context.

Conclusions

Positioned between People and Places

A growing body of research makes it increasingly clear that the built environment has direct and measurable impact on the health and wellbeing of individuals, societies, economies and ecologies across the globe. "Human health depends on society's capacity to manage the interaction between human activities and the environment in ways that safeguard and promote health but do not threaten the integrity of the natural systems on which the environment depends" (WHO, 2012, pp. 103). With neuroarchitecture now positioned at the intersection between the sciences, medicine, humanities and the arts, the field offers the conceptual frameworks and methods required to consider the range of human desires, preferences and perceptions. A basic understanding of neural science provides an essential platform for communication and collaboration between architects and neuroscientists. Whilst neuroscientists readily admit to an incomplete understanding of brain function, lives are saved and enhanced every day based upon this limited knowledge. In a similar manner, neuroarchitectural practice may translate the current knowledge of clinical and neural mechanisms into principles that may also save and enhance lives.

It is vital however, that a rigorous process is applied to avoid errors and risks imposed by misinterpretation, inappropriate generalization or unsuitable applications. While we await the transdisciplinary cohort of neuroarchtiects currently in training, an integrated practice-based research model provides the breadth and depth of expertise required for the interpretation of the best and most comprehensive knowledge base. Architectural and environmental experts would thus define the architectural features that comprise the physical input in the project being considered. Neuroscientists, clinicians, psychologists and sociologists would provide the physiological, clinical and pyscho-social information as required. Importantly, user/experts and ethonographic observations must be included to offer information that informs universal design objectives and addresses specific client and user needs.

Neuroarchitectural principles may thus embrace a diversity of users, uses and contexts, and better serve the most gifted and creative, the most fragile and the most needy. In this way, creative design solutions may enhance design and the health in all of our built environments.

References

Aguirre, G. K. & D'Esposito, M. (1999). Topographical Disorientation: A Synthesis and Taxonomy. *Brain*. 122, 1613–28.

Albright, T.D. (2012). On the Perception of Probable Things: Neural Substrates of Associative Memory, Imagery, and Perception. *Neuron,* 74, 2, 227–45.

Bruno, R., Merzenich, M. & Nudo, R. (2012). The Fantastic Plastic Brain. *Advanced Mind Body Medicine*, 26, 2, 30–5.

Buck, K., Véronique Zimpfer, V., Hamery, P. (2012). Scientific Basis and Shortcomings of EU Impulse Noise Standards. *The Journal of the Acoustical Society of America,* 131, 4, 3531.

Burton, J. (2010). Healthy Workplace Framework and Model: Background Document and Supporting Literature and Practices. World Health Organization. Retrieved May 15, 2014 from www.who.int.

CDC (Centers for Disease Control and Prevention) (2013). Disability and Health Data System (DHDS). Retrieved October 1, 2013, from http://dhds.cdc.gov/?s_cid=dhds_001

Constantinople, C. M. & Bruno, R. M. (2013). Deep Cortical Layers are Activated Directly by Thalamus. *Science*, 340, 6140, 1591–4.

Edelstein, E. (2006). Translational Design: The Intersection of Neuroscience and Architecture. Master of Architecture Thesis. San Diego: NewSchool of Architecture & Design.

Edelstein, E. (2008a). "Understanding Human Needs In Buildings." Invited paper read at the California Energy Commission PIER Lighting and Health Symposium, San Francisco, CA.

Edelstein, E. (2008b). The Laboratory Experiment. In *Developing an Evidence-Based Design Model that Measures Human Response: A Pilot Study of a Collaborative, Trans-Disciplinary Model in a Healthcare Setting* (pp. 63–132). Washington, DC: AIA College of Fellows 2005 Latrobe Fellowship.

Edelstein, E. (2013). Research-based Design: New Approaches to the Creation of Healthy Environments. *World Health Design Journal,* 62–67.

Edelstein, E. (2014). International Benchmarks for Design & Health. *Proceedings of the World Congress on Health and Design*. Toronto, Canada.

Edelstein, E., & Marks, F. (2007). Lab Design and the Brain: Translating Physiological and Neurological Evidence into Design. *2008 Laboratory Design Handbook,* (Special Supplement to R&D Magazine), 26–29.

Edelstein, E. & Sax, C. (2013). Expanding the Universe of Design. *Proceedings of the 28th Annual International Technology and Persons with Disabilities Conference*. California State University Northridge Center on Disabilities, San Diego, CA.

Edelstein, E., Gramann, K., Schulze, J., Shamlo, N. B., van Erp, E., Vankov, A. Makeig, S., Wolszon, L., & Macagno, E. (2008). Neural Responses during Navigation and Wayfinding in the Virtual Aided Design Laboratory—Brain Dynamics of Re-Orientation in Architecturally Ambiguous Space. In *SFB/TR 8 Report No. Report Series of the Transregional Collaborative Research Center SFB/TR 8 Spatial Cognition* (pp. 35–41).

Edelstein-Williams, E. (2000). *Electrophysiologic Diagnostic Protocol to Test Central Control of Perception in Noise. Clinical Applications of Otoacoustic Emissions in the Assessment of Olivocochlear Dysfunction.* (Doctoral dissertation), Institute of Neurology, University College. London, UK.

Fuchs, E. and Flugge, G. (2014) Adult Neuroplasticity: More than 40 Years of Research. *Neural Plasticity*, 2014: article 541780.

Gepshtein, S., & Banks, M. S. (2003). Viewing Geometry Determines How Vision and Haptics Combine in Size Perception. *Currents of Biology,* 13, 6, 483–8.

Gepshtein, S., Lesmes, L. A., & Albright, T. D. (2013). Sensory Adaptation as Optimal Resource Allocation. *Proceedings of the National Academy of Science*, 110, 11, 4368–73.

Kandel, E., Schwartz, J., Jessell, T., Siegelbaum, S., & Hudspeth, A. J. (Eds.) (2013). *Principles of Neural Science* (5th ed.). New York: McGraw-Hill.

Kempermann, G., & Gage, F. H. (2000). Neurogenesis in the Adult Hippocampus. *Proceedings of the Novartis Foundation Symposium*, 231, 220–35.

Koehl, M., & Abrous, D. N. (2011). A New Chapter in the Field of Memory: Adult Hippocampal Neurogenesis. *European Journal of Neuroscience*, 33, 6, 1101–14.

Marquié J. C., Tucker, P., Folkard, S., Gentil, C., & Ansiau, D. (2014). Chronic Effects of Shift Work on Cognition: Findings from the VISAT Longitudinal Study. *Occupational Environmental Medicine*. Retrieved from November 3, 2014 from: pii: oemed-2013-101993. [Epub ahead of print].

Micheva, K., Busse, B., Weiler, N., O'Rourke, N., & Smith, S. (2010). Single-Synapse Analysis of a Diverse Synapse Population: Proteomic Imaging Methods and Markers. *Neuron, 68*, 18, 639-653. DOI: 10.1016/j.neuron.2010.09.024.

Nicolaides, N. C., Charmandari, E., Chrousos, G. P., & Kino, T. (2014). Circadian Endocrine Rhythms: The Hypothalamic-Pituitary-Adrenal Axis and its Actions. *Ann N Y Academy of Science,* 1318, 71–80.

Preiser, W., & Ostroff, E. (Eds.). (2001). *Universal Design Handbook*. New York: McGraw-Hill.

O'Keefe, J., & Nadel, L. (1978) *The Hippocampus as a Cognitive Map*. Oxford: Oxford University Press.

Society for Neuroscience (2012). Global Prevalence of Diseases and Disorders. Retrieved May 15, 2014, from http://www.brainfacts.org/policymakers/global-prevalence-of-diseases-and-disorders/.

Stevens, R. G., Brainard, G. C., Blask, D. E., Lockley, S. W., & Motta, M. E. (2013). Adverse Health Effects of Nighttime Lighting. Comments on American Medical Association Policy Statement. *American Journal of Preventative Medicine*, 45, 3, 343–6.

World Health Organization Regional Office for Europe (2012). The New European Policy for Health—Health 2020. Policy Framework and Strategy—Draft 2. . Retrieved May 15, 2014, from www.who.int.

World Health Organization (2014). Mental disorders. Fact sheet N°396. Retrieved May 15, 2014, from www.who.int.

19

Architecture, Branding, and the Politics of Identity

Mark Foster Gage

On May 31, 2000 the critical satire newspaper *The Onion*, ran a story titled "You Can Tell Area Bank Used to Be a Pizza Hut" (The Onion, 2000). This, of course, requires a few pre-loaded pieces of knowledge to piece together for a reader to get the joke—the first of which is what a "Pizza Hut" is supposed to look like. If someone was to ask a typical American what a "Pizza Tent" or a "Pizza Yurt" would look like, they could likely piece together an approximation of what you think it *might* look like, but not what it *must* look like—as for these fictional places there is no correct answer. A "Pizza Hut" however, is a different story, if you grew up in the United States, particularly in the 1970s or 1980s; odds are you know *exactly* what a Pizza Hut is supposed to look like. A Pizza Hut is a one storey building, with a perversely pitched mansard roof, painted bright red. Its perversity, or strangeness, is what makes it recognizable against a backdrop of multitudes of roof types, particularly on the American suburban landscape. Quite simply, it is identifiable because there is nothing else like it—or because it is strange. It is identifiable because, for Pizza Hut, the architecture is used to not only contain, but establish the brand identity of the company.

The use of architecture in the equation of branding has become far more complex and sophisticated since the housing of the hut, as a proliferation of new forms of media, sensible matter, ubiquitous computing, social media, starchitect statuses and sheer corporate advertising prowess have utterly transfigured the landscape, literally, of branding relative architecture in a mere decade. This text is about this contemporary state, how it emerged, what it means, where it's headed, and how architects can supercharge the profession with new forms of engagement through producing more intense and immersive entanglements of spaces, objects, technologies, and brand identities.

Resistance to these ideas will be levied by proponents of Marxist-cum-critical projects (Hays, 1998) in architecture that insisted, for much of the twentieth century, that architecture act as an equalizing force in the service of social justice and equality—and usually against accumulations of power. This text assumes as an axiom that this is a legitimate and worthy ideological concept, but there are now better tools than architecture available to address such injustices. In a world of Facebook, Instagram, Vine, WhatsApp, Tumblr, Pinterest, and Soundcloud, to name a few, and the ecologies of communication they do and will undoubtedly produce, architecture's power is diminishing, or at least being eclipsed, as a tool for producing sociological equality. Instead, architecture can now be liberated to pursue other endeavors to which it is better suited and, in fact, more productively influential. What we are now encountering in terms of corporations, marketing, and the wholesale acceptance of world economies into the powerful universe of free-market branding, particularly by the American population, demands a new form of action-aggressive, opportunistic, and vigorous engagement by the architectural design community. As we will see, if architecture is to have any power in this new world order it needs to be from a more essential position than rehearsing recent scripts of throwing Marxist rocks from Ivory Towers, or of sticking arrows on diagrams to justify our work to the gullible, or of convincing ourselves that good ways of saving energy necessarily equal good architecture. Architecture no longer needs to be justified by its social performance, or simplistic narratives (the building looks like a mountain against a backdrop of mountains), or by its carbon footprint, or by dumb diagrams that show that its shape was derived from sun angles or zoning envelopes. These are simply weak positions from which to practice, and they relegate architecture to a being a *result of something else important* rather than architecture *itself* being important. The contemporary branded landscape of the global free-market economy offers potent opportunities for a new generation of architects savvy enough to know that the most effective way to influence any system is not from sniping from afar, sleight of hand distractions, or lame metaphors—but rather accumulating and exerting actual power through producing immersive marriages of fresh architectural ambitions with the explosively emerging technologies of the twenty-first century. All of this requires architecture to more intelligently and intensely engage with, and capitalize on, the global economic systems of the new millennium, which are increasingly governed by one of the most powerful forms of dictating human behavior—branding.

> The lack of money is the root of all evil.
>
> (Mark Twain)

Before we get to the contemporary scene of branding we need to know that there is a difference between "branding" and "identity." Identity is "the distinguishing characteristics of an individual or community" (Gove, 1993). "Architecture has been inexorably linked to "identity" from its very beginning. In order to better understand how architecture might operate today it is important to understand the massive historic momentum that it needs to quickly overcome. All great and profitable stories have creation myths, from Bruce Wayne's traumatic experience in a well of bats to Bill Gates notorious garage start-up. Architecture's identity backstory is far, far older than most, perhaps less dramatic but no less interesting or significant. It largely owes its "officially sanctioned" founding narrative to the eighteenth-century Jesuit priest and architectural theorist Marc-Antoine Laugier, who, on the frontispiece of his 1753 "Essai sur l'Architecture," pictured his personal version of the progenitor of all architecture—the "primitive hut." The concept of returning to the primitive hut as a source for disciplinary clarity has guided architects and thinkers ever since. For us it will also be used as a means to better understand the roots of "identity" in architecture. While the exact tectonic or component details will likely be endlessly debated, one thing is for sure, which is that when the "ur-architecture" of the primitive hut was built, using trabeation, tensile structures, found objects, wood, fabric, or any other materials or tectonic methods (as the details don't matter for our inquiry) it was likely improved for one of two reasons—to better protect its inhabitants from the surrounding environment, or, to communicate something about these very inhabitants. The latter is the use of architecture to establish identity. There obviously are no references, artifacts or stories of architectural identity that take us back fifty millennia to this moment, but one can at least speculate that once two or more of Laugiers "primitive-huts" were placed in any sort of proximity, that physical community was born, and the one with the highest peak, the tallest entrance, perhaps the longest span, the most foliage for waterproofing, or the brightest colors inherently conveyed some sort of status to the inhabitant. At this point architecture stopped being about merely shelter and became about identity—that is to say about power, and ultimately about influence. Fifty or more millennia after the formation of our first fictional community this still holds true, perhaps even more so. George Bataille perhaps most directly encapsulates this in his text "Against Architecture," where he writes "Architecture exists only to control and shape the entire social arena. It is constituted by this impulse propelling it to erect itself as the center and to organize all activities around itself" (Hollier, 1989). This "shaping of the entire social arena" now needs to expand more intensely into the territories of branding and identity, and that this invasion should not be abhorred as it is from architecture's default Marxist vantage point, but should be embraced as a new source of architectural empowerment.

Architecture is inherently a discipline about power. In the context of any form of architectural construction, there are limited available resources, and those able to accumulate the most of said resources are those who wield the power to do so. This is an undeniable characteristic of humanity—resources are finite and their expenditure is an act of power. For architecture—the discipline that requires the greatest quantity of sheer resources, the requirements for consolidated power are significant. Powerful, however, is only significant if it becomes influential. A king that gives no orders can be rendered as insignificant as the jester that performs before him. Architectural history is a history of power, and yet in the contemporary landscape of practice, the profession exerts a nearly imperceptible amount of actual influence. The profession of Architecture, by assuming that the forms of influence of operating yesterday are still the forms of influence operating today, has, in short, been neutered.

> The weaker you are the louder you bark.
>
> (Masashi Kishimoto, Naruto, Band 11)

For Laugier's legacy, the *image* of the primitive hut from his frontispiece became at least as influential as the words within. The plate shows a wood structure complete with vertical tree trunks and sloped branches meeting at a peak, which, for Laugier, formed the meta-basis for the architecture of Greek Antiquity. The move from the primitive hut to the systematic development of proto-Doric classicism replete with free standing columns, sloped pediments, entasis and references to wood detailing as found in components such as trigliphs and metopes, was the story of millennia in the development of an identity (Gove, 1993). By the time Laugier's theoretical trajectory from the primitive hut mutated into the emergence of pseudo-canonical classicism, the method of construction had become the de-facto identifier of, for instance, the nation states of Greek Antiquity. Ancient Greece, now as a civilization, is almost entirely represented in the minds of architects and non-architects alike through the architectural identity of the acropolis. This language was an expression of Greek power, precision, religious practices, aesthetic sensibilities, and material preferences. That is to say it had become an identity for a community, and therefore architectural identity had become political.

The exact relationship between identity, architecture, and politics is a subject for a different essay, but by means of summary it is a story of power—a story of community, of identity,

Figure 19.1 Jacques Aliamet after Charles-Dominique Eisen, Frontispiece, in Marc-Antoine Laugier, *Essai sur l'architecture*, Paris 1755

and at times the wholesale erasure of that identity through violence. War is, at its very root, about the systematic erasure of identity, the bombing of buildings that hold that identity and ultimately the creation of new ones that erase it. While these topics such as war, politics, murder, and destruction are typically removed from the narratives of architectural history—they nonetheless have and will continue to exist as part of the backstory of architectural identity.

The contemporary economic landscape, however, and unfortunately for architecture, has rendered this local production of community identity largely mute. Globalization, efficient means of transporting materials, online exchanges about methodologies and techniques, and increasingly mobile workforces have simply erased the establishment of diverse individualized identities in regions, countries, and cities. That is to say the world has become increasingly architecturally generic. A speculative complex of apartments is much the same in Dublin as it is in Houston, as it is in Beijing. Globalized methods of construction and design, though one of very few software programs, has assured a consistently inexpensive, reliable, functioning system of building production used around the world. These gains in accessible shelter for all forms of use have come at the expense of more individualized architectural identity. Architecture's power to produce identity in communities, therefore, has been replaced by an efficient global identity of the generic. As such, architecture no longer has the means to produce regional identity in communities of people, and therefore no longer exerts the same form of power which it has for millennia since Laugier's hut's primitive beginnings.

Branding, however, is the Wild West for architecture's future. Branding is not synonymous with identity, and I propose that it offers the profession the ability to reclaim the cultural influence that architecture once had. Where architecture historically used identity to produce *local* identities, branding allows architecture to go *global*. Branding is relatively new to humanity. It is focused, strategic, and plays many of the same notes as "identity" albeit for solely financial reasons. Terminology for this subject is important; as the word *branding* can be as slippery as the undefined multitude of activities it describes. So we need a clean terminological start: Branding is a concept entirely contingent on commerce and more often than not global corporate entities. Individuals, even architects, can, of course, be brands or branded to some degree (Paris Hilton, Zaha Hadid), but the overwhelming force of influence in the world of branding is exerted through commercial products. As such we will focus exclusively on the latter. A brand, then, as the Merriam-Webster Dictionary simply defines, is "a class of goods identified by name as the product of a single firm or manufacturer", and "branding" is defined by the same organization as "the promoting of a product or service by identifying it with a particular brand." Contemporary readers will hold that this is self-evident, so infused is the activity within our lives, and yet the very concept of branding was not developed until relatively recently—only 250 years ago in a recorded history in a civilization that predates its emergence by, as previously stated, fifty plus millennia. As we will see this trajectory from being a seemingly innocuous process of identifying products has mutated into a force of unimaginable power in the shaping of human events—and architecture is, has, and will continue to need to adjust to address the rise of branding in much the same way it did with the rise of humanism, or modernism, or as it did with the invention of steel, or the elevator. As branding becomes more strategic, more scientific, more influential—so too will its influence on our built environment.

As was the case with architectural identity, the concept of branding requires some historic positioning. The man often credited as establishing the world's first "brands" was a potter named Josiah Wedgwood, (whose antiques my mom actually collects). In 1759 Wedgewood developed a new form of cream-colored glaze for his products that differentiated them from those of his competitors. Queen Charlotte, wife of King George III, was an admirer of this product and used it in the royal court. Wedgewood, in a brilliant first act of branding, renamed this product "Queen's ware" in honor of her patronage. This was not only a name; it was the world's first branded celebrity endorsement. As members of British society at the time sought innovation and novelty in new, rather than inherited, possessions, Wedgewood became relatively affordable luxury—and one that was not only novel but implied a closer relationship between its owners and the Queen of England. In 2005, readers of Forbes ranked Wedgewood as the nineteenth most influential businessman of all time. This was due to his contribution to branding, not his products (Millman, 2012).

This new and even more potent recipe for branding met its most fertile ground in the later industrial revolution. This revolution brought about not only the oft-celebrated sweeping changes in manufacturing methods but also in how products were purchased and consumed. For the first time in history a factory could make identical products in numbers never before conceivable. In order to sell these sheer numbers of goods, consumers needed to be found from much farther afield. This presented a problem for owners of the factories whose products and their reputations were unfamiliar to these new and distant customers. Something needed to be invented that conveyed a sense of not only the quality of the products, but what they were associated with, what they saw themselves as, and most importantly, what they said about the people who bought and used them. From this cauldron of production, distance, skepticism, desire, and identity, our modern concept of branding was born. One could now know about a product without knowing anything about its maker, or method of making, or location of production. Instead, branding was enlisted to replace the story of a product's *actual* making, history, and purpose with a true or even *fictional* story that could be conveyed across vast distances. The activity that was developed to span these distances between producer and consumer was later called advertising. In order to distill these brand identities into signs and symbols, a new language of "logos" was also developed. And to protect logos, a process of trademarking was invented—all in effect today much as they were in 1876—when the world's first trademark, for Bass Brewery's red triangle, was recognized and registered by the British government.

Branding in the early twenty-first century requires some different handling from our historic precedents, primarily because it has mutated from being in an understandable and stable state of postwar consumerism to a nearly indecipherable global industry of influence, power and political will. That is to say twenty-first century branding is a new and ravenous form of historic branding, empowered with the emergence of social media, handheld communications, and a globally networked society where distance has become nearly irrelevant. Accordingly, branding is no longer local, regional, or national, but all brands can be instantly global. Branding today, in this contemporary late-capitalism, corporate strain, is occupying a history-changing force on human individual and social behavior—a territory once reserved, in different times throughout history, for religion or empire. More plainly stated branding is emerging as one of the most powerful forces of the twenty-first century.

A brief online survey of architecture schools globally revealed that there are effectively *zero* courses dedicated to the subject of branding relative to architecture. Mentally compare that to the number of courses dedicated to the Renaissance (rise of humanism), or Modernism (rise of the mechanical age). Architectures respond to, and can even nourish social movements, such the rise of Humanism or Modernism, and yet for reasons unfathomable and mysterious, the academies of architecture are not only late to the game of branding, but are not even on their way to the field. Naturally there will be naysayers that declare what does architecture have to do with branding? (Likely not to have gotten this far in this particular text), so it is important to illustrate the vast swaths of economic and cultural territory that "branding" and its communicatory face, "advertising" occupy in the world today.

Power and influence in contemporary society are largely measured, for right or wrong, by money—so some analysis of the economics of branding as a global activity may help to illuminate the extent of its influence on the behavior of society. According to the economic tracking firm Plunkett Research Ltd, the spending on global branding/advertising, for 2013 topped US$517 billion (Plunkett Research, n.d.). The last reported annual budget for the Chinese Military was US$166 billion, meaning that if "branding" were a country, it could have a military nearly three times larger than that of China, and be second only to that of the United States. Or to describe it in more rarified religious terms—according to a 2012 investigation by the financial publication *The Economist*, the Catholic Church had a 2013 expenditure of US$170 billion. If branding were a religion, it would exert three times the global economic influence of the Catholic Church. Or to take the comparison closer to the academic context, in which this text exists—on October 25, 2011, Dennis Cauchon of *USA Today* reported that the amount of student loans taken out in 2011 crossed the US$100 billion mark for the first time and total loans outstanding will exceed US$1 trillion for the first time this year" (Plunkett Research, n.d.). The annual global resources spent on branding could, by extension, not only eliminate all national United States student debt in two years, but could annually pay for nearly 17 million students to attend private U.S. universities (College Data, n.d.). There are currently only 6 million college students in the United States, meaning that the global expenditures on branding could, only *this* year, not only pay for each of the current 6 million U.S. college students' full tuition, nearly three times, but could hand each one of them US$60,000 in spending money, some of which, naturally, to be spent at Pizza Hut.

> In Globalization 1.0, which began around 1492, the world went from size large to size medium. In Globalization 2.0, the era that introduced us to multinational companies, it went from size medium to size small. And then around 2000 came Globalization 3.0, in which the world went from being small to tiny.
>
> (Thomas Friedman)

To return for a moment to the original concept of "identity," we realize that the tools used by the branding industry are subtle mutations of "identity," to which architecture has always had a close relationship. Identity is about individual people and how they present themselves to the world—but far more powerful than this is the production of identity for communities of people—as previously covered, largely done, historically and locally, through architecture. While this practice has been, as we've established, neutered, communities are also formed *globally* through the branding of things—a territory where architecture can now be at its most influential.

What differentiates this act of forming community identity, which architecture has always done, from a contemporary landscape of branding is manifold, but at its root is that branding is done for the sole purpose of selling products. To brand something in the twenty-first century is to not only give it a singular identity, but to link it with a family of products to which it is related—and link the product to the people who use them, the users to each other, and link all involved into the fictional narrative set by the brand.

These families of products convey information about their quality, their use, and most importantly their users through fictional brand identities. These users of particular products then become related through these fictions, and become clumped into new forms of community not defined by geography, but rather participation in the narrative that the particular brand provides. There are Coke people and there are Pepsi people. Odds are you have, even surprising to you, rather strong feelings about this subject—most people do. This differentiation is one of loyalty, but more significantly participation in a community of like users of these products. Commercials show these communities the great life of being part of them—of drinking with celebrities, playing volleyball on the beach, of being young, in great weather, and enjoying it all the more because of a Coke. If you drink Coke, you are part of this life, this amazing, young, fulfilling, and perfectly constructed life. Register this number: 1.7 billion. This is how many servings of Coca-Cola are consumed daily. That deserves repeating—1.7 billion servings of Coke are served *daily*. If we assume that there are some who are drinking more than one of these servings then we have, by a conservative estimate, perhaps 1 billion *different* individuals who drink Coca-Cola every day. Those who buy and consume Coca-Cola have, globally, made the same decision, bought into the same story, and participate in the manufactured fiction of lifestyle sold by Coca-Cola. This is the formation of a new type of community—Coke drinkers—in this case one that spans continents, classes, genders, races, classes, and every other possible means of human segregation. A community of 1 billion people would form the world's third largest country, falling in line just behind China (1,363,390,000), and India (1,241,690,000).

Even 40 years ago the Coca-Cola Company knew the extent of their global community when they launched their 1971 "Buy the World a Coke" campaign developed by the advertising firm McCann Erikson—which became one of the most successful advertising campaigns in history. If you are over 40 at the time of this writing, you can likely recite the chorus of the song that accompanied the campaign.

There are as many communities as there are products, some larger and more clearly defined than others, but all determined through branding. There are MSNBC people and Fox News people, there are BMW people and Audi people, there are Yale people and Harvard people—all forming vast interconnected networks of varying size and strength—based on the fictional narratives of branding.

And so we recognize that branding is powerful. Very powerful, if not among the most powerful, for better or for worse, influence on the behaviors society today—not only in economic terms but human ones. As such you would imagine that the discipline of architecture would have developed some sort of relationship to the landscape of contemporary branding, seeing how it governs so much of the economic and social landscape across the globe—and architecture is inherently a discipline about identity. You would be wrong.

Branding is big business—a business that barely existed only 250 years ago, and architecture is late to the game. Our tardiness, however, does not mean that we are incapable of eventual engagement—as we've already covered, architecture has a long and storied relationship with brandings' sister, "identity." And branding is certainly about identity, only one that is re-read through a filter of products, loyalty, lifestyle, and mass consumerism. Architecture's oldest function, above and beyond that of mere shelter, is one, in fact, of identity—and if identity is so historically linked to architecture, then there must be some sort of relationship between architecture and branding, right?

So where does architecture currently exist in these equations? Unfortunately, the answer is more often than not, hiding behind the physical detritus of branding—printed or electronic advertisements. Because architecture is large, visible, generally found around larger numbers of people and built primarily from flat vertical surfaces—it, in the late twentieth century, became the ideal scaffold for advertising and branded content. That is to say architecture, historically and today, seems content to merely be *covered* by branding, through signage, but rarely engage it through other means. This mentality continues today with the invention of new LED and LCD technologies that are similarly plastered over buildings in extreme numbers. Environments such as Piccadilly Circus in London, to Shinjuku in Tokyo, to Times Square in New York anticipate a future that, if left unchecked, might devolved into a combination of Rem Koolhaas's "junkspace" married to a language of sophisticated technologies that cover buildings. It is inevitable that proceeding along current trajectories, architectures ultimate end-game is to be conservatively dressed head to toe in a burka of advertising, content to be seen only between accidental eye slits located between screens and signs. If we are not able to retool architecture to better engage the branded landscape, the profession runs the risk of becoming one of lowest-common-denominator construction, unexceptional space making, and a mere provider of the square foot content of cells of Excel spreadsheets.

Instead of selling our large, flat, urban façade surfaces to the brokers of content, architecture as a profession needs a new palette of spatial tools and tactics to enable new forms of participation in the new world order of branding. Fortunately for us, the tools exist; they are within reach, and we can access them—but only with a shifting mentality towards the very foundational root of the profession. In the same way we returned to the ur-architecture, the primitive hut, we must also return for a moment to architecture's "ur-theory" in order to understand a significant disciplinary straitjacket prohibiting us from fully engaging in the newly interconnected and branded world.

And suddenly you know: It's time to start something new and trust the magic of beginnings.

(Eckhart von Hochheim (Meister Eckhart))

The oldest existing text on architecture, *De Architectura*, also known as the *Ten Books on Architecture* was written by the Augustan architect, Vitruvius in approximately 15 BC (Vitruvius, 1960). This text has become a foundation for architectural disciplinarily, defining the extents of the discipline and codifying a series of points to which all architecture must aspire. The importance of this text cannot be overstated, as it later exerted tremendous influence on the Renaissance through Leon Battista Alberti, who sought to replace the Vitruvian text with one of his own. Vitruvius's canonical principles of architecture identified in this book are *firmness, commodity and delight*. These terms have been translated into contemporary terms as *permanent, useful* and *beautiful*—qualities to which architects rarely object.

In the twenty-first century brands change; people change; programs change and styles change—all at a far faster speed than architecture, or people for that matter, has ever before encountered. Therein lies a large component of our problem—our professional obligation to *permanence*, or in our Vitruvius terms, *firmness*. Architecture establishes, if not requires, an ambition for inherent stability over time. Branding is allergic to permanence. Branding today is fast, constantly changing, adapting and mutating. To complicate the equation brands are now transcending categorical barriers and co-branding in ways never before imagined. From fashion icon Karl Lagerfeld's designing a clothing line for the entry-level Swedish fashion brand H&M, then turning around and collaborating with Zaha Hadid on a spaceship for Chanel, to Nike co-branding with Apple to produce computerized sports equipment, branding is no longer even as stable as it was only a decade ago. Horror of horrors, Apple is now even collaborating with its once bitter rival IBM. The ground has shifted, dramatically. Branding has now even more ephemeral, mobile and instantly reconfigurable very difficult qualities for a discipline based on the concept of permanence to address.

Architecture's arsenal is, however changing, and challenges to a disciplinary insistence on permanence are emerging. From shifts in mentality to shifts in technology architecture need not be content to perform as a mere scaffold on which the excitement of the emerging twenty-first century should hang. Architecture is the discipline profession of space, and nowhere has anyone ever determined that a requirement for space is to be stable. Space can move, shift, flutter, breathe and do a vast array of actions it has only never been asked to perform. There are, and certainly will be more, shifts in architectural thinking and technology that offer ways for architecture, using these means, to directly engage with the content of branding.

If architecture, whether a building, pavilion, pop-up store, installation, event space, or residence, is no longer inexorably tied to the concept of permanence, then it can, without shame, be designed with a particular duration in mind. A standard criticism of this mentality is that architecture, among the most resource intensive of human endeavors, must be useful to not only one generation but many, and accordingly must, quite simply, last. This time-honored sentiment is worthy of consideration, but so too is the fact that the way architecture functions in the twenty-first century, which may be to fuse material morality with brands, companies, and individuals that are increasingly nomadic and transitory. The average American, according to U.S. Census data, moves 11–14 times in a lifetime, and brands are no longer architecturally based as they have been in past incarnations where they formed buildings as significant as the Chrysler Building by William Van Alan or the TWA Terminal by Eero Saarinen. Instead the brands of today are cloud based, flowing through the veins

Figure 19.2 Nicola Formichetti Store with Lady Gaga Outfits, Mark Foster Gage Architects, 2011. Image Credit: Mark Foster Gage Architects

of networks, delivering continuously changing content to potential customers through a shifting and transitory landscape of eternally reconfiguring media.

These facts preclude the two largest markets for architecture, residences and offices, from investing in building in any permanent sense, as buildings require location and society is increasingly locationless. These forms of real estate have become temporary financial transactions based on price per square foot and approximate location, whereas in the past they may have been based on architectural form, style, and identity. Architecture must adapt to the new transitory landscape of contemporary life, and engage in rougher, rawer, faster and dirtier forms of practice and construction that may last for far less time than the buildings of yesteryear. They may not be buildings at all, or they may be the development of new design technologies that *overlay or fuse with* buildings, not just cover them up. It may be that the "Junkspace" of Rem Koolhaas is simply too nice, and expensive for a palette for such an endeavor, and new forms of construction need be enlisted to address the desire for disposable architectures.

The industry of branding, especially in fashion, has been a pioneer in this field of architecture and branded experiences through the increasingly ubiquitous typology of the pop-up shop. If the commercial flagship was the architectural project of the 1990s, then the pop-up shop is its twenty-first-century replacement. Pop-up shops are temporary, inexpensive, and frequently allow for the use of far more radical forms, technologies and experiences than a company would allow for in a typical retail environment. From Rem Koolhaas's "pop-up museum" for Prada, to the aforementioned collaboration between Zaha Hadid and Karl Lagerfeld for Chanel to a pop-up shop my own firm designed for Nicola Formichetti that housed a collection of Lady Gaga's outfits, the typology is revolutionizing retail experiences in venues from high-fashion to discount chains, and are designed by architects ranging from Pritzker-prize winners to recently graduated students. This isn't a call-to-arms for architects to build using trash, in the form of discarded tires and shipping containers and to be cobblers of industrial society's junk—but rather we challenge the limited palette of standardized building components to which we have been largely relegated and become free to experiment beyond the disciplines inherited operational lore.

One area that architecture might become further invested in is that of what is previously referred to as the aforementioned architectural "overlay." Sylvia Lavin in the excerpt of "Kissing Architecture," published in the *Issue of Log* (#19) which I guest edited in 2009, describes such a possibility as "pouring mediums together." It may be the case that in order to better address the shifting needs of branded spaces, architecture for a time, turns its attention to the overlaying and pouring together of possibilities including, to name a few, living materials, projection mapping, scent, physical interactivity, responsive touch surfaces, weight registers, infrared tracking, social media, changes in temperature, optical tracking, holographic lighting and other, even more ephemeral means to produce frequent change in architectural forms and spaces.

Another frequency on which the challenge to permanence might occur is that buildings may develop a language of actual movement and reconfigurability, currently championed by figures such as Greg Lynn. Architectural space is mostly unused. Churches sit mostly empty for six days a week. Homes empty for the nine-plus hours of the workday; offices empty for the 15 hours daily that separate workdays, the average car sits idle and unoccupied for 90 percent of its life, in a parking space that is also vacant for a large portion of its own life. Contemporary spatial life is largely one of emptiness and vacancy. Architecture purports to be for function, designed to accommodate the requirement of particular programs, and shelter, yet for a stunning percentage of its life, in most cases, it sits unused, inert, and empty. As urban densities increase and needs for space continually grow, physical motion and reconfigurability will inevitably emerge as a solution, and an opportunity for a shifting, updating and branding of responsive architecture. I am reminded of a joint co-branded space that I used to frequent in Osaka Japan. A local Toyota dealership joined forces with a popular coffee and business lunch chain. For most of the day the interior showroom of the dealership housed a range of Camrys and Corollas scattered around the showroom floor. At lunch the staff backed the cars against the walls, thereby clearing out a large space in the center of the space where the coffee shop would set up chairs to become a temporary restaurant that has apparently been there for years. After lunch the cars would come back and the restaurant would leave a few tables for afternoon coffee scattered throughout the potpourri of automobiles. In this equation the dealership gained as it could use its space to bring in additional people to see their products, and the café gained as it didn't require the overhead of a permanent space. The brand requirements of the spaces were sympathetic to a convergence that, through a logic of movement, allowed them to synergistically accommodate each other. This is, of course, a rudimentary example of reconfigurabilty, but opportunities for co-use, particularly through co-branding, will increase not only as brands become savvier to such opportunities, but as technologies from the robotic architectural movements of Greg Lynn's recent "Room Vehicle" projects to the collapsible structures of Chuck Hoberman continue to evolve. Structures at increasingly massive scales are also participating in the shift away from permanence towards movement. From Rem Koolhaas's "transformer" for Prada that flipped on various sides to accommodate different programs to numerous proposals for rotating towers, actual movement in architecture will continue to take us further from the Vitruvian firmness of yesteryear into new territories where architecture can better address the constantly shifting needs of our dynamically accelerating branded society. These forms of motion, now used primarily for programmatic means will, perhaps, lead to other forms of architectural rippling, fluttering, shifting and twisting that can allow the profession to even better regain new powers of identity production in this branded landscape.

Architectural academia and much of the intellectual edge of the profession is allergic to the idea of working, without cynicism or critique, for corporations, the producers of brands. In fact many of architecture's most inventive and exciting moments have been through revolutionary proposals to counter the status-quo, that is to say "anti" power structure architecture. From Archigram's walking cities to Superstudio's endless grids, architecture will, and should, offer alternate forms of existing and challenges to our inherited notions of habitable space. These were successful in the past because the imagery was powerful, strange, and often haunting, even developing a new genre of "paper architecture" within the profession. In a world buried in limitless fantastic images found online, these moments will continue to have significantly less and less efficacy in the world. If architecture is to have a voice in the world of Facebook, YouTube, Vine, and Google, it will be through its physicality. Physicality, and the impact such physicality has on the senses, is what makes architecture unique, what makes it desirable, what makes it important. To the extent that it can be imagined, the conveyance of constantly changing physicality should be a problem requiring a new form of architecture. There are not many things, including communication, entertainment, shopping, and social interaction, that have not been almost fully absorbed into the digital universe—and architecture's defining characteristic of three dimensional actual space places makes it unique in the world once again, being resistant to digitization. In order to capitalize on this rediscovered uniqueness, and exercise it towards new forms of power, architecture must once again be bravely and radically physical, and not at all required to be permanent or stable. Images of built architecture can be powerful, renderings and speculations less so, but none can compete with the physicality that, increasingly, only architecture can require. If architecture is able to convert the use of emerging technologies into a useful identity-producing language for branding, it will not only allow architecture to reclaim a new form, of an old form of influence, but as brands are, by their very definition, about differences, they ask architecture to be its most experimental, its most radical and its most speculative. The landscape of architecture can thrive like never before. It only takes a shift in mentality towards the extent of what architects produce, and the tools they use to produce it, to be given access to the wealth of spatial opportunities presented in the branded world.

This is no doubt heretical for previous architectural generations that spent decades removing architecture from physicality, consumerism and the reach of corporate business interests—but the truth is we have no other choice. The forces at play in the world are no longer even possibly affected by our utopian or critical speculations, and to think so is nearly comical given the statistics previously presented. We live in a world that operates according to a new economic physics, and architecture must adapt to the new laws or risk becoming a castrated art practice appreciated only by academics and the elite. We're already close.

Branding is among the most promising territories for architectural innovation. As we have already seen it is incredibly well funded, seeks novelty, and prizes creative originality as its existence, literally, depends on the ability to differentiate between products, forms, and spaces. Until now most branding has been two dimensional in the form of billboards, television ads, magazine spreads, computer banners, sides of painted buildings, hung exterior LCD screens, and so on. Architecture is uniquely poised to usher in a new age of advertising and branding by taking it from a logic of stable 2D surfaces into one of 3D spaces that continuously change. With or without our engagement the future urban landscape will be one of drifting between overlapping branded spaces—as the "public" realm increasingly shrinks. The future of cities is one of vulgar 2D signage unless architecture develops a more compelling spatial alternative. Whereas the spatial branding practices of the past were limited to rather conventional means of decoration—color, form, logos, and material palettes, architecture is now being armed with a new generation of technologies that allow us to activate matter in ways only now becoming realizable. Space without atmosphere is flavorless, and whereas architects of the past were limited to a miniscule palette of building materials (timber, brick, wood, concrete), the contemporary architect now has access to a multitude of exotic and smart materials that need to be studied for how they can be used towards the production of new immersive experiences. The creation of images is no longer enough. We must create choreographies of technology and effects in physical spaces that are anything but stable or permanent. Brands are begging for such originality, while the rest of the world seems content to exist on a diet of historic architectural downtowns surrounded by endless rings of the generic. Progressive corporations looking to expand the reach of their brands are the patrons of the immediate future for architecture, asking us to produce spaces that are alive, breathing, interactive, customizable, and globally interconnected. The immediate future offers us the potentials of ubiquitous computing, sensors imbedded in matter; interactive gestures, facial recognition, and choreographies of lighting and sound so that the branded spaces of tomorrow may appear closer to biological entities than the decorated generic spaces of the twentieth century's mechanical paradigm. Architecture could become among the most significant players in the emergence of a new genre of constantly reconfiguring human space, one funded by brands, interactively tuned towards individuals, societally connected to global communities, atmospherically and interactively charged, and, above all, spatial. The alternative is that architecture will, in the face of such massive commercialization expenditures, be increasingly collapsed into inert scaffolds for two-dimensional signage and screens ... and the occasional strange bright red pitched mansard roof.

References

Cauchon, D. (2011). *Student Loans Outstanding Will Exceed $1 Trillion This Year*. Retrieved January 3, 2015 from: http://usatoday30.usatoday.com/money/perfi/college/story/2011-10-19/student-loan-debt/50818676/1.

College Data (n.d.). *What's the Price Tag for a College Education?* Retrieved January 3, 2015 from: http://www.collegedata.com/cs/content/content_payarticle_tmpl.jhtml?articleId=10064.

Gove, P.B. (1993). *Webster's Third New International Dictionary of the English Language, Unabridged*. Springfield, MA: Merriam Webster.

Hays, K.M. (1998). *Architecture Theory since 1968*. Cambridge, MA: MIT.

Hollier, D. (1989). *Against Architecture: The Writings of Georges Bataille*. Cambridge, MA: MIT.

Millman, D. (2012). *Brand Bible: The Complete Guide to Building, Designing, and Sustaining Brands*. Beverly, MA: Rockport Publishing.

Onion, The (2000). You can tell area bank used to be a Pizza Hut. *The Onion*, 31 May. Retreived October 10, 2015 from http://www.theonion.com/graphic/you-can-tell-area-bank-used-to-be-a-pizza-hut-8899

Plunkett Research, Ltd. (n.d.). *Advertising-Branding-Market-Research*. Retrieved January 3, 2015 from: https://www.plunkettresearch.com/advertising-branding-market-research/industry-and-business-data.

Rusbridger, A. (2014). It's essential to be paranoid. *The New York Times Magazine*, 9 March, 12.

Vitruvius (1960). *Vitruvius: The Ten Books on Architecture*, M.H. Morgan, trans. New York: Dover Publications.

Part V
Architectural Design and Urbanism

This part, by looking through a broader lens, will focus into origins of urbanism, and the concerns with the architectonic form of the city. It also brings forth arguments about alternative design strategies with respect to the people's places, and the community residents from various ages, status of living, as well as the critical needs of people toward creating safe and healthful urban environments.

20

Public Health and the Design Process

Dak Kopec

Introduction

Ever since humans ceased to be hunter-gathers wandering the expansive plains of Africa we have relied upon the built environment to meet our daily needs of food, water, and shelter. We formed villages to shelter us, developed systems to bring fresh water to us, and devised ways to keep our food stocks close and easily accessible. In essence, we went from a nomadic people to a stationary society; no longer coping with climate changes through migration. We had to plan for, and endure, the rough times. According to Sir Isaac Newton's third law of motion, "every action has an opposite and equal reaction." The reactions that occurred as we shifted from a nomadic lifestyle to a stationary society were new conditions and circumstances that affected, and continue to affect, our physical, psychological, and social health.

Becoming a stationary society meant that new diseases, conditions, and situations had to be addressed. Some of these changes included the consideration that E-coli from human excrement could contaminate water sources. Food had to be stored in preparation for winter months or times of drought, and the role of family and caregiving became more nurturing as we provided care for longer durations. Additionally, new roles had been created. We now needed people who could construct housing, farm the land, and maintain social order. Hence, we needed to develop a better understanding of the action-reaction process. This action-reaction process within a social construct evolved to include Hammurabi's code, whereby the architect, for example, who designed and built a structure that collapsed, would be held responsible (Trachtenberg & Hyman, 1986).

The Early Days

Early societies such as the Romans understood the relationship between health and the built environment through experience, trial and error, and observation. From this knowledge, architects of the day designed many innovations that would keep the Roman people healthy. For example, aqueducts were built to bring clean water to a series of aesthetically attractive fountains within Roman cities. These fountains supplied the Romans with potable water. Roman architects also designed subterranean canals to transport used grey and black water out of the city (Macaulay, 1974), and ancient courtyard houses to maximize natural lighting throughout the year (Schoenauer, 2000).

For architects of the Roman Empire human health was part of their scope of practice. This meant they had to have some scientific knowledge of engineering and disease transmission in addition to aesthetics. During the Dark Ages, much of human health within the built environment among European cultures was neglected. This is because the sociopolitical climate evolved to embody the concepts of functionalism and fatalism (Amundsen, 1996). Architects of the Dark Ages designed and engineered beautiful structures (mostly cathedrals) that contributed to the rise of urbanism within many European cities. Because of the fatalistic beliefs held by the people, Gothic cathedrals soared into the sky with the hopes of becoming closer to heaven, while death, disease, and infirmity were considered the domain of God's will (Haferkamp & Smelser, 1992), rather than attributed to factors such as poor sanitation and overcrowding.

It was only after the 1880s that indoor plumbing and drainage systems were introduced into the buildings of Europe and some parts of the Western world. Architecture of the late 1800s concentrated on aesthetics and aspects of engineering, while the relationship between design and human health remained perfunctory (i.e. sanitation).

Later, architectural movements focused on human health beyond basic needs. The Bauhaus movement, for example, did not specifically seek to improve human health per se, but the unintended outcomes of many Bauhaus principles did have a positive effect on physical and psychological health (Boubekri, 2008). One Bauhaus concept was the emphasis on air circulation. This principle is still used today. Increased air circulation inside of buildings diffuses carbon dioxide accumulation, and provides better control over the levels and lifecycles of airborne pathogens.

The need for the inclusion of human health within the design process and implementation strategies has been discussed and written about extensively; albeit, mostly from the ancillary professions of public health (i.e. London's Cholera epidemic) (Paneth *et al.*, 1998), psychology (i.e. Jack the Ripper) (Cornwell, 2002), and sociology (i.e. the inquisition) (Woodward, 2008). While these historical events have provided an excellent foundation for the definition of health, they fail to consider the role of design as causal—or cofactor. London's cholera epidemic was linked to a specific well (Paneth *et al.,* 1998). Jack the Ripper who suffered from violent fantasies from an early age (Cornwell, 2002), relied upon poorly lit streets to hunt, and the Spanish Inquisition was centered on mass fear and group-think based on irrational suppositions (Woodward, 2008) often tied to the interaction of natural forces on the built environment (i.e. a sudden flooding).

Simplistic logic has and continues to cripple holistic and comprehensive outcomes. This logic is based on causality by a singular event or source. In the above example the fact that the streets were poorly lit provided an ideal environment for Jack the Ripper to commit mass murder. Similarly, simplistic thinking has resulted in widespread neglect of the built environment as a causal cofactor in human health. This resembles the "Magic Bullet Theory." Coined by Paul Ehrlich, the Magic Bullet Theory is based on a singular leading factor for a particular outcome. For Ehrlich, the factor was mass media messages, and the acceptance of those messages as truth (McLeod *et al.*, 2006). Public health has adopted the term as a negative; arguing that a single intervention will not yield positive outcomes. Hence, public health embraces education, policy, and cultural factors in unison. Unfortunately, much of society has not evolved beyond the singular "Magic Bullet" thought process. This paradigm of reasoning, coupled with a strong culture and a tradition of siloed imperialism, has led to negative situations that might have been avoided by using a more holistic approach. In more recent times, for example, the Centers for Disease Control (CDC) failed to consider animal welfare concerns related to the 1999 sudden and frequent deaths of birds in New York City (American Museum of Natural History, n.d.; Horowitz and Bowers, 2012). This failure to include veterinary sciences within their paradigm of thinking was a contributing factor in the proliferation of the West Nile Virus throughout North America.

Paradigm of Precedence

Within antiquity, the professions of medicine, law, and architecture had much broader scopes of practice than today. This meant issues and concerns were thought of with greater breadth. The profession of architecture, which arose alongside medicine and jurisprudence (law) serves as a fundamental building block for western civilization. Each of these professions depended upon apprenticeships to impart knowledge, and relied heavily on case study to guide outcomes. The act of learning by doing afforded the learner with an opportunity to witness and experience integration from multiple perspectives, thus allowing him or her to be more holistic in their practice.

In the 1980s and into the 1990s medicine coined the term "evidence-based medicine" (Barends *et al.*, 2012). This was a shift in practice away from "best estimations" based on causal comparative analysis derived from case studies. This "guess-work" was replaced with provable facts based on tests. Put another way, if a person had very similar signs and symptoms as their predecessors they were diagnosed with the same condition as their predecessors. Today, the signs and symptoms of the predecessors only guide the tests. It is the test that determines the diagnosis. The test, which is based on science, is the evidence.

The legal system also went through a transformation in paradigm. Scientific methods were embraced by the judicial system as a means to determine guilt or innocence. In law, the supporting factors of the case served as the probability of guilt or innocence. Tests such as DNA testing replaced reasoning by probability. Again, the tests are based on science, and serve as the evidence.

While medicine and law continue to use case study methods in daily practice, this more subjective approach is augmented by objective and definitive outcomes produced by scientific inquiry. In short, the professions of medicine and jurisprudence have evolved from breadth of knowledge to depth of knowledge; or specialization. Today medical doctors can be dermatologists, pulmonologists, vascular surgeons, etc. Likewise, those who graduate with a degree in jurisprudence can be a criminal attorneys, tax attorneys, mergers and acquisitions attorneys, etc. Architecture has yet to make this evolutionary step.

A conundrum unique to the profession of architecture, relative to medicine and jurisprudence, is the relationship between prevention and curative outcomes related to short- and long-term effects. Medicine and jurisprudence, for the most part, concentrate their practice on curing or rectifying a given problem. This after-the-fact model provides significant outcome data. Put another way, it is easy to say that treatment A led to the recovery of X number of patients, or that prosecutor B has a XX percent conviction rate. But we have yet to see a statistic that says for example, XX percent of Renzo Piano's designs have been free of required maintenance upgrades for ABC (Health and Safety) concerns during the first five years of occupation.

Another challenge is that physicians and lawyers tend to only become involved in a situation when there is a clear and present problem that requires an action. The solutions to these problems can then be easily measured and promoted. The "fixing" of problems after-the-fact also ties the profession to an outcome. For example, a physician identifies a treatment, then administers that treatment. A lawyer devises a strategy, then delivers the argument. The architect typically doesn't work from an after-the-fact perspective. Instead they must speculate on the future of the building they design based on past problems. This speculation may or may not manifest, and if it does, may or may not do so as it did in the past. The presence and absence of differing and sometimes competing variables will affect the outcome.

Kopec's Environmental Hierarchy Model

Architecture, and the design professions as a whole, rely upon models and theories to guide practice. Models and theories make up the foundations of social sciences and theoretical disciplines such as Theoretical Physics. When considering the human condition in terms of evolution of cognition throughout human development, a multivariable approach is needed. We might consider human health and the built environment as a symbiotic relationship in terms of hierarchy, similar to Abraham Maslow's 1943 proposal to understand human motivation. Kopec suggested the way in which a society comprehends and understands an environment within the terms of human health is based on a hierarchy (see Figure 20.1) he calls the Environmental Hierarchy Model (Kopec, 2011). This model can be applied to all or one of the trifecta of human environments as they relate to the human experience throughout one's lifetime: home, school/workplace, and community. It should be noted however, that an interesting trend in modern societies is the blending of home, school/workplace, and

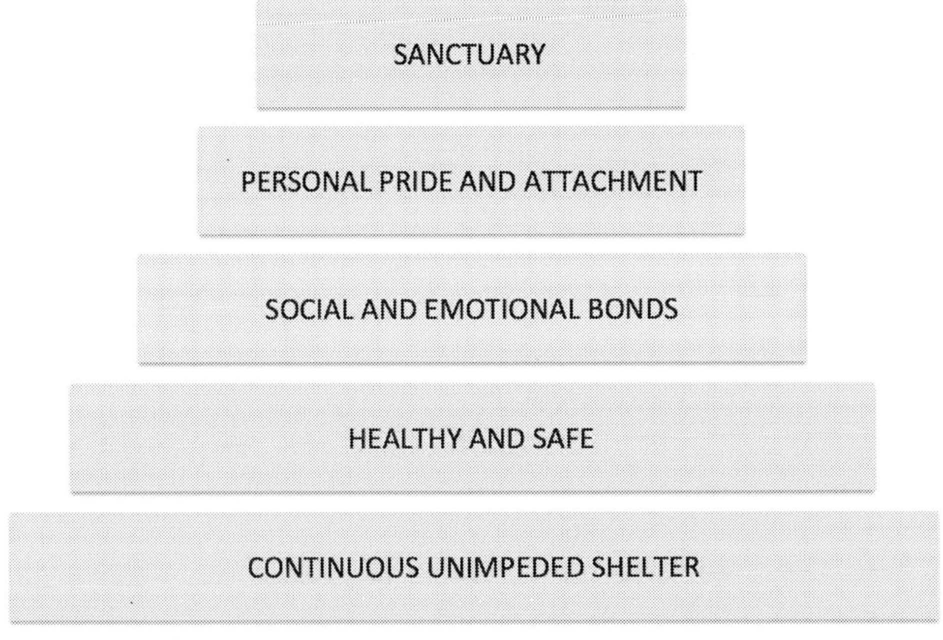

Figure 20.1 Kopec proposes a hierarchy model to achieve optimal health and wellness from the biological, psychological, and sociological perspectives. He asserts that one must achieve the prior level before fully realizing the next level

community as all encompassing, which thus places greater emphasis on the Environmental Hierarchy Model.

In the Environmental Hierarchy Model, Kopec argues that one cannot acquire or maintain health without continued and unimpeded access to a place of refuge. If this place cannot ensure health and safety (safety is an element of health), the occupants will experience discontentment, which will in turn negatively affect social and emotional bonds through learned helplessness and apathy (Goodman *et al.*, 1991). The occupants are then likely to assign blame or withdraw.

If it is possible to retain social and emotional bonds, the occupants will likely start to feel pride in one's community/home. Pride is an essential emotion that helps facilitate place attachment (Manzo & Perkins, 2006). Without pride and attachment people will simply stop caring about their environments, thus compromising health and safety through apathy, dereliction, and negative behaviors. Those who do achieve social and emotional connections will come to regard their environments as a sanctuary.

Early humans accomplished and satisfied their shelter needs with an assortment of one-room huts, teepees, cabins, etc. Within the conceptualization process of the home, these early societies conceptualized home as a territory, not a structure. The next level on the Environmental Hierarchy Model is the refuge's ability to support physical health and personal safety. This was, and continues to be, a difficult step to attain because of the multiple variables involved. To be safe means a structure cannot be penetrated, remains standing through assorted weather conditions, and serves as an effective barrier to moisture and vermin. Even with knowledge and technologies, much of the world's housing stock fails to meet basic health and safety. Likewise, the conceptualization of refuge as a means to support psychological and social health is a fundamental premise throughout all levels within the pyramid, and demands acquiescence to the reality that the physical environment (size, composition, and elements contained within) can, and do, influence collaboration, cooperation, competition, and conflict.

The ability of the physical environment to function in tandem with thought, emotion, and behavior is a significant step on the Environmental Hierarchy Model in relation to social health and the promotion of positive social bonds. Age-specific communities such as retirement villages and residential living on college campuses tend to excel at this level of the pyramid. What makes these living arrangements so successful is the cluster of people who share a developmental stage, and the subsequent age appropriate activities that appeal to a given population cluster. For example, a shallow square or circular swimming pool better accommodates water aerobics and stretching whereas rectangular and deeper swimming pools support diving and sports such as water polo. Hence the former is more appropriate for a retirement campus while the later better accommodates the needs of a college campus. This is not to say that one design must omit the other function; but rather, the design is based on greater probability giving way to the potential for the secondary use; hence, the use of the word hierarchy within the model.

Inspiration of pride and personal attachment denotes yet another phase in the conceptualization of what an environment means. This is the belief that in order for an environment to be healthy, it must inspire individual feelings of security and connectedness; often referred to within psychology as "place attachment" (Manzo & Perkins, 2006). In the context of this discussion, there are no design arrangements that facilitate place attachment per se. It is the provision of design elements for a given activity and subsequent engagement in that activity that leads to place attachment. In other words, a swimming pool designed for water aerobics and stretching activities and then used for that purpose engenders positive associations and the formation of place attachment.

Finally, at the top of the pyramid, is the category of "sanctuary." This level tends to be reserved for spiritual centers where the emphasis is placed on reaching inner peace and complete contentment. This level of conceptualization gives equal consideration to the tangible and intangible, objective and subjective, and the rational and irrational. For an environment to be fully conceptualized as a sanctuary it must first satisfy all needs and desires within an ongoing and continually changing human experience.

Among the fundamental differences between Kopec's Environmental Hierarchy Model and Maslow's Hierarchy of Needs, is the ability for an environment to support or inspire higher levels on the pyramid without first achieving the lower levels; but only for a short period of time. Kopec argues that if the sanctuary status is met without first ensuring health and safety, then the environment's ability to continually support the sanctuary status will diminish over time. He likens the Environmental Hierarchy Model to a building that may have a poorly constructed foundation, frame, or roof. On the surface the building looks good, but the poor construction means that the building will encounter numerous problems over time.

Modern Ideas

Arguably, and with such exceptions as African villages that fight daily starvation, south-east Asian settlements without easy access to clean water, or north American homeless left to wander the streets and sleep in make-shift shelters, the evolution of humanity has seen significant strides in the satisfaction of diverse variables related to the basic human needs of food, water, and shelter. In the second decade of the twenty-first century, select portions of some societies have been able to attain different levels on the Environmental Hierarchy Model, however no society has been able to ensure that all its people are able to meet the first level of the pyramid. The consequences of this social failure are being compounded by the evolutionary pace in medical knowledge, practices, and technologies, which has brought about a rise in overall average life expectancy in western civilizations.

Today, many westerners can expect to live into their late seventies or mid-eighties. By 2025 the average life expectancy is estimated to be late eighties to early nineties, and by 2050 the average westerner will likely live to be over a hundred (Jacobsen *et al.*, 2011). This trend has a two-fold effect; the first is that we will see significant rises in overall population, which will place a significant strain on the planet, make it easier for viruses and bacteria to migrate from one host to another, and place increased psychological demands on individuals related to crowding and personal space violations.

A second effect of longer life spans is that we will see more people plagued with long-term health issues related to the natural aging process, along with the delayed onset or cumulative effects of early and continued exposures to assorted hazards that are inhaled, absorbed, consumed, and injected, leading to more chronic illnesses. If we do not bring about provisions to ensure complete health and safety within our environments then the gap between the poor and wealthy will correspond with the gap between the chronically ill and healthy. This disparity will be mirrored by the quality of the built environment even more than it is today.

Modern Environmental Conditions

Within recent decades we have seen many airborne diseases, such as Tuberculosis, become antibiotic resistant (U.S. Department of Health and Human Services Centers of

Disease Control and Prevention, 2013a), or jump species (i.e. H1N1-Bird Flu) (Howard Hughes Medical Institute, 2006). The consistent variable within such cases is proximity; humans living within crowded conditions and close to livestock. The pathogens that cause Tuberculosis and Bird Flu, like other viruses and bacteria, become stronger each time they are passed from one person to another (U.S. Department of Health and Human Services Centers for Disease Control and Prevention, 2013b). This is because viruses and bacteria adapt and mutate. With continued population growth and spatial densification within our urban cores, we will inevitably see more virulent forms of bacteria and viruses affecting people. Put another way, with more people and higher density levels, it is much easier to pass infectious diseases from one person to another, and with each passing of a virus or bacteria the stronger and more resistant the pathogen becomes.

The emerging high social densification (crowding) phenomena, coupled with worldwide transportation and globalization, means that super-bugs will be introduced into urban cores with greater frequency. Currently, airports, airplanes, and the shuttles that move us about within travel processes experience periods of very high social density. Both Bird and Swine flu penetrated western populations because of high social density loads within airplanes, airports, and shuttles. The probability for a major pandemic will continue to increase as social densities increase within all of our environments. This will lead to skyrocketing healthcare costs. Designers can help to mitigate these issues by increasing the square footage per person within public and private spaces, while concurrently increasing air exchange rates. Ironically, these two initiatives are contrary to some of the modern movements (micro apartments and sustainability) within architecture and design, which are driven by finances, among other social trends.

In addition to issues stemming from basic biology, there are psychological and sociological factors that need to be addressed. A hallmark within an advanced society is the more comprehensive definition of health as going beyond visual infirmities or sets of displayed symptoms to include the complete state of *physical, mental and social* wellbeing. This definition was taken from the World Health Organization's (WHO) preamble to their Constitution, adopted at the International Health Conference in 1946 and subsequently enforced in 1948 (WHO, 1946).

Right, wrong, or indifferent, the majority of the world's societies have traditionally placed great importance on disease and infirmity, and less emphasis on psychological and social health. Disease and infirmity garner more attention because the associated symptoms are often visible and there is a perceived greater threat to life. Health initiatives are often tied to sets of symptoms associated with a specific disease, injury, or illness. Once symptoms have become plainly visible, the solution is some form of medication, surgical intervention, or inclusion of an assistive device. This is known as the curative model. Consequently, we have made great strides in the development of pharmaceutical remedies, mastery of surgical interventions, and the design and development of assistive devices. These initiatives approach disease, injury, and illness from a curative, or after-the-fact, perspective. To this end, consider the growing problem of obesity within the United States. Weight loss pills have been around for several decades, surgical intervention has become a viable solution, and more recently educational messages have promoted greater activity. Each of these solutions attempts to solve the issue after-the-fact.

More recent phenomena within the United States are related to poor psychological and social health. We see people choosing social isolation, suffering burn-out, or engaging in behaviors outside their norm. An example is the frequency of people shooting guns in public spaces. When a person believes that the only solution to their immediate problem is opening fire in a public space it is safe to conclude that individual suffers from some sort of psychological illness. Likewise, communities that suffer from poor social health might justify acts of bullying, discrimination (sexual, racial, age, etc.), or hazing as "rights-of-passage."

As we examine assorted physical, psychological, and social health concerns, one common thread that emerges is the built environment. The built environment is a reflection of society's cultural and behavioral norms. Known within psychology as ideological communication, Kopec & Lord (2010) discussed how the built environment can serve as metaphorical and symbolic representations of a given cultural paradigm within a society at a given time. Consider the segmented clustering of retail, residential, and business districts within a community, or the children's, men's, women's, hardware, and toy sections within a department store. This form of segmentation is prolific within western societies, and is reflective to our management of problems and concerns. For example, we segment approaches to the issue of obesity: pills, surgery, and education. Each segment functions within a vacuum thus failing in the analysis of the opposite and equal reaction of Sir Isaac Newton's third law of motion.

Rather than segmenting human health in relation to the built environment, greater emphasis needs to be placed on a holistic and integrative approach. In other words, if design can include the provisions for a given physical activity (domain of the designer), and if education can promote the engagement of that activity (domain of the health educator), and healthcare can reward engagement in that activity (domain of the business/policy maker) then effects from lack of activity can be reduced. This requires the architect to collaborate with other disciplines, and other disciplines to consult with architects. To be clear, this argument is not promoting a "tossed salad" approach (common to holistic paradigms), but hierarchical approaches that blend one layer into another, thus shifting the weight and credence given to each discipline throughout the process.

Health and Scope of Practice

The discipline of architecture, when compared to other disciplines and professions, is weak on specialization. Whereas many professions promote masters and doctorates as one's area of specialty by delving deeper into some area of interest within the discipline, architecture has yet to systematically transition its graduate degrees beyond the generalist to the specialist. Approaches to these specializations might be typology (healthcare or commercial settings) or idea based (sustainability, human health). Currently, we are seeing some typology-based specialization appear, most notably healthcare. The difference between this typology and idea based specialization is that idea-based approaches can adapt sets of knowledge for application to many typologies.

As a preventative strategy for physical, psychological, and social health concerns, architects with a specialization in human health would be uniquely qualified to address all aspects of health within the initial planning and design of any built environment. Just as the Roman architects devised methods to bring fresh water into the city to prevent water-borne illnesses, many of today's architects have the ability to limit the spread of viruses, increase personal control and empowerment, and facilitate positive social interactions. This understanding stems from the integration of physical (engineering) and biological sciences into the educational pedagogy for the design professions. Continuing with the above example of N1H1 virus (Bird Flu), a person who sneezes or coughs in an airport can infect anyone within a three-foot radius (White County Medical Center, n.d.). If the social density is very high (i.e. crowded conditions), more people will be in that three-foot radius thus increasing the number of potentially infected. Design solutions for this issue might include the development of current and ten-year projections of social density levels throughout the calendar year. From these calculations, the architect can ensure that the building is able to accommodate appropriate levels of population dispersion through ample provision of overall square footage within public spaces. Recall earlier in the chapter that each time a virus spreads from one person to another it becomes more virulent. A second design solution might be based on engineering principles related to airflow. The goal with airborne viruses is to get them out—and keep them out of the primary breathing zones, which are roughly 3 to 6 feet from the floor (Department of Environmental Quality, n.d.). Other types of concerns include those listed in Table 20.1.

Within the built environment there are many considerations that have a direct effect on human health. Items listed in Table 20.1 provide some examples of different potential facets within the scope of architecture that have high-level effects on one or more aspects of human health. It is the role of design studio to identify possible designs that address each of the respective health concerns within their specific and unique geography and climactic conditions.

Physical Health

The profession of architecture has much data gathered throughout the years that can be used for predictive modeling with regard to structural integrity and human health. Being able to use past and current data to predict a probable outcome can apply to many of the diseases that affect

Table 20.1 This table provides examples of how each of the fundamental areas of the WHO's definition of health, and how design can serve, fulfill and address each of these areas

Architect's Scope	*Health Concern*
Architectural Form	Physical: Sturdy and structurally sound. Psychological: Belief in one's safety and security. Social: Positive social bonds within and surrounding the structure.
Material Uses	Physical: Puncture, absorption, inhalation, and consumption of materials and material particulates. Psychological: Personal beliefs about the health effects of a given material. Social: Group or lobbyists' opinion about a given material. That is experts knew about the health hazards of asbestos for a long time, but American companies blocked regulation.
Spatial Density	Physical: Spread of viruses. Psychological: Crowding, personal space, and territorial violations. Social: Aggression, conflict, and withdrawal.
Space Planning	Physical: Unimpeded movement (trip, bump, or clip hazards). Psychological: Visual access and privacy. Social: Choice to collaborate or engage others.
Air Quality	Physical: Indoor air contaminants, and oxygen to carbon dioxide ratios. Psychological: Desire to avoid the environment. Social: Community reputation regarding the belief in a buildings' capacity to support health.
Landscaping	Physical: Asthma and allergies. Psychological: Attention restoration. Social: Criminal activity, maintenance, and human-to-human interactions.

western societies. Chronic Obstructive Pulmonary Disease (COPD), for example, is a chronic lung disease that can affect people exposed to lung irritants such air pollution, chemical fumes, or dust for an extended period of time (National Institutes of Health, Department of Health and Human Services, n.d.). Air pollution is a broad term covering gases, dust and particles, and vapors mixed with oxygen and subsequently inhaled. Air pollutants may occur naturally, such radon and pollen, but most result from human activity related to chemical off-gassing, waste products from fossil fuels, and the decay cycle of synthetic materials. Use of the words "concentration levels" over a "period of time" are important to understand because they are variables that interact with the body's immune system, and that system's coping threshold. Prolonged exposure to high concentration levels often results in a chronic condition. As previously mentioned there are four ways for a hazard to enter the body: puncture, absorption, inhalation, and ingestion. Inhalation of poor indoor air is the cause of many health-related issues stemming from the built and natural environments. To address indoor air quality concerns most heating, ventilaton and air-conditioning (HVAC) systems facilitate air circulation by using filtration devices that have a corresponding Minimum Efficiency Reporting Value (MERV). Table 20.2 exemplifies some of the typical airborne contaminants and the MERV needed to remove that contaminant from the air.

Designers of the built environment need to consider concentration levels of assorted contaminates within ideal and less-than-ideal situations. For example, air circulation patterns are often engineered for optimal exchange rates, thereby keeping indoor concentrations of air pollutants at safe levels. However, upon occupation of a building, people often modify the environment, for example, by stacking storage boxes on top of filing cabinets and impeding air circulation, creating pockets where concentrations of indoor air pollution exceed safe limits. A note of importance with regard to the term "safe levels": numerous contaminants such as tobacco smoke once had levels that were deemed to be safe. Today there are no safe levels for tobacco smoke. Hence, one can argue that there are no safe levels for any airborne contaminant.

Psychosocial Health

The measurements and concern for indoor air quality, along with the effects of artificial lighting within the built environment, continue to receive the greatest attention. However, this paradigm is changing in the United States and other western countries. Greater media attention focusing on accidental and intended deaths resulting from psychological disorders manifesting as violent acts within public spaces, increased incidences of substance abuse, which now affects nearly every westerner in some form, and the killing of one's offspring,

Table 20.2 MERV ratings help to determine a filter's capacity to help prevent the spread of select environmental pathogens through an HVAC system. In this way, the preservation of human health is determined by the designer

MERV Rating	*Particle Size*	*Typical Contaminant*
1–4	>10 micrometers	Textile and carpet fibers
5–8	3–10 micrometers	Mold, spores, hair spray, cement dust
9–12	1–3 micrometers	Legionella, lead dust
13–16	.3–1 micrometers	Bacteria, insecticide dust, copier toner
17–20	< .3 micrometers	Viruses, combustion particulates, radon

all take place within sets of environmental conditions. These forms of social deviance could be related to a physical condition such as a brain tumor, schizophrenia, bipolar disorder, or from sets of social conditions that inspire rage, social withdrawal, or self-medicating. Each of these conditions, either alone or in combination, can cause a person to lose perspective and engage in inappropriate behaviors. As we consider one's physical, psychological, and social health, we must move beyond simplistic functionalist thinking tied only to the visible and provable, and include all that is subjective, intangible, and often irrational, but yet part of the human experience.

Social health can be defined as one's behavioral reactions within person to person, or person to group relations. However, this overly simplistic definition fails to consider precursors or co-variables to a situation. Within western society social health as it relates to the design of the built environment is not given equal attention, and is often addressed only within selected segments of society to a greater or lesser degree. Social workers and public health educators tend to give social health greater emphasis, while design professions tend to only allot cursory attentions. In modern times, issues of social health are increasing by leaps and bounds with terrorism being omnipresent. A society's social health can be compromised when our present and future activities are based on fear derived from a past experience. This is not to say that a society should not learn from past events, but rather learn from past events and implement well considered and rational solutions toward solving the issues. According to *The Washington Post* over 26 million Americans suffer from a form of flight anxiety (Abercrombie, 2013). The causes of this anxiety can range from ochlophobia (fear of crowds) to a fear of crashing, both of which have been exacerbated by the terrorist activities of September 11, 2001. Added airport security features, whether based on reality or a placebo effect, can serve to enhance these fears. Risks for some people are not considered until they are pointed out. Only when the risk is revealed will the subsequent emotion of fear be realized.

The mere act of trying to enhance security can have unintended consequences. Consider airport or airplane rage. High levels of stress related to flying, combined with loss of control to assorted gate keepers (ticket agents, Transportation Security Agency, gate agents, and corridor crowding), and the wait for transportation, are all variables that can influence a person's ability to cope. Each one, or some combination of these processes, can be causal factors resulting in elevated stress and behaviors outside of the norm. When a person has exceeded their coping threshold, subsequent behaviors are often grossly out-of-sync with normal demeanor (e.g. rage), the development of new behavioral norms (i.e. learned helplessness), or social withdrawal (i.e. avoidance). When we add in another variable such as immature cognitive understanding or comprehension of consequences, we see manifestations such as tween or teen school place violence.

As a preventative strategy, design has the ability to keep coping thresholds within tolerable levels by addressing issues of personal control, physical, and social spatial density, and crowding. Several studies in assorted environments demonstrate that incursions into one's personal space inspire excitatory reactions (Kopec, 2012). One design strategy might be the liberal inclusion of respite spaces. A respite space is a place where one can be alone to "calm down." Single occupancy bathrooms, or solid floor to ceiling bathroom stalls, can serve this purpose. Continuing with the airplane example, designers of the Boeing Dreamliner increased window size to allow for greater visual escape, used different materials for the seats to allow passengers more personal space (provided the airliners do not add more rows), changed the overhead configuration to increase perceptions of greater space, and added better air circulation methods to increase the moisture and oxygen to carbon dioxide ratios. The aggregate of these initiatives are intended to help people maintain coping levels at manageable levels.

Psychological Health

Arguably, the least considered aspect for design is psychological health. This is because psychology focuses on an individual's mental state, which is often hard to comprehend for anyone who does not suffer from a psychological condition. Psychological health can be understood from the assorted social psychological perspectives that make up the profession's 56 divisions, identified by part of the American Psychological Association (APA) at: http://www.apa.org/about/division/index.aspx. From the neurobiological/neuroscience perspective, designers would be interested in the effects of decreased serotonin levels (responsible for mood) that result from ultra violet filters found on window glazing, the relationship between the hormone melatonin (responsible for levels of alertness) derived from different forms of lighting, and the release of adrenaline (responsible for panic and anxiety) caused by differing concentrations of social and spatial densities. This area of study also looks at biologically related preferences, which can be over-ruled by socially related preferences, and natural/intuitive measures. The socially based psychological notions related to an individual's ability to navigate assorted environments (personal control and self-determination) for example, motivate positive behaviors. Being lost equates to a loss of personal control. The goals of socially learned behaviors are the retention of moral, ethical, value-based information, and finding inner peace and tranquility. Hence, neurobiology must be considered in tandem with social learning in order to positively contribute to and effect psychological health. In other words, neurobiology provides the line image, but it is social learning that puts color and dimension to that image.

Conclusion

Entire books have been written on the topics of physical health (e.g. Health, Sustainability and the Built Environment), psychological health (e.g. Environmental Psychology for Design), and social health (e.g. Sociology and Architectural Design). The limited attention given to all aspects of health (physical, psychological, and social) in the past by architects and design professionals meant numerous situations, conditions, and consequences arising from the built environment were neglected. This neglect was, and is not, a failure of architecture and the design professions per se. Beginning with the twenty-first century, many scholars and practitioners have recognized the flaws of a highly specialized system and are currently attempting to be more interdisciplinary. Architecture and design are among the professions leading this paradigm shift.

A normal human response to a multidisciplinary approach, however, is based on process ordering along a hierarchy of preference. This means that most of us tend to give preference to a select element or factor within an ordering system, thereby providing unequal attention to all phases. For example, you might ask yourself which you prefer during the course of a meal: appetizer, salad, entrée, or dessert. Our preference will likely translate to the level of attention given to the most desired step in the food serving process. When it comes to our life's work, we are more likely to give emphasis to the portion of the process that we enjoy most.

When we look at human health in relation to the built environment, we see there are four primary professions that include this topic within their scope of practice: architecture and interior design, city planning, public and clinical health, and social services. Within each of these professions, the relationship between humans and the built environment is considered, yet none attribute their primary focus to this factor. Hence, human health in relation to the built environment evolves only as a secondary concern. Of course, building science and industrial hygiene also play a role, but often overlaps with public, environmental, or occupational health, city, community, or urban planning, and architecture and design. Clearly there needs to be a singular profession with a body of knowledge that includes elements of design, biology, psychology, and sociology. During the past two decades architecture and design have given the topic of human health in relation to the built environment greater attention. With this continued attention, significant advancements are likely to ensue. This is because a fundamental paradigm that governs the architecture and design professions is based on futurism and application.

References

Abercrombie, P. (2013, May 23) *Fear of Flying? You Can Get Over It.* The Washington Post.

American Museum of Natural History. (n.d.) West Nile Fever: A medical detective story. *BioBulletin*, Retreived March 28, 2014 from http://www.amnh.org/education/resources/rfl/web/bulletins/bio/biobulletin/story1378.html.

Amundsen, D.W. (1996). *Medicine, Society, and Faith in the Ancient and Medieval Worlds*. Baltimore, MD: Johns Hopkins University Press.

Barends, E., Have, S., & Huisman, F. (2012). Learning from other evidence-based practices: The case of medicine. In D. M. Rousseau (Ed.), *The Oxford Handbook of Evidence-Based Management*. New York, NY: Oxford University Press.

Boubekri, M. (2008). *Daylighting, Architecture and Health Building Design Strategies*. Burlington, MA: Architectural Press.

Cornwell, P. (2002). *Portrait Of A Killer: Jack The Ripper—Case Closed*. New York: Berkeley Books.

Department of Environmental Quality. (n.d.). *Testing for Radon*. State of Michigan website. Retrieved March 26, 2014 from: http://www.michigan.gov/deq/0,4561,7-135-3310_4105_4196-10515--,00.html.

Fien, J., Charlesworth, E., Lee, G., Baker, D., Grice, T., & Morris, D. (2011). Life on the edge: Housing experiences in three remote Australian indigenous settlements. *Habitat International*, 35, 2, 343–349.

Goodman, L.A., Saxe, L., & Harvey, M. (1991). Homelessness as psychological trauma: Broadening perspectives. *American Psychologist*, 46, 11, 1219–1225.

Haferkamp, H., & Smelser, N.J. (Eds) (1992). *Social Change and Modernity*. Berkeley, CA: University of California Press.

Horowitz, B.N., & Bowers, K. (2012). *Zoobiquity: What Animals Can Teach Us About Being Human.* Toronto, ON: Doubleday Canada.

Howard Hughes Medical Institute. (2006, March 16). Evolution in action: Why some viruses jump species. *ScienceDaily*. Retrieved March 28, 2014 from www.sciencedaily.com/releases/2006/03/060316091731.htm.

Jacobsen, L.J., Kent, M., Lee., M., & Mather, M. (2011). America's aging population. *Population Reference Bureau*, 66, 1, 1–18.

Kopec, D. (2011). *Lecture on Housing Hierarchy Needs*. Personal Collection of D. Kopec, Newschool of Architecture of Design, San Diego CA.

Kopec, D. (2012). *Environmental Psychology for Design,* 2nd edition. New York: Fairchild Books.

Kopec, D., & Lord, N. (2010). Scares of communism: Architectural and design remnants of an ideology. *Space and Culture*, 13, 4, 436–454.

Macaulay, D. (1974). *City: A Story of Roman Planning and Engineering*. Boston, MA: Houghton-Mifflin.

Manzo, L.C., & Perkins, D.D. (2006). Finding common ground: The importance of place attachment to community participation and planning. *Journal of Planning Literature*, 20, 4, 335–350.

McLeod, D.M., Detenber, B.H., & Eveland, W.P. (2006). Behind the third-Person effect: Differentiating perceptual processes for self and other. *Journal of Communication*, 51, 4, 678–695.

National Institutes of Health, Department of Health and Human Services (n.d.). *What is COPD?* Retrieved March 8, 2014 from: http://www.nhlbi.nih.gov/health/health-topics/topics/copd.

Paneth, N., Vinten-Johansen, P., Brody, H., & Rip, M. (1998). A rivalry of foulness: Official and unofficial investigations of the London cholera epidemic of 1854. *American Journal of Public Health*, 88, 10, 1545–1553.

Schoenauer, N. (2000). *6000 Years of Housing*. New York: W.W. Norton & Company Inc.

Trachtenberg, M., & Hyman, I. (1986). *Architecture: From Prehistory to Post-Modernism*. Netherlands: Prentice Hall/Abrams.

U.S. Department of Health and Human Services, Centers of Disease Control and Prevention (2013a). *Get Smart: Know When Antibiotics Work*. Retrieved March 28, 2014 from: http://www.cdc.gov/getsmart/antibiotic-use/antibiotic-resistance-faqs.html.

U.S. Department of Health and Human Services, Centers for Disease Control and Prevention (2013b). *Antibiotic Resistance Threats in the United States 2013*. Atlanta GA: U.S. Centers for Disease Control and Prevention.

White County Medical Center (n.d.). *2010–2011 Flu Forecast*. Retrieved March 28, 2014 from http://www.wcmc.org/foundation/flu2010.html.

WHO (1946) Preamble to the Constitution of the World Health Organization as adopted by the International Health Conference, New York, 19 June–22 July 1946; signed on 22 July 1946 by the representatives of 61 States (Official Records of the World Health Organization, no. 2, p. 100) and entered into force on April 7, 1948.

Woodward, I. (2008). Ignorance is Contagious. Paper presented to EIANZ Industry Connect Seminar Series July 2008. Retrieved March 24, 2014 from http://www.forestrytas.com.au/assets/0000/0375/Ignorance_is_Contagious__Ian_Woodward_EIANZ_July_2008_.pdf.

21

To Dwell

The Art of Shaping our Homes and Communities

Michael Pyatok

American Antimonies: Origins of Individualism vs. Communalism

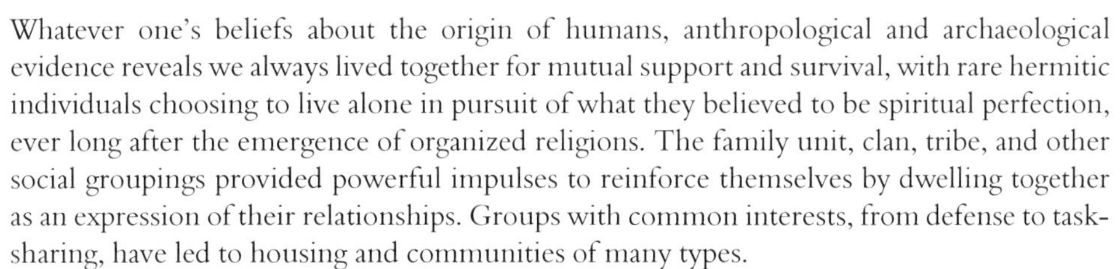

Whatever one's beliefs about the origin of humans, anthropological and archaeological evidence reveals we always lived together for mutual support and survival, with rare hermitic individuals choosing to live alone in pursuit of what they believed to be spiritual perfection, ever long after the emergence of organized religions. The family unit, clan, tribe, and other social groupings provided powerful impulses to reinforce themselves by dwelling together as an expression of their relationships. Groups with common interests, from defense to task-sharing, have led to housing and communities of many types.

From their earliest colonial beginnings, communities in North America experimented with ways to assemble in compact configurations for a variety of reasons such as defense, labor conservation, shared religions, and proximity to neighbors in a strange land. New Amsterdam, Plymouth, and Jamestown all demonstrate the desire to defensively claim territory in new unknown land, occupied by natives with very different cultures, at a time when expansionist countries coveted new lands.

Even in these early and difficult colonial circumstances of necessary communalism, opposing patterns emerged that continue to personify the American landscape: individuals yearning to escape the group and express self-identity and independence, but often within smaller, like-minded splinter groups, and oppositely, those who intentionally pursue the benefits of collective living but within a highly diverse social milieu. Those who splintered away to America from Europe were looking for religious freedom but continued to live among like-minded people. They were not seeking a diversity of neighbors with whom they shared little culturally, religiously or economically.

The solid foundation of the early Puritan Massachusetts Bay Company did not last long. Roger Williams and Anne Hutcheson discovered the limits of oppressive religion and fled, Williams first forming the more religiously tolerant Providence to the south, maintaining a successful and respectful relationship with the local Narragansett tribe. Hutcheson later migrated there also to escape religious persecution from the Puritans. Providence sought to

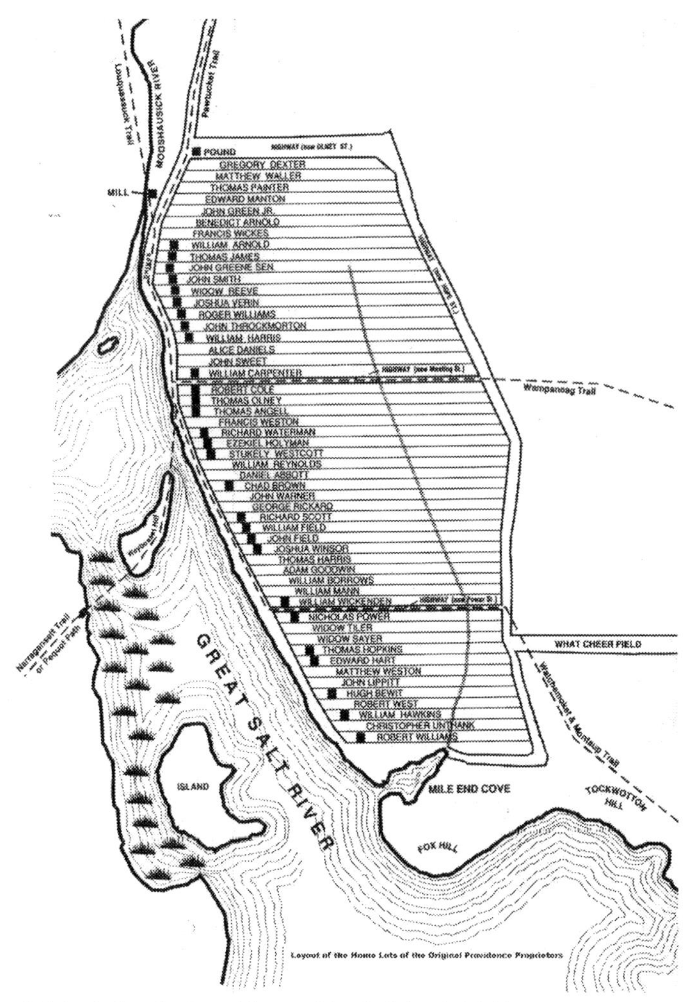

Figure 21.1 Original plan for Providence, Rhode Island, 1664

separate religion and governance, and practiced tolerance. Even its early plan demonstrated respect for individuals where

> each head of household was given a thin tract of land stretching from the cove up the hill from the Towne Street, totaling approximately six acres. Each parcel of land included a bit of the waterfront, a portion of the slope of the hill and some of the flat land at the top of the hill. There was no "big house" at the top of the hill with the poorer households huddled at the waterfront. Each of the settlers would start with the same type and amount of lands, making Providence a settlement of equals.

Conflicts between the mores enforced by the broader community and those emerging from individuals exercising personal freedom were soon a normal part of life in the New World. The French historian and political philosopher Alexis de Tocqueville noted both tendencies in the American character in the 1840s, "Each man is forever thrown back on himself alone, and there is danger that he may be shut up in the solitude of his own heart." Yet he also noted optimistically:

> Americans of all ages, all conditions, and all dispositions constantly form associations ... commercial and manufacturing associations ... associations of a thousand other kinds—religious, moral, serious, futile, general or restricted, enormous or diminutive. Wherever at the head of some new undertaking you see the government of France, or a man of rank in England, in the United States you will be sure to find an association.
> (de Tocqueville, 2003)

De Tocqueville's (2003) observations would hold true about many of today's so-called developing nations where shared housing across generations is both a cultural or religious command, and an economic reality. Whether in India or Latin America or Africa, family economies are such that it is not possible for individuals and couples coming of age to flee the coop, or even for waning generations to live alone in "retirement communities." Those of sound body able to participate in local economies support those too young or too old to fend for themselves. The luxury of individualism, and the resulting fractures between generations, seems a consequence of economically developed societies, where consumption-driven culture creates micro-markets for each age spectrum.

This US tendency to join like-minded people, then uprooting to find more supportive grounds elsewhere within which to flourish, may not be so different from humanity's ongoing quest for a better life instigated with the first migrations out of Africa. In the case of the US it was fueled by the availability of vast lands to the west, occupied by what was perceived to be thinly-populated indigenous peoples with "inferior" cultures and religions. It was simply a continuation of the behavior of the founding colonists—when discontent, just move on. Later generations of immigrants pouring into the US would do the same. Today we see the same pattern with youths escaping the troubles of Central America. The seemingly dualistic struggle between the traditions and troubles of an established community and the emerging norms of adventurous and experimental individuals who have an available geography into which to escape, repeatedly created models of a third option that also typifies the quest to achieve a unique "American Way of Life." It is a pursuit of more individual freedom, but within a new social order, a kind of "associated individualism."

From the middle of the nineteenth century, a series of utopian experiments sought to escape the shortcomings of US society by inventing new forms of association that corrected perceived societal deficits, yet simultaneously purported to offer freer forms of self-expression and individual freedom. The string of "utopian" experiments some heading westward, all heading to rural areas, attempted to create physical settings appropriate to their founding principles, but only a few nineteenth-century examples survived. Founded by visionaries like Robert Owen, Charles Fourier, William Morris, John Noyes (Hayden, 1979) and many others, these communities sought to build mini-societies to free themselves from some aspects of the larger society perceived as either unjust or ungodly.

The Mormons, a Christian branch founded by Joseph Smith and later led by Brigham Young, were looked upon by communities in Ohio, and later in Missouri and Illinois as strange cultists. Both Joseph Smith and his brother were murdered in Illinois in 1844 as tensions with surrounding communities mounted. Under Brigham Young's leadership, they made the westward trek as so many other utopians were doing at the time, eventually settling in Utah where few could interfere with their unique belief system.

The Mormons also had planning principles for physically organizing their settlements:

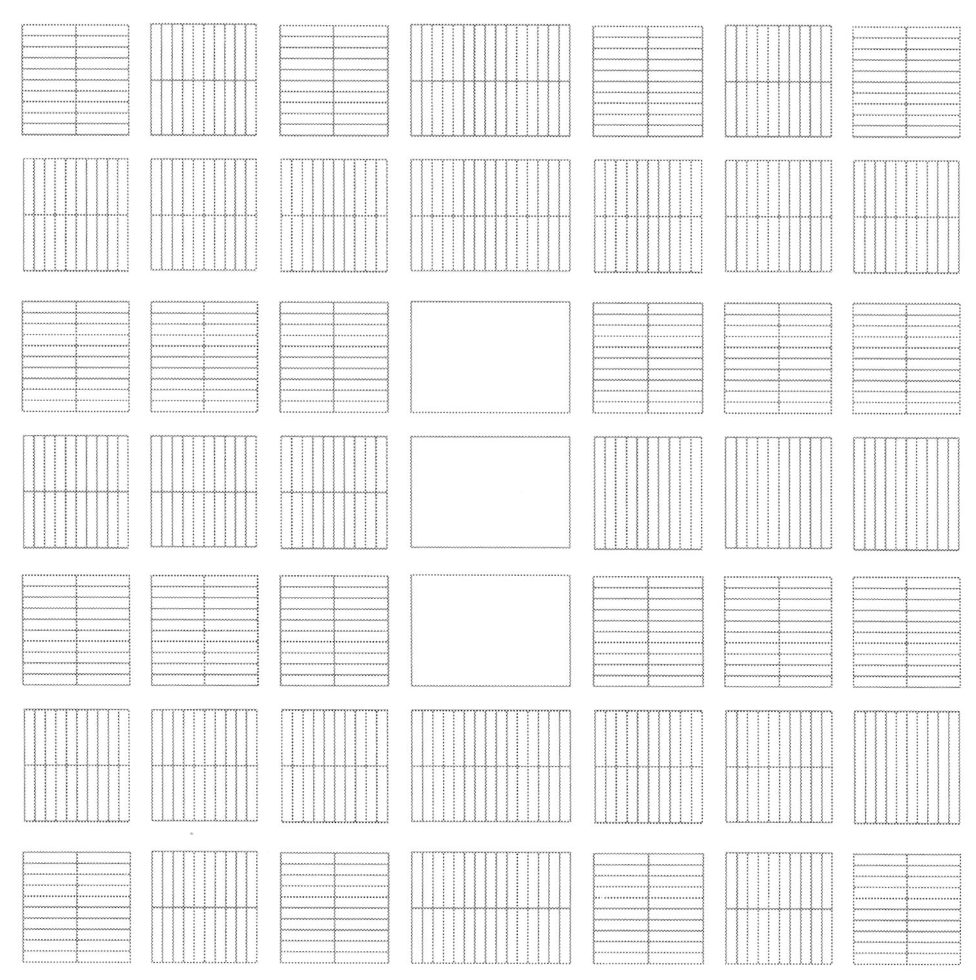

Figure 21.2 Plan for Zion, Missouri, proposed by Joseph Smith, 1833

1 Members should live in a compact village and commute to farming areas outside the village, unlike the individualistic patterns of dispersed homesteaders typical of the time.
2 Like many other utopian experiments of that era, property rights of residents were communitarian, where the interest of the group was more important than the individual.
3 The dedicated duty of the members was to industriously care for, and beautify, the earth.
4 Members should be frugal and achieve economic independence from the broader society.
5 Unity and cooperation were critical cornerstones of the community, allowing them to establish hundreds of settlements in the arid West, based on principles of faith, love, charity, kindness, service, and sharing one another's burdens. In 1833 Joseph Smith presented his ideas about city planning in the City of Zion Plan.

The typical village plan included a regular grid pattern with square blocks, wide streets of 132 feet, presumably to allow a mule train to make a full turn, alternating half-acre lots so that houses face alternate streets on each block, uniform brick or stone construction, homes set back 25 feet from the street with front yard landscaping, vegetable gardens in the backyard, the location of farms outside of town, and central blocks for temples, schools, and other public buildings (Galli, 2005). Contemporary urban planning efforts, such as the New Urbanists, trying to return order to US settlements so damaged by our addiction to the automobile, have resurrected Joseph Smith's gridded villages. Andres Duany recently praised the New Zion Plan not so much for its wide streets, but for its intentions of clearly defining the line between production agriculture on the outskirts and a village of farmers, more compact for easier communication between community members and preservation of the surrounding agriculture, yet ensuring that every household plot was large enough for a family to produce its own food.

Among twentieth-century examples of intentional communities, The Farm founded in Tennessee in 1971 was a reverse migration from west to east by 430 San Franciscan hippies.

It peaked between 1,200–1,600 people, and now has only 175 members, mostly aging Baby Boomers. Unlike previous experiments, The Farm was established within, and surrounded by, a well-developed nation-state. Disagreement with any rules allowed easy return to comfortably survivable settings. Connections between the experiment and the surrounding larger society were inevitable, but retreat from wider society was not the sole purpose of The Farm. Its members wanted to prove certain patterns of life to be superior to the US corporate-run consumption/acquisition model, and wanted to educate the broader society on healthier, more environmentally sound lifestyles. Like the Mormons, this led to creating missions to help developing nations such as Guatemala, or other US communities after disasters, such as New Orleans after Katrina. The intent was not to expand membership in a religion, but to convey practical survival methods utilizing the natural resources available in a region, in conjunction with planet-friendly alternative technologies. The digital age has made these connections even more potent, and those who left continue to be leaders in creating social, environmental, and technological alternatives in keeping with The Farm's founding principles.

Contrary to orderly, intentional communitarian experiments, nothing seemed to promote the opposite quest by self-reliant individuals to create their own destiny within only a loosely-defined, organically emergent social order than the westward expansion. It was promoted by those who claimed that it was America's "manifest destiny" to occupy all the lands between the Atlantic and Pacific oceans. With the Louisiana Purchase, Jefferson doubled the land area of the US, sending Lewis and Clark to the Pacific Northwest to chart new expansion plans. To Jefferson, the more farms, the more self-reliant and lightly governed citizenry, the better for democracy. Farmers were preceded by hunters and fur-traders, another breed of fierce independents.

The federal government continued to commission explorers and the army to map the west. One of these, John Charles Fremont of the Army Corps of Topographical Engineers, wrote exciting reports about his adventures, inspiring many to head West (Jackson & Spence, 1970). The dual personality of the American people was emerging, just as de Tocqueville perceived in his earlier travels. Economics and individual private profit were the motives for much of the westward expansion, not the quest to create a more perfect social order. The resulting settlement patterns were a far cry from the orderly visions of Joseph Smith.

The Homestead Act of 1862 set the ground rules for expansion, allowing each household 160 acres for free after working it for five years. The rush was on and as settlers made their claims, rough-hewn towns sprung up catering to the farmers' needs to resupply, receive mail, engage in banking, and occasionally get off the lonely farm.

Figure 21.3 Deadwood, South Dakota, 1876

Unlike the compact earlier, self-regulated colonial or utopian communitarian efforts, this mid-to-late nineteenth century "free-for-all" version of western settlement spawned the dominant image of what it now means to be American: a rugged individualist under few government or social controls.

The 1850s Gold Rush exacerbated the free-for-all nature of western development. Between 1848 and 1850 San Francisco grew from 1,000 to 20,000. While terms like "squatter settlement," "tent city" or "homeless encampment" were not used at the time for the rapidly-arriving prospectors, images, from the era depict the disorderly array of self-made settlements.

Government presence in mining communities was minimal and miners developed their own ad hoc legal systems. Each camp had its own rules, meting out justice by popular vote and vigilantism. Simultaneous to the hapless development of the West, Eastern citizens were promoting a more refined domestic architecture, considered a sound basis for developing moral character and Christian sensibilities. Gwendolyn Wright summarized these efforts in her book, *Building the Dream: A Social History of Housing in America* (Wright, 1983). The individual dwelling, properly designed, was extolled in the mid-nineteenth century by ministers, teachers, poets and writers of pattern books, who promoted what were thought to be more orderly environments that would support stable family life. Each of these efforts assumed that the family, living alone on its land within its ideal dwelling, should be the building block of a better society.

Immigrants from Europe surging into the country in the late nineteenth and early twentieth centuries reinvigorated the communitarian strain of American dwelling traditions. One of the most notable was the "coops" developed by Jewish immigrant garment workers in the Bronx, New York City.

A mixture of communists, labor organizers, and Zionists, they took advantage of a new State law providing tax breaks to limited-dividend companies that sponsored moderate-cost housing developments. The Amalgamated Clothing Workers completed over 300 dwellings in five brick apartment buildings and within five years the community was thriving with their own clinic, laundry, meat market, library, gymnasium, auditorium, photography club, tailors, nursery school, classrooms, and their own school bus. They were driven by a political ideology that kept them intellectually, culturally, and politically engaged in advocacy on behalf of workers' rights at the local and national levels. Their political commitment to workers' rights drove their activism, and made their housing a desirable destination with long waiting lists.

The coops have evolved over the decades. No longer home to Left-wing activism, they now house a new generation of immigrants from Southeast Asia, Latin America, and the Caribbean. The story of the coops was recently documented by Michal Goldman in his PBS documentary, *A Utopian Bronx Tale,* documenting what communitarian life can be like. The film demonstrates just how much the individualist strain continues to dominate American housing production. The American Institute of Architects annually bestows design awards upon what it considers to be the best architecture. Invariably there are single-family dwellings in the mix, and very rarely if ever are there awards for multifamily housing. This is such a problem that architects specializing in multifamily residences formed another AIA awards program, although it does not receive the attention and status of the main awards.

Ever-splintering the family is the norm, with each generation in its own dwellings and often in different states. Seventy-five percent of US households are now individuals or couples, and as much as 25 percent are single individuals. The push of consumer society has for decades been narrowing definitions of the population by age, race, ethnicity, gender, etc., with each requiring unique social and cultural preferences. Each group must have its own beliefs, forms of expression, music, clothing, language, means of travel, places to live, appliances and furnishings, making multigenerational living intolerable. Only new immigrant households unexposed to the US penchant to fracture on behalf of consumption, Baby Boomers unable to pay for expensive senior care facilities, and singles adjusting to the difficult post-recession economy by remaining with their parents, choose this arrangement. Even with a recent spurt of intergenerational living, only 5.6 percent of all households have such a makeup. Most of these are in the Southeast and Southwest, where cultural traditions and poverty have demanded shared living among Latino, African American, and Native American households (Lofquist, 2012).

An attempt to explain these simultaneous and contradictory tendencies within the US was put forth by Robert Bellah and his colleagues at UC Berkeley some 30 years ago in their book *Habits of the Heart: Individualism and Commitment in American Life* (Bellah, *et. al.*, 1985). They lamented how individualism, in its varying forms, has come to define and measure our success as people and as a nation. But at the same time they optimistically pointed to examples of a continuing tradition of a helping and caring society, now stemming from a "new social ecology" based on community and commitment that restores meaning to work, politics, education, and civic activism. There are physical expressions, in both planning and architecture, of both the dominant cultural framework of individualism and its re-emerging antidote of civic engagement. One example of today's secular and non-ideological expressions of communal tendencies was imported in the late twentieth century from Denmark, referred to as "co-housing." Its largely middle-class adherents are looking for comradery, an environment designed by and for themselves, and more neighborly interaction (McCamant & Durrett, 2011). More often than not, these self-selected enclaves are quite homogeneous—mostly white, with a mix of Masters and PhD degrees. While each household has its own fully equipped residence, all members support a central kitchen and dining facility for some shared meals each week, along with perhaps a shared living area, playroom for children, wood shop, and other multi-purpose areas.

Then there is the suburb, the place between rural and urban designed to support both individuals and communities, but many have argued achieving neither very well. Streets are lined with rows of detached homes, each self-sufficiently equipped, with its own identity and address. Non-residential buildings are excluded from these homogeneous streets and homes are uniformly sized and priced to assure the same economic strata of society reside there. Because these homes are seen as commodities whose sales price is critical to the owner, smaller less expensive homes, or rental apartments on the same street are considered threats to future sales or refinancing expectations. So economic motives limit diversity of social life, and segregated zoning ensures endless hours in automobiles to support household life.

The history of housing design in the US, and the architects who made it, can be seen as a free-swinging pendulum moving in these seemingly contradictory directions. Americans want individuality, yet they also yearn for genuine community. They get sameness because builders use repetition and redundancy to maintain profits, with superficial gestures toward visual differences. They get homogeneous neighbors because ever-rising resale prices exclude the variety of incomes needed to support socio-economic diversity. While the country is still big enough to allow remote rural escape, it is also highly concentrated, driven by the production and consumption efficiencies of cities. But it is the desire to be both, dwelling "rurally," yet within eyesight of a city, that perhaps creates the most difficult architectural design tasks and the most troublesome land use patterns. It is in the suburbs that imitations of these primal tendencies are fabricated so we feel we are deep within the country or in the heart of a "traditional" town when we are, in fact, in neither.

Perhaps the single-most critical choice for families living in cities comes as children reach school age: should they attend steadily declining public schools or expensive private schools? The perception is that suburbs offer an affordable alternative without reducing quality. Depending on the region, another critical factor for families has been the competition for reasonably priced housing. Prices have been skyrocketing in many cities with a resurgence of interest in inner-city living and the resulting rise in housing costs. Empty nesters living on career peak-level incomes are returning from suburbs to cities seeking cultural enrichment, and highly-educated young people looking for excitement team up with roommates, forming multi-income households to pay the rent.

The United States is a big country: there will always be those who want the safety of suburbs, surrounded by like-minded, like-looking, and like-educated people, in well-regulated environs that will keep their economic investments in a stable, rising trajectory. Whether attached or detached, the rules and regulations that govern homeowners' associations are like self-imposed cultural straitjackets, built on the premise that people cannot trust the judgments of their neighbors, even about the color of their homes or the contents of their yards. They seem to express individualistic tendencies by possessing detached dwellings, but in fact more often they live in similar socio-economic and cultural circumstances as their immediate neighbors.

But there will also always be the cauldron of America's cities, where the quest for diversity, the challenges of uncertainty, the excitement generated by mixing with radically different cultures and classes, and the desire for community is fulfilled.

Figure 21.4 Page from a Sears Roebuck Catalogue for a kit-of-parts house

Production Today

The rich US cultural landscape and its demand for local control have prevented the housing industry from establishing a system of centralized production like automobiles, appliances, and home furnishings. Some see this as inefficient, with production each year falling behind the growing need. Meanwhile the mobile home industry flourishes, perhaps the best example of somewhat centralized production. However, it remains a consequence of necessity rather than choice, oftentimes barely tolerated by communities. Yet the pressures to individualize expression, to match historical architectural conditions, and to improve endurance to remain competitive, have dramatically transformed the manufactured housing industry to be equal to, and in some cases, superior to site-built. There has always been a strain of architects pursuing that technological dream of well-designed site-specific manufactured housing for the masses.

Others see fragmentation of the housing industry as a blessing, possessing the potential to respond to unique mixtures of local demographic preferences, history, climate, and available resources. However, with the Internet and universal availability of plans, it is disappointing

Figure 21.5 Porch houses by Lake Flato Architects

that we often see the same house designs in the upper Midwest as in the Southwest. The plethora of small builders relies upon these services because they cannot afford architects. Most of these plan books assume wood-frame construction, yet when applied to the desert climates of Texas, New Mexico or Arizona, wood construction is hardly appropriate.

By contrast to these tendencies, housing architects have worked hard to demonstrate regional histories, climates, physical resources, and cultural tendencies that should produce localized responses. Some architects have succeeded in achieving high quality results without high price tags like Lake/Flato's porch houses in Texas, or homes built with Navaho Flexcrete in Arizona by the Stardust Center for Affordable Homes and the Family.

There are those who argue that "inefficient" production leading to a shortfall of housing is really a matter of political perspective. To this view, each year we produce more than enough housing for our citizens, at least in area, with a growing number receiving 10,000 square feet or more per home, while many live in over-crowded conditions and 3 million receive no housing at all. The problem is not that we under-produce, but that we unevenly distribute. Developers and builders "naturally" cater to those portions of the market that can pay for themselves and ignore those that cannot produce profit. Since the New Deal, government interventions have experimented with every conceivable means to make up for the failure of the market to serve the bottom quarter of our citizens.

Hence, housing production is a sociopolitical enterprise with all of its attendant frictions. Inner cities fear gentrification caused in part by returning wealth, and suburbs are plagued with environmental and agricultural degradation from ever-expanding circles of wealth fleeing inner cities.

Unlike custom home clients, the requirements of multifamily housing thrust architects deeply into the country's sociopolitical and economic malaise. Budgets are rarely "fat," except for high-density luxury living, so exotically novel designs are a privilege for only a few. The design of whole new communities on the urban edge or the transformation of existing ones near the urban center can stir up many environmental and class conflicts, if not race and ethnic frictions, that reach regional if not national proportions. Faced with this level of potential resistance, the design of multifamily housing is often accused of being too "conservative."

When facing this perplexing dichotomy of individualism vs communitarian, architects must deal with four major issues: environmental, cultural, social and economic, and lastly, technological.

Environmental Issues

Since the 1960s, larger scaled developments must be preceded by "environmental impact statements," which attempt to quantify how a proposed development might impact neighboring biophysical, social, and economic systems. By their sheer size and impact, multifamily developments often consume land and material resources in quantities perceived as large when compared to other community additions. Post World War II sprawl, executed prior to awareness of eco-systems, water and air quality, has justified public fears of new developments.

Protests can be intense even when enlightened developments build close to existing infrastructure, in compact patterns, preserve and restore wetlands or other natural conditions, attempt to be "green," or even seek to introduce and support public transit. While sometimes justified, resistance too often seems selfishly focused on preserving existing conditions for those now living in a contested location. Americans cherish family, but are too often unable to see the growth required is in part caused by the offspring produced in their own bedrooms.

Under these circumstances, architects, landscape architects, land planners, and their developer-clients must often work miracles with designs that are more sensitive to environmental and historic conditions. Their work must be guided by informed, careful political maneuvering, and hopefully, by sincere public education campaigns and participatory

Figure 21.6 One of ten groups of neighbors participating in a design workshop with the architects, designing a new, high-density affordable housing development and new park in their neighborhood. Courtesy of Pyatok Architects

design processes that genuinely incorporate public opinion while at the same time informing it. Architects have become critical players in the education process, both in the design and planning, and in the quality of the resulting product.

Cultural Issues

Culture can be described as the summation of a people's beliefs, intellectual and artistic pursuits, and behavioral practices. But it is not necessarily rational, meaning appropriate to survival and perpetuation. It is our fate as humans to develop irrational attachments to places and often American traditions, whether communitarian or individualist, form where humans should never have settled in the first place, resulting in unsustainable self-destructive patterns. As the people of New Orleans have demonstrated, leaving behind buildings, places and memories that became endeared symbols of their ancestors' aspirations, dreams, and artistic achievements is not easy to do. Regardless whether on flood plains, slide-prone slopes, in fire-prone forests, or even wetlands, settlements take on special meanings within human communities because of who lived there before and what they accomplished. This reality of human memory is layered atop other physical realities that are often unsupportive of long-term settlement.

These are conditions that developers, design teams, and environmental activists cannot ignore when designing to suit the images of domesticity and the sense of history that intangibly combine in a region's shared memories and built forms. *Avant garde* custom home experiments, often successful in the service of American individualism in remote locations, when applied to multifamily housing can cause hatred for compact and income-diverse developments so necessary for saving a region's natural and cultural heritage. Non-profit housing development corporations and public housing authorities, when developing high-density housing for low income households, generally eschew avant garde expressions for safer architectural vocabularies to appease nearby higher income homeowners who often have the power to stop projects they dislike.

A book containing 85 successful affordable housing developments completed in the mid-1990s (Jones *et al.*, 1997), demonstrated by its title and contents this tendency to avoid controversy by applying accepted architectural norms and avoiding the language of radical individualism.

Multifamily housing architects often find themselves bringing higher density American communitarian tendencies into neighborhoods where people are clinging to low density rugged individualism, whether real or ersatz. County and municipal authorities may have attempted to resolve these differences in a public process when shaping new comprehensive plans, zoning ordinances, and design guidelines. But invariably the same debates arise again. The larger mission of architects designing high-density, multifamily developments is often to convince locals that they should be living in more compact, transit-served communities, in smaller dwellings and in mixed-use, mixed-income neighborhoods to conserve the very beauty of the land so cherished by individualists. Fear of global warming, conservation of energy, and diminishing material resources are prime motivators.

In the process of making income-integrated communities, architects may even bridge class and race divides, but often face opposition to the basic foundations of their arguments. Locals may not believe in global warming. They may not believe the planet's resources are diminishing and are therefore unconcerned about conserving land and materials. They are uninterested in curtailing desires to procreate, and their reasons for choosing where to live are driven by a desire to separate from people unlike themselves, culturally or

Figure 21.7 Affordable rental townhomes for lower income families in Rancho Cucamonga. Courtesy of Pyatok Architects

economically. All these are major reasons for engaging in calm, deliberate discussions, so architects generally eschew the avant garde pursuits of American individualism. Designing comfortable architectural imagery to help induce cultural changes needed for acceptance of high density far outweigh the short-term design goals of changing consumer preferences for novel designs cherished by the fashion industry.

As with environmental issues, architects have recognized that community design is an intense cultural enterprise and must be collective and inclusive. They develop sophisticated, hands-on group design processes to facilitate public participation in the planning and design of multifamily housing and community development beyond the crude, and often unproductive, series of after-the-fact public hearings and environmental impact reports. From the beginnings of a design all parties must share in the mutual education process, including those who hold the long view of environmental and cultural impacts, those who hold the local view, and those with the short view seeking immediate profits from real estate deals.

While speed and efficiency are critical to housing production, avoiding the collective design process only delays production in the long run. Stubborn, self-serving developers fuel community beliefs that they are victims of private profit, often in collusion with local government. This resistance becomes an immutable force against growth, equally self-righteously stubborn and ignorant of the values of intelligent growth that may underlie some developers' proposals. Recognizing that local populations need to be treated as "partners" in development at the very beginning of design, many developers—for-profit, non-profit, and public alike—are concluding that, in the long run, this is the best way to improve the climate for achieving compact, mixed-use, and mixed-income communities. Architects are filling this new role of public educator in the development process.

Figure 21.8 Assisted by architects, teens participate in the planning and design of a new, affordable, high-density, sustainable community to replace their public housing, San Bernardino. Courtesy of Pyatok Architects

Social and Economic Issues

For all its rhetoric about equality, freedom, and justice, the US is still fundamentally a deeply divided class society, accentuated by racial and ethnic prejudices. High income home owners can hold stereotypical views about low income families. While the previous section dealt with the difficulties of bringing high-density housing into low density communities, "affordable" multifamily rental housing faces an additional challenge when inserted into communities with high incomes. Language for housing for lower-income households is ever evolving to deal with misunderstandings, the latest name being "workforce housing," to inform the broader public that the residents are hard-working Americans like everyone else.

There are several special considerations when designing and programming for lower-income, working families. Some of the more critical points include:

1 An affordable child care program so parents can work or study.
2 On-site services so parents can learn English as a second language.
3 Training in how to shop and cook at home nutritiously on limited incomes.
4 Training in basic parenting skills for young parents in the absence of an older generation.
5 Substance abuse counseling.
6 Financial literacy training.

7 Computer literacy training.
8 Leadership training and the basics of responsible citizenship.
9 After school programs and tutoring, GED assistance.
10 Training in entrepreneurship and small business development.
11 Workers' rights and tenants' rights under current laws.
12 Security to keep out drug dealers, criminals, and harassing ex-spouses.

In addition to the program ingredients outlined above, there are some special design features that should be considered, not the least of which is security. Families should be grouped in secure clusters, each with its own open space or courtyard with only one way in and out, in sufficiently small numbers (ideally six to 25) so that families can get to know each other, and know who belongs in their courtyard and who is a guest or potential intruder. So a development of 100 families should be a collection of four smaller developments of 25 families. These smaller "clans" have a better chance to bond and watch out for each other's interests. When visiting someone in another cluster, people can walk in the public realm such as a street, as they have historically done in cities, and arrive at the front door or gate to another cluster, ringing the bell and waiting to be allowed in. Back walkways only increase the number of ways intruders can enter and escape.

Stereotypical views about lower-income Americans and homeowner fears about property values often get disingenuously expressed as fears of increased traffic, impacts on schools, or crime in the streets. While there are deep familial and societal problems caused by the steady loss of better-paying manufacturing jobs and their replacement by low-paying service jobs, often those with the better-paying jobs of the new economy harbor misperceptions about their less fortunate fellow Americans victimized by these macro-economic shifts.

Figure 21.9 YWCA Family Village, Redmond, WA. Designed for homeless women and children, the facility was unanimously supported by the town. Courtesy of Pyatok Architects

It may be asking too much from architects to mellow middle-class resistance toward mixed-income communities. But when carefully designed with a reverence for the local natural and cultural ecology, executed with a sense of poetry, multifamily housing design for lower-income households can win over even the most hardened nay-sayers.

The YWCA Family Village in Redmond, Washington was designed for homeless families, yet is located in a suburban community that is home to Microsoft. The Y's reputation, well-connected board of directors and mayoral support, provided the architects with a solid foundation upon which to design. Appealing to the local's appreciation for their Northwest Craftsman architectural traditions, the architects designed a residential facility, with a child care center that appeared to be a resort lodge, both contemporary and at the same time imbued with the DNA of local history. The development was and continues to be well received. In fact, the planners of the town attribute this building to changing the general resistance of the community to taller, higher density buildings in Redmond's downtown. Ironically, housing for very low income families became a model for higher density, higher income housing in the redevelopment of Redmond's downtown during the following decade.

Geographic separation by economic class, exacerbated by race and ethnicity, will not dissipate quickly. But as long as economically disadvantaged households are short-changed by inadequate design and planning starved by under-investment, their communities will be shunned and their offspring stigmatized. Some architects have stepped forward with ideas that promote self-help bootstrapping within neighborhoods, even though zoning and building regulations have increased difficulty for those needing to use their homes as income-producing workshops, stores, or other forms of entrepreneurial activity that do not fit the tidy model of residential neighborhood as domestic retreat. A development on the border of Oakland and Emeryville, California, designed by the author's firm with the involvement of local neighbors, includes dwellings specifically designed for first-time homeowners who may be artists or who have other home-based businesses.

Tom Dolan, author of *Live-work, Planning and Design*, reviews many examples for combining work and living, mostly for higher income households. Many strategies are applicable across incomes. Those households not benefiting from today's economy face

Figure 21.10 (Left) Affordable live-work housing for artists and photographers designed with input from neighbors to fit their neighborhood. (Right)Typical interior of live-work housing. Courtesy of Pyatok Architects

similar survival necessities as their predecessor colonists, pioneers, and immigrants. With limited or no markets available, colonists and pioneers had to design and build new communities using their homesteads, with no bureaucracies monitoring and regulating their actions. Later immigrants faced similar conditions, closed out of local economies by language and discrimination. They erected flourishing businesses using their domiciles and neighborhoods to build family-based enterprises. Today's underclasses face insurmountable regulatory obstacles not experienced in the past. Zoning and building codes, insurance policies, lending practices and property management attitudes that, while ostensibly protect the health and safety of everyone, too often stifle entrepreneurial urges of struggling families. Often such families must simply break the law and hope that authorities do not notice or look the other way.

Technological Issues

Every generation of architects dreams of that technological silver bullet that will lower housing costs. Prefabrication has been that savior since the early days of Modernism. Machine-produced modules and materials, and now manufacturing whole dwellings in factories, result in more rapid construction of buildings, thereby lowering costs and making housing accessible to a wider public. This approach denigrated the excessive embellishment of buildings with hand-crafted decoration, which had become associated as symbols of wealthy extravagance promoted by the Beaux Arts Academy in France. But this drive toward prefabrication was really a drive to reduce labor costs, as much as material costs. Not only have we lost hand-crafted buildings, but the number of people engaged in construction, as is true in the manufacturing sector, is lower per square foot than a century ago. So the net result of technological advancements in construction is fewer workers, although higher incomes when unionized.

But this mindset by architects to see technology as the means to make housing more affordable tends to ignore the highly volatile "soft" costs of housing. These include the cost of land, interest on construction loans or permanent financing, and profit margins for developers are all vulnerable to market conditions and can jump up unexpectedly, neutralizing and even reversing cost reductions resulting even from major technological breakthroughs. The hard costs of construction (labor and materials) constitute about 60–70 percent of the total development costs of housing, and depending on developers' profit margins and market conditions, total development costs may represent only 50 percent of final sales prices, so construction could represent as little as 35 percent of sales prices. Assuming that a major new construction method—some combination of execution and material improvements—could lower construction costs by as much as 10 percent, this may represent only a 3.5 percent reduction in sales prices, *if* the developer decides to pass the savings on to buyers. As little as a half-percent jump in the mortgage interest rate could easily wipe out that technological saving.

Does this mean architects are wasting their time in seeking technological improvements in production? Not necessarily, since non-profit corporations pass on savings, lowering mortgages, rents, and long-term operating expenses. Single-family infill homes produced by non-profits for first-time buyers seem easier to introduce innovative systems than multifamily attached housing. Detached homes are less constrained by fire codes than multifamily housing, which is governed by many more regulations that make such innovations somewhat more difficult. But manufactured housing is making inroads into higher density, inner-city neighborhoods, now stacking to three to five storeys. Manufactured housing can claim that it is less expensive than conventionally built housing because it is governed by more liberal HUD codes, uses non-union labor usually located in rural areas, and operates under a roof with controlled conditions. But its production in rural areas will not necessarily help local inner-city economies and construction trades in urban areas where housing is needed.

Looking to the Future

So what will be the main focus for housing architects' in the coming decades? As noted earlier, skills needed to conduct a process for public participation in housing design and community planning will continue to grow to help change both public opinion and that of client-developers. This skill is essential to bring about needed cultural shifts for Americans to accept design innovations if we are to survive on a planet of increasing numbers with diminishing resources. Many examples of participatory design used by academics have been documented because they have the time to record them, but an even wider array are in use among practicing architects, planners, and landscape architects. A brief Internet search reveals many such approaches.

Another innovation includes smaller, higher density units in compact transit-based communities with modest parking and road standards, which include mixed-use neighborhoods designed to easily accept households at all income levels. The Congress for New Urbanism has been a major promoter of these tendencies, as have architects designing affordable housing for non-profit producers serving low income households. Energy-

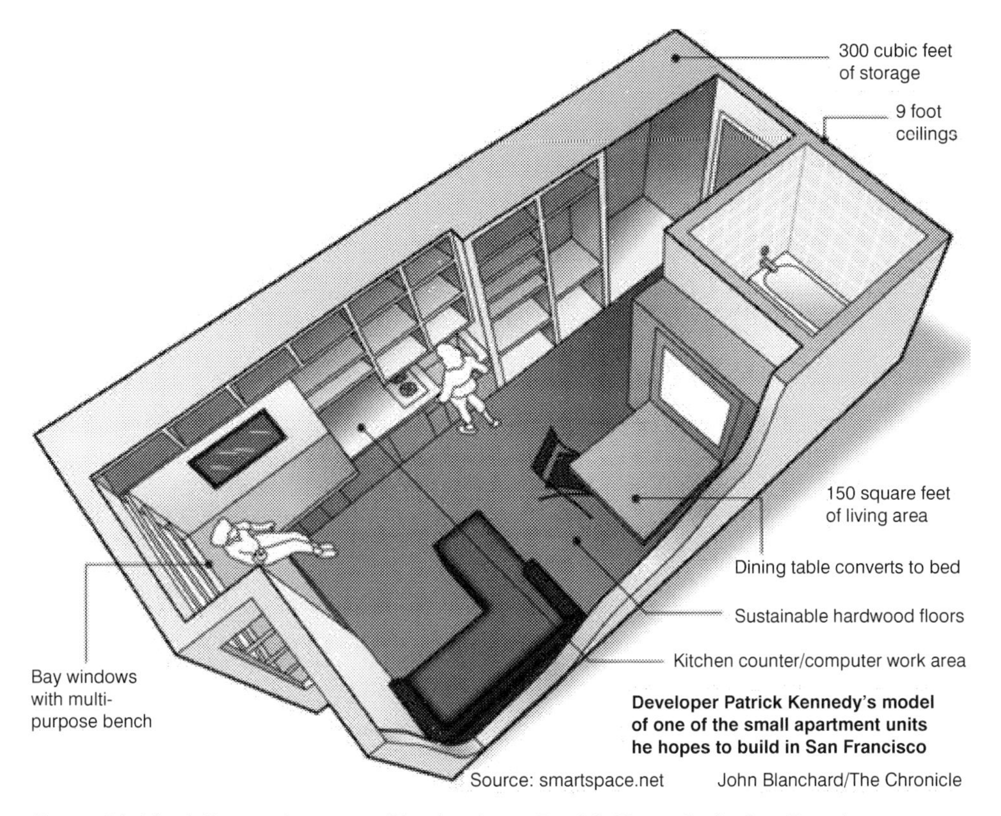

Figure 21.11 Micro-unit proposed by developer Patrick Kennedy for San Francisco

efficient site planning and envelope strategies that utilize greener materials and efficient heating-cooling systems will continue to be major design strategies. Via Verde, a new housing development in the Bronx (Urban Land Institute, 2014), has become a poster child for such best practices, as have a number of projects around the country: Devine Legacy in Phoenix, Tassafaronga in Oakland, Highpoint in Seattle, and many others.

Much has been written recently about the new craze of "micro-units" in cities as the savior for singles, seniors, and couples struggling to get a foothold. This is not unlike the turn of the last century when sons and daughters of small rural towns poured into cities to become clerks, bank tellers or factory workers. The response was a spike in development of residential hotels, some for women only (Groth, 1994). Today's response is coming in several forms, from reincarnations of shared boarding house style living to individual units less than 250–300 square feet, like stacked urban ship cabins. These units are often occupied by college-educated youth, in a temporary stage of their lives. Even at $1000 to $1500 per month, which seems reasonable in high-priced cities, residents are paying more per square foot than for conventional, larger housing units. In effect they are paying for the proximity to desired nightlife, and developers are making record profits.

At last look (National Geographic, 2014), the US is 4 percent of the planet's population, yet consumes almost 30 percent of its resources. We use one quarter of the world's fossil fuel resources—burning up nearly 25 percent of the coal, 26 percent of the oil, and 27 percent of the world's natural gas. New houses in the US were 38 percent bigger in 2002 than in 1975, despite having fewer people per household on average. Overall, National Geographic's Greendex found American consumers rank last of 17 countries surveyed in regard to sustainable behavior, but US consumers are among the least likely to feel guilty about their behavior, and are near the top of the list in believing that individual choices could make a difference. Here again, the misguided myth of individualism dominates and distorts our ability to cope with our problems. Paradoxically, those with the lightest environmental footprint are also the most likely to feel guilty. People in China, India, and Brazil lead the world in sustainable consumer choices, and yet they are among the least confident that individual action can help the environment. They understand the power of collective action, and communitarian obligations.

Regardless of American current events and behaviors, much of the world looks to the US as a cultural model, and its architects are in a unique position to promote lifestyles more appropriate to a shrinking planet. If architects in the next half century can convince the American public to accept living better but with less, on a planet with shrinking resources, in a way that is more than just comfortable, but even elegant and inspiring, then our nation may once again be respected internationally. A future de Tocqueville may say that unlike former empires, we learned to live with our genius—we succeeded in putting our competitive individualism into the service of humanity's collective needs.

References

Bellah, R.N., Tipton, S.T., Sullivan, W.M., Madsen, R., & Swidler, A. (1985). *Habits of the Heart: Individualism and Commitment in American Life*. Oakland, CA: University of California Press.

de Tocqueville, A. (2003). *Democracy in America*. New York: Penguin Classics.

Galli, C.D. (2005). Building Zion: The Latter-day Saint legacy of urban planning. *BYU Studies* 44,1, 111–136.

Groth, P. (1994). *Living Downtown: The History of Residential Hotels in the United States*. Oakland, CA: University of California Press.

Hayden, D. (1979). *Seven American Utopias: The Architecture of Communitarian Socialism, 1790–1975.* Cambridge, MA: MIT Press.

Jackson, D., & Spence, M.L. (1970). *The Expeditions of John Charles Fremont, Volume 1, Travels from 1838–1844.* Champaign, IL: University of Illinois Press.

Jones, T., Pettus, W., & Pyatok, M. (1997). *Good Neighbors: Affordable Family Housing.* New York: McGraw Hill.

Lofquist, D.A. (2012). *Multigenerational Households 2009–2011.* Retrieved February 15, 2015 from: http://www.census.gov/prod/2012pubs/acsbr11-03.pdf.

McCamant, C., & Durrett, C. (2011). *Creating Co-Housing: Building Sustainable Communities.* Gabriola Island, BC Canada: New Society Publishers.

National Geographic (2014). *Greendex, Consumer Choice and the Environment.* Retrieved February 15, 2015 From: http://images.nationalgeographic.com/wpf/media-content/file/NGS_2014_Greendex_Highlights_FINAL-cb1411689730.pdf.

Urban Land Institute (2014). *ULI Case Studies: Via Verde—the Green Way.* Retrieved February 15, 2015 from: http://uli.org/case-study/uli-case-studies-via-verde/.

Wright, G. (1983). *Building the Dream: A Social History of Housing in America.* Cambridge, MA: MIT Press.

22

Design for Disaster Preparation and Mitigation

Adenrele Awotona

Introduction

One of the primary goals of stakeholders who are involved in the provision, design, and construction of safe and secure buildings in any geographic location is to ensure that the built environment is disaster-resistant. These stakeholders include architects, landscape architects, engineers, planners, construction managers, environmentalists, scientists, developers, facilities managers, code officials, fire marshals, building inspectors, national/state/city/county/local officials, emergency managers, law enforcement agencies, disaster relief organizations, civil society organizations (including Non-Governmental Organizations), the private sector, and members of the community as a whole.

Building designs and construction methods must prepare and protect people, resources, and continuity of operations from all forms of disasters, including natural phenomena such as earthquakes, hurricanes, typhoons, tornadoes, floods, landslides, mudslides, and windstorms. They should also respond to shifting contextual community requirements throughout the Disaster Management Cycle that call for innovative multidimensional solutions—social, economic, political, and physical.

Disaster preparedness and mitigation strategies should be integrated into all phases of project planning, design, and construction at the earliest possible stage in order to save lives and property and to continue to function when catastrophes occur, for, as Benjamin Franklin (one of the Founding Fathers of the United States) once counseled, "an ounce of prevention is worth a pound of cure."

Consequently, this chapter looks at the relationship between spatial design and aspects of the Disaster Management Cycle in terms of both process and product. The emphasis, however, is on the need for an all-inclusive program of all-hazard mitigation planning because of its overarching relationships with all phases of disaster management.

Spatial Design

Wikipedia, the free encyclopedia, defines spatial design as:

> a relatively new discipline that crosses the boundaries of traditional design disciplines such as architecture, interior design, landscape architecture and landscape design, as well as public art within the Public Realm. It focuses upon the flow of space between interior and exterior environments [in both] the private and public realm. The emphasis of the discipline is upon working with people and space, particularly looking at the notion of place, [as well as] place identity and genius loci. As such the discipline covers a variety of scales, from detailed design of interior spaces to large regional strategies. ... As a discipline it uses the language of Architecture, Interior Design and Landscape Architecture to communicate design intentions.
>
> (Wikipedia, n.d.)

Thus, whereas architecture and interior design are concerned with such basics as space and people, spatial design integrates sustainability principles into the entire design process (Daw & Wallace, n.d.).

Disasters

According to Chad Berginnis (2012) of the Association of State Floodplain Managers, the United States experienced 14 disasters from natural hazards (floods, earthquakes, hurricanes, winds, and wildfires) in 2011, each costing in excess of US$1 billion, and President Obama issued a record 99 major disaster declarations. Globally, in the same year, disaster losses were a record US$350 billion and six disaster events in the United States were among the top ten costliest worldwide for insurers.

Globally, 231 disasters caused 5,469 deaths, affected a total of 87 million others, and caused US$44.6 billion in economic damages in 2012. Asia continues to be the world's most disaster-prone continent, with floods and storms as the foremost dangers. In China, the economic toll in 2012 exceeded US$10 billion, whilst Asia recorded a spectacular US$300 billion loss in 2011, in large part because of Japan's earthquake and tsunami and Thailand's floods (Awotona, 2014).

Additionally, population trends and climate change are increasing the world's vulnerability, and all stakeholders, especially the public and private sectors, must find ways to reduce risks from all hazards, particularly natural hazards.

The Disaster Management Cycle

As disaster events have increased in both frequency and intensity, the Disaster Management Cycle has served as a mechanism for dealing with them more effectively by a wide array of public and private sector organizations. The notion of the cycle, which was developed to assign order and rationality to various forms of disasters and the human responses to them, is rooted in the early years of disaster phase research in the fields of Sociology, Psychology, Anthropology, and Geography.

Hence, the starting point for examining the interrelationships between the spatial design professions and disaster management is to provide conceptual clarity for the management cycle of a disaster (also referred to as the "disaster life cycle"). For this purpose, this section relies heavily on David M. Neal's seminal 1997 publication, titled "Reconsidering the Phases of Disaster."

Conceptual and theoretical clarification of the management cycle of a disaster is essential for four main reasons. First, disaster phases (e.g., Preparedness, Response, Recovery, and

Mitigation) enable researchers to describe activities and organize their findings and data, as well as to proffer recommendations about disasters in a logical and systematic manner. Second, disaster practitioners rely on the phases to improve their disaster capabilities. Third, there has been little change in the general notion and use of disaster phases since 1932, when Carr first explicitly described them (Carr, 1932). Fourth, academics and practitioners have questioned, observed, or experienced problems with the use of disaster phases since Carr's time.

In promoting a reassessment of the cyclic concept of disaster phases, Neal (1997) provides some critiques from both academics and practitioners. Some of these criticisms include the following:

- A disaster life cycle does not reflect reality;
- The division between phases is arbitrary, since they are random for each event of a certain kind;
- One phase does not follow another in a perfect progressive way;
- The consequence of disasters may go on well beyond the reconstruction phase, especially in poor communities where the resources to undertake reconstruction and mitigation are meagre, resulting in each subsequent disaster further weakening the economic circumstances of the people and undermining their recovery efforts;
- The cyclic notion is not applicable to armed conflicts, droughts, famine, and pestilence;
- The phases of human response to disaster happenings are not a linear development; rather, they are an evolution of events involving complex human behavior in which social, economic, and environmental factors interrelate; and,
- Disaster periods create analytical problems, as the categories often overlap.

So, Are Disaster Phases Really Relevant?

In spite of their limitations, I do agree with Neal (1997) that we should not eliminate the use of disaster phases; appropriately contextualized, the Disaster Management Cycle can be, and has been, adapted by various communities, national and international governance institutions, and international development aid agencies to suit their individual circumstances. Rather, their use should be "recast in a more sophisticated manner."

Definitions of the Four- and Five-Phase Functional Approaches

For the past four decades, policy-makers, practitioners, trainers, educators, and researchers in the United States have defined Emergency Management as a "four-phase" continuous process, encompassing Mitigation, Preparedness, Response, and Recovery. But some sources now refer to five phases (Table 22.1) rather than four, adding Prevention as a separate fifth phase or component of Emergency Management. The United States Department of Homeland Security's Federal Emergency Management Agency (FEMA) uses both "Four Phases" and "Five Phases." According to St. Louis County in Missouri (n.d.), prevention happens when property and lives are protected by those that identify, deter, or stop an incident from occurring. These types of countermeasures can include:

- Heightened inspections;
- Improved surveillance and security operations;
- Investigations to determine the full nature and source of the threat;
- Public health surveillance and testing processes;

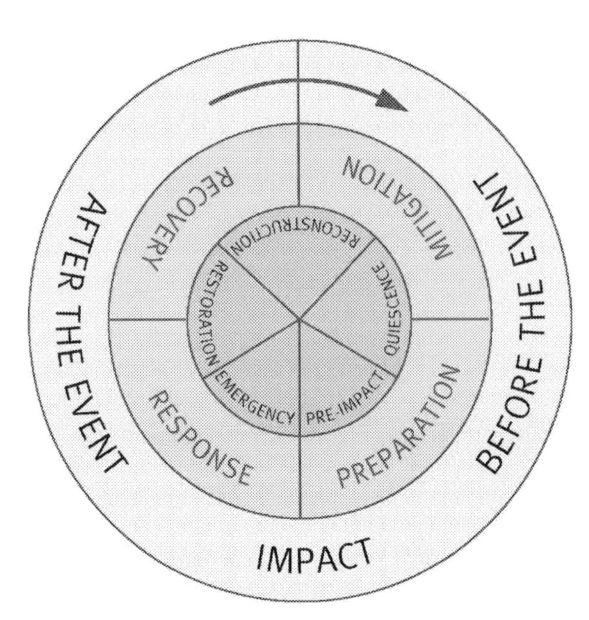

Figure 22.1 The Disaster Cycle (Alexander, 2002)

- Immunizations;
- Isolation or quarantine; and
- Law enforcement operations aimed at deterring, preempting, interdicting, or disrupting illegal activity (Office of Emergency Management, n.d.).

In this chapter, I will be referring to both the four- and five-phase functional (Prevention, Preparedness, Response, Recovery, and Mitigation) and temporal approaches (before a disaster, during a disaster, and after a disaster) (see Figure 22.1).

On the Relationship between Spatial Design and the Disaster Management Cycle

Despite the criticality of spatial design to the Disaster Management Cycle, the relationships between spatial design and disaster management are yet to be fully explored and studied (Murao, 2008). This section will attempt to begin to do so.

Design for Disaster Mitigation

In exploring the bond between disaster phases and design, this chapter places considerable emphasis on disaster mitigation (both pre-disaster and post-disaster, where the former allows ongoing mitigation activities outside of a disaster scenario, especially in communities which are not frequently struck by declared disasters) for five main reasons (Berginnis, 2012). First, it has an overarching relationship with all phases of disaster management. Second, as noted by Murao (2008), "when examined from the spatial point of view, it is not easy to distinguish between Preparedness and Response … [b]ecause making [space] for activity to quickly respond after the disasters should be prepared before disasters." Third, natural hazard mitigation saves money and is also a societal investment, the benefits of which include prevention of loss of life and

Table 22.1a The Phases of Emergency Management: Definitions and Descriptions from Five Sources

Phase	*National Governors' Association (NGA)*	*DHS, Federal Emergency Management Agency (FEMA)*	*DHS, Federal Emergency Management Agency (FEMA)*	*Tennessee Code Annotated 58-2-101*	*National Fire Protection Association*
Mitigation	Mitigation includes any activities that actually eliminate or reduce the probability of occurrence of a disaster (for example, arms build-up to deter enemy attack or legislation that takes the unstable double-bottom tanker off the highways). It includes long-term activities designed to reduce the effects of unavoidable disaster (for example, land-use management, establishing comprehensive emergency management programs, or legislating building safety codes).	Mitigation refers to activities that are designed to: • Reduce or eliminate risks to persons or property; or • Lessen the actual or potential effects or consequences of an incident.	Activities providing a critical foundation in the effort to reduce the loss of life and property from natural and/or manmade disasters by avoiding or lessening the impact of a disaster and providing value to the public by creating safer communities. Mitigation seeks to fix the cycle of disaster damage, reconstruction, and repeated damage. These activities or actions, in most cases, will have a long-term sustained effect.	Reduction of vulnerability of people and communities of this state to damage, injury, and loss of life and property resulting from natural, technological, or manmade emergencies or hostile military or paramilitary action.	Activities taken to reduce the severity or consequences of an emergency. No explanatory material provided for "Mitigation."

Source: Baird (2010), pp. 16–19.

Table 22.1b The Phases of Emergency Management: Definitions and Descriptions from Five Sources

Phase	*National Governors' Association (NGA)*	*DHS, Federal Emergency Management Agency (FEMA)*	*DHS, Federal Emergency Management Agency (FEMA)*	*Tennessee Code Annotated 58-2-101*	*National Fire Protection Association*

Prevention	No definition provided for "Prevention"	Prevention:
		• Means actions taken to avoid an incident or to intervene to stop an incident from occurring.
		• Involves actions taken to protect lives and property.
		• Involves applying intelligence and other information to a range of activities that may include such countermeasures as:
		  • Deterrence operations;
		  • Heightened inspections;
		  • Improved surveillance;
		  • Interconnections of health and disease; and
		  • Prevention among people, domestic animals, and wildlife.
			Actions to avoid an incident or to intervene to stop an incident from occurring. Prevention involves actions to protect lives and property. It involves applying intelligence and other information to a range of activities that may include such countermeasures as deterrence operations; heightened inspections; improved surveillance and security operations; investigations to determine the full nature and source of the threat; public health and agricultural surveillance and testing processes; immunizations, isolation, or quarantine; and, as appropriate, specific law enforcement preempting, interdicting, or disrupting illegal activity and apprehending potential perpetrators and bringing them to justice.	No definition provided for "Prevention."	Activities to avoid an incident or to stop an emergency from occurring.
					Explanatory Material: Activities, tasks, programs, and systems intended to avoid or intervene in order to stop an incident from occurring. Prevention can apply both to human-caused incidents (such as terrorism, vandalism, sabotage, or human error) as well as to naturally occurring incidents. Prevention of human-caused incidents can include applying intelligence and other information to a range of activities that includes such countermeasures as deterrence operations, heightened inspections, improved surveillance and security operations, investigations to determine the nature and source of the threat, and law enforcement operations directed at deterrence, preemption, interdiction, or disruption.

Source: Baird (2010), pp. 16–19.

Table 22.1c The Phases of Emergency Management: Definitions and Descriptions from Five Sources

Phase	*National Governors' Association (NGA)*	*DHS, Federal Emergency Management Agency (FEMA)*	*DHS, Federal Emergency Management Agency (FEMA)*	*Tennessee Code Annotated 58-2-101*	*National Fire Protection Association*
Preparedness	Preparedness activities are necessary to the extent that mitigation measures have not, or cannot, prevent disasters. In the preparedness phase, governments, organizations, and individuals develop plans to save lives and minimize disaster damage (for example, compiling state resource inventories, mounting training exercises, or installing warning systems). Preparedness measures also seek to enhance disaster response operations (for example, by stockpiling vital food and medical supplies, through training exercises, and by mobilizing emergency personnel on a standby basis).	Preparedness is defined as the range of deliberate, critical tasks and activities necessary to build, sustain, and improve the operational capability to prevent, protect against, respond to, and recover from domestic incidents. Preparedness is a continuous process involving efforts at all levels of government and between government and private-sector and nongovernmental organizations to identify threats, determine vulnerabilities, and identify required resources.	Actions that involve a combination of planning, resources, training, exercising, and organizing to build, sustain, and improve operational capabilities. Preparedness is the process of identifying the personnel, training, and equipment needed for a wide range of potential incidents, and developing jurisdiction-specific plans for delivering capabilities when needed for an incident.	Preparation for prompt and efficient response and recovery to protect lives and property affected by emergencies.	Activities, tasks, programs, and systems developed and implemented prior to an emergency that are used to support the prevention of, mitigation of, response to, and recovery from emergencies. No explanatory material provided for "Preparedness"

Source: Baird (2010), pp. 16–19.

Table 22.1d The Phases of Emergency Management: Definitions and Descriptions from Five Sources

Phase	*National Governors' Association (NGA)*	*DHS, Federal Emergency Management Agency (FEMA)*	*DHS, Federal Emergency Management Agency (FEMA)*	*Tennessee Code Annotated 58-2-101*	*National Fire Protection Association*
Response	Response activities follow an emergency or disaster. Generally, they are designed to provide emergency assistance for casualties (for example, search and rescue, emergency shelter, medical care, mass feeding). They also seek to reduce the probability of secondary damage (for example, shutting off contaminated water supply sources, cordoning off and patrolling looting-prone areas) and to speed recovery operations (for example, damage assessment).	Response begins when an emergency event is imminent or immediately after an event occurs. Response encompasses the activities that address the short-term, direct effects of an incident. Response also includes the execution of EOPs and of incident mitigation activities designed to limit the loss of life, personal injury, property damage, and unfavorable outcomes.	Immediate actions to save lives, protect property and the environment, and meet basic human needs. Response also includes the execution of emergency plans and actions to support short-term recovery.	Response to emergencies using all systems, plans, and resources necessary to preserve adequately the health, safety, and welfare of persons or property affected by the emergency.	Immediate and ongoing activities, tasks, programs, and systems to manage the effects of an incident that threatens life, property, operations, or the environment. *Explanatory Material:* The response of an entity to a disaster or other significant event that might impact the entity. Activities, tasks, programs, and systems can include the preservation of life, meeting basic human needs, preserving business operations, and protecting property and the environment. An incident response can include evacuating a facility, initiating a disaster recovery plan, performing damage assessment, and any other measures necessary to bring an entity to a more stable status.

Source: Baird (2010), pp. 16–19.

Table 22.1e The Phases of Emergency Management: Definitions and Descriptions from Five Sources

Phase	*National Governors' Association (NGA)*	*DHS, Federal Emergency Management Agency (FEMA)*	*DHS, Federal Emergency Management Agency (FEMA)*	*Tennessee Code Annotated 58-2-101*	*National Fire Protection Association*
Recovery	Recovery activities continue until all systems return to normal or better. They include two sets of activities: • Short-term recovery activities return vital life-support systems to minimum operating standards (for example, cleanup, temporary housing). • Long-term recovery activities may continue for a number of years after a disaster. Their purpose is to return life to normal, or improved levels (for example, redevelopment loans, legal assistance, and community planning).	The goal of recovery is to return the community's systems and activities to normal. Recovery begins right after the emergency. Some recovery activities may be concurrent with response efforts. Recovery is the development, coordination, and execution of service-and site-restoration plans for impacted communities and the reconstitution of government operations and services through individual, private-sector, nongovernmental, and public assistance programs… Long-term recovery includes restoring economic activity and rebuilding community facilities and housing. Long-term recovery (stabilizing all systems) can sometimes take years.	The development, coordination, and execution of service-and site-restoration plans; the reconstitution of government operations and services; individual, private-sector, nongovernmental, and public-assistance programs to provide housing and to promote restoration; long-term care and treatment of affected persons; additional measures for social, political, environmental, and economic restoration; evaluation of the incident to identify lessons learned; post-incident reporting; and development of initiatives to mitigate the effects of future incidents.	Recovery from emergencies by providing for the rapid and orderly start of restoration and rehabilitation of persons and property affected by emergencies.	Activities and programs designed to return conditions to a level that is acceptable to the entity. *Explanatory Material:* Recovery programs are designed to assist victims and their families, restore institutions to suitable economic growth and confidence, rebuild destroyed property, and reconstitute government operations and services. Recovery actions often extend long after the incident itself. Recovery programs include mitigation components designed to avoid damage from future incidents.

Source: Baird (2010), pp. 16–19.

injury to people; reduction of damage to public and private property; lessening of expenditure of resources and exposure to risk for first responders; reduction in costs of disaster response and recovery; acceleration of recovery of communities and businesses affected by disasters; and enhancement of community resiliency (Berginnis, 2012). Fourth, hazard mitigation is also its "own element and organizationally needs to be recognized as such" (Berginnis, 2012). Fifth, in light of the fact that hazard mitigation is fundamental to disaster resistance, various design approaches and know-hows function in more ways than one by not only preventing or decreasing disaster losses but serving the comprehensive end of lasting community sustainability (WBDG, 2013a).

According to the United States National Institute of Building Sciences (NIBS), when disaster mitigation "is implemented in a risk-informed manner, every dollar spent on mitigation actions results in an average of four dollars' worth of disaster losses being avoided" (WBDG, 2013a). The first step in the design process to mitigate disasters is a comprehensive risk assessment, which takes account of the following:

- Documentation of the hazards existing in the location;
- An assessment of their potential impacts and effects on the built environment based on existing or anticipated vulnerabilities; and
- What the potential losses could be.

(WBDG, 2013a)

As disaster mitigation refers to methods for lessening the impact of disasters on the built environment, the components of risk assessment include: sabotage and terrorist attacks; natural phenomena such as hurricanes and floods; and any force that is likely to destroy, inflict casualties, and cause loss of function in the built environment (WBDG, 2013a).

Techniques that are available to mitigate the consequences of disasters on the built environment should be identified and prioritized before design decisions are made and the mitigation measures are implemented, either during new construction (preventively) or as retrofits (correctively) (WBDG, 2013a).

Mitigation strategies are either structural or non-structural, contingent on three main factors: hazards identified, the location and construction type of a proposed building or facility, and the specific performance requirements for the building (WBDG, 2013a).

NIBS recommends a number of measures that should be taken into consideration when integrating disaster reduction measures into building design for earthquakes, hurricanes, typhoons, tornadoes, flooding, rainfall and wind-driven rains, differential settlement (subsidence), landslides and mudslides, wildfires, tsunamis, and areas of refuge (WBDG, 2013a). It also provides a list of relevant codes and standards when designing for each of these natural phenomena in the United States (WBDG, 2013a; Executive Order 12699, Seismic Safety of Federal and Federally Assisted or Regulated New Building Construction, 1990; Hurricanes, Typhoons, and Tornadoes: Public Law 108–146, 2003). It should, however, be noted that:

> compliance with regulations in building design is not sufficient to guarantee that a facility will perform adequately when impacted by the forces for which it was designed. Indeed, individual evaluation of the costs and benefits of specific hazard mitigation alternatives can lead to effective strategies that will exceed the minimum requirements. Additionally, special mitigation requirements may be imposed on projects in response to locale-specific hazards. When a change in use or occupancy occurs, the designer

must determine whether this change triggers other mitigation requirements and must understand how to evaluate alternatives for meeting those requirements.

(WBDG, 20103a)

Structural mitigation comprises the following:

- Hazard-resistant construction and design (e.g., earthquake-proof structures, engineering systems, and vibration-control systems). Examples of structural mitigation measures include building material and technique selections for all building construction types (*Masonry*—Unreinforced Masonry, Reinforced Masonry; *Reinforced Concrete [RC]*—RC Moment Resisting Frame (MRF), RC MRF with Unreinforced Masonry Infill, RC Shear Wall, Steel and RC Composite Frame, Precast MRF; *Steel*—Steel Frame, Steel MRF with Unreinforced Masonry, Steel-Braced Frame, Light Metal Frame), building code compliance, and site selection.
- Building designs that are fireproof both to prevent fires from occurring and to prevent them from spreading (e.g., fireproof structures and use of unburnable materials).
- Stilted houses to reduce flood damage.
- Seawalls or levees to protect coasts, harbors, or riversides from the force of waves or flooding.
- Stone walls and heavy roof construction to prevent damage from strong winds (caused by typhoons, cyclones, or hurricanes) and salt corrosion.

(Murao, 2008; WBDG Secure/Safe Committee, 2013b)

Design professions and the construction industry play a crucial role in disaster mitigation by improving the standard of practice and the resilience of the built environment to natural and man-made hazards through research into new building materials and construction procedures. Indeed, as noted by NIBS President Henry L. Green, "the building industry has a responsibility to assure that the facilities we design, construct, operate and maintain protect the health, safety and welfare of our nation's citizens." Furthermore, on May 13, 2014, leaders of the United States' construction industry "agreed to promote resilience in planning ... as the solution to making the nation's aging infrastructure more safe and secure" (National Institute of Building Sciences, 2014).

Non-structural mitigation comprises the following:

- Land use (living away from disaster-prone areas; the application of building regulations on active faults to avoid earthquake damage and on coastal areas to reduce damage from tsunamis and hurricanes, etc.) (Murao, 2008).
- Strategies that focus on "risks arising from damage to non-load-bearing building components, including architectural elements such as partitions, decorative ornamentation, and cladding; mechanical, electrical, and plumbing components such as HVAC, life safety, and utility systems" (WBDG Secure/Safe Committee, 2013b). Mitigation actions would include "efforts to secure these elements to the structure or otherwise keep them in position and to minimize damage and functional disruption. These measures may be prescriptive, engineered, or non-engineered in nature" (WBDG Secure/Safe Committee, 2013b).
- Building standards and codes, tax incentives/disincentives, zoning ordinances, preventive health care programs, and public education to reduce risk (Berginnis, 2012).

David R. Godschalk (2007) has also classified mitigation measures into "Voluntary" and "Nonvoluntary." Voluntary mitigation programs

> rely upon individuals, organizations, and communities to recognize the dangers posed by hazards and to reduce their exposure to the risk. Tax incentives, information concerning hazards and how to avoid them, and information on safe building practices, for example, only work if individuals, organizations, and communities decide that the risk of certain behaviors (such as building in wildfire areas) outweighs the benefits. Studies of floodplain management generally find that people will not limit development on the floodplains without strict regulations and the threat of punishment, e.g., withdrawal of eligibility for low cost-flood insurance or eligibility for disaster assistance.
>
> (Godschalk, 2007)

On the other hand, nonvoluntary or mandatory mitigation programs "use the threat of punishment to encourage compliance with established standards, although some individuals, organizations, and communities may risk punishment rather than change their behaviors (such as restricting development in floodplains)" (Godschalk, 2007).

However, a combination of mitigation tools (such as comprehensive and hazard-specific planning, technical assistance, mitigation grant programs, structural measures, and hazard insurance) are necessary to deal with existing older buildings which were constructed before modern building codes and standards were established (Berginnis, 2012).

NIBS has noted that "as a result of the heightened level of interest in homeland security following the attacks of 11 September 2001, the public is even more interested in efforts to protect people, buildings, and operations from disasters" (WBDG Secure/Safe Committee, 2013b), and identified four fundamental principles of all-hazard building design:

- *Plan for Fire Protection*: Planning for fire protection for a building involves a systems approach that enables the designer to analyze all of the building's components as a total building fire safety system package.
- *Protect Occupant Safety and Health*: Some injuries and illnesses are related to unsafe or unhealthy building design and operation. These can usually be prevented by measures that take into account issues such as indoor air quality, electrical safety, fall protection, ergonomics, and accident prevention.
- *Natural Hazards and Security*: Each year U.S. taxpayers pay over $35 billion for recovery efforts, including repairing damaged buildings and infrastructure, from the impacts of hurricanes, floods, earthquakes, tornadoes, blizzards, and other natural disasters. A significant percentage of this amount could be saved if our buildings properly anticipated the risk associated with major natural hazards.
- *Provide Security for Building Occupants and Assets:* Effective secure building design involves implementing countermeasures to deter, detect, delay, and respond to attacks from human aggressors. It also provides for mitigating measures to limit hazards to prevent catastrophic damage and provide resiliency should an attack occur.

(WBDG Secure/Safe Committee, 2013b)

Above all else, it is important to note that buildings and infrastructure should be designed to be resilient to natural and man-made disasters; that is, they should be able to absorb and speedily recover from a disrupting event. Continuity of operations is at the core of resilience; for some of the relevant codes that the construction industry must

Table 22.2 Methods for Local Governments to Implement Mitigation Strategies

Plans	
Land Use	Local Comprehensive Plan
	General Land Use Plan
	Sustainability Plan
	Capital Improvements Plan
	Redevelopment Plan
	Post-Disaster Redevelopment/Recovery Plan
	Regional Development Plans
	Watershed Protection/Enhancement Plan
	Open Space Plan
	Flood Mitigation Plan
	Military Base Development/Redevelopment/Reuse Plan
	College Campus Plans
Emergency Operations	Comprehensive Emergency Management Plan
	Evacuation Plan
Codes, Regulations and Procedures	
Land Use	Zoning Ordinance
	Subdivision Regulations
	Building Code/Permitting
	Landscape Code
	Solid Waste and Hazardous Materials Waste Regulations
	Property Deed Restrictions
	Tree Protection Ordinance
	Site Plan Review
	Architectural/Design Review
	Storm Water Management
	Soil Erosion Ordinance
Programs	
Land Use	Beach Conservation and Restoration Program
	Historic Preservation Program
	Construction/Retrofit Program
	Transportation Improvement/Retrofit Program
	School District Facilities Plan
	Environmentally Sensitive Purchase/Protection Program
	Long-Range Recreation Facilities Program
	Economic Development Authority
	Land Buyout Program
	Downtown Redevelopment Authority
	Local and/or Regional Evacuation Programs
	"Firewise" and other Fire Mitigation
	Fire Rescue Long-Range Programs
	Mutual Aid Agreement
	Temporary Animal Relocation Program

Source: Adapted from FEMA (2008), pp. 70–71.

abide by in order to prepare for disasters in the United States, see WBDG Secure/Safe Committee (2013b).

Table 22.2 contains a wide-ranging list of "methods" for local governments to implement mitigation strategies. It was reproduced by Malcolm Baird (2010) from FEMA's "Local Multi-Hazard Mitigation Planning Guidance" and identifies some specific responsibilities for "mitigation" (FEMA, 2008). Not only does it provide guidelines and requirements for "Local Mitigation Plans" which communities must prepare and adopt as prerequisites for certain FEMA grants, it also illuminates tasks and the interrelationships between phases that need to be addressed in disaster mitigation.

As noted by Robert Wible, there is a need for

> closer coordination between [the] public and private sector in addressing disaster mitigation and resiliency and other emergency codes and standards issues (including sustainability and energy conservation) in a more cohesive manner to increase the cost benefit to building owners and developers to incorporate resiliency into the building construction and renovation projects.
>
> (Fiatech, 2011)

Indeed, I agree with the view expressed by Adham Hany Abulnour (2014), that disaster events should be an opportunity for directed change towards more sustainable development.

An Example of a Successful Post-Disaster Mitigation Strategy

After being subjected to a major flood event in 1995 and repeated floods in previous years, the City of Charlotte and Mecklenburg County in North Carolina developed and adopted a post-disaster approach that integrated hazard mitigation strategies into a recovery plan on a regional level. In order to mitigate the effects of a flood disaster in the future, the city and county were converted on the regional planning level from a flood-prone area to a "safer" one. The specific features of the plan consisted of the following (Abulnour, 2014):

- Increasing the volumetric capacity of the flood watersheds available in the city and county through converting some of the land areas vulnerable to flooding into watersheds themselves.
- Purchasing lands from owners.
- Providing relocation alternatives and applying extensive reconstruction (digging and casing) processes to convert these lands into watersheds.
- Mitigating the probability of future floods by increasing the watershed areas, [which] allows the safe deployment of post-disaster reconstructions (including temporary houses) in the city and county.
- Applying land-use practices and investing in large processes of regional planning.
- A high level of organization on the national level and considerable amounts of funds.

Approaches to Post-Disaster Mitigation Strategies in and for Low-Income Communities

In contrast to the above example of a county in the United States, weak economies, lack of a high level of organizational capacity on the national level, and other contextual circumstances render the development of mitigation strategies on the regional planning

Figure 22.2 Examples of "Katrina Cottage" houses. Designed by Marianne Cusato

level almost impossible to achieve in the poor developing countries of Africa, Asia, and South America, where extensive flooding and other disasters wreak considerable havoc on lives and property every year. Consequently, a more grass-roots, bottom-up approach is employed in developing disaster mitigation strategies which take into account local poverty, level of technical skills, local building materials that are readily available and cost-effective, community participation, and appropriate technology. Architects, planners, and other spatial design professionals work in concert with local communities and NGOs to develop simple and affordable flood-resistant measures that seek mitigation on the design and construction levels to reduce the catastrophic consequences of various forms of disasters on the local population. Similarly, the use of water-thirsty plants, where readily and abundantly available locally, could be a resourceful way of accomplishing flood-resistant constructions though basic, inexpensive, and sustainable methods (Abulnour, 2014).

The "superadobe" technique conceived by the Iranian architect Nader Khalili (Cal-Earth, n.d.) and the work of the Japanese architect and leader in disaster relief design work, Shigeru Ban (Wang, 2014), are examples of the creative use of locally available and inexpensive building materials and methods.

Another example of a housing solution concerned with affordability, sustainability, and the ability to mitigate damage from future storms whilst being appropriate to regional culture and climatic conditions is the design developed by architect Marianne Cusato known as the "Katrina cottage" (Figure 22.2) (Natural Resources Defense Council Staff Blog, n.d.). It is

> assembled using cheap, durable and light prefabricated timber panels specially designed for hurricane conditions, and is able to withstand high wind-loads and excessive moisture without incurring damage or destruction. The roof is covered in tin sheets to protect against rain. Being made from relatively cheap (yet durable) materials, the cost of the "Katrina Cottage" in 2008 was less than 42,000 US$ including bathroom, kitchen and a front porch.
>
> (Abulnour, 2014)

Community Participation in the Design for Disaster Mitigation

Various studies have documented the efficacy and benefits of community participation (and the problems of non-participation) in the design and construction of built environments after disasters (Abulnour, 2014; see also Price *et al.*, 2000; Lawther, 2009; Davidson *et al.*, 2007). Participation is an important component in the overall success of housing and infrastructure redevelopment (to the extent allowed by the scale and context of any given situation and the management and organizational capacities of the community, amongst other factors): it helps to create a sense of communal interaction after a disaster; it strengthens the sense of accountability in regard to the maintenance of the buildings and environment; it reinforces the sense of identity and belonging to the housing solution; and it can speed up the construction process. The lack of community involvement in the post-1999 earthquake reconstruction in Turkey led to, amongst other things, little maintenance accountability and "apparent carelessness regarding the status of the houses ..." (Abulnour, 2014).

Provision of Post-Disaster Temporary Dwellings on a Relocation Site as a Mitigation Strategy

Often immediately after a disaster, temporary dwellings are provided to protect the survivors whilst the impact of the disaster is being evaluated and until more permanent housing (with the associated health and educational services, to name but a few), is available. A temporary dwelling may be either a shelter (public shelter, refuge at a friend's house, shelter under a plastic tent, or any other prefabricated enclosure) or a house (e.g., a rented apartment or a prefabricated home) (Abulnour, 2014). In this chapter, the term "temporary dwelling" refers to any purposely designed and constructed enclosure for the rehabilitation of survivors, either near the original disaster site, or, if the site is disaster-prone, on a new, safer, non-disaster-prone, relocation area. (In the aftermath of the 1999 Marmara and Bolu earthquakes in Turkey, the government initiated a three-step housing strategy for the survivors—provision of temporary shelter, temporary housing, and, later, permanent housing [Johnson, 2007]).

Indeed, depending on the prevailing circumstances (available resources and capacities, level of urbanization, nature of the disaster, dominant cultural values, prompt investments in reconstruction efforts, effective and efficient coordination of the contributions of the stakeholders, the roles of the public and private sectors, housing affordability, funding strategies, and prioritization, amongst other things), temporary dwellings can be designed and planned before a disaster (during the Preparedness phase) to form a nucleus for permanent housing settlements.

In general, however, the design and construction of temporary dwellings are characterized by the following qualitative features (Abulnour, 2014): fast erection using locally available or produced materials; community and occupants' involvement in the construction process which, amongst other benefits, strengthens the sense of community; the use of prefabricated structures and building components which are technologically appropriate and can be easily assembled on-site; availability of housing subsidies with or without the incorporation of the strategy of self-help; and simplification of both the design process and product in order to ensure user affordability. Furthermore, temporary dwellings should: be speedily accessible to the affected people; depend on local resources and suppliers, thereby promoting local employment and the local economy; reflect local living standards and user needs; and be easy to remove from the site in a non-polluting manner (Abulnour, 2014).

Resettling the disaster-affected community to temporary dwellings in a safer, non-disaster-prone area can be considered as a mitigation measure because the central objective of hazard mitigation is to minimize loss of life, property, and function due to disasters by decreasing or eliminating the susceptibility of the built environment to natural or human-made catastrophes.

The "Whole Community" Approach to the Disaster Life Cycle

In recognition of the fact that public assets alone cannot meet all the needs of all the members of a community when a disaster strikes (be it human-made, natural, or another catastrophic event), the United States Government has developed an innovative, all-inclusive, national, all-hazards approach to the five-phase Disaster Life Cycle—Prevention, Protection, Mitigation, Response, and Recovery—with a view to ensuring the development of more resilient Emergency Management plans and capabilities. The goal, as published by FEMA, is: "A secure and resilient nation with the capabilities required across the whole community to prevent, protect against, mitigate, respond to, and recover from the threats and hazards that pose the greatest risk." Presidential Policy Directive (PPD) 8: *National Preparedness* was released in March 2011 with the goal of strengthening the security and resilience of the United States (U.S. Department of Homeland Security, 2013). The National Response Framework (NRF) provides the context for how the whole community (first responders, decision- and policy-makers, and auxiliary bodies) works in concert to achieve the overriding goal of an integrated countrywide response; it categorizes the main response principles (engaged partnerships; a tiered response; scalable, flexible, and adaptable operational capabilities; unity of effort through unified command; and readiness to act), roles, and structures that organize the national response; and it defines how each segment of the community can apply these principles for a coordinated, operative, nationwide response. For a definition of a "whole community," see the U.S. Department of Homeland Security's National Mitigation Framework (2013).

The NRF is one of the five documents in the suite of the National Planning Frameworks, each covering one phase of the Disaster Life Cycle. The other four documents are: the National Prevention Framework; the National Protection Framework; the National Mitigation Framework; and the National Disaster Recovery Framework. The National Planning Frameworks are part of the National Preparedness System, which has six parts: Identifying and Assessing Risk; Estimating Capability Requirements; Building and Sustaining Capabilities; Planning to Deliver Capabilities; Validating Capabilities; and Reviewing and Updating.

Disaster Mitigation in the National Mitigation Framework

Disaster mitigation has always existed at every level in the United States—"from the family that creates a sheltering plan in case of a tornado, to corporate emergency plans for opening manufacturing plants to the community, to local codes and zoning that systemically address risks in a community's buildings" (U.S. Department of Homeland Security, 2013). What is new, however, is that the National Mitigation Framework elevates building widespread resilience throughout communities to a national priority with all the members—individuals, businesses, non-profit organizations, and local, state, tribal, territorial, and Federal governments—working together in a coordinated manner to address how the nation manages risk through mitigation capabilities. This Framework also defines mitigation roles and strategies for increasing risk awareness and leveraging mitigation products, services, and assets throughout the whole community.

Building and land-use codes constitute an important non-structural tool that can be used in hazard mitigation. Consequently, and as a contribution to strengthening the provisions contained in the National Mitigation Framework, the Association of State Floodplain Managers (ASFPM) presented its review of existing codes to the United States House Transportation and Infrastructure Committee Subcommittee on Economic Development, Public Buildings, and Emergency Management on July 24, 2012. Its first observation was the current voluntary nature and wide variability of building code adoption. For example, its recent study of state and local floodplain management programs revealed that in 2010,

> State Floodplain Managers indicated that only 76 percent of states had adopted building codes; that 46 percent of the states that do not require local jurisdictions to administer a building code do allow communities to adopt a building code of their choice; [and] that, even when building codes are adopted in a state, the consensus-based approach means that critical provisions could be omitted from the state code entirely.
>
> (Berginnis, 2012)

The second observation was that state adoption did not necessarily equal local adoption or enforcement of codes. For example, FEMA's Mitigation Assessment Teams (MATs), which had been deployed after major natural disasters to better understand how and why buildings had failed from natural hazards,

> found that [historically] construction often does not meet the level of performance targeted by model building codes. Whether this is a deficiency in the code or lack of enforcement is not known, however the MAT report after Hurricane Ike indicated that residential buildings without adequate elevation, proper construction, and proper foundation selection were found to have widespread failures. Anecdotally, many local floodplain managers indicate that code enforcement can be difficult. Everything from political pressure, misuse of the variance process, to inadequate legal counsel can impact a community's ability to enforce its regulations.
>
> (Berginnis, 2012)

ASFPM recommends the following:

- Steps should be taken to encourage (incent) states and/or communities with unique hazards or [a] long-term vision to implement standards beyond those found in the International Codes.
- Incentives must be created and perverse disincentives must be eliminated. This means that if a jurisdiction has not adopted a building code with natural hazard resiliency provisions, it should not even be eligible for any disaster assistance. Similarly, a community that has adopted and is enforcing such a code should receive the extra incentive. Indeed, ASFPM further recommends an additional incentive—implement a sliding cost share for rewarding those communities doing the right thing, whether for hazard mitigation funding or even disaster relief.
- Local capacity (enforcement training, etc.) is key to successful implementation of building codes. Having a building code is important, but it must be enforced to be helpful. Enforcement training and education for code officials and builders would promote effective enforcement.

- The challenge of jurisdictions that do not have the authority to adopt and enforce building codes needs to be addressed. There is no guarantee that when a state adopts a building code, a community will follow suit. Even worse, some communities have neither the authority to adopt or enforce building codes. This should operate as an incentive for states to grant this authority to all jurisdictions (counties, cities, parishes, etc.). Incentives are key—either for cost share or priority for funding. It is difficult to provide incentives for states with codes, since over half do have them—this may be an instance where disincentives for having no code are appropriate (Berginnis, 2012).

Disaster Mitigation in the National Disaster Recovery Framework

At the behest of the U.S. President in September 2009, the Department of Homeland Security (DHS) and the Department of Housing and Urban Development (HUD) established a Long-Term Disaster Recovery Working Group. One of the key components of the Group's focus is integrating the protection and enhancement of environmental, historic, and cultural resources into Hazard Mitigation Planning. It recommends that for successful recovery to occur, resilience and sustainability should be of primary concern—communities should implement mitigation and resilience strategies that minimize their susceptibility to hazards and strengthen their ability to withstand and recover from future disasters (including those which will occur as a consequence of climate change and global warming).

Climate Change Mitigation and Spatial Design

The United Nations Intergovernmental Panel on Climate Change (IPCC) has noted that "warming of the climate system is unequivocal." It projects that the Earth's surface temperature could rise by as much as 4°C within the next century; that the projected sea level rise could reach 19–23 inches by the year 2100; and that, if left unchecked, the devastating impacts could include increased spread of diseases, extensive species extinction, drought and wildfires, mass human, animal, and plant migrations, and resource wars over shrinking amounts of potable water (The Intergovernmental Panel on Climate Change, 2014).

Climate change mitigation has been defined "as human interventions designed to reduce the sources of greenhouse gas emissions (GHGs) or enhance the capability of sinks to store these gases," while the Intergovernmental Panel on Climate Change (IPCC) defines climate change adaptation as the "adjustment in natural or human systems in response to actual or expected climatic stimuli or their effects, which moderates harm or exploits beneficial opportunities" (The Intergovernmental Panel on Climate Change, 2014).

Buildings account for half of all GHGs, and the Building Sector is the largest contributor to carbon dioxide (CO_2) emissions in the United States. Similarly, the United States, which is home to 5 percent of the world's population, emits one-fifth of global GHGs.

So, how can architects and other members of the spatial design professions reverse global warming? Mitigation strategies could include the design of "smart growth" communities (New Jersey Future, n.d.) and landscape architects working with architects

> to increase the energy efficiency of buildings by strategically placing trees and incorporating green roofs and walls that provide insulation…[and] working with the parks departments and environmental and conservation organizations to manage

sustainable and healthy forests within cities, national parks, and rural areas, thereby enhancing the long-term capability of forests to serve as carbon sinks.

(The American Society of Landscape Architects, 2014)

Sustainable building design concepts are increasingly being incorporated into residential building design and construction in the United States through the green building rating systems. However, as I have already noted earlier, the adoption and implementation of a green building code is not uniform throughout the country. Indeed, not all the buildings that are certified as "green" actually incorporate the necessary standards to withstand the natural hazards to which they are subjected. This matter needs to be addressed as a part of strengthening the National Mitigation Framework. For example, the Association of State Floodplain Managers has noted that "the major national green building standard for both new and existing buildings is the U.S. Green Building Council's Leadership in Energy and Environmental Design (LEED) program. But, LEED itself does not require compliance with any building code..." (Berginnis, 2012).

With regards to sea level rise, it will not only cause the flooding of towns, cities, and other human settlements and destroy "trillions of investments" in housing and infrastructure, it would also "affect freshwater quality by increasing the salinity of coastal rivers and bays and causing saltwater intrusion—the movement of saline water into fresh ground water resources in coastal regions" (The American Society of Landscape Architects, 2014). In order to protect coastal communities, it would be essential to restore, where applicable, "natural systems like wetlands [which] provide critical green spaces and wildlife habitats while playing a central role in blunting the effects of sea level changes," amongst other strategic measures (The American Society of Landscape Architects, 2014).

Similarly, in a February 2006 interview by Deborah Snoonian of the *Architectural Record* magazine, architect Edward Mazria proposes that architects can make buildings carbon-neutral (reducing fossil fuel consumption of buildings by 50 percent by the year 2010, and 10 percent more every five years until we achieve carbon-neutral buildings by 2030) "by designing more energy-efficient buildings and also specifying materials that have low embodied energy and are made with clean energy sources" (Snoonian, 2006).

Concluding Remarks

In sum, a review of the critiques of the phases of disasters leads to the conclusion that they continue to be useful, albeit in a more refined form, by enabling the disaster response community (spatial designers, academics, practitioners, and policy formulators alike) to organize their disaster-focused activities and articulate appropriate policies in a methodical manner. Available evidence demonstrates that innovative integration of disaster phases into spatial design is essential to achieving thoughtful building designs, to contributing to safe and sustainable built environments, and to creating secure and sound living environments. However, design methods and construction techniques must be contextualized, because all disasters are local and each is unique.

Global warming disasters will be adding more momentum and intensity to the traditional disasters of flood and storms, to name but a few. It will also bring new disasters, such as rising seas and disruption to food supplies and human habitations everywhere. But the global effort to mitigate global warming is proceeding at a snail's pace. This, in my view, is because both the political will and political capital are wanting. Many initial goals have already been bypassed. Most notably, the 2°C holding point is already a lost hope. Simply put, we have already lost about half the battle, and spatial designers still need to muster allies among other professions.

So, whatever we declaim, we must acknowledge that global warming is going to be adding more and more disasters and resultant injury to the globe and its inhabitants. The energy realm is the principal culprit. Massive investments have been made in fossil fuel and electricity-generating plants that are designed to last decades more, and more and more gas-fired plants are appearing. Moreover, coal is being consumed at a rate in China that is greater than all other countries in the globe combined (U.S. Energy Information Administration, 2014). Consequently, I propose that the relentless mobilization of support for strategies for combating global warming by spatial designers is imperative.

References

Abulnour, A.H. (2014). The Post-Disaster Temporary Dwelling: Fundamentals of Provision, Design and Construction. *Housing and Building National Research Center (HBRC) Journal*, 10(1), 10–24.

Alexander, D. (2002). *Principles of Emergency Planning and Management*. Oxford: Oxford University Press.

American Society of Landscape Architects, The. (2014). Combating Climate Change with Landscape Architecture. Retrieved July 24, 2014 from: http://www.asla.org/climatechange.aspx

Awotona, A. (2014). Introduction. In A. Awotona (Ed.), *Rebuilding Sustainable Communities after Disasters in China, Japan and Beyond* (pp. xv–xvi). Newcastle upon Tyne: Cambridge Scholars Publishing.

Baird, M.E. (2010, January). The “Phases” of Emergency Management. Background paper prepared for the Intermodal Freight Transportation Institute, University of Memphis, Memphis, TN. Retrieved July 25, 2014 from: http://www.vanderbilt.edu/vector/research/emmgtphases.pdf

Berginnis, C. (2012, July 24). A Review of Building Codes and Mitigation Efforts to Help Minimize the Costs Associated with Natural Disasters. Testimony before the House Transportation and Infrastructure Committee Subcommittee on Economic Development, Public Buildings and Emergency Management. Washington, D.C.

Cal-Earth. (n.d.). About Nader Khalili: Architect and Author. Retrieved January 3, 2015 from: http://calearth.org/about/about-nader-khalili.html

Carr, L. (1932). Disaster and the Sequence-Pattern Concept of Social Change. *American Journal of Sociology*, 38, 207–218.

Daw, C., & Wallace, O. (n.d.). What is Spatial Design? http://www.wisegeek.com/what-is-spatial-design.htm

Davidson, C.H., Johnson, C., Lizarralde, G., Dikmen, N., & Sliwinski, A. (2007). Truths and Myths about Community Participation in Post-Disaster Housing Projects. *Habitat International*, 31(1), 100–115. Retrieved July 25, 2014 from: http://www.sciencedirect.com/science/article/pii/S0197397506000348

Executive Order 12699 (1990, January 5), Seismic Safety of Federal and Federally Assisted or Regulated New Building Construction.

Federal Emergency Management Agency (FEMA). (2008, July 1). *Local Multi-Hazard Mitigation Planning Guidance.* Washington, D.C.: FEMA. Retrieved July 24, 2014 from http://emilms.fema.gov/is318/assets/local_mtgtn_plan_gdnce_0708.pdf

Fiatech. (2011). Mitigating Disaster through Design and Construction Conference Preparing Report to Congress. Press Release. Retrieved January 8, 2015 from: http://fiatech.org/project-management/press-releases/605-mitigating-disaster-through-design-and-construction-conference-preparing-report-to-congress

Godschalk, D.R. (2007). Mitigation. In W.L. Waugh Jr. & K. Tierney (Eds.), *Emergency Management: Principles and Practice for Local Government* (pp. 89–112). 2nd ed. Washington, D.C.: International City/County Management Association.

Intergovernmental Panel on Climate Change, The. (IPCC). (2014). Climate Change 2014: Mitigation of Climate Change. *Contribution of Working Group III to the Fifth Assessment Report of the Intergovernmental Panel on Climate Change,* O. Edenhofer *et al.*, eds. Cambridge: Cambridge University Press.

Johnson, C. (2007). Impacts of Prefabricated Temporary Housing after Disasters: 1999 Earthquakes in Turkey. *Habitat International*, 31(1), 36–52. Retrieved July 25, 2014 from: http://www.sciencedirect.com/science/article/pii/S019739750600018X

Lawther, P.M. (2009). Community Involvement in Post-Disaster Reconstruction—Case Study of the British Red Cross Maldives Recovery Program. *International Journal of Strategic Property Management*, 13(2), 153–169.

Murao, O. (2008). Case Study of Architecture and Urban Design on the Disaster Life Cycle in Japan. Presentation at the 14th World Conference on Earthquake Engineering, Beijing, China, October 12–17. Retrieved July 24, 2014 from: http://www.iitk.ac.in/nicee/wcee/article/14_S08-032.PDF

National Institute of Building Sciences. (2014). CEOs Announce Major Commitment to Promote Resilient Planning and Building Materials. Retrieved July 24, 2014 from: http://www.nibs.org/news/172768/CEOs-Announce-Major-Commitment-to-Promote-Resilient-Planning-and-Building-Materials.htm

Natural Resources Defense Council Staff Blog. (n.d.). Switchboard. Retrieved July 25, 2014 from: http://switchboard.nrdc.org/blogs/kbenfield/

Neal, D.M. (1997). Reconsidering the Phases of Disaster. *International Journal of Mass Emergencies and Disasters*, 15(2), 239–264.

New Jersey Future. (n.d.). Primer on Smart Growth. Retrieved July 25, 2014 from: http://www.njfuture.org/smart-growth-101/primer/

Office of Emergency Management, St. Louis County, MO. (n.d.). The Five Phases of Emergency Management. Retrieved January 7, 2015 from: http://www.stlouisco.com/lawandpublicsafety/emergencymanagement/thefivephasesofemergencymanagement

Price, R., Bieber Gonenc, A., Jacobs, S., & Konvits, J. (2000). *Turkey Post-Earthquake Report*. Ankara, Turkey: OECD Secretariat.

Snoonian, D. (2006, February). How Architects Can Reverse Global Warming: A Conversation with Edward Mazria. Retrieved July 26, 2014 from: http://archrecord.construction.com/features/green/archives/060201mazria.asp

Tornado Shelters Act. (2003). Hurricanes, Typhoons, and Tornadoes: Public Law 108–146.

U.S. Department of Homeland Security. (2013). National Mitigation Framework, May 2013. Washington, DC: FEMA.

U.S. Energy Information Administration. (2014). China Produces and Consumes Almost as Much Coal as the Rest of the World Combined. *Today in Energy*. Retrieved July 24, 2014 from: http://www.eia.gov/todayinenergy/detail.cfm?id=16271

Wang, Lucy. (2014). Innovative Japanese Architect Shigeru Ban Wins the 2014 Pritzker Prize! *Inhabitat*. Retrieved January 8, 2015 from: http://inhabitat.com/shigeru-ban-wins-the-2014-pritzker-prize/

WBDG (Whole Building Design Guide) Secure/Safe Committee. (2013a). Natural Hazards and Security. National Institute of Building Sciences (NIBS). Retrieved July 24, 2014 from: http://www.wbdg.org/design/resist_hazards.php

WBDG (Whole Building Design Guide) Secure/Safe Committee. (2013b). Overview. NIBS WBDG website. Retrieved July 26, 2014 from: http://www.wbdg.org/design/secure_safe.php

Wikipedia (n.d.). Spatial Design. Retrieved July 24, 2014 from: http://en.wikipedia.org/wiki/Spatial_design

23

Defensive Design

Design for Security and Mitigating Potential Terrorist Attacks

Eve Hinman

Security concerns need to be integrated in much the same way as any other design constraint imposed on the project. Ultimately the goal is for the physical security features to maintain an inviting environment and minimize inconvenience to the building users. One of the benefits of aiming for an unobtrusive design is that the building will not attract undue attention of potential attackers. To be successful, the security design needs to be part of an overall multi-hazard approach to the design, so that it does not degrade performance in the event of a fire or natural hazard that is likely to be more prevalent than terrorist attack.

Because of the severity of the damages caused by explosions some levels of damages are permitted provided that it reduces the risk to people inside the building. First and foremost the focus is on saving lives by preventing catastrophic collapse of the building before everyone has been evacuated. We also do our best to reduce injuries by keeping as much of the explosion outside the building through the strength and ductility of the building envelope as well as reducing the hazard presented by flying debris generated by glass, appurtenances, and interior fixtures (e.g., falling lighting fixtures) (Applied Technology Council, 2003). This damage mitigating approach is what is presented in this chapter. In short, the goal is to incorporate reasonable measures that will enhance the life safety of building occupants and facilitate rescue efforts in the unlikely event of attack.

Some of the reasons building owners voluntarily incorporate such concepts not typically included in building codes include:

- Attracting more tenants or a particular type of tenant
- Lowering insurance premiums or obtain high-risk insurance
- Reducing business disruption costs

Protection against terrorist attack is not an all-or-nothing proposition. Incremental measures taken early in design may be more fully developed at a later date. For instance, the space requirements needed to accommodate additional security measures, the protection level may be enhanced as the need arises or the budget permits after construction is complete.

Although many of the concepts presented are intuitive, the design often will entail an engineering expert familiar with these concepts. Also, there are many products on the market which provide tested products which are used on vulnerable buildings. Finally, note that the focus of this chapter is on new construction, but the concepts presented are general enough to provide valuable information for retrofits as well.

Explosive Attack

There are two parameters that define the design threat: the bomb size, typically measured in terms of the equivalent weight of TNT, and the distance from the bomb to the building. The standoff distance is measured from the center of gravity of the bomb to the face of the building (see Figure 23.1).

Vehicle bombs are able to deliver a sufficiently large quantity of explosives to cause potentially devastating structural damage and govern design. The critical location of the vehicle bomb is a function of the site, the building layout and the security measures in place. The critical locations of the bomb are at the closest points that a vehicle can approach, assuming that all security measures are in place. This may be a garage directly beneath the occupied building, the loading dock, or the street curb directly outside the facility, or at a vehicle access control gate where inspection takes place.

Another explosive attack threat is the small bomb that is delivered by hand in a backpack or suitcase for instance. Small bombs can cause the greatest damage when brought into vulnerable unsecured areas of the building, such as the building lobby, mailroom, and retail spaces.

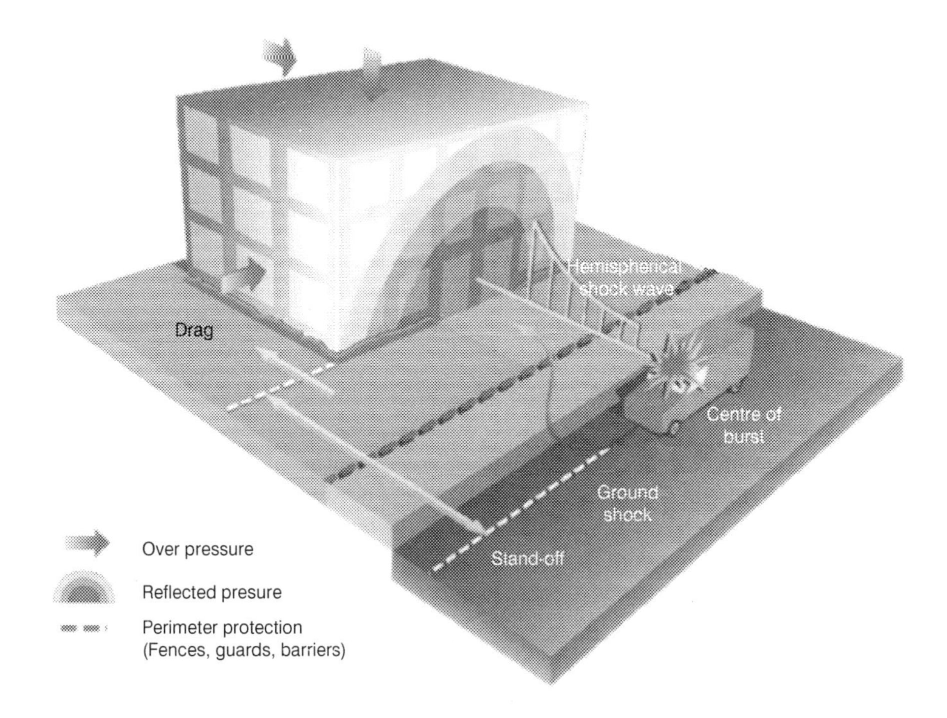

Figure 23.1 Explosive loads acting on a building

Therefore the largest bombs are considered in totally unsecured public space (e.g., in a car or truck on the nearest public street), and the smallest bombs are considered in the most secured areas of the building (e.g., in a briefcase smuggled past the screening station).

The bomb size used for design is usually selected by the owner in collaboration with their security and protective design consultants (i.e., engineers who specialize in the design of structures to mitigate the effects of explosions). Although there are few unclassified sources giving the sizes of bombs that have been used in previous attacks, security consultants have valuable information that may be used to evaluate the range of charge weights that might be reasonably considered for the occupancy. Security consultants draw upon the experience of other countries such as Great Britain and Israel where terrorist attacks have been more prevalent, as well as data gathered from U.S. sources.

The car or truck bomb size considered for design purposes will typically be smaller than the largest credible bomb size. For a truck bomb for instance, the bomb size will be measured in the hundreds of pounds rather than the thousands of pounds of TNT (or the equivalent using another type of explosive) that could be feasibly carried by the truck (Hinman & Hammond, 1997). This bomb size is ultimately translated into lower loads or forces that act on the building. The reason that the bomb is smaller than what has been considered is that the probability of the largest credible bomb size is much lower than for a reduced size bomb. Another reason is that a building designed for a truck bomb would look like a bunker, which is very impractical, expensive and unattractive in a city or town.

Building Damages

Damages due to explosions cannot be predicted with perfect certainty. Past bombing incidents show that indirect effects such as flying debris and fire can significantly affect the level of damage. Despite these uncertainties, it is possible to estimate the extent of damage and injuries in an explosive event, based on the size of the explosion, distance from the event, and assumptions about the construction of the building. Damage due to an air-blast shock wave may be divided into direct air-blast effects and progressive collapse. Direct air-blast effects are damages that may cause localized failure of exterior walls, windows, roof systems, floor systems and columns. In addition to the pressures that explosions exert, there is also a suction phase of the explosion, which is not as lethal as the pressure phase but which could potentially pull the exterior wall of a building off if it is not properly fastened onto the building. The total duration of explosive loads is extremely small compared with, for instance, hurricane winds. The air-blast reduces to zero in a time frame that is much less than a second (durations are measured in milliseconds).

When major columns or other load-supporting structural elements are damaged due to air-blast, it can initiate progressive collapse. Progressive collapse refers to the spread of an initial local failure to other structural elements like falling dominos, ultimately resulting in the collapse of a significant portion of the building relative to the zone of initial damage. Localized damage due to direct air-blast effects may or may not progress, depending on the design and construction of the building and the placement of the weapon. To produce a progressive collapse, the bomb is typically in close proximity to a critical load-bearing element, like a major column (see Figure 23.2). Progressive collapse can propagate vertically upward or downward from the source of the explosion, and it can propagate laterally from bay to bay as well. This damage occurs in less than a minute in most cases.

The pressures that an explosion exerts on a building may be several orders of magnitude greater than the loads for which the building is designed. The explosion may also act in a

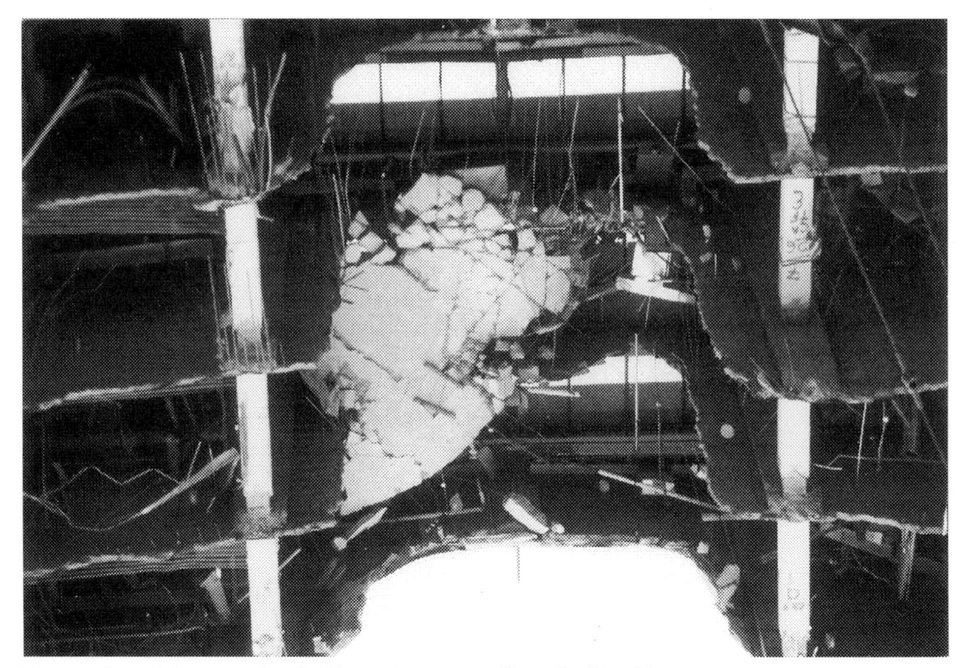

Figure 23.2 Photograph of collapsed portion of bombed building

direction the building may not have been designed for, such as upward on the floor system. Floor failure is common in large-scale explosive attacks, because floor slabs typically have a large surface area for the pressure to act on and a comparably small thickness. This is type of damage particularly common for close-in and internal explosions (U.S. Department of Homeland Security, 2009).

Security Principles

Ideally, a potential terrorist attack is stopped before it ever happens, through intelligence and security countermeasures. If the attack is executed, physical and operational measures are enacted to create layers of security within the facility. The outermost layer is the perimeter of the facility. Interior to this line is the approach zone to the facility between the perimeter line and building exterior. Having multiple lines of defense provides redundancy to the security system, adding resilience to the design. Also, by using this approach, not all of the focus is on the outer layer of protection, which may lead to an unattractive, fortress-like appearance. For a reliable design, each ring must have a uniform level of security provided along its entire length; security is "only as strong as the weakest link."

To have a balanced design, both physical and operational security measures need to be implemented into the facility. Architects and engineers can contribute to an effective physical security system, which augments and facilitates the operational security functions. If security measures are left as an afterthought, expensive, unattractive and makeshift security solutions are the inevitable result.

In the sections below, the physical security of the following is considered individually: site, architecture, building envelope, structure and mechanical/electrical systems. For each, an approach and recommendations are given for enhancing life safety and reducing downtime for the building.

Site Design

Because the pressures generated by explosives decay rapidly with distance, keeping vehicle bombs as far away as possible from the building can be highly effective to increase the protection of the building. The first line of defense to consider is the perimeter line at the curb or property line. The second layer of defense is the buffer zone between the perimeter and the building exterior. The third line is the placement of building on the site. In general the largest credible explosive size is a function of the security measures in place. Each line of security may be thought of as a sieve, reducing the size of the bomb that may gain access.

Sometimes pedestrian access along the perimeter line is limited as well. This is not considered a priority in this chapter because the focus is on publicly accessible buildings, which permit pedestrian access freely. In this section the primary threat considered is a car or truck bomb at the perimeter because of the large pressures generated.

Perimeter Line

The perimeter line of protection is defined as the outermost line, which can be protected by facility security measures (Architect of the Capitol, 2007). The primary threat at the perimeter is a large-scale bomb gaining access to the site. In design, it is commonly assumed that all large bombs (i.e., car-bombs or truck-bombs) are outside the perimeter line. Ideally, a continuous line of security is provided along the perimeter of the facility to control access and keep vehicles as far away from the building as possible. Since it is impossible to thwart all possible threats, the objective is to make it difficult to successfully execute the easiest attack scenarios-like a car-bomb along the curb, or a vehicle jumping the curb and ramming into the building prior to detonation. Gaps in the perimeter security compromise the overall security of the entire perimeter. As the saying goes "A chain is only as strong as the weakest link."

It is recommended that the perimeter line is located as far as practical from the building exterior. However, for vulnerable buildings located in urban areas where site conditions are tight, this is not always possible. In these cases, there is some benefit to pushing the perimeter out to the edge of the sidewalk by means of bollards, planters and other obstacles. Bollards (i.e., concrete filled steel pipes buried into the sidewalk) are the most widely used option for the perimeter. Other solutions include concrete planters, benches, sculptures and other street furniture. To push this line even further outward, restricting or eliminating parking along the curb can often be arranged with the local authorities, but can be a difficult and time consuming effort. In some cases, eliminating loading zones and street/lane closings are an option (NYPD Counterterrorism Bureau 2004).

Perimeter anti-ram barriers are categorized as both passive (or fixed) and active (or operable). Passive or fixed barriers are those that are fixed in place. These are to be used away from vehicle access points and are constructed in place. Active or operable barriers open to permit vehicles through at access points; security personnel often operate these.

Barrier effectiveness is ranked in terms of the weight and velocity of the vehicle at impact and the amount of displacement generated by impact. Barrier manufacturers often will provide information regarding the tested capacity of their products so that it is relatively simple to select a design, which is most appropriate.

For lower risk buildings it may be appropriate to install planters, or to use landscaping features. An example of a simple but effective landscaping solution is to install a large heavy permanent planter around the building with a wall that is as high as a car or truck bumper (see Figure 23.3).

Figure 23.3 Surface mounted planters outside a public building

Individual planters mounted on the sidewalk resist impact through inertia and friction between the planter and the pavement. It can be expected that the planter will move as a result of the impact. For a successful design, the maximum movement of the planter under impact will be less than the setback distance to the building. Also the distance from the stopped vehicle to the building needs to be more than the critical setback distance defined for the project. Also, the structure supporting the weight of the planter must be considered prior to installation.

The closer the anti-ram barriers are to the curb the more effective they will be. However, the property line of buildings often does not extend to the curb. Therefore, to place barriers with foundations near the curb the local authorities will need grant permission, which can be a time consuming effort and needs to be planned for. To avoid this, building owners are often inclined to place bollards along the property line which can significantly reduce the effectiveness of the barrier system.

Access point locations should be oblique to oncoming streets so that incoming vehicles must reduce speed to enter the location. In general, "T" intersections, which allow high run up speeds for cars should be avoided. If the site provides straight-on access to the building, some mitigation options include concrete medians in the street to slow vehicles or, for high-risk buildings, anti-ram barriers along the curb capable of withstanding the impact of high vehicle velocities.

The traditional anti-ram solution entails the use of bollards. Bollards are concrete filled steel pipes that are placed at regular intervals to prevent vehicle intrusion. To resist the impact of a vehicle, typically the bollard needs to be embedded into a continuous reinforced concrete foundation that is buried more than a meter into the soil. The height of the bollard above ground should be higher than the bumper of the vehicle. The spacing of the bollards is typically one half the width of a car. The height of the bollard is to be at least as high as the bumper of the vehicle.

An alternative to a bollard is a continuous knee wall constructed of reinforced concrete with a buried foundation. This design may be used as the base of a fence or fashioned into a bench. To be effective, the height needs to be as high as the vehicle bumper. One approach

Figure 23.4 Bollards along the curb adjacent to a public building

that is effective and unobtrusive is to infill the volume between the wall and the building to create a raised surface, which is protected from ramming attack (see Figure 23.5).

The foundation of the bollard and knee wall system can also present other challenges. Vaults, basements and trees that extend to the property line will need special foundation details. Below ground utilities that are frequently close to the pavement surface also present additional challenges. Their location may not be known with certainty and this often leads to difficulties during construction. This also can be a strong deterrent to selecting barriers with foundations as a solution. However, for vulnerable facilities, it is recommended that these issues are resolved during the design phase so that a reliable anti-ram barrier solution is installed. For lower risk buildings without straight-on vehicular access, it may be more appropriate to install surface mounted systems such as planters, or to use landscaping features to deter an intrusion threat.

At vehicular access points, active or operational anti-ram systems are required. There are off-the-shelf products available that have been rated to resist various levels of car and truck impacts. Solutions include:

- Drop beams
- Sliding gates
- Surface mounted plate systems
- Retractable bollards
- Rotating wedge systems

The first two systems listed above generally have lower impact ratings than the last three listed and look more like traditional solutions. Often these systems are hydraulically operated. It is important that a qualified contractor performs the installation of these to ensure a reliable system that will work properly in all weather conditions.

Also, it is recommended that the manufacturer shows evidence that the system has been tested to meet the impact requirements for your project.

Figure 23.5 Example of a plinth wall adjacent to public street

Landscaping Buffer

Between the secure perimeter line and the building there is a critical buffer which, if thoughtfully designed can serve to facilitate surveillance and control the movement of people and vehicles. The objectives of defensive landscaping are to deter potential attackers from attempting to ram into the building and to delay those who attempt an attack.

If space is available between the perimeter line and the building exterior, much can be done to delay an intruder. Examples include terraced landscaping, fountains, statues, staircases, circular driveways, planters, trees, high strength cables hidden in bushes and any number of other obstacles and devices which make it difficult to rapidly reach the building. Though individually these features are not able to stop a vehicle, in combination, they form a daunting obstacle course. Other ideas for implementing secure landscaping features may be found in texts on Crime Prevention Through Environmental Design (CPTED) (Atlas, 2008). These concepts are useful for slowing down traffic and improving surveillance and site circulation. Natural barriers such as marshes or cliffs along the property lines are useful in mitigating ramming attacks without undue fortification of the site. Water retention pools, fountains and other water features are also effective and attractive methods.

Place parking as far as practical from the building. Off-site parking is recommended for high-risk facilities vulnerable to terrorist attack. If on-site surface parking or underground parking is provided, take precautions to limit access to these areas only to the building occupants and/or have all vehicles inspected in areas close in to the building. If an underground area is used, the garage should be placed adjacent to the building under the plaza area for high-risk buildings rather than directly underneath the building. To the extent practical, limit the size of vehicle that is able to enter the garage by imposing physical barriers on vehicle height.

Figure 23.6 Operable "pop-up" bollards at a vehicle entrance

Building Shape and Placement

At the building exterior, the focus shifts from deterring and delaying the attack to mitigating the effects of an explosion. The building exterior is a critical line of defense for protecting the occupants of the building. Its placement and shape, independent of any structural mitigations, can be surprisingly effective in reducing the damages and associated injuries due to an explosive attack.

Ideally, the building is placed as far from the property lines as possible. This applies not only to the sides that are adjacent to streets, but also to sides that are adjacent to neighboring properties which may change ownership during the life of the building. Ideally the setback is maximized on all sides (i.e., it is in the center of the property).

The shape of the building can have a contributing effect on the overall damage to the structure. Reentrant corners and overhangs are likely to trap shock waves, which may amplify the damaging effect of an air-blast. Terraces, which are treated as roof systems are subject to downward loads, require careful framing and detailing to limit internal damages to supporting beams. Note that large or gradual reentrant corners have less effect than small or sharp reentrant corners and overhangs. In general convex rather than concave shapes are preferred for the exterior of the building (that is, the reflected pressure on the surface of a circular building is less intense than on a flat building).

Generally simple geometries, with minimal ornamentation (which may become flying debris during an explosion) are recommended unless advanced structural analysis techniques are used. If ornamentation is used, it is recommended that it consists of a lightweight material such as timber or plastic which are less likely to become lethal projectiles in the event of an explosion than brick, stone or metal.

Exterior Envelope Design

The exterior envelope is the first line of defense that the building has to offer in defending against an explosive attack. Although heavier stiffer elements do resist more loads, they are also typically susceptible to brittle failure that can be highly hazardous. Lighter materials are able to absorb energy through deformation may fail at lower pressures, but the fragments tend to be less hazardous. The lightweight ductile design approach is generally the preferred solution because the solutions tend to be more cost effective and do not alter the appearance of buildings significantly.

Soil can be highly effective in reducing the impact of a major explosive attack. Bermed walls and buried roof tops have been found to be highly effective for military applications and can be effectively extended to conventional construction. Green roofs also provide protection. Interior courtyards or atriums are other concepts for bringing light and a natural setting to the building while protecting the exterior.

Windows and glass curtain walls consist of a system of components that transfer the blast load back to the structure. In this chapter, the general issues related to blast design of the glazing systems are discussed. Though the glazing design is a primary responsibility of the architect, structural issues will dominate the design once explosive effects are taken into consideration. Glazing designed to mitigate the effects of explosions should first be designed to resist conventional loads before considering explosive load effects.

Balanced or capacity design philosophy means that the glass is designed to be no stronger than the weakest part of the overall window system, failing at pressure levels that do not exceed that of the frame, anchorage and supporting wall system. If the glass is stronger than the supporting members, the window is likely to fail with the whole panel entering into the building as a single unit, possibly with the frame, anchorage and the wall attached. This failure mode is considered more hazardous than if the glass fragments enter the building, provided that the fragments are designed to minimize injuries. By using a damage limiting approach, the damage sequence and extent of damage is controlled.

Windows are typically the most vulnerable portions of any building. Though it may be impractical to design all the windows to resist loads due to a large explosion, it is desirable to limit the amount of hazardous glass breakage to reduce the injuries. Typical annealed glass windows break at low pressure and impulse levels and the shards created by broken windows are responsible for many of the injuries incurred due to large explosions.

Designing windows to provide protection against the effects of explosions can be effective in reducing glass laceration injuries. For a large explosion, this pressure range is expected on the sides of surrounding buildings not facing the explosion, or for smaller explosions where pressures drop more rapidly with distance. Window protection should be evaluated on a case-by-case basis by a qualified protective design consultant to develop a solution that meets established objectives. A number of generic recommendations are given for the design of the window systems to reduce injuries to building occupants.

To limit glass laceration injuries, there are several approaches that can be taken:

- Reduce the area of vision panels.
- Reduce the size of individual glass panes.
- Use transparent materials as part of the cross section that cause less hazard than glass.
- Locate windows in areas where the air-blast is lower.
- Catch the fragments using glass lamination, blast screens/curtains or other method.
- Bring natural light into the building in other ways such as skylights.

Figure 23.7 Protective façade at lower floors of building close to public road

Often several of these concepts will be used in different areas of the façade depending on the use of the interior occupied space and the anticipated location of a potential explosion at the façade.

It is highly desirable for blast resistant walls to be used regardless of the approach used for the glazing design. If blast resistant walls are used, fewer and/or smaller windows will cause less air-blast to enter the building thus reducing the interior damage and injuries.

Specific examples of how to incorporate these ideas into the design of a new building include: limiting the number of windows on the lower floors where the pressures are higher due to an external explosion at the ground level; using an internal atrium design with windows facing inward not outward; and clerestory windows which are above the heads of the occupants; and angling the windows away from the curb to reduce the pressure levels.

Glass curtain wall systems have been determined in explosion tests to perform surprisingly well to low levels of explosive loads. These systems can be designed for large deformations without the glass breaking hazardously compared to rigidly supported punched window systems. Some design modifications may be required to the connections, details and member sizes to optimize the performance.

Glass is often the weakest part of a building, breaking at low pressures compared to other components such as the floors, walls or columns. Past incidents have shown that glass breakage and associated injuries may extend over a kilometer in large external explosions (Norville *et al.,* 1999). High-velocity glass fragments have been shown to be a major contributor to injuries in such incidents. For incidents within downtown city areas, falling glass poses a major hazard to passersby and prolongs post-incident rescue and clean-up efforts by leaving

Table 23.1 Performance Conditions for Windows

Performance Condition	*Protection Level*	*Hazard Level*	*Description of Window Glazing*
1	Safe	None	Glazing does not break. No visible damage to glazing or frame.
2	Very High	None	Glazing cracks but is retained by the frame. Dusting or very small fragments near sill or on floor acceptable.
3a	High	Very Low	Glass cracks. Fragments enter space and land on floor no further than 1 meter from window.
3b	High	Low	Glazing cracks. Fragments enter space and land on floor no further than 3 meters from the window.
4	Medium	Medium	Glazing cracks. Fragments enter space and land on floor and impact a vertical witness panel at a distance of no more than 3 meters from the window at a height no greater than 0.6 meters above the floor.
5	Low	High	Glazing cracks and window system fails catastrophically. Fragments enter space impacting a vertical witness panel at a distance of no more than 3 meters from the window at a height greater than 0.6 meters above the floor.

tons of glass debris on the street. At this time, exterior debris is largely ignored by existing criteria.

As part of the damage limiting approach, glass failure is not quantified in terms of whether breakage occurs or not, but rather by the hazard it causes to occupants. Two failure modes that reduce the hazard posed by window glass are:

- glass that breaks but is retained by the frame
- glass fragments exit the frame and fly into the space

The glass performance conditions are defined based on empirical data from explosive tests performed in a cubical space with a three-meter dimension (ASTM Subcommittee F12.10., 2011). The performance condition ranges from one which corresponds to not breaking to five which corresponds to hazardous flying debris impacting the back wall (see Table 23.1). Generally a performance condition 3a (see Figure 23.8) is considered acceptable for buildings that are not at high risk of attack. At this level, the window breaks, fragments fly into the building but land harmlessly within 1 meter from the window or impact a witness panel 3 meters away no more than 1.6 m above floor level. The window performance conditions are listed in Table 23.1. A typical design goal is to achieve a performance level less than 4 for 90 percent of all the building windows. This is validated by using a 3D model to evaluate all the windows (see Figure 23.9).

The preferred solution for new construction is to use laminated glass adhered with structural sealant at the glass perimeter. For insulated units, only the inner pane needs to be laminated. The lamination holds the shards of glass together in explosive events, reducing its potential to cause laceration injuries. The structural sealant helps to hold the pane in the frame for higher loads. Annealed glass is used because it has a breaking strength that is about one-half that of heat-strengthened glass and about one-fourth as strong

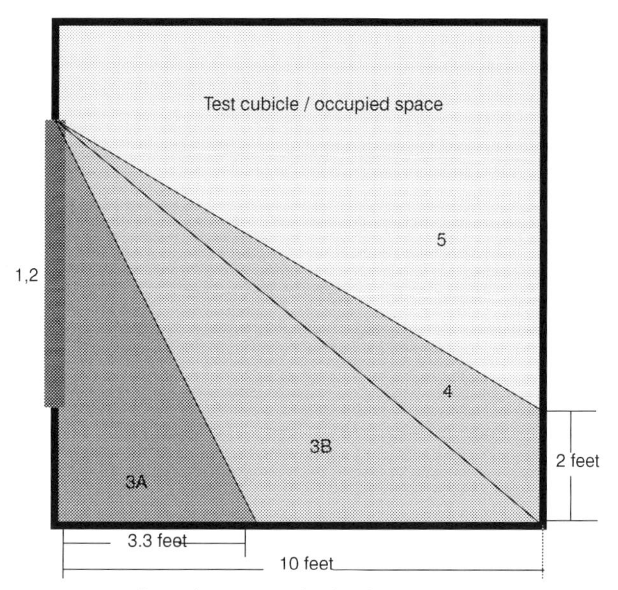

Figure 23.8 Cross-section of window test cubicle showing protection zones

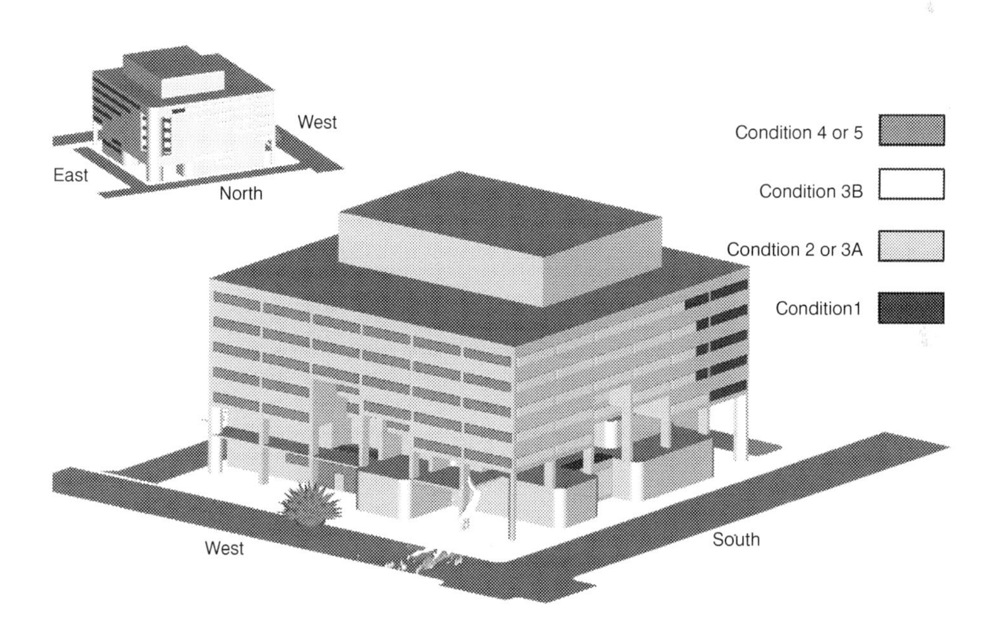

Figure 23.9 Protection zones shown on building façade for a defined explosive threat

as tempered glass. Using annealed glass becomes particularly important for buildings with lightweight exterior walls using for instance, metal studs, dry wall and brick façade. Use the thinnest overall glass thickness that is acceptable based on conventional load requirements. Also, it is important to use an interlayer thickness that is 60 mm thick rather than the 30 mm thick as is used in conventional applications. This layup has been

Figure 23.10 Example of protective windows used on public building

shown to perform well in low-pressure regions. If a 60 mm polyvinyl butyral (PVB) layer is used, the tension member forces into the framing members need to be considered in design (Bush *et al.*, 2004).

Windows designed to mitigate the effects of explosions are most commonly framed as described above. Windows that are not captured in frames or have glass mullions are generally discouraged. If point supported systems and/or butt-glazed solutions are used, it is highly recommended that engineers who are experienced in the design of these systems to resist the effects of explosions be retained.

Other general observations are as follows:

- Wire glass is not recommended because the wire inside the glass may worsen injuries.
- Glass block is vulnerable to failing at the joints, causing the individual blocks to fly in and cause blunt trauma injuries. Only glass block that has been tested to resist explosion loads should be used.
- Insulated panels that use three or more panes through the cross-section are expected to perform better than two panes.
- Layouts using polycarbonate for the inner or outermost layer may be vulnerable to scratching or clouding. A thin pane of glass should be used on the inside and outside to increase its life.
- Window film is similar to polycarbonate but it is also vulnerable to bubbling and peeling and will need to be replaced periodically. As a rule this product should be used only for retrofit.

Figure 23.11 Example of a steel mullion cross-section

The frame members connecting adjoining windows are referred to as mullions. To limit the depth of the mullions, steel inserts are often used (see Figure 23.10). Even with the inserts, the mullion depth is still quite large (see Figure 23.11). The window frames need to hold the glass so that the entire pane does not become a single large unit of flying projectile. It also needs to be designed to resist the breaking stress of the window glass. As with frames, it is good engineering practice to limit the number of interlocking parts used for the mullion.

To retain the glass in the frame, a minimum of a 6 mm bead of structural sealant (e.g., silicone) is used around the inner perimeter of the window. The allowable tensile strength should be at least 20 psi. Also, the window bite (i.e., the depth of window captured by the frame) needs to be at least half an inch thick. The structural sealant recommendations should be determined on a case-by-case basis. In some applications, the structural sealant may govern the overall design of the window systems.

Frame and anchorage design is performed by applying the breaking strength of the window to the frame and the fasteners. In most conventionally designed buildings, the frames will be aluminum. In some applications, steel frames are used. Also, in lobby areas where large panes of glass are used, a larger bite with more structural sealant may be needed.

Inoperable window solutions are generally recommended for air-blast mitigating designs. However, there are operable window solutions that are conceptually viable. Window designs that open about a hinge to the outside will slam shut in an explosion event. If this type of design is used, the governing design parameter may be the capacity of the hinges and/or hardware. For retrofits where replacing the entire façade or adding a blast resistant transparent second façade are not cost effective, there are some cost effective solutions worth mentioning. The simplest is to use a film on the inside face to hold the glass shards together, thereby reducing glass laceration injuries. For "daylight" applications, where the film is attached to the inside of the existing window using an adhesive and not anchored into the supporting framing system, a 30 mm thick film is typically used. For more resistance, the film is anchored into the supporting frame or mullion using a system of battens and anchors. In this case, the film may be thicker and provides greater protection.

To provide additional protection, film retrofits may include a "catchment" system in the form of window treatment on the interior such as a screen or a curtain, which stops the broken glass from penetrating into the space. This solution is particularly desirable for the daylight film application, which provides a relatively low level of protection. For thicker films, a taut cable strung horizontally across the window can also be used to stop the pane from flying into the building.

Building Interior

The final lines of defense are inside the building. Unsecured space is to be located in the outermost bays. These spaces include the unsecured portion of the lobby where people queue to gain access to the secured areas. Other unsecured areas include mailrooms, loading docks and retail spaces. These areas are best designed not without secured space above or below. If this condition is not met, the floor between the two areas needs to be hardened. Similarly for secured areas adjacent to unsecured areas, the walls separating secured from unsecured needs to be hardened. Sometimes, the separation may be in the form of a transitory space, such as a storage area, bathroom or intermittently occupied conference room.

Inside this line are the secured areas where the building tenants are located as well as critical building utilities. Within the secured area there may be additional layers of secured space depending on the occupancy. The advantage of this approach is that it isolates the areas where explicit design for explosion effects needs to be accounted for.

Glass in lobbies used for such items as display cases, railings, skylights or sculptures are discouraged not only because of the potential for injury but the delay in evacuation and rescue that it may cause. Also, it is recommended that the fire control room be hardened to protect against explosions. Similarly the walls adjacent to the lobby will need to be designed to resist explosive loads if the other side is secured. Another situation to watch for is placing desks within 3 meters of the window, due to the likelihood of window failure, which is likely even in modest explosion events.

For smaller bombs brought into the building and placed on the floor away from major columns, the response will be more localized with damages and injuries extending a bay and perhaps to an adjacent floor level. Although the bomb is smaller for hand delivered threats, they can cause lot of damage particularly when they are placed against major columns. When they are placed against major columns the air-blast effects are amplified. Typical damages that may be expected include:

- Localized failure of the floor system immediately below the bomb
- Damage and possible localized failure for the floor system above the bomb
- Damage and possible localized failure of nearby concrete and masonry walls
- Failure of non-structural elements such as partition walls, false ceilings, ductwork, window treatments
- Flying debris generated by furniture, computer equipment and other contents.

More extensive damage, possibly leading to progressive collapse may occur if the bomb is strategically placed directly against a primary load-bearing element such as a column. For this reason, take care to avoid or harden columns in the lobby area, which are supporting secured spaced above, below or adjacent to it.

Conclusion

Architectural measures can be highly effective in protecting buildings to resist the effects of explosive attack. Because protective measures are so integral to many of the decisions made early in the design process and impact so many design elements, the architect implicitly controls the inherent level of protection afforded to the building, if done thoughtfully. Though explosions can be complex and overwhelming, the design measures need not be.

Key points to remember are:

- Impose a controlled setback from streets to keep vehicles away from building.
- Use obstacles to make it more difficult for a vehicle to reach the building.
- Place less window glass in areas close to potential explosions.
- Place most critical areas away from the building exterior or closer to the more protected sides.

References

Applied Technology Council (2003). *Primer for Design of Commercial Buildings to Mitigate Terrorist Attacks* (FEMA 427). Washington, DC: U.S. Federal Emergency Management Agency.

Architect of the Capitol. (2007). *The Site Security Guide*. Washington DC: U.S. General Services Administration Printing Office.

ASTM Subcommittee F12.10. (2011). *Standard Test Method for Glazing and Glazing Systems Subject to Airblast Loadings* (F2912-11). West Conshohocken, Pennsylvania: ASTM International.

Atlas, R. (2008). *21st Century Security and CPTED: Designing for Critical Infrastructure and Crime Prevention*. Boca Raton, FL: Taylor & Francis Group.

Bush, F. J. W., Steinberg, S. & Kaliniak, C. (2004). Security glazing and design applications. In Nadel, B. (Ed.) *Building Security: Handbook for Architectural Planning and Design* (29.1-29.17). New York: McGraw Hill Companies.

Hinman, E. & Hammond, D. (1997). *Lessons from the Oklahoma City Bombing: Defensive Design Techniques*. Reston, VA: American Society of Civil Engineers Press.

Hinman, E. & Arnold, C. (2010). Building envelope and glazing. In Dusenberry, D. (Ed.) *Handbook For Blast Resistant Design of Buildings* (263–299). Hoboken, NJ: John Wiley & Sons.

Norville, H., Harvill, N., Conrath, E., Shariat, S. & Mallonee, S. (1999). Glass-related injuries in Oklahoma City Bombing. *Journal of Performance of Constructed Facilities*, 13(2): 50–56.

NYPD Counterterrorism Bureau. (2004). *Engineering Security: Protective Design for High-risk Buildings*. New York: New York City Police Department.

U.S. Department of Homeland Security (2009). *Bomb Threat Stand-off Chart.* Available from: https://publicintelligence.net/dhs-bomb-threat-stand-off-chart/.

24

New Urbanism and the Economics of Place

What Style is Your Bailout?

Peter Katz

When lecturing to architects in global centers of culture such as London, New York, Sydney and San Francisco—places where I expect to see audience members wearing a lot of black and dark gray clothing—I've learned that it's best to show a few images of modern buildings that exhibit characteristics of good urbanism right up front to address the question of style. If I don't make that point at the beginning of my presentation, I know it will surely be an unstated challenge to all of my subsequent remarks about the New Urbanism.

Indeed, without that preamble, the images of gable-roofed cottages pulled up close to the street, corner stores and newly constructed town squares that I show later on will elicit such strong negative responses that it would hardly be worth discussing the underlying principles and physical configuration of well-planned urban places. For the most part architects who have been "marinated in Modernism," to borrow the historian Vincent Scully's phrase (Scully, 1994), would just stop listening because the level of cognitive dissonance between the images that they were seeing on the screen and what they've come to associate with good design would be too great.

Many architects, of course, would bristle at the notion that their latest high-design creation might actually be less than "state of the art" in the way that it supports the larger community's planning goals. This situation is ironic, especially when one considers that the New Urbanism is a planning movement founded by six architects—Peter Calthorpe, Andres Duany, Elizabeth Moule, Elizabeth Plater-Zyberk, Stefanos Polyzoides and Daniel Solomon—each of whom attained high levels of professional recognition as building designers, all in fairly contemporary idioms, before transitioning to their current focus at the community scale.

At the same time municipal planners, who may have initially been lukewarm to a planning movement instigated largely by architects, now embrace the New Urbanism's promised benefits, at least from a theoretical standpoint. It's important to note that planners typically start with an education that's heavily oriented to either policy or geography. Many see themselves as administrators or facilitators of processes that are most often implemented by outside consultants. Thus they themselves may be less invested in the realm of physical design, and as a result, tend not to focus heavily on matters of style.

The problem, in my opinion, is that many architects cannot see *beyond* the issue of style, which certainly looms large in a profession that concerns itself with the look of things. I understand this, because having been trained as a designer, I too am concerned with the look of things. That's why, for a long time, I had a strong negative reaction to the "retro" appearance of the better-known early new urban communities such as Seaside and Kentlands (see Figure 24.1). However, looks can be deceiving—more importantly—they can mask the larger lessons that professionals need to learn about why a place may look and feel so compelling.

This chapter will attempt to explain why so many architects' fears of New Urbanism are misplaced. Indeed, issues of style associated with New Urbanism that loom so large for the profession can be fairly easily addressed and put aside to enable consideration of more important issues—issues that are key to the long-term social, economic and environmental viability of our communities, and potentially the very survival of our species on a planet with finite resources.

As we tackle the subject of style, it is important to mention that this same concern rarely comes up when speaking to local elected officials, regional business leaders, transportation engineers or any of the other professionals engaged in the planning of our communities. They are comfortable with the idea that a city would be composed of a variety of building types and styles from many previous eras. Indeed, only the architects feel a profound obligation to uphold the tenets of Modernism in the places they design, whether at the scale of a kitchen addition or an entire urban precinct.

Figure 24.1 New urban communities such as Kentlands, located in a suburb of Washington, DC are frequently criticized by architects for being overly nostalgic or "retro" in their style

As mentioned before, I generally respond to this strong concern about style on the part of architects by showing those few extra slides, but I'm not sure, even then, whether most architects actually understand my point. So in my opening remarks, I also emphasize in words that "the New Urbanism is not about style" and continue on to explain that "the movement is more focused on the underlying physical structure of human settlements." Moving on to more specific recommendations, I then explain that one can achieve a more optimal physical form by respecting a few simple principles and dimensional parameters (see Box 24.1).

In the twenty years since the first publication of the "basics" in Box 24.1, my talks have gradually shifted from a focus on physical form to looking at the way we regulate and pay for new development. During that period, two important things changed. First, we now have a much larger portfolio of built new urban examples, particularly in infill locations from which to draw when illustrating the movement's principles; and second, professional planners in local government have come to regard New Urbanism (and its cousin smart growth) as the preferred approach to shaping urban settlements.

Indeed, since the mid-1990s, one would be hard pressed to find a staff planner anywhere in the United States or Canada who openly advocated sprawl—specifically large-lot, single-use, suburban "pod" development. But despite this oft-stated preference, the model remains harder than ever to implement.

When thinking about the emergence of the New Urbanism, it's also important to note that the best-known new urbanist projects of the late 1980s and early 1990s—Seaside, Kentlands and Celebration—were launched amid very different circumstances from that of more conventional master-planned developments. All three projects were greeted with much curiosity by citizens and local officials, and seen by their backers (and to some extent, the local government staffers that processed them) as worthy experiments. The architect-designers of all three communities believed, perhaps naively, that the main things one needed to create a great place were a well-crafted plan, and compelling eye-level images of the future build-out of the plan.

In the case of Kentlands, the development in the Maryland suburbs of Washington, DC, that is now recognized as the first "year round" new urban community, these work products were created in a public charrette, an open community event that garnered considerable local and national media attention. That publicity helped to create a wave of goodwill that made it easier to get the plan approved.

Kentlands was initially processed as a special mixed-use variant of a *planned-unit development*. The street and block layout was a redesign of an earlier, more conventional suburban master plan. Supportive local regulators allowed many new and innovative features, but insisted that the overall unit count and mix of types remain the same, along with two major arterial roads within the development.

Seaside, the resort community that claims the title of America's first new urban community, has a master plan that was initially adopted in early 1980s in the relatively loose regulatory framework of Walton County, Florida. It was a rural area with a rapidly expanding tourist economy. When the county's population reached a key threshold, developer Robert Davis was forced to retroactively submit his plan to state officials for approval. Rick Hall, a former state transportation official and member of Davis' consultant team initially suggested amending the plan to follow the state's "access management" standards. Later Hall came around to enthusiastically support the approach taken by Davis and his planner, Andres Duany. Together the team successfully persuaded state officials to allow Seaside's unique plan to go forward.

Box 24.1 New Urbanism Basics

In the late 1980s, a new approach to the creation and revitalization of communities emerged in North America. Based on community development patterns that were ubiquitous prior to World War II, the New Urbanism seeks to reintegrate the components of modern life—housing, workplace, shopping and recreation—into compact, pedestrian-friendly, mixed-use neighborhoods linked by transit and set in a larger regional open space framework. The New Urbanism is an alternative to suburban sprawl, a form of low-density development that consists of large, single-use "pods," office parks, housing subdivisions, apartment complexes, shopping centers—all of which must be accessed by private automobile.

Initially dubbed "neo-traditional planning," the New Urbanism is best known for projects built in new growth areas. The principles that define New Urbanism can also be applied successfully to infill and redevelopment sites within existing urbanized areas. In fact, the leading proponents of New Urbanism believe that infill development should be given priority over new development in order to revitalize city centers and limit sprawl. An early manifesto by several leading new urbanists states: "we can, first, infill existing communities and, second, plan new communities that will more successfully serve the needs of those who live and work within them." Unfortunately, many of the current social, political and economic realities in the U.S. favor development at the metropolitan edge.

The major principles of New Urbanism are:

- All development should be in the form of compact, walkable neighborhoods and/or districts. Such places should have clearly defined centers and edges. The center should include a public space, such as a square, green or an important street intersection, and public buildings, such a library, church or community center, a transit stop and retail businesses.
- Neighborhoods and districts should be compact (typically no more than one-quarter mile from center to edge) and detailed to encourage pedestrian activity without excluding automobiles altogether. Streets should be laid out as interconnected networks (usually in grids or modified grid patterns), forming coherent blocks where building entrances front the street rather than parking lots. Public transit should connect neighborhoods to each other, and the surrounding region.
- A diverse mix of activities (living, shopping, learning, working and recreation, etc.) should occur in proximity. Also, a wide spectrum of housing options should enable people of a broad range of incomes, ages, and family types to live within a single neighborhood/district. Large developments featuring a single use or serving a single market segment should be avoided.
- Civic buildings, such as such as government offices, churches and libraries, should be sited in prominent locations. Open spaces, such as parks, playgrounds, squares, and greenbelts should be provided in convenient locations throughout a neighborhood.

Developers, planners, local government officials and citizens have all shown great interest in new urbanist design approaches, particularly in regions that are experiencing conflicts related to growth. Many see the New Urbanism as a win-win approach that enables a community's growth to be channeled into a physical form that is more compatible with the scale of existing neighborhoods, that discourages auto use, that is less costly to service and that is less consumptive of land and natural resources.

Adapted from: Katz, P. "New Urbanism" In Willem van Vliet (1998). *The Encyclopedia of Housing.* Thousand Oaks, CA: Sage Publication.

Celebration, in the Orlando region, was built in the Reedy Creek Improvement District, a quasi-municipal entity set up by the Disney Corporation decades earlier, mostly for the implementation of their legendary theme parks and supporting uses. Presumably the autonomy that Disney enjoyed within this district enabled a wider range of development options and an easier approval path than would exist in a more conventionally governed municipality.

Regulatory and Fiscal Challenges

These signature greenfield projects have all reached full build-out and for the most part look and function well. What's mostly unchanged, however, since those pioneering projects were first approved (and the principles in Box 24.1 were written) is a thorny issue that continues to hamper the progress of the New Urbanism movement: the larger regulatory framework (use-based zoning) that prevails in 99 percent of municipalities in the United States and Canada is inherently incompatible with New Urbanism. Because this regulatory framework is so ubiquitous, and because it permeates so many aspects of the development review process, municipalities struggle to deliver such models, even though their planning staffs, and in many cases their citizens prefer them. Worse yet, staff planners are largely unaware of zoning's problematic nature, and rarely consider alternative approaches, mostly because they lack the knowledge of such alternatives and the tools to implement them.

I learned this firsthand when working as a local government planner in three different parts of the United States—Southern California, Southwest Florida and the Washington, DC metropolitan region. From that experience, I now have a much better understanding of both the mechanics of use-based zoning and its operational characteristics. Ironically, my concern with this issue nowadays has less to do with its implications for the physical form of a community (that *was* my chief concern two decades ago) than it does with matters of financial performance.

The problem I'm referencing stems from a characteristic of use-based zoning that's hard-wired into the system. Because zoning focuses primarily on managing the *impacts* of development, and because the typical response to perceived conflicts during the approval process is to lower development densities/intensities to levels that are more "acceptable" to neighbors (thereby reducing the size and scope of a development), the overall economic return on investment (ROI) in the form of property taxes paid by new development to local governments suffers. Increasingly the inventory of properties that government relies on to pay its bills—the tax base—shifts from high-value, close in, compact downtowns and mixed-use neighborhoods that are thrifty in their use of municipal infrastructure and services to land-hungry, low density, and thus low-value sprawl that generates a weak ROI in relation to the costs that municipalities take on when they enable such places to be built.

During the boom years it was easy to ignore the problem. But in the lean times that have followed, such issues are of increasing importance to cash-strapped municipalities. Unlike pension fund obligations, a problem that a municipality can negotiate down to manageable levels in a bankruptcy proceeding, there is no relief for communities from the ongoing costs of maintaining and replacing infrastructure for low-density development.

Municipalities in some states levy impact fees to cover a portion of the up-front costs required for new development. But such fees, paid by developers, cover only capital costs; they are of little help years later when aging infrastructure must be repaired or replaced. With insufficient property-tax revenue to build up needed reserves, local governments resort to local assessments or increased taxes—neither of which are popular with voters.

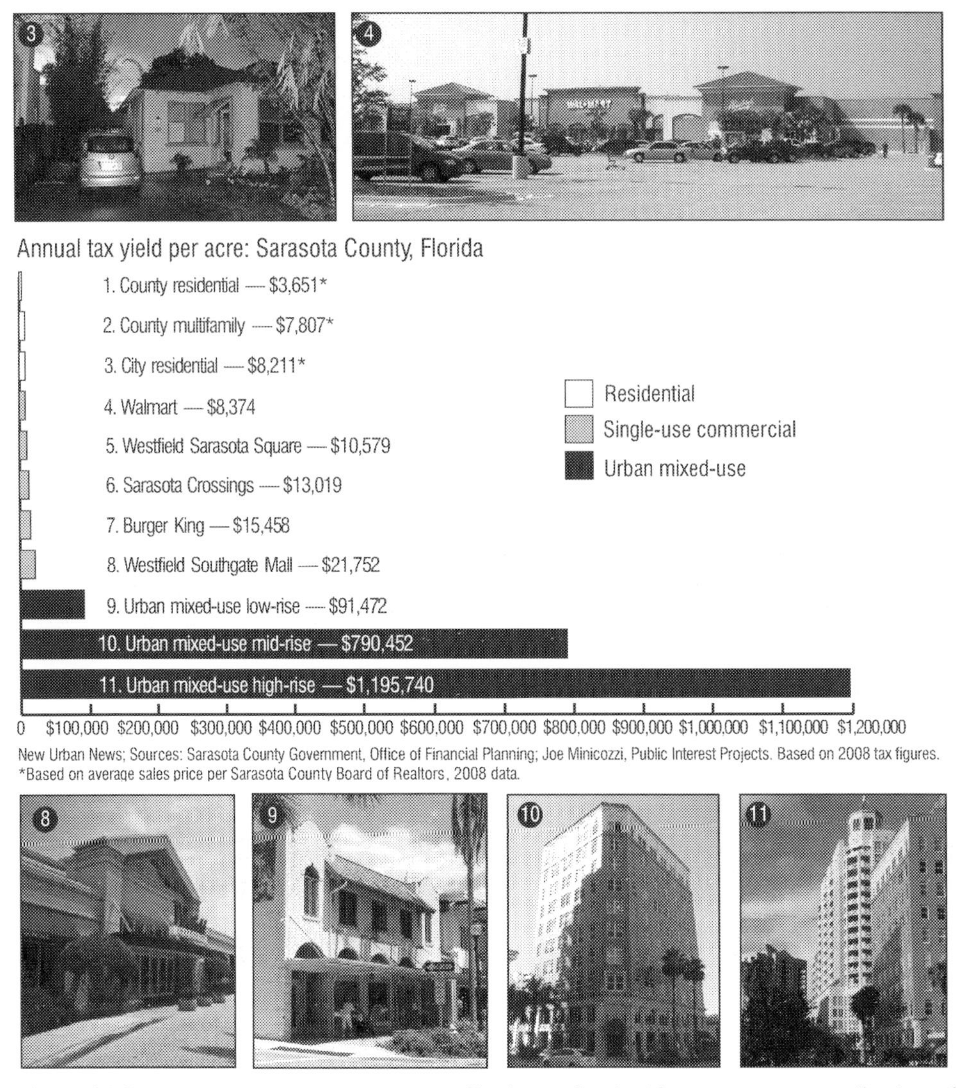

Figure 24.2 Sarasota County's revenue profile shows the significant revenue contribution of mixed-use downtown development (black bars at the bottom of the chart), versus that of other property types. Image provided courtesy of *Better Cities and Towns*

The larger issue is one that I've commented on at length (Katz, 2010) using a tax revenue study looking at the relative contribution of different building types in different locations across Sarasota County, Florida. It was conducted during my tenure in that municipality as Director of Smart Growth and Urban Planning. Among the findings: 1350 Main Street, a recently constructed mixed-use building (see #11 in Figure 24.2) in the City of Sarasota (a separate municipal entity), brought in 142 times more county property-tax revenue in 2008 than the county's newest big-box retail center (see #4 in Figure 24.2). If one combines the property taxes from that development with those of the strongest in-town shopping mall, Southgate (see #8 in Figure 24.2), together occupying 55 acres, the total revenue collected would still be

$350,000 less than the contribution (county *and* city taxes in this comparison) from 1350 Main, which sits on just over two-thirds of an acre.

When comparing a downtown mixed-use building and two suburban malls, an obvious question to ask is: What about sales taxes? It's true that a large, high-volume retailer *can* make a significant financial contribution to a town or city. That's why municipalities expend so much effort to lure strong retailers across town or city boundaries. But at the regional scale, such actions cancel each other out. And in the end, property taxes have a far greater impact on the local economy: Sarasota County's total retail sales from 2008, the year highlighted in the revenue study, brought in just $61 million in sales taxes while property taxes that year (county only) totaled $222 million.

If enhancing revenue is the goal, municipalities are far better off with compact mixed-use development that generates higher property taxes. A hypothetical grouping of 60 buildings like 1350 Main Street would easily fit in a 100-acre land area—about one-sixth of Sarasota's 600-acre downtown. That new development would bring in as much revenue as all of the sales tax collected in the county (per 2008 figures). And it would continue to do so in future years, taking a huge burden off the citizens of the county.

"The Missing Metric" (Katz, 2013), the lead article in a special issue of *Government Finance Review* provides further documentation of the Sarasota study and introduces the concept of a "fiscal impact quotient," a new metric that could be used in granting approvals so that revenue from a proposed development will be sufficient to cover costs of infrastructure and services provided by local government in support of that development.

It's a theoretical proposal, but with municipal budget problems making front-page news across the country, it is the kind of idea that local governments are considering as they look more carefully at the financial implications of the buildings they approve and the plans they adopt. Up until recently, many local government planners have assumed, somewhat naively, that the use-based policies that currently form the backbone of their development regulations, could be modified with a few simple text revisions or the addition of a "character ordinance" to foster great urban places that will also generate the revenue that municipalities need to maintain and expand current programs, services and infrastructure.

While on-the-ground experience is showing the folly of this thinking, little if anything is being done to address this blind spot and establish a regulatory framework to advance better results. Emerging approaches such as form-based codes, where they are successfully spliced into local zoning ordinances, *are* showing great promise, particularly at the neighborhood and district scale. Unfortunately such regulatory practices tend to be implemented in just a few development "hot spots" where the public is engaged and land values are high.

When one looks at the broad sweep of planning policy and regulation across the United States and Canada, there is little to suggest that we will be seeing fundamentally better outcomes any time soon. Worse still is the on-the-ground reality of the places that are currently being built, presumably in full compliance with existing municipal regulations. I am referring here to the thousands of administrative approvals that move through local government planning departments on a daily basis.

Because such actions do not require public hearings, and thus tend to fly beneath the radar, citizens do not notice them. But on a cumulative basis such routine approvals, in my opinion, do the greatest harm to our communities both because of their sheer number and because they're evaluated within a framework of older use-based zoning regulations that are hard-wired to induce sprawl.

The problem of outdated local plans and development ordinances has been on the new urbanist's radar screen for years. In the early years of the movement, leaders of the New

Urbanism frequently spoke of a return to "physical planning." They shunned the typical municipal planners' focus on policy, and use of regulations stated primarily in text that reference detailed listings of use categories. Their criticism—that such regulations failed to define a clear vision of what was being proposed and were far too abstract for most nonprofessionals to understand—was addressed by the more succinct and user-friendly form-based codes. As the name suggests, form-based coding seeks to regulate the *form* of the built environment. By contrast, conventional zoning primarily seeks to control land use and density, but is largely silent on matters of form beyond the most basic height, floor-area and setback limits for individual buildings.

The primary purpose of form-based codes is to shape a high quality public realm. They assign and calibrate a suite of standardized building types that can easily be configured into blocks that form a backdrop for streets, squares and other public spaces within the community. Public buildings such as churches, libraries and city halls typically enjoy special locations within the plan and also a special status. They are generally *not* coded, but instead are designed as special objects meant to stand out from the background fabric of private buildings. This hierarchical relationship, with private buildings in a support role and public buildings in a more special "foreground" role is well established in older cities.

The Tarrant County Courthouse in Fort Worth, Texas, a public building in a context that would be unremarkable in hundreds of other towns and cities across the United States, illustrates this point. An early photo (see Figure 24.3) shows the courthouse, situated on an oversized parcel at the foot of Main Street, towering over nearby buildings that were kept fairly consistent in terms of their form, either by the city's development regulations or simply as a result of planning norms in place when they were constructed. Since then, newer, larger buildings replaced older, smaller ones (see Figure 24.4). But because the courthouse is unique in its form and terminates an important street, a clear and understandable hierarchy remains. The courthouse retains a dominant role in that hierarchy even as surrounding buildings have come to dwarf it in size. This is just one way that a well-configured urban structure provides a high degree of visibility and "legibility" for important public buildings.

If the buildings along Main Street were more varied in their form, and thus able to significantly disrupt the streetscape, as some examples later in this chapter do, the courthouse would stand out less. Form-based codes, as their name implies, are able to regulate such matters, and because of their greater precision they're able to do so in ways that use-based zoning cannot. At the same time, form-based codes are more relaxed when it comes to matters of use. To municipal planners accustomed to a strict separation of public and private concerns, such a notion—that the form of private buildings would serve to "shape" the public realm—seems heretical. Some architects, too, bristle at form-based codes, but for a different reason: They resent the constraints on their creativity (more on this later).

In recent years, form-based codes have come to be regarded as the regulatory tool-of-choice for new urban planning and development. Their greater precision is an important reason why form-based coding has proven so successful when working at the scale of the neighborhood and district. Recently *Miami 21*, and Denver's new citywide form-based code have shown that the approach can also be used to address settlement patterns at the larger, metropolitan scale.

Figure 24.3 Tarrant County's 1895 courthouse towers over commercial buildings on Main Street in this historic photo of downtown Fort Worth

Figure 24.4 Today the courthouse is dwarfed by nearby buildings. Because of its unique form, however, and location terminating the vista at one end of Main Street, the courthouse retains a dominant role in the city's urban structure

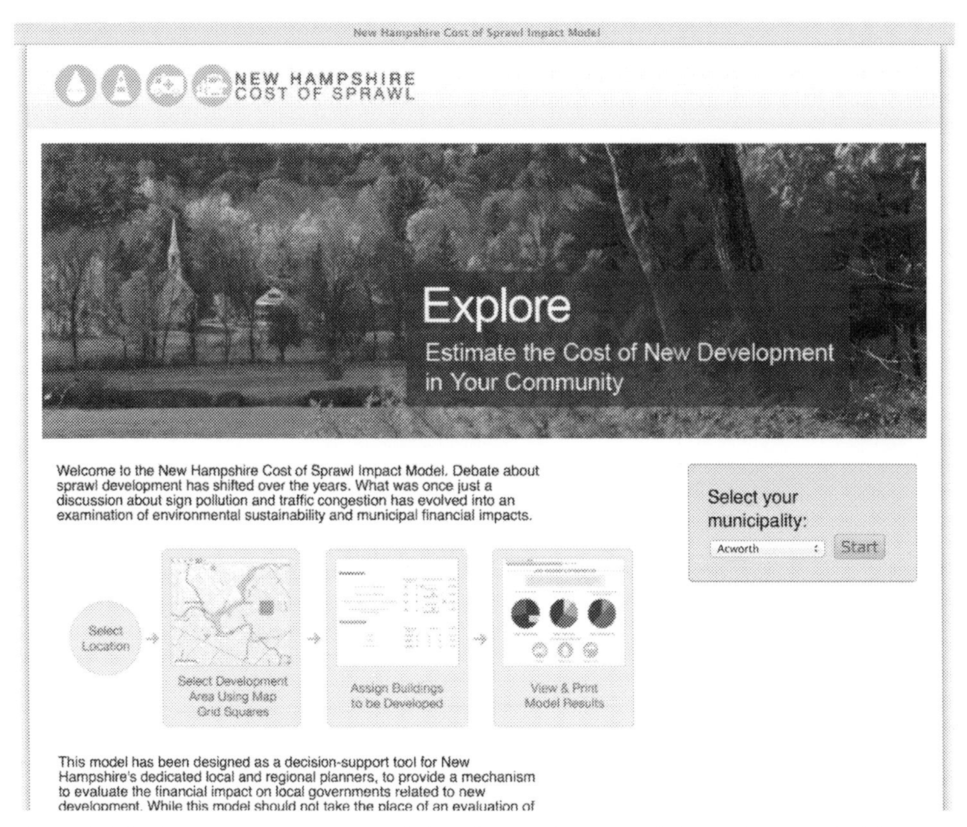

Figure 24.5 Opening screen, State of New Hampshire Cost of Sprawl Impact Model

Planning Meets Analysis

It is at these larger scales where some see great potential to apply the principles of the New Urbanism, coupled with form-based planning and more precise methods of data collection and analysis to achieve better performance in realms that go beyond that of urban form. For example, software that's used to compare scenarios at the regional scale (Envision Tomorrow, n.d.) for infrastructure costs and ROI is now being adapted to assess compliance with adopted policies when granting development approvals at the small-area plan and parcel scale. Another example is the State of New Hampshire's *Cost of Sprawl Impact Model*, an easy-to-use internet-based software tool (see Figure 24.5) that is accessible to the public (New Hampshire Cost of Sprawl, n.d.).

Users can select locations in the state by clicking 40-acre grid squares on a map, and then populate the site with a hypothetical building program. Options include a range of commercial and residential uses, and within the residential use category, a range of unit configurations (single-family, multi-family attached and detached, etc.). The program then analyzes the feasibility of the proposed build-out and provides specific estimates for the miles of roads, water and sewer that will be needed to serve the development along with estimates of the population of additional residents and school children that the development will serve. On the basis of this data, the program then predicts the anticipated municipal infrastructure costs compared with an estimate of the taxes that will be paid by the owners of the development.

The bottom line "score" for each proposal is expressed in dollars—the net loss or gain for the municipality. Personal experimentation with the program, which included a dozen hypothetical scenarios in various locations across the Granite State, yielded none that would generate a positive tax impact until the input parameters were modified to include only commercial uses in close-in urban areas.

Although the software tool is somewhat rudimentary, with results that lack the detail of a project-specific feasibility study, the simple fiscal impact models that it generates often make a strong case for the "no-build" scenario. This results from a phenomenon that's counterintuitive to many: Infrastructure costs tend to decrease at a lower rate than property taxes when the size and scope of a development is reduced. Indeed while a smaller development may need a smaller pipe for water service (Silver, 2014), it still requires a pipe to be installed, and often a new road as well (albeit one with fewer lanes). Local officials, who in the past might have pushed for the compromise of reduced size to allow a favored project to go forward, will be less inclined to do so when they see the actual revenue figures generated by the model.

A more refined version of the New Hampshire tool would stiffen the backs of elected officials who support planning policies in general terms but wilt if it means turning down a project submitted by an important constituent or one that promises "economic development." As in other realms of business and government, better data related to the economics of place brings the prospect of more transparent, accurate analysis and more objective decision-making to local government.

At the state level, fiscal performance evaluation of municipalities is becoming an ever-greater concern, especially in the wake of high-profile bankruptcies in cities such as Detroit, Michigan, and Stockton and San Bernardino in California. States including New York, Rhode Island, Washington and North Carolina have introduced fiscal "stress tests" in the hope of identifying communities at risk for default. By spotting financial problems early on, they hope that corrective action can be taken well before bankruptcy is imminent. Although these stress tests focus almost entirely on managing revenues that are *already* in civic coffers, more comprehensive approaches will look forward—at a community's long-range growth plan—to understand whether projected tax revenue will cover the cost of the infrastructure required to accommodate future development.

Though a prime determinant of fiscal outcomes, a community's physical form is not yet considered in such stress tests. It likely will be in the future software platforms that are more granular in their ability to evaluate data related to the physical layout of a community. Such platforms will be able to accurately project the anticipated cost of a comprehensive plan build-out by linking to records for existing properties that are comparable to what is being proposed. As greater computing power and more sophisticated GIS capabilities become available to local government, screening for fiscal performance should become commonplace. But whether the evaluation is at the scale of a single building or an entire district, the bottom line is based on a simple ratio between the costs incurred by a municipality for "horizontal" infrastructure—streets, water and sewer systems typically constructed or upgraded by local government in order to accommodate new development—and the "vertical" development generally constructed by the private sector that that will pay back government's initial and ongoing costs in the form of property taxes.

There is, of course, a long tradition of local government encouraging private sector investment with actions of its own ranging from the subdivision of land to the provision of streets, parks, public transportation systems and utilities. But in doing so, savvy municipalities knew that their ability to attract the "right kind" of development was key to future prosperity. Shaping the form of that development and limiting its geographic spread was also necessary to keep outlays from becoming excessive. Exercising such discipline would ensure that a virtuous cycle of growth and development could continue uninterrupted—a local government could afford to pay for needed infrastructure and services in the future and attract additional businesses, residents and associated investment as it grew.

In the suburban era this virtuous cycle turned into a vicious one when several important fundamentals changed. With the increasing role of federal and state funding for the construction of highways and large regional roads, a new, highly technical, modeling-driven approach to road funding emerged. This "dialing for dollars" approach—showing which road segments were failing or about to fail in their levels of service (LOS)—came to dominate the business of transportation planning. Regional plans became little more than elaborate order forms, used by municipalities to make their case to state and/or federal transportation agencies to fund favored projects. Amazingly, it is now taking a massive crisis at the federal level—the near depletion of the federal Highway Trust Fund—unfolding as this chapter is written, to shock communities into a better understanding of the true fundamentals of how planning at the local and regional levels shapes their economic destiny.

The problems that now exist at the federal level will, of course, have a huge impact on local government's ability to replace crumbling or obsolete infrastructure. The pain will be felt, not just in older urban areas served by aging roads and bridges, but also in suburban localities where newer infrastructure is stretched beyond capacity by recent waves of "drive till you qualify" houses nested cheek-by-jowl with a range of large-scale, single-use retail and commercial centers.

The strategies that communities employ to deal with fiscal stress will be far from uniform. Many suburban municipalities, wanting to avoid the impact of intensive development, will continue to opt for the low density, mostly residential land uses that created their problems in the first place. If such municipalities conducted a careful study, many would discover that their comprehensive plan actually forces them into a scenario where future property taxes will not come close to covering their plan's anticipated infrastructure costs. In many such areas, commercial revenues have been declining too, the result of a long-term shift in the economy from manufacturing to service businesses.

Other municipalities, particularly those that receive some portion of their revenue from sales tax, will seek to balance their books with automobile-oriented commercial development along arterials in outlying areas. But this strategy, too, is likely flawed. Per the Sarasota fiscal study cited earlier, property-tax revenue from such large-scale commercial development is unlikely to exceed that of single-family residences, and the associated infrastructure costs will certainly be far greater than what would be required for low-density residential uses.

Additionally, a major downside of reliance on sales-tax revenue is the distortion it brings to the physical form of a community. Municipalities encourage retail centers near their edges to gain customers from surrounding communities and also to offload some of the costs of road widening that such centers inevitably require. Although one community might gain advantage over its neighbors by following such a strategy, on a regional basis competition for retail dollars becomes a losing game. It's a loser for many reasons, but mostly because it fosters an automobile-dependent development pattern that creates a weak foundation for long-term growth.

By contrast, more forward-thinking municipalities, especially those that understand the shift to an information-based economy, are consciously laying the foundations for more innovative community models that enhance and revitalize existing under-utilized urban areas. One of the most exciting of these is the science and/or technology-related "innovation districts" (Katz & Wagner, 2014), which are often tied to universities or other institutional anchors. Such places are commonly built on the bones of once thriving downtowns or industrial districts that have been in decline for years.

By reusing existing streets, water and sewer capacity, innovation districts can save significant infrastructure costs. Such districts also foster a range of revenue enhancement opportunities: The physical clustering favored by knowledge workers and their employers is best supported by compact development patterns that are known to return high levels of property tax to the municipality. Other highly desired outcomes associated with such districts include high-paying jobs (and local income tax if levied by the municipality), patents secured by local businesses, and follow-on business activity including sales tax for purchases made in stores, meals consumed in restaurants, and so forth.

That this bouquet of economic benefits connected to "innovation" is taking place in cities—new and old—should be of no surprise to anyone schooled in the economic history of cities. Jane Jacobs made this point repeatedly in her prolific writings (Jacobs, 1961). More recently thought leaders such as Richard Florida and Edward Glaeser have presented research clarifying the link between the settlement patterns characteristic of innovation districts and higher levels of creativity and innovation.

The hard data related to economic performance of such places has proven critical in convincing municipal leaders to adopt policies that direct resources and staff effort toward the creation of physical places meant to nurture innovation. With such policies becoming the norm in larger, more urban municipalities, and increasingly a focus of attention in smaller, more suburban places, many professionals who have traditionally engaged in the craft of urban place-making—planners, economic development officials, engineers, developers, and builders, among them—are enthusiastically signing on to this new innovation-focused urban agenda.

The Architect's Dilemma

My own observation is that many architects—particularly those who work at the cutting edge of design—are increasingly out of step with a set of practices that has been shown to deliver optimal municipal performance within cities and to foster innovation in its wake. This is a serious disconnect for a profession that should be leading the process of reclaiming our cities.

Although architects often see themselves as champions of the city and as agents of urban innovation, or at least its image—in practice many seem unable or unwilling to subsume the form of their own buildings to the larger urban structure of the city. That structure, where buildings combine with other buildings to form blocks, where blocks combine with other blocks to form neighborhoods and districts; and where neighborhoods and districts ultimately combine to form towns, cities and regions, is at its essence, a fairly straightforward physical design proposition. It involves the arrangement of simple geometric forms in a way that is much like what a young child learns to do with a set of toy blocks.

But while the required skills may be basic, there are significant reasons why architects may be reluctant to subject their work to the discipline of the larger urban context. The first, a fairly obvious one, is the fact that architects are generally engaged by their clients to design an *individual* building. The second reason, tied closely to the first, is the way that architects confer recognition on their peers. Awards and media attention are also, for the most part, specific to an individual building. This, of course, is the scale at which the architect's contribution can be seen, photographed, published and evaluated by others, usually as a standalone object, free of context. That is, unless those who are considering the building—

journalists and jury members—choose to focus on matters of context, but in my experience, they rarely do.

The larger plan, if one exists, is usually taken as a given. The building will generally respect property boundaries and in denser urban areas be built out in a way that takes full advantage of the entire zoning "envelope." If a larger plan doesn't exist or is weakly enforced, or if the context is predominantly low-density fabric, the architect may have greater latitude with regard to the form of the building. But when an architect chooses to break with a strong urban plan—an act of hubris, in my opinion—he or she pits one's own creation against an urban framework that provides a range of salient benefits—social, economic and environmental—that are realized at the larger scale.

As I mentioned in this chapter's opening, the matter of architectural style has generated heated debate for years between adherents of the New Urbanism and some architects—hardcore Modernists, in particular, but also others who see themselves as more mainstream. Much of the conflict, in my opinion, is driven by an incorrect perception that new urbanists seek a wholesale return to historic styles. I don't believe this to be the case, although many of my more classically-oriented colleagues do seek such an outcome.

A comment frequently voiced by many on the Modernist side is that today's architecture "should be of its time" and "not mimic the forms of the past." Of course, such a statement presumes that look of today is necessarily a look of gleaming technical precision, like the product design of the smart devices in our pockets. It ignores the fact that the digital camera built into that device employs a shutter sound that is clearly derived from that of an old-style mechanical camera—a quaint sound that is clearly legible to our ear as a shutter, and somewhat different from all the more high-tech sounding beeps and chirps that the same device might emit in the course of a day.

It also ignores the fact that so many of the elements we associate with traditional buildings have deep roots in functionality. Gable roofs, for example, shed water using low-tech materials such as hand-split wood shakes far more effectively than would a flat roof using a high-tech waterproof membrane made from polymers that have been synthesized in the last 25 years. Front porches create a place where occupants of a building can comfortably communicate in conversational tones with passers-by; they are sheltered locations that respect the human proclivity to territoriality by clearly mediating between the private realm of the house and the public realm of the street and sidewalk. It works far better as a mechanism for advancing safety and security in a neighborhood than systems employing electronic intercoms or security cameras. The latter, clearly innovations that are "of our time" do have their uses, but are vulnerable when power systems fail, as they sometimes do in an emergency. And because such high-tech measures replace more direct, human interaction, something important is lost on a social level, as well.

So it often turns out that the simplest, low-tech elements, honed by trial and error and centuries of practice in building design and construction, work the best and prove to be the most reliable over time. That's why such elements tend to recur, and in so doing, impose a certain discipline on those who work in the realm of city making. For example, porches need a certain minimum depth to be usable and they don't work well when they front overly busy or loud streets. Gable roofs need a slope of a certain pitch to effectively shed water, etc.

Vincent Scully (Scully, 1994), the noted scholar and art historian comments on the desire of architects in the early years of the last century to escape any form of discipline or responsibility:

> The Modern architects of the International Style had largely taken abstract painting as their model, and they came to want to be as free from all constraints as those painters

> were, free from everything which had always shaped and limited architecture before, in part from statics itself (forms must float) and from roofs, windows, trim and so on, but most of all from the restraints of the urban situation as a whole: from the city, from the community.
>
> (Jacobs, 1961)

Although the early Modernists certainly realized much of the freedom they sought, the larger profession has, in the meantime, found itself increasingly marginalized. Today, with only a small percentage of the buildings in our communities designed by architects (most are by engineers or non-licensed building designers), one begins to wonder about the larger societal benefits that such freedom has brought. Yes, a handful of exuberant new museums or libraries designed by "starchitects" may dominate the pages of an architecture magazine's special issue on those building types. Such foreground buildings make for great photography, great coverage in the media, and even great postcard images for the cities in which they are situated.

But they don't easily combine with one another to form coherent blocks, neighborhoods, or cities. And while such buildings may sometimes be lauded by local officials as transformative because they bring outsiders and their money to a municipality, I would argue that what our cities need more are the basic background buildings that humbly provide for the functional needs of citizens without drawing undue attention to themselves. When configured into larger units, such buildings provide the backdrop for the standout buildings that today's architects most enjoy creating. More important they are the workhorse buildings that strengthen a community's tax base, per the Sarasota example.

Opportunities for architectural expression don't go away in this scenario—it's not a collectivist city of gray lookalike towers, nor is it the multicolor caricature of New Urbanism that was featured in *The Truman Show*, a movie starring Jim Carrey as the hapless star of a reality show about his own life set in the new urban resort community of Seaside. Rather such opportunities exist in real cities within a regulatory framework that balances architectural expression with the need to maintain *some* level of harmony, for reasons that are both functional and aesthetic. For example, the low-scale historic buildings fronting King Street in Charleston (see Figure 24.6) enable a continuous retail frontage that makes the street a pleasant and efficient place for shopping. Merchandise in store windows can be easily seen within an architectural context that some might call "organic," or even random. While the end result delights us with its range of expression, color, style and unique architectural features, its derivation was likely anything but haphazard. Indeed, the buildings, when constructed, probably hewed to fairly strict standards in terms of building height, width, alignment with neighbors, percentage of building skin that would be glazed versus solid, etc.

By contrast, more recent approaches to development in an urban context, such as New York's Citicorp Center (see Figure 24.7) built in the early 1980s, shows how even the most basic expectations of urban placemaking, such as a street wall next to a sidewalk cannot be presumed. Further underscoring that same point, Frank Gehry's more recent "Fred and Ginger," in Prague (also known as the dancing building; see Figure 24.8) shows why buildings in cities are typically compelled by ordinance to adopt common standards. The photo shows shadows cast by the Gehry structure blocking light from adjacent buildings at certain times of day, and views at all hours. The tangle of support columns branching out from the building has clearly encroached into the public right-of-way, redirecting the path of pedestrian movement into a narrow arcade. Such a strategy may bring tourists and tourism dollars, but ultimately it makes the place far less amenable for neighbors.

Figure 24.6 Buildings on King Street in Charleston, South Carolina, vary in terms of height, color, style and architectural details, yet they adhere to a common frontage line

Figure 24.7 Citicorp Center, in Manhattan, hovers above the sidewalk, creating a condition that some passersby find uncomfortable

Figure 24.8 Frank Gehry's "Ginger and Fred" in Prague encroaches into the sidewalk, forcing pedestrians to navigate through or around a thicket of structural columns

Other examples show where Modernist desires for freedom of expression at the building scale conflict with larger urban goals. The new transit-oriented community of Ørestad (see Figure 24.9) in the Copenhagen region addresses many smart growth priorities: It achieves fairly high densities with a wide range of uses and provides a generous allotment of parks and playgrounds for inhabitants. But it fails to integrate these components in a way that's truly urban. Buildings exist as individual projects; the uniqueness of each is reinforced by an architectural vocabulary that may span several buildings within a complex, but that "look" stops at the property line. Each complex creates its own context and in so doing requires a certain amount of "buffer" space around it before the next project begins. By contrast, mixed-use buildings in the Shirlington district of Arlington County, Virginia (see Figure 24.10), built during the same time period, combine easily into blocks and in so doing define normal streets that support a variety of functions including shopping, access to businesses, residences and institutions as well as socializing. Although transit service of the kind that serves Ørestad has yet to come to Shirlington, the district nevertheless achieves high levels of performance for the municipality.

Return on the county's infrastructure investment, of course, was and continues to be significant, with thousands of square feet of new commercial and residential space added to the tax base along with public buildings including a community theater and library, partly funded by the new development. But fiscal ROI is just one of the benefits that can result from a more efficient urban structure; here are a few others:

- At the *block scale*, they include energy savings that adjacent buildings enjoy when they snug up to each other across a common property line. Such a configuration also delivers

Figure 24.9 Housing (left) in the new precinct of Ørestad, near Copenhagen, achieves urban levels of density. Each group of dwellings, however, exists as a singular project, disconnected from the sidewalk and from each other. A high-rise hotel can be seen in the distance

Figure 24.10 Mixed-use buildings in the Shirlington district of Arlington, Virginia contribute to the making of coherent urban blocks and a main street that is a magnet for social activity and commerce

cost savings from the reduced need for elaborate exterior cladding on common walls, or from more efficient use of parking shared by a range of uses (housing at night, office during the day) at the center of a block. Operational and quality-of-life benefits can be achieved, too, when parking and service functions are located at the center of a block, versus placing them on a street frontage, where they deter pedestrian life.

- At the *neighborhood or district scale*, groupings of larger buildings in proximity enable the use of "district energy," a more cost-effective approach to heating and cooling of buildings than the provision of individual systems within each building. Mixed-use building configurations also offer the opportunity to live, work, shop and meet most of the needs of daily life without the use of a car, or even public transportation to move about, as we are required to do in the sprawl of suburbia.
- At the *regional scale*, more trip origins and destinations in proximity mean that a journey outside of one's neighborhood becomes an elective opportunity, rather than a required obligation. Transportation is a huge consumer of energy, so cutting down on one's daily travel may be the most achievable and cost-effective way to reduce a community's environmental footprint.

But to enjoy these benefits, the physical layout of the community must be urban—again, not in terms of population density, mix of uses, or size, or even in terms of what some might call "urban character," but by incorporating all of these components within a coherent physical structure of blocks and walkable streets. The high-design architect's near maniacal focus at the individual building scale misses much of the context that the New Urbanism has understood and addressed, for the most part successfully.

My sense is that the mainstream architectural profession is gaining a better sense of this context, but still remains unclear on the work to be performed. To be successful, in my opinion, architects need to relearn the craft of designing *background* buildings—what Andres Duany and Elizabeth Plater-Zyberk simply call "normal buildings." These are buildings that generally provide housing and/or workplaces and sometimes incorporate retail at the ground level. Most important, the form of such buildings enables them to combine easily to form coherent blocks. Such blocks, in turn, aggregate with one another to create functional neighborhoods and districts. These, in turn, join with other neighborhoods and districts to form towns, cities and regions that are robust, both economically and in terms of quality of life. In many of the great cities of the world, such as Copenhagen (where I vacationed recently), one can find whole neighborhoods and districts composed of such normal buildings, usually constructed from 1890 to 1930 (see Figure 24.11), but some are more recent (see Figure 24.12). While documenting examples for this chapter in Copenhagen, it was difficult to find one *best* street or group of buildings to photograph. But in seeking such an image, I was reminded that the individual buildings that combine to make up such places are, for the most part, unremarkable. Many are very good, but few are truly exceptional. Again, as background buildings, their primary job is to function as part of the fabric of the neighborhood; a job that many have quietly excelled at for decades and sometimes centuries.

Their architecture is one of "variations on a theme"; larger patterns repeat from building to building, but there is considerable uniqueness in the details of each. In whole cloth, however, as a resident would experience them, the groupings of buildings perform brilliantly in meeting one's daily needs. Such buildings provide a diversity of uses in proximity, they accommodate the density needed to support transit, retail and a vital civic life, and they do all these things while delivering a remarkably high quality of life.

Figure 24.11 Buildings built in the 1890–1920s comprise much of the "fabric" of well-loved and highly functional neighborhoods in many world cities. This street is in one of the close-in neighborhoods of Copenhagen

Figure 24.12 A recently constructed building in an outlying district of Copenhagen shows that similar urban fabric can be created anew. Although the corner tower represents a clear nod to tradition, the rest of the building is fairly neutral terms of architectural style

Most telling, the places described in the previous paragraph have remained relevant both regionally and at the global scale for hundreds of years, despite huge changes in the world around them—a marked contrast to the fragmented urbanism one finds in the failed municipalities mentioned at the start of this chapter. Although it's impossible to know whether the physical configuration was a cause of their success, or merely associated with it, my sense is that places like the close-in Copenhagen neighborhood described have achieved success, at least in part, because success was baked into the community's DNA when it was laid out and the first buildings were designed and constructed.

Although I see little evidence to justify optimism based on the last 50 years of architectural practice—what I've experienced in my own lifetime—my hope is that architects will one day relearn the craft of city making. Doing so, however, will require them to move beyond the current theatrics of style to design buildings that combine with one another to form cities that are habitable, safe, sustainable and prosperous enough to meet the needs of a broad cross section of citizens. Given the diminishing resources of a finite planet, such a turnaround among architects may well be required if their profession, and indeed our entire species, is to survive.

References

Envision Tomorrow (n.d.). *Envision Tomorrow: A Suite of Urban and Regional Planning Tools*. Retrieved October 8, 2014 from: http://www.envisiontomorrow.org/.

Jacobs, J. (1961). *Death and Life of Great American Cities*. New York: Random House.

Katz, P. (2010, December). Sarasota's smart growth dividend: Doing the numbers proves that compact, centrally located, mixed-use development yields the most property taxes. *Planning*, 76, 10, 26–29.

Katz, P. (2013). The missing metric. *Government Finance Review*, 29, 4, 20–32.

Katz, B., & Wagner, J. (2014). *The Rise of Innovation Districts: A New Geography of Innovation in America*. Washington, DC. The Brookings Institution.

New Hampshire Cost of Sprawl (n.d.). *Explore: Estimate the Cost of New Development in Your Community*. Retrieved October 8, 2014 from: http://www.costofsprawl.org/.

Scully, V. (1994). The architecture of community. In P. Katz, *The New Urbanism: Toward an Architecture of Community*, New York: McGraw-Hill.

Silver, M. (2014, March). Metaphor regarding the "size of the pipe." Comment at: New Urbanism in Local Government Initiative Workshop.

Part VI

Architectural Design and Practicing the Profession

The overall tenor of this part expands on the agency of design triggering processes and strategies, which include interaction of various stakeholders involved in architecture as a profession, and refers to the kind of actions which instigate interactive practical processes, and emerging practice models. This part will also expand on the legal dimensions, risks and understanding of the novel formulations, and processes, which objectivize architecture by appreciating realms and ethical responsibilities of practicing with design as a tool.

25

Role of Building Information Modeling in Green Architecture

Phillip G. Bernstein and Aniruddha Deodhar

Sustainable Buildings Crucial to Addressing Critical Environmental Imperatives

The sizable environmental footprint of buildings is now well understood and widely documented. Globally, buildings account for 32 percent of total final energy use, 30 percent of energy-related CO_2, and a third of fluorinated gases (Intergovernmental Panel for Climate Change, Fifth Assessment, 2014). Buildings are also projected to become the fastest growing sector for energy use (U.S. Energy Information Administration, 2013) and therefore the largest emitter of energy-related greenhouse gas. In the United States buildings don't fare much better, where they consume close to 40 percent of total energy, 68 percent of electricity, 12 percent of total water (U.S. Environmental Protection Agency, n.d.c and 60 percent of raw materials during their construction (U.S. Environmental Protection Agency, n.d.c), while creating almost 40 percent of the nation's total carbon dioxide emissions and 26 percent of non-industrial waste (U.S. Environmental Protection Agency, 2009). It's clear that improving building performance is imperative to reducing the dramatic human impact on the environment.

It may also be one of the most cost effective methods of doing so. Amory Lovins proclaimed in the 1990s that a "negawatt" (a term for the amount of energy that never needs to be consumed and hence produced) is far cheaper than an actual watt of energy that needs to be produced, transmitted and distributed to a building (Lovins, 1990). Although a sustainable building may cost a little more upfront to design and construct, integrating cost and environmental strategies at project inception might well reduce the price tag (World Green Building Council, PRP, Skanska, Grosvenor Group, Abu Dhabi Urban Planning Council, 2013). Moreover, these initial investments could pay big dividends over the building's lifetime, and not just in the reduced use of resources. In some studies, sustainable buildings have been shown to outperform traditional buildings financially by offering higher rental and occupancy rates and net operating incomes (Institute for Building Efficiency, an initiative of Johnson Controls, 2012) and ultimately higher resale values (Institute for Market Transformation and Appraisal Institute, 2013). Sustainable buildings also create numerous qualitative benefits such as better brand equity, improved aesthetics, increased productivity, comfort, health and well-being of the occupants (Whole Building Design Guide, a program of the National Institute of Building Sciences, 2012a, 2012b), reduced absenteeism and better talent attraction and retention. Thus buildings that perform sustainably may be not only good for the planet, but also profitable to their owners and inspiring to their occupants. Designing such high-performance buildings will require a different approach by their architects, who must take the long view of the problem at hand and seek to optimize the buildings' design, construction as well as operations for minimal environmental impact.

The mission statement of the US Green Building Council, the leading organization promoting green buildings through its LEED certification, frames the challenge beautifully: "To transform the way buildings and communities are designed, built and operated, enabling an environmentally and socially responsible, healthy, and prosperous environment that improves the quality of life" (U.S. Green Building Council, n.d.a). In this chapter we address the question of how the architect can use digital technology, particularly building information modeling, to achieve this lofty goal.

BIM for Sustainable Design and Building Operation

Building Information Modeling (BIM) is a set of digital processes that support the design, documentation, construction and operation of a building, based on information-rich three-dimensional (3D) models. Unlike the methods of computer-aided drafting (CAD), which merely substituted analog techniques for creating drawings with electronic methods, BIM provides a designer or builder with a 3D digital prototype of the design at full scale and with embedded building attributes and performance characteristics that allow that model to be examined, tested, simulated, optimized and visualized using computerized algorithms.

BIM supports the efficient design, construction and operation of buildings by providing:

1 Transparency of design information by describing the building in 3D in an easily-understood and coherent way that is accessible to the entire design and construction team.
2 A lifecycle view of the project that gives an understanding of the design during its development and construction, and provides a basis for simulation of the eventual behavior of the building during operation.
3 A platform for integrated design and construction processes where the entire design team can participate, collaborate and share the rewards of delivering sustainable design outcomes.
4 A single point of truth for multiple disciplines, where the model can be a common vehicle for consolidating various building performance data—energy and water use, mechanical, electrical and plumbing (MEP) systems, lifecycle analyses of building materials, renewable energy potential, measured data, building management data and asset data.

The potential implications of BIM for sustainable buildings are profound. A 2010 survey by McGraw Hill Construction, concluded that BIM was used on over 50 percent of green retrofit projects and 76 percent of respondents felt that BIM was necessary to achieve their sustainability goals (McGraw Hill Construction, 2010). A BIM-based methodology could accelerate sustainable design and construction and improve the performance of a building in several important ways.

Box 25.1 Case Study: Shanghai Tower

The Shanghai Tower is a 121-story, 632 meter tall glass tower, the largest skyscraper in China as well as one of the most sustainable, according to a 2012 Customer Success Story developed by Autodesk with the help of Gensler and Shanghai Tower Construction & Development Company, titled "Rising to New heights with BIM." The customer story further discusses numerous unique sustainability features such as a double-skinned façade that minimizes heat gain and the spiral shape that maximizes daylighting and views, reduces wind loads and facilitates rainwater recovery. The building reduced energy and water consumption as well as the amount of construction material through the use of BIM-based analysis such as whole building energy analysis and structural analysis. According to the customer story, BIM was also helpful in improving construction efficiency.

According to another case study in McGraw Hill Construction's 2010 GreenBIM SmartMarket Report, modeling the complex structure with BIM streamlined the process between designers and consultants and made it less costly, smoother and faster. The report states that the owners who planned to achieve both LEED® Gold rating and China Three Star rating also planned to use BIM post-occupancy for ongoing facility operations and maintenance and property management.

1 *A better understanding of design and performance criteria for better results*: BIM, as an *intelligent* model, not only incorporates the building's geometry but also information about its structure (e.g. window, wall material, type of construction and insulation), operations (building systems and schedules), building science and additional data (weather, metered consumption or sensor data). These information-rich models enable the team to interact with a common building representation and use its embedded intelligence to evaluate multiple design alternatives, optimize resources, and better predict performance. The inclusion of performance parameters—chunks of data about building geometry, dimensions, relationships or materials—allow the designers to generate and evaluate multiple scenarios that integrate the effects of numerous design decisions, understand their relationships, and create alternatives that can be selected based on measured, optimized results.

   Traditionally, the architect and the engineer have worked in silos and often on different representations of a building. This gave rise to coordination failures between the two camps as "handing off" the BIM caused loss of fidelity and increase in error rate. The result is that client's don't really trust models to accurately predict results. The Rocky Mountain Institute (RMI) found "lack of credibility" to be the biggest barrier to building energy modeling (Rocky Mountain Institute, 2011). Recent advancements (such as those discussed later in this chapter) have made for more streamlined analyses that promise to drastically reduce this friction and make analyses, which used to be the domain of a handful of experts (another barrier cited by the RMI report), available and accessible to everyone.

2 *Early feedback to reduce time and cost:* The digital representation of a building based on BIM can be used for analysis (such as whole-building energy, carbon and water consumption simulation), optimization, error detection and visualization *prior to* construction, giving designers and builders the opportunity to isolate and improve green characteristics of the building in ways never possible with simple drawings and static analysis. Today BIM has been most widely used during the detailed design and construction phases for the production of detailed technical analysis and drawings. But BIM-based conceptual modeling, massing and analysis, generative algorithms and visual programming, are now

possible thereby giving the project team BIM-supported sustainable design strategies in early design.

3 *More efficient construction:* A building designed in BIM can be properly coordinated in three dimensions, eliminating costly wasted material and time that results from clashes and interferences that are common in a building constructed from typical 2D drawings. The model is also a platform for simulating construction, allowing the project team to optimize the build process itself and find the most efficient use of labor and equipment before setting foot on the job site. While builders today are beginning to embrace BIM for these purposes, there are challenges found primarily in the hand-off between architectural and engineering models—which are created to describe the design intent of a project, how it should be configured upon completion—and a construction model, which requires much greater detail and specific descriptions of not just the building itself but the process by which it is made. As model-based design and construction becomes typical for projects, these barriers will begin to fall.
4 *Perpetual dividends through the building's lifecycle:* sustainable design, while necessary, is not sufficient for delivering a sustainable building. Once the building is complete the information that comes from actual performance measurements could be combined with the BIM to allow the building to be run as it was designed while constantly tuning its actual, operating systems like heating or lighting. While such use of BIM is at its early stages today, the eventual connection of design and construction models and facility management software used to monitor and manage the operation of a building is not far away and will likely be a service offered by architects or builders of the future.

Tools and Technologies that Enable BIM-based Sustainable Design

Today's computing environment is rapidly changing from almost complete dependence on desktop computers to mobile devices connected to the cloud that can deliver any digital information anywhere to almost anyone at any time. Such changes are occurring in three broad categories: cloud computation that makes computing power and storage unlimited; small, powerful, internet-connected mobile devices with high-resolution displays that allow very detailed BIM information to be delivered and used in the studio, on the job site or in an operating building; and high-bandwidth internet connectivity through wireless and other transmitters that connects the cloud and all devices with these devices. In the realm of BIM-enabled sustainable design, these technologies in concert create some interesting opportunities for innovation.

Technologies that enable BIM and sustainable design and operations can be classified into four broad categories of use—representation, evaluation, realization and collaboration.

Technologies for representation enable designers and builders create the basic models, drawings and other key data necessary to design and construct a building, and include tools like drafting software, modeling tools and even spreadsheets and word processors. Representation tools are the central instruments needed to really describe the design. CAD and BIM are the most important such tools for architects in this category.

An interesting trend here is that of reality capture (a term used for capturing the analog reality directly into digital form). "3D pictures" of context and existing built conditions can be integrated into design models for simulation, analysis and visualization through the use of laser scanners, sensors, high end mobile technologies, smart devices, wearable computers, robots or unmanned aerial vehicles (also known as "drones") that capture massing amounts of information which can then be processed by sophisticated reality capture software.

Figure 25.1 BIM showing various aspects of a hospital—exterior, glazing, MEP and structure. Source: Autodesk

Technologies for evaluation simulate, analyze and optimize the building's performance based on digital models and related data. The almost infinite computational power of the cloud makes sophisticated analysis such as computational fluid dynamics, whole-building energy analysis, climate studies and seawater rise simulation possible and cost effective. Before the cloud became ubiquitous and cost effective, such studies required special consultants and large numbers of sophisticated, powerful computers and software to complete but these capabilities are now much more available to architects and engineers in their daily work.

As model-based design evolves in the era of the cloud, using digital technologies to simulate entire building systems and context will become the norm, allowing designers to understand and optimize them in relation to one another. Decisions about material selection will have implications, for example, on energy use, construction installation approach, even embedded carbon, and the relationship of those decisions, in context, will be more apparent to the designer. This is the future of "big data" in sustainable design. Other approaches that incorporate massive information collected about human behavior, usage patterns—anything that can be recorded and analyzed—will feed insight about the best sustainable approaches.

Technologies for realization convert the digital descriptions of a design to physical form, or capture high-resolution digital models of existing physical conditions for use during design. These tools operate on the boundary between the virtual and the real. Some examples and their implications for sustainable design might include robotic construction and 3D printing.

Digital models can generate precise geospatial information and instructions to a robot designed to perform construction tasks. Some early experiments in the use of lightweight drones to build simple structures are an early hint of much larger scale robotic construction strategies derived from the digital design process. Machine-assisted construction will be more precise and energy efficient and marshal the use of resources on the project site effectively, important characteristics of green construction.

Additive construction, prefabrication or even 3D printing is also possible by creating production instructions from BIM. While the environmental impact of these trends hasn't been rigorously evaluated at the time of this writing, their potential to reduce cost, construction time and construction waste, improve worker health, and reduce energy and raw material looks promising. An even more fascinating trend is that today's smaller consumer-scale device printing is giving way to 3D printing at building scale.

Technologies for collaboration include tools that capture, manage and share the digital information used by building teams to accomplish their work, and range from simple transactional messaging like email and texting, to social networking, mobile data transmission, and sophisticated data management systems. These technologies are evolving rapidly and ultimately will enable designers to manage and deploy the enormous array of data sources (for example, weather reference, material or embodied energy) necessary for successful sustainable design to occur. Collaboration technologies based on social media and cloud computing will bring "big data" capabilities to the design and construction process.

BIM-based Sustainable Design Across a Building's Development Cycle

A critical difference between drawing-based and BIM-based design processes is the ability to allow the architect to understand the project across its entire lifecycle. It is important for the architect to manage the design implications of sustainability at a proper level of detail as the project design develops over time. Like the design itself, the fidelity of information that comprises the design represented by BIM increases as the design is refined and resolved from concept and overall strategy through detailed information necessary for construction.

- *Feasibility/conceptual design* is where the overall characteristics of the project—its size, general configuration, siting and program are refined should include preliminary analyses of key sustainable design features such as solar orientation, footprint and site coverage. Conceptual building information models can help the architect investigate each of these parameters and create basic approaches that will be developed as the design unfolds.
- *Schematic design* is where plan configuration, enclosure strategy and systems selection begins and where sustainable design means a model-based evaluation of the relationship between the inside and the outside of the project. An excellent example of such a study would be the evaluation of a façade design and its relative level of transparency as it affects daylighting, lighting loads and solar gain. Such analyses are easily prepared in a BIM-based environment.
- *Design development* is where systems are designed and integrated into the project in detail and selection of key materials, mechanical/electrical/plumbing distribution and subsystems (such as air handlers or transformers) are made. This is the time to study and understand the detailed implications of the building design itself. Complex physical and analytical models of building elements and systems, supported by materials databases, complete the picture of the building performance and give the architect her last best chance to optimize building performance before construction.
- *Construction documents* are where final detailed documentation of the design intent is completed prior to construction and when the architect must confirm that all sustainable design strategies and their implementation are properly defined, detailed and coordinated as instructions to the contractor. The integrated view provided by BIM supports proper coordination to the issuing of construction documents.

Construction

While most of the architects' work focuses on the run-up to construction, BIM allows the architect to use digital modeling and analyses to predict, during design, both the construction strategy for the building and its eventual performance post-occupancy. Green construction implications, for example, might include the choice of renewable or recycled materials, building configurations that minimize the need to move earth and disrupt the surface of the site, or even selection of types of systems (concrete, steel or wood) that are more efficient, use less waste during installation, or require less carbon-producing heavy equipment like earth movers, concrete trucks or other diesel-powered engines.

Operations

The models created during a BIM-based design are a simulation—a test bed—for the eventual *in situ* performance of the building itself. That simulation, as described earlier, can be used both for the performance optimization in the development of the design as best choices for sustainability are incorporated into the design, and as the digital "operating template" for the building when it is in use, including operating parameters of mechanical systems, expectations for when daylighting versus natural light is best, or for proper control of air movement, temperature and humidity. Modern green buildings are operated with sophisticated digital control systems, and the parameters that emerge from a BIM-based design process can set the stage for proper use of such systems as predicted and required by the originating design.

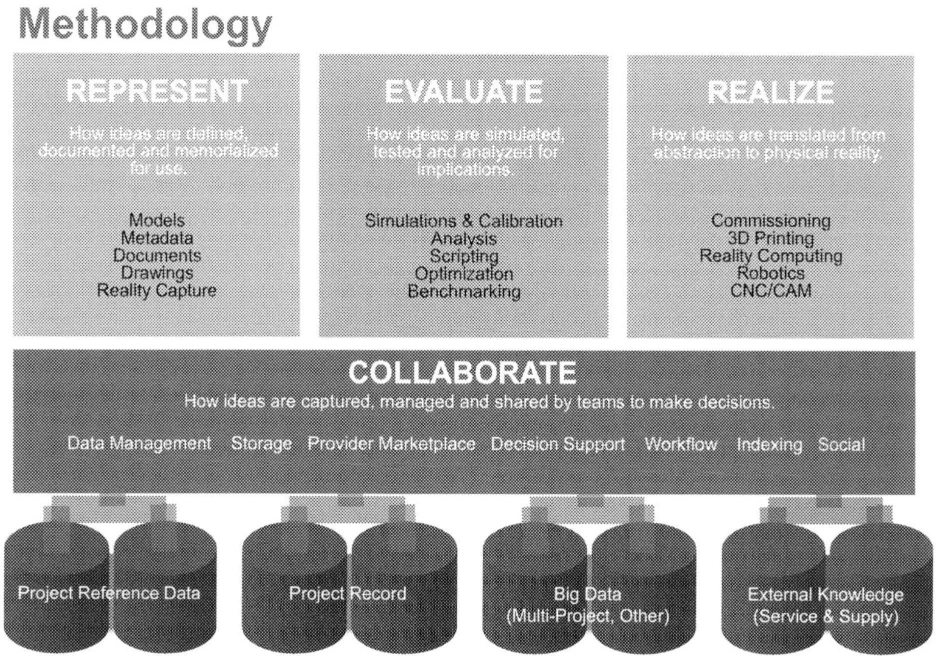

Figure 25.2 Taxonomy of technologies that enable BIM-based sustainable design. Source: Autodesk

BIM-based Sustainable Design Processes

Architects have traditionally focused on the Asset Rating D1 (see definitions of asset ratings in Box 25.4) during the design phase of a building project, a method of certifying the sustainable characteristics of the design rather than the finished building. But 80 percent of greenhouse gases attributable to a building are emitted during its operation (United Nations Environmental Programme: Sustainable Buildings and Climate Initiative, 2009). Many architects and owners are distressed to discover that these supposedly high-performance buildings fail to meet their expected performance, and often fail miserably, using much more energy and water and creating more greenhouse gases than predicted during design.

These failures destroy confidence in green building and certification authorities like the U.S. Green Building Council are starting to take notice. The recent launch of the "dynamic" LEED plaque, for example, not only certifies the building's design as green but also measures the building's ongoing real-time performance (U.S. Green Building Council, n.d.b). So architects now need to change the frame of reference of design and also consider the building's Operational Rating D2 that measures its actual behavior after opening.

And while building operations account for the bulk of its environmental footprint, the implications of the choice of materials—glass, stone, concrete, steel—may take decades to nullify if not chosen carefully. The architect must, therefore, optimize the building's Embodied Rating D3—a measure of the embodied carbon in the building materials themselves—which may comprise the majority of their environmental impact, particularly once buildings become more and more efficient (and in the case of energy, strive towards Zero Net Energy D4).

One way to optimize these environmental ratings through BIM is by connecting three processes in the design process itself: Modeling, Measuring and Managing. Used in concert these processes can optimize all resources (like energy, water, land and materials) and while they are equally applicable at all projects scales (from buildings to cities), the discussion below focuses specifically on building energy as the best example of sustainable design strategy and result.

Modeling

Building information modeling predicts how a building *should* perform, i.e. its potential Asset Rating which is dependent on the building's inherent characteristics that are defined and resolved during design. BIM-based analysis often gives rise to design alternatives that recommend specific design modifications (such as improving the envelope through wall insulation, upgrading windows or adding daylighting controls, or manipulating the building's siting or shading configuration relative to the movement of the sun). Modeling, coupled with Lifecycle assessment (LCA) tools that analyze the effects of materials over time, can help uncover the building's Embodied Rating.

Measuring

The building's day-to-day performance is, however, measured through utility meters, sensors (such as those measuring occupancy, temperature, humidity, CO_2, motion or daylight) and smart thermostats. These measurements and related analysis help calculate the building's Operational Rating. The data helps further revise and refine the BIM and the gap between modeled and measured performance yields useful insights for improving building operations and subsequent designs by the architect. Measures stemming from this approach might include revising operating hours of the building, fixing a damper or changing the temperature set points on thermostats.

Managing

Finally, integrated strategic building performance management in the future will require not only understanding the building's potential (calculated via modeling) and actual performance (obtained via measuring) but also applying controls and project specific information (such as available financing or occupant behavior) to better manage it. The intelligent model that first helped the architect during design and then the contractor during construction could then be used to optimize the building's operations by integrating BIM with electronic building management system (BMS), computer-aided facility management (CAFM), Asset management (AM), Energy management systems (EMS) and numerous other tools and technologies that help the owner with the day-to-day operations of the building. This fledgling research area promises to see more development and market validation in the near future. But the idea of "managing" stems from operational measurements that help operators learn about and eventually optimize building performance, and the baseline expectations that performances are created during design using BIM. Since the architect is responsible for generating the original BIM, her roles and obligations continue deep into building operations accordingly.

A high-performance building needs all three processes in what might be called a "virtuous cycle of activity." The three processes are intertwined because they work in concert to help optimize the operation of the building. For example, you might create the model that you use as a baseline, measure the results of energy conservation measures, continually manage your building's energy footprint and go back and update your model and run the cycle again. Every iteration yields a more effective model that is calibrated to ground conditions and

Figure 25.3 Rendering of various BIM fidelities at architectural, engineering and construction phases. Source: Autodesk

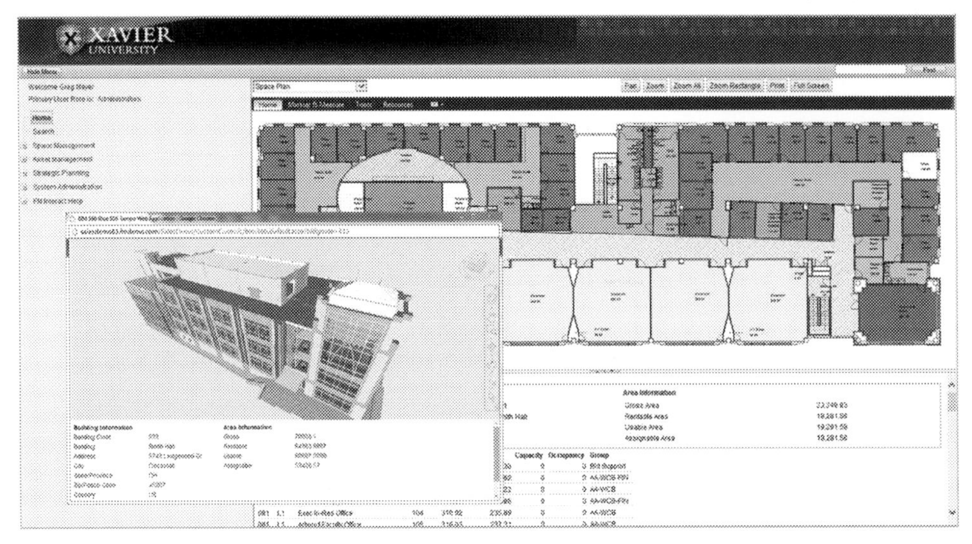

Figure 25.4 BIM-based space planning and utilization. Image courtesy of Xavier University and FM:Systems

that in turn guides the analyses while adjusting building controls. A base of knowledge that provides real insight is the result.

There are significant financial implications of such an approach that the architect should consider at the outset of design. The Appraisal Foundation, in a nod to the increasing market adoption of green building practices, recommended that appraisers learn energy modeling, integrated design process, Net-Zero energy and green building certifications in order to better appraise green buildings (The Appraisal Foundation, 2014) and architects could support such approaches.

To achieve a high-performance building, the architect's role will shift from a "design generator" to that of "master collaborator." Integrated approaches to design and project delivery will be key to realizing aggressive sustainability targets. The architect's ability to synthesize the data streaming from an iterative, multidisciplinary process is of growing importance within the profession. Tomorrow's architect, as the subject matter expert in BIM, will likely be sought by teams who would want to reap dividends from the original BIM investment in perpetuity.

BIM-based Sustainable Design across Project Scales

At the time of this writing, BIM is mostly used by architects to design buildings. But a responsible sustainable design will need to be optimized at a range of scales because every building exists in the overall context of its global ecosystem, city, neighborhood and particular site, particular construction systems, materials and details, as well as processes of construction and, after opening, its operation. Model-based sustainable design can address and connect green strategies at each of these scales assuring explicit and, hopefully, optimal results.

Digital modeling tools are now capable of prototyping the various systems that comprise a building and thereby allowing the architect, engineer or builder to reason about the implications of that design at each scale. Geospatial models describing the city and neighborhood of the project provide information about an increasing number of factors that converge to affect the

Box 25.2 **Case Study: NREL Energy Systems Integration Facility**

The Energy Systems Integration Facility, a 182, 500 square-foot $135 million building on the US Department of Energy's National Renewable Energy Laboratory campus in Golden, CO includes a number of energy saving strategies (such as reuse of waste energy, natural ventilation and daylighting with high efficiency lighting) and achieved LEED® Gold rating, per a case study in McGraw Hill Construction's "Business Value of BIM in North America, 2012" report. According to the case study, the contractor JE Dunn Construction and designer SmithGroupJJR used BIM to meet NREL's strict energy requirements by developing a complex energy model extracted from BIM and leveraging extensive embedded BIM data, to build "one of the most energy efficient data centers in the world."

design, such as weather patterns, biological assets, air movement and traffic. On the site itself, digital models can depict—and allow the architect to manipulate—land form and contours, wind, hardscape, the movement of water, deployment of landscape and vegetation, and even movement of vehicles. Each of these elements impacts the environmental footprint of the project before the building itself is designed, and hence, should have an explicit relationship to the building design itself.

At smaller scales like equipment and building materials or hardware and mechanical components, modeling is also useful. A computational fluid dynamics simulation, for example, can indicate how air might flow through a diffuser, while a product model analysis using mechanical engineering modeling tools can indicate embedded carbon or use of highly impactful materials. By shifting the frame of reference to things that are at a much smaller scale, such as the flashing around a door, the frame of a window, the choice of a specific air diffuser, the architect can understand sustainable implications at fairly low levels of detail and combine various models to synthesize a broad view of the performance if her design can as

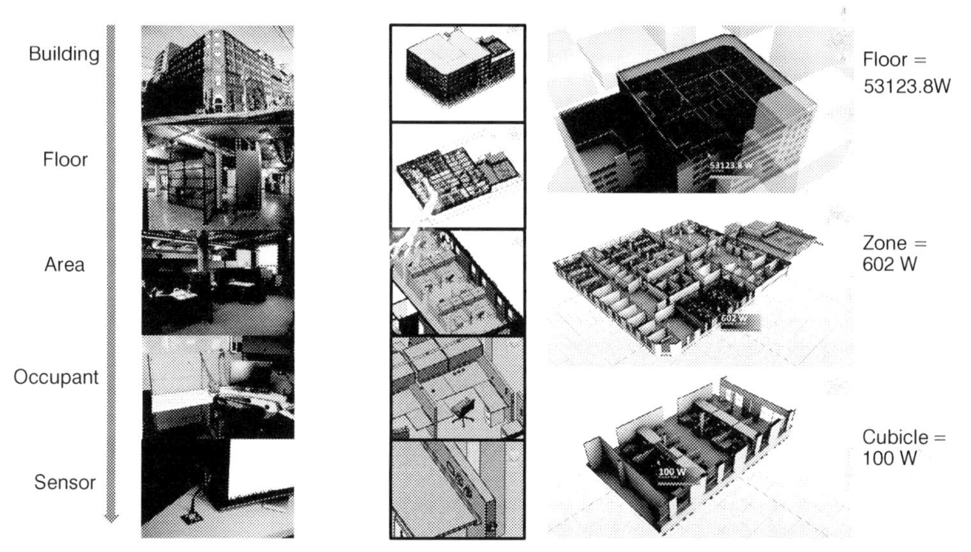

Figure 25.5 BIM use and energy consumption calculation at various project scopes—from building to floor to cubicle to even a cubicle level. Source: Autodesk

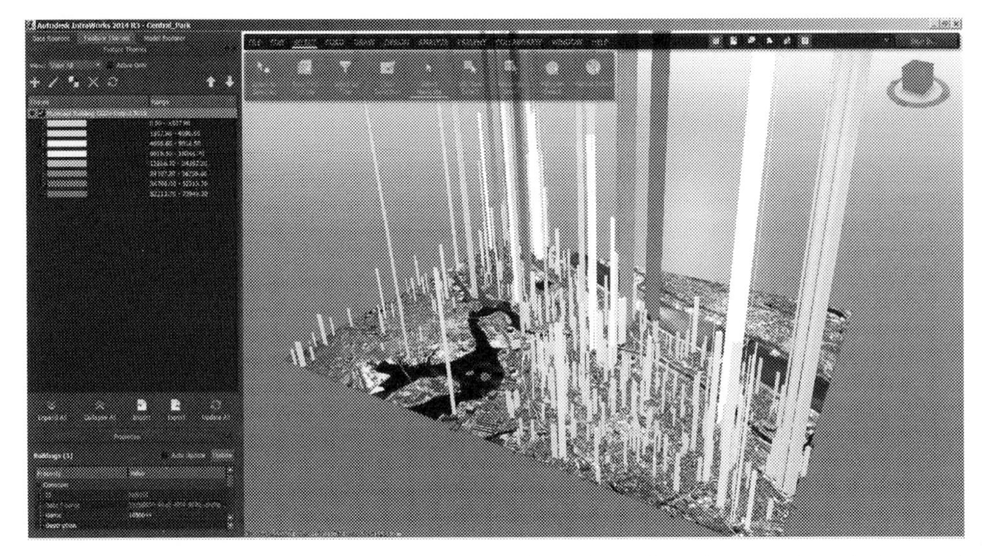

Figure 25.6 Leading cities are now able to track and visualize their GHG emissions and energy and water consumption. Illustrated here is a proof of concept model of the New York Central Park area, with municipal buildings being extruded according to the total amount (in Metric tons of CO_2 equivalent) of greenhouse gases they emitted during 2010–2011. The model was built using publically available data from NYC's Open Data website. Image courtesy of Autodesk

a result empower the architect to predict, control and optimize her project's relationship to the environment.

While BIM has been traditionally used for buildings, there is now a growing adoption of BIM for "non-vertical" construction. A 2012 McGraw Hill's Smart Market Report "Business Value of BIM for Infrastructure" found that almost half (46 percent) of the infrastructure organizations surveyed were using BIM for their infrastructure projects, up from just 27 percent in 2010, since they found that BIM helped reduce conflicts and changes and improve quality thereby lowering the risk and increasing the predictability of outcomes (McGraw Hill Construction, 2012). We expect this trend to continue as a number of technologies apply the principles of BIM and BIM-based analysis (such as parametric design, transparency of information and lifecycle project view) on a larger city scale.

Green Building Codes, Standards and Certifications

Modern building is governed by various codes and standards that assure that projects conform to performance standards deemed necessary by society. Early examples of such requirements are life safety codes that were established to assure the buildings were safe for occupancy and created to assure that occupants were protected during fires and earthquakes. These standards create a common understanding amongst building practitioners about performance criteria, measurement, data structures and approval rules to assure sustainable objectives are met. BIM-based design strategies are an excellent method for creating and understanding the information necessary for such approaches.

As sustainable performance is increasingly understood to be a fundamental characteristic of building, numerous green building codes, standards and certifications are emerging. Legislation is further accelerating requirements for green building. Architects must be well-versed in these regulations and the stringent requirements they establish for building performance. Generally speaking, such requirements fall into several categories:

- *Building Codes* are typically a set of rules, specifications and municipal ordinances and legislations that establish minimum standards to which local buildings must adhere. These include, as examples, the International Green Construction Code (IGCC) (International Code Council, n.d.), a regulatory framework for new and existing buildings, establishing green requirements and sustainability measures for the entire project from design through construction, certificate of occupancy and beyond, Title 24 and CalGreen (California Green Building Standards Code) (Department of General Services, n.d.) that contain the regulations that govern the construction of buildings in California and were touted as the United States' "first green building code" (Department of Housing and Community Development, 2010), and ASHRAE 189.1 (ASHRAE, n.d.), a popular compliance standard for design of high-performance buildings which covers their impact on site sustainability, water usage, energy consumption, indoor environmental quality, materials and resources and also has guidelines for sustainable construction and operation.
- *Green Building Certifications and Ratings* are voluntary ratings and certifications that signify a building's environmental performance or evaluate its various environmental ratings and include Leadership in Energy and Environmental Design (LEED) (United States Green Building Council, n.d.b), a leading voluntary green building certification standard based on specific categories of green building design, construction and operational performance; Green Globes (Green Globes, n.d.), another online green building rating and certification tool primarily used in North America; BREEAM (BREEAM, n.d.) a leading design and assessment method for sustainable buildings popular in Europe; the U.S. Environmental Protection Agency's Energy Star (U.S. Environmental Protection Agency, n.d.a); and the United Kingdom's Energy Performance Certificate (Chartered Institute of Building Services Engineers, n.d).
- *Legislation* in various countries such as the Executive Order 13423 (US) (The White House, 2007) that requires federal agencies to adopt aggressive sustainability goals such as 30 percent reduction in energy intensity and greenhouse gas emissions by 2015; Energy Independence and Security Act (US) (Energy.gov: Office of Energy Efficiency and Renewable Energy, n.d.) that established energy management goals and requirements for federal buildings; and Europe's 20-20-20 targets (European Commission: Climate Action, n.d.), a set of binding legislations that by 2020 aim to reduce greenhouse gas emissions by 20 percent and increase energy efficiency energy from renewable sources by 20 percent.
- *International Energy Efficiency* Standards such as the ISO 50001 (International Organization for Standardization, n.d.) are voluntary international standards that provide a framework for organizations to establish systems and processes necessary to improve energy performance and reduce energy cost, greenhouse gas emissions and other environmental impacts, through systematic management of energy.
- *Data Interoperability Standards* seek to resolve incompatibility and interconnectivity issues between various data and information models as well as to create a common language for meta-data and results and reports. These include the Industry Foundation Classes

Box 25.3 **Case Study: NASA Sustainability Base**

The National Aeronautics and Space Administration (NASA) Sustainability Base is a 50,000 square-foot, $20.6 million research building, touted to be the federal system's greenest facilities. According to a 2010 Customer Success Story by Autodesk, AECOM Technical Services, William McDonough and Partners and Swinerton, titled "Communicate across Barriers," the Sustainability Base was designed to surpass LEED® Platinum standards and approach net-zero energy consumption. The case study also discusses numerous sustainability features such as a unique steel-frame exoskeleton that increases structural performance during seismic events, adaptive building control systems to reduce energy consumption through real-time data, geothermal wells, natural ventilation, high-performance wastewater treatment, reduced potable water consumption and a photovoltaic roof, which will provide 30 percent of the building's power. According to that case study, the team used BIM to evaluate design alternatives and sustainability strategies, perform energy analysis and clash detection, online coordination, reducing material costs and construction time.

(IFC) (BuildingSmart, International home of open BIM, n.d.) an open ISO standard that describes building and construction data in BIM; Green Building XML (gbXML, n.d.) an open standard that specifically helps convert BIM data to energy analysis; and Construction Operations Building Information Exchange (COBie) (Whole Building Design Guide, a program of the National Institute of Building Sciences, n.d.) a data structure for BIM-based asset information with a focus on construction and operational data.

Future of Building Information Modeling

The evolution of building information modeling and associated technologies will continue to enhance the architect's ability to create a sustainable building. As modeling and analysis software becomes more robust (with higher resolution information), more aspects of the design process will become digitized and with them more options for computer-based green design, construction and building operation will become available. More comprehensive models of integrated systems will replace models that today rely exclusively on geometry and meta-data to create abstractions of designed buildings. These model representations will be deeply connected to analysis and simulation software that delivers insight to the architect at the point of a decision, and will be augmented by algorithms that seek answers to computable problems, leaving more time for the designer to focus on the non-computable. The logic of construction will be embedded in models themselves, allowing the constructed implications of the design to be apparent as it is developed. Data flows from technical databases that describe deep characteristics about materials and assemblies are immediately accessible to the designer and integrated into the in-line simulation process. Green building certifications will be evaluated by software and provided, along with full building code compliance analysis and "pre-construction" building inspection, within the architect's design environment.

But like any innovation, BIM and sustainable design face challenges. Standards evolve slowly in a building industry that lacks effective mechanisms for finding consensus on new ways of working. Competition between software vendors to create best practices is fierce making choices of tools and data standards a challenge for architects. Differing standards and regulations that are constantly evolving means technologies have to race to catch up.

Box 25.4 **Definitions of Asset Ratings**

D1: Asset Rating determines the inherent environmental quality of a building based on its design, structure and construction, its location and orientation, and installed systems. The UK Chartered Institution of Building Service Engineers defines Asset Rating as the "design" rating of a building reflected by the CO_2 emissions of a building's design features on an A to G scale. Per the Massachusetts Department of Energy Resources (MA DOER), this metric does not depend on the building's occupancy, tenant behavior or operating schedule, and is often used for financial valuations, appraisals and sale or lease transactions. At the time of this writing, a number of Asset Rating tools are being developed, such as the US Department of Energy's Commercial Building Asset Rating, MA DOER and Northeast Energy Efficiency Partnership (NEEP)'s Building Asset Rating and the UK's Energy Performance Certificate. Asset Rating is also often gauged through proxies such as LEED®, Green Globe and other green building certifications that emphasize design performance.

D2: Operational Rating measures the operational characteristics of a building that are affected by the building's operating schedule, occupant behavior, system performance and equipment and lighting loads. The UK Department for Communities and Local Government defines it as a numeric indicator of the amount of energy consumed during the occupation of the building over a period of 12 months, based on meter readings. It is measured by tools such as the US Environmental Protection Agency (EPA)'s Energy STAR, American Society of Heating and Air-Conditioning Engineers (ASHRAE)'s Building Energy Quotient (be) and the UK's Display Energy Certificates (DEC) or by measuring building performance through sensors, meters, and building management systems.

D3: Embodied Rating (as defined by the authors) measures an asset's embodied attributes such as energy, carbon and water as well as performing lifecycle analyses (LCA) of material used in a building's construction that determines their renewability and recyclability and potential for acidification, eutrophication, global warming, ozone depletion and smog-forming. We foresee a gradual convergence of LCA and BIM in the future.

D4: Zero Net Energy Buildings per the New Buildings Institute (NBI) are buildings with greatly reduced energy loads such that, averaged over a year, 100 percent of the building's energy use can be met with onsite renewable energy technologies.

D5: Integrated Project Delivery defined by the American Institute of Architects (AIA) is a project delivery approach that integrates people, systems, business structures and practices into a process that collaboratively harnesses the talents and insights of all participants to optimize project results, increase value to the owner, reduce waste, and maximize efficiency through all phases of design, fabrication, and construction.

And the real drivers of building—which are fundamentally financial—are just now aligning with social expectations for sustainable design to establish the obligations of the architect to provide it.

Digital technology has empowered designers in new and unexpected ways over the past three decades, and with advent of cloud, mobile and social computing there is reason to expect that this trajectory will continue to empower future architects to incorporate the philosophy and principles of sustainable design into all facets of the practice.

References

Appraisal Foundation, The (2014). *Valuation of Green Buildings: Background and Core Competency: Second Exposure Draft.*

ASHRAE (n.d.). *Standard 189.1.* Retrieved on May 1, 2014 from https://www.ashrae.org/resources--publications/bookstore/standard-189-1.

BREEAM (n.d.). *The World's Leading Design and Assessment Method for Sustainable Buildings.* Retrieved on May 1, 2014 from http://www.breeam.org/.

BuildingSmart, International home of open BIM (n.d.). *Industry Foundation Classes (IFC) Data model.* Retrieved on May 1, 2014 from http://www.buildingsmart.org/standards/ifc.

Chartered Institute of Building Services Engineers (n.d.). *Energy Performance Certificates and Asset Rating.* Retrieved on May 1, 2014 from http://www.cibseenergycentre.co.uk/epc-and-the-assest-rating.html.

Department of General Services (n.d.). *Title 24 Overview.* Retrieved on May 1, 2014 from http://www.dgs.ca.gov/dsa/Programs/progCodes/title24.aspx.

Department of Housing and Community Development (2010). *The California Department of Housing and Community Development Commends the Adoption of the Nation's First Green Building Code.* Retrieved on May 1, 2014 from http://www.hcd.ca.gov/news/release/GreenBuildingCodes11310.pdf.

Energy.gov: Office of Energy Efficiency & Renewable Energy (n.d.). *Energy Independence and Security Act.* Retrieved on May 1, 2014 from http://energy.gov/eere/femp/energy-independence-and-security-act.

European Commission: Climate Action (n.d.). *The 2020 Climate and Energy Package.* Retrieved on May 1, 2014 from http://ec.europa.eu/clima/policies/package/index_en.htm.

gbXML.org (n.d.). *gbXML Open Green Building XML Schema: a Building Information Modeling Solution for our Green World.* Retrieved on May 1, 2014 from http://www.gbxml.org/.

Green Globes (n.d.). *The Practical Building Rating System.* Retrieved on May 1, 2014 from http://www.greenglobes.com/home.asp.

Institute for Building Efficiency, an Initiative of Johnson Controls (2012). *Assessing the Value of Green Buildings.* http://www.institutebe.com/InstituteBE/media/Library/Resources/Green percent20Buildings/Green-Building-Valuation-Fact-Sheet.pdf.

Institute for Market Transformation and Appraisal Institute (2013). *Green Building and Property Value: A Primer for Building Owners and Developers.* https://www.appraisalinstitute.org/assets/1/7/Green-Building-and-Property-Value.pdf.

Intergovernmental Panel for Climate Change, Fifth Assessment (2014). *Climate Change 2014: Working Group III Mitigation of Climate Change.* Chapter 9 Buildings. https://www.ipcc.ch/report/ar5/wg3/

International Code Council (n.d.). *International Green Construction Code.* Retrieved on May 1, 2014 from http://www.iccsafe.org/CS/IGCC/Pages/default.aspx.

International Organization for Standardization (ISO) (n.d.). *ISO 50001—Energy Management.* Retrieved on May 1, 2014 from http://www.iso.org/iso/home/standards/management-standards/iso50001.htm.

Lovins, A.B (1990). The Negawatt Revolution. *Across the Board,* XXVII, 9, 18-23.

McGraw Hill Construction (2010). *Green BIM: How Building Information Modeling is Contributing to Green Design and Construction.* Available from: https://construction.com/market_research/FreeReport/GreenBIM/.

McGraw Hill Construction (2012). *Business Value of BIM for Infrastructure: Addressing America's Infrastructure Challenges through Technology and Collaboration.* Available from: http://download.autodesk.com/us/bim_infra/Business_Value_of_BIM_for_Infrastructure_SMR_2012.pdf.

Rocky Mountain Institute (2011). *Collaborate and Capitalize: Post-Report from the BEM Innovation Summit.* http://rmi.org/Content/Files/BEM_Report_FINAL.pdf.

United Green Building Council (n.d.). *Leadership in Energy and Environmental Design.* Retrieved on May 1, 2014 from www.usgbc.org/leed.

United Nations Environmental Programme: Sustainable Buildings & Climate Initiative. (2009). *Buildings and Climate Change: Summary for Decision Makers*. Retrieved on May 1, 2014 from http://www.unep.org/sbci/pdfs/sbci-bccsummary.pdf.

U.S. Energy Information Administration (2013). *International Energy Outlook 2013: Building Sector Energy Consumption*. http://www.eia.gov/forecasts/ieo/buildings.cfm.

U.S. Environmental Protection Agency (n.d.a). *ENERGY STAR*. Retrieved on May 1, 2014 from https://www.energystar.gov/.

U.S. Environmental Protection Agency. (n.d.b). *Green Building: Frequent Questions*. Retrieved on May 1, 2014 from http://www.epa.gov/greenbuilding/pubs/faqs.htm.

U.S. Environmental Protection Ag:ency. (n.d.c). *Green Building, Choosing Green Materials and Products*. http://www.epa.gov/greenhomes/SmarterMaterialChoices.htm.

U.S. Environmental Protection Agency (2009). *Buildings and their Impact on the Environment: A Statistical Summary*. http://www.epa.gov/greenbuilding/pubs/gbstats.pdf.

U.S. Green Building Council. (n.d.a). *USGBC's Mission*. Retrieved on May 1, 2014 from: www.usgbc.org/about.

U.S. Green Building Council (n.d.b). *LEED Dynamic Plaque*. Retrieved on May 1, 2014 from http://www.leedon.io/

White House, The (2007). *Federal Register: Presidential Documents,* Vol. 72, No. 17.

Whole Building Design Guide, a program of the National Institute of Building Sciences. (n.d.). *Construction Operations Building Information Exchange (COBie).* Retrieved on May 1, 2014 from http://www.wbdg.org/resources/cobie.php.

Whole Building Design Guide, a program of the National Institute of Building Sciences (2012a). *Aesthetics*. http://www.wbdg.org/design/aesthetics.php.

Whole Building Design Guide, a program of the National Institute of Building Sciences (2012b). *Productive*. http://www.wbdg.org/design/productive.php.

World Green Building Council, PRP, Skanska, Grosvenor Group, Abu Dhabi Urban Planning Council (2013). *The Business Case for Green Building: A Review of the Costs and Benefits for Developers, Investors and Occupants*. http://www.worldgbc.org/files/1513/6608/0674/Business_Case_For_Green_Building_Report_WEB_2013-04-11.pdf.

26

Discipline of Architecture versus the Profession

Specialization in Architecture Education and Practice

David E. Miller

Where We Stand as a Profession

The architectural profession is in flux, perhaps even in danger of coming to an end. These concerns are based on many factors in play today—both in society in general, and within the architecture community itself. The profession is challenged by a rapidly changing world due largely to the pressures of powerful global economic forces and the complexities of unsustainable patterns of growth. Over the last several hundred years, architects' influence in the design and construction process has steadily declined. In this Late Modern Age, or "Third Industrial Revolution"—when it is no longer possible to easily move along a pre-determined groove, the complexities of a highly fluid society, fueled by rapidly developing Internet technology—multiple issues both confound the design process and the long-standing tenants of contemporary architecture. The failure of the profession to keep up with the evolving world of the design and construction industry, that is bent on accelerating the process of project delivery, is challenging the core competency of architects to integrate a diverse range of parameters and hyper complexities affecting the performance of buildings—and at a larger scale, the responsiveness of urban communities and the multiple networks that govern commerce and infrastructure.

Coupled with the challenges of the profession are the challenges of the educational programs in schools of architecture. With the rapid changes in the design and construction process questions are asked about the relevancy of our educational models in architecture and whether the emphasis on the discipline of architecture verses more specialized areas is a relevant approach. The search for well-founded, reliable knowledge is what a discipline is about. Schools aim to provide the intellectual instruments by which architecture is advanced with the design studio as the primary instrument or system of the production of knowledge in academic departments of architecture. Unfortunately, in today's mass media environment, schools only provide a fraction of the discourse on design and the intellectual, technical, social scholarship for advancing the knowledge base. Professional and pop-culture journals, on the prowl for star architects' bold gestures and bent on hyperbole, are attracting young impressionable minds toward misguided and elitist architecture. Today the discourse is fueled more by the field of culture than through academic channels.

The dynamic nature of the Internet driven world and the complex set of economic, political and technical parameters within the architectural profession, particularly with large-scale projects, raise questions about how we educate students in schools of architecture to ensure the next generation of architects is fully prepared to practice effectively in the twenty-first century. And given the vast range of issues facing society and the profession—transportation, health, safety, land use, energy, affordable housing and sustainability—have designers convinced constituents, community leaders and the general public that architects can successfully tackle these challenges?

Inevitably, the grand challenges facing contemporary global societies have moved the architectural profession toward the development of specialized expertise as an answer to these complex issues. Now there are architectural specialists in many areas of practice, including but not limited to: sustainability and LEED (Leadership in Energy and Environmental Design) consulting, envelope performance design, curtain wall design, acoustics, economic feasibility analysis, value engineering, project management/owner's representation consulting. The list goes on and on. But is specialization the right path and the correct instrument in which to tackle the human problems posed by twenty-first-century challenges? The interrelated, yet sometimes competing, parameters that come into play with composing building solutions dictates better project management tools and greater technical expertise. As buildings are more complicated than ever to construct, they require more resources to build and operate, which means escalating costs and production challenges. To better manage resources and process efficiencies, more effective tools and information systems are needed to manage the design and construction process.

Historically, each distinct design period required a constituent language or regulating structure. The governing language of design from the Renaissance through neo-classical times was a set of compositional orders. In the modern period it was the tenets of functional order espoused in the United States mostly by Gropius and Mies. The aim of practice in architecture has been comprehensibility—to interpret problems through the clarity of organization. But now—in the Late Modern period—rules are less defined and organizational methodologies are less precise. For architecture to operate effectively in the modern digital age, a new language or regulating structure needs to be formed, as the language of the digital technician is quickly becoming the default language of this era. Regulatory structures, i.e., land use codes, building codes, LEED, today are essentially our information management tools, not the idealized geometrical or mathematical constructs of classical and early modern architecture. Communication tools in digital form enable designers to conceive and understand details before they are produced, assuming the organizational framework to use these tools effectively. More often than not, the leaders of the profession are unable to stay ahead of these new tools, and to guide their development toward integrated strategies of practice.

Today—creating integrated strategies of practice that bring together the vast assemblage of components and energies that form buildings is a Herculean task. Fragmentation seems to be the path that many designers and project teams have taken, resulting in specialization of the various elements of buildings.

From Specialization to Integration

The case for specialization can be compelling, as breaking a problem into identifiable systems with distinct components and operating systems is often quite effective. Understanding and dealing with all of the forces that play into the creation of a building can be challenging; therefore, looking at a structure from a specific perspective can be useful. Certainly training architects to tackle specific components with manageable parameters within more broad headings of site, climate, energy, structure, materials and construction technologies can be effective—particularly in advancing knowledge around these systems. Research efforts—traditionally those funded to university labs but increasingly through advanced practice efforts in architectural firms—have led to significant advances in knowledge around distinct discipline areas, system technologies, materials or individual building components.

Within the building industry, examples of specialized areas of design that have led to significant advances in building systems and even performance are: energy harvesting technologies, water stewardship and management strategies and material science—to name a few. In the arena of energy harvesting, photovoltaic panel development has made great strides toward more efficient conversion of solar gain to electrical power. These advances enable buildings in climates previously ignored for solar projects to gain favor and perform with reasonable payback. Regarding water stewardship, exciting advances in living machines have the potential to take much of the pressure off of taxed wastewater infrastructures. Many new material products are coming on line every day—and traditional materials are becoming more versatile while operating with enhanced performance. An important feature of materials that have seen significant advance is in the area of ductility, with better ability to deform plastically under loads without breaking. The construction industry is becoming increasingly supportive of research in materials and building systems that have higher performance impacts on the built environment. As an example, many of the engineered wood products which are becoming standards in the industry were developed in the Wood Materials and Engineering Laboratory at Washington State University. This long-standing industry-sponsored laboratory is an excellent example of collaborative research efforts between material scientists, structural engineers and architecture professors working with materials and assemblies.

The architectural profession and schools of architecture have increasingly been moving toward specialization. Currently, in academia, the areas of focus are classified fairly broadly; sustainability; design computing or representation; parametric design; fabrication technologies; and preservation and adaptive reuse. Schools are re-structuring to provide advanced post-professional degrees in an array of concentrations, including Master of Science degrees and non-accredited one-year masters degrees. Many of these degrees are highly specialized within broader framed areas. For instance we see degrees in natural daylighting, specialized structures (fabric and suspension systems), materials and components, building envelopes, design and health, biomimicry, etc.

Many of these degree programs are closely tied to research labs in architecture schools. Following the model found in the science disciplines, professors are able to leverage their areas of specialization into lab-based funded research. The development of new research areas has positive impacts on the field of architecture, and are extremely promising for the advancement of knowledge among schools of architecture and within the architectural profession. Now—more than ever—architecture is a collaborative undertaking. Holding more promise, in an age of collaboration and inter-disciplinarity, is the partnering between academic research units and design professionals, along with manufacturers and suppliers.

These partnering endeavors strengthen specialized skills and new knowledge acquisition, thereby advancing design integration and higher quality construction.

A current focus area that is rapidly developing partnering capabilities with great potential is in the field of digital fabrication technologies. Design practices, which are integrated with fabrication research and the building industry, offer new models for the way buildings are conceived and constructed. Architecture schools with state-of-the-art fabrication laboratories are developing highly sophisticated production capabilities for the fabrication of building components and systems. These computer-aided fabrication programs also offer even more specialized areas of concentration in computational software development, manufacturing technologies and material production. An increasing number of architecture schools offer Master of Science degrees in fabrication technologies, many of which include sophisticated field research laboratories. In addition to the highly touted project delivery methodologies developing from these programs, new alliances are also forming between schools and firms in the profession of architecture. Fabrication labs are testing and producing project-based prototypical components and building assemblies for design firms that don't have the in-house capability to produce these elements.

Sustainability is another arena of research and collaboration between architecture schools and the profession. The overall concepts of sustainability are quite broad and are no longer considered an area of specialization within the profession of architecture; but, rather an increasingly mainstream-integrated aspect of the design process. At this point in time, most schools of architecture no longer segregate sustainability into an isolated set of courses woven into all facets of studio teaching and supporting coursework. Many schools offer a Master of Science degree in sustainability in which motivated students that have particular interests within the field of sustainable architecture can investigate specific design practices and conduct independent research.

These areas of specialized focus within the profession and schools are clearly needed and serve to advance knowledge. However, all the elements of architecture are interconnected and require understanding the inter-relatedness of all aspects of building technology at all scales. Addressing these elements through systems thinking is highly important. Seeing the big picture while understanding the individual elements and their interconnectivity is what should be emphasized in education. Problem solving with system-thinking skills will help future architects to practice effectively in the twenty-first century. Seeing systems whole requires more than being "interdisciplinary," if that word means, as it usually does, putting together people from different disciplines and letting them talk past each other (Meadows, 2008). Interdisciplinary communication works only if there is a real problem to be solved, and if the representatives from the various disciplines are more committed to solving the problem than to being academically correct. They will have to go into learning mode. They will have to admit ignorance and be willing to be taught, by each other and by the system. It can be done. It's very exciting when it happens (Meadows, 2008).

Connecting Education and Practice

In thinking about how to advance collaborative design methods, conduct research and educate students to be better prepared for practicing architecture today, it is useful to look at how different schools are integrating design education and direct project experience into team-based comprehensive programs. Many schools are working hard to break away from a disciplinary monoculture to engage students in design thinking and workshop techniques for investigating and addressing larger problems in actual client social, economic and spatial needs. For instance, a large number of architecture schools have community design assistance studios and labs serving under-represented or under-serviced segments of society.

The University of Washington offers a one-year post-professional degree in High Performance Building Design. This degree program targets professional architects or graduates with a degree from an accredited school, who wish to expand their integrated design skills within the fields of sustainable technology and energy performance. Instructors for the program include both University of Washington Department of Architecture faculty and individuals from Seattle-area architecture and engineering firms. Course work is closely tied to research conducted in the UW Integrated Design Lab (IDL) housed in the recently completed Bullitt Foundation building, a targeted net-zero energy "Living Building" located in downtown Seattle.

The Integrated Design Lab in the College of Built Environments at the University of Washington is a self-supported research and integrated building design industry service center that supports the development of high-performance commercial and institutional building design including lighting, daylighting strategies and energy infrastructure. Funding partners include: The Northwest Energy Efficiency Alliance's Better Bricks Initiative, the Northwest utilities, the United States Department of Energy, the National Science Foundation and the New Building's Institute.

The IDL is the final link in the life-long learning chain of state-of-the-art professional education resources offered by the College of Built Environments to regional professional constituencies, alumni and traditional students. The IDL explores increasing building value at no extra project cost to the owner. The goal of IDL research, design and education support is to produce buildings that synthesize a project's context of climate, its patterns of use, with the resulting building loads and systems producing a building that is healthier, more comfortable, productive and 50 percent more energy efficient than today's common best design practice. The University of Washington, through the IDL, assists design teams in meeting those goals. Teams of graduate students and faculty researchers conduct energy and daylighting modeling studies, energy audits of existing buildings and many other services. Functionally, the IDL's goals are to assist in decisions that support 50 percent reductions in a building's loads and 50 percent increases in its system efficiencies, utilizing state-of-the art simulation and verification techniques.

The University of Washington's IDL project-based efforts have included: design assistance to professionals over the last ten years for 2 million square feet/per year in new construction: tracking the energy performance of commercial and institutional building energy use; educating the building industry about integrated team processes; involving faculty and graduate student research to enhance building performance; and communicating key energy efficiency design concepts to market actors and stakeholders via educational outreach, academic course work, and interactive web tools. Over the last three years, the University of Washington Department of Architecture and the IDL have provided these services to the Bullitt Foundation and the Miller Hull Partnership, designers of the Bullitt Center.

When Denis Hayes—founder of Earth Day and President of the Bullitt Foundation—considered creating a net-zero energy office building for his headquarters, University of Washington Professor Rob Pena volunteered to explore the feasibility of a high-performance urban commercial structure by organizing a graduate design studio on the topic. Collaborating in teams, the students produced designs backed by analysis of energy performance and life-cycle payback for several schemes. The studio encouraged systems thinking where the students gained an appreciation for the nature of the interconnections between architectural, structural, enclosure/environmental and mechanical elements of the project. Students

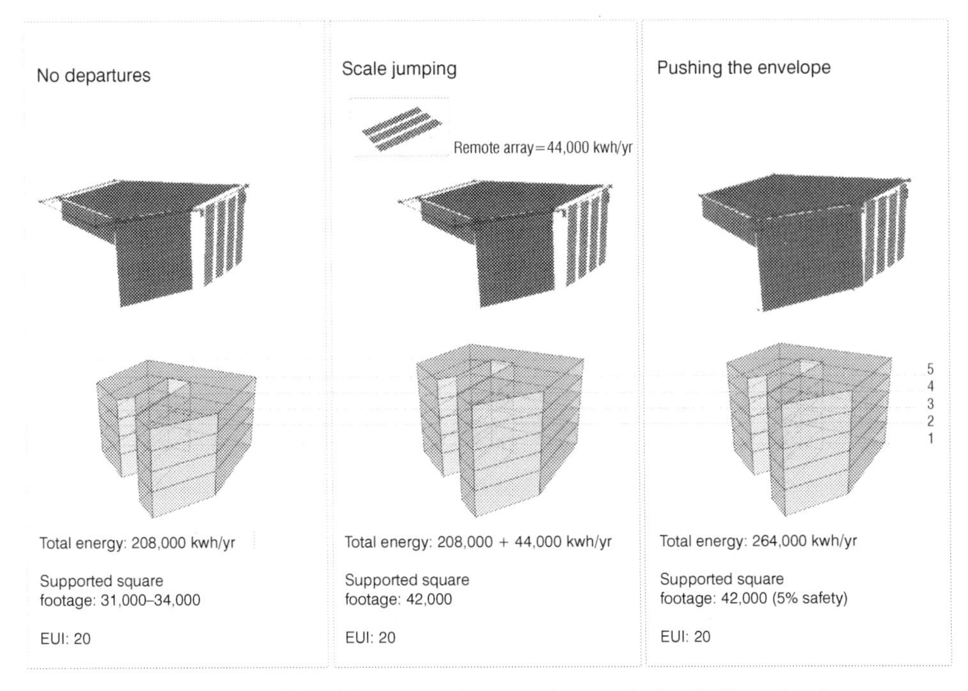

Figure 26.1 University of Washington graduate student analysis of PV production

found that a building's environmental performance goals are influenced by discreet subsystems, i.e., glazing and window systems, but can ultimately dominate at the expense of the building's total system's goals. Students learned about the interconnections of design actions and by testing outcome could ultimately evaluate and substantiate the performance results.

Following the student work for the Foundation which proved the project was feasible, the IDL consulted with the Miller Hull design team to test and model daylighting and energy strategies through all of phases of design. These services by the research faculty and graduate students—which were highly integrated with the design work in the Miller Hull office—played a critical role in the evolution of the design, and are an example of the mutual benefits between educators and professionals that enhance and advance architectural practice.

The early design studies conducted in the graduate studio and the rigorous in-depth analysis that were followed by the IDL at the University of Washington— in collaboration with the client and professional design team at Miller Hull—serves as an example of the advantages to the advancement of architectural education and practice.

Another powerful example of a multi-disciplinary collaborative research project is the Eco MOD Project at the University of Virginia led by Professor John Quale and a group of faculty from various disciplines. This project received the Collaborative Practice Award from the Association of Collegiate Schools of Architecture, which recognizes programs that involve faculty, students and community/civic clients to realize common objectives.

The Eco MOD Project (along with the more recently conceived ecoREMOD studio) at UVA has worked with a large number of affordable housing agencies to create energy efficient and low cost housing units. The design efforts are aimed at producing highly sustainable projects deploying prefabricated construction strategies. The UVA center works closely with the construction industry to develop new technologies for a building type that

Figure 26.2 Bullitt Foundation Building by Miller Hull and Daylighting modeling by UW IDL

Figure 26.3 EcoMOD 4, 2009, University of Virginia

typically has failed to address issues around energy efficiency, water stewardship and long-term life-cycle parameters. Faculty from architecture, engineering, landscape architecture, planning, historic preservation and the business school are involved. The Eco MOD Project also received an Education Honor Award from the American Institute of Architects in 2007. It was awarded by the jury 'for exceptional programs that deal with current issues in cross-disciplinary collaboration that contribute to the advancement of architectural education and that have the potential to benefit or change practice.

Popular predictions are of movement from an economy of mass production and consumption, to one based on mass customization. Prefabricated structures like the Eco MOD projects show promise of customized design utilizing community engagement for specific client requirements, coupled with digital design and fabrication technologies emanating from design integration efforts from schools, professionals and the architecture profession.

Discipline vs. the Profession

In this era of mass disruptive change, where many are questioning the role of the architect, it is important to recognize the vast opportunities, as well as pressures that exist today—and to move beyond the boundaries of traditional regimented thinking within educational and professional constructs. Architects and educators need to challenge conventional thought and leverage the strengths of the new by speculating and investing in new ideas—to reap the benefits of change. Architects have always faced challenges—and moved forward building on the opportunities buried in the realities, histories and complexities of the built environment.

The splintering of education into segregated specialties could be disastrous if we don't continue to teach the integration of the many facets of architecture. Critical thinking within the discipline of architecture that bonds the design process with construction processes involved with assembly, products and materials is essential.

While Master of Science and other advanced degrees in our schools of architecture can focus on specialty areas of the profession and construction industry, the undergraduate and Master of Architecture programs should offer an overview of the range and breadth of the discipline. As Mark Wigley, quoted by Gregory (2011) states, "Architecture Schools should not see their role as places that produce architects, but instead produce new thinking about what architecture is, holding up a mirror of the world for non-architects to look into."

The success of the profession comes from handing off knowledge to those who will carry it forward. The critical knowledge of architecture needs to be developed in both practice and the academy. Architecture firms and schools of architecture need to work hand-in-hand to advance the profession. A greater number of practitioners (who are good teachers) need to teach professional practice courses and advanced studios in schools and architectural offices should run their practices more like studios. European offices, particularly in Scandinavia, have mastered the studio atmosphere. If we create a more fluid and mutually supported relationship between academia and practice we will help save the field of architecture for the future generation that has lost hope and is migrating to other fields of design or other professions as a whole.

To solidify a more stable future the profession needs to achieve a higher level of relevancy by creating greater continuity in the production of architecture. As interdisciplinarity expands the discipline of architecture and as we better connect diverse as well as allied disciplines we will broaden the base of the field in all its dimensions. We can make these connections and integrate multiple systems through building information modeling and other computational tools. The BIM's (Building Informantion Modeling) potential and capacity to connect to a network of interrelated disciplines needs to be developed on a theoretical basis in lieu of a professional tool aimed at production. Theories of practice rather than case studies of practice should be in our core curricula in schools of architecture. At the same time more experimentation and research should happen in offices. We can re-wire the discipline of architecture through greater collaboration and strategic alliances between the academy and the profession. This will help us regain command over the building process in all of its aspects and develop the making of architecture for all involved—the designer, the builder and the consumer.

References

Gregory, R. (2011, August). Mark Wigley calls for more radical thinking at education summit. *Architectural Review,* Available online from: http://www.architectural-review.com/view/segovia-spain-mark-wigley-calls-for-more-radical-thinking-at-education-summit/8617808.article.

Meadows, D.H. (2008). *Thinking in Systems: A Primer.* White River Junction, VT: Chelsea Green Publishing.

27

Project Delivery Systems

Architecture/Engineering/Construction Industry Trends and Their Ramifications

Linda M. Thomas and Hugh D. Lester

> Do not believe in anything simply because you have heard it. Do not believe in anything simply because it is spoken and rumored by many. Do not believe in anything simply because it is found written in your religious books. [...] But after observation and analysis, when you find that anything agrees with reason and is conducive to the good and benefit of one and all, then accept it [...].
>
> (Gautama Buddha)

Introduction

Design/Build is often thought of as a relatively new method that has emerged in the Architecture/Engineering/Construction (AEC) industry, where the design-builder is contracted to both design a project and fulfill construction services. The design/build method can be traced back to the idea of architect as builder from ancient times, the "Master-builder." Proponents of this idea cite the benefits of a single contract, and of risk mitigation for the owner via a guaranteed maximum price, arguing that this should be the preferred methodology for project delivery in the future. This understanding is neither complete nor entirely true; in fact this common misunderstanding of design/build may lead to further adversarial separation of the designer from the builder.

This chapter addresses aspects of, and confusion arising out of, design/build project delivery methods. The aim is to offer a more comprehensive understanding of project delivery systems in general, which will assist those seeking greater control over the process, and better outcomes, especially from the owner's perspective. Although both authors are academics, one has worked in general contracting and the other in architecture. It is hoped that a more holistic viewpoint is presented via this synthesis of perspectives in order to mitigate bias inherent in any single perspective. In construction management circles, contractor-led design/build is overwhelmingly preferred, but when asked about his experiences with design/build the designer, and co-author of this chapter, expressed the following:

> My first experience with contractor-led design/build was a tenant fit-out at a Federal Correctional Institution. The lead firms were in Washington, D.C., but the project was in California. Design was simply another subcontract for the Prime to administer, and it was a low margin affair. Unlike tenant fit-out projects in, say, a spec office building, this was a factory to be inserted into a slab-on-grade prefabricated metal building. The factory was to utilize inmate labor to rehabilitate military vehicles from overseas wars. Many were so extremely damaged from roadside bombs that they had to be dragged off of flatbed trucks before being stripped down. More than thirty equipment vendors had to be coordinated. Existing joist locations had to be avoided for roof penetrations and slabs had to be saw cut for gravity wastewater piping, oil separators, and more. One pre-design site visit was allowed to document existing conditions, and as-built drawings were incomplete, to say the least.
>
> I completed the design, construction documents and specifications without assistance, other than in-house engineering disciplines. Construction proceeded with some difficulty. Unforeseen conditions below slab required redesign to reroute our systems when undocumented conduit runs (between adjacent buildings) were uncovered during excavation. This project remains the only instance in my career where I was over budget on hours. To add insult to injury, the contractor presented a list of errors and omissions to the tune of approximately $50,000 which they expected us to reimburse. Most of these were proven untrue, as documented by project correspondence and a review of the documents and specifications. The remaining few were offset when my PM billed them for the hours redesigning due to unforeseen conditions, as well as researching the disproven errors and omissions. The project still wasn't profitable, but the owner was pleased with the facility. It did leave me with a sour taste in my mouth about contractor-led design/build, but considering how inappropriate the specifics of that project were for the delivery system utilized (all Federal Bureau of Prisons work is mandated design/build) it is a miracle it didn't turn out worse.

Hopefully, by the end of this chapter, the reader will understand that it is the *selection* of the proper project delivery method that is critical, not the roles specific parties play.

Background

To understand design/build the first step is to grasp the meaning of a "project delivery method," or "project delivery system." This is necessary since what is commonly called design/build is actually just one of several approaches that fall under that umbrella. But what is a project delivery system?

Definition

Project delivery is defined as the process used to deliver design and construction services (Construction Management Association of America [CMAA], 1986). Typically the owner chooses which to use, but trusted advisors can inform and influence the decision at the onset. Industry uses "project delivery method" and "project delivery system" interchangeably, but for the sake of clarity, this chapter will refer to the process as the project delivery system, or PDS. This is helpful for the reader because the word "system" is automatically associated with sub-components. It is within such a framework that a more complete understanding can be gained.

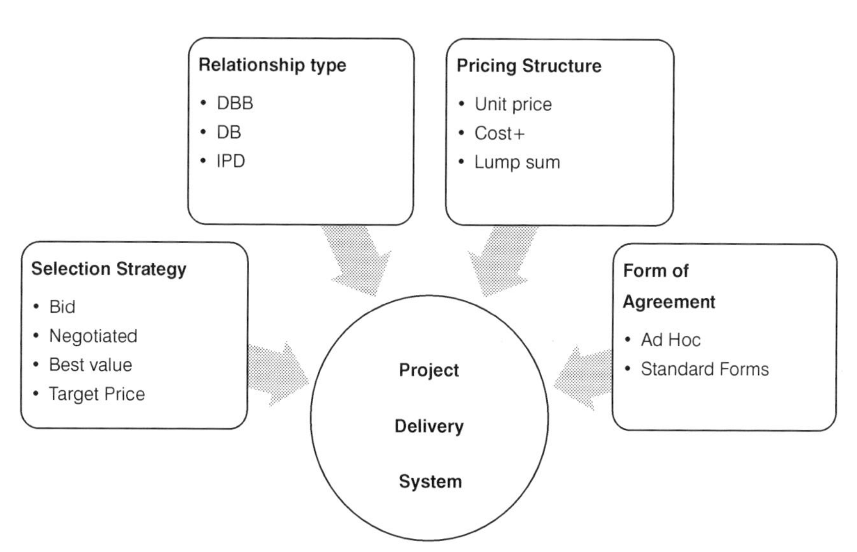

Figure 27.1 The major components of the project delivery system

We can think of a PDS as containing four sub-systems or components: Selection Strategy, Relationship Type, Pricing Structure, and Form of Agreement (Rubin & Thomas-Mobley, 2013). The process of delivering a design is theoretically as varied as the possible combinations of components utilized. When the PDS is carefully selected by the entity commissioning the project at the onset—prior to design—clarity results, various roles become better understood, and the team can function more seamlessly.

To help understand the system components Figure 27.1 is illustrative.

Components

Figure 27.1 depicts the four components with representative types listed. By no means are these lists exhaustive and the industry is constantly innovating, adding types, and exploring variants. The reader is advised to check with the local construction community for the current vernacular. For example, one person's "lump sum" project may be another professional's "stipulated sum" or even "guaranteed maximum price." Knowing that the AEC industry is likewise confused and that definitions of these terms are not consistent will hopefully lead one to ask questions and not assume all stakeholders agree on a common meaning. Additionally, it should be noted that Selection Strategy, Relationship Type, Pricing Structure, and Form of Agreement are all terms adapted by the authors for ease of explanation.

Selection Strategy

Selection Strategy refers to the method the owner or owner's representative will use to select from among the offers tendered by interested companies. Generally, for design services, the gold standard is qualifications-based selection from a short list of firms possessing the desired expertise. The options are more diverse for construction services, when not prescribed by law or professional codes of ethics. Strategies include lowest cost, highest level of expertise, lowest cost amongst the proposers with the highest expertise, highest score based on internally determined attributes, and others. The selection strategy can even be as simple as choosing the offer from a company the owner has a worked with on a prior project. Virtually any scheme that an owner can dream up may be used, as long as it conforms to applicable regulations and legal strictures. Selection Strategies are more limited for projects funded with public resources. This is done to promote fairness and equality of opportunity for respondents to Requests for Proposal, but often include provisions for rectifying historic disparities such as Women Business Enterprise (WBE), Minority Business Enterprise (MBE) and Veteran Business Enterprise (VBE) requirements.

Relationship

The relationship scheme is closely related to the contract type and represents the decision made by the owner about how the designer, builder and other consultants will be contractually related. In the traditional Design-Bid-Build (DBB) method, the owner enters into a contract with the architect and then separately contracts with a builder for implementation of the design. Design/Build (DB) has the owner contract with one business entity that performs both design and implementation. Only the number of participants in the process limits additional combinations and choices, as evidenced by the proliferation of Construction Management (CM) schemes utilized. Integrated Project Delivery (IPD) goes so far as to promote early involvement of facility managers, vendors, and maintenance personnel who are less likely to be included in other PDS.

Pricing Structure

Pricing Structure refers to the agreed upon method of payment for work completed. Typical pricing structures include lump sum, unit price, cost plus, time and material, or target price. Lump sum, unit price, and target price are fixed amounts requiring a change in contract if the figure(s) agreed upon at inception change. These arrangements enable parties to shift the risk of cost overruns from the owner to the builder. The lump sum and unit price are amounts determined by the builder and are included in a proposal to perform the work. The target price is a recent classification of fixed price determined by the owner; it refers to an allowance that reflects the maximum or not-to-exceed price.

Cost plus (a fee) and time and material require the owner to reimburse the builder for the cost of materials, labor and equipment, and pay a predefined fee for professional services, either fixed or some percentage of the total cost of the project. This structure shifts the risk of cost overruns from the builder to the owner. Other pricing structures fall into a pre-agreement upon price, a reimbursement arrangement, or some combination of the two. Terms used in local areas will differ, so it is important to determine the types of pricing structures to be utilized on a project and the contractual obligations of each type.

Form of Agreement

The form of agreement refers to the oral or written contract that the law will enforce. In its simplest form a contract is a promise of some future action, either to perform work or pay for work performed. In practice, parties have the choice of drafting a written contract from scratch, using an industry standard written contract or a hybrid agreement where a standard form is modified with additional language drafted by the parties. The common standardized agreements include those published by the American Institute of Architects, the Construction Manager Association of America, the Associated General Contractors, the Design Build Institute of America, and others. The selection of agreement type and the decision to modify it depends on the desires and goals of the parties and is a major component of the final PDS. For example, the definition of "guaranteed maximum price" under the CMAA standard form may differ from "guaranteed maximum price" as defined in an ad hoc letter contract.

Formulating the Project Delivery System

The Traditional System

The traditional system, primarily referred to as Design-Bid-Build (DBB), is often combined with fixed price or reimbursable-based pricing structures and industry standard contracts to deliver projects. To choose among the bidders, the selection strategy can either be low-bid, negotiated bid or a strategy that includes considering prices from select pre-qualified contractors only, also known as "Best Value." Prototypically, DBB can be executed with the American Institute of Architects (AIA) standard contract between an architect and an owner during the design phase following selection of the architect by qualifications. The architect determines the owner's needs and, along with consultants, designs the project to meet those needs within the owner's budget. Once the construction documents are 100 percent complete, they are used as the basis for soliciting bids for implementation. The owner can use the low-bid selection strategy to select the lowest bidder to perform the work. Without errors or omissions, the traditional system should, in theory, result in the desired facility at the lowest cost.

Unfortunately, DBB does not always work that well in reality. This adversarial arrangement, at its core, results in strategies on the part of both the designer and the implementer that eventually drive cost overruns and schedule extensions. The low bidder attempts to reduce quality during material purchasing and via substitution to make the project more profitable. The architect resists, and the next project typically includes a more restrictive specification to ensure the quality originally intended. Meanwhile, both parties experience increased overhead driven by the high quantity of substitution requests. Contractors are likewise motivated to increase the quantity of Requests for Information in an attempt to lay the groundwork for blaming delays and budget overruns on designer errors and omissions. Instead of working together, both parties actively work against one another, and conduct a covert campaign to influence the owner's perception of the process. Ultimately, the project suffers and the owner pays more and receives less. "Low bidder" becomes synonymous with poor outcomes. Seeking better outcomes, the owner seeks alternate means in order to work with "better" contractors.

One way is to opt for a different Form of Agreement and a Best Value Selection Strategy, analyzing qualifications submitted to generate a short list from which to choose the lowest bidder. This analysis is ideally based on factors such as successful experience with similarly-sized projects of the same type. Success is most often defined via metrics intended to capture whether past projects were "on time" and "on budget."

Finally, the negotiated selection strategy can be used if the owner is satisfied as to the quality of the contractor and the parties meet and arrive at a common agreement on the cost, schedule, and quality of the delivered project. Contractors prefer negotiated selection because all the other schemes involve increased overheads, complexity, and uncertainty.

As one can imagine, changing any of the sub-components in the PDS such as Pricing Strategy or Form of Agreement can change the project significantly. The relationship between the builder and the architect will be drastically different in a lump sum, low-bid situation than in a cost plus, negotiated circumstance.

This basic understanding of project delivery systems with their many moving parts should make it easier to appreciate the confusion that can result when a builder or owner simply refers to their project by base PDS nomenclature, such as DBB. Expectations that nomenclature is congruent among stakeholders can lead to misunderstanding and should, and can be, avoided.

This next section describes PDS—other than DBB, which has already been discussed—with the proviso that outcomes will vary depending on component selection.

Alternative PDS

Construction Manager Agent

The Construction Manager Agent is a form of PDS, but can transcend such distinctions because the CM-Agent can assist the owner with any relationship, pricing structure, selection strategy or contract form. In this sense, the CM-Agent acts as the "owner's representative." The CM-Agent advises for an agreed upon fee, protecting the owner and increasing the probability of a timely project of high quality. Having a secured, fixed fee ensures the CM's advice is decoupled from personal financial gain, in contrast with other PDS. Based upon this, expertise and professionalism, and not profit, predominate.

Construction Manager at Risk

The Construction Manager at Risk form of PDS is executed in two phases. In the first phase, called "pre-construction," the owner hires a professional construction manager (CM) who acts as an agent for the owner in all aspects of the project. During the design phase, the CM assists the owner in deciding among the various alternatives proposed by the designer. In addition, the CM conducts constructability analyses to identify potential issues, such as sequencing issues that might necessitate expensive remobilization by subcontractors. The early design phases are a much easier and cheaper time to modify the design to mitigate such issues.

When the design is almost complete, the CM calculates a "cost to build" based on the drawings and specifications, informed by full knowledge of the owner's needs and objectives. This results in the CM's estimate being more realistic than a "cold" estimate by a third party with no prior knowledge of the project, even when that party is motivated by potential risk. This well informed estimate, combined with the constructor's profit, constitutes the guaranteed maximum price (GMP) and, if accepted, binds the CM to construct the design for the GMP. If the GMP is not accepted, the scope of the project must be reduced and necessary redesign paid for by the owner. The resulting calculus is the final opportunity for the owner to officially direct the project, and "sunk costs" predominate in decision making.

During the second (post GMP) "construction" phase, the Owner/CM relationship shifts from a principal/agent relationship to an owner/contractor relationship. The CM no longer owes a special duty to the owner—to act in the owner's best interest instead of out of self-interest—as once obtained during the pre-construction phase. This change of relationship shifts the risk of completion within budget from the owner to the CM at Risk. This second phase of the relationship is similar to DBB, in that the designer and constructor are in an adversarial relationship, with the designer fighting for the highest quality implementation and the CM at Risk fighting for the best quality implementation within the budget. The owner benefits because the focus is on optimization of the resulting implementation and not profit-taking, since a ceiling for profit was previously established.

The advantage of a more realistic estimate of the final price, combined with latent perspective-taking, allows for more nimble adjustment to the contingencies inherent in complex stick-built construction. The ability of the CM at Risk to intimately understand the project prior to construction lowers the risk of cost overruns, especially when adjustments are made by someone with a vested interest in a successful project.

Design Build

The Design/Build (DB) relationship is characterized by the owner executing one contract with a business entity to both design and construct a project. This entity may be a designer who has hired a construction firm or a designer who self-performs construction. It can also be a construction firm that acquires or enters into a joint venture with a design firm for the same purpose. Leading the DB entity is associated with accepting financial risks and returns. Bonding also becomes an issue. Historically, architects are more financially risk-adverse, so contractor-led DB predominates. DB entities are increasingly firms purpose-built for working with owners who want to contract with one company from design through to the end of construction.

Just as with DBB, selection of the form of agreement can be a standardized contract, such as one authored by the DBIA, or an ad hoc contract written specifically for a project by an attorney. Selection strategies may also be chosen from among the available options. The dynamic of contractor-led versus designer-led DB could not be more different, so owners are advised to inquire with other owners who have experience with both types for help in making an informed decision. Adding to the complexity of the issue is the fact that project type and scope are both differentiators when it comes to making this decision. The Design/Build PDS can be as different as a Biosafety Laboratory Level 4 (most dangerous biological agents) compared to a tilt-up concrete warehouse.

Integrated Project Delivery

The Integrated Project Delivery System (IPD) is the most recent evolution of PDS. IPD's full definition and operation is yet to be fixed in the industry but, as the name implies, the purpose is to integrate the stakeholders in hopes of a cheaper, smoother, schedule adherent project of high quality. This discussion is limited to the IPD as the American Institute of Architects defines it, with little doubt that there will be further refinement of IPD as its use increases.

According to the AIA, there are three levels of IPD, each level becoming progressively more integrated than the last. The three levels are the Transition Form, Multi-Party Agreement Form, and the Single Purpose Entity Form.

The Transition Form was developed for project stakeholders desiring greater integration without changing the traditional relationship or agreement between the owner and the designer, and a separate contract between the owner and constructor. What makes this level unique is the fact that both sets of agreements are linked to a new general conditions section by reference. This new general conditions document has been written to maximize integration by defining the obligations of the owner, designer, constructor, and any consultants used on the project. Having the luxury of using the same general conditions tied to all contractual relationships used in a project reduces conflicts in contract forms, terms, and stakeholders' expectations. Additionally, the general conditions document requires the parties use Building Information Management technologies to the fullest extent practicable, in furtherance of integration.

General conditions, also called "boiler plate," outline the roles and responsibilities of the owner, the builder and any design or specialty consultant used during the process. Having a standard set of rules, notice procedures, and terminology allow contractors to feel comfortable with working for new owners since the basic obligations are already established prior to the work being undertaken.

The Multi-Party Agreement form requires additional commitment from the stakeholders to integration. This level is characterized by a three-party agreement signed by the owner, designer, and constructor incorporating the integrated general conditions. As one would imagine, this multi-party agreement requires a much closer relationship among the three main stakeholders in an effort to generate mutual cooperation. Consultants and subcontractors are not party to this master agreement and subcontract directly with the designer or constructor.

Finally, the Single Purpose Entity is the level with the highest commitment for integration of the parties. As the name implies, the major stakeholders form a unique legal entity in the form of a limited liability company with the project being its sole purpose. This arrangement forces the parties to enter into business with each other. It is thought to be drastic and is not recommended for stakeholders who want to avoid all risk of project failure.

Agreements for design are made between the single purpose entity (SPE) and the designer, who also happens to be a member of the SPE. Likewise the agreement for implementing the design is made via a separate agreement between the SPE and the constructor who then contracts with subcontractors and suppliers to implement the design. Finally, but most importantly, the source of funding for the project is made by the SPE via separate agreement with the Owner. Therefore, the three main stakeholders in a project, the owner, designer, and constructor serve in two capacities, one as a member of the SPE which includes all of the fiduciary duties required of members of an LLC, and as separate entities holding agreements with the SPE. This arrangement is purported to facilitate ultimate integration because the success or failure of the project has a direct fiscal impact on all parties. There can be no winners and losers, only winners, or only losers, with this level of IPD. As IPD projects are completed it will be interesting to see whether parties who have traditionally been at odds can be successfully integrated.

Conclusion

The functioning of the AEC industry is best understood when the project delivery systems available are better understood. Since the terms and approaches used for the various systems vary, effort must be expended by all stakeholders at the beginning of each project. It is hoped that understanding how the various project delivery systems combine and work for specific projects will facilitate greater control over the design process and its eventual implementation in built form.

References

American Institute of Architects. (n.d.). *Integrated Project Delivery: A Guide*. Retrieved from: http://www.aia.org/aiaucmp/groups/aia/documents/document/aiab085539.pdf.

Construction Management Association of America. (1986). *Standards of Practice: CMAA Manual*. Washington, DC: Construction Management Association of America.

Rubin, R. A., & Thomas-Mobley, L. M. (2013). Delivery Systems. In L. Elmore, J. Ralls, & L. Catoe (Eds.), *Fundamentals of Construction Law* (pp. 189–206). Chicago: American Bar Association.

28

The Designed Environment and Deep Ecology

Architects' Rules of Professional Conduct and Ethics for Social Sustainability

Thomas Fisher

Architecture is fundamentally ethical. While clients and communities commission architects for many different reasons, all do so because they want something better than what they have now: more space, rearranged space, upgraded space, new space. And in addressing those needs, every architect confronts the question of what that client or community aspires to, how they see themselves, and what they want for their future. Here, architecture shares with ethics a core question: What constitutes a good life and how should we achieve it?

That question has become particularly relevant at a time when we can no longer sustain the levels of resource consumption and waste that characterize the "good life," at least as defined in the U.S. and other industrialized nations. The environmental impacts as well as the social and economic inequities embedded in our symbols of success—the large single-family house, the heavy gas-guzzling car, the sealed air-conditioned workplace, the sprawling land-gobbling suburb—cannot continue without an ever-increasing number of negative effects on our climate and on our communities. Architects have a role to play here. Because we helped create a built environment that society can no longer sustain, we need to continue to help envision alternatives to it.

Architecture and Survival

There are not just practical reasons for architects to do so; there are survival reasons as well. Human beings first constructed buildings for reasons of survival, creating shelter to protect ourselves from the elements, from predators, and from prying eyes. In our own time, the opposite has become increasingly true. We have become the greatest threat to other species on the planet and the major reason why the earth's climate has begun to change. The rapidity with which these impacts have occurred has left us unprepared not only with how to deal with them, but also in how to think about them. What responsibility do we have to ensure that other species can survive on a planet in which the human population has grown exponentially in less than 100 years, increasing from 2 billion in 1930 to over 7 billion today?

And what obligations do we have to future generations as we consume finite stores of fossil fuels at record rates, leaving little for those who follow us?

Our increasing numbers and growing consumption has not happened intentionally or out of malice, but rather as the result of myriad unintended consequences. Modern buildings can deliver a level of comfort and convenience unheard of in the past, and yet we have so sealed ourselves off from the natural world that the latter has come to seem distant to many people, and for some, almost irrelevant to our day-to-day existence. In our increasingly urban civilization, we rarely experience trees that someone hasn't planted, food that doesn't come wrapped from a grocery store, and heat or cooling that doesn't come from the turn of a thermostat.

This has led, in turn, to a disconnection between our behavior and the impact it has on the natural world. When architects and landscape architects build on a green-field site, for example, we normally remove much of the undergrowth and many of the trees in the way of what we have designed. In doing so, though, we often eradicate the habitat of plants and animals already living on the site in order to create habitat for ourselves. While that overall loss of habitat may not have much of an impact on any one piece of property, done over and over again as our growing population clears land for development has led to a massive disruption of the ecosystems upon which other species need to survive.

And as their survival comes into question, so does ours. As a result of our design decisions related to both urbanization and agricultural production, we have triggered what biologists have come to call the "sixth extinction," in which, for the first time on earth, a massive die off of plants and animals has begun to occur not as the result of an extraterrestrial impact, but instead as the outcome of the actions of one species: us (Kolbert, 2014). This may seem irrelevant to those among us who no longer see the relationship between the survival of other species and our own. But the deleterious effects of this have started to appear.

If, for example, we lose honeybees as a result of "colony collapse disorder," partly caused by the loss of habitat, we will see many of the fruits and vegetables we enjoy and plants such as cotton that we use become prohibitively expensive or no longer available (CCD, 2009). And if we continue to pump greenhouse gases into the atmosphere from the burning of fossil fuels in buildings, factories, and vehicles, we will likely see ever more extreme changes to the global climate that could disrupt everything from the stability of our food production to the safety of our coastal cities.

This, alone, may not seem threatening to our survival. After all, the typical American diet has become so deficient in fruits and vegetables that their disappearance may seem beside the point to some. And so many of the buildings we occupy have such durable wall and roof enclosures and such reliable mechanical systems that extreme weather may seem more of an inconvenience than anything else. What we overlook is that the changes we have brought because of our actions leaves us open to our own colony collapse.

This might most likely happen as the result of climate change combined with rapidly growing informal settlements in cities around the globe creating conditions that make it increasingly likely that a deadly viral disease, against which we have no immunity and no vaccine, can arise and spread around the world via transcontinental air travel. (Fisher, 2010) We all remain one infected person and one plane flight away from a global pandemic against which we have no protection. Ironically, the wealthiest populations, those who travel a lot or live in cities with major airports, will feel the effects of this first. And those humans who manage to survive such a scenario will likely live in small and relatively isolated communities, much as humanity did for most of our history.

No one likes to think of such things, but think of them we must, especially since some in the public health community have begun to talk about such a pandemic not in terms of "if" it will happen, but "when." (Osterholm, 2005) Despite the appearance of invincibility that technology creates for us, the human species has rarely faced a threat as devastating as this one. In the atomic age, humanity seemed as if it might disappear with a bang, something that, of course, could still happen as a few nations retain enough nuclear weapons to annihilate us all. But in the era of climate change and global travel, going out with a whimper seems more likely.

The built environment remains a culprit here, not only because of the poor living conditions in places most likely to give birth to a virulent zoonotic disease, but also because infection will almost certainly occur in indoor spaces as people breathe the same air or touch the same surfaces as someone already infected. The hope lies in knowing that because we have designed our world in this way, we have the ability to design it in other ways to protect us, as architecture has always done, from our greatest threats.

What Ethics Has to Offer

This may seem to have more to do with epidemiology than with architecture and ethics, but the opposite is true. The only way we will protect ourselves from the most likely threats to our survival as a species—which should trump every other concern we might have—involves fundamentally rethinking our responsibility to other people, other species, and to the natural world generally (Fisher, 2008). To do so, let's begin with the ideas of the ethicists Peter Singer and Arne Naess. Singer has argued that we have to enlarge our sense of ethics beyond the effect of our actions on other human beings to include what he calls "all sentient beings": all of the animals that, like us, can feel pain (Singer, 2011). We cannot, from his perspective, view the murder of another human being as wrong and the murder of animals as right.

Naess has made a related argument that we take too superficial a view of protecting the environment (Naess *et al.*, 2008). From that perspective, efforts to save small wilderness areas or to reduce the amount of greenhouse gases we emit represent what he called "shallow ecological thinking," which makes us feel better about ourselves, but does relatively little to affect the environmental damage the modern world continues to do. Instead, he argued, we need "deep ecological thinking," in which we would take into account the wellbeing of all other species—plants and animals—along with our own.

Unfortunately, much of what the architectural community thinks of as sustainable design involves a shallow form of ecology. Designing LEED-certified buildings (Leadership in Energy and Environmental Design) or aspiring to meet the goals of Architecture 2030 represent well-intentioned attempts by architects, clients, and communities, but such efforts, alone, will do little to address the complex interrelated social, environmental, and economic problems that confront us. A "deep ecology" approach to architecture and design would, instead, address issues that most architects tend to avoid, like the amount of space, materials, and resources clients plan to use or the amount of habitat that construction on a site will likely destroy. Architects may not want to raise the question of clients' life-styles for fear of alienating them, but until we do, filling out our LEED checklists will do little.

LEED, as Naess might have argued, may even make it harder to address our real environmental challenges by making everyone involved in the process feel as if they had done all they need to do, while evading the really hard—and necessary—choices they need to make. For all of the power of Naess's idea of deep ecology, his position does have the limitation of all idealist ethics. He makes a compelling argument for deep ecology, but tends to portray it as self-evidently the right thing to do with little sense of how we would achieve it or measure it. His ethics offers great inspiration, but not a lot of clear applications.

That makes Singer's ethics more useful to architects. Singer takes a utilitarian view, measuring the value of an action according to its consequences for the greatest number. Traditional utilitarianism calculated the greatest good according to its results for other people, while Singer enlarges that to include its consequences for all sentient beings. But overlaying Naess's deep ecology with Singer's approach to utilitarianism gets us to where we need to go: assessing our actions according to their impact on every other species—plant and animal—and on the ecosystems upon which they—and we—depend.

What Sets Architectural Ethics Apart

Architecture and its related fields have a special role to play in helping us measure the utility of deep ecology. Because architecture involves the creation of habitat, it offers us the tools we need to create—or preserve—the habitat of other species as well as our own. And, because architecture entails the improvement of living conditions and the attainment of a good life, it allows us to ask what that consists of not just for clients and communities of people, but for other species as well.

Architecture and the other spatially oriented design fields such as interior design and landscape architecture also have a relationship to ethics that differs in a fundamental way from other creative fields. Other art forms address ethical questions all the time. In reading a novel, watching a play, viewing a painting, and listening to music, we experience the ethical dilemmas of others through the interactions of characters in a story, the relationship of forms in a picture, and the drama among the voices or instruments in a composition. Such enactments of the ethical issues we face as human beings can have great power and beauty, and they often move us to see ourselves and the world around us in new ways. But the visual and performing arts remain an indirect way of engaging in ethics. Other than in obeying the rules of a museum or concert hall or in learning the language of the author or dramatist, we don't have to do anything—or more importantly, be anyone—other than who we are.

The spatial arts require more of us than that and affect us differently as a result. Architecture does not just enact an ethical relationship; it puts each of us in ethical relationships as we behave in better or worse ways toward each other in the spaces in which we live and work. We don't just look at architecture; we occupy it for most of our days and nights. And we don't just contemplate the ethical dilemmas of this art form; we enact them through our own actions in and around buildings. As such, architecture requires that we do some things differently than we might have done in the past and that we be someone other than what we might have been before.

The Ethics of the Code of Ethics

That applies to the architectural profession's code of ethics as well. Many professions have codes of professional conduct that pertain to the activities of their members, with consequences for violations of the code that range from reprimands to fines to the loss of membership in the professional organization or loss of the license to practice. The primary code of ethics in architecture, promulgated by the American Institute of Architects, has many of these same characteristics (AIA, 2012).

The current code consists of six "canons" that identify the general areas of architects' responsibilities: nearly 20 "ethical standards" that lay out the expectations of architects' behavior and their obligations to others in the course of practice; and some 25 "rules" that spell out actions that architects must do or not do if they want to avoid discipline by the

AIA. This code, like many others, also enumerates how the AIA handles the serious ethical violations of architects.

At first glance, the AIA's Code of Ethics and Professional Conduct looks like most other professions' codes; architects, on some level, seem no different from, say, accountants or attorneys. All have clients to whom they have contractual obligations, colleagues, and co-workers to whom they have responsibilities, and the general public to whom they must serve in an honest and trustworthy fashion. But architecture differs in that architects not only practice a profession, but also create—as already mentioned—the physical environments in which everyone else practices.

The AIA's code, though, says relatively little about our changing relationship to the natural world. The code's authors have recently added a new canon, Canon VI, having to do with architects' "Obligations to the Environment," which represents a good start in enlarging the ethical responsibility of the profession to the larger natural world. But the standards in this new canon have a vagueness that makes them less than effective and almost impossible to measure. Standard 6.1 urges AIA members to "be environmentally responsible and (to) advocate sustainable building and site design." Standard 6.2 asks that members "advocate the design, construction, and operation of sustainable buildings and communities." And Standard 6.3 advocates that members "use sustainable practices within their firms and professional organization, and … encourage their clients to do the same."

That seems fine as far as it goes, but what constitutes "sustainable" buildings, site design, communities, and practices? If it means the relatively "shallow" ecological thinking that currently comprises much of what the architectural profession considers sustainable design, these ethical standards will do relatively little to address our real obligations to the environment. And by framing these standards within the relatively narrow practice of designing buildings and sites, the authors of these provisions overlook the profession's impact on the larger ecosystems of which buildings remain an inseparable part.

The rest of the AIA's code has a similar tension between overly broad statements in some parts and an overly narrow focus in others. For example, in Canon I, having to do with "general obligations," there occur a number of statements that, from a utilitarian point of view, become almost impossible to measure in terms of their consequences on others. "Members should maintain and advance their knowledge of the art and science of architecture, respect the body of architectural accomplishment, contribute to its growth, thoughtfully consider the social and environmental impact of their professional activities, and exercise learned and uncompromised professional judgment." This passage, like many in the AIA code, evokes a kind of ethical idealism, containing assertions hard to argue with and empty of any sense of what they would look like or result in.

One standard—ES 1.3—also touches upon environmental issues, urging AIA members to "respect and help conserve their natural and cultural heritage while striving to improve the environment and the quality of life within it." But here, too, words like "respect" and "striving" have an idealist emphasis on our intentions to do good, whether or not the results of actions actually "improve the environment and the quality of life." Nor does the code answer the question whose environment and whose quality of life it is. If, as the code seems to assume, it applies to humans only, then as has happened in the past, improving our environment and quality of life of clients can lead to a dramatic decline in those qualities for others, violating the utilitarian goal of doing the greatest good for the greatest number.

Similar questions come up repeatedly throughout the AIA code. "Members should uphold human rights in all their professional endeavors," according to Ethical Standard 1.4. Does that extend to using materials or products manufactured in horrible working conditions or in countries that ignore basic human rights? How far do our obligations extend? Likewise, when Rule 2.104 states that members should "not engage in conduct involving ... wanton disregard of the rights of others," what "others" does that include? If it includes—as it should—the rights of other species and future generations, then most architects now often disregard those rights.

The Consequences of Ethics

There exists a tension in the AIA code of ethics, in other words, between the idealism behind many of its standards and rules and the utilitarian nature of architecture itself, a tension that plays out in ethics between focusing on good intentions versus good results. A further tension in the AIA code occurs between the vagueness of many of its statements and the specificity of designing and constructing particular buildings. That vagueness may reflect a broader skepticism about ethics over the course of the twentieth century. Through much of that century, we heard modern analytical philosophers arguing that ethics represents simply personal preferences and modern artists fearing that ethics constitutes a highly moralistic effort by reactionaries standing in the way of innovative ideas or creative expression.

Such skepticism about and fear of ethics had some benefit. Although ethics is as old as civilization itself, its history shows how powerful people can use it to impose their values and beliefs on others. Two of the dominant ethical ideas that emerged in the late eighteenth century and that prevailed through much of the nineteenth century, for example, had an absolutistic character. Immanuel Kant's ethics, for example, rested on a few "categorical imperatives" that he argued had universal validity and that we should apply regardless of the consequences that doing so might have on other people (Kant, 1993). And Jeremy Bentham's ethics involved quantifying what constituted the good, regardless of the intentions behind an action or the differences that culture or context might make in such a calculation (Bentham, 1907). While these two ethical systems had much to offer, they lent themselves to misuse by autocrats imposing their will on others whatever the consequences, bureaucrats making their distributive calculations without acknowledging exceptions, and plutocrats resisting any challenge to their power despite the often unethical ways in which they got there in the first place.

That misuse of ethics partly prompted a pendulum swing in thinking about ethics during the twentieth century. Dismissing ethics as too subjective to even argue about or as too oppressive to even think about proved salutary after the moralism of the previous century. Unbound from thinking about the good in absolute or quantitative terms, modern artists and thinkers found themselves free to redefine what constituted good work or a good life. But by the end of the last century, we began to see the downsides of this modernist dismissal of ethics. The late twentieth and early twenty-first centuries witnessed a wave of unscrupulous behavior as public- and private-sector leaders engaged in ever more extreme forms of corruption and as artists pursued ever more outrageous forms of expression.

Meanwhile, the ethical dilemmas related to environmental damage and social and economic inequality seemed to demand our attention. As a result, we have seen a revived interest in ethics not only to stem the unethical behavior we have seen around us, but also to guide us as we adjust to the social, economic, and environmental dilemmas we face. In embracing this return to ethics, we need to avoid one mistake that has plagued ethics in the past (Davis & Womack, 2001).

Ethics fundamentally involves looking at any situation from the perspective of others. However most codes of ethics, including that of architects, start from the opposite direction, focusing on what individual practitioners should or shouldn't do. While the AIA's code does look at the architect's responsibility to other individuals or groups, the document nevertheless assumes that ethics begins with oneself and moves progressively outward from those closest to us—clients, colleagues—to those further away—the general public, the natural environment. Those farthest away from us—future generations, other species—get almost no notice in the AIA code or most other professional codes for that matter.

If ethics has any value, though, it should not just reinforce what comes easiest to us, but also persuade us to do what remains the most difficult for us to do, acting on behalf of those who we will never know and who have no way to reciprocate. We naturally care about those who we know best. Caring about those who we will never see represents a much harder task and one that ethics should help us value and help guide our actions accordingly. Ethics that starts with the self and moves outward seems more like self-satisfaction; instead ethics needs to start with our responsibility to those most distant from ourselves and most removed from us in space or time.

A New Kind of Code

What kind of code of ethics would emerge from that approach? And what difference would it make for architects? To answer such questions, let's imagine a code of ethics that, instead of dealing with those closest to us like clients and colleagues, begins at the largest scale and takes into account those most distant from ourselves. At the same time, imagine an architectural code of ethics that, instead of addressing topics that apply to everyone, focused instead on matters specific to architecture and that could apply to no one other than an architect. What would such a code entail and how would it alter what architects might do, what architecture might become, and what the profession might consider that it rarely does now?

In answering such questions, it helps to make the often-misunderstood distinction between morals and ethics. Morals represent the mores or standards of behavior that a community of people expects from others, with the idea that the group has a right to impose its expectations on those who don't conform. Ethics does just the opposite. It generally challenges the complacency that can arise within a community of people and raises questions about the unexamined assumptions they might make. While morality fetters us, ethics frees us.

So let's free ourselves of the assumptions that have so narrowed our sense of what architecture can be. Imagine a designed environment dedicated to deep ecology that did not extinguish the habitat of other species in order to accommodate us, exhaust vital resources that our progeny will need as much as us, or eclipse the very good life that we hope to create and that seems to constantly elude us. Imagine a built world that we could afford, enjoy, and share not just with others we care about, but also with all that cares for us.

In what follows, I have followed the pattern of the AIA code of ethics, with canons and their related standards, and I have included a commentary after each statement to explain the reasoning behind it. See this as the beginning of a new code of ethics for architects, one that urges us to do the hardest things that will have the greatest impact on the greatest number of others.

Canon 1 Obligations to the Planet

It may seem too much to say that we each have a responsibility to care for the planet, since at some level, we can each only control our own behavior. But bridging that gap between what the planet needs and what we control has long been a topic taken up by ethics. For the ancient Greeks and Romans, ethics primarily involved learning such virtues of temperance, courage, fairness, and prudence (Crisp & Slote, 1997). Students of ethics learned self-control and discipline, which in turn, required not only the gaining of knowledge, but also the wisdom to know what to do with that knowledge: respecting what has come before, attending to the consequences of what one has done, and developing good judgment about it. This canon suggests that we need now, more than ever, to respect the natural world we depend on, to have a better sense of the consequences of our actions on that world, and have better judgment as to how we avoid damaging that world to the point where it endangers ourselves.

Standard 1.1 Design in Ways that Do No Harm to the Planet

The medical profession has long had an ethic, captured in the Hippocratic oath, of doing no harm when it comes to patients. This standard suggests that the architectural profession needs a similar ethic with regard to the planet. Few professions—and few activities—have as large an impact on the earth as architecture, when we consider the amount of energy, water, and materials used in the construction and operation of buildings and factories and in the manufacturing and operating of the vehicles that transport us from one place to another. Relatively little of this directly involves architects. But just about everyone inhabits a building and has some involvement either constructing, furnishing, operating, cleaning, or maintaining an enclosure, even if just one's own living or sleeping space.

The AIA code has a number of standards and rules under its first canon having to do with improving professional knowledge, demonstrating reasonable care, and upholding human rights—all worthy goals. The question this standard raises has to do with what boundaries, if any, should exist in how and where we apply our knowledge and demonstrate our care. Does it make any sense to limit that to a particular building or site if the planetary house in which we all live seems so overly stressed, with climate extremes and the resultant suffering happening with greater frequency around us all?

To do no harm locally, we must do no harm globally since we cannot escape the consequences of the latter any more than the former. Which suggests a role for architects that recalls what Buckminster Fuller described as "world man," a person who sees things whole and who makes connections and establishes relationships among local and global systems in ways that enhance life on the planet (Fuller & Lopez Perez, 2013). Here, ethics emerges not as a constraint on our actions, but as a way of opening up opportunities and needs that we haven't always recognized. If we called every living being on the planet our client, and the entire earth our site, architects would become the "world man" that Fuller called for, something the world desperately needs.

Standard 1.2 Design in Ways that Restore Global Ecosystems

Much of modern industrial culture has assumed that we can take finite resources from the planet, if we have the property right or have paid the property owner to do so, and that we can discard the by-products of this process—solid waste, air or water pollution—back to the planet, whether we pay to do so or not. The ethics of this involve what the ecologist Garrett Hardin called "the tragedy of the commons," in which individual self-interest works against the long-term interests of the group (Hardin, 1968).

For much of human history, we needed to maintain the ecosystems upon which we depended since, as hunters and gatherers, we could not destroy the places that we would return to the following season. Practices that we now see as cutting edge, like using only renewable resources to fuel our needs and biodegrading the waste that we did not use, served our distant ancestors well as they thrived for thousands of years on earth. Early agricultural settlements often maintained these restorative practices and the extractive culture that we now have in place arose relatively recently, with the modern, industrialized world of the last few centuries.

The ethical obligation—and design opportunity—we currently face involves recapturing what we once knew as a species and updating that in ways appropriate to what we now know and expect. This means not going back to some primitive existence, but instead going forward in a way that combines the knowledge we now have about the world with the practices that we once knew. For design, this means creating ways in which people can live much more lightly on the land, using far fewer resources, deploying far more ingenuity, and recycling or biodegrading all of the waste we generate.

Canon II Obligations to Other Species

We tend to think of ourselves as the most intelligent species, which in itself shows a certain lack of intelligence. Needing to think of ourselves in this way also reveals a degree of insecurity that I suspect few other species have, since no other animal goes around acting so smart. Indeed, some Native American cultures have it right when they call us the baby species (Nerburn, 1999). We act like children in demanding that other creatures feed and take care of us, while interfering with the ability of those other species, like overworked parents, to care for themselves. That perspective flips the sense of superiority that modern civilization has adopted and points to the need for humanity to grow up or face the fate of an abandoned baby, left by its caregivers to fend for itself.

Standard 2.1 Design to Accommodate Other Species First

This may sound like the opposite of what architects, designers, and planners should do, but this standard has much greater utility than what we do now. Once we stop limiting our ethics to just other humans and include every other plant and animal species, it becomes clear that the latter far outnumber us and that the greatest utility comes with attending to their good above our own. That does not mean that human beings will suffer; quite the contrary. Helping other species thrive—species that we depend on for our survival—remains the most self-interested action we could take. Once we get over the hubris of thinking of ourselves as better than all those who we share this planet with and recognize that we remain just one species among many, then focusing on the greatest good of all will benefit us just as much as every other species.

Architecturally, this means that we should see the removal of habitat, the degradation of ecosystems, or the fragmenting of migration corridors as unethical. And it means designing in ways that we create as much habitat for other species as we do for ourselves, be it with planted roofs, vegetated walls, natural landscapes, wetland restoration, and working within existing tree cover. This also means working from the context of a site in and from the outside of a building in, adapting ourselves to the habitat that already exists in a place and valuing a design according to how many species it accommodates. The utility in doing so lies in seeing that if we don't have enough other species around, we too won't be around much longer.

Standard 2.2 Design as We Would Want Another Species to Do for Us

Reciprocity remains at the core of ethics, embodied in everything from the Golden Rule—"Do unto others as we would want them to do unto us" (Matthew 7:12)—to Immanuel Kant's Categorical Imperative—"Treat humanity … as an end and never simply as a means" (Kant, 1993). However we state it, the idea remains the same: to imagine ourselves trading places with those who we have power over and to act toward them as we would want them to act toward us. That works in human relationships, but we need to expand that reciprocity to include every other species as well. This does not mean that we can never harvest a plant or kill an animal. But it does mean that we need to do so in ways that do not interfere with their species ability to survive or, in the case of animals, inflict unnecessary pain and suffering for our convenience or profit.

In terms of architecture, this means fitting ourselves into the ecosystems that already exist in the places we inhabit, taking up no more room than we absolutely need, and not tampering with the food sources that other species—and ultimately us—depend on. As Geoffrey West, a biophysicist at the Santa Fe Institute, has shown, all plants and animals on the planet exist within a constant mass-to-metabolism ratio, except humans (Lehrer, 2010). While we long lived within this ratio, in which our energy use or metabolism equaled our mass to the three-quarter power, we now live far beyond it, with an energy use roughly equivalent to a blue whale as a result of our fossil fueled technology. That equation offers one measurable way of understanding how we might achieve this standard: we need to once again design in ways in which the energy we use remains proportionate to our mass.

Canon III Obligations to Future Generations

The fact that humanity has used up, in relatively few generations, all of the easily available fossil fuels that took millions of years to stockpile shows how fundamentally flawed—and ultimately unethical—our entire industrial system has become. Whatever claims to property rights individuals might have, we do not have a right to deny future generations the finite resources—oil, natural gas, and fresh water—that they will need too. The inequitable access to resources that occurs now between the wealthiest populations and the rest pales in comparison to that which will occur between our generation and all of those who follow us. It takes a hard-hearted person not to care that our own descendants will curse us.

Standard 3.1 Design with Seven Generations in Mind

People in the past did not do this to their descendants—us. The Native American idea of acting with seven generations in mind shows how deeply our ancestors' sense of ethical responsibility to future generations ran (Nerburn, 1999). That measure of how we pay it forward belies the claim, frequently heard by the most self-interested among us, that we don't know how our actions will affect those 150 years into the future. If Native Americans—and indeed most of humanity prior to the industrial revolution—could figure that out without advanced technology or sophisticated analysis, surely we can as well. We lack not the means to care for future generations, but a willingness to do so. Modern technology may make us feel strong, but never have we shown such weakness of will.

What would it mean for architects to design with seven generations in mind? It would entail using as few finite resources and as many renewable sources as we can; designing assemblies that either have extraordinary durability or allow easy disassembly; and employing materials that we can recycle, reuse, or biodegrade as effortlessly as possible. Design for seven generations also means creating products and environments that allow for a maximum of flexibility, enabling our descendants to repurpose what we have made and re-appropriate as much as they can. This involves real imagination on the part of every designer. Envisioning what else something can be or how else something will be used constitutes one of the great design challenges of our time and one that we would do well to relearn from our oldest ancestors. Design involves seeing what doesn't yet exist, and so acting with seven generations in mind remains something that we, maybe more than most other disciplines, should do well.

Standard 3.2 Design in Ways that Leave No Trace

The idea of intentionally leaving no trace behind in what we design runs counter to almost everything the architectural profession now does. Most practitioners and their clients understandably want buildings to last as long as possible, while the profession likes to recognize and reward those buildings that have the greatest impact on a place or at least on the discipline of architecture. Indeed, the root words of design means to "mark" (sign) "out" (de), which conveys the drive in our field to make our mark (Harper, 2014). The humility inherent in leaving no trace behind seems opposed to almost everything architecture now stands for.

But for most of our history as a species, humans largely did not build this way. Most people lived nomadic or semi-nomadic lives for thousands of years, bringing their shelter with them or constructing it with what they had at hand, leaving little for archeologists to find. The ethics of this have to do with our responsibility to and respect of other species: we remain one of the only species that creates a waste stream that doesn't lend itself to recycling or biodegrading, resulting in the creation of landfills as monuments to our wastefulness. We can—and should—do better than this.

Canon IV Obligation to Others

Over the last few hundred years, at least in the industrialized world, we have largely disaggregated reality, dividing up the world into discrete parts in order to analyze and control them. With that has come a disconnect between our actions and their effects on others. Adam Smith, the father of capitalism, taught and wrote about ethics and he viewed his new economic system as a way of leveraging people's greed in order to do good (Smith, 1909). Smith imagined a world in which producers and consumers largely shared the same locations, incentivizing capitalists to want to help those who lived and worked in their communities and discouraging their damage of the places they too inhabited. We now need to make this happen at the scale of the global economy, reconnecting the cause and effect of everything we do.

Standard 4.1 Design with the Neediest Person in Mind

The ethicist John Rawls argued that we should act as if behind a "veil of ignorance" about our own personal situation, which would ensure that everything we did benefited the most disadvantaged, which might be us (Rawls, 1999). Architects typically work for the wealthy—affluent individuals, successful companies, and thriving communities—and there remain few incentives for thinking about the neediest people. But even if clients do not ask for it, architects still have an ethical responsibility to think about how those without means might benefit from the work.

In terms of design, this can mean providing for those who don't have a voice in a design. It can involve simple moves, like creating a bit of shade along a street, a place to sit along a sidewalk, or a degree of shelter from a passing storm. It might also mean providing accessible landscapes and interiors, recognizing that we all might one day find ourselves on crutches, with a baby carriage, or wheelchair bound. It can mean, as well, taking into account the needs of those charged with building, operating, or maintaining a structure, ensuring that their work does not involve hazards or great difficulty, as we would not want others to do to us.

Standard 4.2 Design to Accommodate Diversity

Healthy ecosystems encompass a diversity of species, with no one so dominant that it extinguishes others or exhausts the resources that all depend upon. From that perspective, the human ecosystem lacks health, which makes it vulnerable to catastrophic failure. This, in turn, suggests that diversity of all sorts has value not only in its own right, but also in terms of enhancing the health of human communities and the resilience of the future generations that spring from a diverse gene pool.

Architecture can embrace diversity in a variety of ways. It can enable people to personalize their physical environment, adapt spaces to their needs, and accommodate the different cultural practices that honor human diversity. Buildings and landscapes can also ensure the greatest possible variety of other species able to live on a site or maybe even in or around a structure. The greater the diversity in our midst, the healthier the ecosystems we all depend on.

Ethics as a Way of Life

These canons and standards outline not just a set of ethical principles, but also a better life for us and for others. They represent an ethic, as well, that deserves reconsideration: the idea that the good life involves learning how to live with less. That idea will eventually get forced on us as we face a future much more constrained in terms of resources than many have had at their disposal in the past, and so we have much to learn from cultures and communities that have long lived with little. We also have much to learn from the ancient Greeks and Romans, whose ethics often revolved around an appreciation of quality over quantity, a valuing of relationships over possessions, and an embrace of moderation over extremes (Aristotle, 2011). Living with less doesn't mean a closing down of options or opportunities for people; quite the opposite. Having less leads to greater freedom and happiness, not just for us, but for every other species with which we share this planet.

References

American Institute of Architects (AIA) (2012). *Code of Ethics and Professional Conduct.* Retrieved from http://www.aia.org/aiaucmp/groups/aia/documents/pdf/aiap074122.pdf

Aristotle (2011). *Aristotle's Nicomachean Ethics*. Robert Bartlett and Susan Collins, translators. Chicago, IL: University of Chicago Press.

Bentham, Jeremy.(1907) *An Introduction to the Principles of Morals and Legislation.* Oxford: Clarendon Press.

CCD Steering Committee (2009). "Colony Collapse Disorder Progress Report." Washington DC: U.S. Department of Agriculture. Retrieved from http://www.extension.org/mediawiki/files/c/c7/CCDReport2009.pdf

Crisp, Roger and Slote, Michael (eds) (1997). *Virtue Ethics.* Oxford: Oxford University Press.

Davis, Todd and Womack, Kenneth (eds) (2001). *Mapping the Ethical Turn, A Reader in Ethics, Culture, and Literary Theory.* Charlottesville, VA: University Press of Virginia.

Fisher, Thomas (2008). *Architectural Design and Ethics, Tools for Survival.* Oxford: Architectural Press.

Fisher, Thomas (2010). "Viral Cities." *Places, The Design Observer.* Retrieved from http://places.designobserver.com/feature/viral-cities/13948/

Fuller, R. Buckminster and López-Pérez, Daniel (eds) (2013). *World Man.* New York: Princeton Architectural Press.

Hardin, Garrett (1968). "The Tragedy of the Commons." *Science.* December 13, Vol. 162, No. 3859, p. 1243–1248. Retrieved from http://www.sciencemag.org/content/162/3859/1243.full

Harper, Douglas (2014). *Online Etymology Dictionary.* Retrieved from http://www.etymonline.com/

Kant, Immanuel (1993). *Grounding for the Metaphysics of Morals, On a Supposed Right to Lie Because of Philanthropic Concerns.* James Ellington, translator. Indianapolis, IN: Hackett Publishing.

Kolbert, Elizabeth (2014). *The Sixth Extinction, An Unnatural History.* New York: Henry Holt.

Lehrer, Jonah (2010). "A Physicist Solves the City." *New York Times, Sunday Magazine.* December 17, p. 46.

Naess, Arne, Drengson, Alan and Devall, Bill (eds) (2008). *The Ecology of Wisdom: Writings by Arne Naess.* Berkeley, CA: Counterpoint Press.

Nerburn, Kent (ed.) (1999). *The Wisdom of the Native Americans.* Novato, CA: New World Library.

Osterholm, Michael (2005). "Preparing for the Next Pandemic," *Foreign Affairs.* July/August, pp. 24–37.

Rawls, John (1999). *A Theory of Justice.* Cambridge, MA: Harvard University Press.

Singer, Peter (2011). *Practical Ethics.* Cambridge: Cambridge University Press.

Smith, Adam (1909). *Wealth of Nations.* C.J. Bullock, editor. Vol. X. The Harvard Classics. New York: P.F. Collier & Son.

29

Legal Dimension of Practice and Regulatory Agencies' Role in Control of Design and Practice of Architecture

Managing Risk and Liabilities for Architects

Robert F. Herrmann

Introduction

From the first day of practice, you as an architect face both potential liabilities and potential risks. Certain liabilities exist just by reason of your being an architect. Other potential liabilities arise or are mitigated by the way in which you manage the risks inherent in any project you undertake. As soon as you put pen to paper or turn on your computer to start drafting, you subject yourself to potential liability, and through the decisions you make (or choose not to make) you expose yourself to possible further liability. If you avoided all risks inherent in the practice of architecture, it would be difficult, if not impossible, to have a successful, let alone challenging practice.

There are many sources of risk to an architect. There are risks you and your firm face if you fail to meet the requirements of regulatory authorities governing your practice. You face risks for claims if you do not know the local codes and ordinances where you are working. Compliance with licensing authorities and local building codes and regulations is within your control and, therefore, those potential risks can be avoided.

Other risks, however, are not within your control but can be managed by contract negotiation, by how you handle your responsibilities during the construction phase, and through insurance. The risk of damages arising from a design error, such as failure to specify adequate insulation, can be managed through limitation of liability provisions. The risk of being held responsible for a contractor's faulty workmanship because, for example, you approved the contractor's application for payment, can be managed through a clear definition of your construction phase responsibilities. The potential claim by an employee for discrimination can be managed by having employer practices liability insurance in place. The risk of a fire in your office can be managed through having property insurance.

Risks can also be managed by transferring them to another party. The risk of being held responsible for costs arising from a structural engineering error can be managed by having your client, instead of you, engage the structural engineer. While you can manage risk through contract negotiation, you can also, regrettably, take on more risk through that very same negotiation. Have you committed to design the project to a certain LEED standard? Have you agreed to a schedule of performance with a financial penalty if you fail to meet the schedule? Have you agreed to unlimited liability for damages arising from a design error? Have you agreed to design to a fixed budget? If the answer to any of these questions is yes, you have taken on a new risk.

Each of these decisions and countless others you make in the course of negotiating an agreement or navigating through the construction phase create the potential for more liability through the risks you assume. As you focus on the potential risks of a particular project, you will need to determine whether you should accept a particular risk if it cannot be managed or transferred. For example, deciding to take on the design of a condominium project may bring with it many risks because of the financial risks your client, the developer, has taken on in pursuit of the prospect of financial reward. Indeed, when you decide to do any new project, you assume some risk. You must then undertake to manage those risks through provisions in your agreement that can limit your liability or transfer potential liability to another party.

How to manage or transfer certain risks through your contract negotiations or during the construction phase is not something easily learned when studying for an architecture degree. You can study the AIA contracts, but only through the experience of negotiating a contract and then working through construction can you really begin to appreciate how the provisions of your agreement apply in the real world and what steps you can take to avoid or manage risks. To have a successful architecture practice, you need to have not only a healthy understanding of the liabilities you face as an architect, but also a recognition that at least some potential risks can be avoided or managed through a carefully negotiated agreement at the outset and through your carefully thought-out conduct during the construction phase of a project. This chapter will explore these risks and how they can be addressed.

Risk Avoidance within Your Control

Compliance with Regulatory Authorities

A design professional is legally obligated to comply with the rules and regulations of the governing authorities in the jurisdictions where he/she works. You not only need to have the appropriate license to practice architecture but, if you have a firm, you must comply with your state regulations for qualifying to do business in the state and for ownership of your business. Should you fail to comply with the rules and regulations, you risk financial loss from non-compliance and potential loss of your project. We are not just talking about the authority in your home state. What many architects do not fully appreciate is that their work in another state, even if they are not the architect of record, can subject them to oversight by governing authorities in that state. You must understand not only whether you as an individual professional need to be licensed in that state, but also whether your firm needs to qualify and register to do business there.

Every state has its own rules and regulations governing the practice of architecture. The professional corporation through which you operate in your home state may not be able to practice architecture in the state just across the border. You may have licensed and unlicensed owners in your firm because it is allowed in your state. But when you take on a project somewhere else you may find that all owners must be licensed. There are no easy answers to what you need to do to practice outside your own state. Laws and regulations governing practice are often broadly written, but interpreted narrowly by the regulatory authorities. Or laws and regulations may be narrowly written but broadly interpreted by the regulatory authorities or courts of law.

The important point here is that you must not only be extraordinarily careful when setting up your firm so that it complies with applicable regulations, but that you must also be sensitive to the requirements of other jurisdictions where you are working.

Compliance with Local Codes and Ordinances

Besides complying with licensing authorities, you are, as a design professional, charged with having knowledge of the local building codes and regulations. Unless you are just serving in a design capacity with no responsibility for construction documents, you must be familiar with the applicable codes and must assure your design will meet those codes. This can be complicated when dealing with some regulations and laws such as the Americans with Disabilities Act, which can be subject to various interpretations. Though no architect is perfect, your clients may expect you to be, and there really are not any good excuses when your plans fail to comply with local building codes and ordinances. Undertaking a review of local laws at the beginning of a project and, if needed, hiring specialists with a thorough knowledge of the codes, are basic steps you can take to assure compliance. But be aware that laws and regulations may be subject to interpretation. The possibility of dispute over regulatory compliance is one of the risks that you as a licensed architect always potentially face.

The Standard of Care

One way you can avoid risk is never to make a design error or omission in your plans. But what is an error or omission? Is the failure to detail the cornice measurements an omission as likely to create a liability for work on a 10 million dollar renovation of a house in Beverly Hills as for a modest home on the prairie? There is not necessarily one legal definition of when an error or omission in a design gives rise to liability. The standard by which you as an architect are judged is generally determined by the locale in which you practice (unless you agree to some different and higher standard). The American Institute of Architects endeavors through its standard agreements to measure an architect's performance by reference to other architects practicing in the same area. The AIA B101-2007 Owner Architect agreement provides in Article 2.2 as follows:

> The Architect shall perform its services consistent with the professional skill and care ordinarily provided by architects practicing in the same or similar locality under the same or similar circumstances.

Coming back to the design of the cornice detail, your potential liability could very easily be different in the two locales. If there was a claim that you erred in your design by omitting a detail, you could refute the claim by having another architect in the same locality testify. As an expert in that particular locale, he/she would explain that architects typically leave out the particular detail. It becomes something the contractor would address in the field.

Professional liability policies typically cover what are described as "wrongful acts" by an architect. But, what a wrongful act is will be determined by a judge, jury or arbitrator based upon the standards within the community where the project is located.

Of course, some owners want to hold you to a higher standard than what might be typically expected within your community. Owners do this by asking you to design to the "highest" standard of care or by requiring you to utilize "your best skill and judgment" in designing the project, or even by asking you to "guarantee" there will be no design flaws. Words like "highest" and "best" create an impossible standard to meet and an expectation as to a level of service which probably cannot be met. This exposes a potential for a claim which cannot be defended on the basis of what is typical in the community. By agreeing to an elevated standard, you have raised your profile and expectations which, if not met, can have dire consequences and increased liability because you cannot deliver on what you promised.

Manage Risk through Contract Negotiation

Contract negotiation provides the best opportunity to define your role and to manage a whole host of risks that may arise on a project. A carefully drafted contract that defines your role and responsibilities will limit the risk of claims later. The standard American Institute of Architects contracts are now lengthy documents packed with provisions designed to define your role and limit your liability. Not all projects are best served by an AIA agreement, and sometimes a simpler letter agreement may suffice. But even a short letter agreement can have provisions defining your role. Be aware, however, that laws and regulations may be subject to interpretation. The possibility of dispute over regulatory compliance is one of the potential risks that you as a licensed architect always face.

The Architect's Relationship with the Client

This relationship requires careful management. Failure to establish a clear understanding of how you and your client will work together poses multiple risks. You can be faulted for making decisions your client never authorized. You can be faulted for creating a design your client never approved in concept. The bottom line is that you can end up in a fee dispute or your client may want to go to another architect.

As independent contractors, architects must exercise their professional judgment in carrying out their contractual responsibilities. They typically act as the representative of their client on a project, but the scope of decision-making authority should be clear and in writing. The standard AIA agreements provide that you "shall have authority to act on behalf of the Owner only to the extent provided in [the] Agreement" (see AIA B101-2007 Art. 3.6.1.2.). Therefore, your responsibility for decision-making needs to be carefully delineated. If it is not clearly spelled out you may find yourself at odds with your client during the course of your work, which could cost you money. What design decisions during construction can you make? Can you tell the contractor to make the closet bigger or do you need your client's approval? Different clients will have different expectations for their architect. Some would love to have you make all the decisions; others want to make all their own design decisions.

In your agreement with your client, be sure to have it clearly stated who speaks for the owner. You need to take direction from someone you can rely upon and not be challenged later that you made a decision which was not properly authorized. Say you are working for both a husband and a wife, both of whom signed the contract with your firm. May you take direction from either one? Do you need both to agree? Get the answer straight upfront and make sure of the scope of authority each owner has. For example, can a designated owner's representative make all decisions regardless of the cost implications? Do all decisions need to be confirmed in writing?

It is critical to set proper expectations with your client. A thorough discussion of the design phases and the work product that the client will be expected to see, and a detailed discussion of your role during construction will go a long way toward avoiding future disputes and contentious meetings. If your client is new to construction, this fact should color how you discuss your role. In contrast, if your client is a seasoned developer who has done multiple projects, your discussions at the beginning will have a different tone. But by all means do not just send out a contract and expect the client to understand fully the scope of your responsibilities. Even if it comes back signed the next day, a meeting to discuss process and procedures is always a sound idea.

Although each contract negotiation is different, certain themes arise in most discussions. These themes include such questions as, who owns the rights to your designs, who will engage the consultants needed for the project, what limitations on damages will be acceptable, what the requirements are for insurance and what is your role during construction. We consider these in turn.

Intellectual Property

Architecture is a creative profession, and the product of your work is intellectual property that has value. By defining your rights to your work product and the rights of others to use your designs you can limit the risk that your designs will be exploited or misused by others. The issues in negotiating this subject with a client are fairly straightforward since clients will often want to know how and when they can use your plans. As a starting point, unless you agree otherwise, you as the design professional own the rights to what you create and can therefore limit what your client can do with your work product. Increasingly, clients believe that, if they have paid you for your services, they should have rights to use your designs should there be a parting of the ways at some point. What often ensues is a negotiation over rights to use plans when there has been either a termination for cause by your client or a termination for convenience, both of which are permitted in the standard AIA agreements.

You should focus on protecting yourself and your firm from claims arising from use of your plans if you are no longer involved with the project. Make every effort to be indemnified and held harmless by your client for claims arising from use of your plans. If you have put your seal on documents issued for construction, then your protection might be limited to circumstances where the client has modified the construction drawings. If you are only 50 percent finished with design development drawings and you are terminated, you should insist on being fully protected from any claims since your plans were never issued for construction prior to your being terminated from the project.

The AIA agreements endeavor to address protection for the architect in the event the client uses the plans without his/her involvement. AIA B101 Article 7.3.1 provides as follows:

> § 7.3.1 In the event the Owner uses the Instruments of Service without retaining the author of the Instruments of Service, the Owner releases the Architect and Architect's consultant(s) from all claims and causes of action arising from such uses. The Owner, to the extent permitted by law, further agrees to indemnify and hold harmless the Architect and its consultants from all costs and expenses, including the cost of defense, related to claims and causes of action asserted by any third person or entity to the extent such

costs and expenses arise from the Owner's use of the Instruments of Service under this Section 7.3.1. The terms of this Section 7.3.1 shall not apply if the Owner rightfully terminates this Agreement for cause.

Managing Consultants

If your project requires consultants from other disciplines, who should hire them? Many owners want one point of responsibility and therefore ask you to hire the structural, mechanical, lighting, acoustic or other consultants. By doing so, you can control their services, but you also risk taking on liability for their errors and omissions and the possibility of being held accountable for someone else's error. If you can get your client to hire the consultants, you have lessened your potential liability, but you will in all likelihood be asked to coordinate their services with yours. If you do and something goes wrong with the work of one of the consultants engaged by the owner, you will probably be blamed for not coordinating with the consultant or simply because you recommended that particular consultant.

If your client is hiring some consultants, you can limit your risk by clearly stating you will rely on the work of those consultants and are not responsible for their errors and omissions. As architect of record there is a good chance you will not only be coordinating your work with the owner's consultants, but also be incorporating their drawings and specifications into the plans you issue for construction. It is critical that you try to limit liability for errors and omissions in plans prepared by your client's consultants. The AIA addresses this in their agreements with a provision as follows:

> The Architect shall be entitled to rely on the accuracy and completeness of services and information furnished by the Owner and the Owner's consultants.
>
> (AIA B101-2007 Art. 3.1.2)

If you do hire consultants, there are two guiding principles to follow. First, make sure each consultant has the appropriate level of insurance and keeps it current for as long as you are required to carry insurance. Second, make sure no inconsistencies exist between your prime agreement with the client and your agreement with your consultants. All too often, consultants are signed up before the prime agreement is finally negotiated, and problems inevitably ensue. For example, the consultant proposal you signed might have an arbitration clause, but your agreement with the client does not. Or the consultant proposal you signed limits the liability of the consultant to their fees, but your agreement with the client has no such limitation. The recommendation here is to keep your agreement with the consultant limited, to the extent possible, to their fees and scope of work. Then make the consultant subject to the terms of your agreement with the client, which can be incorporated into your agreement with the consultant.

Budget

Another area where an architect faces risk is the budget. If you have no clear understanding with your client about the budget, you face the risk of having to do substantial redesign work at no cost or the risk of delay claims because the project has to be rebid. It is critical to determine as soon as possible in discussions with your client whether you are designing to a fixed budget. If you are subject to such limitations and the construction bids come in higher, you could have an obligation to redesign with no reimbursement from the owner. If you are not designing to a fixed budget and changes are required because your client does not like the contractor's bid, you should have no obligation to redesign at no additional cost.

Where the project requires designing to a budget, one way to limit the risk of having to redesign is to require the owner to engage a cost estimator as a consultant. Then, during the course of design, you can confer with the cost estimator to see if your design is consistent with the estimator's budget. If it is and the contractor's bid comes in higher, you should be able to be paid for redesign since the estimated cost of your design was monitored during design. You should have no duty to provide uncompensated services because a contractor came in with higher numbers.

Many owners, particularly residential homeowners, do not have a clear sense of their budget. They may have an idea of what they want to spend, but also want the benefit of new design ideas from you, so they remain flexible on the scope and cost of the project. If this is the case, be sure your agreement provides that there is no fixed limit of construction cost at least in the early phases of a project.

Limitations of Liability

There is typically a huge discrepancy between the fees you receive for a project and the potential liability you face if something goes wrong. Even a large fee bears little relationship to the potential claim if the store you are designing cannot open as planned by Christmas, or the concert hall has to cancel performances because your acoustical consultant failed to meet the performance specification and work had to be redone.

Given the possibility of massive exposure, you have several ways to limit your liability. Some are standard in the AIA agreements; others can be introduced as amendments to the standard form. A critical protection is known as the consequential damages waiver. There are essentially two kinds of damages you face on any project: direct damages and consequential damages. Say the wall you specified fails and needs to be rebuilt. The cost to rebuild is a direct damage flowing from your poor design. On the other hand, if the wall fails and the shop cannot open on time because of it, the lost profits on sales would be consequential damages, and they could be huge. It is important to have in your agreements what is referred to in the AIA documents as the consequential damages waiver.

> The Architect and Owner waive consequential damages for claims, disputes or other matters in question arising out of or relating to this Agreement.
>
> (AIA B101-2007, Art. 8.1.3)

Besides this waiver, or sometimes as an alternative, you should try to limit your liability to the amount of your professional liability insurance. At least some owners will accept this because they understand that most architecture firms do not have deep pockets and there will be little likelihood of recovery beyond the insurance in any case. The owners may then ask you about how much coverage you have and, if it is low, may require you to increase the face amount of your policy.

Another way to limit liability is to have what is called a no-third-party beneficiary clause. You are in contract with your client. You do not want some third party (for example, a purchaser of a condominium unit in the building you design) to claim the same rights that your client, the condominium sponsor, would have against you. A provision in your agreement that limits third-party rights will help you avoid this kind of claim. The AIA B101-2007 Article 10.5 states as follows:

Nothing contained in this Agreement shall create a contractual relationship with or a cause of action in favor of a third party against either the Owner or Architect.

Provisions Governing Termination

As a design professional, you should understand what might happen if your agreement is terminated. By understanding what can occur, you can manage the risk of not getting paid or having someone else take your design and finish the project you started. You need to address what happens if your relationship with the client deteriorates and either one of you wants to get out of the agreement. Typically for architects, as for other professionals, you cannot simply walk away from your commitment unless you are not being paid or your client has, in some other way, violated your agreement. You can, of course, try to include in your contract a provision that you can terminate for any reason, but most owners will not accept such a provision.

Owners will typically want an unfettered right to terminate you, whether for cause or even for no reason at all ("convenience"). If there is a termination for cause, you can expect to receive no further payments under your contract until the project is completed and your client has assessed his or her damages. Naturally, you can challenge the basis of a termination for cause under the dispute resolution procedures in your agreement. If you are terminated for convenience, it is important to have in place contractual provisions which hold you harmless from claims arising out of the use of your plans. You also need to consider whether you want your name associated with the project and whether you will, even though you did not finish the project, be entitled to use images of your design in your portfolio. In addition, it is reasonable to request a provision in the agreement that the owner will pay you a fee to continue to use your plans. These issues all need to be addressed up front during the contract negotiation.

Dispute Resolution

When you sit down to discuss a contract with your client, resolution of future disputes is probably not something you are thinking about, but it is critical to address in contract negotiation how any dispute should be resolved. For many years the AIA contracts had arbitration as the means of dispute resolution. Now, since 2007, the AIA contracts typically offer a choice: arbitration, litigation or some other means of dispute resolution. The agreements also provide for mediation as a prerequisite to the final dispute process. Mediation is a non-binding process where a neutral person agreed to by the parties endeavors to bring the parties together. The neutral person has no authority to make binding decisions. Mediation is increasingly being used in construction disputes. Even if the case is not resolved, mediation often offers the opportunity to narrow the issues in dispute and to give the parties a better idea of what they will face when taking the next step into arbitration or litigation.

There is much debate in the construction world as to whether arbitration or litigation is better for architects who have a dispute with a client. A whole chapter could be written on the pros and cons of one form of dispute resolution over another. Most owners seem to prefer litigation over arbitration. Architects seem to be split as to which is better. A whole host of questions must be considered: is arbitration faster than litigation in your locale? Which is more expensive? Are you better off with a jury or a construction professional appointed as an arbitrator? Do you want to have your case publicly known (arbitration is private)? These questions and others should be discussed with your counsel and insurance broker when considering dispute resolution alternatives.

Means to Manage Risk During Construction Administration

The construction phase of any project poses risks for substantial liability for architects. If you are reviewing shop drawings you can be faulted if there is an error and you do not catch it. If you are reviewing a contractor's applications for payment and a problem arises later, your client may ask you how you could have approved a prior payment. If you are visiting the site weekly and a problem emerges at some point, you may be faulted for not seeing the problem when at the site. Each of these situations and many more can be addressed to some extent by your written agreement and what you agree to do during the construction phase of a project. Risks can also be managed by how you conduct yourself at the site during construction. It is important that once you have defined in writing your scope of services during construction that you do not inadvertently or purposefully take on additional responsibilities by expanding what you have agreed to do. If you take on additional responsibilities at the site, you may become liable if you fail to carry out those responsibilities.

Administration of the Contract between the Owner and the Contractor

The nature of your relationship to the owner's contractor can vary from project to project. The AIA agreements contemplate that you will provide administration of the contract for construction in accordance with the terms and conditions found in the owner/contractor agreements. One such document is the AIA A201 form titled General Conditions of the Contract of Construction. This document has a whole host of provisions governing how a project should be managed by a contractor. Provisions include changes in the work, insurance, dispute resolution, unforeseen conditions and the like. These provisions also involve the architect and help define your role during construction.

Since you will be signing an agreement with your client before your client signs with a contractor, it is a good idea for you to see the owner's contract with the contractor before it is executed. This allows you to advise the owner of any conflicts between the responsibilities you have assumed in your architect agreement with your client and the responsibilities as defined for you in your client's construction agreement with the contractor. Awareness of any such conflicts can help the parties avoid misunderstandings that could lead to a delay in completion of the project and a claim for damages by the contractor. For example if your agreement is silent on the time you have to review a submittal, you do not want to find out after the fact that the contractor has a provision in its agreement with your client that submittals need to be reviewed in three days (a time frame you cannot meet). If such a provision exists and you fail to meet the deadline, the contractor could have a delay claim against your client even though you have complied with the terms of your architect's agreement.

Knowing what expectations the owner and contractor have in their agreement will make your role during construction easier to manage and prevent conflicts that could lead to unhappiness and possible claims during the project.

Review of Submittals

The AIA is very clear that an architect's review of shop drawings and submittals is solely for the "limited purpose of checking for conformance with information given and the design concept expressed in the Contract Documents" (AIA B101-2007 Art. 3.6.4.2.). You are not charged with reviewing accuracy of dimensions, quantities or performance, nor are you responsible for construction means or methods, all of which are left to the contractor.

FILE NO. SUBMISSION NO.

- ☐ NO EXCEPTION TAKEN
- ☐ REJECTED
- ☐ REVISE AND RESUBMIT
- ☐ SUBMIT SPECIFIED ITEM

Review is for general conformance with the design concept of the Project and **general compliance with the information given in the Contract Documents.** Corrections or notations made on Shop Drawings do not relieve the Contractor from complying with requirements of the Contract Documents. Approval of a specific item shall not include approval of an assembly of which the item is a component. The Contractor is responsible for confirming and correlating all quantities and dimensions, selecting fabrication processes and techniques of construction, coordinating its work with the work of others, and performing its work in a safe and satisfactory manner.

By: ______________________________

Date: __________

Architect Proj. No.________ Proj. Name ________________

ARCHITECT'S NAME
Address

Figure 29.1 Sample shop drawing and submittal stamp

Notwithstanding these contractual limitations, two things can happen that create risks for the architect. First, your client may have greater expectations about what you will do than the agreement warrants. Therefore, an early discussion of your limited role in submittal review is critical. Second, it may turn out that you will actually review dimensions or check quantities when presented with a shop drawing, despite such work being outside the scope of your contractual responsibilities. Once you do that, you have taken on a new risk of liability since you have assumed a responsibility that was not in your agreement. And if the dimensions turn out to be incorrect, the owner may seek to hold you accountable for the costs of redoing the work.

All architects have a shop drawing and submittal stamp. Figure 29.1 shows what a typical one might look like. The qualifying language is critical to limiting your liability.

When owners see "Approved" or some similar word, they may think you have reviewed the submission with a fine tooth comb. Your contract and shop-drawing stamp language should protect you unless you do go beyond what you are contractually obligated to do. Resist the temptation to do the contractor's or subcontractor's jobs because you think you can do them better or hope to avoid a delay in the project.

Electronic Transfer of Documents

It is now very common for drawings and other project data to be transferred electronically. In recognition of that fact, the AIA has now developed a form of agreement to govern electronic transfer. Any agreement governing electronic transfer should address liability should the documents become corrupted. The agreement should make clear who owns the documents being transferred and exactly what rights are being transferred in terms of use of the documents. Moreover, with the increasing use of documents transferred electronically it becomes important to establish what are the record drawings for the project. Are they the hard copies or the documents sent electronically? The important point to remember here is that you should not just send off your drawings to your client, a consulting engineer or contractor without giving thought to an agreement governing the transfer.

Site Visits

Your clients often expect you to be their eyes and ears when visiting the site and therefore observe and rectify every problem. That mistaken expectation leads to two risks: the risk that you will not see a serious problem and the risk associated with in fact seeing a problem that is not your responsibility to cure.

First, consider the risk that you will not see a serious problem. You are most likely only going to be at a project site once or twice a week, or perhaps only every other week. And when you are at the project site you may not see everything. A wall may have been closed up so you will not know if the insulation has the requisite value. You may not have seen how a joist was attached. Yet, if there is a problem with the insulation or the joist which emerges later you may well be blamed for not seeing the installation. The risk can be mitigated by making efforts to see critical building components before they are covered up and keeping careful notes of your site visits so it is clear later on what you did or did not see.

Second, when visiting the site you may encounter a situation where the contractor is doing an installation which you believe is being done incorrectly. Say, for example, the contractor is applying stucco but has failed to apply the proper number of coats. What do you do? Do you direct the contractor to stop work? Do you tell the owner to direct the contractor to stop work? Do you let the contractor keep working and simply note the issue in your field notes for the visit? The AIA agreements specifically state that you do not have responsibility for:

> the construction means, methods, techniques, sequences or procedures, or for the safety precautions and programs in connection with the Work.
>
> (AIA B101-2007, Art. 3.6.1.2)

Although the AIA agreements give you the right to reject work that does not conform to the contract documents (see AIA B101-2007, Art. 3.6.2.3), this does not mean you should tell the contractor to stop work. The recommended course of action is to encourage your client to tell the contractor to stop work. If you tell the contractor to stop, you interject yourself into the middle of the owner and contractor relationship and thereby create a potential claim by the contractor for interference with his/her contract with your client. This could result in damages if you were wrong about the need to stop. Of course, if you tell your client and your advice is wrong, then your client may have a claim against you if the contractor asserts a delay claim, but at least you are not fighting both the contractor and the owner in that situation. Although it is best to avoid directly telling the contractor to stop work, what do you do if the owner is unreachable by phone or email? Here you have to use your judgment, particularly if there is a safety issue involved. You just may have to tell the contractor to cease work when you see a dangerous condition, even if such intervention is not provided for in your agreement with the owner.

The importance of careful detailed meeting minutes cannot be overstated. In the absence of minutes you may find yourself at the mercy of others whose memories of what happened are different from yours. Lawsuits can be won or lost based on what field reports or minutes of meetings may say. Many construction disputes arise years after a project is finished. Your project manager may be long gone to another firm or even to another state. The contractor or a critical subcontractor may be out of business. The meeting minutes are the best contemporaneous record of events. Critical decisions reached at a construction site meeting must be documented. If a problem is observed it must be mentioned and the plan to address it also noted. If the client has accepted an as-built condition that is contrary to your plans, note it. Owners sometimes have short memories and later on might suddenly ask you why the ceiling height in the bedroom is only eight feet. A written field report documenting that the condition was discussed and approved should defeat any contention by your client that he or she is entitled to have work redone at your expense.

In between site meetings email communication can also provide a means to record decisions made by your client or in consultation with the contractor. Three years after the project is finished you do not want to have to rely on someone else's memory, particularly since there may not be anyone who remembers what happened.

Although it is typical that you will record the minutes of meetings during the design phase, it is customary that the contractor or construction manager or owner's representative will record the minutes during construction. If you are taking minutes you want to include a sentence to the effect that any corrections should be proposed within a certain period of time (perhaps 72 hours) or the minutes will be deemed accepted. If you are not taking minutes, be sure to review and comment on what is sent to you by another party and do not hesitate to dispute what is written or point out what has been omitted.

Reviewing Applications for Payment

Many architects are charged under their agreements with reviewing and approving applications for payment. By taking on this responsibility you expose yourself to the risk of approving work which turns out to be defective. The AIA documents provide that you represent to the best of your knowledge, information and belief, the work has progressed to the point indicated and that the quality of the Work is in accordance with the Contract Documents. The AIA agreements try to further limit your risk by stating:

> The issuance of a Certificate for Payment shall not be a representation that the Architect has (1) made exhaustive or continuous on-site inspections to check the quality or quantity of the Work, (2) reviewed construction means, methods, techniques, sequences or procedures, (3) reviewed copies of requisitions received from Subcontractors and material suppliers and other data requested by the Owner to substantiate the Contractor's right to payment, or (4) ascertained how and for what purpose the Contractor has used money previously paid on account of the Contract Sum.
>
> (AIA B101-2007, Art. 3.6.3.2)

It is important that you explain to your client early in the engagement how you will go about your review. If the contractor is using a standard AIA application for payment form (Form G 702 and 703) then sit down with your owner and review the form, and explain what it will show each month. Explain how you will look at the stage of completion of the work observed and compare it to the percentage of completion the contractor claims in the application for payment. Then tell your client that you will make a decision and recommendation as to what amount the owner should pay. Also explain that you will not be reviewing invoices from subcontractors or checking quantities that might be reflected in an invoice.

Confusion sometimes arises when the project is billed on the cost of the work plus a fee. In that case, unlike a project where there is a lump sum for the whole project (including contractor's overhead and fee), the contractor should be submitting copies of every invoice to justify and support their costs. You should have no contractual obligation to review every invoice, but be sure to advise your client that you are not going to do that. Otherwise there may be an expectation by your client that you are not going to be able to meet.

Contractors vary in their ability to provide good cost records. Some of the best contractors doing high end residential work simply do not have the back office capabilities to comply with the payment application requirements in an AIA form. Be careful here. Do not try to be the good guy and step in to help the contractor organize his/her records. If you do that, you suddenly take on some responsibility for the contractor's submissions and you expose yourself to unnecessary potential liability.

Project Completion

Architects typically play a very significant role in determining when a project is "substantially" and "finally" complete (separate concepts). Because of the significance associated with each, the risks of liability to the architect are real.

The generally accepted definition of substantial completion is that the project or a portion has progressed to the point that it can be used for its intended purposes. Contractors push for a determination that a project is complete because that determination will often mean funds withheld by the owner during the course of the project will be released. Substantial completion often means that the owner's insurance on the premises kicks in and the contractor's insurance during construction no longer applies. Moreover, upon substantial completion, you as the architect have a duty of oversight that exceeds your normal site visit obligations since you must conduct at this point, according to the AIA agreements, an "inspection" rather than simply a site visit (see AIA B101-2007, Art. 3.6.6.2.). An inadequate inspection at the end of the project can lead to claims if your client later discovers defects in construction.

Typically associated with substantial completion is the creation of a punch-list showing work still to be completed and work that needs correction. It is critical for this punch-list to be accurate and reflect agreement among the architect, owner and contractor. In addition, as items of the punch-list work are completed, they should be noted on updated lists approved by all concerned. You can be exposed to risk if you approve the punch-list work and authorize payment to the contractor and the owner has not agreed.

When determined by the architect, final completion brings with it full payment to the contractor. Before authorizing final payment, be sure that you have complied with your contractual obligations for closing out a project. Typically, owners expect that operations manuals and written warranties and guarantees will be obtained by you from the contractor. Your client may also expect you to obtain lien waivers from contractors (and sometime subcontractors). Contractors may have the right to file a lien against property to protect their right to be paid. If they do not get paid despite the filed lien, they can move to foreclose on the property to collect what is due (subject to the dispute resolution provisions in the agreement). As the architect signing off on final completion, you may have some exposure if you approve payment and then a month later a subcontractor files a lien claiming he/she was not paid in full. The owner may blame you for not making sure all lien waivers had been obtained. Regardless of whether your agreement with the owner requires it, you should make sure all liens have been obtained before authorizing final payment to the contractor.

Additional Services

If, in the performance of your services, you do not properly identify and document additional services, you run the risk of losing out on fair compensation for that extra work. The AIA agreements typically have a laundry list of additional services. They are often the subject of negotiation with the client. Will you be paid for attending public hearings, or is that a basic service? Will you be paid extra should the building code change midway through your design? Identifying additional services and then actually keeping tabs on them and letting your client know when you are going to perform an additional service are two different things. The contract will typically list what is deemed additional services and how those services will be billed (typically at hourly rates). Having your staff know when something is additional is a different issue. All too often architects get caught up in their project and pay no attention to such additional billing. The result can be devastating. You can easily turn a profit-making project into a losing proposition by simply doing hours of additional work that you later find you cannot get paid for.

Insurance

Many of the risks we have identified in this chapter can be managed by having the right insurance in place. This includes not only professional liability insurance to cover errors and omissions in design, but commercial general liability insurance to protect you from claims for personal injury or property damage not related to your professional services, appropriate workers compensation and disability insurance, and even insurance to cover you for employment-related discrimination claims.

Professional liability insurance is issued on what is known as a claims-made basis. In other words, the policy in effect when a claim is actually made applies. Therefore, maintaining coverage while in active practice is critical and, if you retire or move to another firm, maintaining coverage for several years after your retirement or move is also necessary. Each state has its own statute of limitations defining the time period within which your client can sue you for breach of contract or negligence, so be sure to check what is applicable in the states where you work. However, statutes of limitations for claims by a client are different from statutes of limitations for claims by the person who gets injured at one of your projects years later and blames the design, or for third-party claims of damage to property because of a design flaw that only emerges years later. These claims are commonly referred to as third-party claims and have their own statutes of limitations or, in some states, no statutes of limitations.

One important aspect of professional liability insurance is how the policy comes into play when a claim is made. Sometimes your client sends a letter telling you that she has been sued by a neighbor due to damage during construction, and wants you to defend her since your design was at fault. In all likelihood your professional liability carrier will not provide the owner with a defense of a claim at that point. What your carrier will do under normal circumstances, however, is cover any liability that you may have if in fact your design is determined to be negligent. Your carrier may also cover reasonable legal fees the owner incurred defending the underlying claim. What this means in practical terms is that you do not want to have a contractual obligation to defend your client from a “claim” when there has been no finding of a design error or omission. Rather, you should have in your architect agreement a provision that the grounds for holding you liable for damages, losses, costs and expenses (including reasonable legal fees and expenses) will be limited to your negligent acts, errors, and omissions. Agreeing to that should trigger your insurance coverage when claims are made. In contrast, agreeing to defend the owner from claims arising from your services could leave you responsible for having to shoulder the defense of a claim without any help from your insurance carrier.

Commercial general liability policies are occurrence-based policies. This means the policy that covers you is the policy that was in effect at the time of the "occurrence" giving rise to a claim. For example, if an accident occurs at a project site and the lawsuit by the injured party is filed two years later, the policy in effect when the accident occurred applies rather than the policy in effect when the lawsuit begins.

Besides having in place appropriate insurance coverage for your practice, an architect can also take steps to be protected by insurance that an owner or contractor may carry. Owners typically require a contractor's commercial general liability carrier to cover the owner as an "additional insured." This means that the owner in certain circumstances can have the contractor's carrier defend the owner and hold him or her harmless if the owner is sued in a case where the contractor is at fault. Architects can also seek to be named as additional insureds on a contractor's insurance by asking the owner to require this in the contract with the contractor. Most contractors will do this, although occasionally there is resistance. If you are covered by a contractor's insurance, you may be able to avoid having to involve your own carrier and thereby avoid an increase in your premium payments.

Additional insured status is typically reflected in a certificate of insurance issued by a broker. A typical certificate is shown in Figure 29.2

Although it is important to get a copy of a certificate showing your firm as an additional insured, the certificate itself does not bind the insurance company whose policy is listed on the certificate. If you really want to confirm your status as an additional insured, it is necessary to ask to see an endorsement to the actual policy issued by the carrier stating that your firm is indeed an additional insured.

Conclusion

The risks and potential liabilities faced by an architect and discussed in this chapter can appear to be daunting indeed. In this litigious age with ever more complex construction projects, architects are under great pressure to produce product as soon as possible so that a property can get to market.

The AIA has made an increasing effort in its agreements to engage the architects as much as possible with their clients. This in turn raises the potential liabilities. But at the same time, the increased engagement offers design professionals the opportunity to be more involved in the projects. By understanding the potential liabilities that are inherent in the nature of the practice, architects should be able to continue to do exciting, challenging and meaningful work.

Acknowledgments

AIA B101-2007 is reproduced with permission of the American Institute of Architects, 1735 New York Avenue, N.W., Washington, D.C. 20006.

ACORD®

CERTIFICATE OF LIABILITY INSURANCE

DATE (MM/DD/YYYY)

THIS CERTIFICATE IS ISSUED AS A MATTER OF INFORMATION ONLY AND CONFERS NO RIGHTS UPON THE CERTIFICATE HOLDER. THIS CERTIFICATE DOES NOT AFFIRMATIVELY OR NEGATIVELY AMEND, EXTEND OR ALTER THE COVERAGE AFFORDED BY THE POLICIES BELOW. THIS CERTIFICATE OF INSURANCE DOES NOT CONSTITUTE A CONTRACT BETWEEN THE ISSUING INSURER(S), AUTHORIZED REPRESENTATIVE OR PRODUCER, AND THE CERTIFICATE HOLDER.

IMPORTANT: If the certificate holder is an ADDITIONAL INSURED, the policy(ies) must be endorsed. If SUBROGATION IS WAIVED, subject to the terms and conditions of the policy, certain policies may require an endorsement. A statement on this certificate does not confer rights to the certificate holder in lieu of such endorsement(s).

PRODUCER

CONTACT NAME:
PHONE (A/C, No, Ext): FAX (A/C, No):
E-MAIL ADDRESS:

INSURER(S) AFFORDING COVERAGE	NAIC #
INSURER A :	
INSURER B :	
INSURER C :	
INSURER D :	
INSURER E :	
INSURER F :	

INSURED

COVERAGES **CERTIFICATE NUMBER:** **REVISION NUMBER:**

THIS IS TO CERTIFY THAT THE POLICIES OF INSURANCE LISTED BELOW HAVE BEEN ISSUED TO THE INSURED NAMED ABOVE FOR THE POLICY PERIOD INDICATED. NOTWITHSTANDING ANY REQUIREMENT, TERM OR CONDITION OF ANY CONTRACT OR OTHER DOCUMENT WITH RESPECT TO WHICH THIS CERTIFICATE MAY BE ISSUED OR MAY PERTAIN, THE INSURANCE AFFORDED BY THE POLICIES DESCRIBED HEREIN IS SUBJECT TO ALL THE TERMS, EXCLUSIONS AND CONDITIONS OF SUCH POLICIES. LIMITS SHOWN MAY HAVE BEEN REDUCED BY PAID CLAIMS.

INSR LTR	TYPE OF INSURANCE	ADDL INSD	SUBR WVD	POLICY NUMBER	POLICY EFF (MM/DD/YYYY)	POLICY EXP (MM/DD/YYYY)	LIMITS	
	COMMERCIAL GENERAL LIABILITY						EACH OCCURRENCE	$
	CLAIMS-MADE OCCUR						DAMAGE TO RENTED PREMISES (Ea occurrence)	$
							MED EXP (Any one person)	$
							PERSONAL & ADV INJURY	$
	GEN'L AGGREGATE LIMIT APPLIES PER:						GENERAL AGGREGATE	$
	POLICY PRO-JECT LOC						PRODUCTS - COMP/OP AGG	$
	OTHER:							$
	AUTOMOBILE LIABILITY						COMBINED SINGLE LIMIT (Ea accident)	$
	ANY AUTO						BODILY INJURY (Per person)	$
	ALL OWNED AUTOS SCHEDULED AUTOS						BODILY INJURY (Per accident)	$
	HIRED AUTOS NON-OWNED AUTOS						PROPERTY DAMAGE (Per accident)	$
								$
	UMBRELLA LIAB OCCUR						EACH OCCURRENCE	$
	EXCESS LIAB CLAIMS-MADE						AGGREGATE	$
	DED RETENTION $							$
	WORKERS COMPENSATION AND EMPLOYERS' LIABILITY Y / N						PER STATUTE OTH-ER	
	ANYPROPRIETOR/PARTNER/EXECUTIVE OFFICER/MEMBER EXCLUDED? (Mandatory in NH)	N / A					E.L. EACH ACCIDENT	$
							E.L. DISEASE - EA EMPLOYEE	$
	If yes, describe under DESCRIPTION OF OPERATIONS below						E.L. DISEASE - POLICY LIMIT	$

SPECIMEN

DESCRIPTION OF OPERATIONS / LOCATIONS / VEHICLES (ACORD 101, Additional Remarks Schedule, may be attached if more space is required)

CERTIFICATE HOLDER **CANCELLATION**

SHOULD ANY OF THE ABOVE DESCRIBED POLICIES BE CANCELLED BEFORE THE EXPIRATION DATE THEREOF, NOTICE WILL BE DELIVERED IN ACCORDANCE WITH THE POLICY PROVISIONS.

AUTHORIZED REPRESENTATIVE

ACORD 25 (2014/01) The ACORD name and logo are registered marks of ACORD

Figure 29.2 Sample certificate of insurance from ACORD corporation. Permission to reprint the ACORD materials has been given by ACORD. Further reprint or redistribution without the written permission of ACORD is strictly prohibited

Part VII
Architectural Design and Societal Issues

This part focuses on the capacities of architecture in promoting and enriching cultural meaning, as well as scoring of the human interactions and their social and intellectual affairs and activities toward improving the quality of life for people within various groups, fields, and communities. Considering that architectural design transcend beyond building buildings, it has the capacity to invent novel and various forms of relationships between people, places, and their ecosystem.

As a final chapter to the book, this part will promote the thoughts for visionary and futurist way of thinking toward a more reassuring future for architecture, and ultimately for the world we live as its citizens.

30

On Making and Becoming a (Citizen) Architect

Georgia Bizios and Katie Wakeford

Introduction

For those who wish to be an architect, the established path is highly formalized and notoriously rigorous with multiple required thresholds culminating in professional licensure. Knowledge and expertise are accumulated through an accredited academic education, a lengthy and highly regulated internship, and licensing exams. This process has seen only modest modifications in the past fifty years. Social and economic pressures have begun to challenge this homogeneous method and many have begun to question the one-size-fits-all nature of this process.

In particular, from the recent growth of efforts to democratize architectural impacts has emerged a movement of public interest architecture. Public interest architecture is a way of thinking and a way of practicing that emphasizes the importance of social, economic, and environmental factors. This design approach is people-centered and puts a high priority on community participation. Public interest design optimistically strives to use the power of design thinking and practice to tackle significant community challenges and improve lives. Design expertise is partnered with local knowledge to have positive impacts.

Previously the dominant mode of architectural practice served almost exclusively corporate and wealthy clients. The educational system, internship process, and licensing exams aimed to prepare individuals for this narrow definition of architectural practice. With the emergence of public interest architecture, how can the architectural education and training regime better prepare the next generation of practitioners to become creative problem solvers who understand how to collaborate with communities and serve a more diverse clientele?

In this chapter, we will give a brief overview of the history of public interest architecture—what might be called architecture for the common good. We will offer a snapshot of the current education and training system, including progressive methods of preparing students and young professionals to participate in the growing realm of public interest architecture. We will identify salient current events and conditions that are motivating change in the profession, indicators of momentum for public interest architecture, and the potential implications for the path to architectural licensure.

Architecture for the Common Good

It is important to understand the roots of what we are now calling the public interest architecture movement and the history of efforts to prepare "citizen architects" (Mockbee, 2004). In an overview of "Community Engagement" in architectural education in North America, Anthony Schuman traces the origins of architecture's "attention in the collective social condition" to social upheavals in Europe in the early twentieth century (Schuman, 2012). The social agenda of the modern movement in Europe was lost as it was transplanted to North America. Schuman argues the reductive focus on aesthetics happened in spite of the efforts of several distinguished thinkers and progressive educators who tried to sustain the connection of a social and civic agenda with architectural modernism (Schuman, 2012).

In the United States, the golden era of community engagement in architectural education and the profession happened in the 1960s. Political events and social inequities created conditions that inspired the minds and hearts of architecture students and young professionals. They questioned the status quo in architectural practice and sought to put their knowledge and skills to work improving the physical environment and the well-being of all members of society, rather than just an elite few. A number of architecture schools and professional organizations established outreach programs putting design processes, skills, and talents to the service of communities and organizations in need. Interest in such programs declined in the 1970s and 1980s as the discipline became preoccupied with theoretical debates over aesthetics and form such as postmodernism and deconstruction, as well as with explorations of digitally-generated design (Schuman, 2006).

In *Building Community*, a report exploring new directions for architectural education and practice published in 1996, Ernest Boyer and Lee Mitgang concluded that communities both wanted and needed architectural services, and universities and students were eager to participate in service projects, but the climates of many architectural education programs were not sufficiently supportive of these efforts (Boyer & Mitgang, 1996). Still today, community engagement endeavors within architecture schools are not given the resources, revenue, or credit required or deserved, for example promotion and tenure, awards, teaching loads, or salaries.

There is also a dearth of public interest internship opportunities for students and recent graduates which is a disservice to fledgling professionals, the profession, and our communities. Many civic-minded interns are left without the community-oriented jobs they would most desire. The profession is denied an important opportunity to reach out to a wider audience. The shortage of public interest internships also limits the development of public service as a legitimate architectural career track. Most importantly, our communities miss out on the wealth of creativity, design expertise, productivity, and economic development these talented young designers could provide.

A review of the literature and anecdotal evidence clearly indicates that preparation for public interest practice is still sporadic—not systemic—in the curricula and with regard to internship opportunities. There is a sense though that the tide is turning toward a socially and politically conscious practice of architecture. Strong leaders and organizations are encouraging design schools and the profession to better prepare the next generation for a broader understanding of the discipline and to train them in the skills required for community engagement. When we consider the magnitude of the need for design expertise in our communities, the enthusiasm of young designers, and the benefit that engaged learning experiences can provide, the importance of making a public service ethic pervasive in our schools and internships becomes paramount.

Architectural Education and Internship—The Traditional Path

As we consider how best to grow citizen architects, we must first understand the standard path for training an architect. The prescribed route to becoming an architect in the United States is long and demanding, requiring formal education, professional internship, and licensing exams. The process has been evolving over the last century since academic institutions began offering architectural programs and degrees and as states looked for ways to confirm the credentials of architects charged with protecting the public's health, safety, and welfare in the built environment.

Several organizations have the responsibility and the jurisdiction to oversee the process. The collateral organizations, as they are known, are the Association of Collegiate Schools of Architecture (ACSA), the National Architectural Accrediting Board (NAAB), the National Council of Architectural Registration Boards (NCARB), the American Institute of Architects (AIA), and the American Institute of Architecture Students (AIAS).

The first step in becoming an architect is academic study. Approximately 120 institutions of higher education in the United States offer accredited programs leading to professional degrees in architecture. The academic requirements necessitate a minimum of five and up to seven-and-a-half years of study depending on the course of study that students elect. Architecture programs are quite diverse, responding to the context and mission of their academic institutions. The Association of Collegiate Schools of Architecture (ACSA) is the member organization representing the architecture faculties, but each institution maintains independence in determining the curriculum and degree programs they offer. Accredited programs lead to degrees of Bachelor of Architecture, Master of Architecture, and Doctor of Architecture.

The accreditation of these architectural programs is under the auspices of the National Architectural Accrediting Board (NAAB). Academic programs go through a rigorous review in order to establish initial accreditation and then periodic reviews that include thorough program documentation and an extensive visit by a NAAB-appointed visiting team. In addition, accredited programs are required to submit Annual Program Reports to NAAB at the end of each academic year. The conditions, student performance criteria, and procedures by which architecture programs receive and maintain accreditation is assessed and updated on a regular basis with input from all the collateral organizations. This process determines what architecture students are expected to learn in preparation for a professional career, and the context which academic institutions must provide for granting accredited degrees.

The NAAB requirements cover a broad array of topics and skills. Architecture departments are challenged to maintain an atmosphere and culture that fosters leadership, service to the community, and diversity, and prepares students to work in a global economy with an appreciation for design's impact on the environment. Curricula are expected to convey understanding and ability in all areas of architecture including critical thinking, history and culture, sustainability, representation, systems and materials, ethics, and management. Although individual university programs determine how best to meet the NAAB requirements, some would argue that the NAAB criteria and procedures have been shifting towards greater emphasis on the licensure process and professional practice (National Architectural Accrediting Board, n.d.).

Admission to and completion of an accredited academic program is demanding. In addition to general education requirements, the core curriculum of most programs involves a sequence of design studios supplemented by technical courses in areas of building technology such as structures, environmental control systems, and site planning. Courses in architectural theory, urban design, and professional practice are required in addition to elective courses in the major to provide breadth and introduce specialties. Most programs offer foreign travel study and many architecture majors elect to participate in them. Study in and of other cultures and settings as well as visiting significant architectural and urban environments is considered an irreplaceable experience of an architect's educational process. Some programs require study abroad and/or professional internship for completion of the architectural degree program.

The next step for an aspiring architect is completion of the Intern Development Program (IDP). IDP requires 3,740 supervised hours of experience in four Categories: Pre-Design, Design, Project Management, and Practice Management. Within those categories, there are seventeen Experience Areas, with requisite minimum hours assigned to each, to ensure that interns have experience in the broad array of tasks involved in architectural practice. Interns report their progress directly to the National Council of Architectural Registration Boards (NCARB) and supervisors approve the reported hours through an online interface. NCARB reports that in 2012 the average time to completion of the internship phase was 5.33 years, dropping from 6.18 in 2010, after a gradual rise from under 3.5 years in 1983 (National Council of Architectural Registration Boards, 2013).

The architectural registration exams (AREs) are the final step in the licensure process. NCARB administers the exams. The exams are comprised of several parts that test candidates in programming, planning and practice, site planning and design, building design and construction systems, schematic design, structural systems, building systems, and construction documents and services. Upon successful completion of all sections one can register as an architect in her/his state.

Architectural licensing in the United States is regulated at the state level by Architectural Licensing Boards. Each state's board is a member of NCARB, but state boards are not obliged to conform to all NCARB regulations and policies, and may adopt their own regulations and timetables. For example, for many years, California and New York have had different requirements for IDP and licensure than other states. If an architect chooses, she/he may establish a record for NCARB Certification, which certifies reciprocity of the license qualifications, so that she/he can practice in states other than the one where she/he receives her/his initial registration (National Council of Architectural Registration Boards. n.d.).

Architectural Education and Internship—Current Approaches to Preparing a Citizen Architect

Since 2000 we have seen significant reform in the traditional path to licensure. The changes come from demands on—and decisions by—the collateral organizations that have oversight of the process. For instance, until recently the process was quite linear, requiring that the milestones of graduation from an accredited professional degree program and internship completion be accomplished before one could begin taking the registration examinations. Recent changes in most states now allow for significant overlapping of the fulfillment of the requirements for education, internship, and examination, which facilitates a better experience and potentially shorter time to licensure. Undoubtedly the process will continue to evolve, with minor and major changes adjusting to current events and to societal, economic and political pressures.

As stated previously, the overarching goal of the process to licensure is to ensure that professional architects can and will protect the public's health, safety, and welfare. There is now significant pressure to expand the interpretation of the "public welfare." Do architects have a responsibility to more democratically contribute to the public welfare by providing services beyond the typical corporate client or wealthy individual? And if so, how?

Many argue that, yes, architects have additional responsibility and see opportunities for improving the way the profession trains new generations to serve communities. As we reconsider how we educate, how we practice, and whom we serve, it is valuable and feasible for enthusiastic architecture graduates to more directly apply their energy and design skills to current social, economic, and environmental issues. In the introduction to his book *Studio at Large: Architecture in the Service of Global Communities*, Sergio Palleroni questions, "How can architecture and architects become more relevant to society at large? How can architecture education more realistically prepare young professionals for significant, effective practice? (Palleroni, 2004). Enhancements of the architectural education system and early-career experiences will have a powerful influence on the future of our profession and our communities.

University-Based Service Learning

There have been increased efforts at the university level to prepare future architects for public engagement. Service learning experiences are the most common expressions of these efforts. Architecture students enthusiastically participate in public interest-themed summer programs, study-abroad experiences focused on humanitarian issues, and design-build workshops that benefit community partners.

Pedagogically, service learning is growing in importance in higher education. Universities are encouraging faculty to connect the classroom with the community context. Faculty are recognizing the significant level of enrichment that such activities can bring to the curriculum and to the content of coursework. Real-world application of theoretical concepts deepens understanding. Architectural design, by its nature of addressing user needs and requiring special skills such as three-dimensional thinking, problem solving, application of technical knowledge, and drawing, is an ideal discipline to link young practitioners with community needs.

Community-engaged learning offers valuable benefits for all involved. The projects often require teamwork, similar to an architectural practice. Since most coursework in the current architectural curricula is individual, this is a significant asset of service-learning assignments. Additionally, before any structure is framed, the client community is exposed to the design process, learning what architects do and how architecture can positively influence their lives. Students become teachers, sharing their newly acquired knowledge. Our profession, typically perceived as catering to an elite few, demonstrates its capacity to care for and contribute to many.

Summer programs can be productive and rewarding venues for public interest design learning. For example, the Center for Sustainable Development at the University of Texas at Austin School of Architecture recently launched the Public Interest Design Program, a local ten-week design/build experience supported by two seminars. The seminars focus on evaluation, particularly of public interest design efforts, and methods of community engagement. The program's website indicates that the program "challenges students to

Figure 30.1 During the summer of 2010, three NC State University graduate architecture students—Megan Patnaik, Adam Harker, and Courtney Evans—partnered with Sanders Service Center, a nonprofit that provided emergency relief services in four rural counties of North Carolina. The organization's charismatic leader Lillie Sanders desired a storage shed to stockpile relief supplies. The student team agreed to design and build the project. They received independent study credit for their efforts. Images and rendering courtesy of the design/build team.

Figure 30.2 The student team used a physical model and three-dimensional computer renderings to communicate their design to Ms. Sanders, as well as to study the shed's construction system.

Figure 30.3 Ms. Sanders included friends and neighbors in the process, ensuring the shed like her organization would have broad community support.

develop theoretical and practical skills to respond to the ethical complications of engaging the public and its spaces" (University of Texas-Austin School of Architecture, n.d.). Students may seek out this type of program to augment their learning in the traditional curriculum.

Many architectural educators organize study-abroad experiences to expose students to other cultures and highlight the relative privilege many of us enjoy in the United States. The BaSiC Initiative, led by Palleroni and others, employs this strategy to take students out of their comfort zones and open their eyes to new ways for their design education to be applied. Such international experiences often incorporate a service component. Students gain valuable cross-cultural appreciation, often learn about new building systems, and in the best cases acquire new perspectives about our role in the global system. As Palleroni writes,

> I often compare the situation of living in the United States to being in the eye of the storm. When you are standing in the eye of the storm, everything seems calm. But as you step away from the eye of the storm, you realize that this storm you're at the center of is changing the rest of the world dramatically.
>
> (Palleroni, 2008)

We have also seen a rise in the interest of—and opportunities for—architecture students to construct what they design, often small structures for public spaces intended for community use or homes for affordable housing providers. The community of users is often involved in the design process. Public interest objectives combined with the hands-on nature of the architectural training has led to the increase and popularity of these "design/build" programs. The number of schools offering design/build is increasing at an astonishing rate. It is difficult to know how many programs exist at any given time. They vary greatly based on the university and community context in which they exist. Some are established as permanent curricular offerings; others are offered occasionally or informally, for example as independent study projects. Two well-known programs where students are designing and

Figure 30.4 The student team solicited material donations and volunteered their construction time in order to deliver the shed at no expense to their nonprofit partner.

Figure 30.5 Ms. Sanders was an engaged partner—active in the design phase, quick to pick up a paintbrush, and delighted by the enhanced capacity the shed provided.

constructing structures for academic credit are the Building Project at Yale University School of Architecture and Auburn University School of Architecture's Rural Studio.

At Yale, first-year students enrolled in the three-year Master of Architecture program participate in a required first-year Building Project (Yale School of Architecture, n.d.). An innovation in architectural education, the Building Project was instituted in the late 1960s by Charles Moore, then Dean at the school, and is the longest running design/build program in the US. During the program's early years students built community service buildings in Appalachia (community and recreation centers, a health clinic) and then park structures near the campus. For about the last 25 years students in the program have been building affordable housing in and around New Haven, Connecticut where Yale is located.

The best-known design/build program that has inspired many other academic design/build programs is Auburn University's Rural Studio (Auburn University.,n.d.). Established by professors D.K. Ruth and Samuel Mockbee in 1992, students are embedded in Hale County, Alabama. Students learn by designing and building while living in the community, one of the poorest areas in the nation, for a year as undergraduates and/or graduate students. The inventiveness and freshness of the designs, the processes and student experiences, as well as the stories of the structures and the people served, have made the program famous all over the world and have captured the imagination and hearts of architects and the public alike.

Another student-oriented design/build program, the American Institute of Architecture Students (AIAS) Freedom by Design, engages architecture students in improving the accessibility and safety of homes of low-income and disabled community members. Architect Brad Buchanan, FAIA, started the program in 2000 to address accessibility needs in his local Denver area. In 2006, the AIAS expanded the program to the national level (The American Institute of Architecture Students, n.d.a). Students in AIAS chapters design and then build stairs, ramps, bathrooms, and other key accessibility and life safety upgrades for their clients, working under the mentorship of local architects and designers. This integration of real-world architectural experience with dedicated service learning "empowers architecture students to become owners in a process that radically impacts the lives of people" who need architectural design the most (American Institute of Architecture Students, n.d.b).

Changes by NCARB to the regulations regarding IDP experiences instituted in 2013 and 2015 are the most dramatic shifts we have seen in years and could significantly change the landscape of architectural education and internship. These include experience start requirements, work duration, and work and supervisor/mentor settings. Some have the potential to meaningfully affect academic curricula and expand the availability of university-based public interest internships. At NC State University we have taken note of two of these IDP changes: the removal of the "minimum work hours per week" requirement and the new regulation allowing students to earn academic credit and IDP credit in a combined experience. We have formed a pilot studio course, called Public Interest Architecture (PIA), which integrates architectural coursework with real-world experience in architectural offices through design work on community partnership projects, offering valuable academic, workplace, and service-learning experience. This course enriches the architecture curriculum in its response to two strategic goals set by the university: to enhance the success of our students through educational innovation and to enhance community engagement through strategic sustainable partnerships.

The PIA course was first taught by Professor Georgia Bizios who is a licensed architect, as a vertical studio of fourth-year undergraduate and advanced graduate students during the spring

2014 semester. Instead of the traditional architecture studio project, where students design hypothetical buildings with few client or budgetary constraints, the PIA studio included two projects, both with nonprofit partners. Students worked on these projects at the university and at participating local architecture firms, earning academic credit, IDP credit, and monetary compensation (required for earning IDP credit) through grant funding. They were assigned as interns to participating firms through a portfolio review and [mock] interview process, working alongside architects and designers throughout the semester. These practitioners critiqued and mentored the students on their community projects. In return, the students assisted the practitioners with non-billable tasks in the offices for 8–10 hours per week on average, gaining firsthand professional architectural experience on a wide array of projects.

The implementation of this innovative studio was made possible through grants from the NC State University Foundation and the university's Office of Extension and Economic Development Engagement, received by responding to competitive requests for proposals. Additional funding was provided by the community nonprofit partners. The plan is that participating architectural offices will form a PIA Consortium. Consortium membership fees will create a fund to support future student interns and community partnership projects. Through this PIA studio, the students receive real-world professional architectural experience while working on significant community projects, IDP credit towards their licensure, and monetary compensation through grants. The community partners gain design expertise they would otherwise not receive or be able to afford. The participating firms are involved in community design projects and benefit from the assistance of student interns. And NC State University furthers its community engagement goals.

Beyond the University

The training of an architect is far from complete upon receipt of an academic degree. In addition to these university-based public interest experiences, there exist a small but growing number of IDP-accruing opportunities intended to prepare interns for public interest practice. The internship period provides future practitioners with experience and skills that are better acquired in the job place than in a university setting. These public interest internship opportunities are offered by universities, nonprofits, and architectural practices, usually as post-graduation or summer employment. Although such positions are few, a survey of the available options reveals some exemplary models of best practice.

Several schools of architecture have developed opportunities for students to work on community engagement projects and receive payment and IDP credit with faculty supervision. A few such efforts are featured in the essay collection *Bridging the Gap: Public Interest Architectural Internships* (Bizios & Wakeford, 2011). Essays describe various programs and assess their strengths, weaknesses, and results. One example of a successful program that has received recognition and publicity is the Gulf Coast Community Design Studio (GCCDS) in Biloxi, Mississippi. The program grew from the devastation of Hurricane Katrina. It provides local citizens and organizations with design consultation and services as they continue to rebuild their region. The GCCDS hosts one-year interns who work on community-based design and planning projects. This program offers simultaneous coursework culminating in a Certificate in Public Design from Mississippi State University. Interns work alongside GCCDS's professional staff and receive IDP credit. The position gives them exposure to critical elements of public interest practice including community organizing and advocacy planning, nonprofit structures, and fundraising (Gulf Coast Community Design Studio, n.d.).

The Enterprise Rose Architectural Fellowships are prestigious three-year placements for early-career design professionals. Fellows work in partnership with community development organizations to create affordable and sustainable housing and neighborhoods. The program began in 2000. Since that time, 50 fellows have contributed to the development of 8,000 housing units (Enterprise Community Partners, Inc. n.d.). Rose Fellowships are noteworthy for paying competitive wages and providing benefits, attributes that are often missing from public interest architecture positions. Many former fellows hold prominent leadership positions in the public interest design field. Jess Zimbabwe, a fellow from 2003–6, is now executive director of the Urban Land Institutes Daniel Rose Center for Public Leadership. She wrote of her work as a Rose Fellow with Urban Ecology (Oakland, CA), "This amazing project taught me some very technical competencies in architecture, along with dozens of other skills in community organizing, real-estate development, public agency negotiations, and contractor relations" (Zimbabwe, 2011).

Another robust fellowship program is sponsored by the building community Workshop (bcWorkshop) located in Dallas, Texas. Under the leadership of architect Brent Brown, this nonprofit community design center employs young designers to participate in their public interest design efforts. In a powerful TED Talk, Brown describes the goal of providing design justice through community engagement (Brown, n.d.). He outlines the strategy of pairing local experiential social capital with architectural creativity and technical experience. Speaking of the bcWorkshop fellows, he emphasizes their desire to be "relevant," applying their craft of design to pressing community issues.

Interns also find valuable experience at organizations that recruit them as volunteers. Architecture for Humanity (AFH) frequently engages interns, providing a modest stipend in some cases. The organization works nationally and internationally, frequently in response to natural disasters. AFH volunteers gain experience working with non-governmental agencies, displaced populations, and community resilience efforts.

Public Architecture, a San Francisco-based nonprofit advocacy agency, and its program "The 1%" engage summer associates (undergraduate or graduate student interns) to support their advocacy, outreach, and pro bono match-making efforts. "The 1%" organization aims to be a facilitator for alternative practice by helping architecture firms partner with community partners that need pro bono design services. As of 2014, the program has fostered over 400,000 hours contributed annually to community projects by over 1,200 participating firms (The 1%, n.d.). The organization is funded by donations, grants, and foundation support, but volunteering student summer associates are required to secure either funding or course credit from their university (Public Architecture, n.d.). These summer associates gain experience in fundraising, research and writing, public relations, and pro bono design strategies.

Despite the availability of these outstanding programs, the reality is that there are far fewer public interest architecture jobs than interested applicants. As Palleroni writes in the forward of *Bridging the Gap: Public-Interest Architectural Internships*,

> The transition to practice has been difficult for the growing number of students interested in more publicly engaged practice, because training opportunities—true professional training, the kind you get in your first years of practice or in internships—have been scarce to nonexistent. It is in this wasteland of lack of opportunity that we lose so many of our most promising designers, despite all of our efforts as educators to instill in them the skills to make the transition.
>
> (Palleroni, 2011)

We know that architectural internships often influence the direction of a professional life. It will be important to foster additional public internship opportunities as this segment of the profession grows.

No matter what career path they choose, public interest design projects often give students and interns diverse, demanding, and life-changing experiences. The question now becomes how we can scale up existing programs and develop new ones to create enough career opportunities in public interest architecture to meet and expand the demand from students and emerging professionals.

Other Sites of Change Affecting Education and Internship

While future architects are laboring to earn their degrees and accrue IDP credits, the profession is evolving too. A culture of public interest design is swelling and issues of equity and accountability are gaining visibility. There is significant evidence of change, and it is reasonable to assume these recent shifts in the profession have and will continue to influence how we educate and train the next generation of architects.

For example, there is a much-needed body of knowledge growing around public interest design. A welcome library of publications highlights the opportunities and challenges of community-engaged work, international relief efforts, and expanded pro bono models. Notably, *Expanding Architecture: Design as Activism* collects essays from across the design fields with attention to asset-based approaches, affordable housing, prefabrication, and the power of education (Bell & Wakeford, 2008). *Bridging the Gap: Public Interest Architectural Internships* shines attention on the importance and need for early-career public interest design job opportunities (Bizios & Wakeford, 2011). *Design Like You Give a Damn (Volumes One and Two)* document the work of Architecture for Humanity with first-person accounts and case studies (Architecture for Humanity, 2006; Architecture for Humanity, 2012). *The Power of Pro Bono* collects examples of mainstream firms joining with neighborhoods and nonprofits to generate inspiring projects (Cary, 2010). Major magazines such as *Architectural Record* and *Metropolis* have begun to commit annual monthly issues to public interest topics. A lively website and blog, *PublicInterestDesign.org*, founded by design activist John Cary, serves as a clearinghouse for all exhibits, articles, calls for submissions, and newsworthy events in this realm. All of these publications are fueling a vibrant discussion about the present and future of public interest architecture and its impact on the profession.

Assessment and evaluation has been a long-standing challenge for the architectural discipline, and the public interest sector is making significant strides with the emergence of SEED (Social, Economic, and Environmental Design) (SEED Network, n.d.). SEED is a network of practitioners committed to a design process that prioritizes community participation and recognizes the triple bottom line of social, economic, and environmental impacts that designers must consider. The SEED organization has sponsored the development of an "Evaluator" which helps communities and designers to set goals for a project and measure its success with input from a third-party review system. SEED is gathering case studies, another piece of the growing public interest design knowledge base, to provide examples of best practices and lessons learned. SEED has also begun a series of short documentaries as part of their case study efforts.

There is also a strong calendar of events and recognitions related to this movement of public interest design. The annual *Structures for Inclusion* conference, organized by the North Carolina nonprofit Design Corps and its founder Bryan Bell, is particularly geared toward students and young professionals. In recent years, it has been closely coordinated with SEED and has served as a venue for the presentation of SEED Awards for design excellence with an emphasis on inclusivity and impact. The Association of Community Design, founded in 1977, continues to be a fertile professional organization, hosting annual gatherings. ACSA national and regional conferences have hosted a growing number of sessions related to service learning, design/build, and education of the citizen architect.

Many of the recognitions come with financial support. The National Endowment for the Arts has been a generous funder of public interest design publications and projects, including some mentioned above. The 2014 Pritzker Prize was awarded to Shigeru Ban who has committed much of his career to humanitarian design. The prize is arguably the most prestigious international architecture award and comes with a $100,000 purse. Also in 2014, Autodesk, a leading architectural software company, launched the Autodesk Foundation to support what they have coined Impact Design with the goal of funding a "wide spectrum of innovative, scalable, and measurable design solutions that address some of the most epic challenges of our time" (The Autodesk Foundation, n.d.a).

The prestigious AIA Latrobe Prize is awarded biennially for "research leading to significant advances in the architecture profession" (The American Institute of Architects, n.d.). In 2011, the $100,000 grant was given to Bryan Bell, executive director of Design Corps, Roberta Feldman, professor at the University of Illinois Chicago, Sergio Palleroni, professor at Portland State University, and David Perkes, professor at Mississippi State University and GCCDS director. The team proposed to "investigate the needs that can be addressed by public interest practices and the variety of ways that public interest practices are operating" (The American Institute of Architects, n.d.b). It was the first time the grant was given for researching public interest design. In 2013, the team published a comprehensive report of their study and findings entitled *Wisdom from the Field: Public Interest Architecture in Practice—A Guide to Public Interest Practices in Architecture*. In the press release for the report the AIA indicated that,

> Among the findings of the report is that public interest design is transforming architectural practices. This transformation to a more public interest model can be seen as a wide-spread response to the concern that the conventional model of practice responds solely to the paying client, limiting the profession's capacity to address problems of our time.
>
> (The American Institute of Architects, n.d.c)

It is noteworthy that the profession is being transformed by public interest design, and it is natural to assume that this transformation would have implications for architectural internships and education. Portland State University has recently established a Center for Public Interest Design and credits its formation to the Latrobe Prize research and findings (Portland State School of Architecture, n.d.).

We have recently seen significant change in attitudes and rules by the AIA regarding public interest practice. For example, a momentous change by the AIA is the inclusion of public interest design in *The Architect's Handbook of Practice*, the official reference document of the profession's standards of practice. Press releases for the fifteenth edition that became available in December 2013 report that this edition includes up to two-thirds new information. Some of the new content highlights emerging ways of practice deemed to have the potential to become important in the future. The fourth chapter in "Part 1, The Profession" is devoted to public interest design. It provides a thorough overview of socially responsible design. Contributor Rachel Minnery defines a socially responsible architect as one who:

> believes that buildings influence people's lives, that people influence the design of buildings, and that architects are accountable for the impact of their work on people and the environment. Public interest design tends to the common good and advocates for design as a means to help alleviate social distress.
>
> (American Institute of Architects, 2013)

In addition to an overview of socially responsible design, the handbook discusses the role of architects in disaster response and recovery, the nonprofit sector, and in public service and community involvement. The inclusion of public interest design as a chapter in the latest AIA Handbook is an assurance that this way of practice is entering the mainstream in the profession, a fact that is bound to have repercussions on architectural education and internship.

Another example of innovation in the area of emerging professionals and the role they can play in helping communities revitalize and rebuild by providing design services is the National Design Services Act (NDSA). Developed through collaboration by the AIA and the AIAS, the act was introduced by bipartisan support in Congress (H.R. 4205) in March 2014. Upon passage, the bill would give architecture students relief from student loan debt similar to relief granted to students in other professional disciplines such as medicine and law. It would authorize the Department of Housing and Urban Development (HUD) to assist young graduates with the payment of their student loans when they work with community design centers providing design services to underserved communities. In a press release about the bill's introduction AIA CEO Robert Ivy, FAIA, noted, "Millions of young people aspire to help their communities build a better future—but lack of opportunity and the crushing cost of education hold them back" (The American Institute of Architects, n.d.d).

Moving Forward

Certainly, there exists more than one way to train a citizen architect. Schools of architecture as well as the professional and regulatory organizations are recognizing that a more flexible and heterogeneous system will benefit students, the profession, and the public. Curricula and internships will continue to provide a greater number of vehicles for learning about socially, economically, and environmentally responsible design. The academy and the profession cannot afford to miss the opportunity to prepare architects committed to serve their communities and the world by addressing more issues, providing more services, serving more people (Bell, 2008).

Current conditions and recent events in public interest design are worth noting and reflecting upon because they are mainstreaming novel ways of thinking and suggest some meaningful trends regarding educating and training/licensing socially-minded architects. As designers are responding to high profile forces such as global warming, growing economic divides, and natural disasters with a renewed sense of responsibility, relevance, and capacity to contribute to the common good, students and young professionals have the awareness, desire, energy, and skills to grow these efforts.

It is not our goal to conjecture, but we are optimistic that the many changes documented in this chapter, some modest, some significant, are contributing to a new landscape. Thomas Fisher suggests we might see the emergence of a new sector in the profession much like public health developed from medicine and public defense from law (Fisher, 2008). It seems clear the present terrain will continue to evolve. The democratization of architecture will continue to grow and take hold in the profession. This ethic and associated opportunities will become more prevalent and visible. While the values of public interest architecture will hopefully touch all students and professionals, some will want to make this work a career specialty.

Wherever these changes, trends, and movements may lead us, we must set lofty goals for our students, ourselves, and our profession. As ethicist and architect Victoria Beach writes, "We could design our future architects to be leaders beyond the profession— to use the creativity unique to our profession to guide society toward a more humane, engaging, and beautiful inhabitation of the planet" (Beach, 2011). If we can do that, we have indeed achieved the making of a citizen architect.

Acknowledgments

The authors would like to thank NC State graduate architecture student William Sendor for his thoughtful and diligent contributions to this chapter.

References

American Institute of Architects (2013). *The Architect's Handbook of Professional Practice*, 15th ed. Hoboken, NJ: Wiley.

American Institute of Architects (n.d.a). *Pressroom: AIA College of Fellows Awards 2013 Latrobe Prize for "Urban Sphere: The City of 7 Billion"*. Retrieved July 16, 2014 from: http://www.aia.org/press/releases/aiab097878.

American Institute of Architects (n.d.b). *Pressroom: AIA College of Fellows Awards 2011 Latrobe Prize for "Public Interest Practices in Architecture"*. Retrieved July 16, 2014 from: http://www.aia.org/press/releases/aiab087557.

American Institute of Architects (n.d.c). *Pressroom: 2011 Latrobe Prize for "Public Interest Practices in Architecture" Report Now Available.* Retrieved July 16, 2014 from: http://www.aia.org/press/releases/aiab099588

American Institute of Architects (n.d.d). *Pressroom: Architects Issue 2014 "Punch List" for Congress.* Retrieved July 16, 2014 from: http://www.aia.org/press/releases/aiab 101272.

American Institute of Architecture Students (n.d.a). *AIAS Freedom by Design Instructional Manual.* Washington, DC: AIAS.

American Institute of Architecture Students (n.d.b). *For AIAS Chapters*. Retrieved July 16, 2014 from: http://www.aias.org/website/article.asp?id=1585.

Architecture for Humanity (ed.) (2006). *Design Like You Give a Damn: Architectural Responses to Humanitarian Crises*. New York: Metropolis Books.

Architecture for Humanity (ed.) (2012). *Design Like You Give a Damn (2): Building Change from Ground Up*. New York: Abrams.

Auburn University.(n.d.). *Welcome: Rural Studio*. Retrieved July 16, 2014 from: http://www.ruralstudio.org/.

Autodesk Foundation (n.d.). *What is Impact Design*? Retrieved July 16, 2014 from: http://www.autodesk.org/impact-design.

Beach, V. (2011). The Ethical Advantages of Public-Service Internships. In G. Bizios & K. Wakeford (eds.), *Bridging the Gap: Public-Interest Architectural Internships*. Raleigh, NC: Lulu Press. 13.

Bell, B. (2008). Preface: Expanding Design Toward Greater Relevance. In B. Bell & K. Wakeford (eds.), *Expanding Architecture: Design as Activism*. New York: Metropolis Books.

Bell, B. & Wakeford, K. (2008). *Expanding Architecture: Design as Activism*. New York: Metropolis Books.

Bizios, G. & Wakeford, K. (eds.). (2011). *Bridging the Gap: Public-Interest Architectural Internships*. Raleigh, NC: Lulu Press.

Boyer, E. L. & Mitgang, L. D. (1996). *Building Community: a New Future for Architecture Education and Practice: a Special Report*. Princeton, NJ: Carnegie Foundation for the Advancement of Teaching.

Brown, B. (n.d.). *Building Community: Brent Brown at TEDx SMU*. Retrieved April 26, 2012 from: https://www.youtube.com/watch?v=M3nLaTCwEvQ.

Cary, J. (2010). *The Power of Pro Bono: 40 Stories about Design for the Public Good by Architects and their Clients*. New York: Metropolis Books.

Enterprise Community Partners, Inc. (n.d.). *About the Enterprise Rose Architectural Fellowship: Accomplishments*. Retrieved July 16, 2014 from: http://www.enterprisecommunity.com/solutions-and-innovation/design-leadership/rose-architectural-fellowship/about-the-fellowship.

Fisher, T. (2008). Foreword. In B. Bell & K. Wakeford (eds.), *Expanding Architecture: Design as Activism*. New York: Metropolis Books.

Gulf Coast Community Design Studio. (n.d.). *Home Page*. Retrieved July 16, 2014 from: http://www.gccds.org/.

Mockbee, S. (2004). Relating Social Needs to Design: The Role of the Citizen Architect. In B. Bell (ed.), *Good Deeds, Good Design: Community Service through Architecture*. New York: Princeton Architectural Press. 151–156.

National Architectural Accrediting Board. (n.d.). *Home Page*. Retrieved July 16, 2014 from: http://www.naab.org/.

National Council of Architectural Registration Boards (2013). *NCARB by the Numbers*. Retrieved from http://www.ncarb.org/en/About-NCARB/NCARB-by-the-Numbers/~/media/Files/PDF/Special-Paper/NCARB_by_the_Numbers_2013.ashx.

National Council of Architectural Registration Boards. (n.d.). *Certification and Reciprocity*. Retrieved January 26, 2015: from http://www.ncarb.org/en/Certification-and-Reciprocity.aspx.

Palleroni, S. (2004). *Studio at Large: Architecture in Service of Global Communities*. Seattle, WA: University of Washington Press.

Palleroni, S. (2008). El programa de vivienda ecológica: Building the Capacity of Yaqui Women to Help Themselves. In B. Bell & K. Wakeford (eds.), *Expanding Architecture: Design as Activism*. New York: Metropolis Books. 275.

Palleroni, S. (2011). Foreword. In G. Bizios & K. Wakeford (eds.), *Bridging the Gap: Public-Interest Architectural Internships*. Raleigh, NC: Lulu Press, 2011. xi.

Portland State School of Architecture. (n.d.). *Portland State School of Architecture: Center for Public Interest Design | Welcome*. Retrieved July 24, 2014 from: http://www.pdx.edu/public-interest-design/.

Public Architecture. (n.d.). *The Public Dialogue: A Blog by Public Architecture*. Retrieved July 23, 2014 from: http://www.publicarchitecture.org/blog/seeking-summer-associates/.

Schuman, A.W. (2006). Introduction: The Pedagogy of Engagement. In M.C. Hardin (ed.), *From the Studio to the Streets: Service-Learning in Planning and Architecture*. Sterling, VA: Stylus. 8.

Schuman, A.W. (2012). Community Engagement: Architecture's Evolving Social Vocation. In J. Ockman (ed.), *Architecture School: Three Centuries of Educating Architects in North America*. Cambridge, MA: ACSA / MIT Press. 252.

SEED Network. (n.d.). *Welcome to SEED: Social Economic Environmental Design*. Retrieved July 16, 2014 from: http://www.seed-network.org/.

The 1%. (n.d.). *Strengthening Nonprofits Through Design—Participants*. Retrieved July 23, 2014 from: http://www.theonepercent.org/About/Participants.htm.

University of Texas-Austin School of Architecture. (n.d.). *Home Page*. Retrieved July 16, 2014 from: http://soa.utexas.edu/.

Yale School of Architecture. (n.d.). *The Jim Vlock First Year Building Project*. Retrieved July 16, 2014 from: http://architecture.yale.edu/student-life/vlock-building-project.

Zimbabwe, J. (2011). Fitting the Square Peg of a Service-Oriented Internship into the Round Hole of IDP. In G. Bizios & K. Wakeford (eds.), *Bridging the Gap: Public-Interest Architectural Internships*. Raleigh, NC: Lulu Press. 51.

31

Internationalism in Architecture Education and Practice

Sharon Carter Matthews

In April of 2008 representatives of seven architectural quality assurance agencies met in Canberra, Australia, and signed an accord which recognized that graduates of their various institutions had qualifications deemed substantially equivalent by the signatories. The signing marked an important first moment of global cooperation among accrediting agencies from six countries (Canada, the United States, Mexico, China, South Korea, Australia) and the agency validating architecture degree programs in countries of the British Commonwealth. The Canberra Accord is, however, only one example of the many international agreements and events bringing education in the design professions together globally. Design education in Europe is reviewed with respect to educational standards described as national qualifications frameworks rather than by accreditation or validation systems and these frameworks are compared internationally, as another example, for equivalency. Whether the measurement of the quality of architectural education is called validation, or accreditation, or a framework, there is a worldwide movement toward clear, transferable educational standards. The design professions are becoming increasingly globalized and the following text is a report on how the academy and quality assurance agencies are—and may be in the future—responding to that trend. The intention of this chapter is to describe current international networks of design practitioners and educators; to propose opportunities in design education that are relevant to global practices; to comment on current changes in design education; and, to add some observations on the likely international directions design education will take in the near future.

Prior to the 1990s the network of organizations and institutions supporting global interactions that affected architectural education was quite small. Information about accreditation standards, building projects, funding opportunities, curricula, competitions, conferences, practice requirements, and international journals was hard to find and often out of date by the time it was discovered. All this has changed. In order to design your own education, or navigate a career path, or manage a degree program it is critical to understand the vastly expanded network of resources available on the internet.

The largest relevant organizations include higher education as a category of international trade (World Trade Organization, 1995). Regional educational cooperation is supported in the spirit of the North American Free Trade Agreement (Consortium for North American Higher Education Collaboration, 1994). And within the profession of architecture, the International Union of Architects (Union Internationale des Architectes or UIA) published their guidelines for architectural education (UIA, 1996) in the mid-1990s. Since that time, as with other aspects of internationalization, these worldwide aspirations have become actions at local levels. The National Architectural Accrediting Board (NAAB) in the United States now reviews programs outside national boundaries for full accreditation (NAAB, 2014). In Europe, the Bologna Process brings the educational systems of countries within that agreement closer in standards and makes it easier for students to move among national systems. None of these changes has happened without debate and criticism but since the 1990s the trend has been consistently toward international agreements that would encourage mobility and transferability of credentials on the part of students and faculty.

The registration of international architects in the US, and of US architects wishing to practice abroad, is also now facilitated by multi-national agreements. In the US, the regulatory boards have established a process, managed by the NAAB, which serves as a path for architects from other countries to become licensed in the US (NAAB-EESA, 2014). At this time, each domestic and international jurisdiction holding the power to license or register architects acts independently—some with complicated and expensive processes to licensure, some with no requirement beyond holding a degree—and with varying regional accommodations. In the US there are three requirements for the license: education, experience, and examination, although the specifics of each vary by state or territory. In many other countries, however, the only requirement is education. The educational experience in those countries may, but does not always, include professional examinations and internship as part of students' degree programs. As nations work toward stronger participation in various global markets, regulations are changing rapidly. Local regulators are often adding requirements for internships, for examinations, and for continuing education units.

Non-regulatory national associations of architects belong to the only global association of architects—the UIA, based in Paris. The UIA holds a congress every three years and has established several committees to work on issues deemed important for the membership organizations, including education and the validation of professional architecture degree programs. The UIA also hosts a searchable database on their website with information about requirements, by country, for the legal practice of architecture; information which is submitted by, and is the responsibility of, member organizations. National associations, like the AIA, interact globally through the UIA but also directly with other national and regional associations such as the National Council of Architectural Registration Boards (NCARB). The AIA has also now established an "International Region" with representation on the national board of AIA directors and membership composed of American architects working outside the United States in local chapters. International architects with significant bodies of work, either in the built environment or in education, are recognized by the AIA as honorary fellows of the Institute. In the Far East a regional association of architects, the Architects Regional Council of Asia (ARCASIA), performs functions (meetings, awards, competitions, programs for students and practitioners, etc.) for local chapters of national institutes similar to the functions provided by the UIA worldwide.

In the United States the five major collateral organizations important to the educators responsible for accredited architecture programs represent regulatory boards, students, a membership association for architects, the association for schools and faculty, and the association for accreditation. Since the last decade of the twentieth century all of these organizations have decided that it is useful to their members to include programming and services for a global profession. In other design disciplines and in other countries these functions may be organized differently but the importance of international outreach in their programming is the same. For instance, in the field of interior design there exist both the American Society of Interior Designers (ASID) and the International Interior Design Association (IIDA), organizations focused on different geographical areas rather than on membership categories. As in the profession of architecture, interior design membership organizations belong to the global International Federation of Interior Architects/Designers (IFI).

Associations of architectural educators—which in the past have begun as either a group of schools or as part of a practitioner-based organization—until recently had primarily national agendas but have now become players on the international stage. The Association of Collegiate Schools of Architecture (ACSA) in the US welcomes international membership, holds international conferences, and affiliates with other academic organizations outside the US. The Royal Institute of British Architects (RIBA) routinely visits schools for determinations of quality assurance outside the United Kingdom. The Commonwealth Association of Architects (CAA), which began as an association limited to British Commonwealth countries, now validates programs in an expanded list of Commonwealth member countries including Rwanda and Mozambique. Students in the US—and the UK and elsewhere—also have organizations with international agendas.

Beyond the quality assurance reviews of educational degree programs, requirements for internship, examinations of learning, and regulatory requirements for legally practicing architecture, there is an international culture of architectural events which inevitably impacts both higher education curricula and the global public perception of design trends. Each time there is an Olympic sporting event the general public sees buildings demonstrating current architectural imagery and construction techniques. Every other year there is a popular international exhibition in Venice (Biennale di Venezia) presenting the work of leading architectural designers from many countries. And every year there is an influential international design exhibition of furniture and furnishings in Milan (Salone Internazionale del Mobile di Milano). The publicity surrounding these kinds of events and the ability of students and faculty from all over the world to observe them from conception to reality via the internet means we are all often either copying or reacting to, both positively and negatively, a common global culture of design.

Practice

This section depends heavily upon recent articles in Design Intelligence written by Scott Simpson—first Design Goes Global; then Beyond Borders: the ABCs of International Practice; and finally Learning by Design (Simpson, 2013a, 2013b and 2010) He, and his publisher, have kindly given permission to quote broadly from these articles where he summarizes issues to be considered before investing in international practice and taking on international projects. His advice about how to avoid disasters is both direct and comprehensive. His focus is on practice as a successful business—without which great design seldom happens—leaving questions of academic design theory to others. Mr. Simpson, FAIA, LEED AP, is Senior Director at KlingStubbins, a global design firm with offices in the USA and China. He is a Senior Fellow of the Design Futures Council (an organization convened by the Greenway Group, publishers of the Design Intelligence newsletters), has published more than 160 articles on issues of innovation in the design professions, and has co-authored two books: *How Firms Succeed—A Field Guide to Design*

Management, and *The Next Architect—A New Twist on the Future of Design*. The author is very grateful for his kindness in sharing his thinking.

His understanding of how to think about international practice provides a framework for balancing risks and rewards while giving direction to goals for student learning. In Design Goes Global he says,

> Technology, especially building information modeling (BIM), makes borders porous. Outsourcing makes overseas collaboration fast and cheap. Huge international projects provide welcome opportunities for design firms as the domestic market continues to struggle with a spotty recovery.

These comments, basic to considering international practice, are indicative of the assumptions that can be questioned and debated as courses in professional practice and design studios evolve to include international opportunities. Students will need to know in what kinds of circumstances will BIM be effective? How will differing cultural expectations about project management affect the design and construction process? What are the economies, legal requirements, and ethical decisions involved in outsourcing? "Huge international projects" are affected by their social and political environment but it takes an understanding of geopolitics and global economic systems, not just immediate and local personal goals, in order to predict positive outcomes—both built and financial.

In Beyond Borders: the ABCs of International Practice Simpson considers the "shifting, growing markets" that are often reflected in the projects presented in many architecture school lecture series. It is now not even remarked upon that a lecturer would describe perhaps three projects in one lecture, all on different continents. Or, that a one-person practice might be working on a health clinic, to be built by a local client, in another country. Or, that a small-to-medium sized firm engaged in a critical practice will address global issues of climate, conscience, or culture wherever that may take them. Many students today would find an old question, "Where do you intend to practice?" confusing and irrelevant because for their generation the answer is: wherever there is meaningful work in the world. Simpson continues in this article by listing eighteen topics to be addressed if a firm is considering international work, all of which have implications for architectural education.

Approvals

"In the U.S., every jurisdiction has its own unique procedures for obtaining permits and approvals, and the same is true overseas." He recommends taking no shortcuts and, if necessary, hiring a local facilitator. In the US, NAAB-accredited schools are required to have designated faculty or staff to help students understand regulatory practices. These roles could expand to include information on how to proceed with respect to practice regulations in other countries.

The position of the UIA on practicing in a host nation is stated in its "UIA Accord on Recommended International Standards of Professionalism in Architectural Practice" and is quoted here:

> Architects providing architectural services on a project in a country in which they are not registered shall collaborate with a local architect to ensure that proper and effective understanding is given to legal, environmental, social, cultural, and heritage factors. The

conditions of the association should be determined by the parties alone in accordance with UIA ethical standards and local statutes and laws.

(UIA, 1999)

Budgeting

As Simpson points out in this section, there will be larger travel costs, extra time will be needed to accommodate jet lag on both ends of trips, there will be less time available for domestic projects, and larger contingency amounts will need to be budgeted. As noted in other sections of his article there may be unexpected taxes and fees; money should be allowed for IT training and equipment; and there could be additional expense for extended insurance coverage. All these topics could be considered in professional practice classes—especially when crafting business plans.

Codes

Simpson notes that interpretation and enforcement can vary widely—thus knowledge of local practices and key players will be necessary, and that using local professionals with expertise in the appropriate building type can be helpful. Architects who come to the US with international experience must become familiar with US codes before it is possible for them to be licensed in any of the 54 jurisdictions, and US architects need to acquire expertise in codes of other nations. The International Building Code is not commonly used outside the United States and does not guarantee local compliance.

Collaboration

From Simpson: "Some large firms maintain a network of overseas offices, some tap into pre-established consulting networks, and others form project-specific teams that include local professionals with the requisite skills." As the skills necessary for success in architectural projects are so clearly presented in Andy Pressman's recent book on collaboration (Pressman, 2014), these same skills are also critical to success in international teamwork. In many schools they are learned through community service projects.

Construction

Simpson recommends researching the "skill sets that are locally available" and "to seek out the best construction managers and subcontractors." He points out that building techniques can vary widely and gives the example of using bamboo scaffolding on high-rise structures in China. Common building strategies that are different from the prevailing methods in the US could be considered in classes for structures, environmental control systems, and materials and methods content. Students' and practitioners' attitudes about these subjects will benefit from exploring alternative choices based on local practices.

Culture

"Successful international practice requires sensitivity and appreciation of differences." It may be reassuring to dwell on similarities in education ("We both went to Harvard."), or common networks of professionals ("I saw him at the last UIA congress"), or shared language skills ("They speak English!"), but it is more rewarding in the long run to understand and be sensitive to real differences in the use of "language, culture, food, music, social customs, religion, geography, [and] business practices." Respecting differences is key to developing collaborative relationships. Providing students with a multi-cultural academic environment and demonstrating respect in the classroom sends a powerful message to emerging professionals.

Deliverables

Work products and the processes that create them can be very different outside the US. Simpson reports that "firms will provide SD or 'heavy DD' documentation, only with the balance being handled by local firms." Furthermore "specifications are unlikely to be followed to the letter." It is important to think through design priorities and expectations (and business terms) before beginning the work. Programs for studio projects could be designed with these kinds of parameters made explicit so that the students have a chance to confront the inherent frustrations in the field and work through possible alternatives.

Documentation

BIM is recommended by Simpson as a common IT platform and if partners are not equally proficient it makes sense to organize training programs and provide the necessary hardware to bring everyone to the same level of expertise. The use of BIM and consideration of Integrated Project Delivery methods are becoming more common in architecture schools in the US and that expertise will serve students well in international practices. Questioning assumptions about exactly which documents are required is also an exercise that could be included in curricula.

Ethics

There is legislation called the US Foreign Corrupt Practices Act with which firms must fully comply:

> The Foreign Corrupt Practices Act of 1977, as amended, 15 U.S.C. §§ 78dd-1, et seq. ("FCPA"), was enacted for the purpose of making it unlawful for certain classes of persons and entities to make payments to foreign government officials to assist in obtaining or retaining business.
>
> (US Department of Justice, 1998)

As Simpson notes, "It's far better to resign the commission than become involved with any one or anything that would put you or your firm in jeopardy." This legislation could be included in course assignments just as we now include domestic laws and regulations.

Liability

He recommends in this section that firms check for "special provisions or exclusions that may apply to overseas projects," to "arrange for additional coverage as appropriate" and to "consider taking out separate insurance policies so that there is no cross-contamination with your existing coverages." All these topics could be included in professional practice courses and might be presented by representatives of the insurance industry.

Litigation

Legal processes in other countries are often unlike those in the US and very unlikely to have a positive outcome for US architects. Practitioners need to be aware of these differences and talk about them early on with their local partners. When students are reviewing litigation issues in the US, they can also consider what might happen with projects in other countries operating under different legal systems. Simpson advises: "It's far better (and cheaper) to invest extra energy in maintaining excellent client relations to minimize the possibility of problems arising in the first place."

Marketing

Marketing is not a subject commonly taught in architecture programs either in the US or abroad. Whether it should be included in a curriculum is debatable but many practitioners soon learn to budget both time and money for activities in order to build their firms' reputations. Doing this in the international marketplace is, according to Simpson, "expensive, requiring lots of time, travel, and money." His comment in this section is to maintain "a few key relationships and let the practice grow organically." He also says that competitions—common in the awarding of commissions outside the US—are a "high risk, low reward way to pursue work, and they tend to be 'one-off' successes."

Materials

Understanding that your first choice of materials might not be available and might not be of consistent quality means studying "local architecture, building customs, and construction techniques to take full advantage of what's unique (and possible) about building on the given site." This kind of understanding is part of the NAAB requirement for accredited programs to address with their students in meeting the History and Global Culture student performance criterion in the 2014 NAAB Conditions for Accreditation.

Payment

Standard payment arrangements in the US may not be followed in international projects. Simpson recommends requiring a retainer, tracking cash flow carefully, not counting on the last payment, and monitoring fluctuating currency values. These are all topics that could be included in a professional practice class. Students will find this information useful in dealing with domestic projects as well as international ones.

Quality

When the quality of a project depends upon controlling a third-party supplier of materials and the actual construction workers, US architects have little chance of being responsible for a predictable end result. And, if they cannot provide construction administration service, Simpson says that it is "especially important to deal only with reputable construction managers, suppliers, and subcontractors." Students involved in team projects in design schools can develop an awareness of effective team behavior and they could become better judges of expertise and reliability on the part of others.

Taxes

Simpson warns that "it's essential to consider tax consequences when negotiating the contract" and he reminds us "that it may not be possible to move funds easily out of the country." We sometimes don't think of the tax expert as being part of the team of consultants necessary for a building project but this is a good reminder of the range of business expertise it takes to work successfully in a global marketplace.

Technology

Schools of architecture generally have the software and the instructional capability to provide students with the appropriate skills to manage projects online—both domestically and internationally. As courses in Integrated Project Delivery become more sophisticated and more commonplace, this expertise, along with stronger collaboration skills, will make international practice more manageable. Building Information Modeling software is quickly becoming the standard platform for large projects and, Simpson notes, everyone needs to be on the same version and with clearly defined protocols.

Time zones

Working in different time zones can challenge effective project management. As Simpson points out it can be helpful to watch two clocks and it also can extend the time you have to work on a project—earlier in the day for projects to the East and later in the day for those in the West. Time management takes on an expanded meaning.

Travel

And, last on Simpson's list of ABCs is "travel"—which he points out can be expensive, time consuming, and exhausting. It can distract staff from domestic projects and be an "opportunity cost." It does, however, provide the chance to "broaden your perspective" and become more familiar with other cultures. Both aims are consistent with aspirations in current study abroad travel for students, and, we might find adding more student visits to construction sights and international offices rewarding experiences as well.

At the end of Beyond Borders: the ABCs of International Practice, Simpson emphasizes that successful international practices are based on "establishing and maintaining excellent personal relationships." Those relationships all need to be supported by the skills and attitudes described in his list of ABCs. Some of those can be affected by what students learn in school but others will be acquired on the job. Simpson, in another article for *Design Intelligence*—Learning by Design—describes how firms can include life-long learning as a core competency of their organization. He says that "school is not a place—it is an attitude." In the world of international practice there are unlimited opportunities to bring that attitude to bear.

Education

Shifting trends in higher education, combined with a growing sense of the scope and interrelatedness of conditions that affect everyone on the planet, have engaged the imaginations of students and shaped the curricula at almost every school of architecture and design today.

Climate change has implications for higher water levels and intensifying wind and temperature patterns. Wide-spread poverty, the loss of built fabric which represents local cultural heritage, and the disasters of war and of nature are problems that many students and faculty are using as the basis for studio instruction. International websites like www.archiprix.org ask schools to send their best projects—reflecting these global interests—in architecture, urban design, and landscape architecture to share with an international audience. Archiprix schedules biennial presentations of the work, always in a different major city of the world, and maintains a robust website for staying in touch between events. It is their stated intention to be a venue for emerging ideas in design education for the world and students everywhere have access to their design programs and solutions. Other websites like www.sectioncut.com are designed to be an online library of digital resources—another place to share ideas with the world.

The internet makes possible international projects like Archiprix and Sectioncut and it also makes possible international design news coverage. ArchNewsNow at www.archnewsnow.com publishes a newsletter that includes hyperlinks to original sources for stories. There are also current and archived feature stories on its website and links to job information and resources. Publications that recently appeared in its listings include *Architectural Review* (UK), the *Wall Street Journal*, the *San Francisco Chronicle*, *Toronto Star*, *Architecture & Design* (Australia), the *New Zealand Herald*, *South China Morning Post*, and *Gizmodo*. For useful international newsletters with general information about developments in higher education there are the Global section of the *Chronicle of Higher Education* at https://chronicle.com/section/Home/5, *Al-Fanar Media* for news of higher education in the Middle East at http://www.al-fanarmedia.org/, and http://www.universityworldnews.com/ for access to the newsletter from *University World News*.

International conferences of educators happen in a variety of ways. Sometimes they are organized by associations of schools (such as the international conferences of the ACSA), or heads of schools (the annual meetings of the European Network of Heads of Schools of Architecture), and for the past six years there have been biennial meetings of international educators as the result of partnerships with the University of California Los Angeles (UCLA) and schools in Japan, Spain, and Germany. Their International Architectural Education Summits, supported every two years by UCLA, aspire to be "an important chance to evaluate how best to prepare the upcoming generation of architects and city-makers for current and future challenges" and clearly indicate their international scope by the international backgrounds of the participants. (3rd International Architectural Education Summit, 2013).

In all of these conferences, newsletters, websites, and class projects both students and faculty are questioning the appropriate role of the architect early in the twenty-first century. They talk and write about moral and ethical dilemmas, they explore poetic imagery, and they consider the relationship of technique to art. As the work of the profession is now visually available in most parts of the world, one of the more provocative questions has to do with the relationship between local culture and site conditions and the compositional strategies most publicized on the internet. Does the designer have a responsibility to reflect local building traditions even if the client is asking for something else? Is it ethical for architects to be involved in projects that are not making positive contributions to energy usage? Is it possible for a team of designers to be understood as a creative force equal to the powerful image of the master builder? These questions, and others, are posed in schools everywhere.

The context for the internationalization of design education can be understood as a phenomenon driven largely by the globalization of the design professions and the availability of the internet, but it should also be seen as supported and encouraged by institutions larger than individual colleges and universities. The World Bank says on their website:

> Education is fundamental to development and growth. From encouraging higher enrollment, especially for girls and other disadvantaged children, to promoting learning for all, the World Bank Group plays a significant role in education globally.
>
> (The World Bank Group, 2015)

UNESCO says:

> The Organization is committed to a holistic and humanistic vision of quality education worldwide, the realization of everyone's right to education, and the belief that education plays a fundamental role in human, social and economic development.
>
> (UNESCO, 2015)

The Organization for Economic Cooperation and Development publishes the most comprehensive statistics and reports on education in countries around the world, available at http://www.oecd.org/education/. And, the International Monetary Fund has now become a member institution of the consortium that participates in the edX Massive Open Online Courses (MOOCs) platform founded by Harvard and MIT.

Presidents and provosts in higher education go to conferences of their peers; listen to keynote speakers—often from outside the world of academe; debate the prevailing issues in workshops and small groups; then make leadership decisions for their institutions with the intellectual support of, and access to the financial resources of, these associations that operate across national boundaries. The message they bring back to their faculty and staff often reflects the missions and visions of those international organizations. For many schools the goals and values they are sharing today include cultural diversity of their student bodies; international experiences for as many students as possible; the development of skills via cross-cultural collaboration; and, shifting curricular content so that it has an expansive world-view rather than a limited local-view.

The internationalization of any particular design school shares many of the same strategies as other disciplines within their home institutions. Since 1989, US-based ABET (formerly the Accreditation Board for Engineering and Technology) has been a member of the Washington Accord, a recognition agreement among international accrediting agencies for technical and engineering programs, and is now accrediting programs internationally. Schools of engineering throughout the world have been recognized or accredited by ABET and their architecture programs have then petitioned the NAAB, and other accrediting agencies, for similar designations of quality assurance. Partnership agreements sometimes result in joint degrees or certificates, and, Memoranda of Understanding (MOU) define international partnerships and cover agreements on student exchanges, study abroad programs, faculty-led travel, and shared courses. Student exchanges are organized so that each student pays the cost of education at their home campus but actually goes to class at the partner school. This includes tuition but also can include housing and meals. In general the schools are trading students thus making it possible for students from areas with low tuition to attend schools with higher fees. The MOUs make it possible in some countries for students to continue to receive government loans and scholarships for both student exchanges and for study abroad. Study abroad, in this context, means a semester or longer at another school but without the intention to graduate from, or earn a credential from, the second school. For instance, both Mexico and Brazil have programs to support students financially if they are studying outside their home countries in disciplines relative to their home degree programs. In the case of Brazil, the scholarships are the result of a government policy based on a perceived need within the country for expertise in Science, Technology, Engineering, and Mathematics (STEM) fields. Some countries, especially in the Middle East, are giving students full scholarships to pursue degrees outside the region. And, faculty-led travel is the long-standing practice of taking groups of students, either for academic credit or not, on trips to visit historically-relevant sites and/or to visit sites for current studio design projects.

Opportunities for funded international experiences for faculty and students both from the US and from abroad, like Fulbright-sponsored activities, can be found at http://exchanges.state.gov/us/. Funding for partnerships between schools may be available through the US Department of State and are sometimes advertised and supported by embassies abroad as part of their diplomatic initiatives. In the United States, the Institute for International Education (IIE) manages the Fulbright programs and also the recruiting services known as EducationUSA. EducationUSA has over 400 offices around the world where staff interacts with local schools and prospective students who are interested in higher education in the US. They sponsor recruiting fairs, keep libraries of information on US programs, and arrange meetings for traveling representatives of US schools throughout the world. The UK fields a similar organization called the British Council, France supports Campus France, and the Germans have the German Academic Exchange Service (DAAD)—all competing for students in a global marketplace. In the US the Department of Commerce also provides services for US schools in international markets hosting trade missions, providing networking opportunities, and advising on business practices. Other opportunities for funded international faculty development experiences can be found through the Transcultural Exchange at http://www.transculturalexchange.org/.

Representatives of these organizations meet and exhibit annually at the major conferences of international educational organizations. In the Western Hemisphere the major organization is NAFSA: Association of International Educators. In the Far East there are annual meetings of the Asia-Pacific Association for International Education, and in Europe the largest gathering is of the European Association for International Education members. Also based in Brussels is the Academic Cooperation Association, a center for the promotion of the internationalization of education and whose members and associate members are organizations (British Council, Campus France, DAAD, IIE, and others) that share this goal. Higher education institutions now often have, in addition to COOs and CIOs and Provosts and Presidents, Senior International Officers—SIOs—whose responsibility it is to manage and guide the transformation of a school from a local, regional operation to one that students graduate prepared to be citizens and leaders in, and of, the world. The Association of International Education Administrators is the membership organization for professionals in international higher education.

Senior International Officers are involved in many different aspects of colleges and universities and are particularly interested in shifts in the provision of educational environments that expand the diversity of the student body. The biggest changes in recent years have been in the growth of online courses. Schools are experimenting with MOOCs, with hybrid or blended courses, and with onsite courses making limited use of the internet in classrooms. Design programs have been slow to adopt online teaching strategies although they have been quick to incorporate course content related to the use of the internet in professional practices. Instruction in a studio setting with a small group of students and personal attention by the studio instructor has been the successful model for teaching design for generations. A few schools are experimenting with alternatives to the traditional studio methodology by offering courses that are sometimes completely online and sometimes a combination of online and onsite experiences. As students expect more use of social media in classrooms, as faculty becomes more comfortable with relationship-building software, and as the communications among teams in professional offices becomes more software-dependent, it seems inevitable that use of the internet will take on a primary role in teaching design. Mirroring global communication practices in professional settings where teams collaborate from all and any of the time zones will become as common at school as it is at work. This means, with an asynchronous process, courses can be taught with enrollment from anywhere—without the necessity of visas or travel and providing access to higher education to millions of students who otherwise would not have such educational opportunities. This is a change in higher education perhaps more far-reaching than the invention of the printing press and it is too early to predict exactly how it will evolve.

A second, and very different, change in higher education that has an impact on global markets is the rise of for-profit corporations providing not just educational programs but also every service offered in the past by staff in non-profit organizations. The corporate model has been very successful in attracting students in countries where public or private non-profit institutions have been seen as either not rigorous, or sometimes corrupt, or not offering current content in their degree programs that will be useful to students wanting to work in a competitive environment. The quality and intentions of for-profit institutions are often questioned by academics and political groups although they have been extremely successful (based on enrollment numbers as evidence) in offering online degree programs, especially with professional content. Besides offering accredited degrees, there are companies offering to manage student travel trips; help with finding international internships; concierge services for international students needing various kinds of support; pathway programs that include cultural acclimation as well as second-language instruction; and commercial agents representing students as they apply for admission in other than their home countries. The Brenn-White Group, marketing for internationalization in higher education, is an example of the many consulting services available for institutions with international aspirations. With this rise in participation by for-profit entities in the provision of higher education services, there are also organizations managing quality assurance processes for those businesses. An example would be the American International Recruitment Council's work to accredit recruitment agencies.

Current discussions of pressing issues in all accrediting agencies include how to demonstrate and measure learning outcomes. In design programs it has always been the case that student work (evidence of learning over time) was the basis for measuring programmatic quality. This may be the result of the master-apprentice model for studio instruction—where the master assigns the problem, then coaches the apprentice as the solution evolves—rather than an expert-novice model—where the expert shares information and the novice practices until competency is reached. In any case, evaluating the quality of a program based on demonstrable learning and in a collaborative setting is particularly effective in a group of students with diverse cultural backgrounds. As professional design education shifts from the idea of the designer as an individual artist to one based on the strength of a team, the importance of a diverse student body will become obvious. New metrics, in addition to evaluating personal compositional skills, will be useful as programs culturally diversify during this time when international rankings of programs are driving the markets for enrollment.

Examples of how international issues are impacting quality assurance agencies for design education are in the 2014 Conditions for Accreditation resulting from the 2013 Accreditation Review Conference organized by the NAAB. Two of the Student Performance Criteria have evolved from previous editions of the document where they were limited to Western and non-Western distinctions of building types to much more encompassing requirements that students demonstrate an understanding of "parallel and divergent histories," a variety of "cultural norms," and "social and spatial patterns that characterize different cultures." The NAAB has also determined that schools outside the US, without US institutional accreditation, might qualify for full NAAB accreditation with "explicit, written permission from all applicable national education authorities in that program's country or region" (NAAB, 2014).

Future

The challenge in writing a description of the current networks and trends that support and encourage the internationalization of design schools is how to arrange the material in some way that may be useful as the scenarios inevitably change. It is hard to imagine that schools will go back to positioning themselves as relevant only in a certain geographical location, or serving a homogenous student population. It is not impossible that this may happen—there may always be some site-specific or ideologically-based institutions with very focused perspectives and carefully limited enrollment—but considering trends today it seems unlikely. As we consider the changes international influences bring to the curricula and activities at schools of architecture here are some ideas that may be useful in the near future:

- Not only will practitioners need to develop strategies for managing rapid global change, the structure and operations of schools will need to evolve more quickly than in the past.
- In order to keep up with changes, attitudes toward learning will become seamless and extend throughout a professional career, leading to an expanded international mission for existing educational institutions.
- Given current economic forecasts and the shifting opportunities for work globally, the academic intentions of any school will need to be closely aligned with the identity and aspirations of their home institutions or they will not survive larger institutional changes.
- Schools will assume the necessity of becoming "global"—just as they now accept the need to be concerned with issues of sustainability—but there will still be the question of how they balance both global and local issues.
- International institutional partnerships, based on complementary or supplementary statements of mission, will become more common and will transcend national boundaries as global corporations and non-governmental organizations have already done.
- Minimum standards in architectural education, with room for academic variety, will continue to be implemented around the world through the Canberra Accord and through other quality assurance networks. There could be a shift toward describing quality in terms of excelling in the global marketplace rather than in terms of meeting minimum standards but this is a conversation not very far advanced in the field of quality assurance and most organizations do not currently see a need to pursue this as a

standard of achievement. Meetings of the membership of the International Network for Quality Assurance Agencies in Higher Education (INQAAHE) are a possible place to watch for developments in this area.
- Self-assessment practices will become more sophisticated as expectations of transparency and evidence of specific learning outcomes become an international norm.
- In an effort to both broaden markets for design skills through community service and to manage large building projects, interdisciplinary collaboration skills will become a necessary new component in curricula.

This is a moment in the history of the architecture profession and in architectural education when practitioners will look for ways to expand their services in both depth and breadth and educators will debate the appropriate roles of the architect. We have the opportunity to contribute to, and reinforce, each other's quests. To do this with a diversity of student, faculty, and practitioner participation bodes well for the outcome.

Acknowledgments

The author would like to thank Scott Simpson for sharing his writing on global practice, his editing skills, and for his always thought-provoking conversations. Also, thanks to Andy Pressman, Felice Silverman, Phil Bernstein, Vernon Woodworth, Junsuk Lee, Bill Bevins, and Rodner Wright for their insights on the topic. And, of course thanks to Mitra Kanaani for her invitation to join this group of distinguished authors and for her careful reading of drafts of this chapter.

References

Asia-Pacific Economic Cooperation (2012). APEC Architect Project. Retrieved January 3, 2015 from: http://apecarchitects.org/.

Consortium for North American Higher Education Collaboration (1994). Mission. Retrieved January 3, 2015 from: https://conahec.org/mission.

National Architectural Accrediting Board (2014). NAAB Conditions for Accreditation. Retrieved January 3, 2015 from: http://www.naab.org/accreditation/2014_Conditions.

NAAB-EESA (2014). Educational Evaluation Services for Architects. Retrieved January 3, 2015 from: https://www.eesa-naab.org/.

Pressman, A. (2014). *Designing Relationships: The Art of Collaboration in Architecture.* London: Routledge.

Simpson, S. (2010). "Learning by Design," *Design Intelligence*. Belmond, Iowa: Greenway Communications. Retrieved January 3, 2015 from: www.di.net/articles/learning_by_design/.

Simpson, S. (2013a). "Beyond Borders: the ABCs of International Practice," *Design Intelligence*. Belmond, Iowa: Greenway Communications. Retrieved January 3, 2015 from: www.di.net/articles/beyond-borders/.

Simpson, S. (2013b). "Design Goes Global," *Design Intelligence*. Belmond, IA: Greenway Communications. Retrieved January 3, 2015 from: www.di.net/articles/design_goes_global/.

The United States Department of Justice. (1998). Foreign Corrupt Practices Act of 1977. Retrieved January 3, 2015 from: http://www.justice.gov/criminal/fraud/fcpa/.

The World Bank Group (2015). Education. Retrieved January 3, 2015 from: http://www.worldbank.org/en/topic/education.

Third International Architectural Education Summit (September, 2013). New Directions in Architecture Education. Retrieved January 3, 2015 from: http://www.ancb.de/sixcms/detail.php?id=9708635.

UNESCO. (2015). Education for the 21st Century. Retrieved January 3, 2015 from: http://en.unesco.org/themes/education-21st-century.

Union Internationale des Architectes (June, 1996). UIA/UNESCO Charter for Architectural Education. Retrieved January 3, 2015 from: http://www.unesco.org/most/uiachart.htm.

Union Internationale des Architectes (June, 1999). UIA Accord on Recommended International Standards of Professionalism in Architectural Practice. Retrieved January 3, 2015 from http://apaw.uia-architectes.org/ang/compartida/webuia/apaw/pdf/UIAAccordAng.pdf.

World Trade Organization (1995). General Agreement on Trades and Services. Uruguay Round Agreement. Retrieved January 3, 2015 from: http://www.wto.org/english/docs_e/legal_e/26-gats_01_e.htm.

32

Diversity

Taking Steps to Create a Diverse Design Profession

Ted Landsmark

Today's architects and designers are challenged to develop designs that reflect the attitudes and needs of our dense, urban, heterogeneous and rapidly changing global society. An understanding of diversity embodies a sense of *inclusion* and *mutual respect*, empowering all in the environment to feel and be treated as equals. A transformative model of diversity emphasizes understandings of each person's own views of the world, and requires design professionals to look beyond personal viewpoints to understand and engender empathy for the lives, experiences, and viewpoints of others. Diversity in design, designers, and clients, is a mandate for professional success.

In the early twenty-first century, licensed women architects constituted fewer than 20 percent of the American profession, while architects of color constituted just 10 percent. "Diversity," architect John L. Wilson FAIA wrote in 2004, was characterized as

> every architect who is not an able-bodied, straight white male. Even universal design, which implies common design criteria for the human condition, is grouped in this divergent camp...When I look at our profession; there is an opportunity for a different, more holistic idea of diversity that focuses on community.
>
> (Kiisk, 2003)

Diversity *enhances creativity* as diverse perspectives contribute varying visions and design solutions (Hudner *et al.*, 2013). Diversity challenges fixed thinking in a field requiring constant creativity, and can contribute to *workplace efficacy* in meeting clients' needs. Numerous studies by management consultants McKinsey & Company (Barsh *et al.*, April 2013; Barta *et al.*, April 2012; Broderick *et al.*, February 2015; Hunt *et al.*, January 2015), have demonstrated that companies in the top quartile for staff and executive board gender, racial, and ethnic diversity are more likely to have financial returns above their national industry medians.

Why is this? Cross-cultural teams are more likely to bring unique solutions to clients in a competitive marketplace. Empathy for diverse clients, and harmony in the workplace, are enhanced by such teams, enabling the workplace to more ethically mirror the global society served by professional design. The *business development* case for diversity focuses on opening more work opportunities in a competitive marketplace. Diversity in staffing demonstrates a firm's ability to understand the needs of diverse clients (Brown, 2009; Ross, 2011; Young, 1969).

Definitions of Diversity

Traditionally American law has concentrated on reducing or eliminating discrimination on the basis of specific exclusionary policies or practices that isolate groups of individuals based on the following identifiable categories:

- *Race*: the social concept that classifies individuals based on culturally defined groupings with particular ethnic, genetic, linguistic, social, or other identifiable affiliations;
- *National Origin*: the place of origin of an individual, family group, or social grouping of individuals;
- *Gender*: especially as applied to women;
- *Religion;* and
- *Physical disability*: as a basis for isolating a disabled person in workplaces and roles.

Additionally, individuals have been excluded from design schools and workplaces based on other classifications, including:

- *Age*;
- *"Non-Western" cultures* such as Native Americans or Asians which have frequently been treated as "the other," i.e., aberrant client groups with lesser needs and diminished values in relation to those of the dominant society;
- *Gay, Lesbian, Bi-sexual, and Trans-gender (GLBT)* individuals who, for many years, were required to conceal their sexuality in the workplace.

As American society has become more inclusive, new categories of attention have included:

- *Learning and cognitive challenges* that may affect client needs; and
- *Diverse ways of serving diverse clients*, i.e., stepping outside traditional atelier-based ways of engaging working professionals, clients, and wider communities in design development and implementation (Ross, 2011; Tatum, 2007).

The Design Professions Have Legal Obligations to Address Diversity

There are three basic approaches to addressing diversity: avoiding discrimination in the workplace by *adhering to laws* and regulations prohibiting discrimination; passively adopting a position of *benign neglect* on an assumption that long-term demographic trends will inevitably diversify a workplace or marketplace; or *acting affirmatively* to increase diversity. Federal and state laws play a significant role in the first of these areas.

Equality under the law is protected by the Fourteenth Amendment to the United States Constitution, passed in 1866, initially to protect the civil rights of ethnic minorities with particular reference to African Americans. A century of court cases has extended coverage of the Fourteenth Amendment to gender, national origin, sexual preference, religion, and handicaps. The Federal Equal Pay Act of 1963 (Public Law 88-38) was passed to ensure women and men would be compensated equally for equal work. State laws elaborate on and extend the protections assured by the Constitution, and state administrative agencies overseeing employment discrimination are often the first venues for hearing cases of alleged discrimination.

Title VII of the Civil Rights Act of 1964 (42 U.S.C. 2000e *et seq.*) prohibits employers from discriminating against applicants and employees on the basis of race, color, religion, sex, and national origin. It prohibits employers from retaliating against an applicant or employee who asserts his or her rights under the law. Title VII prohibits discrimination in all terms, conditions, and privileges of employment, including hiring, firing, compensation, benefits, job assignments, promotions, and discipline. Title VII prohibits practices that seem neutral but have a disproportionate negative impact on a protected group of individuals, and deems it illegal to harass a person on the basis of a protected characteristic. The law applies to private employers with at least 15 employees, state governments and their subdivisions, the Federal government, employment agencies, labor organizations, and joint labor-management committees or other training programs. It is enforced by the Federal Equal Employment Opportunity Commission.

The *Age Discrimination in Employment Act* (ADEA) (29 U.S.C. 621–634) prohibits discrimination on the basis of age in all terms and conditions of employment including hiring, firing, compensation, job assignments, shift assignments, discipline, and promotions. The ADEA applies to private employers with at least 20 employees, the Federal government, interstate agencies, employment agencies, and labor unions. It is enforced by the Federal Equal Employment Opportunity Commission.

The *Americans With Disabilities Act* (42 U.S.C. 12101–12213) prohibits employers from discriminating against people with disabilities in any aspect of employment, including applications, interviews, testing, hiring, job assignments, evaluations, compensation, leave, benefits, training, promotions, medical exams, layoffs and firing. The laws protect those with disabilities, those who have a history of disability and those who are incorrectly perceived to have a disability. The law applies to private employers with at least 15 employees, local governments and agencies, employment agencies, and labor unions.

Affirmative action policies have been put into place by the Federal government, state governments, private colleges and universities, private employers, professional organizations, and non-profit organizations to diversify employment and educational practices and to redress past practices or instances of unequal treatment.

These laws and policies are supplemented by ethical standards and practices within professions and organizations with social or economic rules of conduct. While legislative action is largely external, ethical action generally emerges from within the self-protective, socially responsible ranks of organizations in order to provide internal accountability. Financial institutions, legal societies, medical organizations, religious orders, and other professional and social groups generally have ethical standards prohibiting discriminatory practices.

A Brief Timeline of Diversity Activities within the Architecture Profession—1968–2005

In 2001 Professor Kathryn Anthony wrote about diversity that, compared with most other professional fields, "the progress of architecture has been nearly glacial" (Anthony, 2001). Prior to 1965, demographic diversity was barely recognized within architecture, apart from occasional mentions of women who had accomplished distinguished work. Among these were *Louise Blanchard Bethune* (1856–1913, first woman accepted into the American Institute of Architects); *Julia Morgan* (1872–1957, designer of William Randolph Hearst's castle at San Simeon); *Eileen Gray* (1879–1956, French architect, theorist, and furniture designer); *Ray Kaiser Eames* (1907–1978, who worked with husband Charles Eames on Modernist furniture icons); *Alison Smithson* (1928–1993, who worked with husband Peter Smithson on Brutalist designs); and *Denise Scott Brown* (b. 1931–, who taught and worked with husband Robert Venturi on Postmodernist theory and designs). Although recognized as leaders in architectural design, many worked in the shadow of their male collaborators (Anderson, 1980; Conway *et al.*, 1996).

Architects of color who received early recognition included *Julian Abele* (1881–1950, designer of the Free Library of Philadelphia); *Norma Merritt Sklarek* (1928–2012, first African American female licensed architect); *Robert Robinson Taylor* (1868–1942, first Black graduate of the Massachusetts Institute of Technology and a leading educator and designer of major buildings at the Tuskegee Institute) (Weiss, 2012), and *Paul Revere Williams* (1894–1980, Hollywood "designer to the stars") (Hudson,1993; Kaplan, 2006). By 2004, Dreck Spurlock Wilson documented 151 African American architects through the end of the Second World War (Wilson, 2004; Travis, 1991). Research remains to be undertaken into other early ethnic minority designers.

The 1968 AIA Convention keynoted by Whitney M. Young Jr. (1921–1971) marked the beginning of efforts to broaden the meaning of diversity in architecture. As Executive Director of the National Urban League, *Time Magazine* described Young as the "most effective man in the nation when it comes to drumming up jobs for Negroes." Young criticized the building trades for freezing Black workers out of higher-paying jobs and chastised the AIA Convention because only 1 percent of American architects were African American. He criticized architects' complacency on racism, and challenged the profession to recruit and educate a new generation of more diverse practitioners to serve a wider range of urban clients (Kiisk, 2003).

In 1970, the AIA responded to Young's challenge by establishing the AIA/American Architectural Foundation Minority Disadvantaged Scholarship, which awarded scholarships to minority students attending architecture programs at primarily Historically Black Colleges and Universities. Over two decades just 20 percent of the scholarship recipients graduated from professional design programs, and there was little evidence that the scholarships had increased the numbers of licensed architects of color. In 1971 the National Organization of Minority Architects was founded to represent the interests of architects of color.

By 2000 African American architects still constituted only 1.5 percent of American architects, up from 1 percent in 1968. Nearly half of all Black architects were graduating from seven Historically Black Colleges and Universities. Architectural educators Bradford Grant and Dennis Mann initiated a *Directory of African American Architects*, Susan Maxman was elected the first woman AIA President, Raj Barr-Kumar FAIA was elected as the first AIA President of color, Gordon Chong became the AIA's first Asian AIA President, and *Arquitectos*, a Chicago-based organization with a focus on Hispanics in the design professions was founded. Seventy-eight percent of architectural interns were Caucasian, and African Americans (4 percent of all interns) then had the highest IDP internship completion rates.

An AIA/NOMA Diversity Summit was convened in 2001, and Kathryn Anthony published *Designing for Diversity: Gender, Race, and Ethnicity in the Architectural Profession*. By 2002, 38 percent of American architecture students were women, while only 16.6 percent of architecture school faculty were women. Anthony compiled extensive data on demographic trends within the profession and found it riddled with discrimination. Her interviews and surveys reported recurrent discriminations: individuals were offered new responsibilities without a commensurate rise in position or compensation; were excluded from client contact, field experience, or construction supervision; and were relegated to narrow fields, specifically public work for racial minorities, interior design for women, and computer-aided technology for Asian Americans working in large firms. Anthony criticized the profession's attitudes toward introducing flexible work schedules, part-time contracts, mentoring, and recognizing family demands. She documented how architects experiencing discrimination tended to leave mainstream firms, establishing their own smaller firms, entering government or corporate service, or abandoning the field altogether. She recommended strategies drawn from progressive employment practices that had helped people of color and women advance within other professions.

The AIA Diversity Committee Summit of April, 2003, brought attention to data collection throughout the profession. A *2020 Vision for Architecture* presented a comprehensive, multi-year effort to achieve a more diverse profession by standardizing and accelerating research, facilitating national and local leadership opportunities, heightening awareness of diversity, and educating all on its value. The Committee also published *20 on 20/20 Vision: Perspectives on Diversity and Design*, bringing together essays by over 20 practitioners, educators, and students. The 2005 AIA Convention passed a resolution to undertake a comprehensive demographic study assessing the status of diversity in the profession, and laying out recommendations for improvement.

The quantitative and qualitative national study, undertaken by law firm Holland & Knight, found that architectural data sources on student enrollments, state-by-state licensure, and Institute membership were disconnected and difficult to cross-correlate. The statistical analysis concluded that women and people of color were significantly underrepresented in the design professions. Two percent of the AIA's members were then Hispanic or Latino, 3 percent were Asian, and 1.5 percent were African American. Only 12 percent of the AIA's members in 2004 were women. The report recommended that the AIA adopt a strategy for obtaining comprehensive data on diversity nationally and develop ways *to expand the path into practice*, including reviewing internship and examination procedures which were slowing the path to licensure, particularly for people of color and women. Holland & Knight recommended steps be taken to *increase licensure rates of people of color and women*, and that efforts be directed toward *ensuring professional equal opportunity* for licensed practitioners. In 2007, Marshall Purnell was elected as the first African American AIA President.

Why Haven't More Diverse People Entered the Design Professions?

By the second decade of the twenty-first century, the AIA and NCARB reported a rise in licensed minority architects, from 11 percent to 18 percent, and NAAB issued reports on diversity in accredited schools. The AIA inaugurated *Diversity Best Practices Awards*, and established GLBT recognition among its diversity priorities. In 2013, 17 percent of AIA members were women, compared with 9 percent in 2000, and ethnic minorities represented 10 percent of members, as compared with 7 percent in 2000. By 2014, a majority of architecture school enrollees were women and students of color.

Design school surveys indicate that many new design school students have been exposed to the design, fabrication (including construction or fashion production) or repair/renovation fields, typically through a family member. Most early exposures occur prior to entering high school.

- Most entrants do not have an architect role model, and few have met an architect prior to applying to design school.
- A majority of entrants are attracted to drawing, building, design, or fashion as their first reason for becoming a professional designer.
- People of color and women often express a desire to make a social or historic contribution to the built environment.
- Women are twice as likely as men to feel they were discriminated against in design school.
- Students of color express the greatest frustrations in design school jury processes, which they consider discriminatory.
- White ARE pass rates were significantly higher than minority pass rates.
- Male ARE pass rates were significantly higher than female pass rates.
- Whites have historically completed the ARE in shorter times than minorities.
- Asians were historically more likely to be project managers than other demographic groups.
- White males have the highest representation among firm principals.
- About one-third of emerging professionals historically felt women and minorities lacked equal opportunities for professional growth.
- One-third of respondents in the 2005 Holland & Knight study indicated they felt overt discrimination or harassment in practice.

"Professional dissatisfaction" (for women and minorities), personal and family circumstances (women), and lack of sufficient compensation (men) in relation to the educational investment made were the primary reasons for not practicing architecture after completing design studies.

Many factors have reduced awareness of design fields as careers where underrepresented individuals can find success and fulfillment:

- A lack of visible role models.
- A lack of exposure to art and design education in public school.
- Workplace discrimination that limits growth opportunities within the private sector.
- Patterns of work that implicitly discriminate against certain categories of employees (e.g., caregivers, who are often women, are often discriminated against in their job development opportunities).
- Discriminatory (i.e., exclusionary) curricula in design schools.
- Exclusion of women and minorities from leadership positions.
- A general lack of public awareness of the design professions.
- High skill requirements coupled with relatively low pay discourage applicants who are not affluent, as women and people of color have tended to be.
- High tuition and few scholarships have historically discouraged diverse students from completing professional studies.
- The traditional lengthy registration process involving three years of private internship discourages diverse interns.
- The lack of a discernible work/life balance in role models discourages emerging employees.
- Pay disparity may reduce the prestige and allure of design as a life-long profession.
- A lack of mentoring within firms has discouraged career growth within design firms.

Challenges to Increasing Diversity in Professional Architecture Practice

Susan Estrich's *Sex and Power* (2001) identified four primary impediments to women gaining and exercising authority in America's top 500 corporate workplaces: *outright discrimination* by men who traditionally exercise such authority; *caregiving responsibilities* usually handled by women; *comfort factors* that tend to isolate cohorts of men and women in workplaces; and *patterns of ambition* that sometimes mitigate against women working together to overcome discrimination in some workplaces.

Kathryn Anthony's *Designing for Diversity* (2001) indicated that traditional rites of passage that serve as gateways to the profession often serve as roadblocks to underrepresented designers. Interviewing, internship practices, local licensing and registration processes, and first job experiences present hurdles to underrepresented minorities and women who are being treated unfairly or differentially.

Dr. Paula Whitman's 2005 study of 550 Australian women in architecture found many women sacrificed career advancement to achieve balanced lives, and were reluctant to undertake formal career planning, preferring to seize opportunities as they presented themselves. Women also rejected advancement opportunities when they questioned whether those opportunities actually met their personal aspirations. Family commitments, lack of time, and poor relationships within the industry impeded women's progress. In this study, women saw competence and relationship building as key metrics of success. In contrast men favored project and firm size, and recognition.

Rosa Sheng's 2014 surveys of women architects (Lau, 2014), identified significant new-hire salary gaps between men and women with 10–15 years of experience, licensure requirements as impediments to retention, and a perceived career growth penalty for architects who take leaves of absence for personal reasons, thus creating challenges (primarily) for women family caregivers.

Ethnic minorities carry additional burdens in achieving professional success. Victoria Kaplan's *Structural Inequality—Black Architects in the United States* pointed to overlapping factors constraining the success of African American architects (2006a). Kaplan identified four key impediments to greater African American participation in architecture. The *profession and its internal organizations* are thought to be interconnected patronage systems favoring white males through self-perpetuating capital and client relationships. Homogenous *architectural school curricula and faculty hiring* patterns perpetuate a bias toward Northern European design aesthetics and teaching pedagogies that marginalize the work of "the other," i.e., non-Western building forms. *Professional practice career advancement hierarchies*, linked to traditional American upper-middle class access to white capital structures, perpetuated a wealth gap between white and non-white practitioners, enabling white architects to obtain connections and resources to work with private corporate clients, while minority and women architects worked primarily with public sector agencies mandating inclusionary hiring and contracting policies. This *political context* created a perception that women and minorities "weren't good enough" to work with private clients, while quietly racist *social networks* around the built environment and building trades implicitly created *de facto* segregation across the profession.

Stephen Kliment FAIA (Anthony, 2001), found that minority-owned firms were likely to be smaller than majority firms, and somewhat more likely to be profitable than comparable white firms (due in part to higher percentages of dependable public work). They were less likely to develop significant private sector patronage or be engaged in cutting edge private work. African American architects Jack Travis, Sharon E. Sutton FAIA, J. Max Bond FAIA,

Darell Wayne Fields, Richard Dozier, and Melvin Mitchell FAIA (Travis, 1991; Anthony, 2001; Fields, 2000; Mitchell, 2003), have written that Black architects tended to find themselves limited to public work where it was sometimes difficult to present distinctive Afrocentric aesthetic forms and values.

Architecture, Kliment concluded, emerges from a social and political context where America's Black architects could weave in African associations and identity, or conclude that they are architects first and Black second, and approach their work in the same spirit as American architects of other racial and ethnic backgrounds. In that regard, Sharon Sutton FAIA concluded that as an African American woman architect she had to "use the common sense (her) ancestors bequeathed to (her) and to feel an urgency to establish an alternative world view… an alternative praxis of architecture with African-American sisters and brothers …" (Kiisk, 2003). Diversity discussions are inevitably transformative for both those in dominant and those in excluded positions (Conway *et al.*, 1996; Ross, 2011; Tatum, 2007).

Diversifying Practice through Alternative Practice Models

A key to increasing diversity within the design profession is the broadening of the definition of what an *architect* is and does. Several studies have indicated that designers of diverse backgrounds may be more inclined to pursue alternative design career paths. Architects of color and women who work outside traditional sectors have gained greater professional success than those who have struggled within private sector firms. Interviews conducted during the studies by Holland & Knight and Kathryn Anthony indicated that smaller firms and government work proved more welcoming to women and people of color than large corporate settings.

American professional definitions have limited the term "architecture" to the process and product of work performed by a graduate of an accredited school, who is licensed to plan, design and oversee the building of structures meeting local health, safety, and welfare building codes. Yet for many years, roughly half of all architecture school graduates have not entered traditional practice, instead designing interiors, landscapes, graphics and products, or working in the fields of real estate, facilities management, software development, urban planning, economic development, and myriad other fields where they could not call themselves "architects." The AIA strictly enforces rules against the use of this term by unlicensed persons working within the built environment, even as other fields such as management, health care, finance, education, and consulting appropriated the term "architect," and the process of "design thinking" to describe the creative work undertaken by practitioners in those fields.

Entreaties from emerging architects began in 1999 with John Cary and Casius Pealer's online *ArchVoices*, calling for a more expansive interpretation of what it means to be an American architect. Among the fields now broadly considered "architecture" by academics and emerging professionals, are those staffed by diverse and unlicensed design professionals working with licensed professionals to provide *pro bono* consultation to non-profit and community-based groups. These alternative practice entities, sometimes based within professional school programs, and established as autonomous non-profit community design entities, have included John Cary and John Peterson's *Public Architecture*, *Architecture for Humanity*, *CityYear*, Habitat for Humanity, and the Community Design Center of Boston. Many have been staffed by more diverse designers, and provide *pro bono* design services to underrepresented, under-served, economically disadvantaged communities. Groups such as the Chicago Architecture Foundation, the American Architectural Foundation, the Charter

High School of Design in Philadelphia, the Design Architecture Senior High School in Miami, and the Baltimore School for Design have involved diverse students in design projects that serve communities and expose a wider range of potential clients to the benefits of good design.

Alternative practice "human centered design" groups work with individuals whose physical handicaps can be alleviated through design interventions. Their work has evolved into programs focused on design, health, and wellness. Accessibility improvements such as wheelchair ramps, lowered bathroom sinks, accessible kitchens, grab bars, and exercise spaces are useful to clients, and often greatly overshadowed by the education of providers, who learn their clients are more diverse than many would have imagined. Yale Architecture Dean Charles Moore, for example, assigned a studio to design a single family home for a blind client; this challenge enabled students to design beyond traditional visual aesthetics, and learn that clients might be shorter, less fit, less nimble, or more diverse than most design school students.

Elaine Martin Petrowski's *Designing for a Diverse Population* (ASID) (2012), and Linda Nussbaumer's *Inclusive Design, a Universal Need* (2012), have focused on public service diversity in putting forth the viewpoint that handicapped individuals should not be marginalized by the profession. Architects have much to learn from the principles of universal interior design and evidence-based design as carried out by groups such as the Institute for Human Centered Design in Boston, or the AIAS *Freedom By Design* initiatives.

The increased interest in meeting the needs of diverse clients encouraged the growth of design research entities, often staffed by environmental psychologists, interior designers, and public health experts engaged with evidence-based design. Dr. Richard Jackson and Stacy Sinclair's *Designing Healthy Communities* (2012), Cynthia Leibrock and Debra Harris's *Design Details for Health—Making the Most of Design's Healing Potential* (2011), Linda Nussbaumer's *Inclusive Design* (2012), Dak Kopec's *Health, Sustainability and the Built Environment*, and *Environmental Psychology for Design* (2006, 2008, 2012), have focused attention on the links between design and improved health outcomes in ways that have raised consciousness about how diverse populations can be better served by evidence-based designers who demonstrate that designs accounting for human differences can make communities healthier.

The emergence of a category of innovative firms with specific vertically-structured research capabilities has provided practitioners with more diverse practices, and increased opportunities to bring diverse trades and individuals into the design process. Such firms combine architects, interior designers, materials specialists, anthropologists, hydrologists, specifications writers, landscape professionals and others within a core group, or through creatively outsourced collaborations to link, for example, computer modeling to innovative materials exploration that is then tied to design-build practices. Research-based practices such as Kieran/Timberlake, Jeanne Gang, SHoP, and OMA have created opportunities for the emergence of new and more diverse practice models.

Some professional design schools have become more diversified by managing community design programs in communities to which students and faculty might not ordinarily be exposed. Yale's Black Studio of the 1960s undertook community service in New Haven's impoverished African American Hill community, and became involved with Black Panther service activities. Tulane's post-Katrina hurricane relief developed design-build skills in students under the direction of the faculty and facilities staff. The University of Arkansas started a highly regarded community design studio, and undertook outreach to a large Hispanic community involved with farm work to expose young agricultural workers to careers in Landscape Architecture. Ball State's Urban Design Studio and Community Based Projects have undertaken over 300 projects in Indiana. The Boston Architectural College's

Gateway programs have provided *pro bono* service opportunities to hundreds of students working with public agencies and non-profit service groups. Auburn's Rural Studio won an AIA Whitney Young Award for using creativity and discarded materials to provide innovative shelter and gathering spaces for Alabama's rural Black population (Dean & Hursley, 2002). Georgia Bizios and Katie Wakeford (2011) documented how public work within the NCARB Internship Development Process could facilitate opportunities for transiting from schools to public service in *Bridging the Gap*. Not all projects have been successful—but most have provided excellent community service.

Some of these projects have continued with particular groups or communities for many years; others have been one-time activities. A key metric of success is whether the community invited the designers back to work on another project. John Cary's *ACSA Sourcebook for Community Design* showcased examples of successful projects. Deborah L. Rhode's 2005 *Pro Bono in Principle and in Practice—Public Service and the Professions* (Rhode), describes the practice-based principles for engaging in such work, and John Cary, Majora Carter, and John Peterson's *The Power of Pro Bono* documents 40 projects (2010). Architecture for Humanity's two compilations by Kate Stohr and Cameron Sinclair of *pro bono* projects around the world, *Design Like you Give a Damn*, inspired many students to undertake alternative design work for under-served populations (2006, 2012), as did the Smithsonian Cooper-Hewitt 2007 exhibition and catalogue, *Design for the Other 90%*.

Recommendations for Improving Diversity Outreach

Steps can be taken to make the profession more attractive to diverse applicants, to recruit more diverse career aspirants, and to support career growth and retention. Recommendations include:

- Increased public awareness of architecture as a profession, particularly in middle and high schools.
- Collaboration between the profession and corporate sponsors, local AIA components, design schools, individual design firms, and public agencies involved with the built environment to expose students to the design professions as potential career paths. Efforts would include field trips to construction sites and design firms.
- Development of principles for highlighting and disseminating examples of equitable workplace policies that specifically recognize differences in the practices of small-, medium-, and large-scale enterprises.
- Establish local recruiting programs where underrepresented individuals and groups with interests in the building trades, the environment, design, and social service through community building are likely to be found (e.g., working with building supply companies on providing educational workshops on weekends in minority communities).
- Diversification of faculty and curricula in architecture schools—a pressing need which can be addressed by schools, professional groups, and firms.
- Identification of designers willing to share their knowledge of their field with young persons through existing local mentoring groups such as Big Brother / Big Sister, 4F, or scouting service, and technology groups.
- Engagement of current design school students in public outreach programs working with communities of underrepresented students. Student demographic diversity has increased more rapidly than design school faculty or administrative diversity, and these students can become ambassadors to other underrepresented groups.

Workplace Diversity Strategies

While *attitudes* largely shape approaches to increasing diversity in academic settings, actual *behaviors* are most readily demonstrated in workplaces. Kathryn Anthony's open-ended interviews with practitioners cited steps that could increase gender and racial equality in workplaces: treating employees equitably; expecting less overtime work; instituting hiring policies to attract talented women and people of color; setting positive examples; placing underrepresented architects in positions of responsibility; and providing on-going equity and diversity training for managers and employees.

Many women and minority individuals found themselves pigeonholed in career tracks which curtailed career growth opportunities. Women and people of color working in large firms reported they were directed to train less experienced white male employees who then "leap-frogged" over their trainers. Women have often been steered into back office, interior design or historic preservation positions, and both women and people of color have complained of few opportunities for direct client contact or field supervision work.

The profession has long been considered not "family friendly". The model architect has been portrayed as a focused, hard-working white male with infinite time to devote to creatively meeting clients' needs. An AIA marketing study indicated that architects had some of the highest divorce rates among all American professions. At the time of Anthony's research, only about half the women interviewed had children, and many admitted to having exchanged a supportive family life for professional success.

Many underrepresented architects found themselves unprepared for the realities of professional practice. Anthony's interviews indicated that, "For the most part, the experiences of underrepresented architects are far more negative than those of their white male counterparts," as pay differentials, promotional possibilities, and opportunities to work directly with clients all lagged behind those of white males. Entering firms or teaching as the only woman or person of color within the work setting was isolating in a field requiring intense collaboration, and numerous individuals failed to find colleagues with the time or inclination to mentor them.

A supportive work environment is fundamental to success in the profession, and mentoring has proven to be an essential component of professional career growth. The fact that the architectural profession depends so strongly on a changing economy has made it difficult for employees to remove themselves from uncomfortable or compromising work situations. This can be said of all competitive professions, but has appeared most compelling within the design fields, where "sink-or-swim" or "survival of the fittest" attitudes are highly determinative of professional success. When faced with unfair treatment or dead-end jobs that suppress professional growth, women and minorities reported they felt they had little flexibility in moving to new work situations. Those who believe they have been discriminated against in hiring, promotion, or performance evaluation are often loath to reveal the circumstances, for fear that disclosing what happened may foreclose job opportunities. Few emerging professionals risked being labeled "trouble-makers" by speaking out against employers. Making confidential complaints was frowned upon, and confidences frequently broken by those hearing the complaints of discrimination or unfairness. "Many underrepresented architects fear a backlash from being labeled whistle blowers." Conferences with anti-discrimination professions can help build the confidence necessary to speak out against such injustices.

While a handful of minorities and women have achieved prominence within major firms, significant numbers have achieved success only after opening their own small firms. This path requires independent access to capital and clients that has proven daunting and limiting to large-scale professional growth in a very competitive marketplace. As a consequence, the majority of architects of color have sought career growth in public sector and government positions; for most of the past few decades, for example, the majority of licensed African American architects have been located in the Washington, D.C. area, where they work with Federal agencies.

Diversity training was historically a human resources approach to enabling a dominant group to better understand the customs and mores of people unlike themselves (Tatum, 2007). This approach to increasing "diversity" meant discussing how women and "minorities" could be better integrated into primarily white male dominated work environments. This often created unnecessary worker insecurity. According to corporate diversity consultant Howard J. Ross, "inclusiveness and cultural flexibility can be learned and developed and … can lead to unprecedented growth and vastly improved productivity, morale, internal communication, leadership, and customer satisfaction" (Ross, 2011).

Dr. Paula Whitman's study of Australian women architects recommended the development of *workplace policies* and flexible working arrangements specifically focused on differences between small, medium, and large-scale firms. She recommended the development of programs for women to start independent businesses as a way to re-enter practice, particularly after an absence.

Architectural firms scoring high in AIA internship training recognition programs have also tended to reflect positive approaches to personnel management, in particular equity and diversity initiatives. Mentoring talented new hires to become long-term employees, and cross-training to expose employees to internal firm cultures, tend to establish a supportive community that relies on multiple viewpoints and talents to assure success.

Work environments that permit family caregivers the flexibility to contribute to firm success without spending all their time anchored to a work station have enhanced diversity efforts. Differing learning styles have been recognized at least since Maslow set forth a multi-tiered formula for assessing *learning styles* and outcomes. Multiple *work approaches* have also been recognized as new technologies have enabled employees to work in real time across virtual spaces and environments.

To proactively embrace diversity, senior management must recognize it as a corporate principle that contributes to financial success (Barsh *et al.*, 2013; Barta *et al.*, 2012; Nivet & Berlin, 2014). Firm principals must initiate training that includes awareness of laws concerning harassment, discrimination, ethics, fairness standards, and disciplinary procedures. Whatever the formal rules and procedures, they must be clearly articulated, frequently stated, and fairly applied. The equitable application of rules must include some form of confidential dispute resolution, before an impartial arbiter, in a climate where a complainant feels no fear of retaliation or retribution.

These processes are found in the public and non-profit sectors, where accountability is assured through self-audits, public disclosure, IRS 990 filings, and third-party reviews conducted by auditors or others. Some firms have adopted one or both of two public disclosure attitudes as firm leadership asks: "how would this behavior be treated by our auditors or our internal accountability committee," and "how would this behavior be perceived by our clients and the outside world if it were revealed online by an employee or by an investigative reporter?" Candid and confidential exit interviews are an excellent tool for the effectiveness of internal staff assessment policies.

The AIA Code of Ethics has been considered by emerging practitioners and educators only marginally effective in addressing issues of sexual harassment and gender discrimination.

Workplace discrimination complainants have often preferred taking grievances to state agencies in order to achieve redress. Interns feeling exploited by under-compensation have similarly had little success in turning to the national professional organization for satisfaction of alleged inequities. As the AIA has minimal workplace equity enforcement power, it has generally referred complainants to external state and Federal agencies.

Perceived favoritism presents challenges to those seeking recognition for their contributions to firm culture, as awards and recognition continue to flow primarily to white males. Recognition of underrepresented groups is a necessary prerequisite to attracting diverse individuals into design. Architecture provides more annual awards than most professions, from Fellowship recognition to Gold Medal, and Pritzker Prizes. Yet virtually all major awards since 1990 have been made to older white males. Awards are rarely made for difficult collaborative successes, although virtually no significant project can be executed as the work of a sole *auteur*. Few of the profession's leading awards have been made to women or people of color, and these representatives of exemplary and most creative work, such as Pritzker Prize awardees, have largely been selected on the basis of their being "a living architect of talent, vision, and commitment who has produced consistent and significant contributions to humanity and the built environment through the art of architecture" (Thorne, 1999).

Workplace initiatives to increase diversity include:

- Effective mentoring programs within workplaces that assess apparently neutral work policies and practices.
- Developing a robust culture of digital communication and new technologies that create a globalized workplace across multiple geographies and time zones. As large American firms have outsourced technical drawing and other tasks overseas, productivity increases throughout the industry and new professional opportunities have emerged for diverse populations.
- Addressing personnel, work flow management and assignments, project management, and internal cultural factors that implicitly support discriminatory outcomes toward women and people of color in design teams. Firms can diversify work assignments so women and people of color are not niched in the public sector, interior design, historic preservation, and similar areas.
- Design firm employees must be selective in choosing the firms within which they start and build their careers. Interns have noted that a lack of supportive mentorship can be accompanied by the emergence of patterns of apparently discriminatory treatment that marginalize and ultimately isolate new and "different" employees within a firm. Outright discrimination can then be difficult to distinguish from engrained patterns of new employee exploitation.
- Recognizing that some groups, such as GLBT or disabled designers, feel socially isolated within firms, and work to maintain collegiality and collaboration on projects.
- Making room within work environments for the expression of viewpoints that are divergent from the established corporate culture.

Government agencies, non-profit and foundation financing sources, colleges and universities, and some corporate entities have stated a preference for working with diverse professionals. These groups can and should be coordinated locally to underwrite the costs and/or participate in developing and supporting underrepresented talent in the design workplace.

Groups such as the Women's Bureau at the U.S. Department of Labor, the EEOC, individual state departments of equal opportunity, and the Department of Civil Rights of the AFL-CIO provide materials and counseling on ways of addressing and avoiding discrimination in the workplace. The Small Business Administration of the U.S. Department of Commerce provides individual guidance and counseling on starting new and small businesses, and the Service Corps of Retired Executives (SCORE) had provided individual counseling to entrepreneurs starting businesses in particular fields.

Academic Initiatives That Support Diverse Learning Environments

Architecture schools have long been admonished to promote and reward greater numbers of underrepresented faculty and provide support, career guidance, and networking systems with their white male colleagues to enable them to excel (Boyer & Mitgang, 1996; Conway *et al.*, 1996; Corroto, 2003). Under-represented minority and women faculty need friendship and support from their white male colleagues. Few professional design schools have demonstrated success in this regard, leading underrepresented faculty to question whether such a commitment to diversity actually exists among established design school faculty.

According to Dr. Mark Paul Frederickson,

> Design educators have been remiss in self-analysis and self-improvement. Unlike educators in many other professions, we employ teaching methodologies that are little changed since the turn of the [twentiethh] century. This reflects an indolent attitude, and one that may be contributing to many of the design professions' current laments.
>
> (Frederickson, 1992)

A thorough examination of design educators' teaching, research, and publication attitudes and practices supports a student learning environment conducive to growing a more diverse student body with cultural values and career goals more diverse than most faculties.

Educational environments can increase diversity and equality in the design professions when they recognize and reward the broad range of skills that contribute to great architecture. Most architects spend a small amount of time actually designing—more time is spent managing a business, procuring goods and services, persuading potential clients of their value, appearing before boards and commissions, obtaining financing, writing reports, and engaging in myriad activities that contribute to design success. Much of this work is done by people who are non-designers. Opening the perception of multiple design career paths available to students expands understanding of how individuals make differing contributions toward success. This wider sense can help reduce structural hierarchies and discriminatory practices, such that interior design, historic preservation, community design, public housing, or landscape architecture, all areas where women and minorities have been more successful than in corporate architecture, are not demeaned as lesser design contributors to the built environment. Wider recognition of the collaborative nature of design may not eliminate discrimination, but it may improve working relationships in ways that support equality across the fields.

Despite efforts by accrediting agencies to encourage gender equity in teaching approaches, design school curricula are frequently male-oriented and exclusionary of material outside Northern Europe. Racial, cultural, and gender-based approaches to incorporating diversity into curricula are often overlooked, and designing for families or the elderly is rarely discussed. Kathryn Anthony (2001), recommends that design school librarians become guest lecturers in architecture classes, and introduce the library as a rich teaching resource beyond what predominantly male studio instructors, or Internet searches, can teach about design perspectives.

Educators Linda Groat and Sherry Ahrentzen pointed to three areas of architectural education needing significant change: diversification of faculty to create widely supportive learning environments; objective standards for evaluating and judging qualitative subjects such as architectural design; and greater emphasis on human and social factors in evaluating designs, with less emphasis on purely formal assessments. Dr. Paula Whitman's study of Australian women in architecture (2005) recommended curricula place greater emphasis on gender, career planning, practice management, and business management. As schools attract mature students, career changers, and students from community colleges, curricular changes sensitize entire categories of students to design for more diverse clients. Design education is a platform for entering diversified career paths such as gamification, applications development, real estate development, robotics, health and well-being, visualization of planning processes, management support, and innovation in product development. Design students can better understand diverse clients and services by absorbing a wide array of materials, tools, and approaches to life-long learning.

All involved with the academy benefit from periodic diversity training.

Higher education can foster demographic change as college and university boards of can ask, in the context of their fiduciary responsibilities:

- Whether the school's diversity initiatives and investments are connected to clearly articulated institutional goals;
- What resources have been applied toward achieving diversity and what has been the return on investment; and
- Whether the school is applying metrics for success to its initiatives, beyond achieving compositional diversity.

Professional design school administrators and design firm principals can ask:

- How many employees across different identity groups rate their managers as treating them fairly and inclusively?
- Are faculty and staff consistently engaged, satisfied, and productive across all populations?
- Does the institution have mechanisms for cultivating a climate of fairness that combats favoritism and tokenism?
- Is the institution's educational or business approach working equally for students and employees across all subpopulations and identity groups?
- Is the institution graduating students with the skill sets needed to succeed in a pluralistic society?
- Do senior executives demonstrate a capacity and aptitude for diversity and inclusion? In addition to questions about prior experience, qualifications, and vision, colleges and firm principals can make a priority to identify senior leaders with training on unconscious bias and diversity.

In addition to questions about prior experience, qualifications, and vision, colleges and firm principals can make a priority to identify senior leaders with training on unconscious bias. Inculcating values that support workplace diversity requires an acknowledgement by faculty and staff of issues of unconscious discrimination. Schools, the profession, and public agencies have an ethical obligation to examine and correct unfairness in design juries, as documented by Professor Mark Paul Frederickson, who found, for example, that female jurors receive less commentary, and speak less than male jurors (1992). Female students facing jurors were interrupted more and had shorter critique sessions than male students. Racial minority jurors are extremely rare. Encouraging authentic dialogue, motivation and trust are crucial elements to the jury process.

Diversity into the Coming Decades of the Twenty-First Century

New models of "community" are constantly coming into being, including digital neighborhoods that are based in social media. Design advocate and *Metropolis* publisher Susan Szenasy has asked,

> What will I hear from those responsible for educating our next generation of citizen designers? After all, this group of students is part of the most globally connected, tech-savvy, environmentally and culturally aware generation our schools have ever seen … Aside from scholarship programs, what are [educators] doing to recruit from the most needy neighborhoods and backgrounds? How do the schools tap into this new human energy?

An answer to this question requires redefining what a "community" is that may include or exclude participants, and redefining what "diversity" means, to incorporate the broadest range of contributors to the design process, particularly in digital environments.

New technologies, changing social mores, and demographic shifts in Western societies have changed workforce dynamics. New definitions of inclusivity are overdue, paralleling the definition employed by Dr. Carla Corroto, who emphasized "social disadvantage" rather than the relative size of a group as the focus for increasing the diversity of the profession. John L. Wilson FAIA similarly called for diversity of *clients*, including low- and moderate-income clients; diversity of *work*, including adaptive re-use and mixed use projects; diversity of *influence,* beyond those presented in design publications; diversity of *involvement* with infrastructure, land use, and streetscape; diversity of *program ideas* that extend beyond traditional spatial programs; and diversity of *voices*, including public users of design.

Cities have become more ethnically, technologically, and age-diverse, and are now understood as catalysts of global cultural diversity, achieving the projected impacts of Marshall McLuhan's *Global Village* (1994).

American society has shifted toward an emphasis on being diverse, rather than merely seeing diversity, i.e., counting numerical increases in minority participation in primarily white-dominated activities. This shift involves making diversity efforts effective beyond quantitative metrics. As America's demographics have diversified, there is an increased focus on addressing *qualitative* measures of diversity, such as acknowledging the impact of gay families on caregiving and employment practices.

The global imperative for designing safe, sustainable, culturally sensitive, accessible, delightful, and affordable places to live and work in, mandates a re-conceptualized sense of what diversity in design means. According to design educator Vibhavari Jani (2011), the twenty-first century's understanding of diversity requires modifying research and design attitudes to better understand how different social and physical influences have affected contributions to architecture and design in the non-Western world, such as the differing design morphologies and urban settlement patterns found by Bernard Rudofsky in *Architecture Without Architects* (Rudofsky,1964). Understanding diversity enables designers to propose culturally appropriate responses to global design problems, to employ design to engender tolerance among all cultures, religions, and races, and to work toward increasing prosperity and social justice (de Botton, 2006; Brown, 2009; van Es, 2009).

All humankind is imbued with a sense of innovation, vision, and a desire for community building and trust. Developing cross-cultural competence, understanding diversity, and incorporating principles of social equity into design solutions are essential components of professional success in the twenty-first century.

References

Anderson, D.M. (1980). *Women, Design, and The Cambridge School.* West Lafayette, IN: PDA Publishers Corp.

Anthony, K. H. (2001). *Designing for Diversity—Gender, Race, and Ethnicity in the Architectural Profession.* Urbana, IL: University of Illinois Press.

Barsh, J., Nudelman, S., & Yee, L. (April 2013). *Lessons from the Leading Edge of Gender Diversity*. New York: McKinsey Quarterly.

Barta, T., Kleiner, M., & Neumann, T. (April 2012). *Is There a Payoff from Top-team Diversity?* New York: McKinsey Quarterly.

Bizios, G., & Wakeford, K. (2011). *Bridging the Gap: Public-Interest Architectural Internships.* Raleigh, NC: www.lulu.com.

Botton, A. de (2006). *The Architecture of Happiness.* New York: Pantheon Books.

Boyer, E.L., & Mitgang, L.D. (1996). *Building Community: A New Future for Architecture Education and Practice.* Princeton, NJ: Carnegie Foundation for the Advancement of Learning.

Broderick, E., Kupper, E.F., Narev, I., & Thodey, D. (February 2015). *Championing Gender Equality in Australia.* New York: McKinsey Quarterly.

Brown, T. (2009). *Change By Design: How Design Thinking Transforms Organizations and Inspires Innovation*. New York: HarperCollins.

Cary, J., Carter, M., & Peterson, J., eds. (2010). *The Power of Pro Bono: 40 Stories about Design for the Public Good by Architects and Their Clients.* New York: Metropolis Books.

Conway, P., Agrest, D., & Weisman, L., eds. (1996). *The Sex of Architecture.* New York: Harry N. Abrams, Inc.

Corroto, C. (2003). Maintaining Their Privilege: A Framework for Assessing Minority Inclusion in Architecture Schools, in *20 On 2020*. Boston: Boston Society of Architects.

Dean, A.O., & Hursley, T. (2002). *Rural Studio: Samuel Mockbee and An Architecture of Decency*. New York: Princeton Architectural Press.

Es, A. van (2009). *Difference on Display—Diversity in Art, Science & Society.* Rotterdam: NAi Publishers.

Estrich, S. (2001). *Sex and Power,* New York: Riverhead Books.

Fields, D.W. (2000). *Architecture in Black,* London: Athlone Press.

Frederickson, M.P. (1992). *Gender and Racial Bias in Design Juries in Architectural Education: Where We Are*. Washington, DC: ACSA.

Hudner, A.S., Busch, A., & Riechers, A. (2013). *Szenasy, Design Advocate—Writings and Talks by Metropolis Magazine Editor Susan S. Szenasy*. New York: Metropolis Books.

Hudson, K.E. (1993). *Paul R. Williams Architect: A Legacy of Style*. New York: Rizzoli.

Hunt, V., Layton, D., & Prince, S. (January 2015). *Why Diversity Matters.* New York: McKinsey.

Huxtable, A.L. (2008). *On Architecture: Collected Reflections on a Century of Change*. New York: Walker & Company.

Jackson, R.J., & Sinclair, S. (2012). *Designing Healthy Communities,* San Francisco, CA: Jossey-Bass.

Jani, V. (2011). *Diversity in Design—Perspectives From the Non-Western World*. New York: Fairchild Books.

Kaplan, V. (2006). *Structural Inequality—Black Architects in the United States.* Lanham, MD: Rowman & Littlefield.
Kiisk, L. (2003). *20 on 20/20 Vision—Perspectives on Diversity and Design*. Boston, MA: Boston Society of Architects.
Kopec, D. (2006, 2012). *Environmental Psychology for Design*. New York: Fairchild Books.
Kopec, D. (2008). *Health, Sustainability and the Built Environment.* New York: Fairchild.
Lau, W. (May 14, 2014). *Rosa Sheng—The Chairperson of The Missing 32% Project wants to Know Why so Few Leaders in Architecture Are Women*. Washington, DC: Architect Magazine.
Leibrock, C., & Harris, D. (2011). *Design Details for Health: Making the Most of Design's Healing Potential*. Hoboken, NJ: John Wiley & Sons, Inc..
McLuhan, M. (1994). *Understanding Media: The Extensions of Man*. Cambridge, MA: MIT Press.
Mitchell, M. (2003). *The Crisis of the African-American Architect: Conflicting Cultures of Architecture and (Black) Power.* Lincoln, NE: iUniverse.
Nivet, M.A., & Berlin, A.C. (2014). Why Boards Must Become Diversity Stewards, *Trusteeship Magazine*, AGB, May/June, 3:22. Retrieved from http://agb.org/trusteeship/2014/5/why-boards-must-become-diversity-stewards
Nussbaumer, L. (2012). *Inclusive Design.* New York: Fairchild.
Petrowski, E.M. (2012). *Designing for a Diverse Population.* Washington, DC: ASID.
Rhode, D.L. (2005). *Pro Bono in Principle and in Practice—Public Service and the Professions.* Stanford, CA: Stanford Law & Politics.
Ross, H. (2011). *ReInventing Diversity—Transforming Organizational Community to Strengthen People, Purpose, and Performance.* Lanham, MD: Rowman & Littlefield.
Rudofsky, B. (1964). *Architecture Without Architects.* Albuquerque, NM: University of New Mexico Press.
Stohr, K., & Sinclair, C. (2006, 2012). *Design Like you Give a Damn{2}: Building From the Ground Up.* New York: Harry N. Abrams.
Tatum, B.D. (2007). *Can We Talk About Race?* Boston, MA: Beacon Press.
Thorne, M. (1999). *The Pritzker Architecture Prize: The First Twenty Years*. New York: Harry N. Abrams, Inc.
Travis, J. (1991). *African American Architects in Current Practice.* New York: Princeton Architectural Press.
Weiss, E. (2012). *Robert R. Taylor and Tuskegee: An African American Architects Designs for Booker T. Washington*. Montgomery, AL: NewSouth Press.
Whitman, P. (2005). *The Career Progression of Women in the Architectural Profession*. Brisbane: Queensland University of Technology.
Wilson, Dreck Spurlock (2004). *African American Architects: A Biographical Dictionary 1865–1945*. New York: Routledge.
Young, W.M. (1969). *Beyond Racism: Building an Open Society*. New York: McGraw-Hill.

33

Architecture to Save the World

The Activist Architect's Social and Humanitarian Role

Mitra Kanaani, Joseph F. Kennedy and Nathaniel Quincy Belcher

> Leading modernist architects once wanted to improve the lives of everyday people; now they hope to astonish and amuse their elite clients.
>
> (Glazer, 2007)

Why Activism in Architecture?

In an era of profound global challenges and unprecedented technical innovation, the need for viable formulas for the ongoing welfare of the human race is ever more urgent. Architecture has a long legacy of activism in pursuit of societal and environmental change. While the very doing of architecture implies an activist stance, a holistic and comprehensive application of professional efforts toward the common good has been largely absent from the global discussion on shelter provision, climate change and other issues impacted by the worlds of design and construction.

In many ways, architecture has lost its moral compass. Economic fluctuations result in architects and designers finding themselves without clear direction. Current models of practice seem provincial and irrelevant when compared to the real problems facing the built environment. Yet there may be paths for architects to pursue activist goals in an effort to serve society.

The impacts of globalization, together with war, drought, hurricanes, and other human and natural disasters, demonstrate that organized humanitarian initiatives are more necessary than at any other time in history. Despite the existence of some organizations in the field, in recent decades most work toward the common good has been through the efforts of passionate individuals. As awareness of humanitarian issues in the design fields has increased, such individuals have been prompted to act. However, efforts are scattered, and relatively little is reported on design for the common good, innovation in activist architectural pedagogy, or the actual projects conducted toward such goals.

How Are Architects Activists?

Architects are trained to contribute to the ongoing welfare of the human race and provide a critical voice in the global discussion on social space, shelter provision, climate change, and other broad issues impacting the built environment. At their best, in collaborative partnership with communities, governments and businesses, architects are able to create robust public-interest approaches through engaged humanitarian praxis.

However, architects must first answer the question of who they work for and how they can ethically serve the needs of the world. This not an idle question, as the profession of architecture is in flux and in danger of fragmentation. Traditional activities of the architect have been usurped by other professions, and architects rarely contribute to core decisions, resulting in inefficient design processes and programs. They have witnessed the marginalization of the profession, as focus has been increasingly limited to form and object-making. However, architects have begun to recognize the need to reposition their role and assert their place in society.

Billions of people will never hire an architect. So how then can architecture impact the planet's majority? Architects have much to offer through the mediating role they perform and the practical solutions they are uniquely trained to create. But these skills have been offered to a very narrow segment of society, for the most part addressing the needs of the elite. As Michael Murphy of MASS Design Group says, "[i]ncreasingly, architecture is serving the wealthy few. We've got to come up with new models to deliver fundamental services to communities that have been underserved" (Hughes, 2012).

Proactive design can be done in partnership with communities, governments, and businesses to facilitate a process that addresses their issues. This is easier said than done, and the past is littered with failures. For example, in post-earthquake Gubal, India in 1993, families had no choice but to accept a donor group's experimental geodesic domes, a purely technical solution that turned out to be "completely inadequate for anything other than storage" (Salazar, 2004). To create robust public-interest approaches, activist architects must be familiar with such failures, and, in contrast, the best practices they can apply to future initiatives.

Lessons from the History of Activist Architecture

Due to its utilitarian aspects, architecture is inherently a social action, and the architect is expected to be a socially responsible member of society. It is a field of thought and practical engagement that encompasses the whole range of human experience and aspiration. At the same time architecture can be used as a literal instrument for change. Due to the integral nature of problem-solving and ethical expectations, architects are inherently prepared to act as social reformers, even in conflicted situations. In an interview by Oosterman and Moore, Malkit Shoshan points out that "[i]t seems that architects can automatically operate as peacemakers" (2010). Architects are indeed charged with the capacity to improve the quality of life for all people, and to be idealists in alleviating societal ills.

Activism toward a social agenda is not new in architecture. Architects throughout the ages have proposed visionary ideas to create a better built environment through responses to aesthetic, social and humanitarian problems that champion social justice and reform. During the Renaissance, scholars employed humanist methods in art and architecture in order to improve society. The nineteenth-century French architect Claude Nicolas Ledoux was an influential social reformer through the design of his rural factory and his proposed social and technical program to manage that factory. Ledoux's early speculations on the relationship of architecture to industrial management serve as an example of an architect championing a social agenda (Anderson & Herr, 2007).

In America the first architect/politician, Thomas Jefferson, was associated with such French visionary architects as Claude Ledoux, Étienne-Louis Boullée, and Charles-Louis Clerisseau. He utilized his formidable intelligence in the search for a new American style by linking the political independence of a new nation with a symbolic architecture of political values (Trachtenberg & Hyman, 1986). Similarly, during the Russian Revolution in the early twentieth century, architecture was used as a means of social comment and inspiration, as exemplified by Tatlin's unbuilt Constructivist tower for the "Monument to the Third International" in St. Petersburg. This idea of a soaring and spiral-like skeleton structure designed with industrial steel and glass, was an exponent of revolution, a symbolic representation of modernity and emblematic of Soviet social reform (Gibberd,1988). In the modern era, architects of the Bauhaus movement followed a structured social pursuit in all art and design endeavors. They believed in the power of design to promote harmony and foster human connection. The Bauhaus design activists followed an agenda which considered "making" an important social endeavor, and design a service to society. They believed in creating practical, economical housing and considered affordability at the forefront of design (Fuad-Luke, 2009).

Activist Architecture in the First Decades of the Twenty-first Century

Activist architecture in the twenty-first century is a multi-pronged approach including areas outside of the usual practice of architecture. Examples include agriculture, business creation, environmental cleanup, emergency shelters, community engagement, political processes, potential conflict or post-conflict situations, catastrophic mitigation, and defensive design. The stakeholders in this process start with the local community, and then include non-profit organizations and local government. Professional designers, either working with a non-profit or on their own initiative, are the third major component of this triangle of social responsibility.

How is *activist* architecture undertaken? The most active architecture takes the form of direct action in a community. This can be an oppositional architecture that challenges those rules and regulations which stifle the greater good. It may appear confrontational or radical, but is ideally the result of a collaborative educational process with local community leaders. Some of these direct actions address underserved populations, or otherwise meet a direct need. The work of City Repair in Portland, Oregon to create neighborhood gathering spaces is one example (City Repair, 2011). Another case in point is the creation of effective informal housing in the peri-urban environments surrounding urban cores worldwide, as described by John Turner (Turner, 2000). Success of these examples stems from long-term engagement where partners build a new social, economic, natural and built ecology over time. Through supporting local innovation and empowerment, the "experts" render themselves unnecessary. To effectively further such work, dedicated field stations can be imbedded in communities of need. These projects can develop new approaches that can be adjusted through a process of "slow prototyping" that will allow a rational and thorough approach to the diverse issues facing the planet (Thorpe & Gamman, 2011).

Much can be learned from the traditions of vernacular architecture, where communities come together to address built environment issues using local skills and materials to support traditional cultural systems. Such bottom-up approaches are based on a societal sense of the greater good and a cohesive group culture to foster design independence and community empowerment. Through assisting the creation of these interconnections using best practices of community design, designers can help knit together splintered societies. However, when working with communities it is important to be clear about the extent of services offered: the old adage to "under-promise and over-deliver" is particularly appropriate.

While it is important to work directly with communities, it is also critical to address top-down issues such as international building codes, government regulations, and macroeconomic strategies. But a critical question still remains: how can professionals effectively do this work and yet afford to pay the bills? Because activist architecture serves those with fewer resources, creative business models are needed to generate the means to pay for it.

The Need for Activist Architecture Now

The twenty-first century continues to unfold its uniquely omnipresent challenges. The influential *Boyer Report* states that

> Perhaps never in history have the talents, skills, the broad vision and the ideals of the architecture profession been more urgently needed. The profession could be powerfully beneficial, at a time when the lives of families and entire communities have grown increasingly fragmented.
>
> (Boyer & Mitgang, 1996)

The many issues driving activist design approaches are complex and quickly evolving. While the need for design for the common good has never been greater, material and design innovation has simultaneously taken unprecedented strides. Accelerating catastrophes, wars and global tensions increase the demand for positive design solutions to these challenges. Architects need to reframe their sense of responsibility to achieve truly "responsive" work that can help achieve "good enough" design that can help more people (Thorpe & Gamman 2011). Architects can be self-directed conduits to help link the needs of the underserved with knowledge and resources. Activist practitioners must leave their offices, engage with communities and seek design opportunities based on community needs.

The good news is that over the past several years an attitude shift has occurred among students, scholars, and practitioners. For example, in the wake of 9/11, interest in activist architecture has surged (Verderber, 2003). While conventional architecture has been particularly hard-hit by the recession, architects have found new ways of doing business and addressing formerly underserved clients. Extreme weather events, the destruction of Syria and Iraq, the BP oil spill in the Gulf of Mexico and other ecological and political imbalances are serious global issues. However, the activities of pioneering architects such as Shigeru Ban and organizations like Architecture for Humanity and Habitat for Humanity have popularized design as a tool to address global problems.

Viable solutions for issues in the built environment are most critical in urban environments, particularly the fast-growing cities of the Southern hemisphere where human and environmental issues are most acute. These cities are beset with a host of environmental and social problems resulting from unsustainable growth. While they are often places of misery and ill-health, the informal settlements surrounding urban cores are also potential test-beds for solutions. The role of the architect as planner and responder in these fast-changing and often dangerous conditions is relatively undeveloped. But the possibilities are rich due to the informal nature of these settlements and the obvious needs that can be directly addressed with relatively modest design inputs (Architecture for Humanity, 2012).

Natural disasters and the threat of climate change must be addressed by the design professions due to the human cost of these epic shifts. While designers are the "second responders" that address systemic issues after emergency crews have left, they can also preemptively address the impacts of droughts, flooding, and increased storms through appropriate structural and envelope design, improving existing buildings, and planning for dangers such as rising sea levels. Based on the latest work of climate scientists, architects and engineers can provide strategies for protection in vulnerable areas through contribution to regional climate adaptation plans. Other ongoing concerns, such as the availability and cost of water, energy, and materials, force architects to radically rethink the scale and performance of buildings so that the inherently destructive act of architecture can be turned toward a net positive. Architects have been asking themselves hard questions about their roles and responsibilities, particularly in the wake of the Indian Ocean tsunami that killed more than 200,000 people in 2004 (Aquilino, 2011). In attempting to answer these questions, it has become clear that architects are largely absent in the effort to protect people from disasters.

Technical innovations can augment social entrepreneurship to scale up good solutions. The radical increase in communications capacity worldwide opens the door for innovative and deeply democratic processes of empowerment and solution building through collaborations supported by social media and increased information access. For example, young African farmers have rapidly adopted low-cost innovations in smartphone technology to improve food security and economic viability (Leny, 2013). These innovations can expand the reach of activist architecture. Advances in materials science can be shared, and innovations in adapting traditional and sustainable building techniques to address local problems, is a new and relatively untapped opportunity for innovation.

Not all need for change stems from emergencies. Some areas of the world are growing quickly while others are depopulating. Architects must pay attention to such demographic shifts as increasingly heterogeneous populations necessitate diverse approaches to the practice and academy of architecture. These changes also prompt the question: who will the architects of the future be and who they will design for? Both the academy and profession must challenge current design decision-making processes to be more reflective of public needs.

The preamble of the "UNESCO/Union of International Architects Charter for Architectural Education" specifies such need for raised awareness in architecture:

> We are aware of the fact that, in spite of many outstanding and sometimes spectacular contributions of our profession, there is a surprisingly small percentage of the built environment which is actually conceived and realized by architects and planners. There is still room for the development of new tasks for the profession when architects become aware of the increasing needs identified and possibilities offered in areas which have not, up to now, been of major concern to the profession. Still greater diversity is therefore needed, in professional practice and, as a consequence, in architectural education and training.
>
> (UNESCO/UIA, 2005)

On the same note in 1996, the report "Building Community: A New Future for Architecture Education and Practice," specified that

> architects and architecture educators, as well as the organizations that represent them, ought to be among the most vocal and knowledgeable leaders in preserving and beautifying

Figure 33.1 While informal housing settlements such as this one in Tijuana, Mexico, are characterized by poor design and inadequate construction using ad hoc materials, they are also dynamic testing grounds for innovative approaches to improving shelter provision using local materials and skills. The important factor to bring to situations like this is the design knowledge of the architect

> a world whose resources are in jeopardy. Graduates should be knowledgeable teachers and listeners, prepared to talk with clarity and understanding to clients and communities about how architecture might contribute to creating not just better buildings, but a more wholesome and happy human condition for present and future generations.
>
> (Boyer & Mitgang, 1996)

To reinvigorate the public sphere of architecture will take leadership, collaborative models, and cross-discipline partnerships. It is important to note that increased interest in activism has arisen in the midst of virtually unprecedented technological advances and possibilities comparable to those of the Renaissance era or the Industrial Revolution of the late nineteenth century. Technologies such as building information modeling (BIM) and sensors in "smart buildings" allow for accurate design for efficiency, energy, and health. While there are limits to technology, there are also opportunities to use it through human-centric processes to increase designers' capacity to address global problems. Indeed these new materials and techniques can be tools for activism, to actualize Buckminster Fuller's notion of ephemeralization, where less and less can be utilized to do more and more (Fuller, 2002).

Architectural Activism for Social Reform

The power of architecture to effect social and cultural transformation is undeniable. Over the past two decades, dedicated activists have instigated creative strategies to improve or eliminate such diverse social and economic issues as economic inequality, poverty, border issues, domestic abuse, and child labor. This work is often most effective by enhancing and strengthening communities rather than focusing on specific issues. Successful efforts, such as that by Purpose Built Communities in Atlanta, solve problems holistically by addressing several issues unique to a community, such as education, health, and housing, simultaneously. However, activity has been sporadic and often incoherent (Cousins, 2013). An active structured presence is necessary for architects to contribute to the alleviation of social ills through design. The activist group Architects, Designers and Planners for Social Responsibility exemplify this approach through such events as "Beyond Resilience: Actions for a Just Metropolis," their commitment to green building with the "Better Envelopes Solutions Showcase" and their ethical commitment to ending design for torture and killing (Breddels & Oosterman, 2010).

This type of approach is also appropriate for reconstruction efforts after conflict situations. Organizations such as Builders without Borders focus on creating long-term sustainable strategies to meet community needs (Kennedy, 2004). This approach is challenging in dangerous conditions where needs are soon forgotten in the next news cycle.

While humanitarian architecture is often the effort of passionate individuals, there are other organizations active in this realm. The United Nations Human Settlement Program is an international organization tasked with this effort by the world's governments. Habitat for Humanity is a faith-based effort comprised largely of volunteers that combines the sweat equity of partner families with fundraising for materials. The non-profit organization Architecture for Humanity places volunteer architects with projects around the world. They also sponsor design competitions and administer the Open Architecture Network, where public interest design solutions can be shared.

One of the most noteworthy attempts to structure architectural activism has been the work of the members of the Social, Economic, Environmental Design (SEED) Network, founded with the mission to advance the right of every person to live in a socially, economically, and environmentally healthy community (Feldman, 2003) Examples of the SEED network's activities include empowering Yaqui women in northwestern Mexico to help their communities, creating urban habitats for poor people in the heart of the major cities such as Oakland, financing public housing in South America and Africa, and creating healthy, safe, and humane transitional housing for refugees. While these efforts are worthy, organizations seeking guidance must be discerning, as untested solutions are sometimes promoted and failures are often underreported (Segal, L., personal communication, April 10, 2012).

The Role of Architect and Activism for Preserving the Planet

Ecological activism in architecture has taken several forms over the past two decades. For example, some architects and organizations have focused on structures that reduce energy use, utilize local renewable materials, reuse existing structures and otherwise reduce design's impact on the planet. The US Green Building Council's LEED rating system exemplifies this approach. The natural building movement and tiny house movement are other examples of this new strain of design. Examples include straw-bale construction, earth and lime plasters and building with bamboo.

Some organizations go further, contending that sustainability is not enough and that architecture must have a regenerative approach that improves soil, water, ecosystems, and human society. Many take the form of challenges, such the Living Building Challenge, Architecture 2030, and the activities of 350.org. These strategies also have the benefit of supporting local economies and culture through community-friendly low-cost techniques. Others advocate building with trash, such as 4Walls International, an organization that cleans Tijuana' streets and uses the trash to create useful building products (4WallsInternational, 2011). Through utilizing such concepts as upcycling, net-plus design, permaculture, and other regenerative design methodologies, architects can bend the problem curve toward a solution-based future.

The Role of Schools, Educators and Students in Activist Architecture

Schools of architecture have sporadically introduced public good as a goal for sustainability. They plant the seed of public interest amongst future architects through developing design-build, rural, affordable housing, or studios with similar objectives such as Auburn University's Rural Studio (Kroiz, 2012). Within a school, individual educators may partner with local or international authorities, policy-makers and NGOs to champion projects, while exposing students to such initiatives. However, this work is largely driven by individual passions, and little concerted effort to develop career paths for future architects in this field has occurred.

Pedagogy is a key place to foster humanitarian architecture. In the 1960s US schools of architecture established "community design centers" which gave students opportunities to gain experience solving community problems. Educators in various fields including architecture have also developed environmental design centers. However, since the publication of Dr. Ernest Boyer's "Building Community" (usually referred to as the "Boyer Report") in the mid-1990s, schools of architecture have done more to instill a commitment to engagement and service in their students through establishing a climate of engagement and public benefit of architecture (Boyer & Mitgang, 1996).

In the decade and a half since the Boyer Report specified a new future for architectural education, the idea of public service has been rekindled in architecture schools. The National Architectural Accrediting Board (NAAB) has adopted "understanding of cultural diversity and social equity" as an accreditation condition, reinforcing the importance of social engagement. According to the NAAB's Realm A, Student Performance Criteria (SPC) A.8, architectural institutions are required to develop in their students the understanding of cultural diversity and social equity. By way of this criterion, students must demonstrate the "understanding of the diverse needs, values, behavioral norms, physical abilities, and social and spatial patterns that characterize different cultures and individuals and the responsibility of the architects to ensure equity of access to sites, buildings and structures" (National Architectural Accrediting Board, 2014). This criterion reinforces the ethical implications of decisions involving built environment, civic engagement, and commitment to professional and public services.

However, active student engagement in public good projects is not yet a required component of architectural programs. In spite of this, increasing numbers of students voluntarily focus thesis projects on resolving society's ills through design innovation. Examples include centers for battered women in underdeveloped countries, centers for abused children, centers for human rights for religious discrimination, and many environmental topics related to the global, ecological and environmental complications of our time. This research signifies an

Figure 33.2 Diploma project of Pegah Roshan, graduated from Baha'i Institute for Higher Education, BIHE, Department of Architecture. Global Associate Faculty Design Advisor: Mitra Kanaani

appreciation for assertive proactive humanitarian sensitivities amongst future architects. An example of social justice in architecture is the development of a school of architecture under the umbrella of Baha'i' Institute for Higher Education (BIHE) by a group of architects and educators in Iran and across the globe. These students and educators were deprived of their right to higher education because of their religious beliefs as Baha'i's (BIHE, 2011).

Social and civic activism has emerged as a vital component of scholastic engagement in architectural academia. But how can this momentum be sustained? Support for faculty to create programs addressing public interest architecture is critical, as is administrative support. Studio courses in particular can partner with humanitarian projects to take advantage of student design energy. Schools can support public interest architecture by applying a certain percentage of studio projects toward such efforts. It should be remembered, however, that

Figure 33.3 Diploma project of Nasim Rowshanabadi graduated from Baha'i Institute for Higher Education, BIHE, Department of Architecture. Global Associate Faculty Design Advisor: Mitra Kanaani

projects undertaken in the context of university programs may not be practical in real world architectural settings (Kroiz, 2012).

As the public demands increased accountability from professionals, evidence-based design research can help identify, define, and support the implementation of best practices in humanitarian design (Kopec *et al.*, 2012). Coordinated research agendas for human-centered development help avoid duplicated efforts, and increase the knowledge base for effective work in the field. Academic partnerships with business and communities could create mechanisms for real projects to germinate and grow. When students are embedded in a community, they can engage in shared co-teaching experiences (Freire, 1970). Informal innovation, ideally through a teacher-training process, is necessary to magnify the positive impacts of a relatively small number of professionals (Norton, 2012). Collaboration through education and design can be a powerful experience.

Schools can encourage and support graduating architecture students to pursue public interest theses and diploma projects, incorporating social agenda and humanitarian concepts, while at the same time articulating with the profession to help students actualize a viable professional life in this field after graduation. However, this type of outside-the-box thinking is complex, given the highly regulated environment of architectural education. Perhaps a way forward is the development of scholastic and professional programs in public interest architecture comparable to those of public interest law and medicine.

Public Interest and Community Design as an Alternative to Traditional Practice

Can public-interest design and humanitarian practice become a viable alternative to traditional practice? If so, what are the implications? For public interest architecture to become a viable profession, change must occur. First, this type of practice must be validated as a career path by the academy, the profession, and the public at large. Professional organizations, governments, and schools must give this architectural approach as much credence as mainstream architecture. While volunteer opportunities are important, these approaches need to be rationalized to maximize positive impact of human and material investments. Simultaneously architects must develop innovative strategies with a wide range of actors, some of whom may not have previously collaborated.

The economics of public interest design challenge the growth of this work. Three economic models comprise the majority of approaches architects have taken. Many projects utilize a combination of two or even all three of these approaches. First, in a service-based model, architects and designers donate their time and energy toward projects. This is usually done alongside conventional practice. Public Architecture's "1 percent" initiative currently strives to get all architecture firms to donate 1 percent of their time to the public interest (Public Architecture, 2015). Second, some firms have found ways to develop fee-paying clients through their pro-bono work or through creative government partnerships (Hughes, 2012). The non-profit model depends on donations and grants for public interest work, with some designers finding volunteer opportunities through organizations such as Architecture for Humanity. Finally, the self-funding model involves projects creating economic opportunities to fund themselves, including sales of goods, micro-loan programs, or crowdfunding such as Kickstarter (Kickstarter, 2015).

To address the problems facing humanity, the study and practice of architecture must become much more proactive. The typical top-down approach is littered with failures, while a "do-gooder" approach is disempowering. Instead, activist architecture could be best

Figure 33.4 Volunteer contractors and architects teach local South Africa builders to construct a shelter using earth tamped into inexpensive polypropylene sacks. This technique, known as "earthbag" construction, was innovated by Aga Khan-award winning architect Nader Khalili, and is now spreading throughout the world as a robust and easy to learn system of construction. Because the earthbag system lends itself to domed structures, it is especially valuable in areas with very little wood

served by a "fraternalist" approach which levels the field to allow for the greatest number of stakeholders to be involved, solve more than one problem at a time, and develop replicable and scalable solutions applicable to similar situations (Thorpe & Gamman, 2011).

Architects and other designers need to find and champion potential projects and communities, and not wait for a client community to find them (Bell & Wakeford, 2008). The architect's role will be radically different in this scenario. This proactive approach demands that architects be more assertive as they insert themselves into the conversation about the future of social, environmental, and built landscapes. Another choice for public interest designers is between domestic and international work. Projects closer to home are desirable because they can build long-term relationships between designers and communities. While international projects are attractive, they can also be fraught with complex problems difficult to solve across long distances. These projects are also more expensive and generally short-term. Many international projects are in post-conflict situations which have their own set of issues and dangers. As these projects are prone to failure, investments of time and effort must be carefully considered (Bell & Wakeford, 2008). It is of key importance to work with a reputable local partner.

Figure 33.5 4Walls International works with communities in Mexico and elsewhere to create energy-efficient systems of construction using such local materials as tires, plastic bottles, and earth. This building utilizes insulating bottles filled with plastic trash in a matrix of cement plaster, which is then plastered over. The glass bottles shown in this building are used for decoration and daylighting

The Future of Activist Architecture: A Manifesto for Action

The need to reorient priorities toward more sustainable and equitable practice is increasing. The profession can aim to do so while also enhancing the global creation of wealth and decent employment in an inclusive frame of freedom, full enjoyment of fundamental human rights, and support for weak and vulnerable populations.

Without proactive research, architects are likely to be working on yesterday's concerns rather than on tomorrow's. Networked anticipatory research can help the architectural community establish a well-defined manifesto for action. Architects can also create alliances with environmental and social activists and business entrepreneurs. Such activist organizations can then call upon the world's governments and peoples to support initiatives and contribute to its processes. The 2012 Rio+20 United Nations Conference on Sustainability "Plan for Activism" provides a viable guide for this process. Architecture is impacted by a consortium of collateral organizations (UIA, AIA, NCARB, ACSA, RIBA, KAAB, and RAIA, etc.) that regulate, educate, and promote the practice and discipline of architecture through geographic, legislated and/or voluntary efforts. The action and goodwill of individual activist architects together with allied organizations will activate this plan. Short of this engagement, practitioners and communities will of necessity continue to self-organize and create autonomous ventures. However, the possibilities of combined resources and collective action remain available to create so much more.

A Five Point Action Plan

1 Establish an information *network* that documents projects, problems, and scenarios of all possible work of activist architects in an open, concerted, and interactive communication platform.
2 Create a fiscal and operational *infrastructure* to facilitate growth of existing and new community-based organizations. Educate and re-educate architecture professionals as well as rally practice to cooperative action in the built environment.
3 *Share* the best available information gathered by non-government and government policy-makers at the national, regional, and global levels in a way that facilitates cooperative action on specific projects in the built environment.
4 *Analyze* viable projects and create a technical plan of action to be implemented by community-level organizations wherever possible, with nongovernmental organizations, governments, and international agencies providing financial and technical capacity.
5 *Mobilize* design professionals in alternative practice models to tackle the tasks identified with community-level organizations and their networks.

This process should reorient the full range of practice activities to encourage flexible patterns and create public awareness and support for a global *apparatus* to monitor the health of the built environment, support human activity, and create better places.

References

4WallsInternational. (2011). The world is littered with opportunity. Retrieved February 10, 2015 from http://www.4wallsintl.org/

Anderson, G. & K. Herr. (2007). *Encyclopedia of activism and social justice*. Los Angeles, CA: Sage Publications Inc.

Aquilino, M. J. (Ed.). (2011). *Beyond shelter: architecture and human dignity*. New York: Metropolis Books.

Architecture for Humanity (Ed.). (2012). *Design like you give a damn [2]*. New York: Abrams.

Baha'i' Institute for Higher Education. (2011). Architecture. Retrieved October 30, 2014. http://www.bihe.org/index.php?option=com_content&task=view&id=56&Itemid=147

Bell, B. & K. Wakeford (Eds.). (2008). *Expanding architecture: design as activism*. New York: Metropolis Books.

Boyer, E. & L. Mitgang. (1996). *Building community: a new future for architecture education and practice,*. Stanford, CA: The Carnegie Foundation for the Advancement of Teaching.

Breddels, L. & A. Oosterman. (2010). The social scientist: did someone say collaboration? Gerd Junne interviewed. *Archis* 4(26), 24–26.

City Repair. (2011). *City repair's placemaking guidebook—creative community building in the public right of way* (2nd ed). Portland, Oregon: City Repair.

Cousins, T. (2013). The Atlanta model for reviving poor neighborhoods. *Wall Street Journal*. September 14. Retrieved February 10, 2015, from http://online.wsj.com/article/SB10001424127887324009304579040862988907966.html

Feldman, R. M. (2003). Activist architecture. In Bell, B. (Ed.), (2003) *Good deeds, good design: community service through Architecture* (pp. 109–114). New York: Princeton Architectural Press.

Freire, P. (1970). *Pedagogy of the oppressed*. New York: Herder and Herder.

Fuad-Luke, A. (2009). *Design activism: a beautiful strangeness*. Abingdon, UK: Routledge.

Fuller, R. B. (2002). *Critical Path* (2nd ed.). New York: Saint Martin's Griffin.

Gibberd, V. (1988). *Architecture source book: a visual reference to buildings around the world*. Wellfleet, MA: Wellfleet Press.

Glazer, N. (2007, March 1). What happened to the social agenda? *The American Scholar*. Retrieved November 1, 2014, from http://theamericanscholar.org/what-happened-to-the-social-agenda/#.VFVAfi7n8y4

Hughes, C. J. (2012). Does "doing good" pay the bills? *Architectural Record 200*(3), 41–41.

Kennedy, J. (Ed.) (2004) *Building without borders: sustainable construction for the global village*. Gabriola Island, Canada: New Society.

Kickstarter. (2015). Kickstarter. Retrieved February 10, 2015 from https://www.kickstarter.com/

Kopec, D., E. Sinclair & B. Matthes (2012). *Evidence based design: a process for research and writing*. Boston, MA: Prentice Hall.

Kroiz, L. (2012). Review: Citizen architect: Samuel Mockbee and the spirit of Rural Studio. *Journal of the Society of Architectural Historians* 71(2), 241–242.

Leny, A. (2013). Social media, mobile apps drive youth to agriculture. Retrieved February 10, 2015, from http://www.scidev.net/sub-saharan-africa/icts/scidev-net-at-large/social-media-mobile-apps-drive-youth-to-agriculture.html

National Architectural Accrediting Board, Inc. (2014). *2014 Conditions of Accreditation*. Washington, DC: NAAB.

Norton, J. (2012). *Woodless construction 3: change and adaption to local needs*. Bourton-on-Dunsmore, UK: Practical Action.

Oosterman, A. & T. Moore. (2010). The architect: small change: Malkit Shoshan interviewed. *Archis 4*(26), 32–39.

Public Architecture. (2015). The 1%. Retrieved February 10, 2015 from www.theonepercent.org

Salazar, A. (2004). Normal life after disasters? Eight years of housing lessons from Marathwada to Gujarat. In Kennedy, J. (Ed.), *Building without borders: sustainable construction for the global village* (pp. 168–174). Gabriola Island, Canada: New Society.

Thorpe, A. & L. Gamman. (2011). Design with society: why socially responsive design is good enough. *CoDesign* 7(3–4), 217–230.

Trachtenberg, M. & I. Hyman (1986). *Architecture, from prehistory to post-modernism*. Upper Saddle River, NJ: Prentice Hall.

Turner, J. (2000). *Housing by people: towards autonomy in building environments*. London: Marion Boyars Publishers Ltd.

UNESCO/UIA. (2005). *Charter of architectural education*. Paris: UIA

Verderber, S. (2003). Compassionism and the design studio in the aftermath of 9/11. *Journal of Architectural Education* 56(3), 48–62.

34

Gender Issues in Architecture

Kathryn H. Anthony

Introduction

Why do we need more women in architecture, and greater diversity among designers? Why has this been, and will it continue to be, such a paramount concern? As I argued in *Designing for Diversity: Gender, Race and Ethnicity in the Architectural Profession*, "The built environment reflects our culture, and vice-versa. If our buildings, spaces, and places continue to be designed by a relatively homogeneous group of people, what message does that send about our culture?" (Anthony, 2001). The built environment is one of culture's most lasting legacies, and women must be included.

This chapter reflects on the current state of women in the architectural profession, how far women in architecture have come and how far they still have to go. We begin by introducing Architect Barbie. Why did she come into being, what did she symbolize, and what issues did she raise? Next is an analysis of some major challenges that women architects in the US and abroad have faced in recent history, including how they have been impacted by the economic recession. We examine some strategies currently in place to promote greater gender diversity in architecture, with a special emphasis on the recognition of women in architecture through awards, prizes, and leadership positions that have met with mixed success.

Space here does not permit an overview of accomplished women architects and their designs, nor does it permit a discussion of issues of sexual orientation in architecture, topics that merit attention elsewhere. Instead our focus is on key controversies related to gender that are still shaping the profession today.

Introducing Young Girls To Architecture: Architect Barbie

The Barbie doll made her debut in 1959, with Ponytail Barbie and a black and white striped swimsuit. Her full name is Barbie Millicent Roberts and she is from Willows, Wisconsin. Since then the toy manufacturer, Mattel, has created over 100 versions of Barbie, from the first teenage fashion model to four runs as a presidential candidate, and almost everything in between.

In 2010 Mattel invited the public to vote on the 125th career of their ever-popular Barbie doll. The vote focused on professions where women were underrepresented, including Architect Barbie, Surgeon Barbie, and Computer Engineer Barbie. Computer Engineer Barbie won.

In an effort to save Architect Barbie, feminist scholar, historian, and professor at the State University of New York (SUNY) at Buffalo, Despina Stratigakos intervened, along with architect, SUNY Buffalo colleague, and 2012 President of American Institute of Architects (AIA) New York State, Kelly Haynes McAlonie. Together they approached Mattel to advocate for an architect's version of the iconic doll. Eventually both were asked to advise on its design. While in real life, architects have a preference for wearing black, young girls would view black in a negative way, more as "villain," "mortician," rather than architect. So instead of providing authentic all-black attire, the designers chose basic colors, clean lines, and simple volumes, along with black ankle boots. Her accessories were a pink drawing tube, a white hard hat, and black glasses.

The doll was launched at the 2011 AIA convention in New Orleans where 400 girls recruited from nearby schools and girls' clubs participated in workshops led by women architects. The architects presented an overview of what architects do, discussed work of past and present women architects, and oversaw an exercise for girls to redesign Barbie's Dream House, a type of first design studio assignment. When the workshop was over, each participant was handed a gift bag with a set of drawing tools and her own Architect Barbie to take home. This workshop served as a prototype for other subsequent workshops held in Boston and Chicago and elsewhere.

As Stratigakos put it, "If Architect Barbie gets us talking, then more power to her. But ultimately she is for kids, not adults, and it is the politics of the sandbox that I hope to influence. I look forward to the day when little girls claim hard hats and construction sites as just another part of their everyday world" (Stratigakos, 2011).

Even the Mattel spokesperson recognized that "The field of architecture is an area where women are underrepresented" (Wischhover, 2011). While women account for about 40 percent of students in architecture schools, the percentage of practicing women architects is less than half that amount. And while the percentage of women in architecture schools has been increasing, according to Stratigakos, "the number of women actually entering the profession and remaining there remains pretty flat" (Wischhover, 2011).

Architect Barbie raised eyebrows in the profession. As John Cary put it in his provocative piece,

> Yet while the AIA and others might hope to inspire a generation of girls and young women to become architects, the systemic problems facing the profession will not be fixed with a doll and a dream. Career pipeline issues must be remedied. Cultural and institutional sexism must be faced. These are matters of retention, not recruitment.
>
> (Cary, 2011)

In her essay "Girl Talk," Alexandra Lange raised the key question: "The world's most popular doll, dressed in architect's garb: friend or foe to a profession already suffering from a pronounced gender gap?" She argued,

> as a design critic and parent, Architect Barbie didn't sit right with me, and I was not alone. Much disquiet on the architecture blogs and in the field focused on her stylized wardrobe: black-rimed glasses, an outdated hot-pink blueprint tube, a skyline-print

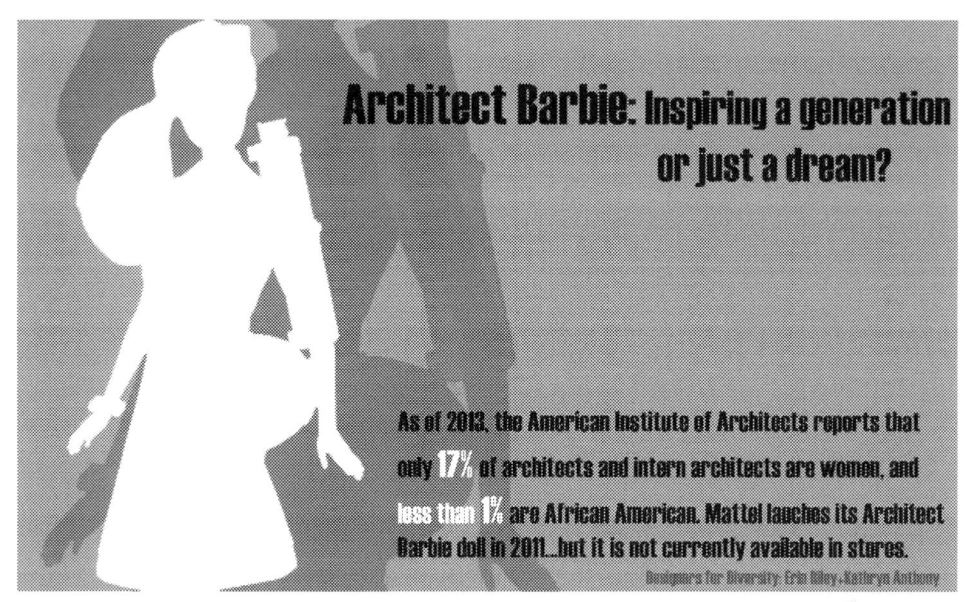

Figure 34.1 A version of the world-famous Barbie Doll, Architect Barbie, launched in 2011, sought to inspire more young girls to pursue architecture as a career

> dress, white hard hat, those oh-so-fashionable high-heel booties. But that was window dressing for a deeper discontent: As the press release that accompanied her debut pointed out, as of November 2010, just 17 percent of AIA members were women. Barbie seemed like a distraction from, not an answer to, an ongoing problem.
>
> (Lange, 2012)

Lange polled a sample of female architects and designers to ask what toys they had played with as children: the computer game, the Sims, make-believe games, crayons, Spirographs, Lincoln Logs, and art supplies. Others sabotaged Fisher Price toys. Those who played with Barbies destroyed her with bleach, Sharpie makeup, and shorn hair. They created dream houses out of shoeboxes, clothes out of fabric scraps, and played with Barbie in their Lincoln Log constructions. Although Lange expressed her dislike for Architect Barbie and pink for pink's sake, she admitted "that Stratigakos is entirely justified in thinking that we have to plant seeds wherever and however we can."

Along with the production of Architect Barbie, in 2011 the AIA and Mattel challenged AIA members to enter the Architect Barbie Dream House Design Competition, drawing 30 submissions from which a panel of jurors selected five finalists. Children and adults alike cast a total of 8,470 votes for their favorite design. The winning design by Ting Li and Maja Paklar was published on the AIA website but Mattel never put it into production (Frank & The American Institute of Architects, 2011).

Why Do We Need More Women In Architecture And Design?

Gender Demographics in Architecture

Gender issues have long posed a tremendous challenge for both architectural education and practice. Compared to the numbers of women in medicine, law, and engineering, the number of women architects and women architecture faculty still remains low. As of 2012, the National Council of Architectural Registration Boards (NCARB) estimated the number of licensed architects in the US at 105,847 and the American Institute of Architects (AIA) included just over 83,000 members. Of all AIA members, including licensed architects as well as intern architects on the licensure path, 17 percent were female, compared to 9 percent in 2000. Underrepresented ethnic minorities such as African American, Asian American, and Latino American comprised 10 percent of AIA membership compared to 7 percent in 2000 (The American Institute of Architects, 2012). African-Americans comprised only 1 percent.

The number of women architects in underrepresented racial groups, such as African American, Latino American, or Asian American continues to remain low. The percent of African-American women architects is minuscule—far less than 1 percent. As Hannah McCann argued in her article, "0.2," in *Architect* magazine: "The number of black women architects has quadrupled in 15 years. But four times a fraction of a percent doesn't amount to much" (McCann, 2007). At that time (2007), the total number of licensed African-American women architects was just 0.2 percent, 196 out of a total of about 91,000 architects, while African-American women comprised almost 2 percent of the legal profession and 4 percent of the medical profession. By 2013, the total number of licensed African-American women architects had increased to 294, while their licensed African-American male counterparts totaled 1,589 (The Directory of African-American Architects, n.d.).

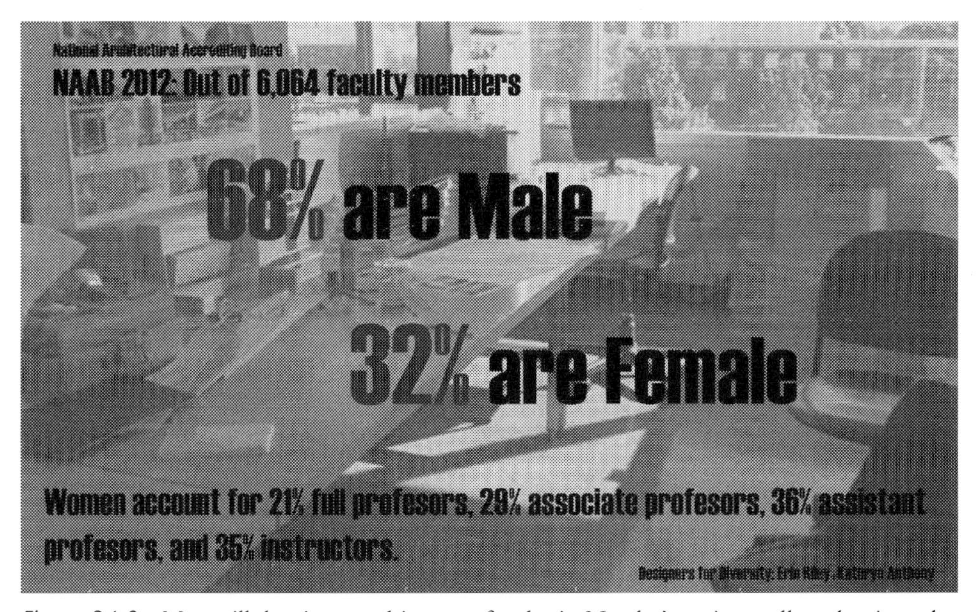

Figure 34.2 Men still dominate architecture faculty in North America at all academic ranks. Women are the least represented at the full professor rank, where men outnumber them about 5 to 1

Despite increasing numbers of African-American women students in architecture schools, many choose to forego licensure and choose alternate career paths. Among the reasons, according to McCann: the high cost of architectural education, lack of role models, and an inflexible model of success that rewards long hours and ignores community design (McCann, 2007).

How does that picture compare with the current status of women in architecture schools? According to the 2012 statistics available from the National Architectural Accrediting Board (NAAB), out of 26,850 students enrolled in accredited architecture programs across the US, women comprised 43 percent while men accounted for 57 percent (The National Architectural Accrediting Board, Inc., 2013). Statistics for graduating students were similar. Of a total of 6,354 accredited degrees awarded during the 2011–12 academic year, women received 42 percent while men received 58 percent (The National Architectural Accrediting Board, Inc., 2013).

According to the NAAB's 2012 report on accreditation, of 6,064 faculty members teaching in NAAB-accredited degree programs, 40 percent were full-time, 15 percent were part-time, and 45 percent were adjunct (The National Architectural Accrediting Board, Inc. 2013). Two-thirds (68 percent) were male faculty while one-third (32 percent) were female, an increase of female faculty from the 2010–11 academic year when males comprised 72 percent and women 28 percent. By 2012, women faculty accounted for 21 percent of full professors, 29 percent of associate professors, 36 percent of assistant professors, and 35 percent of instructors (The National Architectural Accrediting Board, Inc., 2013). Women were less well represented at the higher faculty ranks.

Gender Discrimination In Architecture: In The USA

Many women architects continue to face discrimination on the job. My research that formed the basis of my book, *Designing for Diversity: Gender, Race and Ethnicity in the Architectural Profession,* drew upon surveys and interviews of over 400 members of the American Institute of Architects (AIA) nationwide collected during the 1990s. It was the first study of its kind to compare obstacles and opportunities faced by architects in four demographic groups: white women, women of color, white men, and men of color—under the cloak of anonymity (Anthony, 2001). Here are 12 key findings that emerged from my research:

1 Rites of passage that serve as gateways to the profession often serve as roadblocks to underrepresented architects. Interviewing, internship, registration, and the first job are major hurdles to all architects. But when these experiences go poorly, and if underrepresented architects perceive that they are treated unfairly, they can be driven right out of the profession.
2 The fact that the architectural profession depends so strongly on a changing economy makes it difficult for employees to escape from uncomfortable work situations. When times are tough and jobs are hard to come by, as they are today, architects—especially underrepresented architects—are trapped. When faced with unfair treatment or dead-end jobs that stifle their professional development, they may have nowhere else to turn.
3 Many underrepresented architects are pigeonholed: women as interior designers, African-Americans as government architects, and Asian-Americans as computer-aided designers, thus limiting job mobility and advancement opportunities.
4 The phenomenon of "leap-frogging" occurs all too often. Many women architects told troubling tales of training male underlings who, despite far fewer years of education or professional experience, rapidly surpassed them in rank and salary. These men quickly

Figure 34.3 Designing for Diversity documented a serious workplace leap-frogging phenomenon in architectural practice that drives many women out of the field

climb their own career ladders, leaving the women behind. Subordinates become superiors. Such instances propel many diverse designers right out of the profession, never wanting to return. In fact, my survey revealed significant pay gaps between men and women architects. The gap widened the more experience architects had in the field.

5 Working conditions in many smaller architectural offices make it difficult for those treated unfairly to complain in a confidential manner, and they fear a backlash from engaging in whistle blowing. Large institutions like universities, corporations, and large architectural firms hire human resource personnel to address complex issues like sexual harassment and salary inequities. Small design offices lack such personnel.

6 The profession is not as family-friendly as it should be, a situation that affects both women and men. Long hours and relatively low pay take a toll on family life no matter what gender. But it is even worse for women who must announce pregnancies, request maternity leave, seek flextime or part-time work after childbirth, and find adequate lactation spaces in the workplace. Only about half the women survey respondents had children, and many admitted trading a family life for a career. Male architects, as main breadwinners of the family, did not face this tradeoff.

7 Many underrepresented architects are unprepared for what awaits them in the profession. In school, where both women and men work side by side in studios, lecture courses, seminars, and student organizations, gender issues may simply be off their radar screen. Yet when they transition into the working world where they may be the only woman architect in the office, or the only African-American, Asian-American, or Latina architect in the office, it is a different picture altogether. The phenomenon of standing out while serving as an ambassador for your gender or race presents a new dynamic for many young architects.

8 Gender and racial discrimination still ran rampant in the architectural profession. Over two-thirds of the women and men surveyed had witnessed or heard of gender

discrimination and four out of ten had witnessed or heard about racial discrimination in an architectural office.

9 Significant gender and racial differences were found in which the experiences of underrepresented architects were far more negative than those of their white male counterparts. Most disturbing were inequities in salaries and benefits, with the pay gap widening the longer they remain in the field. Women architects earned significantly less than their male counterparts with comparable levels of professional experience. And women of color, compared to white men, men of color, and white women, reported significantly lower levels of satisfaction with their future career prospects in the field.
10 Although many underrepresented architects have shattered the glass ceiling and achieved great success, they overcame many more obstacles placed in their way. Among the most successful were those who opened their own offices, but not everyone desires or can afford to do so.
11 Compared to those in private practice, underrepresented architects employed in government positions, corporate work, and real estate development, appeared to be significantly better off.
12 For those who triumphed in the profession, finding a supportive work environment—and knowing when to leave an unsupportive work setting—was the key. Management plays a critical role in influencing the success of underrepresented architects, and the "sink or swim" attitude is counterproductive.

Put in a broader perspective, my findings about the status of women architects in the US can be interpreted through the lens of feminist critic Susan Estrich and her broader explanation of why the status of American women is not what it should be: subtle, unconscious discrimination such as the allocation of resources and computer equipment in the workplace, which raises the question: who makes the rules, and how do these rules affect underrepresented groups; motherhood; the comfort factor whereby many middle-aged men are uncomfortable with women in social settings outside work, fearing lawsuits for sexual harassment; and what she calls "traitorism," whereby women in positions of power often fail to help those in the lower and middle ranks (Estrich, 2000).

In her interview with *Architect* magazine, New York firm owner Deborah Berke explained her take on women's absence in the field:

> Family concerns are, of course, part of challenge, but it's more like death by a thousand cuts, including low salaries or the experience of being a young woman architect who is ignored when she's in a room that is 90 percent male…It's the repeated occurrence of several dozen little things, rather than one fixed particular element. … These recurring small blows help drive women and socioeconomic minorities out of the profession.
>
> (Beck, 2012)

But, as Berke admits, as do so many others, "Ultimately, being an architect for me is so profoundly satisfying and fulfilling that it has been well worth the trudge."

Gender Discrimination In Architecture: Across The Atlantic And Across The Pacific

In the early 2000s the Royal Institute of British Architects (RIBA) appointed a research team at the University of the West of England to complete an investigative research report: *Why do women leave architecture? Research into the retention of women in architectural practice* conducted by three faculty members, Ann de Graft-Johnson, Sandra Manley, and Clara Greed (De Graft-Johnson *et al.*, 2003). The troubling situation in the UK, where women students in architecture increased from 27 percent to 38 percent between 1990 and 2002 and yet only 13 percent made it into the profession, whereas in law and medicine women comprised almost half their respective professions, prompted their research. The RIBA-sponsored study was primarily qualitative, eliciting opinions from women who have left the profession as well as those who remained within architecture. A web-based survey along with follow-up interviews formed the major basis of the study. A total of 174 women respondents participated, including 37 who had left architectural practice. Responses were received from around the world, from England, Wales, Scotland, and Ireland as well as from Australia, Canada, Germany, Hong Kong, New Zealand, Singapore, and the USA.

According to findings from the British-based survey, here is why women leave architecture (De Graft-Johnson *et al.*, 2003):

- Low pay
- Unequal pay
- Long working hours
- Inflexible/unfamily-friendly working hours
- Sidelining
- Limited areas of work
- Glass ceiling
- Stressful working conditions
- Protective paternalism preventing development of experience
- Macho culture
- Sexism
- Redundancy and or dismissal
- High litigation risk and high insurance costs
- Lack of returner training
- More job satisfaction elsewhere.

Women who had left architectural practice pursued a diverse set of alternate careers, such as teaching English in Japan, working in a hospital as a client's representative, working in the property section of a bank, project management, running a home improvement agency, specialist roofing contractor, architectural publishing, landscape architect, maternity leave and childcare responsibilities.

Comments about women's perceptions of their career prospects were disturbing. As one woman put it,

> In my previous office, the nature of the work I got to do changed dramatically when I got married, going from competition and design work to suspended ceiling and raised floor layouts. I also believe that this was partially due to the fact that I preferred to get my work done during office hours rather than work evenings and weekends, unlike many people in the practice.

Another stated, "I was offered an associate position within a year, but when I fell pregnant this was forgotten" (De Graft-Johnson *et al.*, 2003). And yet another admitted, "The system is set up for workaholic males. Only women that are prepared to be men have a slight chance of promotion" (De Graft-Johnson *et al.*, 2003).

What does the picture look like for women architects in the UK a decade later? A disturbing headline, "Sexual discrimination on the rise for women in architecture" in an early 2014 issue of *Architects' Journal* heralded the results of its third annual survey of 926 respondents (710 women and 216 men) including architects, architectural assistants, and students (Mark, 2014). An earlier headline covering the same survey released in 2012 read, "Shock survey results as the *AJ* launches campaign to raise women architects' status" (Waite & Corvin, 2012).

Among the more troublesome survey findings released in 2014: when asked "has the building industry fully accepted the authority of the female architect?" two-thirds (66 percent) of women and half (49 percent) of men answered "no." Two-thirds of women suffered sexual discrimination—defined as anything from inappropriate comments to being treated differently because of their gender—a rise from prior surveys. Just under a third (31 percent) reported monthly or quarterly occurrences, and 11 percent reported once a week or more. Over half (54 percent) of women architecture students reported experiencing sexual discrimination in architecture school. Just over a quarter (27 percent) of women reported experiencing bullying while working in architecture; so did just under a quarter (23 percent) of men. Just over three-quarters (79 percent) of women—a significant rise from the first annual survey—and just under three-quarters (73 percent) of men believe the industry is too male-dominated. One woman explained that she has "been interviewed for positions and offered a 30 per cent lower salary than a man with less experience" (Mark, 2014).

Among discriminatory incidents women cited in the first annual survey published in 2012: "being given more secretarial work to do than my male Part 1 colleagues," "difference in treatment on return from maternity leave on part-time basis," and perhaps most shocking of all, "I have been asked if I'm menstruating, been told my salary will be reduced as a result of being pregnant, and have been taken off jobs on site when pregnant." Others found the job site more problematic than the office, for example, "Even if the people in your practice and your client respect you, going on a site visit dressed appropriately and trying to appear professional is somewhat undermined when you are being wolf-whistled at by builders." As another woman put it, "I experienced a lack of willingness to consider flexible or part-time working after I finished maternity leave, effectively forcing me to resign my post and set up as self-employed." Over three-quarters (82 percent) believed that the Royal Institute of British Architects (RIBA) should be doing more to tackle the gender imbalance and improve the retention of women within the profession (Waite & Corvin, 2012).

Even Zaha Hadid, one of the world's leading female architects, admitted that she has faced "more misogynist behavior" in London than anywhere else in Europe and that the situation is not improving for women in architecture (Thorpe, 2013). When interviewed by the *Observer,* Hadid, a British Iraqi and winner of the coveted International Pritzker Prize, stated, "I doubt anything has changed much over the last 30 years," adding

> It is a very tough industry and it is male-dominated, not just in architectural practices, but the developers and the builders too … I can't blame the men, though. The problem is continuity. Society has not been set up in a way that allows women to go back to work after taking time off. Many women now have to work as well as do everything at home and no one can do everything. Society needs to find a way of relieving women.

Some women architects have different priorities from those of their male counterparts. Australia proves a fascinating case in point, where, in 2007, women comprised 43 percent of architecture students but less than 1 percent of firm directors. A 2005 survey of 550 female members conducted by the Royal Australian Institute of Architects found that in measuring their personal success, women architects tended to reject the scale of a project, practice size, awards, and journal coverage in favor of client satisfaction and personal satisfaction—taking on new challenges and finding balance in their lives (McCann, 2007). Gender discrimination among architects is problematic there as well, as Harriet Alexander explained in *The Sydney Morning Herald* (Alexander, 2010):

> Women and men have been graduating with architecture degrees at the same rate, and with the same grades, for at least 20 years but their paths fork from the moment they leave university. Male architecture graduates command an average starting salary nearly $7000 higher than their female counterparts and the profession continues to shed women to the point where it is rare to find a woman directing her own architecture firm ... They are under-represented in major awards and speaking engagements. Those who have remained in the profession say the long hours and intense competition in the large firms are incompatible with the demands of children.

In 2013 the Australian Government's Workplace Gender Equality Agency (WGEA) documented that architecture and building has the worst graduate pay gap of any industry. Median salary for male graduates was $52,000 vs. $43,000 for female graduates. Worse still, the gap increased in successive years, from 12 percent in 2010, to 14 percent in 2011, to 17 percent in 2012 (Clark, 2013). Data from the Australian Institute of Architects Graduate Salary Survey confirms that this pay gap persists over 12 years following graduation (Clark, 2013).

Gender Differences While Riding Out The Recession

Although most architects are more aware of the need to achieve diversity, and demographics are improving ever so slightly, the economic recession has placed a severe strain on all architects across the board. Most are lucky to just to find work. Finding a supportive work environment may be less of a priority than simply finding a job.

As of 2013, 11.7 million Americans were unemployed, and the unemployment rate fell to a four-year low of 7.5 percent. Over 4.4 million Americans had been unemployed for over six months (Rugaber, 2013). Riding out the recession has taken an especially hard toll on architects, whose unemployment rates have long been well above average. Among recent college graduates between the ages of 22 and 26, as of early 2012, the unemployment rate for architecture majors was 13.9 percent, the highest and worst rate of all compared with arts (11.1 percent), humanities and liberal arts (9.4 percent), engineering (7.5 percent), business (7.4 percent), psychology and social work (7.3 percent), education (5.4 percent) and health (5.4 percent) (Censky, 2012). These dire statistics were blamed on the collapse of the construction and home-building industries. Even those architecture graduates aged 30 and more with greater professional experience had an unemployment rate of 9.2 percent. During this same period, architecture majors with graduate degrees, who usually fare better in the employment market, had a jobless rate of 7.7 percent (Rampell, 2012).

A survey of 448 AIA members, published in 2012, revealed that 15 percent of respondents were laid off during the recession and its aftermath. Of this group, 15 percent have moved on to other lines of work. Some optimistic experts predicted a shortage of architects by the time the economy recovers, as many will have left for greener pastures (Hanley, 2012).

High rates of unemployed architects are not just in the US. In the UK, for example, a recent survey revealed that 22 percent of qualified British architects are currently unemployed.

Among those architecture graduates currently in training, 44 percent are unemployed. British architects still employed faced an average 30 percent wage reduction (Stott, 2013).

How do the unemployment rates of male and female architects compare? Depending upon the data sources examined, it is somewhat difficult to tell. To date one of the only available data sources from which to draw this comparison is the U.S. Department of Labor's Bureau of Labor Statistics (Hughes, 2010). As of April 2013, these statistics showed that 113,000 of those in architecture and engineering occupations are unemployed, a rate of 3.8 percent overall, with a rate of 3.2 percent for men and 7.3 percent for women. Just a year before that, in April 2012, statistics were even worse, with a total of 120,000 unemployed, a rate of 4 percent, with 3.4 percent for men and 7.7 percent for women. Compared to men, women were over twice as likely to be unemployed (U.S. Bureau of Labor Statistics, 2013).

Those who are *underemployed* as opposed to unemployed also face special challenges. These include architects who faced sharp salary cuts just to stay on the payroll, who have had to take unpaid furloughs of two weeks or more, or who have been laid off and rehired as short-term contractors for lower pay. Others have taken part-time jobs in unrelated fields just to pay their bills.

The good news, however, is that as campus buildings age, as school districts renovate and replace existing facilities, and as demand for more healthcare facilities continues to increase, the US Bureau of Labor Statistics projects that employment of architects will grow 17 percent from 2012 to 2022, faster than the average for all occupations (U.S. Bureau of Labor Statistics, 2014).

Promoting Greater Gender Diversity In Architecture Through Awards, Prizes and Leadership Positions

Although the AIA has been existence since 1857, it took 135 years for women to achieve significant leadership positions (see Figure 34.4). Susan Maxman was elected as its first female

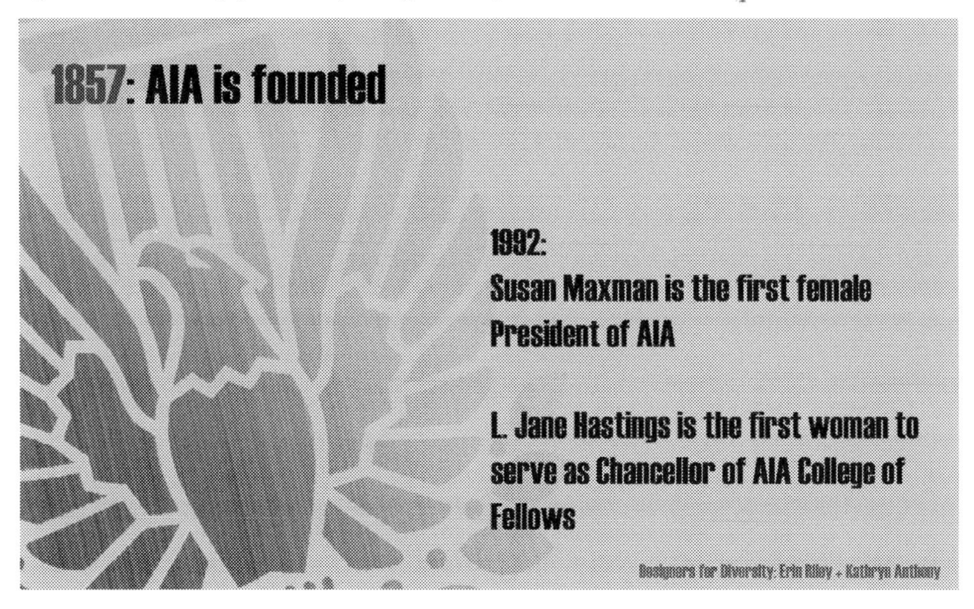

Figure 34.4 It took 135 years before the American Institute of Architects (AIA) elected its first woman President.

President (1992–1993) followed a decade later by Kate Schwennsen (2006–2007). Soon to follow are AIA 2014 President Helene Dreiling and AIA 2015 President-elect Elizabeth Chu Richter, the first time in the organization's history that two women in a row served as AIA President. It took 40 years since the establishment of the AIA College of Fellows in 1952 for L. Jane Hastings to become the first woman to serve as Chancellor of the AIA College of Fellows (1992–1993). Denice Johnson Hunt served as the first woman of color to hold the highest elected office in an AIA local component as AIA Seattle President (1995–1996) (The American Institute of Architects, n.d.b).

Since its founding in 1912, the Association of Collegiate Schools of Architecture, the primary organization for architectural educators, took 74 years to elect its first female President: Blanche van Ginkel from the University of Toronto (1986–1987), soon followed by Diane Ghirardo from the University of Southern California (1988–1989), and Geraldine Forbes-Isais from the University of New Mexico (2007–2008).

The ACSA's prestigious lifetime title of Distinguished Professor was first awarded in 1984, yet as of 2013 only 14 percent (17 of 119) of all ACSA Distinguished Professorships have been awarded to women. Van Ginkel is the first woman to receive the ACSA Distinguished Professor Award (1988–1989). She was followed by Denise Scott Brown (1990–1991), Mui Ho (1995–1996), Patricia O'Leary (1995–1996) and Sharon Sutton (1995–1996), Diane Ghirardo (1998–1999), Maelee Thomson Foster (1999–2000), Sherry Ahrentzen (2002–2003), Georgia Bizios (2003–2004), Anne Taylor (2004–2005), Geraldine Forbes-Isais (2006–2007), Judith Sheine (2008–2009), Kathryn Anthony (2009–2010), Frances Bronet (2010–2011), Marleen Kay Davis (2011–2012), Donna Dunay (2012–2013) and Wendy Ornelas (2012–2013).

Since it was first awarded in 1976, there have only been two female winners of the organization's highest joint award, the ACSA/AIA Topaz Laureate for Excellence in Architectural Education, Denise Scott Brown (1996) and Adele Naude Santos (2009) (Association of Collegiate Schools of Architecture, n.d.b).

The prestigious Pritzker Architecture Prize, founded by Jay and Cindy Pritzker, and modeled after the Nobel Prize, awards laureates a $100,000 grant, a formal citation certificate, and a bronze medallion. Since the prize was first awarded in 1979, as of this writing there have been only two women laureates (2 out of 36 prizes): Zaha Hadid (2004) and Kazuyo Sejima (2010) along with her male partner Ryue Nishizawa.

The Pritzker Architecture Prize caught the design community by storm when Robert Venturi was awarded the Pritzker prize in 1991, while his longtime design collaborator and wife, Denise Scott Brown, was excluded. Although Venturi implored the Hyatt Foundation, who administers the award, to include Scott Brown, his efforts were unsuccessful. The exclusion of Scott Brown sparked a highly publicized controversy culminating by her failing to attend her husband's awards ceremony, a powerful protest.

Over two decades later, at an *Architects' Journal* lunch event in London in March 2013, Scott Brown stated publicly that the Pritzker Foundation still owed her the prize and that it should correct its wrong. Her videotaped comments were posted online and picked up by two Harvard architecture students, Arielle Assouline-Lichten and Caroline James, who launched a Change.Org online petition demanding that Scott Brown retroactively be awarded the prize. The petition created a fury, receiving over 12,000 signatures, including Venturi and nine subsequent Pritzker prize winners. As architecture critic Sarah Williams Goldhagen argued in the *New Republic,* an analysis of their collaboration shows that Scott Brown brought to Venturi a greater capacity for conceptual clarity and precision, interdisciplinarity, ethics, and an urbanist perspective evident in their architectural designs and scholarly publications (Goldhagen, 2013).

Figure 34.5 The 1991 controversy surrounding the omission of Denise Scott Brown from the prestigious Pritzker Prize awarded to her professional partner and husband, Robert Venturi, resurfaced in 2013

Yet in June 2013, Lord Palumbo, Chair of the 2013 Jury of the Pritzker Architecture Prize, responded to the two Harvard students stating that "A later jury cannot re-open, or second guess the work of an earlier jury, and none has ever done so" (Quirk, 2013).

Since it was first awarded in 1907 during the 50th anniversary of the AIA, it took another 107 years for the AIA to bestow its highest honor, the Gold Medal, to a woman. The AIA's 2014 Gold Medal was awarded posthumously to Julia Morgan (1872–1957), designer of California's famous Hearst Castle and over 700 buildings including houses, churches, hotels, commercial buildings, and museums, most which are still standing due to her pioneering use of reinforced concrete, a material that proved resilient in earthquakes (Jacobs, 2013).

My book, *Designing for Diversity* advocated numerous strategies for architectural educators, practitioners, firms, and the profession to promote and achieve diversity. Some of these strategies have since been implemented, including the development of new diversity awards programs.

According to the American Institute of Architects,

> The AIA is committed to increasing diversity and inclusion within the organization and the profession. To that end, the AIA Diversity Council, a presidential-appointed committee, has been established to push diversity and inclusion initiatives forward … Areas of focus for the Council will continue to include women within the profession, multiculturalism, and pathways to the profession.
>
> (The American Institute of Architects, n.d.a)

Starting in 2009, the AIA Diversity Recognition Program has celebrated the contributions of architects, AIA chapters, educational institutions, and individuals with up to 12 annual awards for Diversity Best Practices (The American Institute of Architects, n.d.a). Such positive recognition can go a long way to inspire others to promote diversity in the field. Similarly,

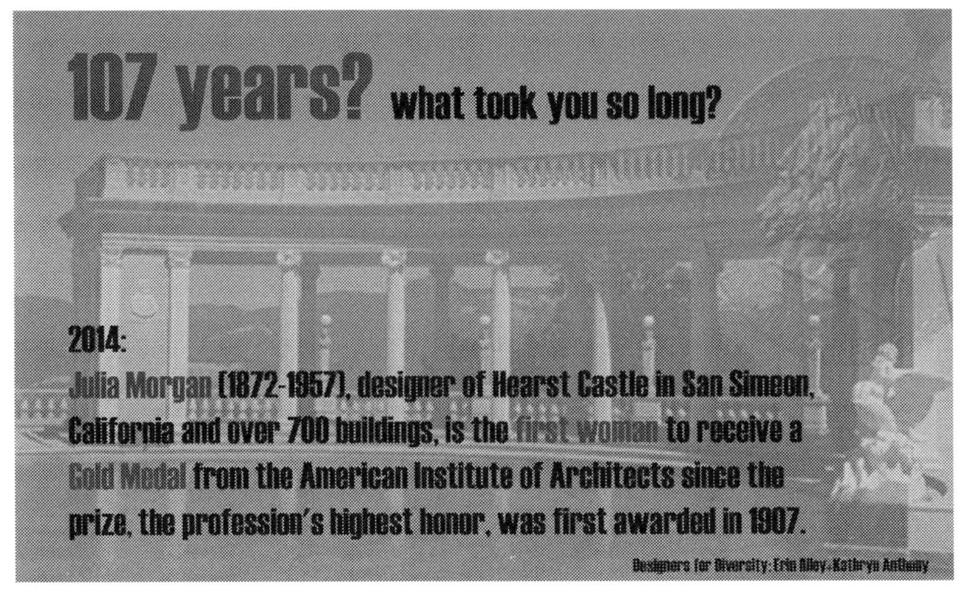

Figure 34.6 It took the AIA 107 years to award its first Gold Medal to a prolific woman architect, Julia Morgan, who had died decades ago.

the AIA's recent publication of its Diversity Timeline, chronicling landmark events, awards, publications, and organizational policies from 1968 to the present, provides an important encapsulated history of diversity in the architectural profession (Hancock, n.d.).

Each year the AIA Diversity Council offers numerous events during the annual AIA convention. On the program for the 2013 convention, for example, was a session on "Equal Roles, Equal Voices," discussing how to transform the profession and increase its value through the full contributions of women at all levels. The annual Women in Architecture Dinner has featured prominent architects Karen Braitmayer, Kim Day, and Billie Tsien. A Multicultural Fellows Diversity Award Honorees' Reception honors those underrepresented architects recently inducted into the AIA College of Fellows.

The Association of Collegiate Schools of Architecture offered its first set of Robert R. Taylor Diversity Awards awarded to seven faculty recipients from 1999–2003. The awards program experienced a hiatus for several years and was reinstated in 2010 as the Diversity Achievement Award. As of 2013 four such awards have been bestowed (Association of Collegiate Schools of Architecture, n.d.a).

Conclusions

In sum, gender issues have continued to play a perplexing role in architectural practice as well as in architectural education. Even though substantial progress has been made along many fronts, and the numbers of women architecture students continue to rise, the profession is still glaringly deficient in others.

For women in architecture in the twentieth and early twenty-first centuries, it has definitely been a rocky road. One can only hope that those who have only recently risen to the pinnacles of their careers, achieving the recognition that they and so many others have long deserved, will pave a smoother path for future women in architecture to follow.

Acknowledgements

The author wishes to thank Ron Corniels for his valuable research assistance as well as Erin Riley for her valuable graphic design assistance.

References

Alexander, H. (2010, October 4). Mind the gap – the gender imbalance in architecture. *The Sydney Morning Herald*. Retrieved July 16, 2014 from: http://www.smh.com.au/executive-style/executive-women/mind-the-gap--the-gender-imbalance-in-architecture-20101004-163vt.html

American Institute of Architects (2012). *Facts, Figures, and the Profession*. Retrieved July 16, 2014 from: http://www.aia.org/press/kit/background/AIAS077761

American Institute of Architects (n.d.a). *AIA Diversity Recognition Program*. Retrieved July 16, 2014 from: http://www.aia.org/about/initiatives/aiab092088

American Institute of Architects (n.d.b). *History of the American Institute of Architects*. Retrieved July 16, 2014 from: http://www.aia.org/about/history/AIAB028819

American Institute of Architects (n.d.c). *About the AIA: programs and initiatives: diversity and inclusion – 2013 AIA Diversity Council*. Retrieved July 16, 2014 from: http://www.aia.org/about/initiatives/AIAB097639

American Institute of Architects (n.d.d). *AIA Diversity History*. Retrieved July 16, 2014 from: https://sites.google.com/site/aiadiversityhistory/

Anthony, K. H. (2001). *Designing for Diversity: Gender, Race and Ethnicity in the Architectural Profession*. Urbana and Chicago, IL: University of Illinois Press.

Association of Collegiate Schools of Architecture (n.d.a). *Diversity Achievement*. Retrieved July 16, 2014 from: https://www.acsa-arch.org/programs-events/awards/DA

Association of Collegiate Schools of Architecture (n.d.b). *Topaz Laureates*. Retrieved July 16, 2014 from: https://www.acsa-arch.org/programs-events/awards/archives/TM

Beck, E. (2012, July 2). *Making the Mold: Architect*. Retrieved July 16, 2014 from: http://www.architectmagazine.com/architects/making-progress-with-diversity-in-architecture.aspx

Cary, J. (2011, August 8). 'Architect Barbie' builds a dream home, but her profession needs a makeover. *The Christian Science Monitor*. Retrieved July 16, 2014 from: http://www.csmonitor.com/Commentary/Opinion/2011/0808/Architect-Barbie-builds-a-dream-home-but-her-profession-needs-a-makeover

Censky, A. (2012, January 4). Unemployment soars for architects. *CNN Money*. Retrieved July 16, 2014 from: http://money.cnn.com/2012/01/04/news/economy/unemployment_college_major/index.htm

Clark, J. (2013, January 13). The graduate gender pay gap part 1 – what do the numbers mean? *Parlour: Women, Equity, Architecture*. Retrieved July 16, 2014 from: http://www.archiparlour.org/the-graduate-gender-pay-gap-part-1-what-do-the-numbers-mean/

De Graft-Johnson, A., Manley, S., & Greed, C. (2003, May). *Why do Women Leave Architecture? Research into the Retention of Women in Architectural Practice*. Bristol: University of the West of England. Retrieved July 14, 2014 from: http://www.architecture.com/Files/RIBAProfessionalServices/Education/DiscussionPapers/WhyDoWomenLeaveArchitecture.pdf

Directory of African American Architects (n.d.). *The Directory of African American Architects*. Retrieved July 16, 2014 from: http://blackarch.uc.edu/

Estrich, S. (2000). *Sex & Power*. New York: Riverhead Books.

Frank, S. & The American Institute of Architects (2011, August 2). AIA Announces the Winner of the AIA Architect Barbie Dream House Design Competition. *The American Institute of Architects Pressroom – Press Releases*. Retrieved July 16, 2014 from: http://www.aia.org/press/releases/aiab090499

Goldhagen, S. W. (2013, May 24). Yes, Denise Scott Brown deserved a Pritzker Prize. *The New Republic*. Retrieved July 16, 2014 from: http://www.newrepublic.com/article/113264/denise-scott-brown-deserves-pritzker-prize

Hancock, M. R. (n.d.). AIA diversity history: AIA diversity/then+now+next. The American Institute of Architects Diversity TimeLine 1968–2013. Retrieved July 16, 2014 from: https://sites.google.com/site/aiadiversityhistory/

Hanley, W. (2012, September 25). Survey predicts architect shortage by 2014. *Architectural Record*. Retrieved July 16, 2014 from: http://archrecord.construction.com/news/2012/09/120925-Survey-Predicts-Architecture-Shortage-by-2014.asp

Hughes, C. J. (2010, October 25). Exactly how many architects in the U.S. are unemployed? *Architectural Record*. Retrieved July 16, 2014 from: http://archrecord.construction.com/news/daily/archives/2010/10/101025real_employment.asp

Jacobs, K. (2013, December 12). Julia Morgan posthumously awarded the AIA 2014 Gold Medal. *Architect*. Retrieved July 16, 2014 from: http://www.architectmagazine.com/awards/julia-morgan-posthumously-awarded-aia-gold-medal_o.aspx

Lange, A. (2012, July/August). Girl talk. *Dwell*. Retrieved July 16, 2014 from: http://www.dwell.com/essay/article/girl-talk

Mark, L. (2014, January 10). Sexual discrimination on the rise for women in architecture. *Architects' Journal*. Retrieved July 16, 2014 from: http://www.architectsjournal.co.uk/home/women-in-architecture/sexual-discrimination-on-the-rise-for-women-in-architecture/8657345.article

McCann, H. (2007, March 12). *Architect: The Magazine of the American Institute of Architects* (March 12, 2007). Retrieved July 16, 2014 from: http://www.architectmagazine.com/architecture/02.aspx

National Architectural Accrediting Board, Inc. (2013). *2012 Report on Accreditation in Architecture Education*. Washington, DC: The National Architectural Accrediting Board.

Quirk, V. (2013, June 16). Pritzker rejects petition for Denise Scott Brown's retroactive award. *ArchDaily*. Retrieved July 16, 2014 from: http://www.archdaily.com/389074/pritzker-rejects-petition-for-denise-scott-brown-s-retroactive-award/

Rampell, C. (2012, January 5). Want a job? Go to college, and don't major in architecture. *The New York Times*. Retrieved July 16, 2014 from: http://economix.blogs.nytimes.com/2012/01/05/want-a-job-go-to-college-and-dont-major-in-architecture/

Rugaber, C. S. (2013, May 3). U.S. employers add 165K jobs, unemployment rate falls to 7.5%. *The Dallas Morning News*. Retrieved July 16, 2014 from: http://www.dallasnews.com/business/headlines/20130503-u.s.-employers-add-165k-jobs-unemployment-rate-falls-to-7.5-percent.ece

Stott, R. (2013, March 8). BD survey reveals 22% of UK architects unemployed. *Arch Daily*. Retrieved July 16, 2014 from: http://www.archdaily.com/341449/bd-survey-reveals-22-of-uk-architects-unemployed/

Stratigakos, D. (2011, June 3). What I learned from Architect Barbie. *Design Observer*. Retrieved July 16, 2014 from: http://places.designobserver.com/feature/what-i-learned-from-architect-barbie/27638/

Thorpe, V. (2013). Zaha Hadid: Britain must do more to help encourage its women architects. *The Observer*, February 16. Retrieved July 16, 2014 from: http://www.guardian.co.uk/artanddesign/2013/feb/17/architecture-misogyny-zaha-hadid

U.S. Bureau of Labor Statistics (2013). *Labor Force Statistics from the Current Population Survey: Household Data Not Seasonally Adjusted. A-30: Unemployed persons by occupation and sex*. Retrieved May 3, 2013 from: http://www.bls.gov/web/empsit/cpseea30.htm

U.S. Bureau of Labor Statistics (2014). *Occupational Outlook Handbook*. Retrieved July 16, 2014 from: http://www.bls.gov/ooh/architecture-and-engineering/architects.htm#tab-6

Waite, R. & Corvin, A. (2012, January 16). *Shock Survey Results as the AJ Launches Campaign to Raise Women Architects' Status*. Retrieved July 16, 2014 from: http://www.architectsjournal.co.uk/news/daily-news/shock-survey-results-as-the-aj-launches-campaign-to-raise-women-architects-status/8624748.article

Wischhover, C. (2011, May 10). Move over, Mike Brady: Now Barbie's an architect too. *Today*. Retrieved July 16, 2014 from: http://www.today.com/id/42976698/ns/today-style/t/move-over-mike-brady-now-barbies-architect-too/#.UW8TmTlRGJU

35

Alternative Futures in Architecture

Jim Dator

In contrast to many people who call themselves "futurists," architects are truly effective in creating the futures—what they design and build often persists for a very long time, shaping, thwarting, and facilitating behavior for generations to come, long after the mortgages have been paid and they themselves are dead and gone. As Winston Churchill is famously quoted as saying, "We shape our buildings and thereafter our buildings shape us." This was expanded by Marshall McLuhan into the wider truth that "we shape our tools, and thereafter our tools shape us."

For most of human history, this was unproblematic. The future was more or less "flat" so that buildings that were erected to shape behavior during the time they were designed and built could be expected to shape similar behavior in the future. Our "tools" had not yet become powerful enough to provoke the kind of massive social and environmental change they do now. For eons, it was not necessary for a designer or a builder to ask, before they built, how might people using this building twenty, thirty, one hundred years from now wish to behave? How might they be able to behave in ways we cannot now? What new options might they have that we do not have? And what options do we have that they might not have? Have we carefully thought of these things and incorporated them into our design, or will future generations struggle to behave as they wish within the confining structure we have built?

While for most of history the life-expectancy of most buildings was very short, many others were intended to last for a very long time. On the assumption that human needs and behavior were not going to (or should not) change, these buildings were expected to be "permanent" and so were built out of substances that could last forever and were difficult to modify or destroy.

We live in a present that is fundamentally unlike that of any past. Behavior that was once common and widespread is rare or regional now. Ways of lighting, ventilating, protecting, heating, cooling, moving, meeting, sleeping, working, eating, defecating—well, almost everything—have changed. Even the physical environment towards which we build has changed. Once, European summers were damp and cool. Now they are becoming hotter and hotter though unpredictably drier or wetter. Air conditioning in most of northern

Europe was an unnecessary luxury—indeed, cross-ventilation was scarcely needed. Now they—or some kind of relief from days of killer heat—are necessities. The future has become fundamentally unpredictable on the basis of the past. Everything about our world now is in flux, some things easily changeable, other things less so, but nothing—not even good old *terra firma*—is expected to last forever, or even to serve the needs of future generations in the same ways they serve the needs of present generations. Thus, we need to design and construct buildings that are fit not only for the present, but also specifically fit for anticipated futures.

And that is tough to do, especially since it is not possible to predict the future as we once could with some confidence.

This new challenge facing architects—and all whose actions persist through time—co-evolved from actions first seriously undertaken only a few hundred years ago when the advent of the scientific-industrial revolution and the emergence of beliefs about progress (or, *vice versa*), development, science, rationality, and continued economic growth became so overwhelmingly powerful that in early twentieth century, the poet Percy Mackaye could proclaim without irony that "The tribes of man are led toward peace by the prophet-engineer" (Mackaye, 1914). Mackaye could very well have said "the prophet-architect," and should more truthfully have said towards "profit" rather than towards "peace." But the mood of the time was confidentially that progress meant both profit and peace (at least for some). The official slogan of 1939–40 New York World's Fair stated it even more starkly: "Science Finds—Industry Applies—Man Conforms." Ah, for the Good Old Days!

In that happy era, great men of great vision could, like Howard Roak, stand, legs spread, arms akimbo, on the top of their unfinished skyscrapers proclaiming their triumph and mastery of the material future from a spire that *THEY DESIGNED AND BUILT ALL BY THEMSELVES*. Futures insight was largely personal, intuitive, utopian, the product of genius, not of serious futures research and extensive consultation, participation, and reflection.

The landscape of the current world is littered with the products of such hubris, with more in the littering. Indeed many established as well as fledgling architects still imagine themselves to be a Howard Roak in captivity, if not an Ayn Rand straining towards the opportunity to proclaim such manly, ego-centric triumphs.

But the future isn't what it used to be. Uncertainties about cheap energy, abundant finance, wholesome food, clean water and clean air are frequently expressed—and even more confidentially denied. If the deniers are correct, and if such fears—that I consider to be well-founded, if not dangerously understated—somehow turn out to be unwarranted so that the present predicts the future well-enough once again, then the architectural profession still cannot surely rest on its laurels. What can an old-fashioned *homosapiens, sapiens* architect do that her emerging artilect companion/competitor cannot do much better, more cheaply, more tirelessly, more creatively, more soundly, perhaps more dynamically, so that even the buildings "we" shape may hereafter be able effortlessly and instantly to re-shape themselves so as to facilitate future preferred behavior of artilects, humans, and transhumans alike?

This chapter will expand on these ideas. It is based on almost fifty years of experience in the field of futures studies, often in the company of architects. It relies on an "Alternative Futures/Preferred Futures" approach—in contrast to the chump's game of "predicting THE future" (Bell, 1997, Dator, 2002, Dator, 2009).

I developed my interest in futures studies during six years (1960–66) of teaching in the College of Law and Politics of Rikkyo University, Tokyo, Japan. I later focused that interest sharply under the influence of two members of the British Archigram Group, David Greene and Mike Webb, who happened to be at Virginia Tech when I moved there and began teaching what is said to be the first course on futures studies officially approved through conventional university procedures, in 1967. I modeled my futures courses then and subsequently on what I observed from the courses taught by David, Mike and other members of the School of Architecture at Virginia Tech. When I moved to the University of Hawaii in 1970, Bruce Etherington, the head of the emerging program in Architecture, engaged me in many activities, as did Deans Elmer Botsai, Ray Yeh, and Clark Llewellyn of the School of Architecture subsequently. So, though not an architect by training I have been strongly influenced, intellectually and pedagogically, by architects for most of my professional life.

In what follows, I will say a bit about what futures studies is and is not. I will discuss the four actually-existing, significantly-different generic images of the futures prominent now, one (or a muddled combination) of which most people have in their heads that influence their beliefs and actions that then help to create the actual future. I will use a body of research, recently completed, to illustrate how the futures of higher education could differ considerably according to the assumptions of each of these four futures, suggesting that this approach, or something like it, should precede all significant attempts of architectural design and construction. I will close by arguing that education for the profession should prepare architects for each of the four and not put all or most of its emphasis on any one future, as, I will show, it does now.

The titles of the four futures, which express their essential perspectives, are *Grow*, *Collapse, Discipline*, and *Transform*. These are titles for categories of images of the futures that were derived from years of empirical research into ideas about the futures that actually exist and are manifest in the plans, policies, reports, movies, games, prayers, and everyday actions oriented towards the futures today. Which is the "real" future? In the world we live in now, we cannot—and certainly should not try to—say for sure. We are no longer able to "predict" THE future. Instead, we must reflect, plan, design, and build on the basis of a "preferred future" that has been determined only after we have undertaken a careful consideration of the challenges and opportunities before us based on our engagement with specific examples of each of the four generic alternative futures.

What Futures Studies Is and Is Not: Identifying the Futures of "X"

There is a common misunderstanding that futurists are only interested in the future—that they hate and ignore both history and the present, and only think about what's new in the futures. Nothing could—or should—be farther from the truth. Futurists are deeply interested in the human experience through time in all dimensions, most certainly including all of the many ways humans lived and acted in the pasts and presents. The more we know about the many diverse ways humans live now and have lived before, the better able we might be to anticipate the many diverse ways humans might live in the futures. Unfortunately, many of these past ways of life are forever beyond our present understanding—there are no surviving records of them that we know of. As a consequence we only do know about a very tiny, and perhaps unrepresentative, sliver of the manifold languages, thoughts, cultures, lifestyles, and architecture of humans before the invention of writing—an invention of only a few thousand years ago—and even then we know only the few written records and physical remains that have somehow survived to the present day—and that are still read/preserved (a smaller fraction yet). Thus before futurists even begin to think about the future of something—anything (let's just call it X)—they should strive to understand the key aspects of the pasts of X.

But what are the "key" aspects? What things must be known among the things that can be known? What facts are vital and what are less central? We cannot expect to know everything about the past of X or we will have no time to think about its futures. We are not historians, anthropologists, or sociologists, but must rely on their work to help us understand past behaviors, structures, and cultures of X and its environments.

Thus before a futurist even begins to think about the past or futures of some specific institution or process, she needs to have articulated or adopted some coherent theory of social stability and change—she needs to have some clear, guiding idea of "how the world works" that tells her what she must have information about, and what information she can safely ignore. There are many existing theories of social stability and change.

In our work, we assume (without denying a role for biology, environment, culture, and agency) that we live during a time when technological change is a fundamental determinant of social and environmental change. Technology is also a "prime driver" of many other factors (such as population, economy, governance, culture, etc.) that then become "independent drivers" on their own that must be identified and tracked. Discussing the details of this theory is beyond the scope of this chapter (Dator *et al.*, 2014). However, understanding the necessity of having some kind of a theory before acting so as to try to influence the future is the key starting point of all futures work, and hence of our discussion here. Overall, the drivers explain why, when, and by whom our X came into being; how and why it came to be structured the way it was; and how and why it changed (or did not change) over time. In order to do all this, we must study not only the history of X itself, but also aspects of the environment of X that contributed to its origin, structure, change, and continuity.

This last sentence makes a very important point. Another mistake that people too often make when studying the futures of some X is to focus only on changes in X itself, and not study also the changes in the environment of X. They seem to assume that the "Earth will stand still" while only their X will change. Unfortunately, it is more complicated than that, and so the co-evolution of both X and its environments need to be studied over time past as well as futures. Now that we have some grasp of the past of the processes shaping X we need to make the same analysis of the present of X and/or its environment, including a review of whatever others have written about the futures of X.

Finally, we are ready to consider the futures.

Our first task is to identifying and project the most significant trends shaping the future. These trends must be based on the historical driving forces. They exhibit aspects of possible futures of the past and present driving forces. Unfortunately many people who call themselves futurists rely almost entirely on the projection of trends (and/or on their imagination) in order to "predict" the future. We hear of "megatrends" or "the most likely future." While the identification of trends is important it is a huge mistake to end our research with the projection of existing trends. This is where the identification of "emerging issues" that might interrupt the trends and/or create new ones comes into play. Emerging issues are unique, rare, sporadic, early events or processes, barely noticed by most people, that might interrupt the other trends or become dominant trends on their own. At the Manoa School, we have learned not to focus too much on well-known trends. Rather we try to identify and develop plausible trajectories for emerging issues that are largely hidden and unnoticed by others. Given the increasing uncertainty and novelty of the futures, emerging issues identification and analysis should be a major part of any futures study.

By this point in our research, we have obtained the information necessary from past, present, and futures to begin to weave them together into alternative futures, according to the four generic futures of the Manoa School. And the drivers do need to be "woven together." One of the weaknesses of many statements about the future is that they are based on the projection of discrete trends, kept separate in the resulting analysis so that contradictions abound and are unrecognized and unaddressed. For example, one trend might be "population will decline." Another trend might be "the economy will recover and grow even faster." A third might be "we are running out of cheap and abundant oil." These are three plausible trends presently, but how can all three be true in the future?

A good futures analysis should interrelate all of the driving forces in systemic ways, and not just project them one-by-one separately. Indeed, it is differing assumptions about the values for each of the driving forces into the future, and of differing impacts of emerging issues, that make each of the four alternative futures separate and different. In the above example, a *Grow* image of the future might assume that we can and will resolve the contradictions by finding new cheap and abundant energy resources and by provoking women to have more children so as to keep the economy growing and the nation strong. A *Collapse* image might postulate that we will not resolve the contradiction, nor even try sincerely to do so. Thus society as currently organized will collapse. *Discipline* might assume we will resolve the contradictions through adherence to frugal and sustainable values and behaviors, but that the economy will not (and should not) grow as it has before, while fertility will be kept low. *Transform* may say that these issues are trivial because of new materials, resources, technologies, and forms of intelligent life that are emerging on Earth and in space.

Once developed, the four alternative futures can be presented and studied in varying ways. Most common is simply reading and discussing a well-crafted written description of each of the four. However, we also stress finding ways by which relevant decision-makers can somehow "experience" the environment of each of the four futures so as better to consider how X might respond to the unique as well as common features of each. Thus we often design four different rooms with "artifacts" from each of the four futures, complete with smells, sounds, and "representatives from the future" who interact with participants in order to help them get a good feel for what each future might be like. Experiential, immersive futures seem better than just passively reading descriptions of futures in order to enable people better to sense what each of the four futures might actually be like, and thus to prepare for them more urgently and effectively.

Having spent some time "in" each of the four futures, the next step is to envision preferred futures for X which probably are not responses to any one of the four generic futures solely, nor necessarily to a combination of all four, but rather are anticipatory responses to all four (rather than to just one). When possible and appropriate, preferred futures visioning is a group process, involving representatives of everyone who will be impacted by the actual futures of X. The wider the participation, the better. Sometimes, if the futures of X process involves only a single futures researcher or research group, and perhaps a few people currently active in or concerned about X, the futures vision is done by only one or a small group of people. But a fundamental aspect of the futures of X process is to arrive at a vision of a preferred future for X that will be used to guide decisions concerning the futures of X itself. The visioning process is very, very important, and should have the widest "buy in" from decision-makers and all stake-holders possible. If it is not already clear, it is important to understand that a futures visioning exercise should not be done until all the prior steps listed here have been done first. Failure to do so is often a reason why a visioning process is not successful in guiding actions towards the preferred future: it is neither sufficiently appreciative of the past nor aware of the futures.

The futures part of the analysis has now been completed, and it is time to design the structures appropriate both for both the present and the futures. If the design is done well, future generations may celebrate our foresight and concern. If not, perhaps our failure will help others to be better.

Example of "Campuses 2060"

From September 2008 through December 2011, advanced architect students in classes taught by Professor Ray Yeh, of the School of Architecture; graduate students in classes on Higher Education taught by Professor Joanne Cooper of the College of Education; and graduate students in futures studies in the Hawaii Research Center for Futures Studies of the Department of Political Science, and myself, all of the University of Hawaii at Manoa, in Honolulu, Hawaii, engaged in research into the history, present, and alternative futures of higher education in various places around the world. We began our historical research by identifying six dimensions of higher education that have persisted across time, though their features and modes of operation have varied considerably. We labeled them *societal assumptions, mission, participants, resources, pedagogy,* and *the physical campus*.

Our historical, present, and futures survey focused primarily on evidence about England, the United States, Korea, and Hawaii. We noted that most studies of the past, present, and futures of higher education focused on only one or two of the following features: 1) what was, is, or should be taught via what modes of delivery; 2) how institutions of higher education were, are, or should be funded and administered; 3) what their mission was, is, or should be (for example, is higher education for personal, societal, or economic enhancement, or for environmental sustainability and the preservation of certain values, behaviors, and beliefs?); and 4) what the physical presence of institutions of higher education were, are, or should be. We believe that our study is one of the very few, if not the only, to have combined these dimensions of higher education in an historical as well as alternative futures context (Dator *et al.*, 2013).

In our historical survey, we observed how the actual responses to the six dimensions of institutions of higher education changed or persisted over time in relation to changes and persistences of four elements of the broader society of which higher education was a part; of the *knowledge and skills* necessary to function in that society; of the *technology,* broadly defined, available in that society; and of the *biophysical environment* within which the society and its institutions of higher education were situated.

In order to have a specific place upon which to base our physical designs we focused on the history, present, and futures of the University of Hawaii at Manoa (UHM). Thus we went into much more detail in understanding when, and how, UHM came to be—the society and physical environment of the time; the original mission and expectations of the founders, who the original participants were, what resources were available; what subjects were taught and researched, and by means of what technology; and what the physical campus and class rooms looked like. We used both typical social science and architectural research methods and modes of presentation. In the process we determined what the driving forces for change (and resistance to change) since the creation of the University of Hawaii in 1907 to the present were.

We then utilized a matrix that conveyed qualitatively the different assumptions made by each of the four generic images of the future about the future of each of the driving

Table 35.1 Seven Driving Forces and Their Implications on Each of the Four Generic Scenarios

Futures:	*Grow*	*Collapse*	*Discipline*	*Transform*
Forces:				
Population	Increasing	Declining	Diminished	Posthuman
Energy	Sufficient	Scarce	Limited	Abundant
Economics	Dominant	Survival	Regulated	Trivial
Environment	Conquered	Overshot	Sustainable	Artificial
Culture	Dynamic	Stable	Focused	Complex
Technology	Accelerating	Stable	Restricted	Transformative
Governance	Corporate	Local	Strict	Direct

forces. We later used this matrix to make quantitative determinations of the qualitative values where possible.

Table 35.1 shows the qualitative matrix we used. This matrix makes clear that each of the four futures (Grow, Collapse, Discipline, Transform) are composed, in this instance, of the same seven driving forces. *What makes each of the futures different is thus the specific values of each of the seven drivers*. For example, population is assumed to continue to increase in Grow, while population is assumed to decline drastically in Collapse; is smaller and more stable than now in Discipline; and is something quite different in Transform where the distinguishing feature is not whether the human population is large or small, but rather the existence of large numbers of artilects, transhumans, posthumans, perhaps ETs, as well as old-fashioned *homo sapiens sapiens*.

Similarly energy is assumed to be sufficient (though perhaps expensive) in Grow; very scarce (except for human and other animal power) in Collapse; limited and rationed in Discipline; and abundant and cheap in Transform—and so on for each of the seven drivers for each of the four futures. Understanding this aspect of the generic four futures is fundamental to understanding and using the four futures method. It is also important to remember that empirical evidence supporting the different values for each driver exists in the literature. *The qualitative differences are not the product of the imagination of the futures researcher*—they exist in statements, plans, and policies made by serious people making serious judgments about the real world. These serious people may each think they are right and that those holding contrary views are not only wrong but stupid, but as futurists, we cannot make that judgment during the generic alternative futures part of the overall futures of X process. We take each of the four seriously and try to present them fairly from the point of view of their advocates. Literature supporting each of the assumptions of the four futures is cited.

At the same time, the specific quantitative values for each of the drivers range widely within the loose qualitative designations, and these values often are the result of judgments made by the researchers. Thus, each specific alternative future is but one possible example of each of the four generic futures. As a consequence, very often, more than just four alternatives will be presented for consideration. There may be two or three versions of Grow, or of Collapse, Discipline, or Transform. For example, historically, during the so-called Cold War (1950–1991), communism and capitalism could be understood as offering alternative visions of Grow, just as libertarianism and liberalism are simply competing visions of Grow in contemporary American discourse. None of them differ on the necessity and possibility of continued economic growth. They only differ on how best to achieve it and how wealth should be distributed. The possibility and desirability of continued economic growth is not questioned at all.

Similarly, there are many bases for collapse. The primary cause may be economic inequities or malfunctions, environmental unsustainability, ethical failures, resource exhaustion, energy insufficiency, nuclear war, asteroid impact, or some combination of these and other causes. Most transformational images of the future spring from optimistic expectations about the impacts of advanced technologies such as robotics, automation, artificial intelligence, nanotechnology, biological engineering, space settlement, and the like, while other bases of transformation are entirely spiritual or otherwise nonmaterialistic.

This matrix and subsequent quantitative judgments were used to make summary statements about the general situation of the world and Hawaii, and more detailed descriptions of the University of Hawaii in 2060. The features of a future University of Hawaii are significantly different for each of the six dimensions in each of the four futures. They are very briefly summarized here:

1. Hawaii Grow 2060: Grow and Succeed!

UHM Grow 2060: Al-Madhi University Hawaii

Assumptions	Hawaii is a thriving, growing community within a prosperous and growing world.
Mission	Al-Mahdi University Hawaii is part of a highly-dynamic global educational and corporate conglomerate focusing almost entirely on developing new technologies, entrepreneurism, and entertainment.
Participants	Many learners, trainers, researchers, business partnersm and supervisors participate remotely from around the world through numerous channels of three-dimensional/multisensory virtual presence.
Resources	Ample financing, and energy from fossil fuels, nuclear energy, and renewable sources. The university operates like a corporation where experts in business and fiscal management are the leading decision-makers.
Pedagogy	A blend of methods that facilitate learning activities in virtual spaces aimed primarily at producing high-tech commercial products. Only courses that sell are offered except for a few loss-leaders or boutique art and humanities courses. The market determines what is taught, and how.
Campus	The University of Hawaii has grown enormously within and beyond the bounds of Manoa Valley. It has branches and applied schools located along the rail mass transit route and wherever client/students congregate throughout the islands. There is also a huge telepresence franchised worldwide.

2. Hawaii Begin 2060: Survival +

UHM Begin 2060: New Beginnings University in Manoa

Assumptions	Hawaii is a thriving, self-sufficient, post-collapse community of new beginnings.
Mission	New Beginnings University in Manoa is a sacred learning center that provides a place for storing, learning, creating, and sharing the old and new knowledge and technologies necessary for a completely self-sufficient Hawaii.
Participants	Teachers and learners play both roles; everyone has something to teach and something to learn. There are also preservers whose duty is to preserve knowledge and technologies; adepts who know how to use knowledge and technologies especially well; and a few creators who strive to create new knowledge or technologies, or combinations of old and new.
Resources	Mainly manual energy, with some bio-fuel and local electricity.
Pedagogy	Learning primarily takes place within the natural environment, where a group or an individual seeks out a mentor to learn and share something necessary or desired.
Campus	The physical campus comprises what is left of the buildings, structures, and resources of the old University of Hawaii at Manoa that were abandoned after the global disaster of 2020 and reclaimed in 2030, plus some new shelters. Manoa is viewed as a special, holy place especially for the preservation and transfer of old knowledge and technologies, and for the creation of new ones.

3. Hawaii Sustain 2060: Slow… but Steady!

UHM Sustain 2060: The Global Green University of the Pacific

Assumptions	Hawaii is struggling towards environmental, energy, and food sustainability.
Mission	GGUP is one of twenty global universities sponsored and funded by the G-20, and focused on research and training for sustainability.
Participants	Outstanding global scientists, leaders, visionaries, engineers, designers, and economists in the fields of ocean, Earth, and space sciences, as well as a few humanists and ethicists. Run by the G-20.
Resources	Limited, expensive fossil fuels. G-20 provides substantial financial support to GGUP which is highly elitist.
Pedagogy	Learners are interns on projects with advanced scientists and engineers, immediately working on practical ways to solve specific energy, environmental, and food problems. Roaming humanists, artists, ethicists comment on the work done.
Campus	The campus features energy-efficient buildings, living quarters, and classrooms that are used for multiple purposes.

4. Hawaii Transform 2060: Beyond Singularity to Dynamic Cosmic Diversity

UHM Transform 2060: Transform You in Manoa

Assumptions	Hawaii is a dynamic part of a changing, diverse inner solar system community.
Mission	Transform You in Manoa is the epicenter of the universe-becoming-self-conscious.
Participants	Humans, posthumans, avatars, and artilects.
Resources	Plentiful and cheap. Resources and information are dispersed and are available anywhere, anyplace, anytime.
Pedagogy	Learners are diverse, and education is universally interdisciplinary and basically for the fun of it. Some education is purposely old-fashioned and arcane; other is practical and futures-oriented.
Campus	Structures are composed of psycho-reactive material that can be configured and re-configured into poly units, based on human interaction and thoughts controlling nanotechnological processes. Nothing is permanent.

With the features of the futures of the world, Hawaii, and the University of Hawaii, determined overall designs for the physical "campus" of the University of Hawaii in each of these four futures were determined and modeled. One prototype building for each future of each campus was designed and modeled as well.

The experience of architects, educators, and futurists working together fully demonstrated the utility and indeed necessity of this kind of cooperation to everyone involved. Students and professors in each of the three disciplines were continuously excited, challenged, and frustrated by the project. Acquired knowledge, learning styles, research modes, and forms of presentation differed enormously among the three intellectual communities and, especially when preparing for public presentations, tensions and tempers ran high with no one quite fully satisfied with what they were able to do. But it is clear the three disciplines (and more) need to work together on similar projects in the future. Academicians focused on each of the dimensions of a subject need to come together if the futures of the subject X are to have a better chance for success.

It is clear to me that courses in futures studies should and can become a routine part of the education of all architecture students. Otherwise, architects will continue to build for the present, past, and unconsciously-fantasized futures without consideration for the needs and desires of future generations who must somehow contend with the persisting structures they have been given. Moreover, futures studies not only alerts people to new problems in the future. Properly done, futures studies also enables people early on to see new opportunities, and solutions to current problems. Futures-oriented architects should have several advantages over architects who are not sensitive to the many facets of the futures.

While neither "the future" nor genuinely "alternative futures" seem to occupy much education, research, thoughts, time, and activities of most architects today, orientation towards the future is by no means missing entirely. A review of some of the recent books about the profession *per se* made this clear.

David Watson, in "Environment and Architecture," has subheadings discussing "Sustainability: The Roots of a Design Paradigm." "Population Growth," "Environments at Risk," "Global Demographics and Politics," "Technology as Problem and as Solution,"

"Human Thought and Culture" (in which he mentions Peter Schwartz as a "futurist"), and "Design of the future" (Watson, 2001). These topics are presented as though offering challenges to what is otherwise a future of continued economic growth.

In the same volume, Sharon Egretta Sutton, in a chapter titled "Reinventing professional privilege as inclusivity: A proposal for an enriched mission of architecture," discusses the "excessive humanizing of the Earth" and in contrast with "conceiving a sustainable approach to humanizing the Earth" noting that "architects can build on the visioning skills they already possess to engage the public in conceiving alternative, more socially just, futures" (Sutton, 2001).

More recently, Lee W. Waldrep asked architects, "What do you see as the future for the architecture profession?" (Waldrep, 2006). Thirty-six responses were published, most expressing views that suggested that there would be no substantial changes in the social and environmental future in which architects will live and work. For example, some said that architects should be "active leaders in their communities" and "serve as the conscience of the built environment," even though "the idea of the master builder will continue to dissolve."

Several suggested that the future will be different from the present, but within the dominant image of continued growth: "the future continues to become more technologically-driven," so architects need to "stay abreast of societal, cultural, and technological change." The "profession will grow more interdisciplinary" and "more collaborative." The "core issues will be the need to focus and manage change." Indeed, one response said that because of rapid change, the profession has two future possibilities: one where "the profession is radically different than it is today and one where the profession does not exist at all." However, with the exception of the mention of technologically-induced change, none of these commentators indicated what is changing, and none suggested why, and to what it will or should change.

Three of the thirty-six said that architects would need to become concerned about "sustainability" and "green design" by becoming "stewards of natural resources," but not even these people suggested any substantially different futures ahead. Overall, the future is projected as one of continued economic growth driven by technological and social change that requires a bit of energy and resource sensitivity on the part of architects leading, but in collaboration with other disciplines.

In the impressive compendium of essays by many of America's most honored architects (Solomon, 2008), Thomas Fisher's contribution stood out by offering a list of some "Challenges Ahead" (Fisher, 2008) among which are "ongoing exponential growth of the world's population"; an "unprecedented amount of instability in the global climate"; and "dwindling natural resources." These would seem to suggest the possibility of collapse or discipline futures. However, while he did mention "sustainability" in passing, he ended up with a kind of transformational view by noting that "we may even come to see buildings not as discrete physical objects but as the intersection of material and energy flows that have existed long before a building's completion and that will continue long afterward" and so design, use, and recycle materials so as "to maintain a balance of matter and energy so that we have enough of both to build in the future." The world is at a tipping point. Fortunately, architects "have, as a profession, two of the skills most needed if we are to achieve healthier and more prosperous lives for all. Architects regularly envision alternative futures in the design of buildings, and there may be no time in which the ability to do so will be more important than now. … Architects also look holistically at problems to propose solutions that address the greatest number of requirements most effectively. This ability, too, is badly needed."

I very much agree with him here.

In 1999, the School of Architecture of UHM began a novel DArch program. By 2013, according to a list in the library of the School of Architecture, 249 DArch theses have been written and approved since the degree became functional. An analysis of those theses shows that slightly more than half of them had some kind of a futures focus. Those that did not were either concerned specifically with the past or present, or with various theoretical or methodological issues with no specific time dimension.

Shortly after the DArch. degree program began, Dean Ray Yeh asked me to lecture on the future and the futures of architects to the first DArch. class in 1999. I also did so for many years after. I also co-taught Architecture courses with Professors Ray Yeh, David Rockwood, and Hyoung June Park, and served on 16 DArch. committees.

One of the very first DArch theses, written by Robert Fielden, "Libraries for the 21st Century" (2000), stated that his interest was sparked by my inaugural lecture, and cited five popular sources of ideas about the future at the time. He also developed an impressive scenario upon which he then based designs for several libraries. While he recognized that electronic technologies were impacting the futures of libraries and their management, he nonetheless implicitly took a conventional continued-growth perspective on the future. This continued-growth orientation is typical of most of the DArch. theses that had an explicit futures orientation.

However, four theses exhibited an explicit high-tech transformational future. Five reflected implicit high-tech transformational future assumptions. Environmental and energy concerns were exhibited by many of the explicitly futures-oriented theses. However, most of them were focused on "sustainability" within an otherwise growth-oriented future. A notable exception was Chad Henderson, *Immersing Architecture: The Features of Undersea Development* (2009) that took a very affirmative view of buildings that eagerly welcome and heartily embrace sea level rise, rather than either ignoring it or trying to fight against it. This welcoming view of sea level rise was also explored by various student teams in several Architecture courses that I co-taught with Ray Yeh and David Lockwood.

The issue of homelessness, of radical and low-tech self-sufficiency, and of learning from squatters— not just in terms of "sustainability," but also mainly as ways of surviving during and thriving after social and environmental collapse—were also expressed by five theses.

How did "the future" fare in each of the contributions to this volume? What images of the futures are portrayed and which are absent? All of the authors exhibited continued-growth images of the future in varying degrees. Most did so implicitly, either by not mentioning the future at all, or by not mentioning any of the energy, resource, environmental, economic, social, or technological challenges found in collapse, disciplined or even transformational images. Seven authors did express some concern about the economy, new technologies, sustainability, climate change, demographics, or energy, but not in a way that suggested any threat to continued economic growth. In an early draft, one author expressed urgent concerns about humanity's negative impact on the ecosphere, saying that architects will be called upon to mitigate those impacts. But those concerns were absent in his final version printed here.

Three authors stated that trends and emerging issues presented substantial challenges to humans, and thus to architects who were facing very different situations in the future than they had experienced in the past

Yeang's chapter, with a forceful introduction by Dent, is entirely devoted to the urgency of solving the deepening energy crisis. He addresses both global warming due to fossil fuel burning and the inability of alternative energy systems to replace energy demand that is now supplied by fossil fuels. He stresses the need for drastic energy conservation and offers many low, mid, high and "eco" tech solutions. His chapter deserves careful reading and consideration. We should not be lulled into complacency when the price of oil goes down as its supply goes up: there may be many such plateaus in the continuing downward slope of supply and the upward slope of price.

Another exceptional essay in this volume is that of Sattler. She focuses on sustainability broadly, accepting the idea that human actions over the past thousands and especially hundreds of years have moved the Earth geologically from the Holocene to the Anthropocene Epoch. This places novel obligations and possibilities squarely on the shoulders of architects. "If architecture is to continue to be relevant, the discipline can no longer afford to address the multitude of contextual forces thrust upon it in a piecemeal manner," she writes. She refers to "the post-growth, post-peak oil context" of "the current developed world." The bulk of her chapters discusses the "3E's: Environment, Equity, and Economics." If I am correct in assuming the absence of this kind of a discussion in the other papers in this volume represents the absence of concern among architects generally for the "3Es," then her paper is one of the most important in the book from my point of view.

Only one contribution here specifically exemplified my contention that, since architects so profoundly influence future behaviors by designing and constructing structures that endure, they should formally assess the environmental, social, energy, and economic future over the lifetime of any construction project they propose before undertaking it. It was inspiring to read Fisher's chapter on architects and ethics for social sustainability:

> [W]hat responsibility do we have to those who have come before us and those who will follow us? In our present-minded culture, the concern about the past or future may not seem to matter much, but here too, architecture has a different ethical role to play. Buildings generally outlive their creators and so every work of architecture must take a stance toward what we have inherited from our predecessors and what we will leave behind for our progeny. And reciprocity—one of the core ideas of ethics—suggests that we should treat the work of the past as we would want future generations to treat our work.

Even more powerfully, Fisher writes in Canon 6:

> Two of the greatest ethical lapses in human history have occurred over the last two hundred years. The first has to do with the fact that humanity has used up, in relatively few generations, all of the easily available fossil fuels that took millions of years to stockpile. The second has to do with the fact that we have so fragmented the habitat and destroyed the food chain of so many other species that we have initiated the largest extinction in human history. Architects and allied fields like engineering and planning have to accept some responsibility for the many energy intensive buildings, auto-dependent communities, and mono-cultural landscapes we have designed. So yes, we need to advocate for sustainable design, but what that entails goes far beyond the tweaking that characterizes most efforts so far.
>
> [...]
>
> This standard may contain the most radical idea of the entire code: we all have to adopt sustainable practices—not just architects, but our clients as well. Unethical behavior eventually comes around to bite those who engage in it, and the unethical actions we have taken not just to fellow human beings, but also to other species have started to come around. Changing how we inhabit this planet and how we define a "good life" is not just a matter of ethics; it has become a matter of survival for us all, as members of one of the most vulnerable species on Earth.

All of the examples I have cited so far revolve around collapse and discipline as alternatives to continued economic growth. And indeed, given the extreme popularity of Ray Kurzweil and his notion of the ever-rapidly approaching "Singularity" when physical, biological, and social technologies all merge into one (Kurzweil, 2005), and the creation of Singularity University to help bring it about, it was surprising to me to find the total absence of high tech, transformational, utopian images of the future that once were the hallmarks of architects—including my old friends in the Archigram Group. There was not even a discussion of what is sometimes called "the ubiquitous society" where we are (for better or worse) "all watched over by machines of loving grace," as Richard Brautigan once phrased it. I read nothing about "architecture as crime control" and the design of global environments based on complete electronic surveillance and control (Katyal, 2002). The closest to it I could find was a brief mention by Gage in his discussion of "branding." Gage said,

> The immediate future offers us the potential of ubiquitous computing, sensors imbedded in matter; interactive gestures, facial recognition and choreographies of lighting, and sound, so that the branded spaces of tomorrow will seem closer to biological entities than the decorated generic spaces of the 20th century's mechanical paradigm. Architecture could become among the most significant players in the emergence of a new genre of constantly reconfiguring human space–one funded by brands, interactively tuned towards individuals, societally connected to global communities, atmospherically and interactively charged, and, above all, spatial. The alternative is that architecture will, in the face of such massive commercialization expenditures, be increasingly collapsed into inert scaffolds for two-dimensional signage and screens… and the occasional strange bright red pitched mansard roof.

Of all authors, Edelstein's essay on "Neuroscience and Architecture" lays the basis for one of the most profound transformations in architecture—and life—while the contributions by Kanaani, Alquist and Menges, and Kolarevic and Parlac also gesture towards something potentially high tech and shape shifting. Kanaani, especially was concerned with how people using a building twenty, thirty, one hundred years from now might wish to behave. Have we carefully incorporated that into our design, or will future generations struggle to behave as they wish within the confining structure we have built?

Similarly, the chapters on social equity, gender, and diversity raise extremely important issues that are too often ignored, but they are largely historical in focus and unfortunately do not alert us to possible new meanings of equity, gender, or cultural diversity which are already at least on the horizon if not well upon us, such as those resulting from the rapid obsolescence of old understandings of sex and gender, as well as the interaction of humans, robots, and other autonomous beings. As Gage writes,

> The forces at play in the world are no longer even possibly affected by our utopian or critical speculations, and to think so is nearly comical given the statistics previously presented. We live in a world that operates according to a new economic physics, and architecture must adapt to the new laws or risk becoming a castrated art practice appreciated only by academics and the elite. We're already close.

Of course, both collapse and discipline images of the future are expressions of doubt about the sustainability of this "new economic physics," which may well have ended its unquestioned reign with the Great Recession in 2007, with nothing yet able to take its place, temporarily low gasoline prices and declarations of renewed growth to the contrary notwithstanding.

In *Utopia Forever* (Feireiss, 2011), Lukas Feireiss writes, that

> architecture … provides the most substantial vehicle to imagine possible futures due to the inherent notion of progress in the discipline, which is naturally linked to the discourse on utopia. In fact, the entire discipline is consequently focused on the future world.

However,

> while it seemed almost compulsory for architects to design a utopian city in the 1960s and early 1970s, it vanished completely from the architectural discourse after the collapse of twentieth century's grand ideologies, and the subsequent disillusionment of the ideas in the decades thereafter. To some it seemed as if the entire Modern Project had failed completely.

And yet, Feireiss declares, "Today, utopia seems to be on everyone's lips."

Perhaps it is, but the concept failed completely to emerge from the word processors of the contributors to this volume for whom the future seems overwhelmingly good, but apparently not good enough for utopias.

And this is fine with me. One of the things I have tried to do over my long career is to make it clear that the "preferred future" of a futurist is "the best possible real world imaginable" and decidedly *not* a utopia. Feireiss himself points out the problematic nature of the term. "Utopia" means "no place": an impossibly good, indeed perfect, place. The history of utopianism is littered with the corpses of people who were killed because they were said to be the reason perfection was not achieved. Feireiss says, "This is the crux of the matter: those who envisage creating 'heaven earth' … Karl Popper denotes in his essay, *The Open Society and its Enemies,* 'will only succeed in making hell'."

The criticism by one of the contributors to this volume of the "high-tech movement" as catering only to the fantasies of a few architects and their well-heeled supporters while being socially and environmentally destructive seems to illustrate this as well.

The opposite of utopia is dystopia—the vision of an impossibly bad place that infects almost all science fiction in all of its genres. Expressions of dystopia are far more widespread and enchanting than are those of utopia. Many of the concerns about energy, the environment, the economy, and so on bristle with the moral enthusiasm of dystopias: it is good that evil humanity be thoroughly thrashed—better, eliminated altogether—so that pure nature can thrive again. Some "environmentalists" seem to relish that thought.

But what we need, what futurists and architects should try to provide, are eutopias—preferred futures that are as good as they can be with imperfect humans imperfectly understanding themselves and their world—not perfectly good or wicked visions of the future that are easy and emotionally satisfying to imagine. We need inspiring, achievable visions of buildings for worlds far better for everyone than are ours now, but not thought to be impossibly perfect and free of all imperfections: just the best that is humanly (and posthumanly) possible. Eutopias are far, far harder to imagine and strive for than are either utopias or dystopias, so only brave, hardworking, and ethical architects are likely to rise to the challenge. It is far easier to engage in irresponsible utopianism, or just keep your nose to the grindstone of the present.

My conclusion from all of this is that architects and especially schools of architecture should take Fisher's Canon 6 seriously; recognize that architects have enormous powers and concomitant responsibilities towards future generations; and see that some kind of serious alternative futures education is provided in all architectural schools and continuing education classes. Like any fundamentally new perspective, it is not easy to acquire an alternative futures perspective, but my experience at the University of Hawaii School of Architecture and elsewhere has demonstrated to me that it can and should be done. Without it, I will join with some of the other authors in this volume who wonder whether there is a future for architects at all.

References

Bell, W. (1997). *Foundations of Futures Studies.* Two Volumes. New Brunswick, NJ: Transaction Publishers.

Dator, J. (2002). *Advancing Futures: Futures Studies in Higher Education.* New York: Praeger.

Dator, J. (2009). Alternative futures at the Manoa School. *Journal of Futures Studies*, 14, 2, 1–18.

Dator, J., Yeh, R., & Park, S. (2013). Campuses 2060: Four Futures of Higher Education in Four Alternative Futures of Society. In Shuib, M., Yunus, A. & Rahman, S. (eds), *Developments in Higher Education: National Strategies and Global Perspectives.* Penang: Universiti Sains Malaysia Press and National Higher Education Research Institute.

Dator, J., Sweeney, J., & Yee, A. (2014). *Mutative Technology: Communication Technologies and Power Relations in the Past, Present and Futures.* New York: Springer Press.

Feireiss, L. (2011). *Utopia Forever: Visions of Architecture and Urbanism.* Berlin: Gestalten, pp. 6–7.

Fisher, T. (2008). Challenges Ahead. In Solomon, N. (ed.), *Architecture: Celebrating the Past, Designing the Future.* Washington, DC: American Institute of Architects, pp. 92–96.

Katyal, K. (2002). Architecture as Crime Control. *Yale Law Journal*, 111, 5, 1039–1139.

Kurzweil, R. (2005). *The Singularity is Near: When Humans Transcend Biology.* New York: Viking Press.

Mackaye, P. (1914). Goethals, in *The Present Hour.* New York: Macmillan, pp. 69–70.

Solomon, N. (ed.) (2008). Ensuring a Healthy and Prosperous Future. *Architecture: Celebrating the Past, Designing the Future.* Washington, DC: American Institute of Architects.

Sutton, S. (2001). Reinventing Professional Privilege as Inclusivity: A Proposal for an Enriched Mission of Architecture. In Pitotrowski, A. & Robinson, J. (eds), *The Discipline of Architecture*, Minneapolis: University of Minnesota Press, pp. 173–207.

Waldrep, L. (2006). The Future of the Architecture Profession. *Becoming an Architect.* Hoboken, NJ: John Wiley & Sons, Inc., pp. 262–270.

Watson, D. (2001). Environment and Architecture. In Pitotrowski, A. & Robinson, J., eds., *The Discipline of Architecture*, Minneapolis, MN: University of Minnesota Press, pp. 158–172.

Index

Note: Page numbers in *italic* indicate figures.